Group Communication

In this comprehensive, advanced introduction to group communication, the field's leading experts summarize theory, methodological advancements, and current research in the field.

This book follows a coherent structure specifying clear objectives and evidence-based practical implications for the management of groups. Each chapter provides case study examples highlighting the role of communication for group functioning. The textbook takes a particular look at recent advancements in the research on virtual teams, the role of technology in group communication, and issues of diversity and inclusion, considering group communication in various situations including health and organizational contexts. It features theory-driven descriptions, an emphasis on empirical findings, and reflections on research methods.

The book is an integrative and coherent textbook for advanced undergraduate and graduate group communication classes and a useful reference for students, scholars, and group communication professionals across different disciplines including communication studies, psychology, life sciences, business administration, management, and engineering.

Online resources include a sample course syllabus, discussion questions, lecture slides, and a test-bank. They are available at www.routledge.com/9781032114712

Torsten Reimer is a Professor of Communication and Psychology and Director of the Communication and Cognition Lab at Purdue University, USA.

Ernest S. Park is a social psychologist and an Associate Professor at Grand Valley State University, USA.

Joseph A. Bonito is a Professor of Communication at the University of Arizona, USA.

Group Communication

An Advanced Introduction

Edited by Torsten Reimer, Ernest S. Park, and Joseph A. Bonito

NEW YORK AND LONDON

Designed cover image: Neliakott/© Getty Images

First published 2024
by Routledge
605 Third Avenue, New York, NY 10158

and by Routledge
4 Park Square, Milton Park, Abingdon, Oxon, OX14 4RN

Routledge is an imprint of the Taylor & Francis Group, an informa business

Library of Congress Cataloging-in-Publication Data
Names: Reimer, Torsten, editor. | Park, Ernest S., editor. | Bonito, Joseph, editor.
Title: Group communication : an advanced introduction / [edited by] Torsten Reimer, Ernest S. Park and Joseph A. Bonito.
Description: New York, NY : Routledge, 2024. | Includes bibliographical references and index.
Identifiers: LCCN 2023026885 (print) | LCCN 2023026886 (ebook) | ISBN 9781032130613 (hardback) | ISBN 9781032114712 (paperback) | ISBN 9781003227458 (ebook)
Subjects: LCSH: Communication in small groups. | Small groups. | Management.
Classification: LCC HM736 .G768 2024 (print) | LCC HM736 (ebook) | DDC 302.34--dc23/eng/20230724
LC record available at https://lccn.loc.gov/2023026885
LC ebook record available at https://lccn.loc.gov/2023026886

ISBN: 978-1-032-13061-3 (hbk)
ISBN: 978-1-032-11471-2 (pbk)
ISBN: 978-1-003-22745-8 (ebk)

DOI: 10.4324/9781003227458

Typeset in Times New Roman
by KnowledgeWorks Global Ltd.

Access the Support Material: www.routledge.com/9781032114712.

Contents

About the Editors

Torsten Reimer (Ph.D. in Social Psychology, Free University of Berlin, Germany) is a Professor of Communication and Psychology and Director of the Communication and Cognition Lab at Purdue University. His research explores the bounded rationality of decision-making processes in individuals, social groups, and organizations. He served as a chair of the Communication and Social Cognition and the Group Communication divisions of the National Communication Association (NCA) and is currently serving as Associate Editor of the journal *Group Dynamics*. For his research on groups, he received several awards, including the Dennis Gouran Research Award and the Golden Anniversary Monograph Award from NCA.

Ernest S. Park (Ph.D., Michigan State University) is a social psychologist and Associate Professor at Grand Valley State University. His research explores a variety of ways in which group contexts influence the motivation, thoughts, feelings, and actions of group members. He is particularly interested in understanding how people communicate and coordinate to make group decisions and perform group actions. He has been awarded funding from the National Science Foundation, was a recipient of the Golden Anniversary Monograph Award from the National Communication Association, and is a Fellow of the Midwestern Psychological Association. He has also served on the Board of Directors of INGRoup, is an associate editor for *Group Dynamics*, and is on the editorial review board for *Small Group Research* and *Frontiers in Social Psychology*.

Joseph A. Bonito (Ph.D., 1997, University of Illinois at Urbana-Champaign) is a Professor of Communication at the University of Arizona. His research focuses on group interaction processes and decision making, with an emphasis on interdependence and mutual influence. He is also interested in the development and application of statistical models to interdependent group processes. He is a former director of the National Communication Association's (NCA) Research Board and served as chair of NCA's Group Communication Division. His research on groups and group processes has received several awards, including the Dennis Gouran Award from the Group Communication Division of NCA and, most recently, the Most Valuable Paper award from the APA journal, *Group Dynamics*.

About the Contributors

Jonas Akpetou (M.Sc. Psychology in Sport and Exercise) is a graduate of the German Sport University Cologne, Germany. Being fascinated by the complexity of communication and its impact on social interaction, in his research, he focused on the effect of nonverbal behavior on impression formation and performance in sports. He currently works in the applied field, promoting teamwork and group communication processes in groups of adolescents and young adults.

Stephenson J. Beck (Ph.D., University of Kansas) is a Professor and Chair of the Department of Communication at North Dakota State University. His research focuses on meeting facilitation, strategic interaction, and social support. His current projects investigate how leaders of school board meetings facilitated conflict during the COVID-19 pandemic, how phone and computer technologies influence participant focus in meetings, and how special education professionals manage tensions in parent/teacher meetings.

Guido Beldi is a Professor of Surgery at the University of Bern and in the Department of Visceral Surgery and Medicine of the University Hospital in Bern, Switzerland. He is a specialist for hepatobiliary and transplantation surgery. Relevant research interests are communication between the different team members of various professions in the operating room. His current and past projects address the question if short briefings during surgery have an effect on patient outcomes.

Bailey C. Benedict is an Assistant Professor in the Department of Management at California State University, San Bernardino. She received her Ph.D. in Organizational Communication from Purdue University in 2021. Her research centers on how individuals and communities organize social networks of support to manage uncertainty and enact resilience, especially when enduring or overcoming hardships like natural disasters. Her work is published in outlets like *Management Communication Quarterly*, *Journal of Applied Communication Research*, and various disaster-related journals.

Leila Bighash is an Assistant Professor of Communication at the University of Arizona. Her research program centers around organizational processes in networks, with a focus on how individuals influence groups and other social networks and vice versa. Leila investigates information-seeking, expertise, and visibility within various contexts, including social media, online communities, and traditional organizations. Leila holds a Ph.D. in Communication from the Annenberg School of Communication and Journalism at the University of Southern California.

Laura W. Black is a full professor in the School of Communication Studies at Ohio University. She is an engaged communication scholar who studies difference and conflict in groups. Her qualitative and discourse-based research helps groups address difficult, divisive issues through collaboration, dialogue, and deliberation. Her research has been published in a wide range of academic journals and scholarly books, and she is the former editor of the *Journal of Deliberative Democracy*. Dr. Black also frequently collaborates with community partners to help understand and improve community dialogue and decision-making processes. She received her Ph.D. from the University of Washington.

Chen-Ting Chang is a Ph.D. student in the Department of Communication Arts at the University of Wisconsin-Madison. Her research interests focus on exploring persuasive communication strategies that can mitigate cognitive and behavioral biases affecting decision-making quality among individuals and groups across various contexts. Her work aims to understand the underlying psychological mechanisms involved in information processing and decision making to develop effective communication interventions that promote well-being, healthy lifestyle choices, and best practices in environmental communication.

Jennifer Woody Collins holds a Ph.D. from Ohio University's Communication Studies program and is a Visiting Assistant Professor at Denison University. Prior to her academic career, Jennifer worked in public health, advocacy, and coalition building and these experiences inform her research on group communication.

Stacey L. Connaughton (Ph.D., The University of Texas at Austin) is a Professor in the Brian Lamb School of Communication at Purdue University and the Director of the Purdue Policy Research Institute (PPRI) in Purdue's Discovery Park District. Her research examines leadership and multi-stakeholder organizing, most recently in the context of political violence prevention initiatives. Dr. Connaughton serves as Director of the Purdue Peace Project (PPP), a locally driven initiative that collaborates with everyday citizens in conflict prone regions of the world to prevent political violence.

Wen Duan is currently a postdoctoral fellow in Human-Centered Computing in the School of Computing, Clemson University. She received her Ph.D. from Cornell University. She conducts research in areas including computer-mediated communication (CMC), human-computer interaction (HCI), computer-supported cooperative work (CSCW), and human-AI teaming (HAT).

Michael Farzinpour is a third-year Ph.D. student in the Department of Communication at the University of Arizona. Michael's research focuses on the social, informational, and privacy implications of communication technology use in different intra-organizational contexts. In particular, he is interested in how communication technology use influences stakeholder communication. He is also a teaching assistant for undergraduate communication courses.

Jeremy Foote is an Assistant Professor in the Brian Lamb School of Communication at Purdue University and holds a Ph.D. in Media, Technology, and Society from Northwestern University. His research focuses primarily on the interaction between individual decisions and group-level processes in online communities. This includes how new communities get started, how people are influenced by the communities they belong to, and why some communities get attention and influence while most do not. Dr. Foote primarily employs large-scale computational approaches and teaches courses introducing students to computational communication research.

Philip Furley is a senior lecturer at the Institute of Training and Computer Science at the German Sport University Cologne, Köln, Germany. He has published extensively in the field of cognitive, social, and performance psychology. He is an international expert on nonverbal communication in sports and received the highest sport science award from the German Olympic

Sports Confederation on his habilitation thesis on nonverbal behavior and person perception in sport in 2023.

Johny Garner is a Professor of Communication Studies in the Bob Schieffer College of Communication at Texas Christian University. Dr. Garner received his Ph.D. from Texas A&M University. His research focuses on groups and teams in organizations. Dr. Garner has also explored the ways in which employees share feedback with supervisors and how those supervisors respond to that feedback.

Kayla J. Gerdes is a Ph.D. student at Purdue University's Brian Lamb School of Communication. Her areas of research include organizational communication, political communication, environmental communication, and critical cultural studies. In particular, Kayla has addressed ranger to visitor communication in the U.S. National Park System, community-based disaster management relief efforts, and leadership in environmental organizations.

Randy Y. Hirokawa (Ph.D., University of Washington, 1980) is a Professor of Communication at the University of Hawaii at Hilo. Hirokawa is known for his expertise in the area of small group communication and group performance. He is the author or co-author of three books and 65 journal articles and book chapters, and has delivered numerous national and international lectures. Prior to joining the faculty at the University of Hawaii at Hilo, he also served on the faculty at the Pennsylvania State University (1980–1984) and the University of Iowa (1984–2005). In 2006, Hirokawa was inducted in the Communication Alumni Hall of Fame at the University of Washington.

Elizabeth H. Hurst, Ph.D., is a research scientist at the University of Oklahoma's Center for Applied Social Research. Hurst specializes in applied qualitative research and text analysis. Much of Hurst's research examines how inter-group discussions, at the interpersonal level, as well as mass media representations, shape how we see ourselves and others. Prior research conducted by Hurst, as well as her dissertation, investigated political conversations among college students. Since 2021, she has been working on NOAA-funded research to bridge partnerships between National Weather Service offices and their partners to better serve vulnerable populations.

Sohyeon Hwang is a Ph.D. student at Northwestern University conducting research on how people organize, govern, and collaborate online. She uses both qualitative and computational methods at the scale of multi-platform and multi-community analyses to understand patterns across diverse, complex, and overlapping online spaces. Focused on large-scale sociotechnical systems and contemporary platforms, her research work centers on questions of accountability, autonomy, and ambiguity, and has been presented and received recognition at top-tier computer science conferences as well as shared with communities, platforms, and in the news.

Payge Japp is a M.A./Ph.D. student in the Industrial Organizational Psychology program at the University of Nebraska at Omaha (UNO). She earned a B.S. in Psychology in 2019 from UNO. Payge's research interests include individual and team creativity, malevolent creativity, and creative problem-solving.

Nathanael Johnson (M.A., Purdue University) is a Ph.D. candidate in interpersonal communication at the Brian Lamb School of Purdue University. His research centers around technology and decision making, especially as it relates to the adoption of new technologies.

Sandra Keller is a post-doctoral researcher at Bern University Hospital (Switzerland), Department of Visceral Surgery and Medicine. Sandra received her Ph.D. in Psychology at the

University of Neuchâtel (Switzerland), where she conducted research on teamwork. Sandra's research interests include communication, distractions, noise and interpersonal tensions during teamwork situations, in particular in surgery. During her first post-doctoral scholarship in the USA, she studied the experience of stress episodes in interprofessional operating room teams. Currently, she is working on a multicentric research project that aims to test the impact of intra-operative short briefings on post-operative patient outcomes and teamwork aspects.

Joann Keyton (B.A., Western Michigan University; M.A., Ph.D., The Ohio State University) is a Professor Emerita of Communication at North Carolina State University. She specializes in group communication and organizational communication. Her current research examines the collaborative processes and relational aspects of interdisciplinary teams, participants' use of language in team meetings, and the multiplicity of cultures in organizations. She received the 2015 Group Communication Career Achievement Award from the Group Communication Division, National Communication Association. Keyton was editor of *Small Group Research*, 2008–2021, and a founder of the Interdisciplinary Network for Group Research.

Nicholas B. Lacy is a Ph.D. student in the Brian Lamb School of Communication at Purdue University. His work in organizational communication addresses ethical and equitable leadership, policy, and decision making with Black communities in U.S. law enforcement and higher education. He is also the Director of Diversity, Equity, and Belonging at Ivy Tech Community College in Lafayette, Indiana.

Seungyoon Lee (Ph.D., University of Southern California) is a Professor in the Brian Lamb School of Communication at Purdue University. Her research is at the intersection of network theory and methods and organizational communication. She typically examines collaboration, social support, and knowledge sharing ties and their implications for individuals' and communities' resilience and well-being. Her recent projects are situated in the context of complex and grand challenges (e.g., natural disasters, violent conflicts intertwined with climate change) and emphasize the interdependence between social, physical, and ecological networks.

Juan Pablo Loaiza-Ramírez, M.Sc., M.A., is a doctoral student in the Brian Lamb School of Communication at Purdue University. His research explores the intersection between communication, decision making, and environmental sustainability. Specifically, his research has examined the effects of companies' sustainable practices, such as green supply chain practices or green energy, on consumers' purchase and adoption intentions. His recent interests focus on how transparent artificial intelligence (AI) systems and machine learning algorithms can help consumers make more ecologically rational and environmentally driven decisions by understanding the role of consumers' perceived trust.

Runzhi Mary Lu is a Ph.D. student in the Department of Communication Arts at the University of Wisconsin-Madison. She is interested in conducting research on the effect of communication technology use on relationship maintenance, psychological well-being, and social influence as a function of individual characteristics and situational demands. Her recent projects examine how attachment style shapes individuals' communication needs, media preferences, and language use when they communicate with romantic partners to seek emotional support and raise complaints.

Stephan Marsch is a Professor of Intensive Care at the University of Basel, Switzerland, and Chairman of the Intensive Care Unit at the University Hospital Basel. He received his medical degree from the University of Zürich, Switzerland, and acquired his MD in Zürich and his Ph.D. in Oxford, UK. He is board-certified in internal medicine, anesthesiology, and intensive care. For over 25 years, his research has focused on human factors relevant to acute medicine. His extensive clinical and research background provides valuable contributions to the book chapter on teams and teamwork in medicine.

Poppy L. McLeod, Ph.D., is a Professor in the Department of Communication at Cornell University where she directs the Group and Interpersonal Communication Research Lab. Her research and teaching focus on social influence in group discussion and decision making especially applied to climate change, task performance and decision making in virtual teams, emotions and language use in intergroup contexts, and how students develop teamwork skills. Her research has been widely published in journals spanning multiple disciplines, including *Academy of Management Journal*, *Journal of Applied Psychology*, *Small Group Research*, *Information Systems Research*, *PLOSOne*, *Healthcare Management Review*, *Creativity Research Journal*, *Group Processes & Intergroup Relations*, and *Communication Research*.

Nathan J. McNeese is the McQueen Quattlebaum Endowed Associate Professor of Human-Centered Computing and the Director of the Team Research Analytics in Computational Environments (TRACE) Research Group in the School of Computing at Clemson University. Dr. McNeese received a Ph.D. in Information Sciences & Technology from The Pennsylvania State University in 2014. His area of expertise is in human-autonomy/AI teaming and human-centered AI. He has been a principal investigator or co-principal investigator for more than 25 research grants and awards, generating more than $35 million in funding. His research has received multiple best paper awards/nominations and has been published in top peer-reviewed HCI and HF venues over 140 times.

Jeonghyun Oh is an Assistant Professor of Communication Studies at the University of Alabama. She holds a Ph.D. in Communication from Purdue University. Her research interest centers on social influence, group decision making, and organizational communication. With a diverse academic background, Jeonghyun also holds an M.A. in Political Science from Shanghai Jiao Tong University in China and a B.S. in Political Science from Ewha Women's University.

Emily A. Paskewitz (Ph.D., North Dakota State University) is an Associate Professor in the School of Communication Studies and the Department of Agricultural Leadership, Education and Communications at the University of Tennessee Knoxville. Her research focuses on relational dynamics in groups and organizations, with current projects exploring family farm communication around mental health and the use of mobile phones in meetings.

Andrew Pilny (Ph.D., University of Illinois Urbana-Champaign) is an Associate Professor in the Department of Communication & Department of Sociology at the University of Kentucky. Pilny studies groups from a systems and network perspective, analyzing how the relationships and interactions they create influence outcomes like performance. Pilny also uses computational social methods like machine-learning to see how we can automate tasks performed by groups.

Stephen A. Rains is a Professor of Communication at the University of Arizona. His research examines health communication, social influence, and communication and technology. He is interested in better understanding how and why messages influence people, particularly in health contexts and when using communication technologies. This includes a line of research investigating social support in online communities and related contexts as a component of digital coping.

Justin Reedy, Ph.D., is an Associate Professor in the Department of Communication at the University of Oklahoma. He studies political communication and deliberation, group dynamics and decision making, and risk and crisis communication. His research focuses on how individuals, groups, and communities make political and civic decisions, in particular on issues involving societal and personal risk. He has worked on and helped lead research projects funded by the US National Science Foundation, the National Institutes of Health, the National Oceanic and Atmospheric Administration, and the National Academies of Science and Engineering.

Roni Reiter-Palmon is a Distinguished Professor of Industrial/Organizational (I/O) Psychology. Her research focuses on creativity and innovation in the workplace, cognitive processes of creativity, team creativity, development of teamwork and creative problem-solving skills, and leading creative individuals and teams. Her research has been published in leading journals in the fields of Organizational Psychology, Management, Leadership, and Creativity. She has published multiple books on the topic of creativity, and served as the editor of the book series "Creativity and Innovation in Organizations" by Palgrave. She has won the system wide research award from the University of Nebraska in 2017.

Julius Matthew Riles researches the interplay between media use and social relationships. Specifically, Dr. Riles explores how exposure to social group portrayals can psychologically influence social perceptions and inclinations pertaining to those groups, the mechanisms by which social relationships influence media use, and the experience of parasocial relationships with figures in the media. Dr. Riles has been published in top-ranked peer-reviewed outlets such as the *Journal of Communication*, *New Media & Society*, *Communication Research*, *Media Psychology*, *Communication Monographs*, and *Health Communication*. He is currently serving as Co-Director for the Media & Diversity Center at the University of Missouri.

Christopher Roland, Ph.D. (Purdue University, 2019), is an Assistant Professor of Communication at the University of Central Arkansas. His research focuses on the role of message features in persuasion and group decision-making processes. He has made prior contributions to books studying small group communication in the context of medicine, organizations, and digital technology.

Rizvan Saeed, a social science researcher, is pursuing a Ph.D. in Health Communication. His research interests encompass masculinities, gender-stigmatized health conditions, interpersonal communication, and digital communication.

Norbert K. Semmer is a Professor Emeritus for the Psychology of Work and Organizations at the University of Bern, Switzerland. He received his Ph.D. from the Technical University of Berlin in 1983. After working at the Federal Health Office in Berlin he became head of the psychology of work and organizations unit at the University of Bern, where he retired in 2014. His research primarily focuses on stress at work, with a particular focus on stress as offense to the self, and teamwork in medicine, notably regarding simulation training as well as communication and coordination in the operating room.

Franziska Tschan is a Professor Emerita of Social Psychology at Work at the University of Neuchâtel, Switzerland. She obtained her Ph.D. and habilitation from the University of Bern, Switzerland and has published in psychological and medical journals. Her research focuses on group processes, communication, and productivity. She collaborated with the University Hospital in Basel to study emergency teams in simulator settings, and with the University Hospital of Bern to examine the relationship between group processes in surgical teams and team and patient outcomes. Her work has shed light on the crucial link between effective communication and improved performance in high-pressure environments.

Lyn M. van Swol (Ph.D., University of Illinois at Urbana-Champaign) is a Professor in the Department of Communication Arts at University of Wisconsin-Madison. Her research examines how groups share and utilize information and advice and how language use in groups affects social influence. She currently edits the journal *Small Group Research*.

Mark E. Willoughby (M.S., University of Tennessee, Knoxville) is a doctoral student in the College of Communication & Information at the University of Tennessee. His research interests include organizational, group, and computer-mediated dissent.

Gwen M. Wittenbaum is an Associate Professor of Communication at Michigan State University. Her research interests in communication, cognition, and performance in small groups and teams are informed by an interdisciplinary approach. She co-founded the Interdisciplinary Network for Group Research (INGRoup) and recently completed a visiting consultantship with Michigan State University's Toolbox Dialogue Initiative Center, which uses philosophically informed dialogue to foster collaboration in cross-disciplinary science teams. Her academic background includes a Ph.D. in social psychology from Miami University and a visiting faculty position in Carnegie Mellon University's Tepper School of Business.

Y. Connie Yuan, Ph.D., is a Professor in the Department of Communication and the Department of Global Development at Cornell University. Her teaching and research explore cultural differences in organizational communication, health communication, and risk communication. Her recent studies explore how cultural differences in communication styles influence expertise recognition in intercultural group collaboration and how information and communication technologies can facilitate intercultural teamwork and social networking. Her research appeared in the *Journal of Applied Psychology, Communication Research, Human Communication Research, Journal of Computer-Mediated Communication, Journal of Communication, Health Communication, JASIST*, and *Group & Organization Management.*

Rui Zhang received a Ph.D. in Human-Centered Computing from Clemson University. Her research focuses on human-AI teaming and AI's communication design in teams. She received her M.S. and B.S. in Aerospace Engineering from Beijing Institute of Technology.

1 Introduction

The Role of Communication in Group Scholarship

Torsten Reimer, Ernest S. Park, and Joseph A. Bonito

Premises and Goals

Groups are the building blocks of human societies and communication is their lifeblood, their *condition sine qua non*. Group membership is integral to the life of an individual as well. Our membership in groups helps to fulfill the basic human need to belong and helps to define who we are. These outcomes can be achieved because of the way in which groups and communication are intertwined: Communication does not only serve important group functions, such as sharing information and the coordination of group actions, but it is also constitutive for the formation and maintenance of groups. It is through the joint understanding of a common bond and the shared agreement to be members of the same group that groups are formed and recognized and people feel accepted (Park & Hinsz, 2006). At the same time, groups are instrumental in the development and practice of human communication by providing a basic form of human organizing – groups provide the building blocks of human societies, which are composed of a web of groups varying in size, boundaries, and the way they are structurally related to each other. Families, work groups, friendship and sports clubs, online communities, and many other groups form the multilevel fabric of societies. Groups do not exist in isolation but are situated within larger entities, such as organizations of a society, which they impact and are impacted by. Like organizations, societies have hierarchical structures with nested levels and overlapping entities, and teams and groups serve as the central building blocks of these structures (Reimer et al., 2017). As societies are presented with a variety of large-scale challenges, people are increasingly asked to work together to solve problems and overcome obstacles. Communication plays a pivotal role in all phases and endeavors of groups as laid out and described in the chapters of this book.

Group Communication provides a state-of-the-art introduction to group communication, summarizing theory, methodological advancements, and current research. A signature characteristic of the book is its three foci: First and foremost, the book introduces a variety of concepts that emphasize the critical role of *communication* for group functioning. Second, the book highlights virtual groups and teams, noting that the COVID-19 pandemic has greatly increased the number of group meetings involving geographically dispersed members. Third, the book reflects on the role of diversity for group functioning and outcomes.

Group Communication aims to fill a gap in the scholarly literature on groups as it provides an *advanced* introduction. Chapters illuminate the fascinating landscape of group communication that are primarily written for advanced readers, including upper-level undergraduate and graduate students. There are excellent handbooks (e.g., Beck et al., 2022; Frey et al., 1999) and books for 100-level introductory courses on group communication (e.g., Hirokawa et al., 2003; Keyton & Beck, 2017). However, there is a dearth of books for upper-level classes on groups and teams that focus on communication. *Group Communication* aims to fill this gap.

DOI: 10.4324/9781003227458-1

The book provides in-depth introductions into major themes, theories, and methods of group communication that are written by scholars in the field. The contributors of this book have many years of experience in teaching group communication on the advanced undergraduate and the graduate level. Different from textbooks for 100- and 200-level courses, this book offers an introduction into group communication that provides depth and breadth appropriate for more advanced students. The book provides more theory-driven descriptions, greater emphasis on empirical findings, and more reflection on research methods without diving into the minutiae of statistical modeling. The book differs from handbooks of group communication in that the individual chapters all have the same basic structure and offer textbook features that are typically not found in handbooks (e.g., summaries of key points and applications). Moreover, the book has a basic section, Part I, that introduces the foundations of group communication.

Structure and Content

The book has three parts. Part I outlines the central themes that undergird theory and research on small discussion groups. Part II addresses components and processes of group communication, and Part III discusses the role of group communication in specific contexts and applications. Chapters can be read and used for instructional purposes in any order, as they reference but do not build on each other in a successive way. However, we recommend reading the foundational chapters first.

Part I: Foundations of Group Communication

The four chapters in the first part provide a general overview of terminology, historical approaches, theoretical frameworks, and methodology that are foundational to the study of group communication. Many of the perspectives and principles that are discussed appear in subsequent chapters.

The foundational overview starts with Chapter 2 by Park that lays out *The Importance of Groups*. As a foundation for upcoming chapters, Chapter 2 provides descriptions of various types of groups including primary and secondary groups, collectives, and social categories. The chapter highlights commonalities and differences among these types of groups and describes how these different groups can form and function. Park argues that one reason we have been able to survive and flourish as a species is because we have a need to belong to groups. However, we often think of ourselves as being unique and distinct individuals and, thus, we do not always appreciate our social nature and the important role that groups play in our lives. The chapter describes what it means for humans to be a social species and reasons we have evolved to be this way. The chapter presents an overview of how our involvement in groups can shape how we think, feel, and act, and how these tendencies of group members also shape aspects of the group. This chapter describes the types of things individuals need to do to become group members and to help a group function.

Chapter 3 by Reimer, Roland, and Oh, *Group Communication Theories: Guidelines for their Application*, focuses on group theories and how they can be applied. This chapter discusses the applicability of group communication theories and emphasizes the role of metacognition in the transfer and application of theories. After providing a short overview of the history of group communication scholarship and basic approaches (the functional, informational, temporal, cultural, and critical perspectives), the chapter summarizes general insights about the role of metacognition in group functioning and communication and formulates five metacognitive principles that inform guidelines for theory application. The chapter closes with a mnemonic that provides guidance and helps readers memorize the main principles for their ready application in groups.

In Chapter 4, *Researching Small Discussion Groups*, Bonito describes general principles of research methods for the study of small discussion groups. The chapter focuses on quantitative approaches, but a brief overview of qualitative research is also provided. The chapter stresses that the research design should reflect the general substantive question of interest. The chapter is structured on the standard APA reporting template in which study participants, materials, task used, and procedure are described. The material on qualitative research addresses the relationship between the researcher and participants, different types of data collection, and options for data analysis. The chapter highlights the fact that, because communication and groups involve more than one individual, specific research methodologies that are suitable for interdependent and group-level data are needed.

Communication in groups and teams is often mediated through technology. In Chapter 5, Paskewitz and Willoughby provide an introduction and overview of various forms of technology use in groups, beginning with a description of the similarities and differences between mediated and face-to-face groups. Paskewitz and Willoughby illustrate how technology use is not limited to geographically dispersed or computer-mediated groups but is becoming more common in all group settings. The chapter describes how groups utilize technology during their meetings and outlines key theoretical perspectives on technology use, including media richness theory, adaptive structuration theory, and approaches on multicommunication (i.e., the participation in multiple conversations at the same time). The chapter also discusses which technologies are available to groups and how groups choose which technologies to utilize. The benefits and costs associated with technology use highlight the challenges for group members.

Part II: Components and Processes of Group Communication

The second major part of this book addresses components of and processes underlying group communication, which is an admittedly complex and broad topic. At base, group interaction is mutually influential; what one says or does is affected by and affects what others say and do (Bonito, 2002; Lehmann-Willenbrock & Allen, 2018; Solomon et al., 2021). In addition, the mutually influential character of group interaction, contextual features and participant characteristics play important roles in how group interaction unfolds and in the outcome of interest (Pavitt, 2014). Although Part II, and the book in general, focuses on decision-making groups, many of the same principles described throughout apply to other types of collectives, for example, social support groups and sports teams (Scheerhorn et al., 1994).

Part II has two sections. The first addresses the emergence and structure of small discussion groups, whereas the second focuses on process features. The circumstances under which a group forms or is created is an important factor in what it does and how it does it (Sanders, 2021). Some groups are created by institutions of various types. For example, the Sixth Amendment of the United States Constitution provides for trial by jury for the criminally accused, which means courts must assemble the requisite number of jurors to hear evidence and testimony, and then render a verdict. And many US universities use committees to determine whether a professor should be promoted and/or awarded tenure. Other groups emerge somewhat more organically, an example of which is a food co-op (Gastil, 1993) or most types of online support groups (e.g., Stack Exchange, which on its homepage states that "each of our 180 communities is built by people passionate about a focused topic").

Specifically, Hirokawa (Chapter 6) addresses group formation and its relationship to whether a group is successful, where success is defined by a goal attainment. Crucially, Hirokawa focuses on structures that either facilitate or hinder group performance and notes that some groups have to deal with the structure provided them (e.g., juries) and others have much more leeway in developing and maintaining structure (e.g., sports teams). In Chapter 7, Pilny and Riles address the system features that characterize groups, and describe how systemic thinking, compared to linear approaches, open new vistas for understanding what groups do and how they do it. McLeod and

Yuan (Chapter 8) address the increasingly important issue of diversity. In many ways, we are all the same and yet we are different, and some differences appear more salient than others in terms of how groups interact and make decisions. Managing differences is a key area for improving group dynamics and outcomes. The first section of Part II concludes with a discussion of leadership (Chapter 9). Connaughton, Lacy, and Gerdes treat communication as constitutive of leadership, which, in contrast to trait approaches (i.e., those who focus on individual characteristics that are more or less likely to result in leadership), assumes that leadership emerges from and is maintained by group interaction.

The second section of Part II focuses on group communication process, which has several dimensions. Black, Collins, and Saeed (Chapter 10) describe aspects of group conflict and note that conflict supports and improves group decision making under the right circumstances. Keyton and Beck's (Chapter 11) concern is with relationship communication, which complements task-based interaction; failure to adequately address the character and quality of intragroup relationships potentially creates problems (e.g., factions and negative conflict) that impede successful group decision making. Chapter 12, by van Swol, Chang, and Lu, evaluates process as the relationship between language and social influence. They describe several approaches to language analysis (e.g., language complexity) and assess whether and how language features persuade to support a given decision alternative. Wittenbaum and Bonito (Chapter 13) describe process in terms of participation and information. It is one thing to have important and valuable information to contribute to discussion, but it's quite another to actually present it during discussion. The chapter explores the conditions under which information quality and quantity might be usefully contributed to discussion.

Another interesting component of group communication process is the collaborative storage and retrieval of information, a topic explored by Bighash and Farzinpour in Chapter 14. In some cases, it makes sense for some members to know and/or remember a subset of necessary information to work on a task, and communication helps members to piece together who knows what about the problem. Reimer, Johnson, and Loaiza-Ramírez describe the contours of group decision making (Chapter 15). The chapter outlines how individuals combine their knowledge and preferences to form a group decision and introduces several combination-based and communication-based decision strategies that are used by groups. They consider a set of task features that make some decision strategies more or less likely.

The remaining two chapters in this part of the book address creativity and social networks. Groups are not often asked to be creative (e.g., juries) but others (R&D teams) exist precisely to generate novel ideas and solutions, a process addressed by Reiter-Palmon and Japp in Chapter 16. Although creativity is often thought of as an individual characteristic, the approach here is how communication facilitates innovation in certain types of groups. Finally, Lee and Benedict (Chapter 17) describe groups in terms of social networks, and show how connections among members influence communication processes and outcomes. Importantly, Lee and Benedict address intra- and intergroup networks, as groups typically do not operate in a vacuum. Instead, groups interact with outside entities in ways that influence communication processes and outcomes within the group.

Part III: Contexts of Group Communication

Groups frequently do things and often convene with an explicit purpose in mind. To explore what groups do, the remaining part of this book provides examples of some contexts in which groups function. While these contexts are just a sample, from these chapters we hope that it will be evident that groups are used for many purposes and are indispensable to our lives. The authors of the seven chapters in this part explain why it is critical for communication to be effective and efficient, and offer insights into how this can be achieved.

In Chapter 18, Garner discusses the central role that groups play in organizational settings. Employees often belong to workgroups that are embedded in organizations. An organization's rules (e.g., norms) and resources (e.g., assets and status) shape a workgroup, and the ways in which workgroup members use these structures during their interactions shape how workplace structures, identities, and experiences are (re)produced and construed. Thus, communication in these groups can be one important way for workers to develop a sense of meaning and identification with the organization. Many people spend much of their lives at work, so it is useful to consider who we become in these settings and how this occurs. Given the time spent working, it is also inevitable group members will experience conflict and tension. In this chapter, Garner describes why it is important to take advantage of conflict rather than to view it as something that must only be managed or avoided.

While Garner describes the reciprocal influence between groups and organizations, in Chapter 19, Reedy and Hurst discuss how groups can shape a democratic society. They describe how the desire for change can promote social movements and inspire collective action. They cover different ways that social movements can form and how collective identities can develop. These shared identities provide feelings of solidarity and unity and help offer members a sense of purpose and direction. Social groups and movements range in size though, so collective action can be difficult to achieve when effective coordination and communication seem out of reach. Fittingly, Reedy and Hurst describe ways that digital technology can be utilized to find likeminded people, organize, and meet online and offline. In their chapter, they also emphasize the importance of group discussions, and provide suggestions for how dialogue and deliberation can be structured to increase participation, offer citizens a voice, and promote feelings of inclusion.

Chapter 20 also goes beyond small groups and focuses on communities. More specifically, Foote and Hwang draw attention to online communities, which are relevant to societies today. The authors describe key attributes of online communities and how people engage and interact in these settings. They also address outcomes that result from involvement in these communities and how the experiences are both similar and different from other types of groups. Given the increasing rates of participation in online communities, Foote and Hwang persuasively make the case that researchers should be invested in studying these groups and offer suggestions for how this can be done.

Rains, in Chapter 21, focuses specifically on online health communities and describes how these groups can be a source of social support for people who are seriously ill. Rains provides an overview of his digital coping model and details how distress and suffering can be reduced through participation in these communities. Importantly, these online communities may be appealing to people who are suffering but cannot connect to others for various reasons (e.g., stigma and inaccessibility).

Chapter 22, by Tschan, Keller, Marsch, Beldi, and Semmer, emphasizes the importance of effective teamwork in medical teams. Medical teams often perform under time constraints with high levels of stress and small margins of error (e.g., ad-hoc emergency teams). Therefore, it is important and useful for scholars to research these teams and to offer insight into how their functioning can be improved. As an example, Tschan et al. provide an overview of different types of teams and outline the challenges and difficulties that they often face. The authors then draw from research on team effectiveness and illustrate how this knowledge can be applied to enhance communication and performance in medical teams.

Clearly, effective and efficient communication is beneficial to a range of groups and teams. In Chapter 23, Akpetou and Furley discuss communication in sports teams. Similar to teams in medicine, in sports it is often the case that group members do not have the time to engage in dialogue during competition. Furthermore, communicating explicitly and verbally at times is ill-advised. Similar to medical teams, sports teams often have to perform under pressure, and at competitive levels there is often a small margin error when performing. And like other groups and teams, it is important for members of sports teams to trust and be familiar with one another. Akpetou and

Furley suggest ways that group members can communicate verbally and nonverbally to achieve these outcomes.

The final chapter of this book offers insight into areas where group communication might be heading. In Chapter 24, Duan, McNeese, and Zhang focus on communication in Human-AI Teaming (HATs). As advances in artificial intelligence (AI) and machine learning are rapidly occurring, AI agents are increasingly being integrated into teams with humans. Therefore, to coordinate and function effectively, there is need to consider how communication between humans and AI agents occurs and how it can be enhanced. In what ways can existing knowledge on groups be applied to HATs, and to what extent is existing knowledge inapplicable? For example, trust between members is important to the functioning of most groups. Is trust between human and AI agents relevant to the functioning of HATs? Does it mean the same thing and is it established the same way?

To increase readability, all chapters of Parts II and III follow the same basic structure of an introduction, the description of objectives, theoretical background, evidence-based practical implications, and a conclusion. The evidence-based practical implications sections are meant to facilitate the application of the concepts described in chapters. Chapters explicitly mention the research methods that are used to study concepts and provide details regarding empirical study designs and findings. Moreover, each chapter addresses implications for technology use and the role of diversity in the development, maintenance, and functioning of groups. Beyond a coherent chapter structure, all chapters explicitly describe chapter objectives, provide an example or case illustrating a central concept displayed in a box, highlight some key terms that are described in a glossary, and list suggestions for further readings.

References

Beck, S., Keyton, J., & Poole, S. (Eds.). (2022). *The Emerald handbook of group and team communication research*. Emerald Publishing.

Bonito, J. A. (2002). The analysis of participation in small groups: Methodological and conceptual issues related to interdependence. *Small Group Research, 33*(4), 412–438. https://doi.org/10.1177/104649640203300402

Frey, L. R., Gouran, D. S., & Poole, M. S. (Eds.). (1999). *The handbook of group communication theory and research*. Sage.

Gastil, J. (1993). *Democracy in small groups*. New Society Publishers.

Hirokawa, R. Y., Cathcart, R. S., Samovar, L. A., & Henman, L. D. (Eds.). (2003). *Small group communication: Theory & practice: An anthology* (8th ed.). Oxford University Press.

Keyton, J., & Beck, S. (2017). *Communicating in groups and teams: Strategic interactions*. Cognella Academic Publishing.

Lehmann-Willenbrock, N., & Allen, J. A. (2018). Modeling temporal interaction dynamics in organizational settings. *Journal of Business and Psychology, 33*(3), 325–344. https://doi.org/10.1007/s10869-017-9506-9

Park, E. S., & Hinsz, V. B. (2006). "Strength and safety in numbers": A theoretical perspective on group influences on approach and avoidance motivation. *Motivation and Emotion, 30*, 135–142.

Pavitt, C. (2014). An interactive input–process–output model of social influence in decision-making groups. *Small Group Research, 45*(6), 704–730. https://doi.org/10.1177/1046496414548353

Reimer, T., Roland, C., & Russell, T. (2017). Groups and teams. In L. Lewis & C. Scott (Eds.), *International encyclopedia of organizational communication* (pp. 1–21). Wiley-Blackwell.

Sanders, R. E. (2021). *The work and workings of human communication*. Wiley-Blackwell.

Scheerhorn, D., Geist, P., & Teboul, J. B. (1994). Beyond decision making in decision-making groups: Implications for the study of group communication. In L. R. Frey (Ed.), *Group communication in context: Studies of natural groups* (pp. 247–262). Lawrence Erlbaum.

Solomon, D. H., Brinberg, M., Bodie, G. D., Jones, S., & Ram, N. (2021). A dynamic dyadic systems approach to interpersonal communication. *Journal of Communication, 71*(6), 1001–1026. https://doi.org/10.1093/joc/jqab035

Part I

Foundations of Group Communication

2 The Importance of Groups

Ernest S. Park

Chapter Objectives

- Provide examples of people working in groups and explain why groups might be utilized in these instances.
- Describe some ways that groups can differ from one another and explain how these differences might impact group dynamics and performance.
- Explain how similarity facilitates the formation and functioning of groups.

Before you read this chapter, I'd like you to pause, and take a moment to reflect and to think about a recent interaction that you had as a member of a group. Now visualize the people in this group and think about how they look, how they sound, and how they might tend to act. Focus on this specific encounter that you had with your group members and even relive the thoughts and feelings you experienced when you were together. What kinds of things were you talking about or doing? How did they end up making you feel?

Why Should People Care About Groups?

Now notice I didn't ask you *if* you could think of a recent group interaction; instead, I just assumed that you could. Why is that? As a species, humans display the attribute of **sociality**. In other words, we are social animals with the tendency to aggregate and to organize activities in groups (Dunbar & Shultz, 2007). So whether you happen to generally enjoy being in groups or not, it is likely that you are currently a member of several groups of different types and sizes. Groups play a prominent role in many domains of life, and it may even seem like they're everywhere. For many of us, when we're first brought into this world, we begin our lives as members of a family. From a young age, we start to play with others in small groups and somehow learn to seamlessly combine our imaginations. We often join teams to play sports or form bands to make music. Groups remain an inherent and prominent feature of our social lives as we age.

Similarly, in the domain of education, groups are utilized across grade levels to facilitate student learning, and to strengthen skills that are relevant to coordination and collaborative work (Calvo-Sastre, 2020). In the workplace, organizations continue to rely heavily upon task groups to generate innovative ideas and to solve pressing problems (Miron-Spektor et al., 2022) (see Chapter 18). Groups are so prevalent that it can be difficult to consume the daily news without encountering stories that feature group actions, whether they come from governmental committees, juries, military units, corporate boards, or various advocacy groups.

DOI: 10.4324/9781003227458-3

Life would be very different if group interactions were the exception rather than the rule. This was made abundantly clear to many people during the COVID-19 pandemic. Due to the highly contagious nature of this respiratory virus that spread across the globe, interactions with those outside of one's household came to be seen as hazardous. The group experiences that were so common in daily life were now a means of viral transmission. To mitigate the rapid spread of this viral threat, many governments decided to implement social distancing measures. This meant that people could no longer freely participate in the types of group interactions that they were accustomed to having on a regular basis.

As routines and regular contact with group members were upended during the pandemic, scholars began documenting a range of ways in which people's ability to function seemed to be disrupted. As one rather curious example, researchers noted that many people were finding it increasingly difficult to identify which day it was (Parks, 2020). Reports of this phenomenon, called "Blursday," has led some to suspect that regular participation in groups might be a thing that people often use to calibrate their internal clocks (e.g., our research group meets on Mondays; Thursday afternoons are for my meetings with co-editors). Group involvement might be so anticipated and integrated into routines that when these social markers are suddenly removed, some people might struggle to find equivalent replacements to represent aspects of time.

For many people who refrained from group activities during imposed lockdowns, the pandemic was also rife with prolonged feelings of isolation and loneliness. Reports from several countries indicated increases in anxiety, depression, stress and substance abuse, along with decreases in well-being and optimism (Marmarosh et al., 2020). So, on one hand, the pandemic made people reluctant to gather in person and to interact in groups. On the other hand, by being deprived of group involvement, the pandemic helped highlight just how much people need and desire group interactions. In the throes of the pandemic, this appreciation for groups could be seen as people of all ages and walks of life took steps to familiarize themselves with the notion of virtual groups. The world witnessed a widespread willingness to seek out and adopt online event platforms such as Zoom or Skype (Parks, 2020). And over time, people started to come up with ways to provide group experiences virtually, like through Zoom meetings, therapy groups, happy hours, and game nights.

In many ways, the negative outcomes associated with disengagement from face-to-face groups is not too surprising. Nor is the gravitation towards highly virtual groups as potential surrogates (Yan et al., 2019). After all, as humans, we have evolved to be social animals with a fundamental need to belong, so group involvement is inextricably linked to our nature and way of life (Baumeister & Leary, 1995). This means people have an innate motivation to form enduring interpersonal relationships, and that this sense of belongingness is often manifested in the desire to affiliate with and be accepted by members of a group. And while people may vary in the general number of attachments that are required to feel sated, it is this universal interpersonal motive that makes humans inherently social. It is this social nature that often leads people to find isolation threatening and quarantining aversive; to seek out and affiliate with others rather than to endure prolonged seclusion.

But why is it important or informative to see ourselves as social animals? And how or why did we get to be this way? When exploring the origins of human nature, it can be useful to draw upon the theory of evolution (Darwin, 1859). Evolution by natural selection suggests that heritable traits that enable organisms to survive and reproduce in particular contexts will generally be passed down to subsequent offspring (Buss, 1995). Put bluntly, when the expression of genetic-based tendencies leads to increased opportunities to mate (e.g., sociality), mating is more likely to occur. And when sexual reproduction does happen, those very same traits that helped make one a more attractive and viable sexual partner are then likely to be inherited by resultant offspring.

To put this into context, try to imagine what life was like for humans long ago. Without the benefits of modern technology and the many conveniences that surround people today, daily life for early humans was probably full of hardships and uncertainty. A lot of work, planning, persistence, and luck would be required for an individual to survive. Even if one could survive, the amount of effort and labor needed to find a mate, procreate, and then raise children in inhospitable environments is hard to really fathom. But given the variability that often exists within populations, some early humans probably had an easier time with survival and procreation than others. More specifically, our early ancestors who had the desire to belong to groups would have been more likely than their less sociable contemporaries to succeed in these ways (Brewer & Caporael, 1990).

Importantly, the concept of belonging goes beyond the initial step of just joining a group; it also presumes the willingness and ability to maintain one's affiliation and meaningful relationships as a group member. A person's place in the group is usually more secure when they are deemed to be a good group member, and relationships will be more fulfilling when they have the acceptance and approval of others. To be a good group member and to maintain satisfying relationships, people need to be accepting of **interdependence**. Interdependence, or mutual dependence, refers to the notion that members are yoked together and depend on one another to some degree (and perhaps to different degrees). This means that group members' outcomes, and their thoughts, feelings, behaviors, and experiences are somewhat influenced by others in the group (Forsyth, 2019). Interdependence connects groups members to one another in various ways and makes people more invested in, interested in, and attentive to one another (Rusbult & Van Lange, 2003).

To understand why interdependence needs to be accepted to belong to groups, it's helpful to start with the assumption that people join groups for a reason. People often have motives or goals that they can't satisfy or meet by themselves (e.g., social approval and acceptance; and safety from large predators), so they need to enlist the help of other people. In this sense, a group forms and a group exists because the group members are reliant on one another to fulfill various needs and to achieve various goals. When joining groups, people are entering an implicit social contract that acknowledges that their outcomes will necessarily be affected to some degree by their group members and the interactions they have together. They accept that they will necessarily be influenced by others in the group. This is what group members are signing up for. After all, if one doesn't have to depend on others to meet their needs and goals, and if one doesn't want to be affected by others in any way, why bother being in a group? So, group membership inherently requires a willingness to be mutually dependent and mutually influenced.

For some people, interdependence is not necessarily easy to tolerate because it requires group members to sacrifice some degree of freedom or autonomy (Eidelson, 1980). As individuals, people might be completely independent and have freedom from control by another person. But while being completely free and unconstrained by others may feel liberating at times, a downside of being untethered is that one must forgo the benefits of group involvement (e.g., sense of belonging and shared resources). You might imagine if people long ago were extremely resistant to interdependent arrangements, they probably would have been undesirable group members. They would have rejected connectedness and refused to endorse group goals when these conflicted with their personal goals. They would rarely accommodate or compromise. People who were unable or unwilling to enter interdependent relationships would have had little interest in belonging to groups and would have likely been expelled rather quickly after joining.

People who were not willing to be interdependent or cooperative would not have survived for very long on their own. Furthermore, they wouldn't be desirable mates or responsible caregivers if they had any offspring. This line of reasoning suggests that the genetic make-up of people who were not sociable or cooperative would gradually become less represented in the human gene pool, and early humans like this would not be our primary source of ancestry (Boyd & Richerson, 1992).

In contrast, humans long ago who had the need to belong and who had minds that were suited for ongoing and interdependent relationships – those predisposed for empathy, social interaction, communication, and cooperation – would have had survival and reproductive advantages (Levinson, 2006). By forming and utilizing small groups, people who were social and cooperative could coordinate their efforts to accomplish laborious survival tasks that might be exceedingly difficult for a lone individual (e.g., hunting or foraging for food when availability is scarce) (Kameda & Tindale, 2006). People who were sociable, or gregarious, would have inevitably had more access to potential mates and mating opportunities than those who preferred a completely independent or solitary life. Furthermore, the former would have had access to the resources of "a village" to help raise their offspring to eventual maturity. This would only increase the likelihood that the genes underlying these adaptive traits would be passed on from one generation to the next.

Since sociality seems to have been adaptive, it should be expected that people today have a desire to belong and are equipped for interactions and interdependence (Kurzban & Leary, 2001). People should be susceptible to the influence of others and cooperative tendencies should emerge readily. Some support for this evolutionary narrative can be found in theory and research on the "social brain" (e.g., Adolphs, 2009). This line of work proposes that many mental processes and corresponding neural circuits were shaped by the social lifestyle of our species, and that their functions can be interpreted accordingly.

Perhaps one way to observe our uncanny receptiveness to the influence of others is through phenomena like interactional synchrony or mimicry. Interactional synchrony occurs when the movements of interacting individuals become organized in time and space. When this occurs in groups, members become coordinated temporally, whether their actions are similar or complementary (e.g., a crew team where rowers alternate strokes). Mimicry refers to replication, and instances when two or more interacting individuals perform the same or similar actions (e.g., marching in step). There are nuanced differences between these concepts that make them distinct, but that discussion is beyond the scope of this chapter (see Richardson et al., 2005, for details). For current purposes, the similarities between these phenomena are more relevant.

Interactional synchrony and mimicry often occur spontaneously and readily, and often without conscious intention. For example, when people walk alongside each other, they often adopt similar strides and often do so without awareness (Semin & Cacioppo, 2008). A similar effect was shown in a study that had participants seated side by side with pendulums attached to each of their wrists. They were instructed to each swing their pendulums at their own preferred, comfortable tempos while looking directly at each other. Despite these instructions to maintain their own tempos, a spontaneous self-organizing dynamic emerged and movements of their pendulums became synchronized (Richardson et al., 2005). Research also shows that during conversations, interacting individuals tend to converge in dialect (Giles et al., 1991), speaking rate (Street, 1984) and pausing frequency (Cappella & Planalp, 1981) (see Chapter 12 for more examples). Furthermore, when two people are engaged in dialogue, they also often mirror or mimic each other's facial expressions or gestures (Condon & Sander, 1974).

When people have a desire to affiliate, behavioral matching is more likely to occur. But interestingly, as people reflexively influence each other in these ways, they experience increases in rapport, liking, trust, and the willingness to help one another (e.g., Miles et al., 2009; Wiltermuth & Heath, 2009). Moving and thinking together in time binds people together and fosters cooperation, empathy, and reciprocal exchange (Haidt et al., 2008). If humans evolved to be social and group-oriented, it makes sense that we would have the innate tendency to be so receptive to the input of interaction partners and to coordinate movements so readily. It also makes sense that convergence would be associated with bonding and cohesion.

In addition to movements, communication patterns, and gestures, research has also shown that physiology and brain activity can spontaneously align as people interact. For example, research shows that a coupling of parent's and child's physiology and behavior occurs during early parent–child interactions, and this bio-behavioral synchronization is associated with social bonding (Feldman, 2012). More recent research has documented neural (brain-to-brain) synchrony in parent–child dyads when they are mutually engaged in a task (e.g., Reindl et al., 2018). This is theorized to reflect similar cognitive processes in both brains and is thought to promote not only bonding but also learning and cooperation during tasks with a common goal.

So, even from infancy, humans reflexively display a range of tendencies that promote collaboration and coordination. We have evolved to be sociable and are inclined to be open to others' influences. When we communicate, we display a truth bias or rely on a default presumption that what people are telling us is true (Levine, 2014). We are psychologically and biologically equipped for a social life that involves interdependence and cooperation. And because we have evolved to value groups and our group memberships, we tend to be hypersensitive to threats of social rejection.

If we have evolved to be social, it would be adaptive for humans to know when their membership or good standing in a group is in jeopardy. It would be advantageous to be vigilant to cues of social disapproval because if someone was in jeopardy of being removed from the group, knowing this would allow someone to respond in ways that make expulsion less likely.

If, on the other hand, one was oblivious or aloof to the disapproval of others, one would be less likely to enact the type of changes that might secure or improve their social standing. So as social animals, we can expect that when we face the prospects of isolation or expulsion from groups, our initial responses will be automatic and reflexive. Reactions are likely to be visceral and negative to alert us of this pressing situation that requires our attention.

Empirical evidence supports this reasoning. Research shows that when people feel ignored by group members, the cardiovascular, hormonal, and immune systems reflexively activate in ways that allow one to confront social rejection (Stroud et al., 2000). When group members say mean things, express disapproval, or make others feel left out, the recipients of these exclusion messages often feel *hurt* or *wounded*. These targets of social rejection show increased activity in the dorsal anterior cingulate cortex (dACC) and the anterior insula, two areas of the brain that are also associated with the sensation of physical pain (Eisenberger et al., 2003). These biological reactions perhaps explain why we commonly use descriptors like "sore," "hurt feelings," or "heartache" to express sentiments of social rejection, disconnection, and isolation.

More recent research using electroencephalography (EEG) recordings found that when participants were exposed to a series of statements, including verbal insults featuring their name (e.g., "[participant's name] is an idiot"), brain activity in areas related to emotional attention was greater than when participants were exposed to compliments (Struiksma et al., 2022). This effect was robust over repetition, suggesting that participants did not become less alarmed or desensitized to the lexical "slaps in the face" that they encountered. Findings across studies show that people are "wired" to be sensitive to rejection, and that we respond to these types of insults and threatening communication with heightened attention and negative arousal. In contrast, when people receive messages of inclusion and social acceptance, heart rate and blood pressure decrease, and levels of oxytocin (a neuropeptide and hormone that among other things, is associated with feelings of trust and the desire for social bonding) rise in some people (Taylor, 2006).

I began this chapter asking, "Why should people care about groups?" Well, a wide range of evidence suggests that we are genetically predisposed to belong to groups and are inclined to be cooperative group members. These drives are defining features of who we are as human beings. We would not be here if we did not belong to groups and we would not have a future if we cease to utilize groups. With their prevalence and inherent connections to human life, people should be invested in knowing how to make groups thrive. From a scholarly standpoint, I would argue that it behooves us to study groups, and to try to thoroughly understand how groups operate, how groups influence us, and how we influence the groups that we belong to. By knowing groups, we can know more about ourselves. But how do we go about deepening our understanding of these important social entities? What types of things should we learn and know?

From the perspective of a social animal, one reasonable approach to addressing such questions involves a focus on communication. It is hard to imagine how individuals can come together and form a group and exist as a group without communication. Even if this were possible, it hardly seems desirable or worthwhile. But as you will see, throughout this book the collection of authors will demonstrate how groups and communication are integrally intertwined. To appreciate the role that communication plays throughout a wide range of group experiences, I will use the remainder of this chapter to offer an overview of foundational concepts that will provide some context for the remaining chapters. I will start with definitions and will then describe select features of groups that may help set the stage for the more substantive chapters that follow.

What Is a Group?

Perhaps unsurprisingly, different scholars have different views on how to define a group. Still, it can be useful to attend to the commonalities that emerge across viewpoints and to the ways in which the varying conceptualizations tend to complement one another. Rather than trying to determine if a particular definition is right or wrong, it might be more productive to appreciate the different facets of groups that are being highlighted and to notice how multiple paths can be taken to address the same question.

So, starting with its most basic form, a group can be defined as "two or more individuals who are connected by and within social relationships" (e.g., Forsyth, 2019, p. 3). But because different dynamics and meaningful distinctions have been noted to exist between dyads and groups (e.g., dyads cannot have subgroups, or numerical majority and minority factions), some theorists find it is useful to maintain a distinction between a dyad and a group. Thus, some see a group as having at least three members (e.g., Moreland, 2010; Tasca, 2020).

While size may matter at times, the number of members is clearly not the only aspect that people consider. For example, some believe that for a group to exist it is important for the group members to "… perceive themselves to be members of the same social category" (Turner, 1982, p. 15). If we are in a group, we should be able to know who "we" are and who is one of "us." Along these lines, scholars also suggest that these people who are bonded with a common social identity and exist as a group should be able to be recognized as such by others (Brown, 2000). In other words, "they" should be able to tell that "we" are in a group and "they're" not one of "us."

As discussed previously, *mutual dependence* is also often emphasized and thought to be a prominent feature. So, a group could be seen as "three or more people who work together interdependently on an agreed-upon activity or goal" (e.g., Keyton, 2002, p. 5). Having a shared purpose, goal or fate is arguably one feature that makes a group different from a mere collection of individuals (e.g., several strangers waiting at the same bus stop). Importantly, to pursue a shared goal or to complete a shared task, communication is often required. Thus, some scholars see communication as being inherently linked to groups and define a group as "three or more people … who (a) think of themselves as a group, (b) are interdependent (e.g., with regard to shared goals or behaviors that affect one another), and (c) communicate (interact) with one another (via face-to-face or technological means)" (Frey & Konieczka, 2010, p. 317).

When people see themselves as a group and care about their group membership, they become even more susceptible to the influence of other group members. In other words, when group membership has psychological significance, people are motivated to maintain their status of inclusion – they want to remain a group member. As discussed previously, to belong to a group it's important that people accept the conditions of interdependence. It also helps to be accepted by group members, which means gaining their approval and avoiding their disapproval. To the extent that people cannot act freely because they are concerned about how other group members will respond, those group members have influence. They are exerting some degree of control and are influencing what someone in the group does or doesn't do. But if this is what group members are signing up for, perhaps another major feature of a group is *mutual influence.*

In this sense, a group can be characterized as "two or more persons who are interacting with one another in such a manner that each person influences and is influenced by each other person" (Shaw, 1981, p. 454). A group exists when a bond connects group members to one another and to the group itself, but it should be noted that these links and potential paths of influence do not need to be equally strong across members or relationships. For better-or-for-worse, sometimes specific members might display an outsized amount of influence, like when someone occupies a leadership position or when a few group members are involved in an escalating conflict that disrupts the ability of the entire group to function.

Are There Different Types of Groups?

To help organize our knowledge, some scholars have developed specific labels that can be used to distinguish different types of meaningful groups from one another. The term, primary group, is used to describe a small, enduring group whose members are relatively intimate and closely connected (Cooley, 1909). Some groups are designated as primary because these groups often exert substantial influence on the lives of their members (e.g., offer protection, care, and sustenance; and transmit beliefs and ideals), and they are thought to play a vital role in transforming individuals into social beings (i.e., one's sense of self expands and incorporates the concept of "we"; language is often introduced) (Forsyth, 2019). Common examples of primary groups often include families and sets of close friends. Members of primary groups are highly interdependent and tend to interact frequently and for relatively long periods of time. As in the case of families, membership in a primary group is not necessarily voluntary or something that is chosen.

As noted, earlier generations of humans survived by banding together in relatively small primary groups. As these groups lived in proximity to one another, they probably took on the form of tribes or small communities. Presumably, living in these ways made it easier for humans not only to survive but also to thrive. That said, as the size of communities grew some aspects of life probably became more complex and complicated. To maintain a larger community, some type of social structure is generally required. As a consequence, the need to interact and work with others outside of one's primary group would have increased, and interactions with a wider range of people would have become more frequent. To help structure and organize these interactions with less familiar others, some suggest that people started to form social groups (also called secondary groups or task groups) (Forsyth, 2019).

Compared to primary groups, social groups are more formally organized and structured, and members are less committed to the group and their relationships. Membership tends to be more transitory, and boundaries for these groups tend to be more porous and fluid than those of primary groups. Examples of social groups might include work groups, committees, medical units (see Chapter 22), and sports teams (see Chapter 23). When group research is conducted on a college campus using a student sample, the researcher often tries to simulate relevant "real-world" conditions and dynamics in their laboratory setting. They often do this so findings from their student sample can be generalized to some type of target social group (e.g., hiring committee and jury) (see Chapter 4).

While primary and social groups tend to be relatively small, a collective often describes a larger assemblage or gathering of individuals. Collectives can form when people congregate for some event or activity (e.g., protesters gathering for a march). Members of collectives are often bonded through some common interest or shared action, but bonds and commitment tend to be weaker in comparison to smaller groups. With the latter, members are more likely to interact directly and be familiar with one another. But because collectives are often large and can dissolve quickly and rather easily, members of collectives are not expected to all know each other. A social movement (e.g., BLM; see Chapter 19) would qualify as an example of a collective. These larger groups form and act in response to some shared purpose, but then often dissipate once the defining activity terminates or their shared cause becomes obsolete.

It is important to note that despite having weaker relational ties, larger groups like collectives can still have a profound impact on their members. A range of theoretical frameworks suggest that groups both small and large can influence their members and prompt them to think and act in ways that seem "out of character" for the individual (e.g., Hogg & Terry, 2000; Park & Hinsz, 2006). For example, during the insurrection that occurred at the U.S. Capitol on January 6, 2022, large numbers of Americans gathered to attend a protest under the banner of "Stop the Steal." Most of the attendees were thought to generally be law-abiding citizens. Yet as they gathered en masse, they seemed to influence one another in what are generally undesirable ways and collectively stormed and ransacked the U.S. Capitol (Winget & Park, 2022).

The last type of a group that will be discussed here is called a social category. A social category might be more accurately described as a perceptual grouping of people rather than a group. In essence, it simply refers to a collection of individuals who seem to share something in common, such as a feature or attribute (e.g., people enrolled in classes are called students and citizens of the United States are called Americans). But a social category can become the basis of group when it has social significance and prompts a personal or interpersonal process. For example, if Eve goes to class or does her homework because she is a student, or if Adam generally prefers Americans to Canadians, the respective categories of student and American are socially meaningful. When applied, social categories can systematically shape how people think, feel, and behave. But how and why do some social categories have these types of influences?

Categories offer people a way to assign a sense of meaning to their experiences. One way this occurs is by allowing people to make distinctions between those things that belong to the category and those things that do not. So, for categories to have utility they need to have boundaries that can be used to make these perceptual decisions. Imagine Adam has formed a conceptualization of what it means to be an American. This mental representation will only be useful if some people in the world can be perceived to be Americans while others are not. If everyone was always and only seen as being American, the term would serve no purpose. It wouldn't offer the ability to make functional distinctions between members of our species. But if Adam has a representation of this category called American, this infers he has some basis for deciding who does and does not belong to this grouping. On some level, he has devised a way to define what it means to be an American or what Americans are like.

When people are members of a social category, they have a sense of who is in their category and who is not, and to some degree, they have a sense of what they and the other people in their category are like. When people are members of the same social category (e.g., American), they often share a common identity (e.g., we are Americans). And when people perceive themselves to be members of the same group or social category, they may develop a social identity. A social identity represents a person's sense of self that is rooted in their relationships and memberships in groups (see Chapter 8). It reflects the aspects of the self that are thought to be shared by most of the other members of that same group or social category (Tajfel, 1974).

So, if Adam has a social identity as an American, he is likely to see himself as possessing the defining qualities that he associates with Americans. And if American is an important aspect of who he is, Adam will be inclined to have a favorable view and bias towards fellow Americans compared to non-Americans. To Adam, fellow Americans would be included in the self-aspect that he references when he says "we" and "us" (while non-Americans would be represented as "they" and "them").

How Do Groups Operate and Function?

While there are different types of groups, there are some similarities that can be found across the variations. For example, like anything that can be categorized, groups have some type of boundary that is used to distinguish who belongs to the group and who does not. Those who belong to the group are often referred to as ingroup members, while those who do not are often called outgroup members. A group's boundaries can vary and be open or closed.

With open groups, group membership is more fluid and members are relatively free to stay or leave as they wish. A group can also be open when members are voted in or out, or when membership is determined on the basis of meeting some performance criterion (e.g., a player is cut from a baseball team). Given the relative fragility of membership status, open groups tend to be lower in cohesion than closed groups. This is in part because the types of forces that tend to keep members attracted to the group (e.g., relational bonds between members, perceived unity as a group, clarity of roles, shared commitment to achieve the group's task, perceived ability of the group to coordinate, and accomplish group goals) are not as strong.

On the other hand, closed groups are those with more stable compositions, whose memberships change more slowly (e.g., a city council; Barge & Keyton, 1994). Stable membership offers opportunities for members to become more familiar with one another and to form stronger social bonds. Since membership in the group is more secure and predictable, people are not as distracted by concerns about expulsion. So unhealthy competition and conflict between members tend to be lower in closed versus open groups, and members are freer to devote more of their attention and energy towards advancing the group's goals. Since members anticipate working together for longer periods of time in closed groups, their members are also more likely to identify with the group and tend to focus more on the collective than members of open groups. Communication and interdependencies tend to be more routinized, and the clarity that this provides for members helps to increase their attraction to the group.

As mentioned, groups are often assembled to perform tasks that individuals would struggle to complete by themselves. In order to create a group product or perform as a group, group members need to reach some degree of consensus in how they understand things. One reason group members are thought to develop social identities is because groups produce and have a shared psychological reality (Hogg & Abrams, 1993). So, group members often share an outlook or viewpoint and often hold particular attitudes in common. This may not be the case when members are assigned to groups (e.g., juries), especially when a quota system is used to select a diverse composition of group members.

But when groups are self-organizing and form more freely, people tend to seek out others who are similar in relevant ways. One reason this occurs is because people assume that interactions with similar others will be more cooperative and less contentious (e.g., Insko & Schopler, 1972). Similarity is also associated with connectedness and liking (Arkin & Burger, 1980). So, when people are free to self-organize into groups, **homophily** is often exhibited. Homophily refers to the tendency for individuals to associate and bond with others who are similar in some way ("birds of a feather flock together").

When groups are formed to complete tasks, group members often have a shared sense of purpose or common goals. These types of commonalities and sense of social sharedness are functional and can serve to unify the group. Even in cases where members are assigned to groups, social forces can accentuate sources of similarity across members as they interact. For example, when groups are newly formed and members are getting acquainted, they are often reluctant to exacerbate any existing awkwardness or tension by introducing conflict. Instead, group members often display consensus-seeking tendencies, are relatively compliant, and may focus discussion on areas of agreement and commonality (see Chapter 6). Likewise, group members might mention and repeat shared information that is known by all members, which can lead people to adopt similar views and preferences (see Chapter 13). These types of tendencies allow group members to converge so they are "on the same page" and group decisions and actions can then be easier to produce (e.g., Park et al., 2012).

To function effectively as a group, it is also important for members to develop shared mental models. Mental models are cognitive representations of a given construct. They are organized knowledge structures that allow individuals to interact with their environment and to describe, explain, and predict events. For example, a musician might have of mental model of a particular tune she has learned. This model serves as a cognitive representation of things she knows about the song and how to play it (e.g., what to do and when and anticipated challenges). Now imagine a musician is in a band and her group plans to play this song. Before this can happen, the other group members need to each have their own mental model of the tune as well.

Because the group members may have different histories and experiences with the song (e.g., heard different versions of it), at the individual level it's possible that the group members have different mental models of the piece. Group members might differ in their views or understandings of the song and how it should sound and be played (e.g., different expectations about tempo and tone and role of instruments). If members' mental models vary widely, it's likely they will have disagreements and misunderstandings. The group will experience difficulties coordinating and performing. So, to play this tune effectively as a group it's important that the band members develop shared mental models. Shared mental models are the knowledge, expectations, and representations that members of the group have in common.

There are several different types of shared mental models that are relevant to effective group performance (Cannon-Bowers & Salas, 2001). For example, it is often useful for group or team members to share mental models of the equipment or technology they might be using (e.g., how the equipment interacts with the input of team members) (see Chapter 5). It's useful for people to have shared mental models of the task (e.g., how to accomplish the task in terms of procedures and strategies). It is also important for group members to have a shared understanding of how the team interacts (e.g., roles, responsibilities, interaction patterns, and interdependencies) and shared mental models of group members (e.g., knowledge, skills, attitudes, preferences, strengths, weaknesses, and tendencies of individual members) (see Chapter 15). As one might imagine, communication and group interactions often play a vital role in fostering familiarity and the development of shared mental models. While it may take time and intention to develop shared mental models, when these are achieved, group members can be on the same page and coordinate. They can see and experience things in similar ways.

Importantly, when group members operate under a shared reality and pursue shared goals, their social identity is more likely to serve as a self-guide and basis of esteem. Group goals are likely to become prioritized over individual ones, and members are more likely to conform to group norms and adhere to the group's values. With the production of uniform and coherent group behaviors, the shared and social attributes that help unify the group become more noticeable. When group members converge and come together in this fashion, the group is characterized as being high in **entitativity**. Entitativity refers to the extent to which a group is perceived to be a single, unified entity rather than a collection of individual members. For example, a school of fish would be high in entitativity. When the observer perceives a school of fish, they are seeing and describing a single entity rather than perceiving all of the individual fish that make up this school.

Like a school of fish that moves in unison, entitativity for human groups also increases when members appear similar, move similarly, are close in proximity, and appear to act in pursuit of a common fate. For example, imagine a group of construction workers who are all intensely surveying a building's blueprint together to determine where additional support structures are needed. Are the people you're visualizing all wearing hard hats, or similar clothing? Are they all looking at the same piece of paper? Is it clear the people you're imagining are a group? If so, this group would appear high in entitativity. A unit of uniformed soldiers who are synchronized as they march in unison would be high in entitativity, as would a team of athletes who are huddled and swaying and chanting together before a game. When groups are perceived in this way, not only is cohesion increased, but in adversarial contexts they also appear more formidable and daunting to opponents and foes.

For groups to function and perform, group members have to not only be unified to some degree but they also have to interact and coordinate. To facilitate success, group members engage in task interactions and relationship interactions (Bales, 1950). Task interactions refer to the group behaviors that are focused on the work that the group must do to achieve its goal. For example, group members often have to define the problem or their goals, develop plans, and share information so that they can form shared understandings of their task and how they plan to accomplish it. When group members exchange information, they also often assist one another by detecting and correcting each other's errors and mistakes. As group members encourage and affirm one another and support one another through these types of interactions, their commitment to the group often increases.

However, when group interactions are only task-focused, groups become at risk for dissolution. Therefore, relationship interactions (sometimes called socioemotional interactions) also serve a vital function (see Chapter 11). These interactions serve to maintain or strengthen interpersonal bonds within the group. For example, when members feel dejected or experience evaluation apprehension, relationship interactions can be a source of validation and boost morale. Compliments and expressions of appreciation are common examples of relationship interactions.

In some groups with a division of labor, members take on specific roles. For example, one group member might adopt the position of task leader to move the group forward so tasks can be accomplished. Another might occupy the position of socioemotional leader to promote cohesion and diffuse tension, which ultimately reduces interpersonal conflicts (see Chapter 9). In some groups, a member might be assigned the role of devil's advocate. Given the tendency for group members to conform and converge, this position can be useful to implement. With this role, a group member is asked to be an active dissenter during group discussions so that arguments that are counter to the group's prevailing position are more likely to be expressed and can be considered. By being assigned this formal role, the group member does not have to be concerned with social disapproval when expressing healthy criticisms or dissent.

So as group members interact and identify with the group, tendencies converge and group actions become easier to perform. Commitment to the group and group goals increase and the group members resemble a single entity that can act in unison. This ability of individual group members to transform and act as a coordinated unit could not occur without a "social brain" – one who is adapted for cooperation and effective communication. In the remainder of this book, the central role that communication plays in the life and functioning of groups will be revealed.

Further Readings

Forsyth, D. R. (2021). Recent advances in the study of group cohesion. *Group Dynamics: Theory, Research, and Practice*, 25(3), 213–228.

Hinsz, V. B., Tindale, R. S., & Vollrath, D. A. (1997). The emerging conceptualization of groups as information processors. *Psychological Bulletin*, 121(1), 43–64.

Levine, J. M., Resnick, L. B., & Higgins, E. T. (1993). Social foundations of cognition. *Annual Review of Psychology, 44*, 585–612.

Glossary

Entitativity   The perception of being a single, unified entity rather than a set of independent and unrelated pieces.

Homophily   The tendency to seek out or associate and bond with similar others.

Interdependence   A state of mutual dependence or reliance; the ways in which individuals influence each other through their interactions.

Sociality   The urge or tendency to aggregate, associate in groups, and develop social connections.

References

Adolphs, R. (2009). The social brain: Neural basis of social knowledge. *Annual Review of Psychology, 60*, 693–716. https://www.doi.org/10.1146/annurev.psych.60.110707.163514

Arkin, R. M., & Burger, J. M. (1980). Effects of unit relation tendencies on interpersonal attraction. *Social Psychology Quarterly, 43*(4), 380–391. https://www.doi.org/10.2307/3033958

Bales, R. F. (1950). *Interaction process analysis: A method for the study of small groups.* Addison-Wiley.

Barge, J. K., & Keyton, J. (1994). Contextualizing power and social influence in groups. In L. R. Frey (Ed.), *Group communication in context: Studies of natural groups* (pp. 85–105). Lawrence Erlbaum Associates, Inc.

Baumeister, R. F., & Leary, M. R. (1995). The need to belong: Desire for interpersonal attachments as a fundamental human motivation. *Psychological Bulletin, 117*(3), 497–529. https://www.doi.org/10.1037/0033-2909.117.3.497

Boyd, R., & Richerson, P. J. (1992). Punishment allows the evolution of cooperation (or anything else) in sizable groups. *Ethology & Sociobiology, 13*(3), 171–195. https://www.doi.org/10.1016/0162-3095(92)90032-Y

Brewer, M. B., & Caporael, L. R. (1990). Selfish genes vs. selfish people: Sociobiology as origin myth. *Motivation and Emotion, 14*(4), 237–243. https://www.doi.org/10.1007/BF00996182

Brown, R. (2000). *Group processes* (2nd ed.). Blackwell.

Buss, D. M. (1995). Evolutionary psychology: A new paradigm for psychological science. *Psychological Inquiry, 6*(1), 1–13. https://www.doi.org/10.1207/s15327965pli0601_1

Calvo-Sastre, A. (2020). Teaching social education with and through groups. *Social Work With Groups, 43*(3), 227–240. https://www.doi.org/10.1080/01609513.2019.1593918

Cannon-Bowers, J. A., & Salas, E. (2001). Reflections on shared cognition. *Journal of Organizational Behavior, 22*(2), 195–202. https://www.doi.org/10.1002/job.82

Cappella, J. N., & Planalp, S. (1981). Talk and silence sequences in informal conversations III: Interspeaker influences. *Human Communication Research, 7*(2), 117–132.

Condon, W. S., & Sander, L. W. (1974). Neonate movement is synchronized with adult speech: Interactional participation and language acquisition. *Science, 183*(4120). https://www.doi.org/10.1126/science.183.4120.99

Cooley, C. H. (1909). *Social organization.* Scribner.

Darwin, C. (1859). *On the origin of the species by means of natural selection.* Murray.

Dunbar, R. I. M., & Shultz, S. (2007). Evolution in the social brain. *Science, 317*(5843), 1344–1347. https://www.doi.org/10.1126/science.1145463

Eidelson, R. J. (1980). Interpersonal satisfaction and level of involvement: A curvilinear relationship. *Journal of Personality and Social Psychology, 39*(3), 460–470. https://www.doi.org/10.1037/0022-3514.39.3.460

Eisenberger, N. I., Lieberman, M. D., & Williams, K. D. (2003). Does rejection hurt? An fMRI study of social exclusion. *Science, 302*(5643), 290–292. https://www.doi.org/10.1126/science.1089134

Feldman, R. (2012). Oxytocin and social affiliation in humans. *Hormones and Behavior, 61*(3), 380–391. https://www.doi.org/10.1016/j.yhbeh.2012.01.008

Forsyth, D. R. (2019). *Group dynamics* (7th ed.). Cengage.

Frey, L. R., & Konieczka, S. P. (2010). Group identity. In R. L. Jackson (Ed.), *Encyclopedia of identity* (Vol. 1, pp. 316–319). Sage.

Giles, H., Coupland, N., & Coupland, J. (1991). Accommodation theory: Communication, context, and consequence. In H. Giles (Ed.), *Contexts of accommodation: Developments in applied sociolinguistics* (pp. 1–68). Cambridge University Press.

Haidt, J., Seder, J. P., & Kesebir, S. (2008). Hive psychology, happiness, and public policy. *Journal of Legal Studies*, *37*(2), 133–156.

Hogg, M. A., & Abrams, D. (1993). Towards a single-process uncertainty-reduction model of social motivation in groups. In M. A. Hogg & D. Abrams (Eds.), *Group motivation: Social psychological perspectives* (pp. 173–190). Harvester Wheatsheaf.

Hogg, M. A., & Terry, D. J. (2000). Social identity and self-categorization processes in organizational contexts. *The Academy of Management Review*, *25*(1), 121–140.

Insko, C. A., & Schopler, J. (1972). *Experimental social psychology*. Academic Press.

Kameda, T., & Tindale, R. S. (2006). Groups as adaptive devices: Human docility and group aggregation mechanisms in evolutionary context. In M. Schaller, J. A. Simpson, & D. T. Kenrick (Eds.), *Evolution in social psychology* (pp. 317–341). Psychosocial Press.

Keyton, J. (2002). *Communicating in groups: Building relationships for effective decision making*. McGraw-Hill.

Kurzban, R., & Leary, M. R. (2001). Evolutionary origins of stigmatization: The functions of social exclusion. *Psychological Bulletin*, *127*(2), 187–208. https://www.doi.org/10.1037/0033-2909.127.2.187

Levine, T. R. (2014). Truth-default theory (TDT): A theory of human deception and deception detection. *Journal of Language and Social Psychology*, *33*(4), 378–392. https://www.doi.org/10.1177/0261927X14535916

Levinson, S. (2006). Cognition at the heart of human interaction. *Discourse Studies*, *8*(1), 85–93. https://www.doi.org/10.1177/1461445606059557

Marmarosh, C. L., Forsyth, D. R., Strauss, B., & Burlingame, G. M. (2020). The psychology of the COVID-19 pandemic: A group-level perspective. *Group Dynamics: Theory, Research, and Practice*, *24*(3), 122–138. https://www.doi.org/10.1037/gdn0000142

Miles, L. K., Nind, L. K., & Macrae, C. N. (2009). The rhythm of rapport: Interpersonal synchrony and social perception. *Journal of Experimental Social Psychology*, *45*(3), 585–589. https://www.doi.org/10.1016/j.jesp.2009.02.002

Miron-Spektor, E., Emich, K. J., Argote, L., & Smith, W. K. (2022). Conceiving opposites together: Cultivating paradoxical frames and epistemic motivation fosters team creativity. Organizational Behavior and Human Decision Processes. Advance online publication. https://www.doi.org/10.1016/j.obhdp.2022.104153

Moreland, R. L. (2010). Are dyads really groups? *Small Group Research*, *41*(2), 251–267. https://www.doi.org/10.1177/1046496409358618

Park, E. S., & Hinsz, V. B. (2006). "Strength and safety in numbers": A theoretical perspective on group influences on approach and avoidance motivation. *Motivation and Emotion*, *30*(2), 135–142. https://www.doi.org/10.1007/s11031-006-9024-y

Park, E. S., Tindale, R. S., & Hinsz, V. B. (2012). Interpersonal cognitive consistency and the sharing of cognition in groups. In B. Gawronski & F. Strack (Eds.), *Cognitive consistency: A fundamental principle in social cognition* (pp. 445–466). Guilford Press.

Parks, C. D. (2020). Group dynamics when battling a pandemic. *Group Dynamics: Theory, Research, and Practice*, *24*(3), 115–121. https://www.doi.org/10.1037/gdn0000143

Reindl, V., Gerloff, C., Scharke, W., & Konrad, K. (2018). Brain-to-brain synchrony in parent-child dyads and the relationship with emotion regulation revealed by fNIRS-based hyperscanning. *Neuroimage*, *178*, 493–502. https://www.doi.org/10.1016/j.neuroimage.2018.05.060

Richardson, M. J., Marsh, K. J., & Schmidt, R. C. (2005). Effects of visual and verbal interaction on unintentional interpersonal coordination. *Journal of Experimental Psychology: Human Perception and Performance*, *31*(1), 62–79. https://www.doi.org/10.1037/0096-1523.31.1.62

Rusbult, C. E., & Van Lange, P. A. M. (2003). Interdependence, interaction, and relationships. *Annual Review of Psychology*, *54*, 351–375. https://www.doi.org/10.1146/annurev.psych.54.101601.145059

Semin, G. R., & Cacioppo, J. T. (2008). Grounding social cognition: Synchronization, coordination, and co-regulation. In G. R. Semin & E. R. Smith (Eds.), *Embodied grounding: Social, cognitive, affective, and neuroscientific approaches* (pp. 119–147). Cambridge University Press. https://www.doi.org/10.1017/CBO9780511805837.006

Shaw, M. E. (1981). *Group dynamics: The psychology of small group behavior* (3rd ed.). McGraw-Hill.

Street, R. L. (1984). Speech convergence and speech evaluation in fact-finding interviews. *Human Communication Research*, *11*(2), 139–169. https://www.doi.org/10.1111/j.1468-2958.1984.tb00043.x

Stroud, L. R., Tanofsky-Kraff, M., Willfley, D. E., & Salovey, P. (2000). The Yale Interpersonal Stressor (YIP): Affective, physiological, and behavioral responses to a novel interpersonal rejection paradigm. *Annals of Behavioral Medicine*, *22*(3), 204–213. https://www.doi.org/10.1007/BF02895115

Struiksma, M. E., De Mulder, H. N. M., & Van Berkum, J. J. A. (2022). Do people get used to insulting language? *Frontiers in Communication*, *7*, 1–21. https://www.doi.org/10.3389/fcomm.2022.910023

Tajfel, H. (1974). Social identity and intergroup behavior. *Social Science Information*, *13*, 65–93.

Tasca, G. A. (2020). What is group dynamics? *Group Dynamics: Theory, Research, and Practice*, *24*(1), 1–5. https://www.doi.org/10.1037/gdn0000115

Taylor, S. E. (2006). Tend and befriend: Biobehavioral bases of affiliation under stress. *Current Directions in Psychological Science*, *15*(6), 273–277. https://www.doi.org/10.1111/j.1467-8721.2006.00451.x

Turner, J. C. (1982). Toward a cognitive redefinition of the social group. In H. Tajfel (Ed.), *Social identity and intergroup behavior* (pp. 15–40). Cambridge University Press.

Wiltermuth, S. S., & Heath, C. (2009). Synchrony and cooperation. *Psychological Science*, *20*(1), 1–5. https://www.doi.org/10.1111/j.1467-9280.2008.02253.x

Winget, J. R., & Park, E. S. (2022). Discharged in D.C.: The role of disinhibition in the behavior of insurrection group members. *Group Dynamics: Theory, Research, and Practice*, *26*(3), 252–262. https://www.doi.org/10.1037/gdn0000182

Yan, B., Kim, Y. J., Hollingshead, A. B., & Brandon, B. P. (2019). Conceptualizing online groups as multidimensional networks. In A. Attrill-Smith, C. Fullwood, M. Keep, & D. J. Kuss (Eds.), *The Oxford handbook of cyberpsychology* (pp. 306–327). Oxford University Press.

3 Group Communication Theories

Guidelines for Their Application

Torsten Reimer, Christopher Roland, and Jeonghyun Oh

Chapter Objectives

- Reflect upon the role of metacognition in the application of group communication theories in everyday groups and teams.
- Identify and describe the processes and functions of monitoring and control processes in groups.
- Apply the META mnemonic (*M*onitor, *E*xplain, *T*est, and *A*ssess) in group communication contexts.

Introduction

The study of group communication has a long history, with roots in several fields of research, including communication, psychology, and sociology (Frey, 1996; Gouran, 1999). Group communication scholarship has generated a number of highly influential and well-studied approaches, such as the input-process-output framework (Hinsz et al., 1997; Ilgen et al., 2005; Reimer et al., 2017; see Chapter 12), structuration theory (Poole et al., 2022; see Chapter 7), and social network approaches (Pilny & Poole, 2017; see Chapter 17), which are described and compared in several overviews on group communication theories (e.g., Frey et al., 1999; Gouran, 1999; Poole, 1999; Poole et al., 2022; see also Forsyth, 2018). Rather than summarizing successful individual research programs, frameworks, and theories, this chapter lays out some guidelines for the *application* of group communication theories, including the theories and models that are covered in this textbook. We would like to invite readers to approach the chapters of this book by asking several theory-related questions that highlight different vantage points: On what theoretical assumptions is a given chapter based? Which methods were used to test the theoretical assumptions or hypotheses? What empirical evidence supports the described theories? What contributions does the described research add to the theoretical body of knowledge about group communication? In addition – and this is the focus of this chapter – we would like to invite readers to think about ways the theories they read about can be applied in their daily group lives. The quest is to find ways to utilize the described theories in a way that improves group communication and helps groups achieve their goals. In line with Kurt Lewin's famous saying that *there is nothing so practical as a good theory* (Lewin, 1951), knowledge about group communication scholarship can help group members improve the functioning of their groups by providing the foundation for structuring group processes and informing interventions that are based on sound principles and evidence-based research.

In the remainder of this chapter, we will briefly describe some basic considerations of what constitutes a theory. One way to approach the body of scholarship in an area is to learn about the jargon that is used and the topics that have been studied. We emphasize this aspect by referring to some key concepts of group communication research that have been developed over a long period

DOI: 10.4324/9781003227458-4

of time and by outlining some basic approaches to group communication scholarship. Looking at theories from a practitioner's perspective begs questions about their *applicability*. The main part of our chapter discusses the application of group communication theories from the vantage point of **metacognition**, which plays a pivotal role in theory application. Metacognition in groups may be construed as the knowledge group members have about their group and their task, and as the way group members monitor and control their group discussions and actions.

We summarize some general insights about the role of metacognition in group functioning and communication and formulate five principles that inform guidelines for theory application. Some of the provided guidelines are general and apply to other fields of inquiry, whereas others are specific to the domain of group communication. The chapter closes with a summary of the main points and a mnemonic that provides guidance and helps readers memorize the main principles for their ready application in groups.

Studying and Applying Theories

Kurt Lewin's saying that nothing is as practical as a good theory invites the question, *What is a theory and what are the criteria of a good theory?* A theory refers to a set of claims that attempt to describe and explain patterns in the world. For theories of small group communication, this could take the form of explaining a host of diverse observations including how groups share information, create meaning, make good decisions, build identities, deal with conflict, and coordinate action. However, as the saying goes, hindsight is 20-20 and merely explaining past phenomena is not enough. Theories must also make predictions about future observations to provide guidelines for interventions. Accordingly, small group theories may offer insights into how groups can modify their behavior to communicate, decide, or relate more effectively.

Despite the common goal of explaining and predicting phenomena in the world, not all theories are created equal. This begs the question: What is a *good* scientific theory? A good scientific theory is not defined by a single feature, but rather a collection of distinguishing characteristics. One characteristic of a good theory is that it is *accurate* – the theory's propositions should be supported by empirical evidence from existing studies (Kuhn, 1977). For example, early research comparing risk taking in groups and individuals suggested that groups have a general inclination to form riskier decisions and take riskier actions than individuals, an observation that was dubbed the *risky shift phenomenon*. Risky shift in groups was explained by the assumption that members expect that other members would support their risks and by a diffusion of responsibility, that is, members' lower sense of responsibility for the group decision than for their individual decisions (Park & Hinsz, 2006). These explanations were inconsistent, though, with the eventual observation that some groups form more cautious decisions than individuals and demonstrate a *cautious shift*. Thus, arguably, the diffusion of responsibility assumption cannot provide an accurate explanation of risk-taking tendencies in groups.

Another theory appears to be more accurate in that it can explain risky as well as cautious shifts. It assumes that members compete with one another in advocating positions that are valued by the group, which results in *group polarization* (Park & Hinsz, 2006): If a group is predominantly composed of members who tend towards a risky decision and, thus, being risky is valued by most members, groups demonstrate a risky shift. By the same token, if a group is predominantly composed of members who value cautious decision, a cautious shift is likely to occur in the group (also see Chapter 15).

While good theories aim to accurately reflect the world, they should also be *falsifiable* or capable of having claims contradicted by the available evidence (Popper, 2014). A good scientific theory is also *parsimonious* and seeks to provide an explanation that is as simple as possible. While no theory can explain everything, scientific theories should be *broad in scope* – predictions should apply beyond the observations that were originally studied. The most useful theories make concise and testable predictions that can be generalized across many situations, contexts, and groups, while also specifying boundaries and describing contexts to which the theory does not apply (e.g., typically, explanations of flaming only apply to computer-mediated groups, but not to face-to-face groups). Moreover, good theories often generate controversy and trigger considerable discussion about their explanations (Fiedler, 2004; Gigerenzer, 1991).

Even though these are not standard characteristics that are used to evaluate theories, such as accuracy and falsifiability, from a practitioner's perspective, it is also important to understand how difficult it is to learn about a theory and apply it to different contexts. Likewise, in a group context, it makes a difference how well a theory and research testing the theory can be explained and communicated to others. Theories with applications that are transparent, explainable, and can be well demonstrated are promising candidates for theories that can be applied in groups (see Chapters 4, 13, and 15 for the concept of demonstrability). We do not claim that applicability is the most important characteristic of a theory, as it is very important for a discipline to do basic research without looking at the immediate applicability of a theory. The history of scientific discoveries has seen various instances showing that basic research can *eventually* be transformational and highly applicable and change the way we think about a phenomenon or enable the development of new technologies. This holds in particular in the natural sciences, in which many basic discoveries had to wait a long time before they saw an application. For example, the concept of radio waves was used by James Clerk Maxwell in the 1860s but not practically applied until the early 20th century with the invention of radio communication technology. Basic discoveries often require further research, development, and refinement before they can be applied in practical ways, a process that can take many years or even decades. Typically, theories of group communication are much easier to apply. However, even in the social sciences, some theories can be more readily applied than others.

Some relevant considerations of the applicability of theories in social scientific contexts such as group communication are as follows: Have the main propositions of a theory been supported many times and have the predictions of the theory been replicated across varying samples of participants, measures, and materials (see Eysenck, 1987; Lakatos & Musgrave, 1970; Open Science Collaboration, 2015)? Theories are often developed with the goal of explaining a specific phenomenon (e.g., in a specific problem context or using a specific task). Beyond these *paradigmatic* applications, theories also have *intended* applications, that is, applications that are envisioned by the authors of a theory and that have not been tested yet (see Balzer et al., 1989). Intended applications typically refer to questions of generalizability and transferability. Thus, it is important to ask, does a theory likely hold in my specific case? What are boundary conditions of the theory (i.e., conditions or contexts where the theory does not apply)? For example, information sharing behavior may be different in groups in which group members know each other and have a history of successful task completions than in a newly formed team in which members focus on relationship building and avoid conflicts. Psychological safety may be considerably higher in the former groups in which members know each other well. Psychological safety refers to the extent that group members feel accepted and respected for who they are and what they think, and free to engage in constructive conflict and experimentation without fear of rejection or negative consequences (Edmondson, 1999; Newman et al., 2017). Findings about information sharing in established groups (with high psychological safety) may not apply to a newly founded team in a company, unless additional actions are taken to enhance psychological safety in the team (Park & Hinsz, 2006). Teams with low psychological safety not only exchange fewer messages but also generate fewer ideas (see Chapter 16).

Knowing the main claims of a theory is key for understanding its applications. Also important in this regard is being knowledgeable about the relevance of a theory for a specific application and a theory's boundary conditions, including situations in which the theory likely does not apply (see Balkwell, 1994). As there are many different theories, it is helpful to organize and structure the body of knowledge to enhance accessibility. Two basic organizing principles for group communication theories used here are identification of classic themes that have evolved and been studied in depth (the history of group communication research) and acknowledging major perspectives of group communication scholarship (classic perspectives on group communication).

History of Group Communication Research

The history of group communication scholarship can be described as a continued evolution of ideas, knowledge claims, and methods (Keyton et al., 2022). Some concepts have been studied and refined over decades, including research on leadership, information processing, network structures and communication channels, the role of communication media and technology, and decision making and problem-solving in groups. Early developments in related disciplines in the 20th century were pedagogical in nature and illuminated group discussion as an instrument of democracy (e.g., Albert Craig Baird, 1928, *Public Discussion and Debate*). In social psychology, Kurt Lewin and his successors' work on the *systems perspective*, which considered a group as a complex social system consisting of interdependent individuals, laid a foundation for group communication research in the 1930s and 1940s (see Gouran, 1999; Poole, 1999; also see Chapter 7). Lewin's insights on group dynamics and field theory continue to have an impact on current scholarship (see Forsyth, 2018), including his seminal work on leadership styles (Lewin et al., 1939).

Empirical research in group communication largely grew in the 1950s. Bales's (1950) interaction process analysis (IPA) was groundbreaking as it systematically delved into the interactions among group members (see Chapters 11 and 12). Bales established a category system of group interaction and examined associations of message types with various output variables, thereby establishing conceptual and empirical links between group processes and outcomes (for recent advancements on group interaction analyses, see Brauner et al., 2018). In the 1960s, a large volume of research dealt with functional and developmental perspectives (see Gouran, 1999). Functional perspectives are concerned with what communication accomplishes in terms of task-related and relational-related processes and outcomes (Gouran & Hirokawa, 1996; Wittenbaum et al., 2004). Developmental perspectives center on group interaction as a process that emerges and evolves, influenced by both, internal relationships and the external environment (e.g., Anderson et al., 1999; Poole & Baldwin, 1996).

In the 1970s and the 1980s, group communication research expanded broadly by emphasizing factors beyond message and interaction characteristics. Studies dealt with topics such as conflict, leadership, discussion procedure, deviance, and conformity. The expansion of theoretical groundings included systems approaches such as structuration theory. Structuration theory focuses on the underlying structures of systems, such as group norms and roles, and emphasizes how structures affect members' communicative behaviors, which, in turn, result in alterations of the structures (Poole et al., 1996; also see Chapter 7).

The diversification and application of research continued in the 1990s when research activities examined issues and methods that had not been explored previously. While early research emphasized the dynamics of face-to-face communication among members of small groups, in the last three decades, research expanded to include the study of communication technology and virtual teams and larger groups such as online communities (Beck et al., 2022; Gouran, 1999; see Chapter 5).

Today, group communication is a well-established interdisciplinary field of study with theories and applications spanning many fields, including communication, psychology, and sociology, as well as management, business, engineering, medicine, and education.

Classic Perspectives on Group Communication

Group theories cover a wide range of perspectives on group communication, each with its own unique point of view in understanding communication within a group (see Poole et al., 2005; for overviews, see Forsyth, 2018; Gouran, 1999; Poole, 1999; Poole et al., 2022). Some of the key approaches of group communication include the functional, informational, temporal, cultural, and critical perspectives (for other classifications, see Poole et al., 2005). Each of these perspectives provides a vantage point to evaluate theories and how group theories can be applied. The perspectives are not mutually exclusive but highlight different aspects of group communication. Many theories tap into and integrate more than one perspective (e.g., theories that look at the development of cultural differences).

The **functional perspective** of group communication (Gouran & Hirokawa, 1996; Wittenbaum et al., 2004) focuses on the ways in which communication serves important purposes within a group, such as coordination, decision making, and social support. Two techniques that were born out of the functional perspective are the nominal group technique and conflict framing. The nominal group technique identifies four discussion stages that groups might use or go through, which are problem identification, brainstorming of solutions, evaluation of ideas, and idea selection (see Chapter 16). This technique of structured deliberation has the goal to help groups pool their ideas and generate high-quality alternatives and solutions to a given problem. Conflict framing sheds light on how groups communicate during a conflict, including verbal and nonverbal expressions and how it impacts their conflict management (see Chapter 10).

The **informational perspective** of group communication (Bonito, 2007; Hinsz et al., 1997; see Chapter 13) emphasizes the role of communication in sharing, processing, and interpreting information within a group. One concept from Chapter 18 discusses how information sharing (and the lack thereof) affects organizational processes. Information silos occur when communication becomes insular within parts of an organization, resulting in organizations being unable to share their expertise or relevant knowledge that is critical to the function of the organization. For example, a sales team that perceives themselves as being superior to other parts of the organization may not request and share information as needed with other organizational units (see Chapter 18).

Transactive memory systems provide another concept that emphasizes information processing in groups. Transactive memory is a group-level memory system that exceeds the memory of individuals in quantity and quality. When a transactive memory system is developed, members can rely on other members and retrieve information from them efficiently (Hollingshead, 1998; see Chapter 14).

The **temporal perspective** of group communication (Anderson et al., 1999; Moreland, 1987; Poole & Baldwin, 1996) looks at the ways in which group communication evolves and changes over time. Tuckman's (1965) model of group development provides a framework for understanding the stages a successful group moves through from inception to maturity. Weick's (1979) theory of sensemaking highlights the evolutionary process through which groups collectively develop plausible explanations for their environment (see Chapters 6 and 9). Similarly, McGrath emphasizes group development stages and group performance phases in what he calls a *time-based theory of functional groups* (McGrath, 2014). He suggests that group behavior is temporally patterned and that temporal matters affect social psychological processes and human behaviors (McGrath & Tschan, 2004; also see Ballard et al., 2008).

The **cultural perspective** of group communication (Oetzel, 2002; Yuan et al., 2019) emphasizes the role of culture and context in shaping group communication. For example, research on the cultural perspective revealed that low-context communicators, which characterize Westerners, tend to speak directly and explicitly, whereas high-context communicators, mostly found in East Asia, tend to speak indirectly and rely more on the context for interpretation (Hall, 1976; see Chapter 8). The cultural perspective also includes studies that look at the development of organizational cultures. For example, research indicates that technological affordances such as anonymity facilitate communication in online advice-seeking networks by increasing disclosure, thus, shaping the development of communities of support for health-related issues (Rains, 2018; see Chapter 21).

The **critical perspective** of group communication emphasizes the ways in which communication can be used to challenge and transform power dynamics within a group. Critical theory aims to make factors visible that constrain group members' ability to act and to establish structures that enable members to control their groups (Poole et al., 2022). An example refers to leadership studies: Critical leadership literature suggests that inclusive leadership provides justice, equity, and feelings of belongingness to marginalized groups (Ashikali et al., 2021; see Chapter 9).

Perspectives like these help organize the topics that have been studied and themes that have been addressed in research on small group communication. Having adequate knowledge about groups provides an important foundation for the application of evidence-based interventions. Knowing the main propositions of a theory, however, is not sufficient. To be able to apply a theory and improve group functioning, the gained knowledge about groups must be transferred by identifying situations that can be explained by a theory and changed through interventions. The next section looks at the application of theories from a metacognition perspective. Group scholarship has identified a variety of ways how group members' metacognitions affect group functioning and communication in groups, including the role of **monitoring and controlling** that are particularly important for the application of theories.

Metacognition in Groups: Tools to Apply Group Communication Theories

Metacognition in groups may be construed as the knowledge group members have about their group and their task, and as the way group members monitor and control their information processing and actions. The term *metacognition* refers to the process of thinking about what others and we think and know, as well as our metaknowledge. *Metaknowledge* includes the representations, beliefs, and thoughts about our own thoughts and the thoughts of other group members.

Nelson and Narens (1994) argue that cognitive processes are split into two interrelated levels, the meta-level and the object-level. The object-level includes all types of first-order cognitions about the world. In a group context, this may include, for example, members' task-related knowledge. The meta-level contains second- and higher-order cognitions about the object-level, that is, cognition about our cognitive processes. Examples for meta-level cognitions in a group context include group members' perception of the knowledge that other group members possess or assessments about contributions and thoughts that are shared by members during group discussions. Importantly, the two levels are connected by two metacognitive processes, monitoring and controlling. Monitoring informs the meta-level through introspection or observation on the object-level. Controlling includes initiating, continuing, or terminating actions. An important function of controlling consists in changing a group's goals or tasks, if possible, and the structure of their group discussions (e.g., determining discussion time) or the choice of group-decision strategies (see Chapter 15).

Some metacognitions may be descriptive beliefs about how groups work, such as the belief that groups follow the majority rule when forming decisions, while others may be normative beliefs about how groups should work, such as the belief that applying categorical or stereotypical information to judgments about individuals is inappropriate (see Gastil, 2008).

There are various cognitive processes that depend on accurate perceptions and lay theories about the extent and nature of other people's knowledge. These include perspective-taking, empathy, and effective communication. Communication, persuasion, coordination, and understanding are all reliant on the accuracy of perceptions and theories about the nature of other people's knowledge and beliefs. Metacognition in groups is intertwined with communication. Perhaps, the most basic difference between problem-solving and decision making in groups and individuals consists in the opportunity for members of a group to interact and communicate with other members. Group discussions provide the opportunity to exchange information and to propose different courses of action. Groups negotiate and set goals and discuss how tasks can be divided among group members. Groups offer opportunities to correct each other when a member makes an error and provide feedback (see Chapter 22 for various examples). All these activities involve group communication and can be described as antecedents, processes, or consequences of metacognition.

Metacognitive Principles for the Application of Group Communication Theories

The application of group theories in a group can be construed as a regulatory problem-solving process (see Davidson et al., 1994). Metacognition can help groups recognize that there is a problem, figure out what exactly the problem is, and reach a solution. The following four metacognitive processes are important for problem solving: (1) identifying and defining the problem, (2) representing the problem, (3) planning how to proceed, and (4) evaluating what group members know about the group's performance. To be able to apply theories in a fruitful way, it is important to have or gain adequate knowledge about groups and the ways in which groups communicate, to identify situations to which a theoretical approach applies, to understand boundaries of the approach, and to account for the complexities of real-world situations, including the possibility of unintended effects. In the following, we introduce five principles that are relevant for the application of theories (see Box 3.1 for an overview). The principles are meant to inform guidelines that can facilitate

---

Box 3.1   Metacognitive Principles Guiding the Application of Group Communication Theories and the META Mnemonic

Metacognitive Principles

Principle 1: *There is a continuum between lay theories and scientific theories about groups.*
Principle 2: *Group members' lay theories about groups affect their perception and behavior.*
Principle 3: *Monitoring and controlling are central for the application of theories.*
Principle 4: *Theories about groups can be used to inform the planning, action, and post-action phase of group processes and interactions.*
Principle 5: *Group members' vigilance can be improved through deliberate practice, training, and feedback.*

The META Mnemonic: *Monitor, Explain, Test,* and *Assess*

The practice of theory requires group members to go through a continuous process to *monitor* the specific situation and group behaviors, *explain* this situation in terms of a group concept, *test* out an intervention informed by the theory, and *assess* the impact it has on group functioning. Thus, the application of theory to practice requires groups to engage in META communication.

theory applications. Even though several of these principles are general and apply to other fields of inquiry, we focus here on group communication.

Principle 1: *There is a continuum between lay theories and scientific theories about groups.*

Groups are ubiquitous. Everyone has experience interacting in many types of small groups, one's family, work-related groups and teams, and groups that we join in our free time, such as friendship networks and sports clubs. As a consequence, most people have developed concepts, expectations, and explanations pertaining to groups and teams and the role of communication in groups.

Group members' general concepts, assumptions, and expectations regarding groups can be described as *lay theories*. A lay theory refers to the informal assumptions that laypersons have about the world (Furnham, 1988), including assumptions about group processes. Lay theories can be construed as a form of declarative and procedural metaknowledge (see Brand et al., 2003). Declarative metaknowledge refers to knowledge about our own knowledge and thinking (Kluwe, 1982), whereas procedural metaknowledge refers to the process by which a problem can be solved (Flavell, 1979; Metcalfe & Shimamura, 1994).

Arguably, most people have some accurate and some inaccurate declarative and procedural metaknowledge about groups with great variation in their *group-related expertise*. As with other areas of expertise, knowledge about groups is gained through learning, including first-hand experience and feedback, observations of other groups, and through the study of group-related concepts and theories. Empirical studies found that perceived self-expertise and knowledge does not always match actual differences in knowledge (Yang et al., 2013). On the one hand, research suggests that basic assumptions about cognitive processes are widely shared among individuals. For example, research on intergroup relations found that lay theories share some overlap with predictions of scientific theories (Levy et al., 2006).

On the other hand, there is empirical evidence suggesting that group members' knowledge about groups greatly varies. For example, Ladbury and Hinsz (2009) presented hypothetical scenarios to their participants in which groups had to make a choice, such as picking a student for an award, predicting the outcome of a coin flip, or discussing a mathematics problem and choosing the correct answer. Ladbury and Hinsz (2009) asked groups varying in size to complete the tasks. In addition, a separate sample of individuals were asked to predict what decisions groups most likely form in each of these scenarios. In the prediction study, participants were told the distribution of preferences within each group, that is, what fractions of a group were in favor of each alternative. For example, respondents were told that three out of five members of a group preferred Student A for an award and two members preferred Student B. Group size and preference distributions were systematically varied. Participants in the prediction condition correctly predicted that groups would apply a majority rule most of the time. However, this perception matched actual group behavior better in some tasks than in others; at times, participants were not as sensitive to differences in tasks as real groups. Participants varied in their ability to predict actual group behavior.

One important requirement for the application of group communication theories consists in gaining adequate, state-of-the-art knowledge about group theories. Reading through this book and learning about the theories that are described in each chapter provide opportunities to gain new knowledge about groups and to correct and inform one's lay theories about group communication. This also includes encountering and learning new jargon (e.g., the construct of a shared mental model, see Chapter 2) and understanding how important concepts are used. Terms in group research (as in other areas of scholarship) often have more specific meanings than the respective terms in everyday language. Learning about and understanding nuances in these terms and differentiating the terms from related concepts helps apply the accompanying theories. For example, research differentiates among various types of expertise, concepts of power, and forms of diversity (e.g., see Bonner et al., 2022; Phillips et al., 2014). Describing a team as diverse without specifying the dimension of diversity can be misleading, as research suggests that it matters what characteristics of the group are diverse (e.g., diversity in values vs. diversity in expertise and knowledge; see Chapter 8). Having a diverse team may be a goal in itself; however, the expected group interactions may greatly vary depending on whether a team is diverse in terms of the expertise that group members bring to the table or their tenure and basic values. These different dimensions of diversity affect group processes and outcomes in different ways (see Chapters 8 and 15). Knowing relevant distinctions and even subtleties in key concepts that are used in the literature on group communication and correcting one's lay theories and idiosyncratic assumptions about groups is an important part of the successful application of theories.

Principle 2: *Group members' lay theories about groups affect their perception and behavior.*

There is ample empirical evidence that our lay theories about other individuals and communication influence our perceptions, expectations, and behavior in our interactions with others (Baumann & Bonner, 2013; Reimer, 2001; Thompson & Cohen, 2012). For example, there is evidence that people expect at times to be biased in their judgments, which they try to correct. Among others, studies reported self-correction processes in judgments related to impression formation, affect, stereotyping, persuasion, and court rulings (Mussweiler & Strack, 2001; Wegener et al., 2000; Yzerbyt et al., 1998).

Some individuals tend to overcorrect their perceived biases, leading to an opposite bias. Research has demonstrated that people make adjustments for biases they assume exist, even when there is no actual bias present (Wegener & Petty, 1995), which can result in the development of a contrasting bias. For instance, correcting for perceived negativity towards a disliked source can make that source more convincing than a likable one (Petty et al., 1998; Schul & Goren, 1997).

Research suggests that people may not always be more accurate in their assessments of their own thoughts and feelings compared to those of relevant others (Jost et al., 1998). For instance, Vesonder and Voss (1985) examined the accuracy of students' predictions of their own ability to learn paired associations of adjectives compared to their predictions of another person's ability to learn the same associations. The study found that predictions about oneself were no more precise than predictions about the other person, as long as predictions about the other person's abilities were made after observing their initial attempt to learn the items. It appears that individuals follow an implicit metacognitive principle that allows them to infer the cognitions of others based on their own cognition (Jost et al., 1998).

Group members share a host of expectations and knowledge about how groups work, including memory processes and decision making in groups. Research indicates that group members' metacognitive beliefs about the group and the task can affect their subsequent behavior and performance (Hinsz, 2004). Members in groups bring their lay theories about groups and group communication to their groups. Group members vary in their expertise and knowledge about groups, and their lay theories include imperfect or wrong assumptions about groups (Principle 1). Even wrong lay theories about groups form and shape group members' expectations, perceptions, and behaviors in groups (Principle 2). Thus, important guidelines that follow from Principles 1 and 2 are based on the insight that group members should learn about group communication theories and correct or improve their inaccurate beliefs. However, having accurate knowledge about theoretical propositions is not enough to utilize theories. The theories also have to be applied accurately, which requires monitoring and controlling.

Principle 3: *Monitoring and controlling are central for the application of theories.*

Monitoring refers to assessment and controlling refers to regulating. Monitoring is the process by which the meta-level is informed by the object-level. Subsequently, the meta-level's model of the object-level will be updated and adjusted. Central monitoring processes in groups can refer to the (1) tasks and goals on the individual and the group level, (2) self and other group members within the group (i.e., their knowledge and beliefs), and (3) processes and technologies that are used by the group to interact and to achieve their goals. Monitoring operates through introspection or observation, and through interaction with other group members and one's environment.

Monitoring affects one's metaknowledge and representations on the meta-level. For example, a group member may observe changes in the task environment that require to adapt strategies and behaviors (DeRue et al., 2008; Ilgen et al., 1979; Reimer et al., 2005). For instance, Reimer et al. (2005) taught their participants one of two strategies that could be used to solve the Tower of Hanoi puzzle. One strategy (the goal-recursion strategy) could be applied to a transfer problem, whereas the second strategy (the move-pattern strategy) could not be used to solve the same transfer problem yielding negative transfer – participants who had learned the move-pattern strategy, performed worse on the transfer tasks than participants who had not learned any strategy. Performance in dyads, in which one or both problem solvers had learned the move-pattern strategy, depended on problem solvers' ability to recognize that the transfer task required a change in strategy. The earlier in the problem-solving process participants recognized that their move-pattern strategy was not useful anymore, the better they performed. Moreover, Reimer (2001) found that participants' metacognitions affected their motivation and accuracy in taking their partner's perspective. The more they attributed the breakdown of their developed routine to their own behavior, the better they were able to predict forthcoming moves of their partner. Because monitoring affects group members' metaknowledge, the way group members monitor information processing and group behavior can strongly affect the commonality and accuracy of their metaknowledge. Using the Tower of Hanoi and structurally similar tasks, Brand et al. (2003) demonstrated that problem solvers performed better with these tasks when they were stimulated to engage in metacognitive monitoring by thinking aloud about their next moves and evaluating each move. Taken together, these studies demonstrate that reflexive thinking and monitoring can affect problem solvers' metaknowledge and subsequent performance.

Effective metacognition in groups is most achievable when members share an understanding of relevant theories, cooperate, strongly identify with, and pursue the same group goals (Tjosvold, 1998). Monitoring and controlling have been shown to have positive effects on the development of shared knowledge and transactive memory systems (see Chapter 14). Shared knowledge is crucial for group functioning, but research indicates that group members tend to overestimate the sharedness of knowledge and opinions within their groups (Nickerson et al., 1987). For example, people often assume others know a fact if they know it. This exaggeration may hinder groups' ability to monitor distributions of information within the group, the consequence being that important information may not be contributed to discussions as group members assume that other members of their group have access to and know the same information as they. Monitoring enables the assessment of whether there is an overestimation of agreement and shared knowledge within the group and helps control the false consensus effect, which is the erroneous belief that others share our own judgments and perspectives when they do not (see Chapters 13 and 15).

Principle 4: *Theories about groups can be used to inform the planning, action, and post-action phase of group processes and interactions.*

Group theories can be used in all phases of a group's life and tenure. For practical reasons, it is useful to distinguish between the planning, action, and post-action phase of group interactions. The planning phase includes all activities prior to a group meeting and may even include the formation of a group. For instance, if we think about a hiring committee in a company, several decisions are needed. Who should be on the team? Should the team have a formal leader? How often should the team meet? How should team members prepare for their meeting? Should team members review the material and develop individual decisions before they come to the meeting? The answers to these questions and the related decisions can be informed by evidence-based research on team development (e.g., see Chapter 6), leadership (see Chapter 9), and decision making (see Chapter 15).

Monitoring plays a central role during the action phase as well as for feedback during the post-action phase (e.g., after a sport competition, see Chapter 24). Monitoring is an important part of self-regulation that is integral to the functioning of all types of teams, including fast-paced settings as in sports, health, and business settings. Marks and Panzer (2004) conducted a study that speaks to the role of monitoring during the action phase in a fast-paced environment. The study aimed to examine the significance of monitoring in a flight combat scenario. According to the authors, effective team monitoring is a crucial element of team regulation that can increase the likelihood of achieving team performance goals by enabling better coordination and feedback among team members. In their study, they employed three-person teams in a simulated flight combat team exercise to investigate how team monitoring can facilitate coordination and intra-team feedback. Marks and Panzer (2004) found that teams that monitored their performance better were more adept at evaluating their groups' actions and were better able to time and coordinate their independent actions. Effective monitoring also led to more accurate assessments of team members' current state and needs, which facilitated better feedback provision. Overall, the study highlights the importance of monitoring and feedback as a means of enhancing team performance in complex tasks that require coordination and collaboration among team members.

At times, groups tend to review their actions in an unsystematic way (Wilson, 2011) and deny responsibility when their actions were not successful (Leary & Forsyth, 1987; Reimer, 2001). Yet, it is important that groups dedicate a significant effort to evaluating their actions and outcomes in the post-action phase. Group theories can also help groups determine to what extent their members' involvement is needed. The normative model of decision making (Vroom, 2003; Vroom & Yetton, 1973), for example, distinguishes five levels of member participation in decision making, from the leader deciding to the group deciding to predict the effectiveness of each level across different group settings (also see Chapters 13 and 15).

Principle 5: *Group members' vigilance can be improved through deliberate practice, training, and feedback.*

Vigilant group members recognize when their group behaves in a problematic way and intervene. Vigilance can be construed as a form of group awareness (Schneider et al., 2022). Monitoring for and identifying signs of problems can be learned through observation and feedback. Feedback may be evaluative (and refer to the performance level) or descriptive (and refer to actions and behaviors). To be most effective, feedback should be accurate and relevant (Ashford & Cummings, 1983; Klein, 1989).

In groups, social learning provides an important source of learning (Schneider et al., 2022) that is based on the observation and imitation of group members. Group members who exert effective monitoring and controlling may be seen as role models and be imitated by their group. At times, it can be effective to invite group members to monitor each other's monitoring behavior as an important source for intra-group feedback (Wiedow & Konradt, 2011).

Several authors have argued that monitoring and controlling can be learned and improved through deliberate practice, training, and feedback. For example, Uitdewilligen and colleagues (2013) studied how teams evaluated a fire crisis situation in terms of the fire's intensity, rate of spread, and how it can be extinguished (i.e., their *mental models*). Teams that discussed how to create similar and accurate mental models were able to respond to the fire crisis more effectively. Developing shared mental models helps teams coordinate their actions in fast-paced environments, monitor for errors, and increase members' attention and vigilance (Kozlowski, 1998; Reimer et al., 2006; Salas & Fiore, 2004).

Importantly, at least the monitoring part of metacognition does not necessarily require high cognitive load. Correction processes related to biases, for example, have been shown to become less effortful and occur automatically if highly practiced (Wegener & Petty, 1995; Maddux et al., 2005). One can learn to apply theories and get better at applying theories. As a person learning to drive a car gets better not only in steering the car but also in cognitive multitasking by monitoring a variety of cues (other cars, oncoming traffic, pedestrians, and traffic signs), one can learn to monitor group processes for relevant cues that signal faulty group processes.

The META Mnemonic: *Monitor, Explain, Test,* and *Assess*

To say there is nothing as practical as a good theory invites the question: How does one translate theory into practice? The described principles inform guidelines to help group members rely on the valuable if sometimes elusive insights described in theories of small group communication. To adapt theory to practice effectively, group members must communicate at times *about* their communication and engage in meta-communication. The practice of theory requires group members to go through a continuous process to *monitor* the specific situation and group behaviors, *explain* this situation in terms of group concepts, *test* out an intervention informed by the theory, and *assess* the impact it has on group functioning. Thus, the application of theory to practice requires groups to engage in **META** communication.

Monitor

To monitor the situation, group members should ask: What about the situation needs to be explained? Group members may seek to explain how to have effective group discussions, share information, identify with each other, engage in productive conflict, or make good decisions. Groups should critically discuss the characteristics of group members such as expertise, preferences, traits, or limitations to examine their role in past group exchanges or decisions that they hope to explain. Just as groups monitor where they start, they should evaluate where they are headed, such as emergent tasks, goals, problem solving, or decision making. Finally, groups should consider how they will achieve these goals by looking at their information sharing, conflict management, coordination, or modes of communication.

Explain

While group members can create explanations on their own, theories provide guidelines based on scientific evidence. The explanations described in group communication theories provide direction and focus amid the uncertain, complex, and dynamic situations where groups operate. Consequently, a central task for groups is to identify what theory can explain the situation. Each theory will advance a set of key claims or propositions that provide an explanation for how the relevant factors in a group's situation are related to each other. Additionally, groups should look to the scope of a theory: What group phenomena can the theory explain and what are the situations when it can explain them best?

Test

The practicality of a theory consists not only in the ability to explain past group situations but also in providing direction for improving group processes in the future. With an explanation for the process underlying a phenomenon, theories provide guidance concerning how group members can implement corrective action. If groups tend to underestimate the amount of time required to achieve a task, then focusing on a highly coordinated procedure should alleviate the problem. It is this experimentation of theory-informed change that provides the necessary direction to improve.

Assess

Monitoring group characteristics, tasks, and processes does not end once a question has been asked or a problem identified. Groups should continue to review how a particular change altered a group's information sharing, coordination, influence, decision making, or other processes and outcomes. Individuals should likewise provide feedback to their collaborators in the group and evaluate the effectiveness of theory-informed interventions.

META in Practice

While the application of theory to practice may be relevant in many situations, applying META to practice is particularly useful in fast-paced, stressful environments such as an intensive care unit (ICU) of a hospital (Reimer et al., 2015; also see Chapter 23). Certain medical situations that are difficult to resolve often require pooling the expertise of physicians of internal medicine, infectious disease, oncology, or toxicology to arrive at an accurate diagnosis. Consider a case where a diverse team of experts discusses a patient's mysterious symptoms. Despite reviewing information intensively and discussing extensively, the team of physicians circles the same issues and is unable to identify the source of the symptoms – only able to rule out one disease. Under such urgent conditions, how can this team use group theory to manage an effective discussion and maximize the chance of an accurate diagnosis?

Through engaging in META communication, the team may use insights of group theory to conduct a more effective discussion. First, the group should account for what problem in this situation needs to be explained. If the group of physicians with such diverse expertise seems to be discussing the same elements of the case, they may be experiencing *shared information bias*. That is, the tendency to discuss information that is common to group members at the expense of potentially important, unique information (Reimer et al., 2010). Through *monitoring* this tendency, the group can work towards identifying a root cause based on the guidance of group theory. The *explanation* for this group behavior can be found in research on the *hidden-profile* effect wherein groups that pool relevant information that is unique to each member can arrive at accurate decisions (Larson et al., 1996; see Chapters 13 and 15). Through *testing* this insight, the team can deliberately structure discussions to pool the important, and potentially critical, information from each medical professional. The diagnostic team should still be vigilant and carefully evaluate or *assess* if the change in discussion structure assists in deriving an accurate diagnosis. Through embracing the idea that theory can be practical, applying META communication can support groups in addressing real-world problems.

Conclusion

There is nothing as practical as a good theory. Applying group communication theories requires that group members have adequate knowledge about the theory (including metaknowledge regarding what they do not know) and know when and how to apply a theory. Metacognition in groups can be construed as the way members perceive their group and their task and the processes by which they monitor and control group interactions. Group members' metacognitions are central for the application of theories. As reflected in the *Recommendations for Practice* sections of each chapter in this book, some theories and robust findings about groups can be easily applied. For example, as pointed out in Chapters 8, 10, 13, and 16, diversity in expertise and knowledge and access to opposing pieces of information is a pre-requisite to engage a group in an open-minded debate, in which groups discuss different standpoints on an issue. Diverse opinions can result in better decisions and reduce the risk of group polarization, thus, intellectual diversity and diversity in opinions should be considered when coordinating teams to work on tasks that require divergent thinking such as the generation of creative problem solutions (see Chapters 15 and 16). Boundary conditions of these claims refer to situations that require convergent thinking and to other dimensions of diversity including differences in basic values (see Chapters 8 and 15). At the same time, differences in prior experiences and knowledge (e.g., in an organization with great turnover) can be a source of conflicts and misunderstandings that can challenge the implementation and execution of problem-solving solutions. Developing shared cognitions and a shared mental model (Cannon-Bowers et al., 1993; Cannon-Bowers & Salas, 2001), as well as shared cognitive representations pertaining to the group, members, tasks, procedures, and resources, can facilitate the group's communication and performance, including the development of an effective transactive memory system (see Chapter 14).

As another example of highly applicable research that is relevant in many groups, Chapter 5 provides clear guidance regarding the use of technologies in groups by recommending setting clear policies and expectations regarding the use of technology during group meetings and for group task performance. Initially, groups may need richer media in order to define their task and members' roles. Rich media, according to media richness theory (Daft & Lengel, 1986), refers to communication channels that have a high capacity to convey information and provide immediate feedback, such as face-to-face communication or video conferencing. Over time, the use of media may change and reliance on technology may shift to more asynchronous types of communication to complete tasks while remaining effective.

As a caveat, group interactions are more complex than has been addressed in any single study. The focus on one theory or aspect may have unintended and detrimental effects on other aspects. For example, choosing the most knowledgeable member as the leader of a group may not be in a group's best interest if this member does not also have good relationship and communication skills (see Chapters 9 and 11). We invite readers to explore how the theories described in this book can be utilized to improve group communication and help groups achieve their goals.

Further Readings

Gouran, D. S. (1999). Communication in groups: The emergence and evolution of a field of study. In L. R. Frey, D. S. Gouran, & M. S. Poole (Eds.), *The handbook of group communication theory and research* (pp. 3–36). Sage.

Keyton, J., Beck, S. J., Poole, M. S., & Gouran, D. S. (2022). Group communication: A continued evolution. In S. Beck., J. Keyton, & S. Poole (Eds.), *The Emerald handbook of group and team communication research* (pp. 7–24). Emerald Publishing.

Poole, M. S. (1999). Group communication theory. In L. R. Frey, D. S. Gouran, & M. S. Poole (Eds.), *The handbook of group communication theory and research* (pp. 37–70). Sage.

Glossary

Metacognition   Metacognition in groups refers to knowledge group members have about them-selves and other group members, about their group, their task, and their group interactions, and the way group members monitor and control their information processing and actions.

Monitoring and controlling   Metacognitive processes that are important for the application of group communication theories. Monitoring refers to the assessment of group processes and controlling refers to regulating and changing processes and group interactions and behavior.

The META mnemonic   META stands for *M*onitor, *E*xplain, *T*est, and *A*ssess. The application of group communication theories requires group members to go through a continuous process to *monitor* the specific situation and group behaviors, *explain* this situation in terms of a group theory, *test* out an intervention informed by the theory, and *assess* the impact it has on group functioning.

References

Anderson, C. M., Riddle, B. L., & Martin, M. M. (1999). Socialization processes in groups. In L. R. Frey, D. S. Gouran, & M. S. Poole (Eds.), *The handbook of group communication theory and research* (pp. 139–163). Sage.

Ashford, S. J., & Cummings, L. L. (1983). Feedback as an individual resource: Personal strategies of creating information. *Organizational Behavior and Human Performance, 32*(3), 370–398.

Ashikali, T., Groeneveld, S., & Kuipers, B. (2021). The role of inclusive leadership in supporting an inclusive climate in diverse public sector teams. *Review of Public Personnel Administration, 41*(3), 497–519.

Baird, A. C. (1928). *Public discussion and debate.* Ginn & Company.

Bales, R. F. (1950). *Interaction process analysis: A method for the study of small groups.* Addison-Wesley.

Balkwell, J. W. (1994). Status. In M. Foschi & E. J. Lawler (Eds.), *Group processes: Sociological analyses* (pp. 119–148). Nelson-Hall.

Ballard, D. I., Tschan, F., & Waller, M. J. (2008). All in the timing: Considering time at multiple stages of group research. *Small Group Research, 39*(3), 328–351.

Balzer, W., Moulines, C. U., & Sneed, J. D. (1989). *The architectonic for science: The structuralist program.* D. Reidel Publishing Company.

Baumann, M. R., & Bonner, B. L. (2013). Member awareness of expertise, information sharing, information weighting, and group decision making. *Small Group Research, 44*(5), 532–562.

Beck, S., Keyton, J., & Poole, S. (Eds.). (2022). *The Emerald handbook of group and team communication research.* Emerald Publishing.

Bonito, J. A. (2007). A local model of information sharing in small groups. *Communication Theory, 17,* 252–280.

Bonner, B. L., Soderberg, A. T., Meikle, N. L., & Overbeck, J. R. (2022). The effects of experience, exper-tise, reward power, and decision power in groups. *Group Dynamics: Theory, Research, and Practice, 26,* 309–321.

Brand, S., Reimer, T., & Opwis, K. (2003). Effects of metacognitive thinking and knowledge acquisition in dyads on individual problem solving and transfer performance. *Swiss Journal of Psychology, 62*(4), 251–261.

Brauner, E., Boos, M., & Kolbe, M. (Eds.). (2018). *The Cambridge handbook of group interaction analysis.* Cambridge University Press.

Cannon-Bowers, J. A., & Salas, E. (2001). Reflections on shared cognition. *Journal of Organizational Behavior: The International Journal of Industrial, Occupational and Organizational Psychology and Behavior, 22*(2), 195–202.

Cannon-Bowers, J. A., Salas, E., & Converse, S. (1993). Shared mental models in expert team decision making. In N. J. Castellan (Ed.), *Individual and group decision making: Current issues* (pp. 221–246). Lawrence Erlbaum Associates, Inc.

Daft, R. L., & Lengel, R. H. (1986). Organizational information requirements, media richness and structural design. *Management Science, 32*(5), 554–571.

Davidson, J. E., Deuser, R., & Sternberg, R. J. (1994). The role of metacognition in problem solving. In J. Metcalfe & A. P. Shimamura (Eds.), *Metacognition: Knowing about knowing* (pp. 207–226). The MIT Press.

DeRue, D. S., Hollenbeck, J. R., Johnson, M. D., Ilgen, D. R., & Jundt, D. K. (2008). How different team downsizing approaches influence team-level adaptation and performance. *Academy of Management Journal, 51*(1), 182–196.

Edmondson, A. (1999). Psychological safety and learning behavior in work teams. *Administrative Science Quarterly, 44*(2), 350–383.

Eysenck, H. J. (1987). "There is nothing more practical than a good theory" (Kurt Lewin) – True or false? In W. J. Baker, M. E. Hyland, H. van Rappard, & A. W. Staats (Eds.), *Current issues in theoretical psychology* (pp. 49–64). Elsevier Science Publishers B.V.

Fiedler, K. (2004). Tools, toys, truisms, and theories: Some thoughts on the creative cycle of theory formation. *Personality and Social Psychology Review, 8*(2), 123–131.

Flavell, J. H. (1979). Metacognition and cognitive monitoring: A new area of cognitive–developmental inquiry. *American Psychologist, 34*(10), 906–911.

Forsyth, D. R. (2018). *Group dynamics*. Thomson Wadsworth.

Frey, L. R. (1996). Remembering and "re-membering": A history of theory and research on communication and group decision making (R. Y. Hirokawa, & M. S. Poole, Eds.; Vol. 2, pp. 19–51). Sage.

Frey, L. R., Gouran, D. S., & Poole, M. S. (Eds.). (1999). *The handbook of group communication theory and research*. Sage.

Furnham, A. (1988). *Lay theories: Everyday understanding of problems in the social sciences*. Pergamon Press.

Gastil, J. (2008). *Political communication and deliberation*. Sage.

Gigerenzer, G. (1991). From tools to theories: A heuristic of discovery in cognitive psychology. *Psychological Review, 98*(2), 254–267.

Gouran, D. S. (1999). Communication in groups: The emergence and evolution of a field of study. In L. R. Frey, D. S. Gouran, & M. S. Poole (Eds.), *The handbook of group communication theory and research* (pp. 3–36). Sage.

Gouran, D. S., & Hirokawa, R. Y. (1996). Functional theory and communication in decision-making and problem-solving groups: An expanded view. In R. Y. Hirokawa & M. S. Poole (Eds.), *Communication and group decision making* (pp. 50–80). Sage.

Hall, E. T. (1976). *Beyond culture*. Doubleday.

Hinsz, V. B. (2004). Metacognition and mental models in groups: An illustration with metamemory of group recognition memory. In E. Salas & S. M. Fiore (Eds.), *Team cognition: Understanding the factors that drive process and performance* (pp. 33–58). American Psychological Association.

Hinsz, V. B., Tindale, R. S., & Vollrath, D. A. (1997). The emerging conceptualization of groups as information processors. *Psychological Bulletin, 121*, 43–64.

Hollingshead, A. B. (1998). Communication, learning, and retrieval in transactive memory systems. *Journal of Experimental Social Psychology, 34*(5), 423–442.

Ilgen, D. R., Fisher, C. D., & Taylor, M. S. (1979). Consequences of individual feedback on behavior in organizations. *Journal of Applied Psychology, 64*(4), 349–371.

Ilgen, M., McKellar, J., & Tiet, Q. (2005). Abstinence self-efficacy and abstinence 1 year after substance use disorder treatment. *Journal of Consulting and Clinical Psychology, 73*(6), 1175–1180.

Jost, J. T., Kruglanski, A. W., & Nelson, T. O. (1998). Social metacognition: An expansionist review. *Personality and Social Psychology Review, 2*(2), 137–154.

Keyton, J., Beck, S. J., Poole, M. S., & Gouran, D. S. (2022). *Group communication: A continued evolution.* In S. Beck, J. Keyton, & S. Poole (Eds.), *The Emerald handbook of group and team communication research* (pp. 7–24). Emerald Publishing.

Klein, H. J. (1989). An integrated control theory model of work motivation. *Academy of Management Review, 14*(2), 150–172.

Kluwe, R. H. (1982). Cognitive knowledge and executive control: Metacognition. In *Animal mind–Human mind: Report of the Dahlem workshop on animal mind–Human mind, Berlin 1981, March 22–27* (pp. 201–224). Springer.

Kozlowski, S. W. J. (1998). Training and developing adaptive teams: Theory, principles, and research. In J. A. Cannon-Bowers & E. Salas (Eds.), *Making decisions under stress: Implications for individual and team training* (pp. 115–153). American Psychological Association.

Kuhn, T. S. (1977). Objectivity, value judgment, and theory choice. In T. S. Kuhn (Ed.), *The essential tension–Selected studies in scientific tradition and change* (pp. 320–339). The University of Chicago Press.

Ladbury, J. L., & Hinsz, V. B. (2009). Individual expectations for group decision processes: Evidence for overestimation of majority influence. *Group Dynamics: Theory, Research, and Practice, 13*(4), 235–254.

Lakatos, I., & Musgrave, A. (Eds.). (1970). *Criticism and the growth of knowledge: Volume 4: Proceedings of the international colloquium in the philosophy of science,* London, 1965. Cambridge University Press.

Larson, J. R., Jr., Christensen, C., Abbott, A., & Franz, T. (1996). Diagnosing groups. Charting the flow of information in medical decision-making teams. *Journal of Personality and Social Psychology, 71,* 315–330.

Leary, M. R., & Forsyth, D. R. (1987). Attributions of responsibility for collective endeavors. In C. Hendrick (Ed.), *Group processes* (pp. 167–188). Sage Publications, Inc.

Levy, S. R., Chiu, C. Y., & Hong, Y. Y. (2006). Lay theories and intergroup relations. *Group Processes & Intergroup Relations, 9*(1), 5–24.

Lewin, K. (1951, reprinted 1964). Problems of research in social psychology. In D. Cartwright (Ed.), *Field theory in social science–Selected theoretical papers by Kurt Lewin* (*Chapter 7*). Harper and Row.

Lewin, K., Lippitt, R., & White, R. K. (1939). Patterns of aggressive behavior in experimentally created "social climates". *Journal of Social Psychology, 10,* 271–299.

Maddux, W. W., Barden, J., Brewer, M. B., & Petty, R. E. (2005). Saying no to negativity: The effects of context and motivation to control prejudice on automatic evaluative responses. *Journal of Experimental Social Psychology, 41*(1), 19–35.

Marks, M. A., & Panzer, F. J. (2004). The influence of team monitoring on team processes and performance. *Human Performance, 17*(1), 25–41.

McGrath, J. E. (2014). Time matters in groups. In *Intellectual teamwork* (pp. 37–76). Psychology Press.

McGrath, J. E., & Tschan, F. (2004). *Temporal matters in social psychology: Examining the role of time in the lives of groups and individuals.* American Psychological Association.

Metcalfe, J., & Shimamura, A. P. (Eds.). (1994). *Metacognition: Knowing about knowing.* MIT press.

Moreland, R. L. (1987). The formation of small groups. *Review of Personality and Social Psychology, 8,* 80–110.

Mussweiler, T., & Strack, F. (2001). Considering the impossible: Explaining the effects of implausible anchors. *Social Cognition, 19*(2), 145–160.

Nelson, T. O., & Narens, L. (1994). Why investigate metacognition? *Metacognition: Knowing About Knowing, 13,* 1–25.

Newman, A., Donohue, R., & Eva, N. (2017). Psychological safety: A systematic review of the literature. *Human Resource Management Review, 27*(3), 521–535.

Nickerson, R. S., Baddeley, A., & Freeman, B. (1987). Are people's estimates of what other people know influenced by what they themselves know? *Acta Psychologica, 64*(3), 245–259.

Oetzel, J. G. (2002). The effects of culture and cultural diversity on communication in work groups. In L. R. Frey (Ed.), *New directions in group communication* (pp. 121–137). Sage.

Open Science Collaboration. (2015). Estimating the reproducibility of psychological science. *Science, 349*(6251), aac4716.

Park, E. S., & Hinsz, V. B. (2006). "Strength and safety in numbers": A theoretical perspective on group influences on approach and avoidance motivation. *Motivation and Emotion, 30*, 135–142.

Petty, R. E., Wegener, D. T., & White, P. H. (1998). Flexible correction processes in social judgment: Implications for persuasion. *Social Cognition, 16*(1), 93–113.

Phillips, K. W., Medin, D., Lee, C. D., Bang, M., Bishop, S., & Lee, D. N. (2014). How diversity works. *Scientific American, 311*(4), 42–47.

Pilny, A., & Poole, M. S. (Eds.). (2017). *Group processes: Data-driven computational approaches*. Springer.

Poole, M. S. (1999). Group communication theory. In L. R. Frey, D. S. Gouran, & M. S. Poole (Eds.), *The handbook of group communication theory and research* (pp. 37–70). Sage.

Poole, M. S., & Baldwin, C. L. (1996). Developmental processes in group decision making. In R. Y. Hirokawa & M. S. Poole (Eds.), *Communication and group decision making* (pp. 215–241). Sage.

Poole, M. S., Dobosh, M. A., & Keyton, J. (2022). Group communication theory: New theories and perspectives. In S. Beck, J. Keyton, & S. Poole (Eds.), *The Emerald handbook of group and team communication research* (pp. 45–52). Emerald Publishing.

Poole, M. S., Hollingshead, A. B., McGrath, J. E., Moreland, R., & Rohrbaugh, J. (2005). Interdisciplinary perspectives on small groups. In M. S. Poole & A. B. Hollingshead (Eds.), *Theories of small groups: Interdisciplinary perspectives* (pp. 1–20). Sage.

Poole, M., Seibold, D., & Mcphee, R. (1996). *The structuration of group decisions*. Sage.

Popper, K. (2014). *Conjectures and refutations: The growth of scientific knowledge*. Routledge.

Rains, S. A. (2018). *Coping with illness digitally*. MIT Press.

Reimer, T. (2001). Attributions for poor group performance as a predictor of perspective-taking and subsequent group achievement: A process model. *Group Processes & Intergroup Relations, 4*(1), 31–47.

Reimer, T., Bornstein, A.-L., & Opwis, K. (2005). Positive and negative transfer effects in groups. In T. Betsch & S. Haberstroh (Eds.), *The routine of decision making* (pp. 175–192). Lawrence Erlbaum Associates.

Reimer, T., Park, E. S., & Hinsz, V. B. (2006). Shared and coordinated cognition in competitive and dynamic task environments: An information-processing perspective for team sports. *International Journal of Sport and Exercise Psychology, 4*(4), 376–400.

Reimer, T., Reimer, A., & Czienskowski, U. (2010). Decision-making groups attenuate the discussion bias in favor of shared information: A meta-analysis. *Communication Monographs, 77*, 121–142.

Reimer, T., Roland, C., & Russell, T. (2017). Groups and teams. In L. Lewis & C. Scott (Eds.), *International encyclopedia of organizational communication* (pp. 1–21). Wiley-Blackwell.

Reimer, T., Russell, T., & Roland, C. (2015). Decision making in medical teams. In T. R. Harrison & E. A. Williams (Eds.), *Organizations, communication, and health* (pp. 65–81). Routledge.

Salas, E., & Fiore, S. M. (Eds.) (2004). *Team cognition: Understanding the factors that drive process and performance*. American Psychological Association.

Schneider, S., Beege, M., Nebel, S., Schnaubert, L., & Rey, G. D. (2022). The cognitive-affective-social theory of learning in digital environments (CASTLE). *Educational Psychology Review, 34*, 1–38.

Schul, Y., & Goren, H. (1997). When strong evidence has less impact than weak evidence: Bias, adjustment, and instructions to ignore. *Social Cognition, 15*(2), 133–155.

Thompson, L., & Cohen, T. R. (2012). Metacognition in teams and organizations. In P. Briñol & K. G. DeMarree (Eds.), *Social metacognition* (pp. 283–302). Psychology Press.

Tjosvold, D. (1998). Cooperative and competitive goal approach to conflict: Accomplishments and challenges. *Applied Psychology, 47*(3), 285–313.

Tuckman, B. W. (1965). Developmental sequence in small groups. *Psychological Bulletin, 63*(6), 384–399.

Uitdewilligen, S., Waller, M. J., & Pitariu, A. H. (2013). Mental model updating and team adaptation. *Small Group Research, 44*(2), 127–158.

Vesonder, G. T., & Voss, J. F. (1985). On the ability to predict one's own responses while learning. *Journal of Memory and Language, 24*(3), 363–376.

Vroom, V. H. (2003). Educating managers for decision making and leadership. *Management Decision, 41*(10), 968–978.

Vroom, V. H., & Yetton, P. W. (1973). *Leadership and decision making*. University of Pittsburgh Press.

Wegener, D. T., Kerr, N. L., Fleming, M. A., & Petty, R. E. (2000). Flexible corrections of juror judgments: Implications for jury instructions. *Psychology, Public Policy, and Law*, *6*(3), 629–654.

Wegener, D. T., & Petty, R. E. (1995). Flexible correction processes in social judgment: The role of naive theories in corrections for perceived bias. *Journal of Personality and Social Psychology*, *68*(1), 36–51.

Weick, K. (1979). *The social psychology of organizing*. Random House.

Wiedow, A., & Konradt, U. (2011). Two-dimensional structure of team process improvement: Team reflection and team adaptation. *Small Group Research*, *42*(1), 32–54.

Wilson, T. D. (2011). *Redirect: Changing the stories we live by*. Hachette UK.

Wittenbaum, G. M., Hollingshead, A. B., Paulus, P. B., Hirokawa, R. Y., Ancona, D. G., Peterson, R. S., Jehn, K. A., & Yoon, K. (2004). The functional perspective as a lens for understanding groups. *Small Group Research*, *35*, 17–43.

Yang, J. H., Kennedy, Q., Sullivan, J., & Fricker, R. D. (2013). Pilot performance: Assessing how scan patterns & navigational assessments vary by flight expertise. *Aviation Space and Environmental Medicine*, *84*(2), 116–124.

Yuan, Y. C., Liao, W., & Bazarova, N. N. (2019). Judging expertise through communication styles in intercultural collaboration. *Management Communication Quarterly*, *33*(2), 1–34.

Yzerbyt, V. Y., Dardenne, B., & Leyens, J.-P. (1998). Social judgeability concerns in impression formation. In V. Y. Yzerbyt, G. Lories, & B. Dardenne (Eds.), *Metacognition: Cognition and social dimensions* (pp. 126–156). Sage.

4   Researching Small Discussion Groups

Joseph A. Bonito

Chapter Objectives

- Connect research questions about small discussion groups with appropriate research designs.
- Identify what design characteristics produce credible research findings.
- Understand the broad distinction between quantitative and qualitative research.
- Assess features of quantitative small group research, including sampling, participants, materials, and task.
- Introduce basic concepts related to qualitative research on small discussion groups.

Introduction

Search Google Scholar for research studies on decision-making groups and you'll find that most of the returned reports will have a section named "Method," which describes procedures used to collect and process data. The method section usually follows the part of a research article that contains the study's warrant, which presents the rationale for conducting the study, identifies a set of constructs (characteristics that cannot be directly observed, e.g., satisfaction), plausible covariates (variables that aren't central to the study's research question but help explain the relation among those that are central, e.g., age), and presents one or more hypotheses, which are testable statements about the relationships among constructs. The final part of the standard research report discusses the study's findings and their implications for theoretical development and practical implementation. The method section then functions as the link between a study's conceptual framework and what to make of the study's findings.

In this chapter, I address methodological issues related to the study of small discussion groups.[1] I focus primarily on quantitative approaches (i.e., ones that represent observations as numbers and evaluate hypotheses using statistical techniques) but also address aspects of qualitative research, in which observations take many forms, including field notes, interviews, and audio/visual recordings. Although there are variations on the theme, the method section for quantitative studies describes the study's design, which, among other things, includes a description of participant recruitment and characteristics, study materials, and the procedure by which data were collected from the participants using the described materials (American Psychological Association, 2020). Study design is usually carefully planned and adjustments during data collection are rare, though sometimes necessary. Qualitative studies report similar information, although the design (i.e., **fieldwork**) itself is often fluid (i.e., changes as the researcher's understanding and interpretation of and access to the data evolves). Of primary importance to qualitative analysis is the researcher's relationship with study participants and how that relationship affects data collection and analysis (Levitt et al., 2018).

DOI: 10.4324/9781003227458-5

I note from the outset that scientific inquiry usually begins with a question, followed by the gathering of data to answer it. Questions for which data are not currently or ever available are philosophical in nature. Researchers choose a particular method because it addresses or answers a research question of interest.[2] It is helpful to pose a well-framed question, as doing so suggests both an appropriate design and type of data needed. The study of small discussion groups is no exception. One might begin by asking how groups make decisions, but the question is too broad because it doesn't suggest what kind of data is needed or identify the context in which data collection might appropriately occur. Such questions are akin to asking a mechanic why your car isn't running like it used to or wanting to know, when consulting with your physician, why you don't feel right. Those types of questions aren't terribly helpful to either the mechanic or physician, but "why am I hearing a clicking noise when I turn left?" and "why am I dizzy when I stand?" are much more informative and provide those professionals with a starting point for collecting relevant data (e.g., from both further prodding and diagnostic tests) and solving the respective problems. Similarly, asking whether group outcomes reflect the preference of the most frequent speaker, for example, points to the kind of data needed, which likely include information about speaking frequency, individual preferences (regarding what the group should do or choose), and group outcomes.

A study's method describes choices made to measure or observe the constructs in question and the context in which data are collected. If done well, the chosen method implements the conceptual framework in a sensible and defensible manner, and if done poorly, calls into question the basis for the study and its results. The issue, as Robert Abelson (1995) noted, is credibility:

> Credibility refers to the believability of a research claim. It requires both methodological soundness, and theoretical coherence. Claims based on sloppy experimental procedures or mistaken statistical analyses will fall victim to criticism by those with an interest in the results. Clues suggested by funny-looking data or wrongly framed procedures provide skeptics with information that something is amiss in the statistical analysis or research methodology.
>
> (p. 13)

I focus first on quantitative methods and then address qualitative approaches. Regarding quantitative research, note that I do not address statistical analysis for several reasons. First, method is a distinct problem unto itself, although choice of method has implications for analytical choices; it is unusual for a method to be chosen to fit a statistical model. For example, one might ask whether the amount of time a group spends working on a task is related to productivity (e.g., quality of decision making and number of ideas generated), which implies a correlation-based analysis of some sort (i.e., as the value of one variable increases, the value of the other reliably or consistently increases or decreases), depending on the level of measurement of productivity. The second reason for not addressing statistical methods in this chapter is because, in most cases, group data present difficult analytical challenges, and there simply isn't enough space to address all the issues here (Bonito, 2021; Poole et al., 1999). As a case in point, consider the problem of participation and influence on group outcomes. It might be that higher rates of participation are positively associated with influence, but most statistical models assume independence of observations (i.e., that one person's data are unrelated to that from others in the study). It should be obvious that both participation and influence within groups are not independent – one's speaking frequency usually affects how much others in the group speak and one member's influence often comes at the expense of another (Bonito, 2002). Data of this type usually require advanced statistical analyses that consider the nonindependence of the data (Kenny et al., 2002), and are beyond the scope of this chapter.

Quantitative Methods for the Study of Small Groups

Most quantitative methods sections describe three main features of the study in the following order: *participants*, *materials*, and *procedure*. The participants section, as the name implies, addresses relevant characteristics of the people from whom data were gathered, and materials provide details about, among other things, what measurements were used and features of the task on which groups worked. As an example, assume that relatively equal participation among members leads to higher levels of satisfaction with the group (Bonito, 2001). The question then is what are the relevant antecedent characteristics (i.e., factors that precede and often influence discussion) that are likely to produce similar participation rates? One approach is to assume that status differences privilege the verbal contributions of some (Balkwell, 1994), which implies that groups composed of members with similar status should display more equal rates of participation than status-differentiated groups, which should then produce higher levels of satisfaction. Thus, we expect the researchers to tell us, among other things, who participated in the study; how participation, status, and satisfaction were measured; what task the group worked on; and the design (i.e., the steps involved in data collection from beginning to end) the researchers used. This information gives us a sense of how credible, to use Abelson's (1995) term, the results are given the means by which the data were collected and how the method fits with the research question.

Participants

In a perfect world, researchers could measure everyone for whom a study's results are relevant or meant to apply (i.e., the *population*). Examples of populations include all decision-making groups, all cancer support groups, all married couples, all adults, all registered voters, all organizations, and so on, though one could restrict or trim the populations as needed (e.g., all decision-making groups in the United States, all nonprofit organizations in Canada). Of course, it's nearly impossible to measure everyone in a target population so most researchers resort to using a *sample* of participants who are *representative* of the population with the goal of *generalizing* results from the sample to the population.[3] The trick is obtaining a representative sample and in what follows, I describe two main procedures for doing so, the first of which is *random* or *probability* sampling and the second is *nonprobability* sampling.

The ideal approach, in most cases, to obtaining a representative sample is random sampling, in which every member of the population has an equal likelihood of being selected for the sample. The benefit of large random samples is that their representativeness can be estimated probabilistically, which gives a sense of how similar they are to the population. Random sampling is often difficult to perform successfully for a variety of reasons, not the least of which is obtaining a list of units in the population which, of course, likely numbers in the tens of millions. Professional political pollsters perhaps come the closest to this ideal (more or less; see Prosser & Mellon, 2018) though most vary in some crucial aspects that affect how well their sample estimates (i.e., polls conducted prior to an election) match up with actual voting (see the pollster ratings at https://projects.fivethirtyeight.com/pollster-ratings/). Most other quantitative social science researchers, including those who study small groups, use one of several nonprobability techniques, the most common of which is the *convenience sample*. As the name implies, a convenience sample consists of participants to whom the researcher has easy and direct access, for example, undergraduate students in a university researcher's home academic department.

The preceding begs the question of whether convenience samples are representative of the population given the research question of interest, and this is where describing participant characteristics and recruitment really comes into play. As an example, consider the question of whether a group adopts the solution that receives the most support during discussion (Hoffman & Kleinman, 1994). This seems a basic or universal phenomenon that applies to all small decision-making groups, so using a sample of undergraduate students seems reasonable in terms of generalizing to the population of all groups. But even here care would have to be taken regarding, among other things, gender and racial representation in the groups, whether friends were permitted in the same group, age distributions, and so on. Bales's seminal work on group discussion, which took place in the 1950s, used all-male groups, which makes one wonder whether his findings, which still influence the field today, might look a bit different if women were represented in the study.[4]

It is standard, at the very least, for quantitative studies in general, that participants should be described in terms of age, gender, race, and nationality, and for studies of small discussion groups specifically, some statement about group composition is in order. Notice that, in the example above regarding groups adopting the solution with the most support, gender, age, and race are not mentioned as predictors or covariates of either support or decision making. And yet this information seems crucial to judge whether and how the results generate to a population in which groups vary on all sorts of dimensions. If a sample's characteristics seem too different from the population of interest, then one might question the validity of the results.

It is worth noting a recent and important shift away from undergraduate samples toward "crowdsourced" participants. In general, participants of this type are more or less professional research participants who sign up or register with one of several companies that provide the service online. Examples include Amazon Mechanical Turk (commonly referred to as "MTurk"), the online survey provider Qualtrics, and a company called Prolific. Researchers pay the company for the service, usually based on the number of participants needed and the time required to complete the study, and the company makes the study available to an appropriate sample of participants. Crowdsourced samples are not based on random sampling; rather, crowdsourced sampling relies on self-selection, which means some participants are more or less likely to participate than others. Regardless, a benefit of crowdsourced samples is that they tend to be more representative of the population than student convenience samples, and the extent to which they provide better quality data than undergraduate samples appears related to the question of construct of interest (see Chmielewski & Kucker, 2020; Goodman et al., 2013).

Because crowdsourced participants are online and work independently of one another, most studies that make use of such participants employ standard **survey research** techniques. Group decision-making studies usually require sets of interacting participants, which seems to eliminate crowdsourced participants or severely limits how they might be used. It turns out that some researchers have made innovative use of crowdsourced participants in group decision-making studies. For example, Teschner and Gimpel (2018) examined negotiation strategies during a simulated investment task using MTurk participants, who were provided a link to the study. Participants were randomly paired to work on the task. Of interest is that MTurk participants can be screened in a variety of ways, some of which are common (age and gender), whereas others are less so, for example, performance in previous studies (e.g., whether the participant provided valid data rather than simply clicking the same response for each question). It is likely that researchers will find more ways to incorporate crowdsourced participants in groups decision-making studies because (a) the samples are often more representative than undergraduate ones, (b) participants can come from many countries if desired, and (c) pandemic concerns that, as of this writing, make laboratory research on small groups somewhat risky in terms of health.

Materials

The materials section of a study provides details regarding what instruments the researchers used to collect and process data, which includes everything that participants experience in a study. Returning to the example above regarding status, participation, and satisfaction, the researchers should describe, among other things, measurement issues (i.e., how were status, satisfaction, and participation observed and/or measured) and the task on which participants were asked to work. In what follows, I address those two broad areas of the material section in a quantitative research report.

Measurement

Empiricism is central to the study of groups and group processes, which for quantitative researchers requires the measurement of some aspects of group inputs, process, and outcomes, depending on the research question. I address each in turn.

Measuring Inputs

Regarding inputs, it is common to use self-reports, usually in the form of a questionnaire, to collect relevant attitudinal, experiential, cognitive, and demographic information. Most questionnaire items employ a closed set of responses (e.g., strongly agree to strongly disagree) from which participants must choose.[5] For example, Staggs et al. (2018) asked participants to provide attitudes regarding capital punishment before they engaged in mock jury discussions. And Marcus (Marcus & Leatherwood, 1998; Marcus & Lehman, 2002) asked participants to evaluate each other on a series of personality characteristics prior to discussion. In some cases, open-ended responses are used, as when Bonito (2006) gave participants a set of statements about a fictitious person and asked them to provide a "psychological profile" in writing, under the assumption that one's profile predicts what one might say when asked to discuss and come to a consensus about that fictitious person's characteristics in a group.

Measuring Process

Many studies of groups evaluate process either because it is of interest in and of themselves or because of the relationship to either/both inputs and outputs. I discuss two forms of process here, discussion characteristics and other types of actions.

When discussion characteristics are of interest, researchers figure out a way to capture them for subsequent processing. If face-to-face groups are used, the researcher usually records the interactions with audio-visual equipment.[6] Things are simplified somewhat if groups that use synchronous meeting technologies with audio-visual capabilities (e.g., Zoom or Skype) are of interest, as those technologies have the option to record meetings baked in. It is common for such recordings to be transcribed. Other types of communication technologies (e.g., messaging software) require participants to type their contributions, which are easily captured and require no transcribing (e.g., Poole et al., 1993). Once discussion has been transcribed (if needed), it is common for it to be segmented and coded to examine the distribution of comment types, as Lehmann-Willenbrock et al. (2013) did. Researchers, not participants, categorize discussion comments, with categories derived from theory or inductively.[7] As examples of a theoretically driven approach, Meyers and Brashers (2010) developed a coding system based on features of argument and Weingart et al. (2007) used conceptual notions of negotiation to categorize discussion among participants who were instructed to collaborate on the design of a new building. An inductive approach to categorizing group interaction is found in Mansbridge et al. (2006), who specifically recruited coders (from a list of professional facilitators) who were interested in "watching four hours of tape from a deliberative session, and coding it for particularly good deliberative moments and more problematic ones (p. 11)." Mansbridge et al. justified their approach by noting that there was no literature that identified in any meaningful way good and problematic deliberation. In fact, inductive coding often occurs exactly because research on a given domain is in early stages such that the development of a deductive, theoretically driven approach would be premature.

A current and evolving approach to coding group interaction is to use computer-based text processing. Two broad approaches are worth nothing, the first of which is *unsupervised machine learning*. In essence, the software searches for patterns in the text and identifies, based on a range of input parameters, a set of topics that are distinguished by word co-occurrence (Hvitfeldt & Silge, 2021) – it is comparable to inductive category generation described above.[8] In contrast, *supervised machine learning* is deductive in nature – the researcher uses coded data as input from which the machine learns the relationship between content and codes. Once the machine codes the training set acceptably (although there is no consensus on what the proportion of correctly coded units should be), the researcher might then use the software to code new and uncoded data. For example, Bonito and Keyton (2018) used supervised methods to evaluate performance on a set of data that had been previously coded using the interaction process analysis (IPA; Bales, 1950). One issue is the extent to which the training and new data should come from comparable tasks and/or whether the coding system should be context independent (i.e., apply to a wide range of tasks or discussions) or be sensitive to features of the task or problem (e.g., whether it makes sense to use the same trained software to code data from a promotion and tenure committee and a self-managed work team). There is much promise in the use of computers to code interaction data, but more work is needed to see how current algorithms match issues of importance to group scholars and whether new algorithms can be developed from theory and research on groups.

In some cases, discussion is not the only or primary process of interest. For example, Pilny et al. (2020) examined team coordination during multi-player computer game simulations, which was operationalized as capturing "participant screen actions and interactive behavior in real time" (p. 560). As more types of data become available from virtual teams, other types of process measure are likely to become of interest (see Pilny & Poole, 2017).

Measuring Outputs

Researchers often observe and measure outputs, though it is worth noting that outputs exist at either or both the group and individual levels. At the group level, a common outcome of interest is the group's choice, which in some cases is fixed (e.g., a jury) or quite variable, for example, a group's consensus on a psychological profile as described earlier (Bonito, 2006). And other outputs might be of interest, for example, efficiency, in terms of the time and effort needed to work on a task (Luciano et al., 2018), and productivity (e.g., the number of ideas generated by a brainstorming group). Many options are available at the individual level. Park (2008), for example, measured satisfaction after discussion with a set of items based on Keyton's (1991) conceptualization and operationalization of the construct. Because persuasion and influence are important concepts related to group performance, scholars have asked participants to identify the most influential group members (e.g., Bonito, 2006; Marcus et al., 2000) after having completed the discussion task.

The preceding highlights the "level of analysis" problem when researching small discussion groups, which means that it is possible to collect data from either individuals or groups, or both. This choice, as is true of any methodological decision, is or should be based on conceptual issues.[9] In the example about participation and group outcomes, one would have to count the unit of participation for each person in each group, as well as determine the group's choice; the former constitutes individual-level data and the latter a group-level measure. One "tell" is that individual-level data vary (or has the potential to vary) within groups and group-level data does not (i.e., each person must have the same score for that variable).[10] If the question concerns the relationship between participation and satisfaction, then both variables are at the individual level (participation and satisfaction likely vary within groups), and if the association between the amount of time a group takes to complete its task and the quality of the outcome (e.g., whether the decision is correct or assuming the task has a correct answer) is of interest, then both variables are at the group level. Finally, it is common, when circumstances dictate (e.g., when data are nonindependent) to aggregate individual-level data, a common example of which is to take the group mean. In the example about participation and group outcomes, analysis is simplified if both variables are at the level of the group. The problem with aggregation is that the aggregate might not well represent the scores that comprise it (Bliese, 2000). Imagine a four-person group in which participation scores/counts are 10, 12, 40, and 50; the mean is 28, which isn't very close to any of the scores. In such cases, it might make sense to capture or use the dispersion of the scores, for example, the standard deviation (i.e., the average distance of scores from their mean), which for the four participation counts above is approximately 20. A measure of dispersion like the standard division gives a sense of similarity among scores within a group, but other options are available (see Coulter, 1989).

I conclude this section by noting that a given construct is often credibly operationalized (i.e., converted to an observation and corresponding measurement) in several ways. Consider the problem of speaker frequency or participation that I used in the aforementioned example. One might record groups discussing a problem and then count the number of times each participant speaks. But this approach begs many questions, including what to do about interruptions, nonverbal behavior (e.g., a head nod, which often means "yes" or signals agreement), and when one person starts a sentence but another finishes it (Goodwin, 1981). Beyond those issues, another problem is whether to use the speaking turn, sentence, phrase, or word as the unit of analysis (Tsai, 1977). An interesting approach to measuring speaking frequency is to use a computer to measure whether and when participants produce verbal sounds (Dabbs Jr. & Ruback, 1987). But not all sounds indicate speaking, which means the data are likely sprinkled with both verbal communication and other types of behavior (e.g., coughing). The bottom line is a given method is not judged in terms of correctness but by validity – does the described method capture an aspect of the construct in a way that is defensible?

Task

When a researcher develops or poses a question about group processes and/or outcomes, he or she is faced with the problem of choosing, assuming a laboratory study, a task that compels members to interact in ways that are relevant given the research question. And if the study involves observations of natural groups (Frey, 1994), ones who work on a task or problem as a function of occupational or other types of obligations (e.g., developing a budget for a school district in the US; Tracy, 2007), task choice is still relevant. There are countless tasks on which groups work but it is helpful to identify relevant characteristics or dimensions on which tasks vary that, among other things, (a) provide insight into what types of processes one might expect to observe, (b) whether and how process is related to outcomes, and (c) generalize findings from a given task to others with similar characteristics.

McGrath (1984) posed a relevant and important question regarding the relationship between tasks, interaction, and outcomes.

> If we want to learn about groups as vehicles for performing tasks, we must either (a) assume that all tasks are alike, in regard to how groups of various kinds can and do perform them; or
> (b) take into account differences in group performance as they arise from differences in tasks.
> (McGrath, 1984, p. 53)

Clearly, all tasks are not alike – rendering a verdict in a criminal case seems different from preparing a budget or hiring a new football coach. But we can approach the problem in a slightly different way (one implied in McGrath quote above) by asking whether it makes sense to compare different groups working on the same task or have groups work on different tasks. The answer is it depends on the research question of interest. The first approach (i.e., many groups work on the same task) seems relevant if the task lends itself to different problem-solving approaches, which are important to document and evaluate (e.g., Poole, 1983). The second approach, often used in experiments, allows one to examine the correspondence between task features and problem-solving interaction, though field studies might also evaluate differences in interaction and outcomes for a set of tasks (Keyton & Beck, 2009).

Although there are several approaches to conceptualizing tasks (including Chapter 13 and 15 in this volume), I focus on the task circumplex (McGrath, 1984; McGrath & Hollingshead, 1994), which arrays tasks on two dimensions, the first the extent to which the task requires cognitive or behavioral performance and the second the degree of collaboration required. Four general types of tasks can be derived from combinations of the two dimensions. The four task types are *execute, generate, choose, and negotiate*. Execution tasks (e.g., sports contests) require little collaboration but a fair amount of coordination and are largely behavioral (see Chapter 23 in this volume), whereas generation tasks, for example, brainstorming, are somewhat cognitive and collaborative in nature but usually do not require the group to make a choice (Straus, 1999). Negotiation and choice tasks do typically involve group-level choices but vary in whether conflict resolution is involved (e.g., Weingart et al., 2007). Though there are exceptions to the rule, most studies of small decision-making groups use some version of choice or negotiation tasks. As Straus (1999) notes, choice tasks are interdependent, which implies that any given contributions to discussion influences what gets said and by whom, which in turn has some bearing on group choice.

An important feature that distinguishes among choice problems is *demonstrability*, which is the extent to which a task has a correct answer that can be shown as such (Laughlin & Ellis, 1986). Demonstrability is a continuum, with *intellective* tasks at one end and *judgmental* tasks at the other. An intellective task has a correct answer and judgmental tasks do not, at least in any obvious way. An example of an intellective task is a mathematical problem (e.g., solving a differential equation) and another is diagnosing a computer network glitch – both have correct solutions that can be demonstrated (e.g., the network returns to normal operating conditions). An instance of a judgmental task is hiring a new basketball or football coach for a university or college. Conceptualizing tasks in this way creates an interesting set of questions, especially concerning judgmental tasks. If the problem or task does not have a correct answer, then on what basis does the group make a choice? How does a university administration, for example, know which coaching candidate to choose? The answer is that justification for a choice is the group's collective wisdom or judgment, and even then, it's hard to know after the fact if the group made the best choice. For some universities, hiring a football coach whose teams occasionally qualify for mid-level bowl games is an indicator that the hire was a good one and for other schools such a record would be an abject failure. Unlike an intellective task, for which the correct solution is or should be obvious, the potential outcomes and criteria on which an outcome is evaluated are subject to debate.

The preceding suggests that intellective tasks tend not to foster discussion or debate whereas judgmental tasks do, which is partially true. All things being equal, one is likely to observe variation in process and outcomes with judgmental tasks and less so with intellective tasks. As is often the case, there is more to the story. Some judgmental tasks, under the right conditions, appear to have correct answers and some intellective tasks not so much. Evidence presented during a criminal trial, for example, might leave little doubt regarding the defendant's guilt, and the academic record for a university professor far exceeds the minimum requirements for promotion and tenure. Some intellective tasks might not appear on the surface to point to the correct solution, for example, a medical team's initial diagnosis based on a set of symptoms typically associated with a given illness or malady might be wrong or lead the team down a path that risks the health and well-being of the patient.

Let's return to the problem of whether to observe groups working on the same task and using multiple tasks. If the goal is to produce different interaction patterns and problem-solving approaches, some sort of judgmental task that does not point to an obvious solution or outcome seems appropriate. And if one suspects participant characteristics or group composition, for example, is related to group interaction patterns and outcomes, then one must use a task that produces variation in process and outcomes – if interaction patterns or outcomes do not vary, then it is impossible to establish a statistical association with any predictor variables. Conversely, if one assumes that interaction patterns vary with task type, then one should choose tasks that produce different interaction trajectories, as Stasser and Stewart (1992) did when comparing tasks that compelled groups to either make a judgment or solve a problem.

Although there is much more to the story, a related aspect of tasks indicates whether and how discussion is essential for decision making – whether members initially agree on a solution. As an example, consider a criminal jury that hears evidence and testimony, and then heads to the jury room to deliberate. It is important to note that all federal and most state criminal trials in the US require unanimous verdicts. Imagine the jurors take a straw poll shortly after sequestration, the results of which show complete unanimity on the verdict. As there is no minimum deliberation time for juries, and without disagreement there is very little to discuss (cf. Bonito & Sanders, 2011), the jury might choose to notify the court that it has reached a verdict. But if the straw poll reveals disagreement, then discussion seems in order, and there is some evidence that the size of the factions advocating each verdict option influences what is discussed and for how long (Tanford & Penrod, 1986). For intellective tasks, however, as long as one member knows the correct answer and is motivated to demonstrate it (and the other members are motivated to hear it), the problem is likely solved quickly with little discussion, but if two members claim to know the correct answer and both propose different solutions, discussion might take on a different trajectory. It is worth nothing that disagreement can be artificially created in the laboratory – see Chapter 13 in this volume.

Procedure

It is common, when describing quantitative research, to make a broad distinction between experiments and descriptive designs. I use that approach here, although I note at the outset that overly broad distinctions hide or obscure relevant nuances that factor in conclusions drawn about a study's results. The study of groups makes things even more challenging because many issues involving interacting discussion groups are beyond the researcher's control, though my contention is that such "loose ends" are precisely what makes the study of small groups compelling and interesting.

Experiments

The term **experiment** is often used indiscriminately to describe any type of research, though not all (and probably the minority of) studies on small discussion groups are "true" experiments. An experiment has two defining characteristics, the first of which is the manipulation of the independent variable, which the researcher does to essentially change the conditions of the study for a subset of participants (Maxwell & Delaney, 1990). The second defining characteristic of an experiment is random assignment to condition, which means that each participant has an equal likelihood of being in the treatment or control condition. A classic case is a drug treatment study, for example, whether a medication reduces pain, in which some participants are randomly assigned to the treatment condition (they receive the medication) and others the control condition (participants are given a placebo or nothing at all). There are variations on the theme, but the point of such studies is to show conclusively that the medication caused the observed differences in the outcome between the treatment and control groups (e.g., the participants in the treatment group experienced less pain than those in the control group).

A simple but effective way to think about causation is in terms of the relationship between variables X and Y.[11] A claim of causation is warranted if (a) X and Y are correlated, (b) X precedes Y in time, and (c) some third variable Z is not responsible for the association between X and Y (Kirk, 2012). In the case of the drug treatment design described earlier, the first two conditions are met, as (a) Y (the outcome of interest) is related to X (participants who received the medication are observed to be in less pain compared to those who received the placebo) and (b) the medication was given prior to the measurement of the outcome. Evaluating the third criterion, that another variable Z isn't responsible for the association between X and Y, requires more information about the design. Perhaps the most important element is whether participants were randomly assigned to conditions. What does random assignment buy us? It provides evidence, or at least makes it quite plausible, that the level of the dependent variable (pain, in the example) is comparable across groups prior to the administration of the treatment. In short, randomization controls for confounding variables (which lead to alternate explanations for the results) and adds a sense of validity to the findings. If the dependent variable changes as expected after the administration of the treatment (e.g., mean reported pain of individuals in the experimental group is lower than that for the control group), then one might rule out other competing explanations for the results.

Experiments provide the same general set of assumptions regarding causality and alternative explanations for studies of small discussion groups. Imagine a study in which 100 four-person discussion groups work on a task and the question is whether knowing the task has a correct answer affects whether the group makes the right or best choice (Stasser & Stewart, 1992). This design is akin to the drug treatment example described earlier: a treatment-control design. Participants are randomly assigned to groups (which reduce the likelihood that groups of friends work on a task, which eliminates that as a potential confound) and groups to the treatment or control condition. The treatment group receives the experimental manipulation (informed that the task has a correct answer) and the control group does not. Assuming that groups in the treatment condition do correctly solve the problem more frequently than those in the control, then the first two criteria of causation are satisfied: X (whether a group is told that the task has a correct answer) and Y (whether the group solves the problem correctly) are associated and X precedes Y in time (the treatment was administered before groups worked on the problem). And if participants were randomly assigned to groups and groups to condition, then there is sufficient evidence for causality.

If an experiment is the "gold standard" because it establishes causation if done well, then one is right to wonder why researchers would use other types of designs. The answer is threefold. First, in some cases it's not always possible or desirable to randomly assign participants to groups and groups to conditions; second, finding or creating a control group is not feasible, possible, or desirable (Laughlin, 2012); and third, the researcher cannot or is unable to manipulate the independent variable. Consider the study by Cohen and Ledford (1994) in which self-managed and "traditional" (i.e., contained a leader or manager with decision-making authority) teams in a telecommunications company (a term that used to describe delivery of analog services, e.g., landline telephones) were compared in terms of effectiveness. The researchers identified a set of self-managed and traditional teams within the company; each team was created by management to support the company's needs and functions and not for the study. Thus, participants were not randomly assigned to either of the two conditions. Study designs of this type are included under the umbrella "quasi-experiments" which, as the name implies, contain at least some elements of a true experiment (e.g., attempts to control extraneous variables) but not randomization to condition. Though the study did find differences in efficiency as predicted, one might wonder if the results would be different if participants were randomly assigned to groups and groups to condition. At the very least, it is reasonable to suggest that the results might tell us something about the benefits of self-managed teams, but the fact that the company assigned employees to self-managed teams precisely because those employees displayed greater ability to work independently than other employees might account for the results.

Another type of quasi-experiment includes multiple observations of groups, in which prior observations serve as a control for comparison with subsequent ones. One version of this design is to observe one set of groups under one condition and another set of groups under a different condition, as Alizadeh et al. (2018) did when evaluating leadership identity development. Some groups were assigned to a reflection and feedback condition, which occurred between measurements of leadership identity; the other groups were measured twice, too, but not given the feedback intervention. Changes in leadership identity could be due to the intervention or some other mechanism related to time (e.g., members getting to know each other and/or the task better).

One other type of quasi-experiments with a time component worth mentioning is when all groups are observed multiple times under the same conditions or process. To make this design type more concrete, let's return to the example of pain reduction, in which (a) all participants are measured for pain level, (b) all are given the medication, then (c) all are measured for pain level again after some suitable period has passed. Furthermore, assume that the level of observed or reported pain after administration of the medication was less than that reported prior to the administration. What alternative explanations for the results are plausible? One might argue that pain tends to decrease on its own over time, or that high levels of pain tend to reduce over time (however temporarily) or that the initial measurement of pain had some bearing on reported pain after the treatment. This type of design, referred to as a pretest/posttest, one-group experiment, leaves enough room to cast doubt on at least some percentage, if not all, of the results, simply because of what is known to be true of the effects of time on pain in the absence of the treatment.

Group and team training studies often use designs like the one-group pain medication quasi-experiment described earlier (Salas et al., 2007). Many training studies involve participants and teams that provide professional services, for example, medical teams, and it often isn't possible or desirable to recruit or compose groups for a control condition. In such cases, groups are measured on the outcome variable of interest (e.g., effectiveness and productivity) and then are asked to participate in a training program, which can be administered by the researcher in person or via a webpage that walks teams through the training steps. Following the training, groups are again measured on the outcome variable of interest. Assuming improvement from the pretest to posttest, one might argue, among other things, that some other factor, either in concert with or in lieu of the factor (e.g., natural tendency of groups to improve performance over time) is responsible for results. In such cases, if it is not feasible to include a control group and/or random assignment, one is well advised to take multiple measures both prior to and after the training to determine whether the type of natural improvement occurs and whether it persists.

Descriptive Studies

Descriptive quantitative studies, as the name implies, focus on numeric assessments of a population, based on sample data, examples of which include (but are not limited to) frequencies, means, standard deviations, and correlations (Keyton, 2018). Descriptive quantitative studies are often quite useful but offer none of the characteristics associated with experiments or quasi-experiments, which means that the criteria for causality do not apply in the same way, if at all. In most cases, descriptive studies do not include or involve, intentionally, at least, observations made under different conditions. A classic example is a survey (most of which are online) in which a sample of participants responds to the same set of questions (although it is common to set up surveys to skip questions based on previous responses if needed – it makes little sense, for example, to ask a never-married respondent about marital harmony). Results are often modeled with sophisticated statistical techniques to demonstrate associations among relevant variables and, although causal relationships are difficult to establish in such designs, researchers often include control variables to "remove" their influence on the variables of interest. For example, Killumets et al. (2015) examined the effect of professional familiarity and organization commitment on team effectiveness, and included, among other things, sex, age, and education as covariates – doing so effectively renders participants as "equal" on those variables by removing their association from the focus variables. What's left are estimates of the relationship among the variables of interest, in this case familiarity, commitment, and effectiveness, that account for whatever influence the covariates might have on those relationships. Even then, one is hard-pressed to make causal inferences, based on the rules of causality described earlier; because the design offers no control, it is likely that many other unmeasured variables ("Z" variables) have some bearing on the results.

Descriptive studies need not be surveys; they can involve laboratory and field studies. An example of a laboratory study is Parker (1988), who had participants in four-person groups get to know each other. (Participants were told that the task was important for understanding how job applicants were selected.) Parker's objective was to examine sequences of speaking turns for some type of order. In turns out that discussion consists largely of pairs of speakers taking turns, such that Persons A and B address each other for several turns while Persons C and D remain quiet, which led Parker to conclude that the "floor" (a metaphor based on public speaking forums in which a person is given or obtains the right to speak to those assembled) is an interdependent, interpersonal process in groups. Floors can be broken (e.g., Person C says something) which almost always resolves to another floor state (e.g., Persons C and B say a few things in sequence); rarely is speaker order random, an important finding that stimulated others (Stasser & Taylor, 1991) to identify mechanisms that explain floor processes. Similarly, Lehmann-Willenbrock et al. (2013) examined sequential properties of group interaction by recording meetings from teams whose members were employed by one of several German companies.

Qualitative Methods for the Study of Small Discussion Groups

Unlike quantitative approaches to the study of small groups, qualitative research preserves, as much as possible, the content and context in which discussions take place. As such, the point of qualitative research is less about generalizing to some larger population, as is true of most quantitative studies, and more about developing a deeper and richer understanding of group communication processes and decision making, often from the participants' point of view. I address three issues related to the qualitative study of small discussion groups. The first issue concerns the metatheoretical underpinnings of qualitative research, in general, and the second, methods of data collection. Finally, I address how scholars evaluate and interpret qualitative data.

Metatheoretical Issues

The most obvious difference between qualitative and quantitative research is that the latter converts observations to numbers whereas the former does not, but that is an oversimplification and misses the larger point. In essence, qualitative researchers are interested in observing behavior in context, which generally involves the researchers traveling to places where the behaviors in question are likely to be found. For example, Sigman (1984) observed a private nursing home's admission board as they carried on their work in their offices and meeting rooms, and Kramer (2004) studied the interactions and workings of a community theater group in the American Midwest. Observing group meetings in context underlies a more central assumption of most qualitative work; it is difficult, if not impossible, to understand behavior without observing it in context, over time, and with people and groups working on real problems that have some relevance to their lives. Artificial settings, such as student groups working in a laboratory under contrived conditions, so the story goes, offers fairly superficial accounts of how groups work through problems and make decisions. Thus, one is quite unlikely to find anything resembling an experimental manipulation in qualitative research because most do not resemble or look anything like what one finds in the real world.

Another issue is objectivity – quantitative researchers often strive for it and many qualitative researchers reject it or, perhaps more accurately, recognize and often embrace implicit and explicit biases carried into research settings and interpretation of data. An example is critical ethnography, in which the researcher's goal is to apply a lens that questions key assumptions about the people and behavior of interest (Conquergood, 1991). I agree with Trochim (2023) in that both points raised by qualitative researchers, context and subjectivity, are valid concerns, and their consideration is vital to understanding the results of and implications for all research. Similarly, objections raised concerning qualitative research, most notably issues of **generalizability** (among other things) should be considered when evaluating findings based on that approach.

Data Collection

All sorts of data gathering techniques are possible with qualitative research. A simple, and perhaps overly broad, approach to describing qualitative research is the extent to which the researcher interacts with and affects the behaviors of the group in question (cf. Kramer & Zanin, 2021). In some cases, researchers assume the role, by design or not, of participant observer which, as the name implies, situates the researcher as both a "player" in and an observer of the unfolding stream of communication and behavior. An interesting case is Conquergood's (1994) ethnographic study of gangs and gang culture, which he began by moving into a building in the neighborhood of interest and developing relationships with the young men and women who would become both his subjects and collaborators.[12] Yet another case, noted above, is Kramer's (2004) observations of a community theater group, in which the author worked and performed. Studies of this type typically fall under the umbrella ethnography, which involves a researcher's immersion into the culture or group of interest over a relatively long period of time. Not all, however, require participation observation; Sigman (1984), for example, observed but did not participate in the decision-making efforts of the nursing home's admission board. Studies of this type cast the researcher as an observer-participant – although the researcher does not directly play a role in the behaviors under observation, he or she indirectly affects such observations by his or her presence.[13]

Other options for qualitative research include interviews and focus groups. Both methods provide opportunities for those studied to weigh in on a researcher's interpretations of the behaviors and events in question (Sigman, 1980). In both cases, one might employ unstructured or loose protocols that allow the participant to describe assumptions, rules, and norms without being "steered" by the researcher's perspective or interpretation. One other option is retrospective or archival studies (Kramer & Zanin, 2021). For example, Raven (1998) applied the concept of groupthink (Janis, 1972) to decisions made by the Nixon white house to (a) break in to the Democratic National Committee's headquarters in the Watergate Hotel and (b) cover up the break in, both of which led to Nixon's resignation. Raven worked with transcripts of Nixon's recorded meetings (and many of those caught on tape were unaware of being recorded), the televised hearings, interviews, and other sources to reconstruct whether and how groupthink set in. (One would be hard pressed to ascribe such a monumentally and historically bad decision to anything else, but Raven offers some interesting alternative assessments.) Finally, Kramer and Zanin (2021) describe conditions under which one might interview individuals away from their groups in order to ascertain perspectives that might not otherwise emerge in group interview settings.

Data Analysis

As is evident from the preceding, qualitative research usually produces mountains of data in a variety of formats, including recordings, archival documents, text, and field notes. Analysis is often iterative, with the researcher forming initial impressions of the data at some level of abstraction and then checking those impressions with other data, including participant interpretations. Trochim (2023) notes that it is something of a canard to say that qualitative research and data analysis is inductive and that quantitative data analysis is deductive – there are plenty of examples to the contrary. But it is true to say that the deductive approach (sometimes called or linked with a positivist orientation) allows examination of whether data support theoretical claims and/or hypotheses, but doing so often creates unreasonable assumptions or findings of questionable validity. The inductive approach, to some extent, allows the data to suggest more abstract assessments of the processes and behaviors under examination, an example of which is Adelman and Frey's (1994) study of an AIDS hospice and the emotional challenges faced by a team of volunteers in caring for the terminally ill. A well-known inductive approach often used by qualitative researchers is grounded theory, which, among other things, produces theoretical claims based on observations. Analyses based on grounded theory often start with some level of data coding, which means looking for patterns or commonalities among observations, and then assessing those associations as they evolve throughout the study and data analysis. (Many qualitative studies continue observations while examining data already collected.) This approach produces a level of detail regarding group processes that often lead to conceptual avenues and illumination that could not have been anticipated at the study's planning and inception.

Finally, it is worth noting that findings from qualitative research are held to similar standards as those produced by quantitative researchers, though the evaluative criteria are necessarily different. Whereas reporting quantitative research often follows a fairly standard format (which for most is based on the APA publication manual), there is some leeway for qualitative researchers to report results. A recent article, however, produced by an APA task force (Levitt et al., 2018), provides a set of guidelines that, for better or worse, propose a more standardized reporting format for qualitative research, which might make things easier in terms of assessing the quality of the results. Whereas one might evaluate quantitative design and measurement in terms of validity (i.e., whether observations measure or correspond to the construct of interest) and reliability (i.e., if similar results are obtained using the same or similar measures and design), the value of qualitative studies is assessed on different grounds. For example, qualitative research is often judged on credibility, in terms of whether results provide some insight into participants' perspectives, and dependability, which is whether and how a researcher accounts for the fluid and changing nature of context. In short, qualitative and quantitative studies address important but usually different questions – they should be viewed as complementary rather than competing.

Conclusion

The study of small discussion groups employs many methods to address different aspects of what is a rich and varied phenomenon. The method chosen is based on the question asked, and if the match between the two is appropriate, then the results have some level of validity. Asking good questions about small group discussion helps address what is arguable the primary function of group research, which is understanding how groups make decisions, including what groups do well and poorly, and using results to provide guidance for real life groups about best decision-making practices.

Notes

1 There are two senses of the term "methodology." The first refers to the study or analysis of methods within a particular domain and the second is the accepted or prescribed set of data gathering procedures in a given field. I use the latter sense of the term throughout, but the first sense is also relevant, as the study of methods highlights what procedures typically work and those that do not.

2 Most academic departments train budding scholars in either quantitative or qualitative methodologies, a choice which reflects a historical perspective on the phenomenon in question. Though there are exceptions, quantitative scholars ask questions that suggest designs that produce numeric data and qualitative scholars form their inquiries to examine data that are not meant (and in some cases are impossible) to be quantified. The point is that choices exist within each methodological domain, and most designs reflect the research question of interest.

3 The US Constitution requires a census (i.e., everyone is measured or accounted for) every 10 years for the purposes of congressional representation. But the census is rarely perfect—some groups are more likely than others to be undercounted for a variety of reasons. In practice, a census is extremely rare.

4 Two items are worth mentioning. First, Bales's participants were Harvard undergraduates, and Harvard did not admit women until 1975. Before then, women matriculated at Radcliffe College and were taught by Harvard faculty (Walsh, 2012). Second, most professional and academic groups of the time likely contained only or mostly men, so Bales's findings might have generalized then.

5 Participants have the option not to respond to a question and/or researchers offer an option along the lines of "prefer not to say." All studies conducted by university-affiliated researchers must be approved by an institutional review board (IRB) which, among other things, exists to protect the rights of participants. One of those rights is not to be coerced or forced to answer any item in a given survey.

6 It's hard to believe now, but the original Bales's (1950) studies had to make do with real-time scoring of discussion, as recording devices of the time were expensive and not widely available. My dissertation data were recorded using "camcorders," which was state of the art and not terribly expensive. Of course, today one might use smart phones to record groups and upload the recordings to the cloud.

7 In either case, researchers are generally agnostic about whether a given coding scheme captures what participants intended when a given comment was made. Poole and Folger (1981) used the term "representational validity" to describe the (mis)match between a researcher's coding and a participant's intent.

8 AI bots are based on unsupervised methods—OpenAI, the organization that developed the ChatGPT platform, trained the system on millions of Reddit conversations (https://www.nytimes.com/2023/04/18/technology/reddit-ai-openai-google.html).

9 There are also statistical issues to consider. Sample size is related to statistical power, which is the likelihood the null hypothesis is rejected when it (the null hypothesis) is not true of the population. Greater sample size leads to more power, all things equal. Using the inappropriate level of analysis has implications for power by either amplifying or attenuating it. For example, as study with 25 four-person groups has 100 participants but, if the analysis is (or should be) at the group level, then $N = 25$. It would be tempting to analyze the data at the individual level because power would be much greater, but doing so would be wrong.

10 It is possible for scores to vary within groups but not between (Kenny et al., 2006). For example, if each group has two males and two females, then gender varies within but not between groups—at the group level, the score is the same (e.g., the proportion of males and/or females to group size is .5) for all groups.

11 Symbols of this type are common in statistics because they allow generalization without getting bogged down with the features of a specific set of variables.

12 I had the good fortune to hear Conquergood give a guest lecture when I was in graduate school. He was still doing his fieldwork and the results of the study had yet to be widely distributed. I was struck by his commitment to the work and research participants, and quite moved by the points he made regarding mainstream perceptions of gangs. Interested readers should watch the documentary of his work, titled "Heart Broken in Half," that he and his research participants produced. It is available as of this writing on YouTube.

13 In most cases, participants must consent to being observed and studied. In some older studies, researchers would mask or conceal their identities as researchers so that participants would act "normally." Such practices are currently (and appropriately) not allowed by institutional review boards because of ethical and perhaps legal issues.

Further Readings

Bonito, J. A. (2002). The analysis of participation in small groups: Methodological and conceptual issues related to interdependence. *Small Group Research, 33*(4), 412–438. https://doi.org/10.1177/104649640203300402

Hewes, D. E., & Poole, M. S. (2012). The analysis of group interaction processes. In A. B. Hollingshead & M. S. Poole (Eds.), *Research methods for studying groups and teams: A guide to approaches, tools, and technologies* (pp. 358–385). Routledge.

Poole, M. S., Keyton, J., & Frey, L. R. (1999). Group communication methodology. In L. R. Frey, D. S. Gouran, & M. S. Poole (Eds.), *The handbook of group communication theory and research* (pp. 93–112). Sage.

Glossary

Experiment A specific type of study that in base form compares control and treatment groups. Participants are randomly assigned to either the treatment or control. The researcher manipulates the independent variable, which changes the conditions under which participants experience the study.

Generalizability Is the extent to which study results obtained from a sample can be used to describe characteristics of a population.

Survey research A study technique that captures self-reports from participants using a set of questions that measure a construct (e.g., satisfaction), experiences (e.g., time spent working in small groups), or demographic information.

Fieldwork Research that takes place away from the laboratory. In most cases, the purpose is to observe groups as they go about their normal activities on any given day.

References

Abelson, R. P. (1995). *Statistics as principled argument* (1st ed.). Psychology Press.

Adelman, M. B., & Frey, L. R. (1994). The pilgrim must embark: Creating and sustaining community in a residential facility for people with AIDS. In L. R. Frey (Ed.), Group communication in context: Studies of natural groups (pp. 3–22). Erlbaum.

Alizadeh, M., Mirzazadeh, A., Parmelee, D. X., Peyton, E., Mehrdad, N., Janani, L., & Shahsavari, H. (2018). Leadership identity development through reflection and feedback in team-based learning medical student teams. *Teaching and Learning in Medicine, 30*(1), 76–83. https://doi.org/10.1080/10401334.2017.1331134

American Psychological Association. (2020). *Publication manual of the American Psychological Association 2020:* The official guide to APA style (7th ed.). American Psychological Association.

Bales, R. F. (1950). *Interaction process analysis: A method for the study of small groups.* Addison-Wesley.

Balkwell, J. W. (1994). Status. In M. Foschi & E. J. Lawler (Eds.), *Group processes: Sociological analyses* (pp. 119–148). Nelson-Hall.

Bliese, P. D. (2000). Within-group agreement, non-independence, and reliability: Implications for data aggregation and analysis. In K. J. Klein & S. W. J. Kozlowski (Eds.), *Multilevel theory, research, and methods in organizations: Foundations, extensions, and new directions* (pp. 349–381). Jossey-Bass.

Bonito, J. A. (2001). An information-processing approach to participation in small groups. *Communication Research*, *28*(3), 275–303. https://doi.org/10.1177/009365001028003002

Bonito, J. A. (2002). The analysis of participation in small groups: Methodological and conceptual issues related to interdependence. *Small Group Research*, *33*(4), 412–438. https://doi.org/10.1177/104649640203300402

Bonito, J. A. (2006). A longitudinal social relations analysis of participation in small groups. *Human Communication Research*, *32*(3), 302–321. https://doi.org/10.1111/j.1468-2958.2006.00277.x

Bonito, J. A. (2021). Quantitative analysis of group data: Multilevel latent variable models. In S. J. Beck, J. Keyton, & M. Scott Poole (Eds.), *The Emerald handbook of group and team communication research* (pp. 55–72). Emerald Publishing Limited. https://doi.org/10.1108/978-1-80043-500-120211006

Bonito, J. A., & Keyton, J. (2018). Introduction to machine learning. In E. Brauner, M. Boos, & M. Kolbe (Eds.), *The Cambridge handbook of group interaction analysis* (pp. 387–404). Cambridge University Press. https://doi.org/10.1017/9781316286302.020

Bonito, J. A., & Sanders, R. E. (2011). The existential center of small groups: Member's conduct and interaction. *Small Group Research*, *42*(3), 343–358. https://doi.org/10.1177/1046496410385472

Chmielewski, M., & Kucker, S. C. (2020). An MTurk crisis? Shifts in data quality and the impact on study results. *Social Psychological and Personality Science*, *11*(4), 464–473. https://doi.org/10.1177/1948550619875149

Cohen, S. G., & Ledford, G. E. (1994). The effectiveness of self-managing teams: A quasi-experiment. *Human Relations*, *47*(1), 13–43. https://doi.org/10.1177/001872679404700102

Conquergood, D. (1991). Rethinking ethnography: Towards a critical cultural politics. *Communication Monographs*, *58*(2), 179–194. https://doi.org/10.1080/03637759109376222

Conquergood, D. (1994). Homeboys and hoods: Gang communication and cultural space. In L. R. Frey (Ed.), *Group communication in context: Studies of natural groups* (pp. 23–55). Erlbaum.

Coulter, P. (1989). *Measuring inequality: A methodological handbook*. Westview Press.

Dabbs, J. M., Jr., & Ruback, R. B. (1987). Dimensions of group process: Amount and structure of vocal interaction. *Advances in Experimental Social Psychology*, *20*, 123–169. https://doi.org/10.1016/S0065-2601(08)60413-X

Frey, L. R. (1994). The naturalistic paradigm: Studying small groups in the postmodern era. *Small Group Research*, *25*(4), 551–577. https://doi.org/10.1177/1046496494254008

Goodman, J. K., Cryder, C. E., & Cheema, A. (2013). Data collection in a flat world: The strengths and weaknesses of Mechanical Turk samples. *Journal of Behavioral Decision Making*, *26*(3), 213–224. https://doi.org/10.1002/bdm.1753

Goodwin, C. (1981). *Conversational organization: Interaction between speakers and hearers*. Academic Press.

Hoffman, L. R., & Kleinman, G. B. (1994). Individual and group in group problem solving the valence model redressed. *Human Communication Research*, *21*(1), 36–59. https://doi.org/10.1111/j.1468-2958.1994.tb00338.x

Hvitfeldt, E., & Silge, J. (2021). *Supervised machine learning for text analysis in R* (1st ed.). Chapman and Hall/CRC.

Janis, I. (1972). *Victims of groupthink*. Houghton-Mifflin.

Kenny, D. A., Kashy, D. A., & Cook, W. L. (2006). *Dyadic data analysis*. Guilford Press.

Kenny, D. A., Mannetti, L., Pierro, A., Livi, S., & Kashy, D. A. (2002). The statistical analysis of data from small groups. *Journal of Personality and Social Psychology*, *83*(1), 126–137. https://doi.org/10.1037/0022-3514.83.1.126

Keyton, J. (1991). Evaluating individual group member satisfaction as a situational variable. *Small Group Research*, *22*(2), 200–219. https://doi.org/10.1177/1046496491222004

Keyton, J. (2018). *Communication research: Asking questions, finding answers* (5th ed.). McGraw-Hill Higher Education.

Keyton, J., & Beck, S. J. (2009). The influential role of relational messages in group interaction. *Group Dynamics: Theory, Research, and Practice*, *13*, 14–30. https://doi.org/10.1037/a0013495

Killumets, E., D'Innocenzo, L., Maynard, M. T., & Mathieu, J. E. (2015). A multilevel examination of the impact of team interpersonal processes. *Small Group Research*, *46*(2), 227–259. https://doi.org/10.1177/1046496415573631

Kirk, R. E. (2012). *Experimental design: Procedures for the behavioral sciences* (4th ed.). Sage Publications, Inc.

Kramer, M. W. (2004). Toward a communication theory of group dialectics: An ethnographic study of a community theater group. *Communication Monographs, 71*(3), 311–332.

Kramer, M. W., & Zanin, A. C. (2021). Qualitative methods for studying group communication. In S. J. Beck, J. Keyton, & M. S. Poole (Eds.), *The Emerald handbook of group and team communication research* (pp. 73–88). Emerald Publishing Limited. https://doi.org/10.1108/978-1-80043-500-120211007

Laughlin, P. R. (2012). Experimental designs for research on small groups: The five Ps. In A. B. Hollingshead & M. S. Poole (Eds.), *Research methods for studying groups and teams* (pp. 30–40). Routledge.

Laughlin, P. R., & Ellis, A. L. (1986). Demonstrability and social combination processes on mathematical intellective tasks. *Journal of Experimental Social Psychology, 22*, 177–189. https://doi.org/10.1016/0022-1031(86)90022-3

Lehmann-Willenbrock, N., Allen, J. A., & Kauffeld, S. (2013). A sequential analysis of procedural meeting communication: How teams facilitate their meetings. *Journal of Applied Communication Research, 41*(4), 365–388. https://doi.org/10.1080/00909882.2013.844847

Levitt, H. M., Bamberg, M., Creswell, J. W., Frost, D. M., Josselson, R., & Suárez-Orozco, C. (2018). Journal article reporting standards for qualitative primary, qualitative meta-analytic, and mixed methods research in psychology: The APA publications and communications board task force report. *American Psychologist, 73*(1), 26. https://doi.org/10.1037/amp0000151

Luciano, M. M., Bartels, A. L., D'Innocenzo, L., Maynard, M. T., & Mathieu, J. E. (2018). Shared team experiences and team effectiveness: Unpacking the contingent effects of entrained rhythms and task characteristics. *Academy of Management Journal, 61*(4), 1403–1430. https://doi.org/10.5465/amj.2016.0828

Mansbridge, J., Hartz-Karp, J., Amengual, M., & Gastil, J. (2006). Norms of deliberation: An inductive study. *Journal of Public Deliberation, 2*(1).

Marcus, D. K., & Leatherwood, J. C. (1998). The interpersonal circle at zero acquaintance: A social relations analysis. *Journal of Research in Personality, 32*(3), 297–313. https://doi.org/10.1006/jrpe.1998.2222

Marcus, D. K., & Lehman, S. J. (2002). Are there sex differences in interpersonal perception at zero acquaintance? A social relations analysis. *Journal of Research in Personality, 36*, 190–207.

Marcus, D. K., Lyons, P. M. Jr., & Guyton, M. R. (2000). Studying perceptions of juror influence *In Vivo*: A social relations analysis. *Law and Human Behavior, 24*(2), 173–186. https://doi.org/10.1023/A:1005406902505

Maxwell, S. E., & Delaney, H. D. (1990). *Designing experiments and analyzing data: A model comparison perspective*. Wadsworth.

McGrath, J. E. (1984). *Groups: Interaction and performance*. Prentice-Hall.

McGrath, J. E., & Hollingshead, A. B. (1994). *Groups interacting with technology: Ideas, evidence, issues, and an agenda*. Sage Publications, Inc.

Meyers, R. A., & Brashers, D. E. (2010). Extending the conversational argument coding scheme: Argument categories, units, and coding procedures. *Communication Methods and Measures, 4*(1), 27. https://doi.org/10.1080/19312451003680467

Park, H. S. (2008). The effects of shared cognition on group satisfaction and performance: Politeness and efficiency in group interaction. *Communication Research, 35*(1), 88–108. https://doi.org/10.1177/0093650207309363

Parker, K. C. (1988). Speaking turns in small group interaction: A context-sensitive event sequence model. *Journal of Personality and Social Psychology, 54*(6), 965–971. https://doi.org/10.1037/0022-3514.54.6.965

Pilny, A., Dobosh, M., Yahja, A., Poole, M. S., Campbell, A., Ruge-Jones, L., & Proulx, J. (2020). Team coordination in uncertain environments: The role of processual communication networks. *Human Communication Research, 46*(4), 385–411. https://doi.org/10.1093/hcr/hqz020

Pilny, A., & Poole, M. S. (Eds.). (2017). *Group processes: Data-driven computational approaches* (1st ed.). Springer.

Poole, M. S. (1983). Decision development in small groups III: A multiple sequence model of group decision development. *Communication Monographs, 50*, 321–342. https://doi.org/10.1080/03637758309390173

Poole, M. S., & Folger, J. P. (1981). A method for establishing the representational validity of interaction coding systems: Do we see what they see? *Human Communication Research, 8*(1), 26–42. http://dx.doi.org/10.1111/j.1468-2958.1981.tb00654.x

Poole, M. S., Holmes, M., Watson, R., & DeSanctis, G. (1993). Group decision support systems and group communication: A comparison of decision making in computer-supported and nonsupported groups. *Communication Research, 20*(2), 176–213.

Poole, M. S., Keyton, J., & Frey, L. R. (1999). Group communication methodology. In L. R. Frey, D. S. Gouran, & M. S. Poole (Eds.), *The handbook of group communication theory and research* (pp. 93–112). Sage.

Prosser, C., & Mellon, J. (2018). The twilight of the polls? A review of trends in polling accuracy and the causes of polling misses. *Government and Opposition, 53*(4), 757–790. https://doi.org/10.1017/gov.2018.7

Raven, B. H. (1998). Groupthink, Bay of Pigs, and Watergate reconsidered. *Organizational Behavior and Human Decision Processes, 73*, 352–361.

Salas, E., Nichols, D. R., & Driskell, J. E. (2007). Testing three team training strategies in intact teams: A meta-analysis. *Small Group Research, 38*, 471–488.

Sigman, S. J. (1980). On communication rules from a social perspective. *Human Communication Research, 7*, 37–51.

Sigman, S. J. (1984). Talk and interaction strategy in a task-oriented group. *Small Group Research, 15*(1), 33–51. https://doi.org/10.1177/104649648401500102

Staggs, S. M., Bonito, J. A., & Ervin, J. N. (2018). Measuring and evaluating convergence processes across a series of group discussions. *Group Decision and Negotiation, 27*(5), 715–733. https://doi.org/10.1007/s10726-018-9560-3

Stasser, G., & Stewart, D. (1992). Discovery of hidden profiles by decision-making groups: Solving a problem versus making a judgment. *Journal of Personality and Social Psychology, 63*(3), 426–434. https://doi.org/10.1037/0022-3514.63.3.426

Stasser, G., & Taylor, L. A. (1991). Speaking turns in face-to-face discussions. *Journal of Personality and Social Psychology, 60*(5), 675–684. https://doi.org/10.1037/0022-3514.60.5.675

Straus, S. G. (1999). Testing a typology of tasks—An empirical validation of McGrath's (1984) group task circumplex. *Small Group Research, 30*(2), 166–187.

Tanford, S., & Penrod, S. (1986). Jury deliberations: Discussion content and influence processes in jury decision making. *Journal of Applied Social Psychology, 16*(4), 322–347.

Teschner, F., & Gimpel, H. (2018). Crowd labor markets as platform for group decision and negotiation research: A comparison to laboratory experiments. *Group Decision and Negotiation, 27*(2), 197–214. https://doi.org/10.1007/s10726-018-9565-y

Tracy, K. (2007). The discourse of crisis in public meetings: Case study of a school district's multimillion dollar error. *Journal of Applied Communication Research, 35*(4), 418–441. https://doi.org/10.1080/00909880701617133

Trochim, W. M. K. (2023, February). *The research methods knowledge base.* https://conjointly.com/kb/cite-kb/

Tsai, Y. (1977). Hierarchical structure of participation in natural groups. *Behavioral Science, 22*(1), 38–40. https://doi.org/10.1002/bs.3830220106

Walsh, C. (2012, April 26). Hard-earned gains for women at Harvard. *Harvard Gazette.* https://news.harvard.edu/gazette/story/2012/04/hard-earned-gains-for-women-at-harvard/

Weingart, L. R., Brett, J. M., Olekalns, M., & Smith, P. L. (2007). Conflicting social motives in negotiating groups. *Journal of Personality and Social Psychology, 93*(6), 994–1010. https://doi.org/10.1037/0022-3514.93.6.994

5 The Use of Technology in Groups

Emily A. Paskewitz and Mark E. Willoughby

Chapter Objectives

- Understand how FTF and CMC group research provided a foundation for group technology research.
- Explain these theoretical perspectives of group technology use: media richness theory, adaptive structuration theory, and multicommunication.
- Describe different types of technology available to groups in today's world.
- Help your groups determine which technology(ies) to use based on your unique context.
- Evaluate the costs and benefits to technology use in groups.

Introduction

Traditionally, group communication researchers focus on groups meeting in face-to-face (FTF) or computer-mediated communication (CMC) settings. Though these two settings are important and still common, the advent of technology has shifted research to explore how group members utilize technology in FTF or CMC meetings. Most groups in today's organizations utilize technology during meetings. From laptops to take notes, mobile phones to check in with absent individuals or find needed information, group members continue to utilize technology to manage group projects. As a result, most groups vary in their level of virtuality and cannot be defined by one context and one communication medium (Gibbs et al., 2017). Many groups utilize multiple **information and communication technologies** (ICTs) throughout group work that aid their ability to work on tasks and complete assignments (Straube et al., 2018).

The increase of technology use in groups has many impacts. Some researchers find many benefits to technology use in groups, including being available to talk with others (Stephens, 2012), improved productivity (Cameron et al., 2016), and the ability to "invisibly whisper" with other members during the meeting (Dennis et al., 2010). Others point to challenges with technology use in groups, such as distracting participants (Piercy & Underhill, 2021), and poor evaluations of individuals' focus and contribution, and group meeting effectiveness and satisfaction due to assuming the technology use is unrelated to the meeting (Paskewitz & Beck, 2019, 2021). However, the positive or negative impact of technology use in groups has less to do with the medium used and has more to do with the norms and rules groups create for utilizing and managing technology use.

This chapter begins with a review of research on FTF and CMC groups as a foundation for understanding groups and technology use. The rest of the chapter focuses on how groups utilize technology in their everyday work. First, three theoretical perspectives researchers use

DOI: 10.4324/9781003227458-6

to explore group technology use are introduced: **media richness theory** highlights how group members select specific technologies, **adaptive structuration theory** focuses on whether group members utilize technology as intended, and **multicommunication** researchers explore how technology is used to participate in multiple conversations simultaneously. Second, the discussion turns to technologies available to groups and how groups choose which technologies to utilize. Next, the benefits and costs associated with technology use highlight the challenges for group members. Finally, recommendations for practitioners are offered to help managers as they guide group efforts.

Early Research View: Face-to-Face Versus Computer-Mediated Groups

Starting in the early 2000s, group researchers began exploring communicative differences between FTF and CMC groups. In this work, CMC groups were typified by a limited ability to send communication cues (cues-filtered-out [CFO] perspective; Bordia et al., 1999; Dennis et al., 1999), and occurred almost exclusively via text-based chatting in laboratory settings (e.g., Hobman et al., 2002; Zornoza et al., 2002). This early work highlighted the unique challenges associated with CMC group interaction, specifically focusing on the lack of nonverbal cues available to participants. For example, Barrett and Murphy (2021) found participants in both FTF and CMC 12-Step meetings preferred the FTF setting due to the personal nature of in person meetings. In another study, Dennis et al. (1999) found females felt the loss of nonverbal cues more than male participants did, which impacted female team performance.

This lack of nonverbal cues common in CMC research was termed by Walther and Burgoon (1992) as social information processing, whereby CMC group members had limited nonverbal cues to facilitate relational development. Instead, CMC groups need more time to build relationships with other group members due to the limitations of the text-based medium (Walther, 1996). Social information processing informed many CMC studies going forward, with researchers replicating Walther and Burgoon's (1992) assertions. Further work led to the development of a hyperpersonal CMC framework (Walther, 1996) which explained that CMC may be more desirable for relationship building due to the idealized identities group members presented in CMC settings. For example, Hian et al. (2005) found CMC groups were able to form relationships at a faster rate than FTF groups. This rapid development of relationships was likely due to members being able to create idealized versions of themselves that appear attractive to other group members.

However, this idealized identity creation can also cause problems in CMC groups. As Walther (1996) notes, group members are likely to create inflated versions of their group members when they do not have nonverbal cues to fill in their impression. Though the anonymity provided with verbal only messaging can help reduce the impact of diversity on groups (Krebs et al., 1996), other studies highlight how members make errors in perceptions when in CMC groups. Peña et al. (2007) found that group members formed more extreme impressions of dominance among group members when they lacked nonverbal cues. In a more recent study, Rains et al. (2019) found that when CMC group members are anonymous, members who ask for help are evaluated more negatively than in FTF and CMC identified conditions. Both of these studies point to the challenges of working without nonverbal cues to guide impressions and relational development.

In addition to this work on relational development in groups, researchers have explored differences in task accomplishment between FTF and CMC groups. Generally, FTF is seen as the better group setting, with studies finding FTF groups were more effective (Barrett & Murphy, 2021), had better performance (Becker-Beck et al., 2005; Li, 2007), and were more conducive to facilitating discussion (Cortese & Seo, 2012). Task accomplishment studies note the importance of time. CMC groups can often reach the same performance level as FTF groups but require more time to do so. For example, Dennis et al. (1999) found CMC groups took longer to make decisions and complete the task but were able to reach the same level of performance of FTF groups that took less time. In another study, Adams et al. (2005) found CMC groups where members were familiar with others were able to decrease the time needed to complete tasks and make decisions.

A series of papers has explored communicative differences in decision-making processes for groups, finding FTF groups exchanged more messages than CMC groups and were more effective in their communication. First, Li (2007) noted FTF groups exchanged more communication messages than CMC groups, and were significantly better at problem analysis and establishing criteria for a decision than CMC groups. Additionally, FTF groups performed communication decision-making functions better than CMC groups, but in contrast to most findings, FTF groups did not have significantly better outcomes. Becker-Beck et al. (2005) also found FTF groups exchanged more messages than CMC groups. Their work also highlights communicative differences between FTF and CMC groups, with anonymous CMC groups using more task-related messages. However, similar patterns of interaction were found between FTF and synchronous CMC groups (members typing messages at the same time).

The research on FTF and CMC groups highlights many important features of communication, but also presents challenges for understanding groups in today's world. Most of the studies focus on text-based chatting only, which does not capture the number of ICTs available today. Though FTF versus CMC group research utilizes similar theories as contemporary research on technology use in teams (Schiller & Mandviwalla, 2007), the ways group members interact via technology have advanced to capture more nonverbal cues and reshape the communicative potential ICTs carry for group members (Gibbs et al., 2017). Second, as noted by Gibbs et al. (2017), groups cannot be defined as only FTF or CMC; rather, group virtuality ranges on a continuum to capture how all groups can be virtual to some extent. As a result, the remainder of this chapter highlights group technology use from a continuum of virtuality perspective, highlighting the multiple ways all groups can utilize technology.

Theoretical Perspectives of Communication and Technology Use in Groups

Researchers studying group technology use different perspectives to guide their research, impacting how much we know about group technology use. This section introduces three theoretical perspectives commonly used in group technology research today. The first is media richness theory, which focuses on the consistent characteristics of technology and how those characteristics impact group interaction. The second is adaptive structuration theory, which considers both the characteristics of the technology, and the impact of group member interaction and context on group outcomes (DeSanctis & Poole, 1994). Finally, multicommunication focuses on how individuals perceive technology use in groups. Table 5.1 provides an outline of the three theoretical perspectives.

Media Richness Theory

Posed by Daft and Lengel (1986), media richness theory focuses on how communication media have varying levels of richness for carrying messages, and that certain technologies have set characteristics that do not change. Richness refers to "the ability of information to change understanding within a time interval" (Daft & Lengel, 1986, p. 560). Some media allow for more information to be shared with group members and can change understanding in a timely fashion, while other media limit what can be shared due to technology characteristics and require more time to reach understanding. FTF conversation is the richest media since the most information (verbal and

Table 5.1 Theoretical Perspectives of Communication and Technology Use

	Media Richness Theory	Adaptive Structuration Theory	Multicommunication
Central assumption	Technologies differ in level of richness or the amount of verbal and nonverbal information that can be conveyed. Leaner media convey less information and are better for unambiguous messages, while richer media convey more information and work well for ambiguous messages.	Technologies have specific characteristics that can be utilized in many ways. The impact of technology on groups depends on how faithfully group members utilize these characteristics.	Group members can use technology to engage in multiple conversations simultaneously. As a result, group members must distinguish between two sets of conversational norms.
Description of technology	Technology has fixed properties that group members must consider when sending messages.	Technology contains specific structural features that group members can choose to utilize as intended or in different ways.	Technologies afford group members' opportunities to work on other tasks and remain available to other individuals.
Key concepts	Richness Equivocality Approbation	Structure Spirit Appropriation	Multicommunication Attention Presence
Potential research questions	Which medium is best for sending this message to group members? How do teams adapt their communication when required to use leaner media?	How do group members balance group norms and technology characteristics when deciding how to send a message? Do groups utilize technology as intended by the creator?	Why do group members choose to multicommunicate? How do group members adapt their communication with members who multicommunicate?
Key citations	Daft & Lengel (1986) Handke et al. (2018)	DeSanctis & Poole (1994) Rains & Bonito (2017)	Reinsch & Turner (2019) Cameron et al. (2018)

nonverbal) can be conveyed and interaction is synchronous. Lower levels of richness include written documents (e.g., letters, emails, and text messages) and phone calls. Straube et al. (2018) found groups utilizing richer communication tools avoided problems with demographic fault lines and infrequent communication, while using leaner media increased misunderstanding and attribution biases in another study (Cramton, 2001). Additionally, considering the richness of the medium is important for managing group interpersonal processes and for handling social phenomena during group life (Maruping & Agarwal, 2004).

In addition to technology richness, media richness theory discusses how the characteristics of the message function in the selection of media. Relational messages are best shared via richer media (FTF), while more process messages can be communicated clearly via leaner methods (Daft & Lengel, 1986). The amount of ambiguity in the message and how well a certain media can communicate that message influence the choice of media for communication (Handke et al., 2019). For example, group members may decide to utilize a leaner text message approach when confirming meeting times, but a richer FTF conversation when managing conflict. One way group researchers capture this selection of media process is through the input-mediator-output-input model (IMOI). This model recognizes the selection of media is based on past team experiences, tasks, and the characteristics of the medium (Handke et al., 2019). By also considering the team and the task at hand, media selection becomes a complex task that asks individuals to evaluate the appropriateness of the media for the current situation.

Adaptive Structuration Theory

DeSanctis and Poole (1994) present adaptive structuration theory as a way to understand why specific technologies (**group support systems** [GSSs] in their case), even with advanced capabilities, do not always lead to the desired group and organizational outcomes. The first two primary concepts focus on the technology itself: structural features and spirit. Structural features refer to the characteristics, capabilities, and rules associated with the technology, such as document sharing, recording tools, or voting mechanisms (DeSanctis & Poole, 1994; Rains & Bonito, 2017). Related to structural features, spirit focuses on the intended values and goals that underline the structural features present in technology. For example, anonymity within a GSS captures the spirit of allowing all members to participate in discussions and evaluating contributions based on merit and not only status or social cues (Rains, 2007). The spirit of a technology is a property of the technology and is not based on individual or designer intentions, but "is the preferred set of actions and interpretations of the technology stemming from the technology itself" (Rains & Bonito, 2017, p. 34).

Whereas structural features and spirit focus on the technology, DeSanctis and Poole (1994) move a step further to focus on how the technology is utilized (or not) by groups. Structuration refers to how individuals take rules and resources from any source (e.g., technology characteristics and social structures) and put them into practice in a given situation. As groups utilize certain rules and resources, they may end up creating new rules and structures to guide their work. For example, group members may utilize the poll feature in Zoom during virtual meetings (feature of the technology) and continue to use anonymous voting in FTF meetings. In another example, group members who meet FTF regularly and prefer knowing how members vote may utilize anonymous polling in Zoom, but then encourage group discussion to share viewpoints as they go forward. In both of these scenarios, the characteristics of the technology and social structures come together to impact group work processes.

As groups create underlying structures to guide their process, the visible manifestations of structures occur as appropriations. Appropriations refer to the specific actions by groups that reflect deeper structuration processes (DeSanctis & Poole, 1994), and are unique to each group based on their choice of operating practices (Poole & DeSanctis, 1990). Technology may not always be used in the intended ways (faithfulness in appropriation) and may be avoided if group members are uncomfortable with the system (group attitudes; see DeSanctis & Poole, 1994 and Rains & Bonito, 2017, for a discussion of appropriation dimensions).

Though not as common as media richness theory, adaptive structuration theory highlights the importance of group member perceptions in determining the impact technology has on group processes. "Although the properties or characteristics can be important, the way that these properties are perceived and used is central to determining the technology's effects" (Rains & Bonito, 2017, p. 38). Even if a technology offers many benefits to groups, those benefits are only potential benefits unless the group decides to utilize that feature. As Markus and Silver (2008) note, the technical features of technology can only offer so much support to a group; rather, it is how the group chooses to interpret and potentially utilize those technical features that can impact group function.

Multicommunication

Multicommunication is "using technology to participate in more than one conversation simultaneously" (Stephens, 2012, p. 196). Though multicommunication can occur in FTF interaction, most research focuses on multicommunication via ICTs. Multicommunication occurs in many conversational settings, but is most commonly studied in group or organizational meetings (e.g., Cameron & Webster, 2011; Cameron et al., 2018; Stephens, 2012).

Many organizations encourage or even require multicommunication from employees to maintain efficiency. Multicommunication allows employees to offer social support, direct meetings, participate in parallel meetings, and be available to others who may need them (Stephens, 2012). In addition, multicommunication during meetings between meeting members can improve meeting efficiency since fewer follow-up meetings will be needed (Dennis et al., 2010). Organizations may also emphasize multicommunication as more groups are geographically distributed and reliance on virtual work increases (Cameron & Webster, 2013). As a result, many employees are forgiving of multicommunication behavior and errors if others can explain why they need to multicommunicate, apologize for the interruption, or do not see multicommunication negatively impacting either conversation (Cameron & Webster, 2011).

Though some individuals are forgiving of multicommunication, others struggle with multicommunication. For example, Cameron and Webster (2011) shared one participant's insights: "I did not know with whom X was communicating, but it irritated me, particularly because she phoned me. If she was too busy, she could have phoned at a more convenient time" (p. 764). In many group situations, multicommunication is perceived negatively by other group members, impacting both individual and group perceptions. In one study, the mere presence of a phone raised concerns from other group members, even if the phone was used to ask people questions about issues raised during the meeting (Paskewitz & Beck, 2021). Other research found acknowledging the on-task nature of mobile phone use did not change perceptions, though positive managerial policies did (Piercy & Underhill, 2021).

Technologies Used by Groups

Increased availability of ICTs continues to shape group work. Early group technology research focused on GSS, networked computer information systems that facilitated group work through structured communication (e.g., information exchange, planning, problem solving, decision making, and conflict resolution; Poole & DeSanctis, 1990). GSS helped facilitate group work since members could enter comments directly for others to see, participation was anonymous, and messages and materials were stored for later use (Ackermann, 2021). Communication scholars extended GSS work by focusing on three factors that impact communication: physical arrangement (group size and whether the group is FTF or dispersed), level of communication intervention (amount of communication structure provided by the system; Poole & DeSanctis, 1990), and restrictiveness (system flexibility; DeSanctis et al., 2008). Laboratory GSS studies found GSS helped with complex decision making and facilitated the generation of multiple courses of action, but only when groups were confident in using the system (DeSanctis et al., 2008). Field studies reported similar findings, though researchers noted field use of GSS equalized participation among members which did not occur in laboratory studies (DeSanctis et al., 2008). Ironically, though GSS received some support for helping groups, most groups do not like using them (DeSanctis et al., 2008).

Though GSS can help structure group discussion and facilitate group decision making, most groups do not have access to the systems due to cost (Lewis, 2010). Instead, today's groups primarily utilize ICTs, a broad term to capture all the devices, media, applications, hardware, and software that allow users to distribute, receive, process, store, retrieve, and utilize digital information (Rice & Leonardi, 2014). Examples of ICTs include options such as email, mobile phones, video conferencing tools (e.g., Zoom, Skype, and Facetime), cloud storage systems (e.g., Google Drive, Dropbox, and OneDrive), and intelligent assistants (see Box 5.1 for an example). One technology used by many groups is instant messaging. Instant messaging is often viewed positively as group members can communicate more frequently, with multiple people inside and outside the meeting, and receive quicker feedback (Tang & Bradshaw, 2020). Instant messaging also allows group

---

Box 5.1   Planning a 16th Birthday Party with Intelligent Assistants

We often think about technology as a tool we use in groups to help us make decisions, share information, and complete group tasks. But what if that technology has its own information to share? Shaikh and Cruz (2019) explored how groups used intelligent assistants (e.g., Amazon Echo, Cortana, and Siri) when working on a task. In contrast to other technology forms that rely on user operation, intelligent assistants come with algorithmic systems that help them process verbal commands and questions. In the study, groups were planning a 16th birthday party. Half of the groups had access to an intelligent assistant to ask questions and gather information while planning, while the other groups brainstormed together with no technology resources. Interestingly, groups that had access to the intelligent assistant had fewer interactions with other group members and instead relied on the information the intelligent assistant could provide. This effect was heightened when groups had limited amounts of time to complete the task. As Shaikh and Cruz (2019) noted, Alexa had never attended a 16th birthday party, but the participants likely have. This raises a lot of questions for group work going forward as we wonder how useful intelligent assistants can be when working on group tasks.

---

members to gather information needed to make decisions in real-time (e.g., directing meetings, offering support, clarifying information, participating in subgroup meetings, and providing social support; Dennis et al., 2010).

Recent communication research has also focused on the use of email, mobile phones, and video conferencing to facilitate group work. Email is considered a lean medium that does not include as many communication cues (no nonverbals, no immediate feedback, and no visual or auditory cues; Straube et al., 2018). However, email has many benefits for group work as it allows for asynchronous communication, editing, documentation of messages, and replicability (Erhardt et al., 2016). In one study focused on email between group members, researchers found email was beneficial because it allowed group members to have control over their communication and more time to process the message due to their asynchronous nature (Erhardt et al., 2016). In addition, email is adaptable to the communication situation and members can alter their messaging to ensure comprehension of content (Straube et al., 2018).

Mobile phones are also common in most groups as members can utilize text messaging, email, storage systems, and more. Researchers find many student groups (Guo et al., 2010; Handke et al., 2019; Reychav et al., 2016) and workplace teams (Paskewitz & Beck, 2019, 2021; Piercy & Underhill, 2021) rely on mobile phones for project coordination. Using mobile phones during group meetings can be helpful for finding needed information for discussion (Reinsch et al., 2008), increasing meeting efficiency (Dennis et al., 2010), and connecting with members who are not present (Stephens, 2012). However, many group members take issue with the use of mobile phones during meetings, even if the user is trying to help with the task at hand (Paskewitz & Beck, 2021). Mobile phone use during group discussion is viewed by other group members as impolite, incivil (Cameron & Webster, 2011), and annoying (Paskewitz & Beck, 2019). However, clear group norms around acceptable use of mobile phones can mitigate the negative perceptions and maximize the positive benefits (Piercy & Underhill, 2021).

Finally, though video conferencing has been available for years, more organizations are offering video conferencing software for group collaboration. Video conferencing software (e.g., Zoom, Google Meet, and Microsoft Teams) offer inexpensive ways for groups to coordinate activity without needing to meet in person. Additionally, this software offers more nonverbal cues than most other ICTs as members can see each other and respond to nonverbals (Standaert et al., 2021). However, there are challenges when using video conferencing as group members may miss out on understanding social dynamics and eye contact (Kuzminykh & Rintel, 2020), and employees reported a higher likelihood of multitasking (Cao et al., 2021). Though these challenges can be frustrating for meeting members, many group members see the benefit of video conferencing for meetings, including using chat for conversations, polling tools as ways to assess group member positions, and a chance to get to know other group members in more personal ways (e.g., personal lives, home environment; Karl et al., 2022).

Deciding What Technologies to Use

Choosing a technology to use relies on considering many different characteristics: individual and group, technology, task, and situational (Brown et al., 2010). These characteristics provide a holistic view of how technology is used in groups and which technology is chosen to be used. Most theories take a singular perspective to the use of technology (e.g., media richness theory focusing on characteristics of the technology for accomplishing the task at hand). However, how group members choose technology is a dynamic process that is explained by four characteristics (Handke et al., 2018; Handke et al., 2019).

First, individual and group characteristics play an important role in how and what collaborative technologies are used. Most individuals come to groups with different perceptions of specific technologies (Müller & Antoni, 2021). These perceptions can be based on positive or negative past experiences (e.g., Guo et al., 2010), or no prior experience, and play a huge role in group decisions about ICTs use (Handke et al., 2018). For example, individuals with high computer self-efficacy are likely more comfortable working with technology since they are confident they can collaborate and accomplish their communication goals (Brown et al., 2010). In addition, individuals need a positive evaluation of the new technology before they will consider changing their habits and adopting the system (Kroenung et al., 2017).

However, as individuals work in groups, members' individual factors combine and compete to create a group level understanding for what technology to use and how. One way this happens is through shared mental models, or the group members' shared understanding of the task, the roles and skills of group members, and recognition all group members have this knowledge (Fiore & Schooler, 2004). Müller and Antoni (2021) noted members come to groups with different expectations and mental models for technology use. As members interact, group members blend their individual perceptions of technology use with others and through communication form a group-level shared mental model for technology use. For example, group members may take time during a meeting to discuss how best to contact each other (e.g., texting, email, and GroupMe). During this discussion, individual perspectives of these three ICTs emerge and group members can assess whether members agree or disagree on the medium. The more agreement shows higher similarity in mental models. These decisions become part of the group norms and inevitably help the group perform better (Guo et al., 2010; Müller & Antoni, 2021). Some groups revisit these norms and modify technology norms, especially since different technologies may be more helpful at different points in group life (Handke et al., 2019).

Second, characteristics of the technology impact group members' choice of technology. Each technology comes with different characteristics (Erhardt et al., 2016) and each individual or group sees those characteristics differently. Researchers take one of two approaches: CFO or affordances. The CFO perspective focuses on how certain technologies filter out important communication cues (most often nonverbal or socioemotional cues such as body language and facial expressions;

Handke et al., 2019). Common CFO theories, such as media richness theory, argue that different technologies come with specific characteristics that vary in the amount of communication cues shared. The second approach, affordances, shifts focus away from set characteristics for media and instead focuses on what each media could accomplish for the group (Erhardt et al., 2016). The affordances approach considers the characteristics of the media, as well as the subjective perceptions of the individual or group using the media. For example, from a CFO perspective email would have very limited nonverbal and social emotional cues. However, from an affordances perspective, groups may enjoy using email due to its asynchronicity, editability, and replicability for text-based tasks (Erhardt et al., 2016).

Third, task characteristics can impact the choice of media (Brown et al., 2010). For example, media richness theory focuses on matching the message to the appropriate media given the nature of the task at hand (Straube et al., 2018). Media appropriation is how individuals compensate for media challenges by adapting their communication behavior in order to accomplish the task at hand (Straube et al., 2018). As individuals work in groups, certain tasks may be more challenging to complete via technology (Brown et al., 2010). Some groups may choose to wait until an FTF meeting to interact, while others may adapt the technology available to meet the communication need at the time. Group members may send messages through multiple media (e.g., email and a phone call; Straube et al., 2018) or individuals may take more time to craft an email (fewer cues) to ensure the message is communicated clearly (Handke et al., 2018). Though certain aspects of a task may be harder to manage via technology, through media appropriation group members are able to complete tasks.

Finally, technology use relies on an assessment of the situational characteristics. As Brown et al. (2010) note, situational characteristics play an important role in technology use. In organizations with specific software programs in place, groups may be required to use specific media as they work together (Brown et al., 2010). Other organizations may have rules against technology use that limits what groups and individuals can do (Piercy & Underhill, 2021). Technology use may also be limited by group member familiarity and relationships among group members. If group members have strong relationships, they can use CFO technology and still be successful (Brown et al., 2010; Handke et al., 2019). Another important factor is diversity, especially in today's global workforce. Group members may have different levels of comfort with technology based on their experiences (Müller & Antoni, 2021). Additionally, certain media may work better for global teams. Shachaf (2005) found email worked best for diverse global teams due to improved language accuracy, reduced miscommunication, and eliminated nonverbal differences. In another study, Shachaf (2007) noted global teams that utilized ICTs mitigated the negative impact of diversity on decision-making effectiveness, and that cultural diversity influenced choice of media due to the limited range of potentially effective channels. Other important situational factors for determining technology use include gender (Gopal et al., 1997), fault lines (Straube et al., 2018), group project phase (Handke et al., 2019), and technology enjoyment (Reychav et al., 2016).

Benefits and Costs of Technology Use

Benefits of Technology Use

Numerous studies have found benefits to the use of technology in groups. One major benefit is increased flexibility and information sharing (Darics & Gatti, 2019; Dennis et al., 2010; Erhardt et al., 2016; Stephens, 2012; Tang & Bradshaw, 2020). Technologies have allowed groups to be more flexible in their interaction. For example, Darics and Gatti (2019) noted technology allowed group members to connect from a variety of spaces. In one example, a group member sent a picture from an airport lounge, but using technology still allowed them to be present in the meeting and discussion. Most technologies allow group members to interact more often, with multiple members quickly (Tang & Bradshaw, 2020), gather needed information, provide social support to members (Dennis et al., 2010), and adapt messages to clearly communicate within the technological limitations (Erhardt et al., 2016). For example, Hassell and Limayem (2020) found information sharing was not significantly different between rich and lean media groups. Whether groups utilized rich media or lean media, the same amount of information was shared, and effective decisions were made due to group members flexibility with their assigned medium.

Another benefit of technology use in groups is frequent and timely communication between group members coordinating tasks across space, cultures, and time. For example, within virtual groups, performance and communication frequency improved when members gave and received weekly feedback (McLarnon et al., 2019). Frequent peer feedback throughout the process offers members a chance to self-regulate their performance to align with group expectations (McLarnon et al., 2019). Technology can also help groups respond more thoughtfully when they maximize the technology features. Erhardt et al. (2016) highlighted that asynchronous communication (e.g., email) allowed group members more time to reflect on others' messages and provided responses (or forward to other recipients) leading productive team learning. In addition, Dennis et al. (2010) found that group members were able to provide more timely information through multicommunication to others helping increase efficiency and likely impact decision-making quality.

Finally, the use of technology among groups also has an impact on members' sense of belonging and identity creation. Darics and Gatti (2019) found that members' use of technology blurred the lines of personal and professional space. Members of the group used the technology to communicate that they were available and accessible, even when away from their office space, sharing pictures of themselves in personal settings. Being available and ready for online communication allowed group members to feel a greater sense of belongingness to the group (Darics & Gatti, 2019). In another study, Ge and Lang (2020) linked media richness to the development of transactive memory systems (the process of encoding, storing, and retrieving information held by groups and group members). Richer media (e.g., video conferencing) helped group members learn about the skills and knowledge other group members had, thereby building a transactive memory system, which in turn helped foster relationships among group members.

Costs of Technology Use

Technology use in groups can also cause challenges or hindrances, including decision making, performance, effectiveness, and satisfaction. One cost is the delays in decision making. In one study, the richness or leanness of the media did not impact performance or decision-making quality, but leaner media required more time for communication (Hassell & Limayem, 2020). While communication was prolonged due to using lean technology, the impact did not reveal a higher quality decision, and the authors noted group members were less satisfied with the communication process (Hassell & Limayem, 2020). Technology can also delay decision making in short-term groups. Ortiz de Guinea et al. (2012) posited that short-term groups (i.e., ones that exist less than several days) might experience more negative costs of using technology than longer term groups (i.e., numerous days or weeks) due to more time needed to transmit information and allow for conversation. Ortiz de Guinea et al. (2012) suggested that virtual group members using lean technology be given opportunities to form better relationships, build a strong group identity, and ensure members are familiar with the task.

Another cost groups face are potential process losses from technology use. One major cost is miscommunication between group members regarding task performance. In a virtual group study, Newman et al. (2020) noted virtual group members perceived leaders were very effective at communicating via technology and trustworthy, and also felt group performance was high. However, Newman et al. (2020) found misalignment between group member perceptions of effectiveness and organizational standards, pointing to issues in how leaders communicate performance measures and organizational expectations to members. Miscommunication can also occur as members are overwhelmed with the number of messages at any given time. For example, Dennis et al. (2010) noted that group members, when managing two conversations, overlooked important details, misunderstood instant messages that they read too quickly, or replied inappropriately to instant messages. The increased number of messages also can negatively impact information sharing, as group members often decrease text-based or complicated messages when overloaded, and instead relied on emoticons, compressed text messages, or withdrawal from the interaction (Nematzadeh et al., 2019).

Finally, in some group situations, the use of technology can be perceived negatively and impact perceived performance and satisfaction among members. For example, mobile phone use leads to many negative perceptions of group members and the overall meeting, with women viewing multicommunicators more negatively in respect to focus, incivility, contribution, performance, effectiveness, and satisfaction (Paskewitz & Beck, 2019). Similarly, Piercy and Underhill (2021) noted mobile devices (i.e., phone, laptop, or notepad) are seen as distractions and that newcomers should consider that the use of mobile devices will be perceived negatively. Group members multicommunicating may be distracted from the group conversation or splitting their focus between two conversations leading to negative perceptions. However, as the cellphone relevance hypothesis highlights, if the mobile phone conversation is integral to the discussion topic, the negative perceptions can be minimized as other group members recognize the relevance of mobile phone use (Cummings & Reimer, 2021).

Evidence-Based Recommendations for Practice

There are numerous implications to consider for the use of technology in groups for managers. One challenge, however, is the experimental design utilized in most group technology studies. Most prior studies do not capture the organizational context, including norms, policies (Piercy & Underhill, 2021), relationships (Cameron & Webster, 2011), and rules, which can impact how technology is utilized by groups. However, though these recommendations come largely from experimental study results, they do highlight crucial steps for groups that utilize technology in their work.

The first, and probably the most important consideration, is setting clear policies and expectations regarding the use of technology during group meetings and for group task performance. Setting organizational norms toward the use of technology will help to create appropriate technology use, ultimately leading to greater task performance (Guo et al., 2010). Using multicommunication as an example, group members might need to communicate via text message or instant message with others in order to get information necessary to answer immediate questions to continue task performance, engaging in on-task communication outside of the group conversation. When group members acknowledged the task and the multicommunication aligned with a technology-supported policy, perceptions were more positive of the individual's behavior (Piercy & Underhill, 2021).

Throughout the group process, technology is likely to play different roles as the group functions. Initially, groups may need richer media to define the task and members' roles. Over time, the use of media may change and reliance on technology may shift to more asynchronous types to complete the task to remain effective. Handke et al. (2019) highlighted that as groups moved from one task phase to another, the increased use of leaner media was more appropriate to coordinate duties and facilitated group functioning. The group's use of different media types might require additional training, time, or interaction for group members to acclimate to the different media being used. Sharing technology experiences, both positive and negative, with other group members will help others assimilate and remain flexible to technology uses (Darics & Gatti, 2019). Additionally, management may help effectiveness and flexibility by offering training in encoding and decoding of messages using leaner media to help with understanding and relationships (Handke et al., 2018).

While technology use can allow for richer feedback, it is important to acknowledge when a message is received and when a group member might get a response with more information and details. Using email as an example, a recipient might be reflecting on the sender's message and understanding of the task situation or sharing with other members involved for more feedback and information. In replying to the sender, the recipient might say, "I've received your message and am gathering needed information from another group member" in order to acknowledge the message and show that the recipient is acting on the request, potentially alleviating the dissatisfaction with the leaner medium due to longer decision times (Hassell & Limayem, 2020). The use of asynchronous-type communications affords group members more time to ponder the message and provide enhanced feedback, leading to greater decision making (Erhardt et al., 2016). This highlights that while the use of technology has opened communication to 24/7, taking time to reflect on messages might impact task performance and rapid, quick-fire responses might not always be the most effective.

Conclusion

As technology continues to evolve, groups will also need to adapt to the changing availability of technology. New technologies such as artificial intelligence, intelligent assistants, virtual reality, and Google Glass offer many new ways for groups to collaborate, lessen perceived distance between geographically dispersed members, and add new sources of insight to groups. In addition, many organizations are shifting to virtual workplaces where technology will be essential to all group work. For group members to be successful in the ever-evolving world of technology will require them to continually evaluate their communication needs at that time and what technology can best help them communicate the message.

Further Readings

Handke, L., Schulte, E., Schneider, K., & Kauffeld, S. (2019). Teams, time, and technology: Variations of media use over project phases. *Small Group Research*, *50*(2), 266–305. https://doi.org/10.1177/1046496418824151

Paskewitz, E. A., & Beck, S. J. (2019). Exploring perceptions of multicommunicator texting during meetings. *Computers in Human Behavior*, *101*, 238–247. https://doi.org/10.1016/j.chb.2019.07.032

Straube, J., Meinecke, A. L., Schneider, K., & Kauffeld, S. (2018). Effects of media compensation on team performance: The role of demographic fault lines. *Small Group Research*, *49*(6), 684–722. https://doi.org/10.1177/1046496418796281

Glossary

Adaptive structuration theory   A theory that focuses on how organizations and groups utilize technology, focusing on the structures of the technology and the way users appropriate those structures.

Group support systems   Networked computer information systems that facilitate group work through structured communication (e.g., information exchange, planning, problem solving, decision making, and conflict resolution).

Information and communication technologies   A broad term referring to the devices, media, applications, hardware, and software that allow users to distribute, receive, process, store, retrieve, and utilize digital information.

Media richness theory   A theory that focuses on how communication media have varying levels of richness for carrying messages, and that certain technologies have set characteristics that do not change which must be considered.

Multicommunication   A behavior occurring when individuals simultaneously engage in two or more conversations that require speaking turns.

References

Ackermann, F. (2021). Group support systems: Past, present, and future. In D. M. Kilgour & C. Eden (Eds.), *Handbook of group decision and negotiation* (pp. 627–654). Springer. https://doi.org/10.1007/978-3-030-49629-6_47

Adams, S. J., Roch, S. G., & Ayman, R. (2005). Communication medium and member familiarity: The effects on decision time, accuracy, and satisfaction. *Small Group Research*, *36*(3), 321–353. https://doi.org/10.1177/1046496405275232

Barrett, A. K., & Murphy, M. M. (2021). Feeling supported in addiction recovery: Comparing face-to-face and videoconferencing 12-step meetings. *Western Journal of Communication*, *85*(1), 123–146. https://doi.org/10.1080/10570314.2020.1786598

Becker-Beck, U., Wintermantel, M., & Borg, A. (2005). Principles of regulating interaction in teams practicing face-to-face communication versus teams practicing computer-mediated communication. *Small Group Research*, *36*(4), 499–536. https://doi.org/10.1177/1046496405277182

Bordia, P., DiFonzo, N., & Chang, A. (1999). Rumor as group problem solving: Development patterns in informal computer-mediated groups. *Small Group Research*, *30*(1), 8–28. https://doi.org/10.1177/104649649903000102

Brown, S. A., Dennis, A. R., & Venkatesh, V. (2010). Predicting collaboration technology use: Integrating technology adoption and collaboration research. *Journal of Management Information Systems*, *27*(2), 9–54. https://doi.org/10.2753/MIS0742-1222270201

Cameron, A.-F., Barki, H., Ortiz de Guinea, A., Coulon, T., & Moshki, H. (2018). Multicommunicating in meetings: Effects of locus, topic relatedness, and meeting medium. *Management Communication Quarterly*, *32*, 303–336. https://doi.org/10.1177/0893318918759437

Cameron, A.-F., & Webster, J. (2011). Relational outcomes of multicommunicating: Integrating incivility and social exchange perspectives. *Organization Science*, *22*(3), 754–771. https://doi.org/10.1287/orsc.1100.0540

Cameron, A.-F., & Webster, J. (2013). Multicommunicating: Juggling multiple conversations in the workplace. *Information Systems Research*, *24*, 352–371. https://doi.org/10.1287/isre.1120.0446

Cameron, A.-F., Webster, J., Barki, H., & Ortiz de Guinea, A. (2016). Four common multicommunication misconceptions. *European Journal of Information Systems*, *25*, 465–471. https://doi.org/10.1057/ejis.2016.8

Cao, H., Lee, C.-J., Iqbal, S., Czerwinski, M., Wong, P., Rintel, S., Hecht, B., Teevan, J., & Yang, L. (2021). *Large scale analysis of multitasking behavior during remote meetings* [Paper presentation]. ACM CHI 2021, Yokohama, Japan. https://hci.stanford.edu/publications/2021/cao_remote/CHI2021-RemoteMeetingMultitask.pdf

Cortese, J., & Seo, M. (2012). The role of social presence in opinion expression during FtF and CMC discussions. *Communication Research Reports*, *29*(1), 44–53. https://doi.org/10.1080/08824096.2011.639913

Cramton, C. D. (2001). The mutual knowledge problem and its consequences for dispersed collaboration. *Organization Science*, *12*(3), 346–371. https://doi.org/10.1287/orsc.12.3.346.10098

Cummings, R., & Reimer, T. (2021). Cellphone relevance in face-to-face interactions: The effects of cellphone use on conversational satisfaction. *Mobile Media & Communication*, *9*(2), 274–292. https://doi.org/10.1177/2050157920958437

Daft, R. L., & Lengel, R. H. (1986). Organizational information requirements, media richness and structural design. *Management Science*, *32*(5), 554–571. https://doi.org/10.1287/mnsc.32.5.554

Darics, E., & Gatti, C. M. (2019). Talking a team into being in online workplace collaborations: The discourse of virtual work. *Discourse Studies*, *21*(3), 237–257. https://doi.org/10.1177/1461445619829240

Dennis, A. R., Kinney, S. T., & Hung, Y.-T. C. (1999). Gender differences in the effects of media richness. *Small Group Research*, *30*(4), 405–437. https://doi.org/10.1177/104649649903000402

Dennis, A. R., Rennecker, J. A., & Hansen, S. (2010). Invisible whispering: Restructuring collaborative decision making with instant messaging. *Decision Sciences*, *41*(4), 845–886. https://doi.org/10.1111/j.1540-5915.2010.00290.x

DeSanctis, G., & Poole, M. S. (1994). Capturing the complexity in advanced technology use: Adaptive structuration theory. *Organization Science*, *5*(2), 121–147. https://doi.org/10.1287/orsc.5.2.121

DeSanctis, G., Poole, M. S., DeSharmais, G., D'Onofrio, M., Gallupe, B., Holmes, M., Jackson, B., Jackson, M., Lewis, H., Limayem, M., Lee-Partridge, J., Niederman, F., Sambamurthy, V., Vician, C., Watson, R., Billingsley, J., Kirsch, L., Lind, R., & Shannon, D. (2008). The Minnesota GDSS research project: Group support systems, group processes, and outcomes. *Journal of the Association for Information Systems*, *9*(10/11), 551–609.

Erhardt, N., Gibbs, J., Martin-Rios, C., & Sherblom, J. (2016). Exploring affordances of email for team learning over time. *Small Group Research*, *47*(3), 243–278. https://doi.org/10.1177/1046496416635823

Fiore, S. M., & Schooler, J. W. (2004). Process mapping and shared cognition: Teamwork and the development of shared problem models. In E. Salas & S. M. Fiore (Eds.), *Team cognition: Understanding the factors that drive process and performance* (pp. 133–152). American Psychological Association. https://doi.org/10.1037/10690-007

Ge, H., & Lang, C. (2020). The effect of media richness on transactive memory system in virtual teams: The moderating role of team identity. *International Journal of Science*, *7*(2), 132–142.

Gibbs, J. L., Kim, H., & Boyraz, M. (2017). Virtual teams. In C. R. Scott & L. Lewis (Eds.), *The international encyclopedia of organizational communication* (pp. 1–14). Wiley & Sons, Inc. https://doi.org/10.1002/9781118955567.wbieoc215

Gopal, A., Miranda, S. M., Robichaux, B. P., & Bostrom, R. P. (1997). Leveraging diversity with information technology: Gender, attitude, and intervening influences in the use of group support systems. *Small Group Research*, *28*(1), 29–71.

Guo, Z., Tan, F. B., Turner, T., & Xu, H. (2010). Group norms, media preferences, and group meeting success: A longitudinal study. *Computers in Human Behavior*, *26*, 645–655. https://doi.org/10.1016/j.chb.2010.01.001

Handke, L., Schulte, E., Schneider, K., & Kauffeld, S. (2018). The medium isn't the message: Introducing a measure of adaptive virtual communication. *Cogent Arts & Humanities*, *5*(1), 1–25. https://doi.org/10.1080/23311983.2018.1514953

Hassell, M. D., & Limayem, M. (2020). Media impacts and performance in dispersed teams. *Journal of Computer Information Systems*, *60*(1), 18–25. https://doi.org/10.1080/08874417.2017.1383864

Hian, L. B., Chuan, S. L., Trevor, T. M. K., & Detenber, B. H. (2005). Getting to know you: Exploring the development of relational intimacy in computer-mediated communication. *Journal of Computer-Mediated Communication*, *9*(3). https://doi.org/10.1111/j.1083-6101.2004.tb00290.x

Hobman, E. V., Bordia, P., Irmer, B., & Chang, A. (2002). The expression of conflict in computer-mediated and face-to-face groups. *Small Group Research*, *33*(4), 439–465. https://doi.org/10.1177/104649640203300403

Karl, K. A., Peluchette, J. V., & Aghakhani, N. (2022). Virtual work meetings during the COVID-19 pandemic: The good, bad, and ugly. *Small Group Research*, *53*(3), 343–365. https://doi.org/10.1177/10464964211015286

Krebs, S. A., Hobman, E. V., & Bordia, P. (1996). Virtual teams and group member dissimilarity: Consequences for the development of trust. *Small Group Research*, *37*(6), 721–741. https://doi.org/10.1177/1046496406294886

Kroenung, J., Eckhardt, A., & Kuhlenkasper, T. (2017). Conflicting behavioral paradigms and predicting IS adoption and non-adoption – The importance of group-based analysis. *Computers in Human Behavior*, *67*, 10–22. https://doi.org/10.1016/j.chb.2016.09.058

Kuzminykh, A., & Rintel, S. (2020). *Classification of functional attention in video meetings* [Conference session]. *2020 CHI Conference on Human Factors in Computing Systems*, Honolulu, HI, United States. https://doi.org/10.1145/3313831.3376546

Lewis, L. F. (2010). Group support systems: Overview and guided tour. In D. Kilgour & C. Eden (Eds.), *Handbook of group decision and negotiation* (Vol. 4). Springer. https://doi.org/10.1007/978-90-481-9097-3_15

Li, S.-C. C. (2007). Computer-mediated communication and group decision making: A functional perspective. *Small Group Research*, *38*(5), 593–614. https://doi.org/10.1177/1046496407304335

Markus, M. L., & Silver, M. S. (2008). A foundation for the study of IT effects: A new look at DeSanctis and Poole's concepts of structural features and spirit. *Journal of the Association for Information Systems*, *9*(10/11), 609–632.

Maruping, L. M., & Agarwal, R. (2004). Managing team interpersonal processes through technology: A task-technology fit perspective. *Journal of Applied Psychology*, *89*(6), 975–990. https://doi.org/10.1037/0021-9010.89.6.975

McLarnon, M. J. W., O'Neill, T. A., Taras, V., Law, D., Donia, M. B. L., & Steel, P. (2019). Global virtual team communication, coordination, and performance across three peer feedback strategies. *Canadian Journal of Behavioural Science*, *51*(4), 207–218. https://doi.org/10.1037/cbs0000135

Müller, R., & Antoni, C. H. (2021). Effects of ICT shared mental models on team processes and outcomes. *Small Group Research*. Advance online publication. https://doi.org/10.1177/1046496421997889

Nematzadeh, A., Ciampaglia, G. L., Ahn, Y.-Y., & Flammini, A. (2019). Information overload in group communication: From conversation to cacophony in the twitch chat. *Royal Society Open Science*, *6*(10), 191412. https://doi.org/10.1098/rsos.191412

Newman, S. A., Ford, R. C., & Marshall, G. W. (2020). Virtual team leader communication: Employee perception and organizational reality. *International Journal of Business Communication*, *57*(4), 452–473. https://doi.org/10.1177/2329488419829895

Ortiz de Guinea, A., Webster, J., & Staples, D. S. (2012). A meta-analysis of the consequences of virtualness on team functioning. *Information & Management*, *49*(6), 301–308. https://doi.org/10.1016/j.im.2012.08.003

Paskewitz, E. A., & Beck, S. J. (2021). "Put the phone away!": Does text message content influence perceptions of group member texting? *Computers in Human Behavior*, *115*, 1–9. https://doi.org/10.1016/j.chb.2020.106591

Peña, J., Walther, J. B., & Hancock, J. T. (2007). Effects of geographic distribution on dominance perceptions in computer-mediated groups. *Communication Research*, *34*(3), 313–331. https://doi.org/10.1177/0093650207300431

Piercy, C. W., & Underhill, G. R. (2021). Expectations of technology use during meetings: An experimental test of manager policy, device use, and task-acknowledgement. *Mobile Media & Communication*, *9*(1), 78–102. https://doi.org/10.1177/2050157920927049

Poole, M. S., & DeSanctis, G. (1990). Understanding the use of group decision support systems: The theory of adaptive structuration. In J. L. Fulk & C. W. Steinfield (Eds.), *Organizations and communication technology* (pp. 173–193). Sage.

Rains, S. A. (2007). The impact of anonymity on perceptions of source credibility and influence in computer-mediated group communication: A test of two competing hypotheses. *Communication Research*, *34*(1), 100–125. https://doi.org/10.1177/0093650206296084

Rains, S. A., Akers, C., Pavlich, C. A., Tsetsi, E., & Appelbaum, M. (2019). Examining the quality of social support messages produced face-to-face and in computer-mediated communication: The effects of hyperpersonal communication. *Communication Monographs*, *86*(3), 271–291. https://doi.org/10.1080/03637751.2019.1595076

Rains, S. A., & Bonito, J. A. (2017). Adaptive structuration theory. In C. R. Scott & L. Lewis (Eds.), *The international encyclopedia of organizational communication*. Wiley. https://doi.org/10.1002/9781118955567.wbieoc003

Reinsch, N. L., & Turner, J. W. (2019). Multicommunicator aspirational stress, suggestions for teaching and research, and other insights after 10 years of multicommunication. *Journal of Business and Technical Communication*, *33*(2), 141–171. https://doi.org/10.1177/1050651918816356

Reinsch, N. L. Jr., Turner, J. W., & Tinsley, C. H. (2008). Multicommunicating: A practice whose time has come? *The Academy of Management Review*, *33*(2), 391–403. https://doi.org/10.5465/amr.2008.31193450

Reychav, I., Ndicu, M., & Wu, D. (2016). Leveraging social networks in the adoption of mobile technologies for collaboration. *Computers in Human Behavior*, *58*, 443–453. https://doi.org/10.1016/j.chb.2016.01.011

Rice, R. E., & Leonardi, P. M. (2014). Information and communication technology use in organizations. In L. L. Putnam & D. K. Mumby (Eds.), *The Sage handbook of organizational communication* (pp. 425–448). Sage.

Schiller, S. Z., & Mandviwalla, M. (2007). Virtual team research: An analysis of theory use and a framework for theory appropriation. *Small Group Research*, *38*(1), 12–59. https://doi.org/10.1177/1046496406297035

Shachaf, P. (2005). Bridging cultural diversity through email. *Journal of Global Information Technology Management, 8*(2), 46–60. https://doi.org/10.1080/1097198X.2005.10856396

Shachaf, P. (2007). Cultural diversity and information and communication technology impacts on global virtual teams: An exploratory study. *Information & Management, 45*(2), 131–142. https://doi.org/10.1016/j.im.2007.12.003

Shaikh, S. J., & Cruz, I. (2019). "Alexa, Do You Know Anything?" The Impact of an Intelligent Assistant on Team Interactions and Creative Performance Under Time Scarcity. In *arXiv*. http://arxiv.org/abs/1912.12914

Standaert, W., Muylle, S., & Basu, A. (2021). How shall we meet? Understanding the importance of meeting mode capabilities for different meeting objectives. *Information & Management, 58*(1), 103393. https://doi.org/10.1016/j.im.2020.103393

Stephens, K. K. (2012). Multiple conversations during organizational meetings: Development of the multi-communicating scale. *Management Communication Quarterly, 26*(2), 195–223. https://doi.org/10.1177/0893318911431802

Tang, C. M., & Bradshaw, A. (2020). Instant messaging or face-to-face? How choice of communication medium affects team collaboration environments. *E-Learning and Digital Media, 17*(2), 111–130. https://doi.org/10.1177/2042753019899724

Walther, J. B. (1996). Computer-mediated communication: Impersonal, interpersonal, and hyperpersonal interaction. *Communication Research, 23*(1), 3–43. https://doi.org/10.1177/009365096023001001

Walther, J. B., & Burgoon, J. K. (1992). Relational communication in computer-mediated interaction. *Human Communication Research, 19*(1), 50–88. https://doi.org/10.1111/j.1468-2958.1992.tb00295.x

Zornoza, A., Ripoll, P., & Pieró, J. M. (2002). Conflict management in groups that work in two different communication contexts: Face-to-face and computer-mediated communication. *Small Group Research, 33*(5), 481–508. https://doi.org/10.1177/104649602237167

Part II

Components and Processes of Group Communication

6 Characteristics of Successful Groups and Teams

Randy Y. Hirokawa

Chapter Objectives

After reading this chapter, you should be able to:

- Identify and elaborate on the properties that distinguish successful from unsuccessful groups.
- Identify and elaborate on the processes by which these properties emerge and develop in successful groups.

Introduction

Suppose you were asked to name a successful sports team? What would your answer be? If you are a football fan, you might say the New England Patriots, Tampa Bay Buccaneers, or the Kansas City Chiefs because they recently won NFL Superbowl championships. If you are a baseball fan, you might say the Atlanta Braves, Los Angeles Dodgers, or Boston Red Sox because they are recent World Series champions. If you are a basketball fan, you might say the Los Angeles Lakers or Golden State Warriors because they are recent NBA champions. If you are a hockey fan, you might say the Tampa Bay Lightning or the St. Louis Blues because they have recently won the NHL's Stanley Cup championship. Obviously, there are many successful sports teams, just as there are many successful groups and teams in government, corporations, and educational settings.

Defining Team Success

What makes a group or team successful? For many, a "successful" team is one that reaches its goal, accomplishes a task, or otherwise achieves what they set out to do. In competitive sports, this usually means winning games and championships. Others define success in terms of a team's process – or the way the group goes about doing things. Legendary basketball coach, John Wooden, defined success as " … knowing you did your best to become the best you are capable of becoming" (Wooden & Johnson, 1997). Noble laureate Maya Angelou defined team success as " … liking what you do and liking how you do it" (Hardy, 2021). Still others define success in terms of the effort that the group, and its members, put forth in trying to accomplish its task. The famous American educator and author, Booker T. Washington, said that "success is not measured by the heights one attains, but the obstacles one overcomes in its attainment" (Washington, 1901).

Over the years, various researchers have examined the differences between successful and unsuccessful groups with varying results. Larson and LaFasto (1989) studied 75 high-performance executive and managerial teams and found that successful groups and teams possess the following features: (1) a clear, elevating goals, (2) a results-driven **structure**, (3) competent members, (4) standards of excellence, (5) a **collaborative climate**, and (6) principled leadership (pp. 24–26).

DOI: 10.4324/9781003227458-8

Hackman (1990) observed that successful groups (1) exert sufficient effort to accomplish the task well, (2) bring adequate knowledge and skills to bear on the task work, (3) employ task performance strategies that are appropriate to the work and the setting in which it is being performed, (4) have a group structure that promotes competent work on the task, and (5) have a context that supports and reinforces excellence. Hirokawa et al. (2000) used narrative analysis to study 522 written stories of successful or unsuccessful group performance. The researchers divided the stories into two groups – those that described group success, and those that described group failure – and then identified explanations for the success or failure that were embedded within the narratives. Their analysis revealed seven general influences on group performance: (1) relationships, (2) group structure, (3) group **process**, (4) member emotions, (5) group communication, (6) member attributes, and (7) external forces. Of those, a comparison of standardized frequencies revealed significant differences between the group success and failure stories with regards to relationships, member emotions, and member attributes. In a follow-up study of health care teams, Hirokawa et al. (2003) reported five general factors that were perceived to affect health care team success or failure: (1) member attributes, (2) relationships, (3) process, (4) structure, and (5) external support. Of these, member attributes, process, and structure were found to distinguish the stories of health care team success and failure most consistently. In short, successful groups and teams appear to succeed or fail because they have qualities that enable them to be successful, or qualities that prevent them from succeeding. I elaborate on some of these characteristics in the next section of this chapter.

Characteristics of Successful Groups and Teams

Although previous studies have identified different characteristics of successful and unsuccessful groups and teams, there are six that are common to those studies. They are: (1) Clear goals, (2) Facilitative structure, (3) Competent members, (4) Standards of excellence, (5) Collaborative climate, and (6) Effective process.

Clear goals. All successful teams have a clear understanding of the goal they want to achieve and, equally importantly, believe that the goal is important and worthwhile achieving. According to Larson and LaFasto (1989), **goal clarity** "implies that there is a specific performance objective, phrased in such concrete language that it is possible to tell, unequivocally, whether or not that performance objective has been attained" (p. 28). Locke and Latham (1990) found that clear goals not only affect group behavior and job performance, but also help mobilize energy which leads the group exert greater overall effort and success. In short, team success depends on its members not only knowing what they want to achieve, but also believing in the importance of that goal. Kiefer and Senge (1984) use the Apollo Moon Project is an example of a clear, elevating goal. They write:

> By committing themselves to "placing a man on the moon by the end of the 1960s," the leaders of the project took a stand. The clarity and conviction they generated touched people at all levels of the enterprise. One can imagine how much less spectacular the results might have been if they had adopted an alternative mission statement, such as "to be leaders in space exploration."
>
> (p. 112)

Facilitative structure. A second component of successful teams is that they possess a structure that helps the group achieve its goals (Hackman, 1990; Hirokawa et al., 2000, 2003; Larson & LaFasto, 1989). Group structure refers to the **norms** and **roles** of the group (MacPherson & Howard, 2011). Norms are the rules or standards of behavior that are shared by members of the group, whereas roles are the specific behaviors expected of group members who occupy specific positions in the group. When a team has structure, its members know exactly what is expected of them – both as a group, and as individual members of the group. In the case of high-performance teams, the norms and roles of the group are results-driven; they function to maximize performance outcomes. That is, every rule, and every expected behavior, exists to ensure that the team is successful (Larson & LaFasto, 1989, pp. 39–40). For example, successful sports teams have results-driven norms that place the needs of the team above those of its individual members. The "sacrifice bunt" in the game of baseball is an example of a results-driven norm. During a game, a batter is occasionally expected to hit ("bunt") the ball softly to deliberately get him/her out at first base to allow the runner already on base to advance to the next base. When successfully accomplished, the batter is applauded by his/her teammates for his "sacrifice."

Another important aspect of a facilitative structure are clear roles and responsibilities for group members. In their study of successful and unsuccessful health care teams, Hirokawa et al. (2003) report that the success and failure stories underscore the importance of clear roles and responsibilities. The success stories contained frequent references to the importance of the team members knowing precisely what they are supposed to do, whereas the failure stories contained equally frequent references to ambiguous roles and duties as explanations for team ineffectiveness. As one respondent, a member of a military surgical field team, explained:

> Our success was based on the fact that each one of us had a very specific job with clearly specified responsibilities and assignments (that we were) efficient and competent at. We could move in, set up, and be performing surgery within a day. The only way this was possible is if each of us performs our jobs precisely and, collectively, nothing is neglected or overlooked.
>
> (p. 153)

Another important aspect of a group's facilitative structure is its leadership. Research shows that effective groups and teams possess principled leaders (Larson & LaFasto, 1989). A *principled leader* is one who is (1) committed to the team's goals, (2) is fair and impartial to all team members, and (3) is open to new ideas and information from team members (p. 123). Perhaps most importantly, a principled leader serves as a daily example of how group members should act and interact in the group. Kirk Ferentz, the winningest, and longest-tenured, football coach at the University of Iowa, attributes his teams' success to the leadership that his coaches and players provide (see full interview in this chapter). According to Ferentz, good leaders are ones who "live up to the expectations of others on the team … they live the standards that we expect from all of our players on a daily basis … they do things, even the small things, the right way at all times … (because) they are actively responsible for making sure that everyone on their team is doing everything in a quality manner (and) are expected to hold others accountable if they aren't, or at least try to convince them of the importance of doing things in a quality manner at all times" (see Box 6.1).

Competent members. A third component of all successful teams is *competent members*. A competent team member is one who (a) possesses the knowledge, skills, and abilities needed to successfully accomplish the task of the group (Hackman, 1990), (b) have the personal characteristics required to work well with others to achieve excellence (Larson & LaFasto, 1989), and (c) are able to exert the effort required to perform at a high level (Hackman, 1990). Successful teams have highly competent members, and the efforts of those members usually contribute directly to the success of the team. The University of Connecticut women's basketball team is widely regarded as the most successful teams in the history of women's collegiate basketball. While most collegiate basketball teams are happy to win 20 games in a season, the Connecticut women's basketball team has won 30 (or more) games 18 times in the last 20 years, including back-to-back 39-0 records in 2008–2010, and three other years with only one loss per season. When Connecticut's

Box 6.1   Interview with Iowa Football Coach Kirk Ferentz

This is the transcript of an interview with Kirk Ferentz, head football coach at the University of Iowa. Coach Ferentz is considered the "Dean" of college football coaches because he is currently the longest tenured head coach in college football, and the winningest football coach at the University of Iowa. As you read the transcript, think about the six characteristics of successful groups and teams that we presented in this chapter: (1) clear, elevating goals, (2) a results-driven structure, (3) competent members, (4) standards of excellence, (5) a collaborative climate, and (6) effective process. Can you point to specific statements that Coach Ferentz makes in reference to these six characteristics?

Dr. Hirokawa

Of all the teams you have coached at Iowa, which ones would you say were your most "successful" teams? Why?

Coach Ferentz

Record-wise, the 2015 team was arguably the most successful because it was our only undefeated team with a record of 12-0. But there are other teams that stand out too. The 2002 and 2004 teams were remarkable. The 2002 went undefeated in the Big-10 season and were co-champions that year. The 2008 team was special because started of 3-0, and then lost 3 straight, and everyone was throwing dirt on us, but they came back to win 6 of 7 games to finish the season strong. The way that team came together and rallied at the end was really impressive. The 2013 team is one of my favorites even though they finished the season with a good, but not spectacular, 8-4 record. But that team really did things first class from start to finish, from January through the bowl game. And last year (2022) was really a gratifying year because we started the season 6-0, rose to #2 in the country, and the expectations were unrealistic, and then we lose two straight, and they were ugly two losses, but then we scratched and clawed and fought back to win the final four games to get ourselves into the Big-10 title game. Those are all different examples of successful teams, but in a nutshell, I judge a team's success in terms of how well they maximized their potential, how well they took advantage of the opportunities that presented themselves, and how they handle the challenges that came their way.

Dr. Hirokawa

You've identified several successful teams. Did those teams share the same characteristics? Or were they different and unique?

Coach Ferentz

I think there are certainly characteristics that they all share. One is that they prepare well. They tend to compete well. And then there is also a level of togetherness that they demonstrate. In football, that togetherness is powerful. In order to display that togetherness, they have to have mutual respect for each other; a respect for their likenesses and differences. The better they understand those things, the more together they tend to act.

Dr. Hirokawa

Are there some differences? For example, when you compare the 2004 team to the 2015 teams, were there some uniqueness?

Coach Ferentz

The circumstances and challenges in front of you tend to play themselves out differently. In 2004, for instance, we went into season with what we thought would be a stout defensive group that was pretty experienced, but offensively, we thought it would be a bit of challenge, and then we lost a bunch of players to injuries, and at one point we were down to our 4th or 5th string running back. That really made the mountain that much higher to climb on the offensive side. But the thing that that team learned to do was to work around the challenges that we had. So, whether it was winning games with special teams, or winning games with defense, we found ways to win despite the challenges on offense. But even the offense found ways to contribute even if they weren't good enough to carry the team week to week. In 2015, we never experienced the adversity of losing, but we played in a lot of close, tough games, and they found ways to win every game.

Dr. Hirokawa

You have also had some less successful teams. Did those less successful teams have different characteristics from the more successful teams that you have been talking about?

Coach Ferentz

Talent is always an issue when you are not as successful as you would like. With one of our less successful teams, the senior class of players wasn't especially strong. In other cases, complacency was the issue. We had been having great success, and then complacency set in and the players began to feel some entitlement. Our first two years, we didn't have the talent to compete and there was a need for education so the players knew what would be needed to compete, and have the buy-in to do it. But when you look at the difference between more successful and less successful teams, preparation is such a key factor. The preparation that the team does, from January through the season to the bowl game, is so crucial for success. It's doing even the little things right. The teams that we had that were successful better understood, or comprehended, the importance of everyone doing everything, even the little things, right. Not everyone buys into the idea, but the more players that buy into the idea of doing things right, the better your chances are of having a successful team. In addition to preparation, is the importance of teamwork. Everyone on the team needs to understand that everyone has a role on the team, and everyone needs to do their role well, for the team to be successful. Whether it is on offense, defense, special teams, or on the scout team, everyone has an obligation to do their best in whatever role they have. We don't expect as much from a first- or second-year guy, as much as a fifth-year senior, but everyone needs to understand that they have to do their best in whatever role they have in order to have a successful team and season.

Dr. Hirokawa

Earlier, you mentioned that the lack of talent can explain why a team is less than successful. Does that also apply in reverse? In other words, does superior talent trump good preparation?

Coach Ferentz

When the two go together, you have a greater chance of success. That's why Alabama has been consistently good. They probably have the best talent, or at least the top 5% of talented players in college football. But they also do a very good job of preparation and doing things the right way, even the little things. Their players are well trained and well coached – in and out of season. Other teams may have as much talent as Alabama, but their preparation may not be as consistent on a year-to-year basis, and that may be why their level of success is not as consistent as Alabama's.

Dr. Hirokawa

When I listen to your players being interviewed after a game, regardless of whether they won or lost, they talk about the importance of meeting standards. What are they referring to?

Coach Ferentz

Some of the standards refer to tangible goals. So, for defense, points allowed is always a big one. If the ball gets down in the red zone, we're trying to keep them out of the end zone. Offensively, one of the big ones is ball security. When we don't turn the ball over, we usually win. Those are basic axioms, goals if you will, that we strive to achieve every game, regardless of the score or situation. Other standards are less tangible but just as important. We constantly talk to our players about being smart, tough, and physical. We talk to them about playing together. We talk about being prepared. We talk to them about doing their best. These are the expectations that we have for all of them, whether they are first-year players or fifth-year seniors, whether they are on scholarship or are walk-ons, whether it's in the training room, during practice or during games, those are the standards that they are expected to live up to. Standards refer to the way we want to operate; not so much what we do, but how we do things.

Dr. Hirokawa

Where do these standards come from? How do they become a part of the fabric of your teams and program? Do they come from you as the head coach?

Coach Ferentz

I think we all mutually agree that this is the way we want to go about it. And you have to have buy-in at every level of your team from coaches to players to training staff on down. We have a fifth-year senior who has never played a down in any meaningful game, but he lives up to the standards and does everything the right way. He is a walking billboard of what we expect from all of our team members. If everyone is like that, then you have a chance of having a successful team.

Dr. Hirokawa

In post-game interviews, especially after your team has won the game, you often attribute success to the leadership on the team, and especially your senior leadership. What are you referring to? Can you give me some examples of the kind of leadership you're talking about that makes a difference in the success of the team?

Coach Ferentz

You don't have to be a senior, or even an upper classman, to be a leader. Leaders are the ones who live the standards that we expect from all of our players every day. They have to do things the right way at all times. They don't have to, but it sure helps if they have the ability to connect, or at least try to connect. One of the things we have currently is the Hawkeye Championship competition that starts in January and goes till the start of training camp in August. Part of the competition involves their football training, but it also includes academics and community service. The competition emphasizes the importance of doing everything, even the little things like being punctual, in the right way. The team elects 12 captains. We have six teams, with two captains per team. Most of those captains are seniors, but not all. The captains are actively responsible for making sure that everyone on their team is doing everything in a quality manner. The captains have to live up to their expectations of others on their team. They have to do things the right way at all times, and hold others accountable if they aren't, or try to convince them of the importance of doing things in a quality manner at all times. That kind of leadership from January to August is what paves the way for success on game days.

head coach, Geno Auriemma was asked about his team's long-running success, he stated that "We have a tradition of success because some of the best players who have ever played the game have played here … We keep trying to attract the right kind of players and coach them the best we can so we can sustain this level of success" (2022). Simply put, the Connecticut Huskies women's basketball team is more successful than their competition in large part because they have better (more talented) players than their competition. Of course, it certainly helps that they also have a head coach who can consistently recruit those talented players and get them to work well together.

In addition to having knowledgeable and skilled members, successful teams also require highly motivated individuals. In their study of health care teams, Hirokawa et al. (2003) found that the success stories of health care teams contained frequent references to team members who were willing to do whatever is necessary to help the group succeed (e.g., "We did well because we had members who quite simply worked their butts off"), and who had high levels of dedication and commitment (e.g., "Each member of the team was a consummate professional with total dedication and commitment to the success of each transplant procedure"). In contrast, the authors found that failure stories often indicated a lack of motivation (e.g., "Team members were just tired, burned out, I guess, so no one had the desire or energy to put forth the effort necessary to get the job done"). As a member of an emergency room critical care team puts it:

When someone is "crashing," nobody says, "sorry that's not my job." Everyone is motivated to do whatever needs to be done. It also happens in less critical situations. Success of a team depends on … a great deal of respect for all duties that contribute to the successful functioning of the team. Everyone has to be good at what they do, but they also have to be motivated to back each other up so that no matter how hairy it gets, we can provide the best care possible for the patient.

(pp. 150–151)

Standards of excellence. Standards of excellence can be thought of as expectations that emphasize high-level performance or achievement. Players on highly successful sports teams often talk about the expectations that are placed on them. Carol Hutchins, Hall of Fame coach for the University of Michigan's softball team, tells her players that "you better raise your standards, because we are not going to lower ours" (Girandola, 2019). Bill Walsh, the legendary football coach of the San Francisco 49ers said "if you were lucky enough to receive a 49er paycheck, it meant you were part of an organization that had high expectations of itself and of you, whether you were a superstar or a secretary, manager or maintenance man, athlete, executive, or head coach" (Janssen, 2015). Kirk Ferentz constantly reminds his players about the importance of "being smart, tough, and physical ... about playing together ... about being prepared ... about doing their best." Ferentz says that these "are the expectations that we have for all of them, whether they are first-year players or fifth-year seniors, whether they are on scholarship or are walk-ons, whether it's in the training room, during practice or during games, those are the standards that they are expected to live up to" (see Box 6.1). Rorke Denver (2013), a former Head of Advanced SEAL Training states that special forces units like the U.S. Navy SEALS, have uncompromisingly high standards because lives depend on them. If a member of a SEAL team fails to meet a necessary standard, he/she could jeopardize the success of the mission, their own life and lives of their colleagues. As he puts it:

A boat race isn't just a boat race. It's a way of teaching the culture of winning. A room inspection isn't just a room inspection. It's an excuse for the instructors to get all over the students and teach the life-or-death importance of sweating every last detail. It actually does matter if your knife is fully sharpened and sitting just so by the bed. It matters if your dive vest is freshly safety-checked and your fins are resting at a precise 45 degrees. All our lessons are written in blood.

(p. 46)

Collaborative climate. The *climate* of a group pertains to the feelings, emotions and perceptions that group members have when they are participating in the group. For example, in some groups, we feel "welcomed" and "comfortable," while in other groups, we feel "unwelcomed" and "uncomfortable." In some groups, we perceive ourselves to be "valued" and "appreciated" by others in the group, while in other groups, we believe that we are being "used" and "unappreciated" by others. A collaborative climate is one where group members share positive feelings, perceptions, and relationships that make them want to work together to achieve a common goal or objective. When a team lacks a collaborative climate, its members lack the motivation or desire to work together. Sports psychologists use the term "team chemistry" to refer to this collaborative climate. Mukherjee et al. (2019) found that positive relationships among team members (i.e., "team chemistry") significantly improves the likelihood of team success across all sports beyond the talent of individual team members. In fact, research has found that team chemistry and team success exist in a dual relationship where team chemistry fosters team success, and team success strengthens team chemistry.

In their study of healthcare teams, Hirokawa et al. (2003) found that many stories of team success talked about the importance of climate and relational factors. Success stories often referenced the importance of mutual respect (e.g., "We were successful because we all respected and affirmed each other's value and contribution to the team") and group cohesiveness (e.g., "I would attribute our success to the fact that we were a tight-knit team ... we covered for each other, and picked each other up, so that even if someone was having a bad day, we were able to get the job done as a team"). In contrast, stories of team failure illustrated how negative relationships, and culture, can adversely affect team performance. As a psychologist on an interdisciplinary health care team put it:

> At our very first meeting, the doctor immediately took charge and said, "Look, if anything goes wrong and the patient sues, I pay the malpractice insurance, so we're going to do things my way." At that point, the rest of us figured why put in any effort since the doctor is going to do what he wants regardless of what we say.
>
> (p. 152)

Effective process. Perhaps the most important characteristic of successful groups and teams is their **process**; that is, how they go about doing their work and completing their task(s). An important aspect of process is the amount of effort group and team members put forth in completing their task. Tim Notke, a high school basketball coach, is credited with saying "hard work beats talent, when talent doesn't work hard" (Mohamad, 2022). Renowned author, J.K. Rowling, said "I believe in hard work and luck … the first often leads to the second" (Loftus, 2012). There is no question that hard work and vigilant effort are important aspects of successful team process.

Another important aspect of process is the quality of communication among group or team members. Hirokawa et al. (2000) found that the stories of healthcare team success and failure highlight the importance of effective group communication. The success stories contained numerous references to the importance of effective listening, open exchange of ideas and information, and the timely sharing of information to team members who were most in need of it. For example, one respondent wrote:

> Our success was due to good communication – we discussed each case thoroughly, really listened to each other's ideas and suggestions, and made sure we understood what others were saying and opened [ourselves] up to understanding the viewpoints of the other people.
>
> (pp. 153–154)

In contrast, failure stories contained nearly twice as many references to the detrimental effects of poor listening, close-minded interaction, and the absence of proper information flow among team members. The authors point to one story that illustrates the detrimental effects of poor communication:

> I was a member of a purchase team for an MRI scanner. Basically, the hospital administrator, behind closed doors with a vendor, made the purchase without consulting with any of us. After we found out, we tried to talk to talk the administrator, but he wouldn't listen to us. As a result, the hospital ended up purchasing an MRI scanner that was soon obsolete … (and) to make matters worse, it was discovered that we didn't have adequate space to install the MRI because the administrator never consulted with the building engineers and just assumed that the MRI would fit in the existing CT suite. All of these problems could have been easily avoided if the administrator had taken the time to talk with various members of the team before making the purchase.
>
> (p. 154)

Evidence-Based Recommendations

Thus far, we have noted that successful groups and teams are characterized by six qualities that facilitate high performance: (1) clear goals, (2) a facilitative structure, (3) competent members, (4) standards of excellence, (5) a collaborative climate, and (6) effective process. Now, suppose you are assigned to be the chair of an important decision-making or problem-solving group in your organization, or are hired to be the head coach of a college or professional sports team, how would you go about ensuring that your team possessed the characteristics of a high-performance group. Where would you start first, and how would you proceed?

Let us begin with the question of where to start? Which of the six characteristics that I talked about in this chapter would you focus on first? Would you begin by trying to ensure that your group had the most competent members possible? Or would you first focus on establishing clear goals? Or perhaps your first task would be to establish a facilitative structure? Or would establishing standards of excellence and building a collaborative climate be your first order of business? Or perhaps establishing an effective process, with effective communication, would be what you would try to accomplish first? Research on the relationship between group development and group performance (see, e.g., Hirokawa, 1983; Poole, 1983; Poole & Roth, 1989a, 1989b) clearly show that the order in which the characteristics of a group emerge or develop is less important than the fact that they emerge or develop in the first place. In other words, you should not be concerned about the order or priority in which the six characteristics of successful groups are developed in the groups – what is ultimately important is that they all develop over time because each characteristic is very important for successful group and team performance.

Now, let's turn to the question of how to establish these six characteristics in your group or team? Research indicates that few, if any, groups and teams possess all six characteristics of successful teams right away (Larson & LaFasto, 1989). Most groups require time to develop them fully, and many never achieve them at all (Brown, 2013). Bruce Tuckman's (1965) model of group development can help us understand how the characteristics of successful groups develop over time. Tuckman proposed that groups and teams move through four stages of development from inception to maturity. He called them "forming, storming, norming, and performing.[1]

When a group or team is first formed, its members are generally unsure about all aspects of their groups, including what is expected of them. As such, Tuckman suggests that the first stage of a group's development is called "forming," where group members interact with each other to gain some clarity about their tasks, goals, roles and responsibilities, rules and expectations, and the like. It is in this first stage of group development that goal(s) of the group are first introduced to, and begin to gain traction in, the group (Larson & LaFasto, 1989). My daughter's high school volleyball team provides an example of this. In their senior year in high school, her volleyball team won the Iowa state championship with an undefeated record. The success of the team can be traced back to the formation of the team when they were in the seventh grade. During the team's first practices, the coach told the players that their goal was to "be the best team they could be." Eventually, as the team developed and experienced success, the goal of "being the best team they could be" evolved into a higher-level goal of "being a championship team." The goal of "being a championship team" superseded the goal of "being the best team they could be" because "being the best team you can be" does not necessarily result in "being a championship team." Each team member embraced the higher goal of "being a championship team" and it motivated them to work harder in practices and games, make a commitment to attend camps and clinics in the summer, and play in highly competitive tournaments throughout the year. The desire to be a "championship team" was not introduced by the coach when the team was first formed and, quite frankly, would have been seen as an unrealistic goal by the team, until they experienced enough success for the goal to become realistic. This is often the case with high-performance teams – their clear, elevating goals usually emerge over time.

The second stage of Tuckman's model is called "storming." In this second stage, the goal(s) of the group become clearer to group members, but they are unsure about, and may even disagree over, and compete for, preferred roles and responsibilities in the group (MacPherson & Howard, 2011).

For example, on my daughter's volleyball team, when the team was first formed, the girls were unsure of who would play the roles of "setter," "middle blocker," "outside hitter," and "defensive specialist" (aka "libero"). As might be expected, several girls wanted to play the same positions, and so there was a certain amount of tension among them as they competed for preferred positions and roles on the team. It was in this second stage of the team's development that the coach introduced the foundations of a facilitative structure. She told the players that in order for the team to achieve its goal of being the best it could be, each player had to assume a role that was best suited for her physical characteristics and athletic skills. She told the team that the "middle blockers" and "outside hitters" need to be taller people, but the "libero" needed to be quick and agile because her job was to "dig" balls that were served or spiked (i.e., prevent them from hitting the ground). She also explained that the "libero" needed to be shorter in height because she was often required to dive to the ground to dig balls and this was easier for a shorter person to do that than a taller one. By carefully explaining the various positions and roles on the team and explaining why specific players were assigned to them, the players were able to accept their roles on the team, and as such, the coach was able to begin building a facilitative structure in the "storming" stage of the team's development.

The third stage of group development in Tuckman's model is called "norming." In this third stage, the group continues to work on its facilitative structure by establishing group norms. As explained earlier, group norms are behavioral expectations that group members are expected to follow and abide by in the group. For example, on my daughter's volleyball team, one of the first norms introduced during the norming stage was the importance of being on time, and putting in 100% effort, for all practices and games. The coach explained that when players are late, it disrupts the team's preparation and can contribute to poor team performance. Likewise, not putting in 100% effort can adversely affect the team's performance.

Norms related to a facilitative structure of the group, also lead to the development of standards of excellence in the "norming" phase of the group's development. As noted earlier, standards of excellence are expectations that emphasize high-level performance or achievement. These expectations are usually directly related to the norms of the group. For example, a common norm of sports teams is to prioritize the needs of the team ahead of the needs of the individuals. This norm leads to the standard of excellence that the team members should make personal sacrifices for the sake of the team. For example, in the game of football, the performance of a punter is usually measured in terms of the average distance of his punts (kicks). In professional football (NFL), the average distance of a punt is approximately 45 yards. The higher a punter's average, the "better" he is assumed to be. However, there are times in a game when the punter is expected to sacrifice his average for the sake of placing the ball in a disadvantageous field position for the opposing team. For instance, the punter will choose to make a 30-yard punt so that the ball ends up at the opposing team's one-yard line. In short, the punter sacrifices his average distance to meet the standard of excellence of doing what is best for the sake of the team.

The 2005 movie, "Coach Carter," provides a good illustration of how team norms and standards of excellence are related to each other and emerge in the "norming" stage of a group's development. The story begins with Coach Carter being hired to coach the Richmond High School basketball team. The team initially consists of rowdy, rude, disrespectful, and undisciplined players, who are doing badly in school. On the first day of practice, Coach Carter gives each player a team contract to sign and follow without fail. The contract consists of a set of attitudinal, behavioral, and academic standards, including the expectations to attend all their classes daily, sit in the front row of all their classes, and maintain a 2.3 (C+) grade point average. The team initially rebels against the contract, and some players refuse to sign the contract and quit the team. Even the school's principal questions the contract, telling the coach that his expectations are unreasonable and unrealistic. Over time, though, the players come to understand that the contract consists of norms and standards of excellence that, if followed, will lead to team success. The players sign and follow the contract, and the team begins winning games, and completes the season undefeated. The movie ends with Coach Carter expressing his pride that the team lived up to the standards or excellence, and the film ends with the team celebrating with the community despite losing by two points in the state tournament. The closing graphics explain that six players went on to attend college. This movie shows that norms and standards of excellence take time to develop in a group, but once they are established, often lead to group or team success.

In addition to norms and standards of excellence, effective processes also begin to form in the "norming" stage of the group's development. As noted earlier, having an effective process for achieving their goals and objectives is something that groups and teams learn to do. Very few, if any, groups immediately begin by doing things effectively and efficiently. The student government group that I advise is an example of this. The group follows *Robert's Rules of Order* to conduct their meetings, facilitate discussion, and make group decisions. The process described in Robert's Rules is very specific and detailed, and it takes time for the members of the group to learn the process. New members are provided with instructions prior to the first meeting, and the group has a "Parliamentarian" (an expert on Robert's Rules), who reminds the group of what to do, or corrects them when the improperly deviate from the Robert's Rules process. Over the course of a year, the group eventually becomes very proficient in following the process of Robert's Rules.

University of Iowa football coach, Kirk Ferentz, says that when new players first join the team as freshmen, they must learn the process of becoming a good football player. They must learn how to lift weights properly; they must learn how to eat properly; they must learn how to practice properly; they must learn how to communicate effectively both on and off the field; and so forth. Ferentz says that very few players enter the program already knowing "how to do things the right way." Most must learn how to do it, and some take longer than others to do it. Typically, these aspects of effective process begin to emerge in the "norming" stage of a group development.

The fourth stage of a group's development is called the "performing" stage according to Tuckman. In this stage, the group knows what needs to be done, and how to go about doing it. Group members know their roles and responsibilities, as well as what is expected of them, and the group performs its task with a high degree of autonomy and relatively little conflict among group members. It is in this fourth stage that successful groups and teams focus on developing competent members and a collaborative climate.

Group members bring a certain level of competence to the group. Over time, particularly during the "performing" phase, their competence can be increased through training and learning experiences in the group. And finally, in some groups, the overall competence in a group can be increased by replacing members of lesser talent with new members who bring greater competence to the group. Iowa football coach Kirk Ferentz admitted that when he first took over the University of Iowa football program in 1999, the overall level of talent on the football team was considerably less than the talent on the teams they competed against. Not surprisingly, the Iowa football team only won one game in 1999. Coach Ferentz said that the immediate first step was to elevate the overall talent on the team through coaching, teaching, and training, as well as through the recruitment of new players who brought to the team more talent than the ones they were replacing. In 2000, the team won three games; in 2001, they won seven games; and in 2002, they won 11 games. In four years, Iowa went from being the worst team in the Big-10 to the co-champions of the league largely be increasing the overall talent and competence on the team. Coach Ferentz said that there are very few football teams that are blessed with instant and inherent talent every year. Most teams must develop their talent over time through hard work and the careful recruitment of new players.

Of course, while the competence of group members is important to team success, the effective integration and utilization of the talent and skills of group members is also important. In his book, *The Boys in the Boat* (2013), Daniel James Brown succinctly summarizes the importance of integrating the skills of the eight rowers on an Olympic-caliber rowing team:

> There is a thing that sometimes happens in rowing that is hard to achieve and hard to define. Many crews, even winning crews, never really find it. It's called "swing." It only happens when all eight oarsmen are rowing in such perfect unison that no single action by any one is out of synch with those of others. It's not just that the oars enter and leave the water at precisely the same instant. Sixteen arms must begin to pull, sixteen knees must begin to fold and unfold, eight bodies must begin to slide forward and backward, eight backs must bend and straighten all at once.
>
> (p. 161)

Building a collaborative climate also begins to take place in the "performing" stage of a group's development. Very rarely does a team have "instant chemistry" among its players. Often, a collaborative climate takes time to develop in a group or team. In their study of healthcare teams, Hirokawa et al. (2003) provide a story that shows how a team's collaborative climate develops over time.

> I think the secret to our success was the motel hot tub. Our health care team was sent to a really remote part of the state. It was a six-hour drive to the clinic so rather than driving back and forth 3 times a week, we would go up there and stay for two nights then come back. The town we were in had nothing to do and after work we'd go back to the motel and sit in the hot tub and just talk. We really developed a close bond doing that and we became a really close-knit group. We respected each other and trusted each other and communicated well with each other. We just really clicked as a team and I think it all started with us spending time together in the hot tub.
>
> (p. 155)

Our local high-school baseball team provides another good example of how a collaborative climate develops over time. The team recently won the state championship, and after the championship game, the TV media interviewed the coach and some of the players who starred in the game. To a person, they all gave credit to the "chemistry" on the team. When asked how the team's chemistry developed, the coach said that most of the players on the team had "played together since they were in youth leagues." He said that many of them "had developed close friendships over the years" and those "friendships helped to develop close bonds among the players that made them enjoy playing with, and for, each other." According to one of the players, his team's chemistry was "started when they started playing together in the 5th grade … (it) wasn't something that developed overnight."

Conclusion

Researchers have found that successful teams have certain characteristics that less successful teams seem to lack. In this chapter, I have identified six characteristics: (1) clear goals, (2) a facilitative structure, (3) competent members, (4) standards of excellence, (5) a collaborative climate, and (6) effective process. I have noted that none of these qualities are instantly present in a group or team. Rather, they emerge and develop over time as a group moves through the "forming," "storming," "norming." and "performing" stages of its development. In some groups, these characteristics develop rather quickly; in others, more slowly; and in still others, they fail to develop at all. These six characteristics – however slowly or quickly they emerge and develop – are crucial for group and team success because they enable group/team members to perform the essential functions needed for group success (Hirokawa & Laybon, 2022).

In his book, *Groups That Work (and Those That Don't)*, J. Richard Hackman (1990) concludes that the factors that affect the performance of a group or team are like the "backlash on a fishing reel." If you have ever used a fishing reel, you know that a "backlash" occurs when the line in the reel gets tangled together such that there are so many tangles and knots to untie that it is difficult to tell where to start. The six characteristics that I have discussed in this chapter essentially intertwine with each other in such a way that each characteristic can lead to, and influence, another characteristic. As such, much like trying to unravel the many tangles in the backlash of a fishing reel, knowing what characteristic of a high-performance group we should begin with is a difficult undertaking. In the end, all we know if that we need *all* six because they serve as the building blocks for creating a successful group or team.

Note

1 Tuckman later added a fifth stage called "adjournment." By that fifth stage is less relevant to this chapter so we will not discuss it here.

Further Readings

Brown, D. J. (2013). *The boys in the boat*. Penguin Books.
Hackman, J. R. (1990). *Groups that work and those that don't* (No. E10 H123). Jossey-Bass.
Larson, C. E., & LaFasto, F. M. J. (1989). *Teamwork: What must go right/What can go wrong*. Sage Publications.

Glossary

Collaborative climate   Climate where group members share positive feelings, perceptions, and relationships that make them want to work together to achieve a common goal or objective.
Goal clarity   Clear understanding of the performance objective the group wants to achieve, phrased in a concrete way such that it is possible to tell whether or not that performance objective has been met.
Norms   Rules or standards of behavior that are shared by members of the group.
Process   How group members go about doing their work and completing their task.
Roles   Specific behaviors expected of group members who occupy specific positions in the group.
Structure   It refers to the norms and roles of the group.

References

Allison, G. T., & Zelikow, P. (1999). *The essence of decision: Explaining the Cuban missile crisis*. Addison-Wesley.
Auriemma, G. (2022). Masterclass: How to attract and keep top talent. https://www.masterclass.com/classes/geno-auriemma-teaches-leading-winning-teams/chapters/how-to-attract-and-keep-top-talent#
Denver, R. (2013). *Damn few: Making the modern SEAL warrior*. Hachette Book Group.
Girandola, C. (2019). The values that shape the life and legacy of Carol Hutchins. Flosoftball.com. https://www.flosoftball.com/articles/6547661-the-values-that-shape-the-life-legacy-of-carol-hutchins
Hackman, J. R. (1990). *Groups that work and those that don't* (No. E10 H123). Jossey-Bass.

Hardy, S. (2021). Maya Angelou quotes of wisdom and hope. Independently published. ISBN: 979-8766932970.

Hirokawa, R. Y. (1983). Group communication and problem-solving effectiveness: An investigation of group phases. *Human Communication Research*, 9(4), 291–305. https://doi.org/10.1111/j.1468-2958.1983.tb00700.x

Hirokawa, R. Y., DeGooyer, D., & Valde, K. (2000). Using narratives to study task group effectiveness. *Small Group Research*, 31(5), 573–591. https://doi.org/10.1177/104649640003100504

Hirokawa, R. Y., DeGooyer, D., & Valde, K. (2003). Characteristics of effective health care teams. In R. Y. Hirokawa, R. S. Cathcart, L. A. Samovar, & L. D. Henman (Eds.), *Small group communication: Theory and practice* (pp. 148–157). Oxford University Press. ISBN: 9780195330007

Hirokawa, R. Y., & Laybon, A. (2022). Communication and group decision-making process. In S. J. Beck, J. Keyton, & M. S. Poole (Eds.), *The emerald handbook of group and team communication research* (pp. 191–208). Emerald Publishing Limited. doi:10.1108/978-1-80043-500-120211013

Janssen, J. (2015). Five ways standards define and differentiate your program. https://coachad.com/articles/five-ways-standards-define-and-differentiate-your-program/

Kiefer, C. F., & Senge, P. M. (1984). *Transforming work*. Miles River Press.

Locke, E. A., & Latham, G. P. (1990). *A theory of goal setting and task performance*. Prentice-Hall, Inc.

Loftus, G. (2012). Two magic lessons from J. K. Rowling. Forbes. https://www.forbes.com/sites/geoffloftus/2012/08/01/2-magic-leadership-lessons-from-j-k-rowling/?sh=33d323662769

MacPherson, A. C., & Howard, P. W. (2011). The team perspective: Promoting excellence in performance teams. In D. Collins, A. Button, & H. Richards (Eds.), *Performance psychology* (pp. 121–137). Churchill Livingtone. https://doi.org/10.1016/B978-0-443-06734-1.00009-2.

Mohamad, Z. (2022). Leading life: Talent versus hard work. *New Straits Time*. https://www.nst.com.my/lifestyle/sunday-vibes/2022/03/779505/leading-life-talent-versus-hard-work

Mukherjee, S., Huang, Y., Neidhardt, J., Uzzi, B., & Contractor, N. (2019). Prior shared success predicts victory in team competitions. *Nature Human Behavior*, 3, 74–81. https://doi.org/10.1038/s41562-019-0581-y.

Poole, M. S. (1983). Decision development in small groups III: A multiple sequence theory of decision development. *Communication Monographs*, 50(4), 321–341. https://doi.org/10.1080/03637758309390173

Poole, M. S., & Roth, J. (1989a). Decision development in small groups IV: A typology of group decision paths. *Human Communication Research*, 15(3), 323–356. https://doi.org/10.1111/j.1468-2958.1989.tb00188.x

Poole, M. S., & Roth, J. (1989b). Decision development in small groups v: Test of a contingency model. *Human Communication Research*, 15(4), 549–589. https://doi.org/10.1111/j.1468-2958.1989.tb00199.x

Tuckman, B. W. (1965). Development sequence in small groups. *Psychological Bulletin*, 1965, 63(6), 384–399.

Washington, B. T. (1901). Booker T. Washington: An autobiography. Independently published. ISBN: 979-8622953842.

Wooden, J., & Johnson, S. (1997). *Wooden: A lifetime of observations on and off the court*. Contemporary Books.

7 Groups as Systems

Andrew Pilny and Julius Riles

Chapter Objectives

This chapter approaches group communication from a systems perspective. The chapter has several objectives. First, readers should be able to understand the difference between (a) conventional thinking and (b) systems thinking through the explication of systems concepts. Next, they should be able to identify and tell what are known as *systems stories* about various group communication anecdotes. Finally, they should be able to identify the practical applications of systems thinking for managing and being a part of groups.

Introduction

Complexity is at the heart of **systems thinking**. Rather than trying to reduce social phenomena into simplified concepts, systems' thinking embraces the messiness and chaos of human interaction. Although this might paint a more realistic picture of some social phenomena, it comes at the cost of a higher likelihood of obfuscation. To help reduce such ambiguity, this chapter is organized into three parts.

The first part introduces fundamental systems concepts and principles by contrasting it with what can be called **conventional thinking**. We will categorize differences between systems and conventional thinking with respect to differing views on (1) causality, (2) accountability, (3) outcomes, and (4) time. The second part puts many of these concepts into action through the idea of recognizing and telling *system stories*: (1) vicious cycles, (2) fixes that backfire, and (3) conflicting goals. Finally, the third part of this chapter concludes with some general practical recommendations for managing life inside groups from a system perspective. These include suggestions on how to create system maintenance (i.e., restoring stability) and adapting (i.e., dealing with change) communication mechanisms.

Part I: Conventional and System Thinking

We can view *conventional thinking* as dividing social phenomena "into their components under the assumption that we can best address the whole by focusing and optimizing the parts" (Stroh, 2015, pp. 25–26). This sort of thinking is sometimes called reductionist and atomistic. For instance, if we know that groups perform better when their members are hard-working, then each member just simply needs to work harder. As we navigate our lives in a complex world, such thinking can be incredibly useful as a heuristic to make decisions. Consider conventional thinking in more primitive human tribal times. If somebody from the tribe hears a scary animal noise, it is probably a good sign for that person to tell the group to seek shelter.

DOI: 10.4324/9781003227458-9

On the other hand, *systems thinking* is the study of the whole, constituted by various "sets of elements standing in interrelation" (Von Bertalanffy, 1968, p. 38). Based on the principle of **holism**, the system is viewed as more than the sum of its parts. Systems thinking can be thus defined as "the ability to understand these interconnections in such a way as to achieve a *desired* purpose" (Stroh, 2015, p. 28, emphasis in original). However, this is still a little vague and even semi-mystical. As such, to help flesh out systems thinking, we will describe it and contrast it with conventional thinking across the familiar concepts of (1) causality, (2) accountability, (3) outcomes, and (4) outcomes.

Causality

Causality in conventional thinking is often simple and linear. By simple, we mean thinking of how one variable (i.e., X) might have a direct influence on another (i.e., Y). By linear, we mean a "straight line" relationship between X and Y. That is, the more you increase X, the more you will increase/decrease Y (and vice versa). For instance, consider collective action groups who have the goal of preserving a public good (e.g., maintaining a free online Encyclopedia like *Wikipedia*). Olson's (1965) famous thesis is that the larger the group, the more difficult it will be for members to cooperate. In other words, increasing the group size (X) decreases the likelihood of preserving the public good (Y).

Causality in systems thinking can be a bit messier. Here we will point to two features common in systems thinking on causality: (1) multiple levels and (2) complex causality. Regarding the former, Kozlowski (2012) argues that systems theory complicates conventional X $\rightarrow$ Y causality because it forces researchers to think about how groups are coupled across *levels* (e.g., think of a Russian doll). As such, we have to specify the levels across macro (i.e., X_g, group level) and micro (i.e., X_i, individual level) dimensions in order to get a better understanding of what might be going on. Opp (2009) reframes Olson's theory of group size and public goods in this way. Here, we have group size (X_g) as a macro level variable that influences group member incentives (X_i) at the individual level. More specifically, the larger the group (X_g), the less noticeable (X_i) one's contributions are to the public good. In turn, the less noticeable (X_i) a group member's contributions are, the less likely that group member will contribute to a public good (Y_i). After all, people generally like to see their contributions get recognition and acknowledged according to Olson's thinking. Finally, the less likely a group member will contribute to a public good (Y_i), the less likely a public good will be preserved (Y_g).

Re-specifying conventional X $\rightarrow$ Y relationships can also open the door to specifying other relationships, particularly the second feature of *complex causality*. Complex causal situations are phenomena in which "due to feedback loops (sometimes multiple loops), it is impossible to distinguish cause and effect, because each variable in the loops are both" (Poole, 2013, p. 53). For instance, if a system is only defined by **positive feedback** (i.e., factors that continuously amplify each other), causality is better understand as a result of the structure of the system. For instance, if a work team gets a poor evaluation (X_1), they might then go out and party together (Y_1) to blow off steam. However, such partying (Y_1) might cause work members to perform poorly because they are tired and hungover and thus, receive another poor evaluation (X_2). Here, the cycle perpetuates over and over again. To counteract such cycles, what is needed is **negative feedback**, which is when a factor influences another factor in a counteracting way (i.e., corrective feedback). For instance, we might create a rule that the group is only allowed to party together if they receive a positive evaluation, which is akin to the "work hard, play hard" motto. However, negative feedback can be a double-edged sword because systems defined only by such corrective feedback will tend to remain stagnant and likely never grow/innovate. For instance, the sociologist Max Weber famously thought of highly bureaucratic groups as an *iron cage* because they were so entrenched in corrective rules and regulations that stifled creativity.

To sum things up, systems thinkers tend to treat simple and linear notions of causality (e.g., X causes Y) as (1) multilevel and (2) complex. Answering two simple questions is a good first step to engaging in systems explanations for things:

1   Can the relationship among variables in question be converted into a micro-macro model?
2   Are any of the variables in question interdependent through feedback loops?

When tackling these questions, it becomes evident that our notion of causality shifts a bit. That is, rather than trying to explain why a dependent variable (Y) is distributed the way it is (i.e., *variance*), systems thinkers are more interested in explaining *equilibrium*, the "condition of the system in which competing influences are balanced" (Poole, 2013, p. 53). For *Wikipedia*, this mean juggling different factors that keep group incentives high enough to main a critical mass of contributors to keep the public good alive over time. As such, if we can get a better picture of how things are related to one another and specify complex causal mechanisms in systems, we might logically ask who or what should be held accountable in groups.

Accountability

When things go wrong in groups, conventional thinking tends to emphasize things like individual responsibility and personal accountability rather than situational or environmental factors. An example of this is known as the fundamental attribution error (Ross, 1977), Put another way, there is nothing wrong with the group, per se, but it is victim to a few bad apples. This view emphasizes *agency*, which can be viewed as group members' ability to (a) respond to information, (b) monitor actions of themselves and others, (c) deliberatively engage in problem solving, (d) be aware of other group members and environmental factors, (e) meaningfully interpret their actions, and (f) be aware of their own agency (Poole, 2013).

On the other hand, systems theories do not discard agency, but also put varying degree of emphasis on what might be called *structure*, which is often seen as existing in tension with agency (i.e., the heavier the influence of structure, the less influence of agency). Giddens (1984) notably described structure as the rules and resources that individuals draw upon in interaction and behavior. For instance, in group Zoom meetings, there are formal structures (e.g., a group member has to request control to share his or her screen) and sometimes informal structures (e.g., keeping your mic on mute when not talking) in place. Structuration is an example of a *recursive* theory that is common among many theories of systems (Giddens, 1984). Recursive theories are a lot like recycling symbols in that past actions set the conditions for future actions, linking together concepts like agency and structure. Structuration posits that group members are enabled and constrained by structure in interaction and, as a result, either challenge or reproduce said structures. In this case, a group might have some bad apples (agency), but the barrel where they come from may also be rotten (structure). For instance, some tech-startup groups (e.g., Uber) had issues with individuals who were sexually harassing fellow group members (Fowler, 2017). However, if the larger group culture (i.e., the structure group members are drawing from) explicitly and implicitly encourages such behavior, it is likely that the problem will persist even if a few bad apples are removed.

However, what are some structures that create rotten barrels? To place more accountability on system structures, Rice (2008) developed a theory of *unusual routines*. Some key symptoms of such unusual systems include *catatonic non-responsiveness* (i.e., lack of any feedback), *denial* (i.e., ignoring complaints), *pathological rigidity* (i.e., inability to change any rules), *psychopathic manipulation* (i.e., secretly retaliating/gas-lighting whistleblowers while publicly appearing to do the opposite), and *suspicion/secrecy* (i.e., hiding and concealing information).

Whenever somebody says something is *systemic* (e.g., systemic racism), they are usually referring to issues dealing with structure (i.e., rules and resources) rather than agency. For instance, in 2016, work group members of Wells Fargo were caught opening millions of fake savings and checking accounts for existing clients. Then CEO John Stumpf blamed it on a few bad apples. For systems thinkers, this explanation is incomplete. Instead, they might look as systemic structures that enable such behavior in the first place. These structures include things like the Wells Fargo Incentive Compensation Program that incentivized workers with bonuses for new accounts, insufficient ethics training that enabled working to bend rules (as parodied by comedian John Oliver[1]), and accusations of retaliations against whistleblowers calling the Wells Fargo ethics hotline reporting such illegal behavior.

Outcomes

Typically, the main function of any system is to generate some sort of outcome relevant the goal of the system, whether it be *explicit* or *implicit*. For instance, an intended outcome of a college study group might be to do well on the final semester project, while an unintended outcome might be creating friendships. But where do these outcomes come from?

In group communication, there is a question of how much of group outcomes emerge from what are called *input* or *process* factors (Bonito et al., 2014). Input factors include (but are not limited to) attributes that individuals bring into groups (e.g., work ethic, personality), characteristics of the specific group task (e.g., complex or simple), and modalities of technologies used to get work done (e.g., richness of the medium), while process factors are the interaction dynamics during group activity. Imagine a soccer team. Does the soccer team win a lot of games (outcome) because they have a lot of highly skilled players (input) or because they play well and have good chemistry together on the field (process)? Of course, the real answer is probably a bit of both, but systems thinking tends to focus more on process and what types of processes should be enacted to generate outcomes consistent with the objectives of the system (e.g., win the soccer game). For instance, Grund (2012) found the decentralized ball passing patterns (process) predicted soccer team performance in the English Premier League even after controlling for team quality (input). This clearly has implications for how we train and coach soccer teams. For instance, how much should the focus be on optimizing input features like helping the players become faster, stronger, more flexible, and healthier (e.g., the Tom Brady 12 diet), versus process features like having the players play and scrimmage each other, and in so doing handling interpersonal conflicts and developing camaraderie.

The emphasis on system processes has several implications for how to look at groups and teams. Because groups can engage in a variety of processes, systems can display what is called *equifinality*, the idea that multiple different system processes can lead to the same outcome. For instance, some successful work groups might have a decentralized "divide-and-conquer" strategy, where each group member takes equal share of responsibility. Other groups might have a more centralized "strong-leader" strategy, in which a small number of group members have the most responsibility and delegate smaller tasks to others (e.g., Pilny et al., 2020). Moreover, one basic rule of systems is that their various processes must be as complex as the environment that they face, otherwise known as *requisite variety*. For instance, soccer teams in more popular leagues like the English Premiere League have to routinely engage in media training on how to handle questions and scrutiny from the media, something soccer teams in lower divisions may not have to worry about.

Marks et al. (2001) theorize three key processes for groups and teams: (1) transition processes (e.g., planning activities and defining goals), (2) action processes (e.g., monitoring progress and coordinating tasks), and (3) interpersonal processes (e.g., conflict resolution and emotions management). The first two have been widely studied by group and team researchers (e.g., Gouran &

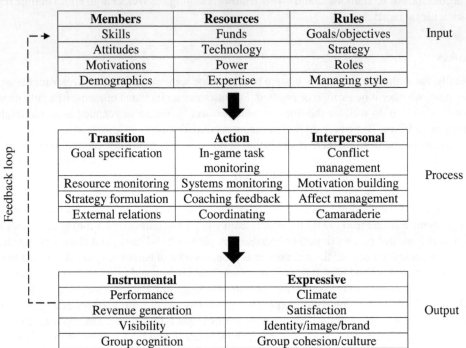

Figure 7.1 Input-Process-Output Framework for Groups.

Hirokawa, 1996), but it is important to not neglect the more social/interpersonal processes as well (see Figure 7.1). For instance, consider the ambitious 2012 Google project code-titled Project Aristotle. The goal was to study hundreds of its work teams in a quest to find out what makes the perfect team. To their surprise, they found that the individual attributes of the team members had little to do with successful teams. Instead, it was *how team members interacted* to create psychological safe environments that explained things. Woolley and colleagues (2010) similarly found that aspects of psychological safety, such as equal communicative participation rates and social sensitivity (i.e., being able to recognize other team members' emotions), were the best predictors of team success. As the *New York Times* profile summarized a point systems thinker have long been making:

> Project Aristotle is a reminder that when companies try to optimize everything, it's sometimes easy to forget that success is often built on experiences – like emotional interactions and complicated conversations and discussions of who we want to be and how our teammates make us feel – that can't really be optimized.

> (Duhigg, 2016)

Time

Speaking of Greek philosophers, Plato once summarized a thought from Heraclitus by saying, "Heraclitus, I believe, says that all things pass and nothing stays, and comparing existing things to the flow of a river, he says you could not step twice into the same river." Indeed, when we describe systems as *dynamic* and *evolutionary*, we are viewing them akin to a flowing river, always ongoing and passing through time. The implication here is to resist the urge to learn everything about a group from a single snapshot.

For instance, think about how individuals make relationships in groups and if such relationships influence their attitudes and behaviors. This has been the focus of research on online groups, where we often wonder how people can believe very strange things (e.g., politicians who drink blood from babies). On one hand, individuals can be influenced to change their attitudes and/or behavior by their group, or on the other hand, they can join groups that share that same attitudes/behavior. Whereas the former is referred to as a social influence effect, the latter is referred to as a social selection effect. It is a real chicken or the egg dilemma that needs a dynamic systems perspective to tease out.

Time is a special feature in many different strands of systems theory. For instance, consider Luhmann's (1995) theory of social systems. Here, the argument is that past decisions set the context for and enable/constrain future decisions. For instance, the decision to include a new group member might influence the future trajectory of that group (e.g., a football team signs a great quarterback, which means they might turn into a passing, rather than a running, team).

Likewise, many of the *new science of systems* approaches emerging in the late 20th century also highlight the dynamic nature of time. For instance, time is anything but static in *self-organizing systems (SOS)* theory (Contractor, 1994). In SOSs, groups are constantly drawing upon various rules and resources to organize with each other over time; there is no man behind the green curtain controlling things. One aspect of SOSs is called *autocatalysis*, which is like a self-generating group effect on how a past factor influences the same factor in the future. For instance, when team members direct many messages to one person, it is very likely that person will be even more popular as time unfolds (Schecter et al., 2018). This is often known as *preferential attachment*. Time is also apparent in *chaos theory*. Chaos can be described as systems that are characterized by highly continuous (e.g., groups varying their levels of communication over time) and discontinuous (e.g., group members coming and going, changes in group rules, changes in group outputs) behavior (Gregersen & Sailer, 1993). For example, Miller (1998) studied how a team of nurses operated on the *edge of chaos* over time. Groups at the edge of chaos are defined by such highly continuous and discontinuous behavior and are on the "edge" of creating a new group form.

When time is not considered by researchers, conventional thinking might also assume that group interventions designed to garner *short-term success will persist in the long-term*. As the earlier descriptions of **cybernetic** systems demonstrated, time is perpetually in motion and groups need to continuously analyze how their actions are meeting goal parameters. For instance, one reason why we might be skeptical of conventional approaches is sometimes called the *butterfly effect*. The butterfly effect is an example of how *unintended consequences* can emerge from very small changes in an otherwise stable system. For example, Watson et al. (1988) studied how introducing a computer-based group decision support system (GDSS) influenced how groups made decisions. The GDSS was intended to promote democratic deliberation, increase the likelihood of consensus, and improve overall group satisfaction. However, although several benefits were found, there were also some unintended consequences, such as how the newness of the technology led to perceptions that conversations during deliberation were trivial, and that GDSS simply confused many group members over time.

Part II: Telling Systems Stories

As Stroh (2015) notes, stories are a powerful way to make sense of the world and understand dense concepts. In general, systems stories are meant to shift the focus from characters as central to the story to the system itself. In other words, the system is the star of the show. In a *Medium* post, Wolske (2012) argued that the HBO TV show *The Wire* (2002–2008) exemplified a great example of systems storytelling. As such, let us take a deeper look at the groups portrayed in the series and how we can see common types of systems stories.[2]

The Wire was a crime drama series based in Baltimore, Maryland in the United States. Each of the five seasons uniquely positioned the show around a different set of groups and institutions. The key groups are (1) the team of Baltimore Police officers responsible for decreasing drug trafficking, (2) the Barksdale group, a gang involved in drug trafficking, (3) the city port authority, another team of blue-collar workers also involved in drug and human trafficking, (4) the mayor's election team, which is responsible for promoting different laws on drug trafficking enforcement, (5) a Baltimore public school-affiliated group responsible for researching and mentoring at-risk youth, and (6) a group of journalists and editors at the *Baltimore Sun*, who are responsible for what stories get visibility and how they are framed.

In the following, we will demonstrate some common *systems plot lines* and how they emerge in the *The Wire*. In particular, we will focus on plot lines that depict (1) vicious cycles, (2) fixes that backfire, and (3) conflicting goals.

Vicious Cycles

Vicious cycles are defined by recursive cycles of positive feedback. Visually, vicious cycles look like the recycling symbols you see on repurposing containers. They are systems that lack negative feedback needed to reach equilibrium. Here, continuing processes of positive feedback never go unchecked and eventually escalate out of control. For instance, Hebel-Sela et al. (2022) theorize a vicious cycle between intergroup conflict and conspiracy theories. That is, the more group A has a conflict with group B, the more likely group A will adopt negative conspiratorial beliefs about group B. As such, if group A espouses conspiratorial beliefs about group B, group B will also have increased conflict with group A and adopt their own conspiratorial beliefs about group A. The cycle goes on and on.

Consider the *The Wire* episode titled, *The Bigger the Lie, the More They Believe.* In season 5 of *The Wire*, reporter Scott Templeton of the *Baltimore Sun* begin receiving national attention for his coverage of a serial killer that is supposedly operating in the Baltimore area. A primary issue is that this killer was fabricated by a police detective seeking additional funding for other murders and Scott, who is unaware of this fabrication, begins falsifying stories about his contact with the killer. Scott's false stories are vivid, and he obtains notoriety and recognition from his publisher, as his publisher is receiving the same from the broader public. However, with every new story, Scott is continuously positively reinforced: each story had to be more salacious than the last to generate more viewership and acclaim for him and the news outlet. In other words, it leads to a classic vicious cycle that keeps going and going. Eventually, Scott becomes unable to substantiate his false accounts until both his, and his outlet's reputations are ruined.

Fixes that Backfire

This system plot line largely describes unintended consequences. That is, because systems are nested across levels and characterized by **interdependence**, any change to an input could have a variety of different outcomes. In other words, quick fixes could have long-term consequences that only exacerbate the original problem in the first place.

Consider the episode called *They Used to Make Steel There, No?"* In season two of *The Wire*, unions affiliated with the Baltimore port authority are losing money because of changing political and business dynamics on the city's waterfront. Frank Sobotka, as head of his local union, decides to subsidize his worker's official streams of income by permitting illegal trafficking from an Eastern European crime syndicate (i.e., the quick fix). This move works and keeps the union alive. Moreover, with the extra cash flow, Frank was able to expand the influence of his group through political contributions, hired lobbyists, and church donations. However, with the reputation of being a failing port, this new group influence begins to raise suspicions on how so much money is being generated, an unintended consequence of an illegal scheme going right. In other words, the success of the money coming in from illegal trafficking communicated an image of the group that conflicted with the truth of a port that was losing money, eventually leading to Frank's downfall.

Competing Goals

Individual embedded in various social systems typically have goals in mind, both explicit and implicit. Sometimes, these goals can conflict with one another, resulting in unusual routines that often create undesirable systems (Rice, 2008). When goals conflict, it can often be the case that group members try to satisfy all goals, but really only end up end satisfying one or none. Indeed, Eisenberg (1984) argued that competing goals often motivated groups to create ambiguous messaging strategies that often never fully satisfy any individual goals.

For instance, in season one of *The Wire*, the Barksdale crime group is introduced, as are its two founders, Avon Barksdale and Stringer Bell. Though there were various ebbs and flows in this organization's success, by season three, the organization was at its zenith and even forayed into legitimate businesses. However, the goals of Avon and Stringer were in deep conflict. While Avon prioritized the tough image and street credibility of his group, Stringer increasingly made decisions based primarily on what would bring them the most money and legitimate opportunities to generate income legally. When the competing Marlo Stanfield group began to challenge the Barksdale Group, the inability to reconcile the conflicting goals of these two leaders led to the downfall of both figures and the larger group. That is, it became hard to be a legitimate group while still committing underground crimes, and it became hard to continue to be an underground group while trying to become legitimate.

Part III: Evidence-Based Recommendations for Practice

Various academic books have provided a set of practical recommendations stemming from systems perspectives (e.g., Meadows, 2008; Rice, 2008; Stroh, 2015). However, how do concepts and stories from systems translate into tactics that can be applied to groups and teams? Any suggestion is primarily based on the claim that system theory is largely a descriptive theory, meaning that systems thinking will not typically advocate a one-sized-fits-all way to manage groups. After all, do so would violate the principle of equifinality (i.e., more than one way to reach an end goal). However, this does not mean that systems thinking is nihilistic. There are some basic tenets that can be suggested to avoid some of the reoccurring problems in groups and teams. Here we discuss two that focus specially on the role of communication in complex systems. As a framework, we can follow Almaney's (1974) argument that communication has two key systems mechanisms: (1) maintenance and (2) adaptation. Here, communication can be conceived of as a *binder*, linking various processes together to make sure the group is accomplishing its goals and adapting with changes in the environment.

Maintenance Mechanisms: Regularly Soliciting Group Feedback

If you are a car owner, you probably know some of the basic maintenance procedures like changing the oil every 3,000 miles, rotating tires every six months, inspecting the brakes every year and so on. These procedures are maintenance mechanisms because they are meant to keep the car functioning as it should. In systems terminology, this is the ability for systems to engage in *negative entropy*, fighting the forces that create disorder and chaos. But how can groups take advantage of communication to ensure the group does not spiral into entropic chaos?

Here, feedback is the key maintenance mechanism. Indeed, the basic tenet of cybernetics is that systems depend on feedback in various forms to ensure they are meeting their goals. Rice (2008) advocates feedback from a multiple stakeholder perspective, meaning that groups should regularly encourage feedback from components in the environment such as their own group members, customers, investors, local community, suppliers/partners, and governments. The goal here is to identify how relationships between components can be improved on a routine basis. Gabelica et al.'s (2012) review of the effectiveness of feedback on teams has shown positive associations of feedback with important outcomes like team cohesion and performance. However, there are a few caveats.

First, the specific content of the feedback is important and often overlooked. Most of the time, feedback is limited to the performance of the group (e.g., our group only accomplished 50% of its goals). Gabelica et al. (2012) noticed that other types of feedback, what they call *process* feedback, is not very well understood. This includes things like (1) interpersonal feedback (e.g., how are group members getting along?), (2) cognitive feedback (e.g., do group members agree with each other?), and (3) task-related feedback (e.g., do group members understand their jobs?). Indeed, Geister et al. (2006) found that teams that engaged in process feedback had positive associations with team performance. As such, we would recommend that group and teams regularly solicit feedback from one another along issues related to (1) performance, (2) interpersonal relations, (3) cognitive understandings, and (4) task-based problems.

Second, feedback cannot be merely symbolic. Often groups will give the impression that they are listening to stakeholders, but simply discard the information. Here, the performance of garnering feedback is more important than listening to it. Put simply, "team feedback will only demonstrate performance improvement if teams actively process and thus reflect upon this feedback" (Gabelica et al., 2014, p. 88).

To encourage authentic processing of feedback, Rice (2008) suggests that systems need to (1) co-construct a shared vision (e.g., create a clear and agreed upon mission), (2) increase psychological safety to learn from feedback (e.g., allow group members to voice vulnerable and honest opinions), and (3) be open to new approaches (e.g., be flexible to changing leadership and group structure). Indeed, Gabelica et al.'s (2014) experiments found that team feedback is only effective if teams have a chance to reflect on that feedback, what they call *team reflexivity*. More specifically, they asked teams to discuss (1) why they achieved success, (2) why they encountered problems, (3) any alternatives that could have improved success, and to (4) set goals and strategies for the future.

Adapting Mechanisms: Making Sense of the Environment

Adapting mechanisms are any type of communication that functions to "detect environmental changes and deal with them appropriately" (Almaney, 1974, p. 38). In other words, it is how group members interpret and respond to the external environment outside of the system. One key systems perspective involving how groups communicate about the environment is Weick's (1979) theory of sensemaking. Sensemaking is the "intersubjective, improvisational communication process through which teams attempt to reduce ambiguity collectively by developing increasingly plausible explanations of problem situations, their causes, and the actions needed to resolve them" (Scott, 2021, p. 498). Sensemaking unfolds in three steps: (1) variation, (2) selection, and (3) retention. Here, variation simply means that because groups *enact* their environments (i.e., by simply existing and acting, a variety of different events and information will confront groups), groups must *select* which interpretations make the most sense and *retain* those interpretations as heuristics for the future. The key outcome here is the reduction of *equivocality* (i.e., abundance of possible interpretations of the same information and events).

As such, how exactly do groups accomplish sensemaking? This is not a simple or easy task, as gaining consensus is often a difficult communicative accomplishment (e.g., see Weick's, 1993, treatment of the Mann Gulch fire disaster). At the bare minimum, *double interact* cycles are needed where group members meaningfully communicate, respond, and adjust their interpretations. Double interact cycles are the opposite of what Hewes (1996) calls *egocentric* speech, meaning that group members come into conversation with pre-existing beliefs and simply reiterate them (i.e., talking *at* group members, rather than talking *with* group members). One way to think of this is as the difference between an improvised jazz group where members are closely listening and responding to each other and a scripted symphony orchestra where members have pre-planned compositions that they are supposed to play at a specific time in the concert. In this sense, double interact cycles are more like spontaneous and unscripted back-and-forth conversations between group members.

Reviewing the literature on sensemaking, Ancona (2011) provides three key suggestions for group leaders to accomplish collective sensemaking. First, group members need to *explore the wider system*. This includes mixing various types of informational data (e.g., performance data, group member testimony), including participatory decision making (e.g., every group member gets input on decision), and avoiding stereotypes (e.g., reducing group members to attributes). Second, group members need to try and *create a map of the situation*. This essentially involves the construction of a shared explanation of why things are happening the way they are. Ancona suggests that for this to happen, members must (1) not overly impose their existing maps and (2) use existing images, metaphors, and stories to adapt equivocal events into meaningful interpretations. Finally, group members need to *act to change the system to learn from it*. Here members can (1) learn from small experiments by trying something new and (2) create an awareness that they themselves enact their environment that can enable and constrain behavior. In sum, Ancona suggests that to achieve sensemaking, groups need to be open to (1) all information, (2) competing plausible explanations, and (3) understanding how they create their environment.

Conclusion

Understanding groups as systems means shifting from looking at them as sets of individual actors that need to be optimized to a set of dynamic and interdependent actors that interact together to create emergent outcomes. A deep understanding of group interactions and interdependencies is the primary task of a group systems thinker. In Box 7.1, we have included a brief survey to gauge your level of systems thinking. In the end, systems thinking can be quite the paradox. It does not provide all the answers to a group problem. Instead, it gives you the tools to understand how those group problems emerged. From there, answers to the problem might be obvious.

Box 7.1   Are You a Systems Thinker?

The following survey is meant to gauge your level of systems thinking in groups. Imagine you are in a group and are thinking of making improvements. Write down your score for each item using the following prompt:

"When you think about making improvements in my group…"

Score: 1 = *Never*, 2 = *Seldom*, 3 = *Some of the time*, 4 = *Often*, 5 = *Most of the time*

Item	Score

I seek everyone's view of the situation
I look beyond a specific event to determine the cause of the problem
I think understanding how the chain of events occur is crucial.
I include people in my work unit to find a solution.
I think recurring patterns are more important than any one specific event.
I think of the problem at hand as a series of connected issues.
I consider the cause and effect that is occurring in a situation.
I consider the relationships among coworkers in the group.
I think that systems are constantly changing.
I propose solutions that affect the work environment, not specific individuals.
I keep in mind that proposed changes can affect the whole system.
I think more than one or two people are needed to have success.
I keep the mission and purpose of the group in mind.
I think small changes can produce important results.
I think about how different group members might be affected by the improvement.
I try strategies that do not rely on people's memory.
I recognize system problems are influenced by past events.
I consider the past history and culture of the group
I consider that the same action can have different effects over time, depending on the state of the system.

Total

Scale adapted from Dolansky et al. (2020). Add up your scores. If you scored at least 70, odds are you are a systems thinker.

Notes

1 Last Week Tonight with John Oliver (Season 3, Episode 23).
2 For a brief summary of *The Wire*, see https://www.youtube.com/watch?v=IZyROkfOb7s

Further Readings

Agazarian, Y. M., & Gantt, S. (2005). The systems perspective. In S. Wheelan (Ed.), *The handbook of group research and practice* (pp. 187–200). SAGE Publications.

Poole, M. S. (2013). Systems theory. In L. Putnam & D. K. Mumby (Eds.), *The SAGE handbook of organizational communication: Advances in theory, research, and methods* (pp. 49–75). SAGE Publications.

Salazar, A. (2002). *Self-organizing and complexity perspectives of group creativity: Implications for group communication*. In L. R. Frey (Ed.), *New directions in group communication* (pp. 179–200). SAGE Publications.

Glossary

Systems thinking   The idea that social phenomenon-like groups can be best understood by looking at and optimizing their complex interactions (e.g., relationships between group members, interactions with other groups).

Conventional thinking   The idea that social phenomenon like groups can be best understood by looking at and optimizing their individual parts (e.g., group member attributes, technologies, etc.).

Interdependence   The mutual reliance and influence that exists between two or more individuals, groups, or systems. In interdependent relationships, the actions and decisions of one group member have an impact on the outcomes of the other group member involved.

Cybernetics   An interdisciplinary field of study that explores the communication and control mechanisms in systems. Some core concepts include feedback (i.e., information about a system's behavior), communication (i.e., exchange of information between components of a system), and control (e.g., adjustments to behavior based on feedback). Cybernetics provides a framework for understanding how systems work, how they can be designed and controlled, and how they interact with their environment.

Positive and negative feedback   Positive feedback is deviation amplifying in that such communication leads to further behavior reinforcement (e.g., past success of groups creates future success). Negative feedback is deviation reducing feedback in that such communication leads to a change in behavior (e.g., an information sharing intervention leads to group success).

Holism   Because groups as systems consist of complex and interdependent webs of relationships, they cannot be reduced to the sum of its parts (i.e., reductionism). Holism is based on the idea that such complex interactions in groups will create a higher-level entity that needs to be understood by analyzing such interactions rather than individual components of the groups.

References

Almaney, A. (1974). Communication and the systems theory of organization. *The Journal of Business Communication, (1973)12*(1), 35–43. https://doi.org/10.1177/002194367401200106

Ancona, D. (2011). Sensemaking: Framing and acting in the unknown. In S. Snook, N. Nohria, & R. Khurana (Eds.), *The handbook for teaching leadership* (pp. 3–21). SAGE Publications.

Bonito, J. A., Gastil, J., Ervin, J. N., & Meyers, R. A. (2014). At the convergence of input and process models of group discussion: A comparison of participation rates across time, persons, and groups. *Communication Monographs, 81*(2), 179–207. https://doi.org/10.1080/03637751.2014.883081

Contractor, N. S. (1994). Self-organizing systems perspective in the study of organizational communication. In B. Kovacic (Ed.), *New approaches to organizational communication* (pp. 39–66). State University of New York Press.

Dolansky, M. A., Moore, S. M., Palmieri, P. A., & Singh, M. K. (2020). Development and validation of the systems thinking scale. *Journal of General Internal Medicine, 35*, 2314–2320. https://doi.org/10.1007/s11606-020-05830-1

Duhigg, C. (2016). What Google learned from its quest to build the perfect team. *The New York Times Magazine*. https://apastyle.apa.org/style-grammar-guidelines/references/examples/magazine-article-references

Eisenberg, E. M. (1984). Ambiguity as strategy in organizational communication. *Communication Monographs, 51*(3), 227–242. https://doi.org/10.1080/03637758409390197

Fowler, S. (2017). Reflecting on one very, very strange year at Uber—Susan Fowler. Retrieved from https://www.susanjfowler.com

Gabelica, C., Van den Bossche, P., De Maeyer, S., Segers, M., & Gijselaers, W. (2014). The effect of team feedback and guided reflexivity on team performance change. *Learning and Instruction, 34* 86–96. https://doi.org/10.1016/j.learninstruc.2014.09.001

Gabelica, C., Van den Bossche, P., Segers, M., & Gijselaers, W. (2012). Feedback, a powerful lever in teams: A review. *Educational Research Review*, *7*(2), 123–144. https://doi.org/10.1016/j.edurev.2011.11.003

Geister, S., Konradt, U., & Hertel, G. (2006). Effects of process feedback on motivation, satisfaction, and performance in virtual teams. *Small Group Research*, *37*(5), 459–489. https://doi.org/10.1177/1046496406292337

Giddens A. (1984). *The constitution of society: An outline of the theory of structuration*. Polity

Gouran, D. S., & Hirokawa, R. Y. (1996). Functional theory and communication in decision-making and problem-solving groups: An expanded view. In R. Y. Hirokawa & M. S. Poole (Eds.), *Communication and group decision making* (pp. 55–80). SAGE Publications.

Gregersen, H., & Sailer, L. (1993, 1993/07/01). Chaos theory and its implications for social science research. *Human Relations*, *46*(7), 777–802. https://doi.org/10.1177/001872679304600701

Grund, T. U. (2012). Network structure and team performance: The case of English Premier League soccer teams. *Social Networks*, *34*(4), 682–690. https://doi.org/10.1016/j.socnet.2012.08.004

Hebel-Sela, S., Hameiri, B., & Halperin, E. (2022). The vicious cycle of violent intergroup conflicts and conspiracy theories. *Current Opinion in Psychology*, 47, https://doi.org/10.1016/j.copsyc.2022.101422

Hewes, D. E. (1996). Small group communication may not influence decision making. In R. Y. Hirokawa & M. S. Poole (Eds.), *Communication and group decision making* (pp. 179–212). SAGE Publications.

Kozlowski, S. W. (2012). Groups and teams in organizations: Studying the multilevel dynamics of emergence. In M. S. Poole & A. Hollingshead (Eds.), *Research methods for studying groups and teams* (pp. 260–283). Routledge.

Luhmann, N. (1995). *Social systems*. Stanford University Press.

Marks, M. A., Mathieu, J. E., & Zaccaro, S. J. (2001). A temporally based framework and taxonomy of team processes. *Academy of Management Review*, *26*(3), 356–376. https://doi.org/10.5465/amr.2001.4845785

Meadows, D. H. (2008). *Thinking in systems: A primer*. Chelsea Green Publishing.

Miller, K. (1998). Nurses at the edge of chaos: The application of "new science" concepts to organizational systems. *Management Communication Quarterly*, *12*(1), 112–127. https://doi.org/10.1177/0893318998121004

Olson, M. (1965). *The logic of collective action*. Harvard University Press.

Opp, K. D. (2009). *Theories of political protest and social movements: A multidisciplinary introduction, critique, and synthesis*. Routledge.

Pilny, A., Dobosh, M., Yahja, A., Poole, M. S., Campbell, A., Ruge-Jones, L., & Proulx, J. (2020). Team coordination in uncertain environments: The role of processual communication networks. *Human Communication Research*, *46*(4), 385–411. https://doi.org/10.1093/hcr/hqz020

Rice, R. E. (2008). Unusual routines: Organizational (non) sensemaking. *Journal of Communication*, *58*(1), 1–19. https://doi.org/10.1111/j.1460-2466.2007.00371.x

Ross, L. (1977). The intuitive psychologist and his shortcomings: Distortions in the attribution process. In L. Berkowitz (Ed.), *Advances in experimental social psychology* (pp. 173–220). Academic Press.

Schecter, A., Pilny, A., Leung, A., Poole, M. S., & Contractor, N. (2018). Step by step: Capturing the dynamics of work team process through relational event sequences. *Journal of Organizational Behavior*, *39*(9), 1163–1181. https://doi.org/10.1002/job.2247

Scott, C. (2021). Emergency team communication: Adaptive sensemaking in turbulent environments. In S. J. Beck, J. Keyton, & M. S. Poole (Eds.), *The emerald handbook of group and team communication research* (pp. 493–504). Emerald Publishing.

Stroh, D. P. (2015). *Systems thinking for social change: A practical guide to solving complex problems, avoiding unintended consequences, and achieving lasting results*. Chelsea Green Publishing.

Von Bertalanffy, L. (1968). *General system theory: Foundations, development*. George Braziller.

Watson, R. T., DeSanctis, G., & Poole, M. S. (1988). Using a GDSS to facilitate group consensus: Some intended and unintended consequences. *MIS Quarterly*, *12*(3), 463–478. https://doi.org/10.2307/249214

Wolske, J. (2012). What is "Systems Storytelling," and how can it help us learn? "The Wire" as gateway drug. *Medium*. https://medium.com/caseworx/what-is-systems-storytelling-and-how-can-it-help-us-learn-the-wire-as-gateway-drug-e4f9a8cc5be6

Woolley, A. W., Chabris, C. F., Pentland, A., Hashmi, N., & Malone, T. W. (2010). Evidence for a collective intelligence factor in the performance of human groups. *Science*, *330*(6004), 686–688. https://doi.org/10.1126/science.1193147

8   Diversity in Groups

Poppy L. McLeod and Y. Connie Yuan

Chapter Objectives

- Recognize different conceptualizations and definitions of diversity.
- Understand two major theoretical approaches to studying diversity: (a) information processing and (b) social identity and categorization.
- Identify factors that influence how diversity affects team communication processes and task outcomes.

Introduction

What exactly do people mean when they use the term ***diversity***? The connotative and denotative meanings of this term have changed significantly since it has commonly appeared in academic research, organizational practices, and educational materials. The origins of the interest in diversity can be traced to social justice activism and legal reforms in the early 1960s in the U.S. This early phase can be characterized by an *affirmative-action* approach to diversity. At that same time, the reforms brought about demographic changes to the U.S. workforce due to large influxes of previously underrepresented groups – primarily women and racial minorities. These changes are associated with a *demographic inevitability* approach to diversity. These two approaches – diversity as a legal mandate through affirmative action and thus inevitable – represent a relatively negative outlook on diversity as a problem to be managed. In contrast, the *value-in-diversity* approach which focused on the inherent benefits resulting from a demographically diverse workforce, arose partially in response to this negative perspective (Cox & Blake, 1991; Nkomo et al., 2019). It is fair to say that the central concern of academics and practitioners has been to understand how to extract the benefits of diversity while minimizing difficulties. The eruption of racial tensions in 2020 sparked, for example, by tragic incidents of anti-Black and anti-Asian violence (Bell, 2020; Man, 2020) starkly highlights how far this research still needs to go.

Today, the approach has evolved to one of *promoting and celebrating* diversity, and this basic concept has expanded to encompass *equity, inclusion, and justice*. This expanded perspective on diversity has coincided with advances in communication technology that enable direct contact between people from disparate backgrounds. In companies with a global presence, for example, work teams frequently consist of members located in different countries who may differ along a variety of dimensions such as nationality and ethnicity. It may be especially challenging for all members in such teams to feel included, due, perhaps, to time zone differences or differences in local contexts in addition to differences in communication norms (Hung et al., 2021). Moreover, close contact through communication media may reveal disparities in resources and other circumstances, thus bringing issues of equity and justice to the fore (Hakonen & Lipponen, 2008).

DOI: 10.4324/9781003227458-10

This chapter discusses the various meanings of diversity that have appeared in the literature and the different dimensions along which groups can be considered diverse. For example, should diversity be defined by how similar members are on a given dimension, by the number of dimensions represented in the group, or by some other criterion? What determines which dimensions are important, and how does the importance change? What are the theoretical approaches to the central question of how to harness the benefits of diversity while minimizing adverse effects?

What Do We Mean by Diversity?

Despite the widespread use of the term *diversity*, Harrison and Klein (2007) note that formal definitions rarely appear in the literature. There is nevertheless convergence that at its most basic, the term *diversity* refers to the *heterogeneity among members of a group* with respect to some attribute, and we thus think of groups as diverse with respect to that attribute. Ethnicity, race, sex, nationality, and organizational function have traditionally been, and continue to be, the most frequently examined attributes (Nkomo et al., 2019) though significant attention to other attributes such as age (e.g., Wegge & Meyer, 2020), sexual orientation and identity (e.g., Cunningham, 2011), personality (e.g., Anglim et al., 2019), and communication styles (Hall, 1976) can also be found. Considerable attention has focused on identifying underlying dimensions to categorize the heterogeneity in member attributes. One widely used dimension is the degree of job-relatedness. Social identity attributes such as race or sex generally have been classified as non-job-related, whereas attributes such as professional training have been classified as job-related (Guillaume et al., 2012). A second common classification is the degree of visibility – that is, surface-level, visible attributes such as sex and race versus deep-level, less visible attributes such as personality and values. Some have argued that surface attributes are less directly job-related than deep-level attributes (e.g., Nishii & Mayer, 2009). Challenges to these traditional categorizations (e.g., van Knippenberg et al., 2004) will be discussed later in the chapter.

Equally important as identifying which attributes may differentiate group members from each other is determining how heterogeneity should be characterized conceptually. Harrison and Klein (2007) proposed an influential model of heterogeneity comprising three dimensions of separation, variety, and disparity. *Separation* refers to the horizontal distance between group members on a continuous attribute, such as age. So, for example, separation diversity increases as the difference between the oldest and youngest group members increases. *Variety* involves categorical attributes, such as ethnicity, and refers to the number of categories represented in the group. Here, the larger the number of different ethnicities present, the higher the group's variety diversity. Finally, *disparity* refers to the vertical difference between members on a socially valued attribute associated with power or status, such as hierarchical position. The concentration of high status and privilege among one or a few, compared to all other group members, would constitute high disparity diversity. It should also be noted that the same attribute could be defined along all three dimensions. For example, age could also represent variety if people are placed into age groups, or it could be defined as disparity as high status is correlated with age in many organizations.

Bell et al. (2011) used this model to conduct a meta-analysis based on 92 empirical studies of the relationship between diversity and team task performance. They coded each study's operationalization of diversity as variety, separation, or disparity. Across the studies included in their analysis, categorical attributes (e.g., race, sex, and functional background) were exclusively operationalized as variety-based diversity, whereas continuous attributes (e.g., age and organizational tenure) were most frequently operationalized as disparity-based diversity. Further, the studies within their sample generally *conceptualized* diversity on race as separation (i.e., how much people differ on this attribute), yet *operationalized* diversity on race as variety (i.e., the number of racial categories present in the team). Bell et al. suggested that such mismatches between conceptual and operational definitions may be one explanation for inconsistent research findings about the effects of diversity on communication processes and team task performance.

How Diversity Operates: Theoretical Approaches

From its earliest roots, research on group diversity has grappled with the tension between the task quality benefits derived from the variety of perspectives and knowledge on the one hand, and interpersonal difficulties on the other hand (Phillips et al., 2014). The frequently seen *doubled-edged sword* metaphor (Milliken & Martins, 1996) describes this tension. The two major theoretical perspectives used to explain the positive and negative effects of diversity, respectively, are **information elaboration**, and **social identity and categorization**. We next discuss these two theoretical approaches and relevant empirical evidence, discuss proposed integrations between the approaches, and review contingency factors that shape diversity effects.

Information Elaboration Processes

The foundational idea for the value-in-diversity perspective is that variety in knowledge, ideas, and expertise is beneficial to groups (Cox & Blake, 1991; Phillips et al., 2014). This perspective is based on the assumptions that (a) the resources associated with member attributes, in the form of knowledge or perspectives, are relevant to a group's work, and that (b) the group can and does make use of those resources. The information elaboration model thus predicts that a group's access to a variety of task-relevant knowledge, combined with high-quality communication and information processing, should improve performance on a variety of tasks (van Knippenberg et al., 2004). That is, performance will be enhanced to the extent that group members communicate their knowledge, attend to each other's contributions, and understand the implications of that knowledge for their task.

Several meta-analytic reviews have provided weak support for this expectation. Bell et al. (2011) found, for example, that diversity in functional background (e.g., marketing vs. finance), was positively related to innovation and creativity. Similarly, Horwitz and Horwitz (2007) and Joshi and Roh (2009) found a positive relationship for a variety of tasks between diversity in functional expertise and decision-making, problem-solving, creativity, and the volume of work accomplished. Critical for support of the information elaboration model is evidence showing that performance depends on how thoroughly groups exchange, analyze, and integrate the information that members contribute. For example, van Knippenberg et al. (2004) described a study showing that decision-making quality was higher in groups in which members emphasized information elaboration than in groups without such an emphasis. It must be noted, however, that the average effect sizes reported in these meta-analyses are small. That is, despite the general finding that task-related diversity has a positive impact on performance, that impact may be hard to detect. Further, some reviews have failed to find any significant effects of task-related diversity, positive or negative (e.g., Bowers et al., 2000; Webber & Donahue, 2001).

Social Identity and Categorization Processes

The theories under the umbrella of social identity processes generally predict that diversity among team members is associated with negative effects such as low trust and social cohesion, communication difficulties, low team identification and attraction, and low member satisfaction (Harrison & Klein, 2007). These theories, largely influenced by social identity and social categorization theory (Tajfel & Turner, 1986), share a focus on socially relevant identity dimensions. The central argument is that people derive their identities partially through their memberships in meaningful social groups. By definition, one's own group is the ingroup and all others are outgroups. This sets the stage for ingroup bias – the tendency to show favoritism toward ingroup members. Ingroup bias is strengthened by similarity-attraction processes involving people's preference for interacting with others whom they perceive as sharing common characteristics (Berscheid & Hatfield, 1969). Further, biases can lead to expectations of others' capabilities which then shape the structural patterns of group interaction that eventually solidify into status hierarchies (Ridgeway et al., 2009). Research on the *self-fulfilling prophecy* (Rosenthal & Jacobson, 1968) shows that such expectations are conveyed through communication cues such as tone of voice or amount of airtime, which in turn induce behaviors in line with the expectations.

It has been argued that the negative effects predicted by social identity processes are associated with attributes that are not necessarily related to task performance – chiefly the surface-level attributes of sex, race, ethnicity, and age. The empirical evidence related to this argument is equivocal. Results from several major reviews range from showing no effects to small negative effects of surface-level diversity (also categorized under other labels such as relational or bio-demographic diversity). For example, meta-analytic reviews by Webber and Donahue (2001) and Horwitz and Horwitz (2007) found no effect of surface-level diversity on social cohesion or task performance. In contrast, Bell et al. (2011) and Joshi and Roh (2009) found small negative effects of surface-level diversity on task performance, but neither of these reviews examined social cohesion.

One area of research that has consistently found negative effects of diversity is based on the theoretical construct of faultlines. *Faultlines* are "defined as hypothetical dividing lines that split a team into relatively homogeneous subgroups based on the team members' demographic alignment along multiple attributes" (Thatcher & Patel, 2011, p. 1119). *Faultline strength* is related to the degree of homogeneity within the respective subgroups on one or more attributes. For example, on a global team in which members differ by age and job function, a strong faultline could result if all the members from marketing were under 30 and located in the U.S., while all those from finance were over 50 and located in Europe. The faultline could be weakened by adding older people to marketing or younger people to finance.

Empirical evidence generally supports the primary prediction that strong demographic faultlines will negatively affect group interaction processes and task performance quality (Thatcher & Patel, 2011), but two studies suggest that the relationship may be curvilinear. Thatcher et al. (2003) reported that lower conflict, and higher morale and task performance were seen in groups with moderate strength faultlines (based on work experience, education, sex, race, and nationality), than in groups with either absent or strong faultlines. Similarly, Gibson and Vermeulen (2003) found that team learning behaviors ("experimentation, reflective communication and knowledge codification," p. 222) were higher within teams with moderately strong than non-existent or strong faultlines (based on sex, ethnicity, functional background, and tenure in the team). An important consideration for future research based on faultlines is that the alignment of identity categories may depend on the salience of group members of various attributes (Thatcher & Patel, 2012). For example, having the youngest members all in marketing and the oldest members all in finance may not necessarily produce a faultline if age differences are not relevant to the members of a team. Further, because people may ascribe to themselves multiple social category memberships (Crenshaw, 1989; Roccas & Brewer, 2002), it may not be clear how categories in a given team align to form faultlines.

Integrating Competing Perspectives

The weight of the empirical evidence supports the general conclusion that diversity can be associated simultaneously with positive and negative effects. The association is extremely complex, however, depending on factors such as conceptual and operational definitions of diversity, type of team and task, or organizational climate – to name but a few examples. Therefore, the most important research questions must focus on explaining the circumstances surrounding the differential effects of diversity (van Knippenberg & Schippers, 2007). That is, which factors and processes are likely to help groups benefit from the breadth of resources that comes from inter-member heterogeneity, and which are likely to impede constructive communication and task coordination? Addressing such questions requires theoretical models that integrate the competing information elaboration and social categorization perspectives, based on the central idea that to take advantage of the potential benefits of diversity, groups must manage the potential disruptions to interpersonal interactions that may also be associated with diversity.

One influential example is the category elaboration model (CEM; van Knippenberg et al., 2004), which provides a strong integration of the information elaboration and social categorization perspectives. The central idea of the CEM is that the key benefit of diversity stems from high-quality processing (exchange, discussion, evaluation, and integration) of a wide range of task-relevant knowledge, but that interpersonal biases stemming from social categorization processes can disrupt processing. A critical argument to this model is that *any* category of diversity can be associated with information elaboration or with social categorization bias. For example, differences in job function, traditionally classified as a task-related type of diversity, can also be a source of social identity, thus leading to social categorization dynamics. Their model proposes, therefore, that the likelihood of positive or negative effects on task performance outcomes depends on three contingencies: (a) the salience of demographic differences (e.g., due to unbalanced composition such as a group composed of one man and the rest, women), (b) conditions that can provoke or attenuate interpersonal bias (e.g., threats to members' social identity through overt or subtle derogatory comments), and (c) conditions that promote or prevent information elaboration (e.g., group members' motivation or ability to process task information).

Carter and Phillips (2017) propose a *dual-pathway model* that similarly seeks to integrate the two paths leading to positive and negative effects. Like the CEM, their model proposes that social categorization processes can disrupt the positive effects achievable through information elaboration. An important distinction Carter and Phillips make between their model and the CEM is that: "social categorization and resulting forces of similarity-attraction are *necessary prerequisites* for eliciting beneficial information and decision-making processes" (p. 9, emphasis in original). Their model thus rejects the dichotomy of social categorization *versus* information processing and implies instead that social categorization processes are always present, but their effects depend on the level of intergroup bias (i.e., ingroup favoritism and outgroup denigration). Thus, in the absence of intergroup bias, social categorization processes would influence group members' assumptions about each other's task-relevant knowledge, and these expectations would facilitate productive information exchange.

Contingency models such as these propose mechanisms that *mediate* the effects of diversity (i.e., explain how diversity effects occur) and factors that *moderate* the effects (i.e., change the direction or strength of diversity effects). Empirical evidence regarding the effects of these contingency factors on group communication processes and task outcomes will be discussed next.

Contingency Factors

Mediators

Consistent with our discussion in the previous sections of this chapter, empirical evidence generally supports the expectation that the quality of information exchange and communication mediates the positive effects of group diversity on outcome variables, and social categorization processes mediate negative effects of diversity on outcome variables. For example, Kooij-de Bode et al.

(2008) found that in ethnically diverse teams, decision-making quality depended on the extent of exchange and integration of task-relevant information, whereas Curşeu and Schruijer (2010) found that negative effects of gender and nationality diversity on perceived team effectiveness were mediated by trust and task and relationship conflicts.

Moderators

Type of diversity, usually defined by the degree of task-relatedness and visibility, is one of the most frequently studied moderators, but empirical evidence about its moderating effects has been mixed. For example, whereas some reviews have found task performance to have a weak positive relationship with task-related diversity and a weak negative relationship with non-task-related diversity (e.g., Bell et al., 2011), other reviews found no relationships at all (e.g., Webber & Donahue, 2001). In fact, van Knippenberg et al. (2004) have suggested that researchers should abandon the effort to use fixed typologies to explain diversity effects, arguing that any dimension of diversity can affect group processes and outcomes.

Group member characteristics have also received significant attention as moderators. One individual difference variable that has been found to be important for how diversity affects a team is how strongly the members see diversity as valuable for task performance. For example, in an experiment, Homan et al. (2007) found that the negative effects of faultlines on decision-making quality could be reduced when members were given information about the value of gender diversity. Hentschel et al. (2013) argued that not only is belief in the value of diversity important, but it also matters how diverse the members perceive their group to be. For example, they found that perceived degree of diversity was related to high conflict and low group identification, primarily among those with negative beliefs about the general value of diversity.

Another individual difference that is receiving increasing research attention is *intercultural competence*, "an individual's ability to function effectively across cultures" (Leung et al., 2014, p. 490). This characteristic comprises traits such as tolerance for ambiguity, and attitudes toward intercultural interactions. Moon (2013), in a longitudinal study of student teams, reported that the team-level cultural competence attenuated the negative effect of cultural diversity on team performance on case analysis assignments. A closely related trait is communication style. Hall (1976) proposed that Westerners, for example, are *low-context* communicators because their direct, explicit communication styles reduce message receivers' reliance on the context to understand a message. In contrast, East Asians are *high-context* communicators because their preference for indirect, implicit communication styles increases the message receivers' reliance on the context to help interpret a message. An example of how such differences can affect interaction in work teams is how members can recognize each other's expertise. One study found that Americans tend to equate talkativeness with competence, and thus may significantly under-estimate the competence of East-Asian teammates if they are not as talkative as their American counterparts (Yuan et al., 2019).

The double-edged sword metaphor implies that groups and organizations benefit from a variety of intellectual resources, but difficulties in communicating across differences can hinder resource exchange. Group members hence need to rise above categorical separations to reap the benefits of expertise diversity. The irreversible trend of globalization urges us not just to manage or accept but rather to celebrate diversity because doing so offers unprecedented growth opportunities for everyone. Take Starbucks' success in China as an example. Attracted by the enormous Chinese market, many Western companies poured in colossal amounts of money to gain a foothold. But most failed due to their inability to recognize local companies' knowledge of the market as valuable expertise. When Howard Schultz, the founder of Starbucks, decided to enter the Chinese market, he faced a more significant challenge because China has had a tea-drinking culture for centuries. But Schultz was committed to understanding the culture and rising above the them-versus-us mentality. He disclosed in an interview his belief that people from the two countries share more similarities in values than differences (https://www.youtube.com/watch?v=sBKL9752NWw). He reached out to Jack Ma, the founder of Alibaba, one of the largest e-commerce companies in China. Software engineering, marketing, and sales teams from both companies worked closely together in creating Starbucks' online store on Alibaba's shopping platform. Reaping the benefits of Alibaba's deep knowledge of Chinese consumers, Starbucks sold almost $2 million worth of merchandise in 48 hours, even before the official opening of Starbucks Reserve – Shanghai Roastery, Starbucks' largest store in the world. Starbucks' success in China would not have been possible if neither party considered diversity in expertise and knowledge about another culture as growth opportunities, despite East-versus-West, or the U.S.-versus-China categorical differences. Starbucks ended with the creation of its fastest-growing market; and China, a new coffee-drinking culture.

The moderating effects of *team leader characteristics* have also received considerable attention. The conceptualizations of leadership within this research area are markedly heterogeneous. Indeed, Homan et al. (2020) identified "over 30 different leadership behaviors and leader characteristics" (p. 1103) in a recent review of the leadership and diversity literature. Among these, the most studied is *transformational leadership*, which involves "inspirational motivation, idealized influence, individualized consideration, and intellectual stimulation" (Kark et al., 2003, p. 247). Transformational leadership should thus be expected to enhance the effects of multiple dimensions of diversity on group outcomes by motivating high-quality information processing and creating a climate for constructive communication.

Empirical evidence largely supports these expectations, but not consistently so. For example, Kearney and Gebert (2009) found a positive relationship between nationality and education diversity and efficiency, innovativeness, and overall quality of task performance in the presence of high transformational leadership but no relationship when transformational leadership was low. Greer et al. (2012), on the other hand, point to circumstances when visionary leadership – a facet of transformational leadership – can be harmful. They found that when visionary leaders also showed the cognitive tendency to categorize team members into groups rather than to consider them as individuals, ethnic diversity had a negative effect on the thoroughness of team communication and team financial performance. They argued that the tendency to categorize group members can – inadvertently or not – create perceptions of divisions among the group members, an effect intensified under visionary leaders.

Leaders' intercultural competence has also been found to moderate the effects of diversity. For example, Groves and Feyerherm (2011) found that leaders' extent of cultural intelligence was more positively related to how they were perceived by followers as the cultural diversity of their groups increased.

The *nature of a group's task* has also been thought to moderate the relationship between diversity and performance. The most studied task characteristics include task complexity (i.e., degree of structure, routineness, and ambiguity) and task type (e.g., brainstorming vs. decision-making). In meta-analyses, Horwitz and Horwitz (2007) found no moderating effect of task complexity on the relationship between any measures of diversity and performance for any tasks, whereas Wang et al. (2019) found a negative relationship between surface-level diversity and team creativity for simple tasks but no relationship for complex tasks. van Dijk et al. (2012) presented meta-analytic evidence that the way task performance is measured moderates the relationship between diversity and performance. Specifically, they showed that the negative relationship between non-task diversity and performance was seen only when the performance criterion was based on subjective ratings from team members or leaders. They argued that the negative relationship between diversity and performance was therefore due to rater bias rather than to the effects of diversity *per se*.

The social, temporal, and physical *contexts* can also moderate the relationship between diversity and a group's interaction and outcomes. An example of the social context is occupation-level demographics of a team's environment (Joshi & Roh, 2009), such as the relative number of males and females typical for the occupation. Joshi and Roh argued that in occupations dominated by people of a certain category, stereotyping of people in the numerical minority on that category is likely to occur (e.g., females in male-dominated occupations such as production engineering), and negative team outcomes are likely to result. In support of this reasoning, their meta-analysis showed that gender diversity in groups was negatively related to performance in occupations with predominantly male populations, but positively related for occupations with a balanced gender makeup (e.g., insurance underwriter). Organizational culture is another important social context factor that can interact with group diversity. For example, Nishii (2013) found that a positive diversity climate reduced interpersonal bias and interpersonal conflict associated with gender diversity, which ultimately was associated with reduced turnover.

The amount of time a group works together has also been thought to be important, though again findings have been inconsistent. For example, a study by Harrison et al. (2002) found that the effect of deep-level diversity (e.g., in task meaningfulness) on social integration became more negative the more time groups spent collaborating, whereas surface-level diversity (e.g., race) became less important. On the other hand, the meta-analysis by Joshi and Roh (2009) found that the negative effect of surface-level diversity on task performance was stronger in long-term teams than in short-term teams. They argued that differences and conflicts based on surface diversity become more entrenched over time.

Geographic configuration is an important physical context factor. Culturally diverse global virtual teams (GVTs) are now commonplace, a trend greatly accelerated by the tremendous increase in virtual teamwork seen during the COVID-19 pandemic (Newman & Ford, 2021). Geographic configuration comprises both how team members are dispersed through space (*geographic dispersion*), and the extent of face-to-face synchronous communication versus mediated communication (*virtuality*). Like the previous factors, the questions regarding the interactions of diversity, geographic configuration, and group outcomes are complex, and the empirical evidence is mixed. Polzer et al. (2006) reported experimental evidence that virtual teams with strong faultlines experienced more conflict and less trust than did teams without strong faultlines. Polzer et al. did not report findings on task performance, but in a follow-up experiment, Chiu and Staples (2013) did find a negative effect of faultlines on decision quality and replicated Polzer et al.'s findings on conflict and trust.

In a survey study of virtual teams across several companies, Mortensen and Hinds (2001) studied the relationships between national culture diversity, intra-team conflict, and the efficiency, quality, and innovation of task performance. Contrary to expectations, they found a *negative* relationship between diversity and conflict. They suggested the explanation for the decrease in conflict with greater diversity was due to the diversity training that some of their respondents received. They speculated that the salience of an attribute like nationality may have motivated team members to apply tools from this training.

In addition to training, certain qualities of communication behaviors may help virtual teams manage challenges related to intercultural diversity they might face. Chiu and Staples (2013) found that perceived faultlines could be reduced by stimulating social attraction across the subgroups, for instance, by members engaging in self-disclosing communication. A review by Han and Beyerlein

(2016) also points to the importance of frequent communication, task-oriented communication especially, in helping virtual teams establish trust, common ground, and group identity.

Evidence-Based Recommendations for Practice

Despite the inconsistencies in research findings discussed here, empirical evidence tends to show that team members' perceptions and how they behave toward each other have a more direct effect on outcomes than does the extent of their differences. This evidence offers some suggestions which we believe would be most usefully directed toward diversity training programs. Perhaps the most important is for team members to understand that diversity is *fluid* and *dynamic* (Li et al., 2018). Member attitudes toward diversity and how they think about and value each other's social identities change over time and circumstances. For example, deep-level attributes such as values may become more visible, or their perceptions of how different they are from each other may change as teammates communicate with each other. Moreover, team members simultaneously occupy multiple identity categories, and which of those categories is important for diversity can vary across multiple factors. A specific recommendation, therefore, is for diversity training programs to help team members recognize these dynamics.

A closely related recommendation is that training programs need to help group members develop the communication skills reflective of these dynamics. This implies that training should increase attention on inclusion – behaviors that help foster an "individual's sense of being part of the organizational system" (Mor Barak et al., 2016, p. 309) – relative to attention to representation. For example, despite increased representation, women in some organizations are still faced with a double-bind dilemma in that they are deemed unlikeable when they behave as assertively as men but are deemed lacking leadership qualities when they do not (Kramer, 2020). Expectations of their behaviors become self-fulfilling prophecies through subtle communication cues (Rosenthal & Jacobson, 1968).

Conclusion

The effective management of diversity challenges is vital to ensure that all group members feel treated fairly, but the perception of diversity as something to be managed can nevertheless be constraining because it takes focus away from diversity as a resource. The *double-edged sword* metaphor should be re-thought, and perhaps even retired. The sword analogy implies that diversity is a dangerous weapon that demands careful handling. It also invites the unfortunate allusion to the feeling of helpless inevitability captured by the Greek myth of Damocles' experience with the sword hanging by a hair over King Dionysus' throne. How team leaders feel about diversity matters. Instead of perpetuating an image of fearful resignation, research and practice should focus more on how to celebrate the life-giving promise of growth that comes from exposure to and sharing of diverse perspectives.

Further Readings

McLeod, P. L., & Yuan, Y. C. (2021). Diversity and team communication: A critical review and call for broadened representation. In S. Beck, J. Keyton, & M. S. Poole (Eds.), *The handbook of group and team communication research* (pp. 391–405). Emerald. https://doi.org/10.1108/978-1-80043-500-120211025

Nkomo, S. M., Bell, M. P., Roberts, L. M., Joshi, A., & Thatcher, S. M. (2019). Diversity at a critical juncture: New theories for a complex phenomenon. *Academy of Management Review*, *44*(3), 498–517. https://doi.org/10.5465/amr.2019.0103

van Knippenberg, D., De Dreu, C. K., & Homan, A. C. (2004). Work group diversity and group performance: An integrative model and research agenda. *Journal of Applied Psychology*, *89*(6), 1008–1022. https://doi.org/10.1037/0021-9010.89.6.1008

Glossary

Diversity   Diversity is heterogeneity among members of a group with respect to some attribute. It is a multidimensional concept that can imply variety, separation, and disparity. Some diversity dimensions are surface-level and visible, while others are deep-level and less visible.

Double-edged sword metaphor   This metaphor is frequently used in diversity research to capture the simultaneous existence of opportunities and challenges of diversity.

Information elaboration   Information elaboration refers to systematic exchange, discussion, and examination of the content of communication. Group task performance is thought to benefit from diversity through the elaboration of knowledge contributed by members.

Social categorization   People's tendency to place themselves and others into different social groups based on socially meaningful categories such as demographics, professional or personal interests, political, religious, or professional affiliations, among others. Social categorization processes can lead to intergroup bias, which can disrupt knowledge-sharing processes and task performance.

References

Anglim, J., Sojo, V., Ashford, L. J., Newman, A., & Marty, A. (2019). Predicting employee attitudes to workplace diversity from personality, values, and cognitive ability. *Journal of Research in Personality*, *83*, 1–14. https://doi.org/10.1016/j.jrp.2019.103865

Bell, M. P. (2020). Anti-blackness, surface-level diversity continues to matter: What must we do? *Equality, Diversity and Inclusion: An International Journal*, *39*(7), 749–759. https://doi.org/10.1108/EDI-06-2020-0160

Bell, S. T., Villado, A. J., Lukasik, M. A., Belau, L., & Briggs, A. L. (2011). Getting specific about demographic diversity variable and team performance relationships: A meta-analysis. *Journal of Management*, *37*(3), 709–743. https://doi.org/10.1177/0149206310365001

Berscheid, E., & Hatfield, E. (1969). *Interpersonal attraction* (Vol. 69, pp. 113–114). Addison-Wesley.

Bowers, C. A., Pharmer, J. A., & Salas, E. (2000). When member homogeneity is needed in work teams: A meta-analysis. *Small Group Research*, *31*(3), 305–327. https://doi.org/10.1177/104649640003100303

Carter, A. B., & Phillips, K. W. (2017). The double-edged sword of diversity: Toward a dual pathway model. *Social and Personality Psychology Compass*, *11*(5), 1–13. https://doi.org/10.1111/spc3.12313

Chiu, Y.-T., & Staples, D. S. (2013). Reducing faultlines in geographically dispersed teams: Self-disclosure and task elaboration. *Small Group Research*, *44*(5), 498–531. https://doi.org/10.5465/amj.2006.22083024

Cox, T. H., & Blake, S. (1991). Managing cultural diversity: Implications for organizational competitiveness. *Academy of Management Perspectives*, *5*(3), 45–56. https://doi.org/10.5465/ame.1991.4274465

Crenshaw, K. (1989). Demarginalizing the intersection of race and sex: A black feminist critique of antidiscrimination doctrine, feminist theory and antiracist politics. *University of Chicago Legal Forum*, *1989*, 139–167. https://chicagounbound.uchicago.edu/uclf/vol1989/iss1/8

Cunningham, G. B. (2011). The LGBT advantage: Examining the relationship among sexual orientation diversity, diversity strategy, and performance. *Sport Management Review*, *14*(4), 453–461. https://doi.org/10.1016/j.smr.2010.11.003

Curşeu, P. L., & Schruijer, S. G. (2010). Does conflict shatter trust or does trust obliterate conflict? Revisiting the relationships between team diversity, conflict, and trust. *Group Dynamics: Theory, Research, and Practice*, *14*(1), 66. https://doi.org/10.1037/a0017104

Gibson, C., & Vermeulen, F. (2003). A healthy divide: Subgroups as a stimulus for team learning behavior. *Administrative Science Quarterly*, *48*(2), 202–239. https://doi.org/10.2307/3556657

Greer, L. L., Homan, A. C., De Hoogh, A. H., & Den Hartog, D. N. (2012). Tainted visions: The effect of visionary leader behaviors and leader categorization tendencies on the financial performance of ethnically diverse teams. *Journal of Applied Psychology*, *97*(1), 203–213. https://doi.org/10.1037/a0025583

Groves, K. S., & Feyerherm, A. E. (2011). Leader cultural intelligence in context: Testing the moderating effects of team cultural diversity on leader and team performance. *Group & Organization Management*, 36, 535–566. https://doi.org/10.1177/1059601111415664

Guillaume, Y. R. F., Brodbeck, F. C., & Riketta, M. (2012). Surface- and deep-level dissimilarity effects on social integration and individual effectiveness related outcomes in work groups: A meta-analytic integration. *Journal of Occupational and Organizational Psychology*, *85*(1), 80–115. https://doi.org/10.1111/j.2044-8325.2010.02005.x

Hakonen, M., & Lipponen, J. (2008). Procedural justice and identification with virtual teams: The moderating role of face-to-face meetings and geographical dispersion. *Social Justice Research*, *21*(2), 164–178. https://doi.org/10.1007/s11211-008-0070-3

Hall, E. T. (1976). *Beyond culture*. Doubleday.

Han, S. J., & Beyerlein, M. (2016). Framing the effects of multinational cultural diversity on virtual team processes. *Small Group Research*, *47*(4), 351–383. https://doi.org/10.1177/1046496416653480

Harrison, D. A., & Klein, K. J. (2007). What's the difference? Diversity constructs as separation, variety, or disparity in organizations. *Academy of Management Review*, *32*(4), 1199–1228. https://doi.org/10.5465/amr.2007.26586096

Harrison, D. A., Price, K. H., Gavin, J. H., & Florey, A. T. (2002). Time, teams, and task performance: Changing effects of surface-and deep-level diversity on group functioning. *Academy of Management Journal*, *45*(5), 1029–1045. https://doi.org/10.5465/3069328

Hentschel, T., Shemla, M., Wegge, J., & Kearney, E. (2013). Perceived diversity and team functioning: The role of diversity beliefs and affect. *Small Group Research*, *44*(1), 33–61. https://doi.org/10.1177/1046496412470725

Homan, A. C., Gündemir, S., Buengeler, C., & van Kleef, G. A. (2020). Leading diversity: Towards a theory of functional leadership in diverse teams. *Journal of Applied Psychology*, *105*(10), 1101–1128. https://doi.org/10.1037/apl0000482

Homan, A. C., van Knippenberg, D., Van Kleef, G. A., & De Dreu, C. K. W. (2007). Bridging faultlines by valuing diversity: Diversity beliefs, information elaboration, and performance in diverse work groups. *Journal of Applied Psychology*, *92*(5), 1189–1199. https://doi.org/10.1037/0021-9010.92.5.1189

Horwitz, S. K., & Horwitz, I. B. (2007). The effects of team diversity on team outcomes: A meta-analytic review of team demography. *Journal of Management*, *33*(6), 987–1015. https://doi.org/10.1177/0149206307308587

Hung, S. W., Cheng, M. J., Hou, C. E., & Chen, N. R. (2021). Inclusion in global virtual teams: Exploring non-spatial proximity and knowledge sharing on innovation. *Journal of Business Research*, *128*, 599–610. https://doi.org/10.1016/j.jbusres.2020.11.022

Joshi, A., & Roh, H. (2009). The role of context in work team diversity research: A meta-analytic review. *Academy of Management Journal*, *52*(3), 599–627. https://doi.org/10.5465/amj.2009.41331491

Kark, R., Shamir, B., & Chen, G. (2003). The two faces of transformational leadership: Empowerment and dependency. *Journal of Applied Psychology*, *88*(2), 246–255. https://doi.org/10.1037/0021-9010.88.2.246

Kearney, E., & Gebert, D. (2009). Managing diversity and enhancing team outcomes: The promise of transformational leadership. *Journal of Applied Psychology*, *94*(1), 77–89. https://doi.org/10.1037/a0013077

Kooij-de Bode, H. J., van Knippenberg, D., & van Ginkel, W. P. (2008). Ethnic diversity and distributed information in group decision making: The importance of information elaboration. *Group Dynamics: Theory, Research, and Practice*, *12*(4), 307–320. https://doi.org/10.1037/1089-2699.12.4.307

Kramer, A. (2020, Jan. 22). Why Asian American women aren't advancing into senior leadership positions. *Forbes*. https://www.forbes.com/sites/andiekramer/2020/01/22/why-asian-american-women-arent-advancing-into-senior-leadership-positions/?sh=23e43cb573d2

Leung, K., Ang, S., & Tan, M. L. (2014). Intercultural competence. *Annual Review of Organizational Psychology and Organizational Behavior*, *1*(1), 489–519. https://doi.org/10.1093/acprof:oso/9780190218966.003.0006

Li, J., Meyer, B., Shemla, M., & Wegge, J. (2018). From being diverse to becoming diverse: A dynamic team diversity theory. *Journal of Organizational Behavior*, *39*(8), 956–970. https://doi.org/10.1002/job.2272

Man, S. (2020). Anti-Asian violence and US imperialism. *Race & Class*, *62*(2), 24–33. https://doi.org/10.1177/0306396820949779

Milliken, F. J., & Martins, L. L. (1996). Searching for common threads: Understanding the multiple effects of diversity in organizational groups. *Academy of Management Review*, *21*(2), 402–433. https://doi.org/10.5465/amr.1996.9605060217

Moon, T. (2013). The effects of cultural intelligence on performance in multicultural teams. *Journal of Applied Social Psychology*, *43*(12), 2414–2425. https://doi.org/10.1111/jasp.12189

Mor Barak, M. E., Lizano, E. L., Kim, A., Duan, L., Rhee, M. K., Hsiao, H. Y., & Brimhall, K. C. (2016). The promise of diversity management for climate of inclusion: A state-of-the-art review and meta-analysis. *Human Service Organizations: Management, Leadership & Governance*, *40*(4), 305–333. https://doi.org/10.1080/23303131.2016.1138915

Mortensen, M., & Hinds, P. J. (2001). Conflict and shared identity in geographically distributed teams. *International Journal of Conflict Management*, *12*(3), 212–238. https://doi.org/10.1108/eb022856

Newman, S. A., & Ford, R. C. (2021). Five steps to leading your team in the virtual COVID-19 workplace. *Organizational Dynamics*, *50*(1), 1–11. https://doi.org/10.1108/eb022856

Nishii, L. H. (2013). The benefits of climate for inclusion for gender-diverse groups. *Academy of Management Journal*, *56*(6), 1754–1774. https://doi.org/10.5465/amj.2009.0823

Nishii, L. H., & Mayer, D. M. (2009). Do inclusive leaders help to reduce turnover in diverse groups? The moderating role of leader–member exchange in the diversity to turnover relationship. *Journal of Applied Psychology*, *94*(6), 1412–1426. https://doi.org/10.1037/a0017190

Phillips, K. W., Medin, D., Lee, C. D., Bang, M., Bishop, S., & Lee, D. (2014). How diversity works. *Scientific American*, *311*(4), 42–47. https://doi.org/10.1038/scientificamerican1014-42

Polzer, J. T., Crisp, C. B., Jarvenpaa, S. L., & Kim, J. W. (2006). Extending the faultline model to geographically dispersed teams: How co-located subgroups can impair group functioning. *Academy of Management Journal*, *49*(4), 679–692. https://doi.org/10.5465/amj.2006.22083024

Ridgeway, C. L., Backor, K., Li, Y. E., Tinkler, J. E., & Erickson, K. G. (2009). How easily does a social difference become a status distinction? Gender matters. *American Sociological Review*, *74*(1), 44–62. https://doi.org/10.1177/000312240907400103

Roccas, S., & Brewer, M. B. (2002). Social identity complexity. *Personality and Social Psychology Review*, *6*(2), 88–106. https://doi.org/10.1207/S15327957PSPR0602_01

Rosenthal, R., & Jacobson, L. (1968). Pygmalion in the classroom. *The Urban Review*, *3*(1), 16–20. https://doi.org/10.1007/BF02322211

Tajfel, H., & Turner, J. C. (1986). The social identity theory of intergroup behavior. In S. Worchel & W. G. Austin (Eds.), *The psychology of intergroup relations* (pp. 7–24). Nelson-Hall.

Thatcher, S., & Patel, P. C. (2011). Demographic faultlines: A meta-analysis of the literature. *Journal of Applied Psychology*, *96*(6), 1119.

Thatcher, S. M., Jehn, K. A., & Zanutto, E. (2003). Cracks in diversity research: The effects of diversity faultlines on conflict and performance. *Group Decision and Negotiation*, *12*(3), 217–241. https://doi.org/10.5465/amr.2015.0396

Thatcher, S. M., & Patel, P. C. (2012). Group faultlines: A review, integration, and guide to future research. *Journal of Management*, *38*(4), 969–1009. https://doi.org/10.1177/0149206311426187

van Dijk, H., van Engen, M. L., & van Knippenberg, D. (2012). Defying conventional wisdom: A meta-analytical examination of the differences between demographic and job-related diversity relationships with performance. *Organizational Behavior and Human Decision Processes*, *119*(1), 38–53. https://doi.org/10.1016/j.obhdp.2012.06.003

van Knippenberg, D., & Schippers, M. C. (2007). Work group diversity. *Annual Review of Psychology*, *58*(1), 515–541. https://doi.org/10.1146/annurev.psych.58.110405.085546

Wang, J., Cheng, G. H. L., Chen, T., & Leung, K. (2019). Team creativity/innovation in culturally diverse teams: A meta-analysis. *Journal of Organizational Behavior*, *40*(6), 693–708. https://doi.org/10.1002/job.2362

Webber, S. S., & Donahue, L. M. (2001). Impact of highly and less job-related diversity on work group cohesion and performance: A meta-analysis. *Journal of Management*, *27*(2), 141–162. https://doi.org/10.1016/S0149-2063(00)00093-3

Wegge, J., & Meyer, B. (2020). Age diversity and age-based faultlines in teams: Understanding a Brezel phenomenon requires a Brezel theory. *Work, Aging and Retirement*, *6*(1), 8–14.

Yuan, Y. C., Liao, W., & Bazarova, N. N. (2019). Communication styles and expertise recognition in intercultural collaboration. *Management Communication Quarterly*, *33*(2), 238–271. https://doi.org/10.1177/0893318918824674

9 Leading Groups and Teams

Stacey L. Connaughton, Nicholas B. Lacy,
and Kayla J. Gerdes

Chapter Objectives

- Demonstrate that leadership of groups is constituted by communication. Show that perceptions of leadership as either effective or ineffective is tied to leaders' communication.
- Illustrate that effective group leadership is related to group effectiveness.
- Emphasize the importance of infusing justice, equity, diversity, and inclusion (JEDI) into how we view and "do" leadership.

Introduction

We all have been members of groups. Take a moment and imagine one of the groups to which you belong. Now, imagine the individual(s) who lead that group. That leader might be you. Think about what makes that individual effective (or perhaps, ineffective). We anticipate that if responses to these questions were pooled together, one common feature that would emerge is how the leader(s) communicated.

Leadership is communicative. That is, leadership is constituted by and through communication. How people perceive you, as a leader, is inextricably tied to your communication with those you seek to lead. Group leadership takes place in multiple contexts, across multiple cultures, and in different organizing forms. First, leadership occurs in varied contexts since work occurs in either times of relative stability, or in times of crisis. Leading, therefore, requires adaptability. Second, groups are often made up of people from various ethnic, religious, and race identities, and different genders, sexual orientations, and nations of origin. Leadership necessitates being aware of and inclusive of group members' varied backgrounds and frames of reference. And, lastly, groups are nestled within a host of different organizations.

In this chapter, we underscore that leadership is not only a matter of position or title. In fact, an individual can be a leader without having a formal leadership title at all. Group leaders often emerge. Regardless, leadership is a communicative act, one that has profound consequences for people's behavior and feelings, and for the success of group development and effectiveness. This responsibility cannot be fulfilled without a commitment to "JEDI" principles: Justice, equity, diversity, and inclusion, as well as belongingness, ethics, and integrity. You will see why these principles matter as we integrate literature and examples that illustrate justice, equity, diversity, and inclusion (JEDI) commitment throughout this chapter.

Notions of Leadership

So, what is leadership? This section begins to answer that question by explaining five notions of leadership that are popular in the academic and practitioner literatures: transactional, transformational, discursive, relational, and inclusive leadership.

DOI: 10.4324/9781003227458-11

Transactional and Transformational Leadership

Picture this: Tetyana is interning with a manufacturing company. Her supervisor gives her clear directions and a livable wage and makes her feel like she is a part of the workgroup. Tetyana finds herself wanting to complete her tasks and please her supervisor.

Transactional leadership theory (Bass, 1981; Weber, 1947) is grounded in the concept of exchange. The theory assumes that individuals act in self-interest and that their basic needs must be met. Leaders and members' relationship is based on rewards and punishments. In this way, a group leader's relationship to their members is based on a series of exchanges. The formal authority of the leader over their group members is central to members' motivation and the achievement of group goals.

Now, picture this: Kamlesh works in the Office of Human Resources at his university. His supervisor, Bianca, has invited him to workshops and has gotten to know his ambitions. Bianca also learned from Kamlesh about Indian students' experiences at the university. Together, they are developing an orientation program they hope will support Indian students' transition to campus.

Transformational leadership refers to a leader's ability to motivate individuals – in this case, group members – to do something they never thought they could do. Transformational leaders go beyond mere transactions with their members; they seek to address higher level needs, lifting members up to greater levels of motivation and ethicality. In this way, leadership is a mutual relationship that changes both leaders and followers for the better. Originating in part from James MacGregor Burns' (1978) concept of transforming leadership and the work of Robert House (1977), the research on transformational leadership holds that, for the most part, transformational leaders are highly effective (Bass & Avolio, 1994). Their members tend to be more satisfied and engaged (Piccolo & Colquitt, 2006), and the teams tend to be high performing (Charbonneau et al., 2001). So how do transformational leaders communicate? Johnson and Hackman (2018) suggest that they communicate creatively, are interactive, visionary, and passionate; and they empower others. Think about people you know who exhibit these qualities. It seems obvious that they would inspire leadership, but there also is a dark side to transformational leadership. Warning against the tendency to put too much power in the transformational leader, Tourish (2013) alerts members to be sure to exhibit agency ourselves when he states:

> If power corrupts, then the same might be said of powerlessness. It corrodes our ability to act purposively, take responsibility for our actions and manage our own destiny but it enhances our tendency to ridicule the imperfect efforts of others, to little positive effect.

> Members must actively interrogate why, toward what end, and through what means transformational leaders are motivating us to act.

(p. 5)

Emergent Leadership

As described by Hanna et al. (2021), emergent leadership is distinct from other types of leadership based on three characteristics: First, emergent leadership is lateral, meaning that certain individuals are leaders only perceptually. They do not have a formal leadership role; rather, they use communication to establish influence. Second, since emergent leadership tends to focus on a particular person within a group, it is considered an individual-level phenomenon. Third, emergent leadership is temporary, as leaders can emerge for unknown amounts of time in a group (Hanna et al., 2021). For example, previous research into emergent leadership has noted that even in children's groups, leaders can emerge. In Sun et al.'s (2017) study of fifth-grade students in Mideastern China, students were able to observe and practice leading and following as they discussed stories with their group, in accordance with what their peers saw as acceptable. Taking these three features collectively, **emergent leadership** can be described as a group's temporary perception that a certain individual appears to be a leader, despite a lack of formal authority.

Emergent leadership can help improve virtual collaboration, which requires employees to organize their actions for effective outcomes over physical distance (Sutanto et al., 2011). Self-managed teams also require emergent leaders to help them navigate changing demands across the team's life cycle (Gerpott et al., 2019). Additionally, emergent leaders can aid in the communication and implementation of diversity. House et al. (2004) state how implicit leadership theories suggest members from dominant identities are more likely to be perceived as emergent leaders and cultural influencers. This phenomenon creates a criticism for emergent leaders who do not acknowledge diversity, just as Cox et al. (2014b) criticized emergent leadership for its lack of attention to the role of race, sex, and gender in determining who is seen as a leader. Moreover, researchers Jansen et al. (2016) found that marginalized and underrepresented team members are more likely to value emergent leaders who use multicultural approaches in their communication, whereas majority groups tend to value colorblind communication in leadership approaches. With these empirically backed findings, we strongly recommend emergent leaders communicate diversity-related initiatives and goals to diverse groups and teams.

Discursive Leadership

Discursive leadership has shifted our perspective from considering communication as a conduit for leadership to seeing communication as the starting point for creating leadership and organizational life (Jian, 2019). Fairhurst (2007) explains that discursive leadership occurs through interactions, and considers how context (what is happening/where), identities (who), and relationships (between members in an organization) influence leadership.

Sometimes, who we perceive as a leader is based on formal, structured categories, such as roles. Whittle et al. (2014) argue that organizations categorize people in the company based on their role (e.g. sales) or positions (e.g. manager). As we talk to other people in our groups or teams, we think of them in terms of these categories (Whittle et al., 2014). But it is also important to note that discourse happens at different levels. Small 'd'iscourses concern day-to-day language and interaction, while large 'D'iscourses refer to larger systems of thought (Fairhurst, 2009). For example, we perform our gender every day. The things we say about our gender and the routine ways we behave (like putting on makeup in the morning or selecting particular clothing) constitute 'd'iscourses. Most frequently, the way we enact gender is dependent on larger 'D'iscourses that define gender relations as a whole (Fairhurst, 2009). These 'D'iscourses include historical and cultural definitions of what a body is and how it should act, typically based on the gender binary (Butler, 1988). Such 'D'iscourses can also be resisted through leaders' communication, but they tend to be more permanent and less flexible.

Relational Leadership Theory

Relational leadership theory (RLT; Uhl-Bien, 2006) positions leadership less within an individual and more so within the relationship between people. RLT enables us to view leadership as a phenomenon that emerges by and through social relations and, for communication scholars, by and through communication.

Picture this: Jorge and Naja are members of the same workgroup at a non-profit organization. Their supervisor is Daniel. Jorge and Daniel meet frequently during work and non-work hours.

Daniel knows Jorge well. Jorge goes to Daniel directly with work-related issues and Daniel turns first to Jorge to learn what is happening in the group. Contrarily, Daniel and Naja rarely interact. When they do, they talk about work-related topics. Naja rarely discusses issues openly with Daniel, as she is afraid of how he will respond. Naja sees how open Jorge and Daniel are in their interactions. Naja finds herself starting to resent Jorge.

Leader-member exchange (LMX) theory is one of the first relationally oriented leadership theories. Over four decades, LMX has emphasized that leaders develop unique relationships with each of their (team/group) members and that those relationships have different features and qualities. Research utilizing LMX approaches has demonstrated that the nature of a member's relationship with their leader influences their friendships, their relationships with peers, and their general position in the team/group (Bakar & McCann, 2016).

Inclusive Leadership

Including team/group mates in decisions and goals is vital to leadership. However, making every voice valued and heard is no easy feat. Nembhard and Edmondson (2006) define **inclusive leadership** as "words and deeds exhibited by leaders that invite and appreciate others' contributions" (p. 941). The reference to "words" and "deeds" indicates a need to communicate and act inclusively. Randel et al. (2018) argue that "doing" or leading inclusively means that you will need to effectively: (1) support team members, (2) ensure justice and equity are present in each experience, and (3) provide opportunities for collaborative decision making when important issues arise.

Think about King Arthur. His "round table" was significant because it broke the mold in a time when only "head" tables were used. The round table signified that the knight's input at the table was equal to that of the king.

Today, many identities are not welcomed to the "table," so to speak. Although such exclusions are commonplace, allowing everyone to be part of the conversation makes groups better. Ashikali et al. (2021), for example, found that inclusive leadership improves negative ethnic-cultural climates. Furthermore, inclusive leadership is needed in particular contexts (like academic departments). By responding to the many racial and social injustices (like the deaths of George Floyd and many more), inclusive leaders provide justice, equity, and feelings of belongingness to underrepresented students. Research has shown that in academic departments: (1) underrepresented students are oppressed and (2) the culture is one of whiteness (Chakravartty et al., 2018). All too often, college and university departments' leaders forget to include and center the voices of their diverse students. Inclusive leadership eventually shifts from silence to communicative acknowledgement to action. In the following section, we discuss different types of teams you might lead.

Types of Teams

All organizational life encompasses change, but some teams are set up to exist for only a short period of time. These teams, which meet to complete a certain goal, during a set time period, are called temporary teams (Massaro et al., 2019). As Lv and Feng (2020) argue, "the most significant difference between normal teams and temporary teams is whether members are still together after the tasks are over" (p. 1). In Lee et al.'s (2019) research on support after natural disasters, some individuals without strong personal support networks needed to improvise, and find support in other places. After natural disasters, temporary teams like those organized by the American Red Cross can be an answer for those without strong support networks, as they provide community members with support they may not have otherwise had (Wegmann, 2020). Leadership on these teams requires clear communication about assignments, along with formal meetings to create cohesion (Wegmann, 2020).

In addition to temporary teams, leading teams from afar has become a norm in organizations of all kinds. The recent pervasive move toward remote work – prompted by the COVID-19 pandemic – has made virtual organizing more prevalent across sectors. Regardless of your organizational associations, you are likely to find groups being led by someone who is not physically present with the group. In some cases, group members are each located in a different place. We call these organizing forms virtual teams, distributed teams, and/or dispersed teams. Connaughton and Shuffler (2007) point to virtuality as a continuum; teams range from low to high in degree of virtuality as opposed to being merely virtual or non-virtual. Team members are separated by some degree of time and space, are constituted by nationally diverse members, tend to communicate via digital/technological means, and are often temporary in existence.

Communication is central to leading all teams, especially virtual ones (Connaughton & Daly, 2005). When we are physically collocated with our team leader and members, we often chat with them. When we are not physically collocated, this sort of social interaction may be absent (Connaughton & Daly, 2003). Trust may be swift and fleeting (Jarvenpaa & Leidner, 1998), conflict among team members may be hard to pinpoint and manage (Hinds & Mortensen, 2005), and communication may be strained due to team members' and their leader's diverse backgrounds (Cascio & Shurygailo, 2003). Yet, team leaders who devote time to learning each other's preferred ways of communicating tend to develop cohesive, better functioning teams (Gibbs & Connaughton, forthcoming); and Jarvenpaa and Leidner (1998) report that employee satisfaction with leaders can be maintained when members feel like everyone knows each other on a personal level.

Communicative Behaviors and Processes

Thus far in the chapter, you have begun to see how leading groups involves communication. In the paragraphs that follow we will build that argument further by noting that leading groups is about communicating vision/goals, managing conflict, being emotionally intelligent, encouraging feedback, framing, embracing intersectional identities, facilitating participation and voice, and leading ethically and with integrity.

Communicating Vision/Goals

As a leader, the last thing you want to do is communicate in a way that is confusing, or create an environment where people feel uncomfortable asking for clarification. When communicating your vision and goals as a leader, it is important to be clear and concise. Sull et al. (2018) provide us with a six-step process for leaders to communicate strategic vision/goals effectively. We have included examples of their recommendations in Table 9.1.

In addition to clear, concise communication of vision and goals, as a leader empathy must be prioritized. For example, Mayfield et al. (2015) studied top leaders of successful organizations and found that many include empathetic phrases in their strategic messages. For example, Mayfield et al. (2015) point to the founder/former CEO of Southwest Airlines, Herb Kelleher, who exemplified empathetic language toward both employees and customers in a video where he said, "[t]he business of business is people" – thus, putting people first through empathetic language. The addition of empathetic statements used by leaders when communicating strategic visions and goals creates an environment of trust and loyalty.

Managing Conflict

Let's face it: When dealing with different groups of people, conflict is inevitable, but the key is how we respond to and deal with conflict. Always use caution! Conflict will reveal truths about the leader.

Table 9.1 Leading Goals and Visions

What to Do	Why	Examples
Limit visions/ goals to a handful	Narrowing goals shows that leaders have done the work to weigh competing objectives and recommend a course of action.	The restaurant operator Darden has over 1,800 restaurants, but they have narrowed down their goals/values to seven key ideas for all the restaurants to follow (Darden Concepts, Inc., 2022).
Provide concise explanations of each visions/ goal's meaning	It is a communication myth that more communication is always better. Excessive communication can be unproductive and confusing.	Instead of reading an entire sample essay when explaining directions for a paper, a good teacher/leader might give an overview of key instructions (the prompt, word count, and any key objectives).
Clarify how goals will be accomplished	This assures group members and any company stakeholders that goals will eventually be met.	A business leader explains, in detail, how a five-step process will be completed by certain individuals, under a particular protocol, with new software.
Explain why visions/goals matter	Offering members an explanation of "why" you are set on a particular goal/vision helps them to recognize why it is important.	A leader in the church pushes members to sign up for a new small group, and shows them why the lessons will be meaningful and helpful in their family relationships.
Ensure progress toward visions/ goals	Monitoring progress keeps visions/ goals prioritized and increases the credibility of the leaders' commitments.	Electronic Arts, a video game producer, tracks its annual digital sales annually to see if there has been growth.
Set specific targets for the future	Managers' credibility is increased with company stakeholders and/or with members of the team when they set targets for the future.	At the end of a successful football season, a coach reminds the team of summer goals/ his vision for their practices, hoping to motivate them for the upcoming season.

Note: These data were largely conceived from Sull et al. (2018) unless otherwise noted.

Bradley et al. (2015) reveal that task conflict arises based on priorities for methods used to achieve or the distribution of tasks. It can have a positive effect on team/group outcomes because of: (1) the level of task complexity, (2) the level of individual and group information processing, and (3) the level of intensity of conflict expressions. Task conflict enables leaders and participants to consider the best "matching" of tasks per group/team member, giving them the ability to align tasks with each assignee's strengths and abilities. This process of managing task conflict can also help influence **role coordination** between team members, which occurs when people's different roles, subcultures, and expertise work together to facilitate organizational performance (Grant et al., 2018).

You may be wondering about team conflict that arises outside of tasks – say, relationship conflict? Or personality clashes?

Relationship conflict, unrelated to tasks, differs as it is more of a relational struggle, disagreement, argument, or debate that takes place between two or more people, which is often highly emotional and harms team outcomes (De Wit et al., 2012). Intragroup conflict occurs when two or more members have incompatible goals or interests (either real or perceptual) (Korsgaard et al., 2008). Given these different types of conflict, we look to Behfar et al.'s (2008) study of 57 independent teams to better understand how leadership and communication can help in the face on conflict. Behfar et al. (2008) assert that leaders of groups and teams should work on the clear interpersonal conveyance of: (1) the content of interactions and not delivery, (2) logic/reasoning behind decision making, and (3) distributing tasks based on team member prowess and ability. Through transparent leader communication, Behfar et al. (2008) suggest that successful groups and teams are proactive in anticipating the need for conflict resolution.

Emotional Intelligence

Emotional intelligence (EI) has long been considered as a person's ability to accurately understand and express emotion, facilitate thoughts and feelings, and regulate emotional processes (Chen & Guo, 2020). As a leader, it is imperative to know and communicate through EI's five key components: (1) self-awareness, understanding your own personal feelings; (2) self-regulation, the ability to manage your own impulses; (3) motivation, the ability to connect with emotion to reach goals; (4) empathy, awareness of the feelings of others; and (5) social skills, being able to invoke a certain desirable response (Sadri, 2012, p. 537). In other words, leaders should well know their own EI and understand their group/team's emotions. Leaders who possess this knowledge are perceived as more socially skilled and can motivate others to reach their goals.

Consider: For years, autism has been portrayed as a disorder. A presumption is made that non-autistics (allistics) have the ability to understand others' emotional states, while autistics have little to no emotional intelligence (Milton, 2012). Instead of viewing autistics as less communicative, less empathetic, or less aware, Milton (2012) suggests that we acknowledge the double empathy problem, which says that just as autistics may experience difficulty communicating with allistics, allistics also struggle to understand autistics (Mitchell et al., 2019). The problem is that allistics misinterpret social cues from autistics as a lack of desire for social connectedness.

It can be easy to misuse or misinterpret the idea of EI. Recent attempts to measure EI in businesses come from a place that is not neutral, but political (Fambrough & Hart, 2008). Emotions are politicized because they are made into commodities, valuable "things," that can be exploited by employers. EI is defined by employers, and certain characteristics are ranked as more important than others, thus limiting the range of emotions accepted in the workplace, benefiting some workers over others, and capping personal growth (Fambrough & Hart, 2008). While it is important to consider what we define EI to be and who we think can be emotionally intelligent, research has shown that EI does have important implications in groups and teams. Maamari and Majdalani (2017) found that if leaders have higher EI, they also communicate better, increase workplace performance, help to maintain stability in hiring, have better social relationships at work, lead others toward more effective decision making, and use creativity in making unique, new reward incentives.

Encouraging Feedback

At some point in our lives, we will all receive constructive feedback in an evaluation. Leaders who supply feedback at inappropriate times (e.g. in a public setting) risk embarrassing team members or creating a critical environment (Willemyns et al., 2003). However, when leaders provide feedback in a way that is empathetic and convey the value of the person's work, feedback can actually increase trust. Although constructive feedback is powerful and meant to make us all better (Besieux, 2017), as a leader, poor delivery of feedback can often be more memorable than the feedback itself (Brown et al., 2016). Delivering effective feedback is perhaps one of the most powerful tools you can possess as a leader, since it can communicatively guide positive behaviors toward goal achievement (Besieux, 2017). Though, the timing of when to deliver feedback depends on the leader's context. For example, Lechermeier and Fassnacht (2018) reviewed 64 empirical articles surrounding feedback and its delivery timing and found that a delayed approach is more conducive for leaders in education contexts, while it is advantageous for leaders in (non-education related) organizational contexts to provide immediate feedback.

Brown et al. (2016) identified three foundational concepts for leaders to remember when communicating positive/negative feedback. First, remember to stick to evidence-based communication when providing feedback in an evaluation, that is, only address what can be factually and/or statistically backed. For example, leaders could use one of the organization's benchmarks to show how an employee is falling short of a particular performance goal. Or, they could compare one group member's performance to that of their peers, encouraging them to look at the objective facts. Second, as a leader, or group/team member, do not allow negative emotions to run away in the evaluation; instead, pause, consider your options, and engage in mindful communication. According to Brown et al. (2016), one common communication tactic is to "sandwich" feedback, by providing positive feedback first, then offering a recommendation for change, and finally following up with another compliment. Third, select communication tactics and delivery based on the setting and context. This last method requires a leader to understand both the social dynamics of the organizational space and the personality of members, so that leaders can know what form of feedback will be most effective.

A recent study examined 300 Chinese employees and found that feedback had an influence on employee behavior, and in instances where supervisors did not provide feedback, peer feedback served as a supplement (Eva et al., 2019). Through two studies (one panel study of working adults and a sales team), Harvey and Green (2022) found that the level of agreeableness in a leader influences the emotional tone of their feedback. That is, agreeable leaders provide feedback with higher levels of positive emotional tone, which in turn makes providing constructive feedback increasingly difficult, as this limits team reflexivity in response to the feedback (Harvey & Green, 2022). However, in mixed teams, if poor performance is not addressed, good performers may not feel their efforts are worthwhile (Brown et al., 2016). Still, Besieux (2017) emphasizes that as a leader, communicating feedback is dependent on your team and your ability as a leader to hit the pause button and reflect.

Framing

Oftentimes, leaders need to decide how to share news with their organization. Framing allows leaders to shift the perception of bad news, moving it into a more positive light (Minei et al., 2018). For example, your instructor might tell the class, "I know you've had a hard exam and your essay is due in just a week, but you'll have a break once you've completed it." In this example, framing helps the leader to achieve support when they share their message (Minei et al., 2018). There are three main types of framing tasks. First, in diagnostic framing, actors define the problem, assign blame, and suggest whether the issue is good or bad. For example, in their study on Twitter activists in the #March For Our Lives (MFOL) movement concerning gun violence in schools, Zoller and Casteel (2021) found that although the public is often divided about diagnosing "guns" versus "individuals" as the reason for gun-associated deaths, activists in MOFL reframed the question, focusing on *why* shooters had *access* to guns. Prognostic framing uses communication to outline strategies and goals (Park et al., 2013). Leaders may use prognostic framing when they are attempting to instill new visions or motivate members to achieve new goals. MFOL activists used Twitter to both (1) promote gun safety and (2) demand that the NRA be defunded (Zoller & Casteel, 2021). Finally, with motivating framing, action is encouraged and a rationale is offered (Park et al., 2013). The MOFL activists in Zoller and Casteel (2021), for example, identified with both (1) responsible gun owners (including military veterans and gun activists) and (2) promoted the idea of "shared victimhood" as a result of gun violence such as mass shootings, criminal actions, or accidental shootings.

In Park et al.'s (2013) study of the implementation of data-driven decision making (DDDM) in schools, they found that leaders were able to frame reform ideas in ways that provided useful insights about what would support or hinder the school during its reform period. For example, leaders supported DDDM when they reappraised a situation where students performed poorly on tests. Leaders suggested that the data could help create objective assessments, but teachers could still practice good instructional practices to increase their own classroom efficacy. Teachers and administrators stated directly that framing shifts such as this helped them view DDDM practices favorably, as they were still able to engage with the data after it was collected/shared. In Andersson's (2020) study with Swedish school leaders, it was found that leaders acted as representatives for their respective programs, situating proposed reforms within the wider context of the organizational identity. Sometimes, this prevented beneficial changes from being made. For example, when school leaders were attempting to solve problems in their educational *program,* they tended to frame the problem in terms of the education *system*, since they perceived the identity of their program as one of "low priority." Their framing left the blame with higher sections of management and prevented the program itself from solving their own policy issues (Andersson, 2020).

Embracing Intersectional Identities in Groups and Teams

In recent years, the term *intersectionality* has become a popular way to describe layers of our identity that creates who we are. Our identities are ever so important when leading others and when participating in teams and groups. The concept of intersectionality emanated from Black feminist thought (Agosto & Roland, 2018). Black feminists saw differences between their goals and the goals of white feminism; most significantly, they sought not only gender equality but also racial equality. Black feminist and legal scholar, Kimberlé Williams Crenshaw (1989) showed that in legal discrimination cases, identity tended to be viewed from a single perspective: sex, or class, or race alone, never in combination. Crenshaw gave the idea of multi-layered identities a name: intersectionality. Today, intersectionality can be understood as multiple, interconnected identities of a person that are not fixed, and are performed differently in each social context (Collins, 2019). Intersectionality teaches us that (1) race, class, and gender are intersecting systems of power, (2) each setting will reflect social inequality differently, (3) individual and collective identities are socially constructed within systems of domination, and (4) all social problems, and their solutions, are also intersecting phenomena (Collins, 2019). Categories including "race, class, gender, sexuality, ethnicity, nationality, age, and ability" are particularly important as they relate to social inequity in global and local contexts (Collins, 2019, p. 22). Leaders can pay attention to needs to underrepresented populations by acknowledging specific factors impacting their inclusion.

Who are you? When we introduce ourselves, we quickly explain who we are to others. Yet, we are more than what we explain in 30 seconds, and what we say could easily change the next day.

Research coming from an intersectional approach has often called for diversification of companies, institutions, or schools. McGee et al. (2021) discuss how several diversification efforts have led to targeted recruiting and retaining underrepresented populations in STEM, but have failed to consider specificity, grouping "women of color" together as one singular group. McGee et al. (2021) argue that diversification efforts must be approached from a perspective that recognizes difference as being multi-layered. For example, in their interviews, McGee et al. (2021) found in their interviews that Black women expressed being inspired by other faculty of color, and by spiritual or faith-based support. In contrast, Latinas found a lot of support in ethnic-based professional organizations. Grouping women of color together fails to attend to true diversification efforts; and as you can see, who we are matters when we participate in groups, teams, and especially in leadership.

Facilitating Participation and Voice Through Ethical Leadership

Leadership communication is a diverse, global phenomenon that is relational (Fairhurst & Connaughton, 2014). Facilitating participation and voice in groups requires leaders to communicatively create spaces for multiple identities and their counter narratives. For example, Asante (2020) argues for Ghanaian/African church leaders to reform their treatment of queer communities, wherein, LGBTQIA+ voices are marginalized and not included as participants in national discourses. Similarly, a Black-African female, Pindi (2020) states academic leaders need to disrupt "colonial gatekeeping" and (re)center marginalized identities and knowledge at the core of the communication. Here, academic leaders can lead diverse populations by modeling communication that facilitates open spaces that invite differing perspectives.

Additionally, Chen (2018), an Asian immigrant woman, illustrates creative forms of leadership in academic settings in her autoethnography. Chen (2018) found that members in her institution were intentionally refusing to hear her, and she refused the racialization of Asian women as silent and (in)content or silent and hardworking. Instead, Chen relied on silence to: (1) stop conforming to the standards of speaking in the department while not being heard, (2) using ambiguity to complete personal goals, and (3) showing how silence itself is an interactive form of communication. Chen's reframing of silence serves as an example to others experiencing ostracism, racism, gender-based oppression, xenophobia, and racism in groups or teams.

Therefore, leaders should facilitate voice and not leave group members/team members to their own devices. Leading in this way (re)centers identities and knowledge(s) that are often marginalized and creates an environment that supports participation and voice of all team/group members. According to Brown and Treviño (2006), ethical leadership, in a broadened sense, is the socially accepted behavior of how leaders "ought" to behave. Integrity refers to the quality of a person's character (Cox et al., 2014a). Integrity is key to leadership, as character and behavior are used to judge the effectiveness and integrity of a leader (Storr, 2004). We maintain that a leader who encourages participation and voice is one who resists and rejects the urge to label people based on stereotypes that create ongoing harm (Rosette et al., 2016). Building on Agosto and Roland (2018), encouraging participation and voice entails at least three things: (1) supporting solutions for inequities on the micro- and macro-levels; (2) focusing on individuals' leading practices; and (3) acknowledging all members' identities and serving as an ally. Participation and voice in leadership is no small feat; yet, the aspiration to communicatively support group members and their participation is a necessary part of leading groups.

Evidence-Based Recommendations for Practice

Globalization has led to an increase in cultural diversity in businesses all around the world (Wang et al., 2019). We emphasize that leaders of groups and teams must focus on JEDI. If leaders are open to diversity and have high levels of multicultural experience, diversity can be a great strength (Wang et al., 2019). Tadmor et al. (2012) reported that dyadic creativity (creativity in pairs), or teams' fluency, flexibility, and novelty is greater when partners each have high levels of multicultural experience. Martinez et al. (2017) also found that in research and development, diversity is a valuable asset, as it allows for greater cognitive diversity, enhancing innovativeness. All of this success, however, depends on how you, as a leader, attend to your groups and teams. We hope our chapter provided more information on the relationship between communication and leadership as well as strategies of leadership and will help you understand how to enact JEDI principles as a leader.

Box 9.1   Global Leadership in Action

Dr. Yea-Wen Chen is a full Professor in the School of Communication (The School of Communication, San Diego State University, 2023). She also serves as the Director of the Institute for Dialogue and Social Justice, and Core Faculty for the Center for Communication, Health, and the Public Good at San Diego State University (Author #2, Personal Experience). In her 2018 article "'Why don't you speak (up), Asian/immigrant/woman?'": Rethinking silence and voice through family oral history" she discusses the nuances of leadership in higher education spaces through autoethnography, featuring her perspective as an Asian/immigrant/woman faculty. Chen uses vivid descriptions that invite readers to consider how racial and cultural microaggressions can affect dedicated/passionate workers who may come from different backgrounds (Chen, 2018). Personally, Dr. Yea-Wen Chen had a tenure track position at her institution; however, when leadership and peers created multiple invisible storms, she drew on her family's oral history of silence. Dr. Chen's ultimate decision to leave her institution was an excellent one, as she not only regained tenure at a new institution, but she is also now a full professor. Through her research, pedagogy, and activism, Dr. Yea-Wen continues to raise critical consciousness of intercultural communication, cross-cultural communication, and ethical leadership in a myriad of ways. Dr. Chen is committed to investigating racialized acts of "speaking up," barriers for international students, women's rights advocacy, racial equity, and the persistence of social justice. If her first department seriously considered the effects of racism, xenophobia, and anti-Asian actions, they would perhaps still have a decorated faculty member in Dr. Yea-Wen Chen. It is noteworthy that Dr. Chen now has 18 top papers from regional, national, and international communication conference, is a co-recipient of the 2020 Western States Communication Association Exemplary Teacher Award by the Communication and Instruction Interest Group, and has co-authored "Teaching social justice: Critical tools for the intercultural communication classroom" (The School of Communication, San Diego State University, 2023). We highlight Dr. Yea-Wen Chen because she is a great example of why facilitating participation and voice through ethical leadership is important. Ethical leadership would have facilitated Dr. Chen's voice, ideas, and input, and mitigated non-inclusive environments as opposed to disregarding team members' differences and lived experiences. Under new leadership, Dr. Chen is excelling at her new institution as full professor, director, and core faculty, and we wish her continued success!

Conclusion

Leadership is, indeed, about communication. As you have seen, the various notions of leadership and various types of teams that one leads are each grounded in communication. As we suggested at the beginning of this chapter, leading groups is inextricably tied to communication. Leadership of groups is constituted by communication. Whether individuals are perceived as effective or ineffective leaders depends partly on how and what they communicate.

The nature of communication when leading groups not only has ramifications for how an individual is perceived by others; it also is related to the effectiveness of the group itself. As we continue to think about the ways in which communication is tied to the leadership of groups, let us also keep at the forefront of our minds the importance of infusing JEDI into how we view and "do" leadership.

Further Readings

Cogliser, C. C., Gardner, W. L., Gavin, M. B., & Broberg, J. C. (2012). Big five personality factors and leader emergence in virtual teams: Relationships with team trustworthiness, member performance contributions, and team performance. *Group & Organization Management*, *37*(6), 752–784. https://doi.org/10.1177/1059601112464266

Kossek, E. E., & Buzzanell, P. M. (2018). Women's career equality and leadership in organizations: Creating an evidence-based positive change. *Human Resource Management*, *57*(4), 813–822. https://doi.org/10.1002/hrm.21936

Kuhn, T. (2012). Negotiating the micro-macro divide: Thought leadership from organizational communication for theorizing organization. *Management Communication Quarterly*, *26*(4), 543–584. https://doi.org/10.1177/0893318912462004

Glossary

Discursive leadership   A perspective that sees communication as the starting point for creating leadership and organizational life.

Emergent leadership   A group's temporary perception that a certain individual appears to be a leader, despite a lack of formal authority.

Inclusive leadership   Words, deeds, and communication from leaders that invite and appreciate others' contributions.

Role coordination   Occurs when group members' different roles, subcultures, and expertise work together to facilitate organizational performance.

Transformational leadership   Refers to a leader's ability to motivate group members to do something they never thought they could do.

References

Agosto, V., & Roland, E. (2018). Intersectionality and educational leadership: A critical review. *Review of Research in Education*, *42*(1), 255–285. https://doi.org/10.3102/0091732X18762433

Andersson, R. (2020). Contextual influence on school leader problem framing: The role of perceived organizational image and identity in making sense of policy-related problems. *Leadership and Policy in Schools*, Ahead-of-Print, 1–16. https://doi.org/10.1080/15700763.2020.1836232

Asante, G. A. (2020). Anti-LGBT violence and the ambivalent (colonial) discourses of Ghanaian Pentecostalist-Charismatic church leaders. *Howard Journal of Communications*, *31*(1), 20–34. https://doi.org/10.1080/10646175.2019.1590255

Ashikali, T., Groeneveld, S., & Kuipers, B. (2021). The role of inclusive leadership in supporting an inclusive climate in diverse public sector teams. *Review of Public Personnel Administration*, *41*(3), 497–519. https://doi.org/10.1177/0734371X19899722

Bakar, H. A., & McCann, R. M. (2016). The mediating effect of leader–member dyadic communication style agreement on the relationship between servant leadership and group-level organizational citizenship behavior. *Management Communication Quarterly*, *70*, 32–58. https://doi.org/10.1177/0893318915601162

Bass B. M. (1981). *Handbook of leadership*. Free Press.

Bass, B. M., & Avolio, B. J. (1994). *Improving organizational effectiveness through transformational leadership*. Sage.

Behfar, K. J., Peterson, R. S., Mannix, E. A., & Trochim, W. M. (2008). The critical role of conflict resolution in teams: A close look at the links between conflict type, conflict management strategies, and team outcomes. *Journal of Applied Psychology*, *93*(1), 170–188. https://doi.org/10.1037/0021-9010.93.1.170

Besieux, T. (2017). Why I hate feedback: Anchoring effective feedback within organizations. *Business Horizons*, *60*(4), 435–439. https://doi.org/10.1016/j.bushor.2017.03.001

Best, K. C. (2011). Holistic leadership: A model for leader-member engagement and development. *The Journal of Values-Based Leadership*, *4*(1), 1–19. https://scholar.valpo.edu/jvbl/vol4/iss1/5

Bradley, B. H., Anderson, H. J., Baur, J. E., & Klotz, A. C. (2015). When conflict helps: Integrating evidence for beneficial conflict in groups and teams under three perspectives. *Group Dynamics: Theory, Research, and Practice, 19*(4), 243–272. https://doi.org/10.1037/gdn0000033

Brown, M., Kulik, C. T., & Lim, V. (2016). Managerial tactics for communicating negative performance feedback. *Personnel Review, 45*(5), 969–987. https://doi.org/10.1108/PR-10-2014-0242

Brown, M. E., & Treviño, L. K. (2006). Ethical leadership: A review and future directions. *The Leadership Quarterly, 17*(6), 595–616. https://doi.org/10.1016/j.leaqua.2006.10.004

Burns, J. M. (1978). *Leadership*. Harper & Row.

Butler, J. (1988). Performative acts and gender constitution: An essay in phenomenology and feminist theory. *Theatre Journal, 40*(4), 519–531. https://doi.org/10.2307/3207893

Cascio, W. F., & Shurygailo, S. (2003). E-leadership and virtual teams. *Organizational Dynamics, 31*, 362–376. https://doi.org/10.1109/EMR.2008.4490142

Chakravartty, P., Kuo, R., Grubbs, V., & Mcilwain, C. (2018). #CommunicationSoWhite. *Journal of Communication, 68*(2), 254–266. https://doi.org/10.1093/joc/jqy003

Charbonneau, D., Barling, J., & Kelloway, E. K. (2001). Transformational leadership and sports performance: The mediating role of intrinsic motivation. *Journal of Applied Social Psychology, 31*, 1521–1534. https://doi.org/10.1111/j.1559-1816.2001.tb02686.x

Chen, J., & Guo, W. (2020). Emotional intelligence can make a difference: The impact of principals' emotional intelligence on teaching strategy mediated by instructional leadership. *Educational Management Administration & Leadership, 48*(1), 82–105. https://doi.org/10.1177/1741143218781066

Chen, Y.-W. (2018). "Why don't you speak (up), Asian/immigrant/woman?": Rethink silence and voice through family oral history. *Departures in Critical Qualitative Research, 7*(2), 29–48. https://doi.org/10.1525/dcqr.2018.7.2.29

Collins, P. H. (2019). Intersectionality as critical inquiry. In *Intersectionality as critical social theory* (pp. 21–53). Duke University Press.

Connaughton, S. L., & Daly, J. A. (2003). Long distance leadership: Communicative strategies for leading virtual teams. In D. J. Pauleen (Ed.), *Virtual teams: Projects, protocols, and processes* (pp. 116–144). Idea Group Inc. https://doi.org/10.4018/978-1-59140-166-7.ch005

Connaughton, S. L., & Daly, J. A. (2005). Leadership in the new millennium: Communication beyond temporal, spatial, and geographical boundaries. (In P. Kalbfleisch (Ed.), *Communication yearbook*, Lawrence Erlbaum Associates). Annals of the International Communication Association, 29(1), 187–213. https://doi.org/10.1080/23808985.2005.11679047

Connaughton, S. L., & Shuffler, M. (2007). Multinational multicultural distributed teams: A review and future agenda. *Small Group Research, 38*(3), 387–412. https://doi.org/10.1177/1046496407301970

Cox, D., La Caze, M., & Levine, M. (2014a). Integrity. In *The handbook of virtue ethics* (pp. 208–217). Routledge.

Cox, D., La Caze, M., & Levine, M. (2014b). Integrity. In S. Van Hooft (Ed.), *The handbook of virtue ethics* (pp. 200–209). Acumen Publishing.

Crenshaw, K. (1989). Demarginalizing the intersection of race and sex: A Black feminist critique of antidiscrimination doctrine, feminist theory and antiracist politics. *University of Chicago Legal Forum, 1*(8), 139–167. https://chicagounbound.uchicago.edu/cgi/viewcontent.cgi?article=1052&context=uclf

Darden Concepts, Inc. (2022). *About us: Company information*. https://www.darden.com/our-company

De Wit, F. R., Greer, L. L., & Jehn, K. A. (2012). The paradox of intragroup conflict: A meta-analysis. *Journal of Applied Psychology, 97*(2), 360–390. https://doi.org/10.1037/a0024844

Eva, N., Meacham, H., Newman, A., Schwarz, G., & Tham, T. L. (2019). Is coworker feedback more important than supervisor feedback for increasing innovative behavior? *Human Resource Management, 58*(4), 383–396. https://doi.org/10.1002/hrm.21960

Fairhurst, G. T. (2007). Discursive leadership: A communication alternative to leadership psychology. *Management Communication Quarterly, 21*(4), 510–521. https://doi.org/10.1177/0893318907313714

Fairhurst, G. T. (2009). Considering context in discursive leadership research. *Human Relations, 62*(11), 1607–1633. https://doi.org/10.1177/0018726709346379

Fairhurst, G. T., & Connaughton, S. L. (2014). Leadership: A communicative perspective. *Leadership, 10*(1), 7–35. https://doi.org/10.1177/1742715013509396

Fambrough, M. J., & Hart, R. K. (2008). Emotions in leadership development: A critique of emotional intelligence. *Advances in Developing Human Resources*, *10*(5), 740–758. https://doi.org/10.1177/1523422308323542

Gerpott, F. H., Lehmann-Willenbrock, N., Voelpel, S. C., & Van Vugt, M. (2019). It's not just what is said, but when it's said: A temporal account of verbal behaviors and emergent leadership in self-managed teams. *Academy of Management Journal*, *62*(3), 717–738. https://doi.org/10.5465/amj.2017.0149

Gibbs, J. L., & Connaughton, S. L. (forthcoming). Distributed collaboration. In V. Miller & M. S. Poole (Eds.), *Handbook of organizational communication* (pp. x–x). De Gruyter.

Grant, J. L., Taylor, A., & Wheeler, C. (2018). Planners' perceptions of the influence of leadership on co-ordinating plans. *Environment and Planning, C, Politics and Space*, *36*(4), 669–688. https://doi.org/10.1177/2399654417720798

Hanna, A. A., Smith, T. A., Kirkman, B. L., & Griffin, R. W. (2021). The emergence of emergent leadership: A comprehensive framework and directions. *Journal of Management*, *47*(1), 76–104. https://doi.org/10.1177/0149206320965683

Harvey, J. F., & Green, P., Jr. (2022). Constructive feedback: When leader agreeableness stifles team reflexivity. *Personality and Individual Differences*, *194*(1), 111624–111634. https://doi.org/10.1016/j.paid.2022.111624

Hinds, P. J., & Mortensen, M. (2005). Understanding conflict in geographically distributed teams: The moderating effects of shared identity, shared context, and spontaneous communication. *Organization Science*, *16*(3), 203–225. https://doi.org/10.1287/orsc.1050.0122

House, R. J. (1977). A 1976 theory of charismatic leadership. In J. G. Hunt & L. L. Larson (Eds.), *Leadership: The cutting edge* (pp. 189–207). Southern Illinois University Press.

House, R. J., Hanges, P. J., Javidan, M., Dorfman, P. W., & Gupta, V. (Eds.). (2004). *Culture, leadership, and organizations: The GLOBE study of 62 societies*. Sage publications.

Jansen, W. S., Vos, M. W., Otten, S., Podsiadlowski, A., & van der Zee, K. I. (2016). Colorblind or colorful? How diversity approaches affect cultural majority and minority employees. *Journal of Applied Social Psychology*, *46*(2), 81–93. https://doi.org/10.1111/jasp.12332

Jarvenpaa, S. L., & Leidner, D. E. (1998). Communication and trust in global virtual teams. *Journal of Computer-Mediated Communication*, *3*(4). https://doi.org/10.1111/j.1083-6101.1998.tb00080.x

Jian, G. (2019). Transforming the present moment through conversation and narrative: Toward a hermeneutic leadership theory. *Communication Theory*, *29*(1), 86–106. https://doi.org/10.1093/ct/qty016

Johnson, C. E., & Hackman, M. Z. (2018). *Leadership: A communication perspective* (7th ed.). Waveland Press, Inc.

Korsgaard, M. A., Soyoung Jeong, S., Mahony, D. M., & Pitariu, A. H. (2008). A multilevel view of intra-group conflict. *Journal of Management*, *34*(6), 1222–1252. https://doi.org/10.1177/0149206308325124

Lechermeier, J., & Fassnacht, M. (2018). How do performance feedback characteristics influence recipients' reactions? A state-of-the-art review on feedback source, timing, and valence effects. *Management Review Quarterly*, *68*(2), 145–193.

Lee, S., Sadri, A. M., Ukkusuri, S. V., Clawson, R. A., & Seipel, J. (2019). Network structure and substantive dimensions of improvised social support ties surrounding households during post-disaster recovery. *Natural Hazards Review*, *20*(4), 1–12. https://doi.org/10.1061/(ASCE)NH.1527-6996.0000332

Lv, M., & Feng, S. (2020). Temporary teams: Current research focus and future directions. *Quality & Quantity*, *55*(1), 1–18. https://doi.org/10.1007/s11135-020-00990-y

Maamari, B. E., & Majdalani, J. F. (2017). Emotional intelligence, leadership style and organizational climate. *International Journal of Organizational Analysis*, *52*(2), 327–345. https://www.emerald.com/insight/content/doi/10.1108/IJOA-04-2016-1010/full/html#sec006

Martinez, G. M., Zouaghi, F., & Marco, G. T. (2017). Diversity is strategy: The effect of R&D team diversity on innovative performance. *R & D Management*, *47*(2), 311–329. https://doi.org/10.1111/radm.12244

Massaro, M., Dal Mas, F., Bontis, N., & Gerrard, B. (2019). Intellectual capital and performance in temporary teams. *Management Decision*, *58*(3), 410–427. https://doi.org/10.1108/MD-02-2019-0219

Mayfield, J., Mayfield, M., & Sharbrough, W., III. (2015). Strategic vision and values in top leaders' communications: Motivating language at a higher level. *International Journal of Business Communication*, *52*(1), 97–121. https://doi.org/10.1177/2329488414560282

McGee, E. O., Main, J. B., Miles, M. L., & Cox, M. F. (2021). An intersectional approach to investigating persistence among Women of Color tenure-track engineering faculty. *Journal of Women & Minorities in Science & Engineering, 27*(1), 57–84. https://doi.org/10.1615/JWomenMinorScienEng.2020035632

Milton, D. E. M. (2012). On the ontological status of autism: The "double empathy problem." *Disability & Society, 27*(6), 883–887. https://doi.org/10.1080/09687599.2012.710008

Minei, E., Eatough, M., & Cohen-Charash, M. (2018). Managing illegitimate task requests through explanation and acknowledgment: A discursive leadership approach. *Management Communication Quarterly, 32*(3), 374–397. https://doi.org/10.1177/0893318918755506

Mitchell, P., Cassidy, S., & Sheppard, E. (2019). The double empathy problem, camouflage, and the value of expertise from experience.. *The Behavioral and Brain Sciences, 42*(1), 1–3. https://doi.org/10.1017/S0140525X18002212

Nembhard, I. M., & Edmondson, A. C. (2006). Making it safe: The effects of leader inclusiveness and professional status on psychological safety and improvement efforts in health care teams. *Journal of Organizational Behavior, 27*(7), 941–966. https://doi.org/10.1002/job.413

Park, V., Daly, A. J., & Guerra, A. W. (2013). Strategic framing: How leaders craft the meaning of data use for equity and learning. *Educational Policy, 27*(4), 645–675. https://doi.org/10.1177/0895904811429295

Piccolo, R. F., & Colquitt, J. A. (2006). Transformational leadership and job behaviors: The mediating role of core job characteristics. *Academy of Management Journal, 49*(2), 327–340. https://doi.org/10.5465/amj.2006.20786079

Pindi, G. N. (2020). Speaking back to academic colonial gatekeeping: The significance of intercultural performance studies works in promoting marginalized knowledges and identities. *Journal of Intercultural Communication Research, 49*(5), 442–457. https://doi.org/10.1080/17475759.2020.1801487

Randel, A. E., Galvin, B. M., Shore, L. M., Ehrhart, K. H., Chung, B. G., Dean, M. A., & Kedharnath, U. (2018). Inclusive leadership: Realizing positive outcomes through belongingness and being valued for uniqueness. *Human Resource Management Review, 28*(2), 190–203. https://doi.org/10.1016/j.hrmr.2017.07.002

Rosette, A. S., Koval, C. Z., Ma, A., & Livingston, R. (2016). Race matters for women leaders: Intersectional effects on agentic deficiencies and penalties. *The Leadership Quarterly, 27*(3), 429–445. https://doi.org/10.1016/j.leaqua.2016.01.008

Sadri, G. (2012). Emotional intelligence and leadership development. *Public Personnel Management, 41*(3), 535–548. https://journals.sagepub.com/doi/pdf/10.1177/009102601204100308

Storr, L. (2004). Leading with integrity: A qualitative research study. *Journal of Health Organization and Management, 18*(6), 415–434. https://doi.org/10.1108/14777260410569984

Sull, D. N., Turconi, S., & Sull, C. (2018). *Six steps to communicating strategic priorities effectively.* MIT Sloan Management Review. https://sloanreview.mit.edu/article/six-steps-to-communicating-strategic-priorities-effectively/

Sun, J., Anderson, R. C., Perry, M., & Lin, T.-J. (2017). Emergent leadership in children's cooperative problem solving groups. *Cognition and Instruction, 35*(3), 212–235. https://doi.org/10.1080/07370008.2017.1313615

Sutanto, J., Tan, C.-H., Battistini, B., & Phang, C. W. (2011). Emergent leadership in virtual collaboration settings: A social network analysis approach. *Long Range Planning, 44*(5), 421–439. https://doi.org/10.1016/j.lrp.2011.09.001

Tadmor, C. T., Satterstrom, P., Jang, S., & Polzer, J. T. (2012). Beyond individual creativity: The superadditive benefits of multicultural experience for collective creativity in culturally diverse teams. *Journal of Cross-Cultural Psychology, 43*(3), 384–392. https://doi.org/10.1177/0022022111435259

The School of Communication, San Diego State University. (2023). *Dr. Yea-Wen Chen: Professor, Director of Graduate Studies.* https://communication.sdsu.edu/faculty_and_staff/profile/dr.-yea-wen-chen

Tourish, D. (2013). *The dark side of transformational leadership: A critical perspective.* Routledge.

Uhl-Bien, M. (2006). Relational leadership theory: Exploring the social processes of leadership and organizing. *The Leadership Quarterly, 17*(6), 654–676. https://doi.org/10.1080/03634523.2020.1811362

Wang, J., Cheng, G. H.-L., Chen, T., & Leung, K. (2019). Team creativity/innovation in culturally diverse teams: A meta-analysis. *Journal of Organizational Behavior, 40*(6), 693–708. https://doi.org/10.1002/job.2362

Weber, M. (1947). *The theory of social and economic organization*. The Free Press.

Wegmann, R. N. (2020). A grounded theory for the performance of temporary disaster response teams. *Journal of Organizational Effectiveness: People and Performance*, *7*(2), 155–172. https://doi.org/10.1108/JOEPP-04-2020-0059

Whittle, A., Housley, W., Gilchrist, A., Mueller, F., & Lenney, P. (2014). Category predication work, discursive leadership and strategic sensemaking. *Human Relations*, *68*(3), 377–407. https://doi.org/10.1177/0018726714528253

Willemyns, M., Gallois, C., & Callan, V. (2003). Trust me, I'm your boss: Trust and power in supervisor–supervisee communication. *The International Journal of Human Resource Management*, *14*(1), 117–127. https://doi.org/10.1080/09585190210158547

Zoller, H. M., & Casteel, D. (2021). #March for Our Lives: Health activism, diagnostic framing, gun control, and the gun industry. *Health Communication*, *37*(7), 813–823. https://doi.org/10.1080/10410236.2020.1871167

10 Managing Conflict Within Groups

Laura W. Black, Jennifer Woody Collins, and Rizvan Saeed

Chapter Objectives

- Define conflict, describe how conflict occurs in groups, and explain how conflict has been studied by group scholars.
- Understand how diversity, power, and identity are related to conflict in groups.
- Describe different approaches and practical advice on conflict engagement and de-escalation.
- Understand how dialogic communication is used to manage conflict in groups.

Introduction

How do you feel about conflict? Conflict is something most people are not eager to experience. Yet, some degree of conflict is inherent in social life and group scholars have long argued that healthy group processes should include diverse perspectives, opinions, and information. Therefore, this chapter approaches conflict as inherent to group communication.

The chapter illustrates how conflict is constructed, shaped by group membership and communication processes, and can be positive for successful group functioning.

This chapter begins by explaining some key ideas to help you understand how conflict occurs in groups, and then considers the communication processes that group members use when managing conflict. It explains how individual group members can develop conflict management skills, and how groups can manage conflicts on their own or through formal processes like mediation. The chapter also highlights the role that diversity plays in group conflict and explains how group members can develop intercultural conflict competence. We end by describing dialogue as a practical method for engaging in and transforming conflicts, and we provide an example of some workshops in Pakistan that use dialogic methods to manage conflict in a diverse group.

Understanding Conflict in Groups

Communication scholars define conflict as involving three components: interaction, incompatibility, and interdependence (Jehn, 1995; Nicotera & Jameson, 2021). Putnam and Poole (1987) connect these components with their definition of conflict as "the interaction of interdependent people who perceive the opposition of goals, aims, and (/or) values, and who see the other party as potentially interfering with the realization of these goals (aims, or values)" (p. 552). Communication is integral to conflict because it is used to identify issues, frame something as a conflict, develop perceptions (i.e., intensity or intractability of the conflict), and engage in the conflict itself as it unfolds (Putnam, 2013).

DOI: 10.4324/9781003227458-12

Garner (2022) explains that there are three overarching approaches to researching group conflict: developmental, instrumental, and political. Each approach focuses on a different aspect of conflict in groups. Developmental approaches situate conflict as a normal, inevitable, and necessary part of group development over time. Instrumental approaches view conflict as unavoidable and consider whether and how conflict helps or hinders a group's ability to achieve its goals. Political perspectives consider power dynamics within groups, foregrounding how social class, race, sex, age, and a wide array of other identity-based differences can lead to conflict.

Many scholars use Jehn (1995) as a starting point for understanding the types of conflict that occur in groups. Jehn's conflict types are **task, process, and relationship conflict**. Task conflicts have to do with perceptions about what the group is or should be doing; process conflicts involve the how of task accomplishment, such as the distribution of work among group members, timelines, meeting structures, and so on. Relationship conflict has to do with interpersonal (dis)harmony within the group, or how people are getting along with one another and the factors that shape those relationships. These different conflict types may require different conflict management strategies. While task conflicts can often be resolved through negotiation, or sometimes simple clarification, relational conflict requires interpersonal conflict management processes such as apologizing, acknowledging emotion, and peacemaking.

Task, process, and relational conflict make sense as conceptually distinct. But in real groups they can become intertwined. For example, in a student group, Luis and Petra might agree that the group should create a survey for their research methods class, and that Luis will do the literature review and Petra will set up the survey in the online form. At first glance, it seems like this group is working well together. However, Luis, thinking there is no further discussion needed to get the work done, begins feeling resentful about having to attend group meetings, treating them as an inconvenience. Conflict could arise between Luis and Petra, as Petra sees value in the group's meetings. Ostensibly, this is a process conflict, since they disagree about what process is best for the group to accomplish its goals. However, it could easily develop into a relationship conflict. Importantly, relationship conflicts may not be obvious or verbally expressed; however, they can have outsized impacts on group function. If Petra becomes resentful of Luis's attitude, she may stop reaching out to him to share information or discuss ideas (Meng et al., 2015).

Conflict is often studied in dyads, for example between two friends, colleagues, or relational partners. Even when only two people are involved, conflict can be complicated and challenging, as the example of Luis and Petra illustrates. But in a group setting, conflict is even more complex. Because group members are interdependent, conflict between two group members often ripples out and involves others. Interdependence is easy to see in a student group all of whom receive the same grade for their project, but members of other groups such as juries, committees, and work teams also rely on each other. In a conflict, group members might take sides or form coalitions. They might feel pressured to either join or try to resolve the conflict. Group members might discuss aspects of the conflict outside of group meetings, which can lead to members having different understandings of what is happening. This can exacerbate the conflict and undermine trust. In these ways, conflicts that begin with two members can easily spread throughout the group.

The group's history also impacts conflict. Group members might see a disagreement, such as the one between Petra and Luis, as a continuation of some previous conflict; history can shape how people understand and respond to conflict events. Sometimes conflict can have a chilling effect in the group with members feeling like the negative aspects of conflict are unavoidable. Conflict can feel threatening to group members. It brings uncertainty and can feel very stressful. If unresolved, conflict can breed resentment and leave group members feeling on edge because they cannot predict when someone might become angry or aggressive. Some conflict situations can be so awkward that groups can avoid discussing important topics in an effort to keep the peace. This can lead groups to develop norms of conflict avoidance, which have a negative impact on group members' relationships and the group's ability to function well.

As the aforementioned description highlights, emotion is inherent to conflict. Bodker and Jameson (2001) argue that traditional definitions of conflict have sidelined emotion, treating it as secondary to more "rational" dimensions of conflict like perceptions on interference in achieving one's goals. In contrast, they argue that conflict is inherently emotional. Emotions influence attributions and interpretations, which impact group members' communication and can intensify or help de-escalate conflict. So, to understand conflict interaction, scholars should study group members' emotional experience. Additionally, research has shown that diversity and emotion are related because group members' social identity categories (such as gender and cultural background) are linked to how they experience conflict and emotion in groups (Garcia-Prieto et al., 2003).

Another approach to understanding emotion's role in group conflict is offered by Affect Theory, which is starting to be used to study conflict in groups (e.g., Woody Collins, 2021). Affect Theory examines the emotional dynamics of individuals and groups in a holistic way. Affect, in part, is about considering the prevailing mood of a group and the ways it evolves over time. Returning to the aforementioned example, Luis and Petra's conflict influences the affective tone of the group, perhaps shifting it from amicable to adversarial. This shift in affect may lead Luis and Petra's group to make different choices or think of their work differently. Affect Theory asserts that what individuals or groups see as reasonable, possible, or important is influenced by affective forces. Examining affect can help understand why one group views conflict as something to learn from while another sees conflict as unbearable enough to make members stop participating. In sum, emotion is a key part of how people experience conflict in groups and studying emotion and/or affect can help group scholars understand how people reflectively engage in, manage, and transform conflicts (Jameson et al., 2010).

Managing Group Conflicts through Communication

Developmental approaches to studying conflict note that disagreement is a normal part of group development (Garner, 2022). Conflict tends to develop over time and follow some predictable patterns in groups. High functioning groups learn to recognize conflict development and communicate in ways that treat conflict engagement as an opportunity for learning and growth rather than a hindrance. There are several areas of group research that investigate how communication relates to conflict development, management, and outcomes.

Group conflict affects both task and relational outcomes. Group scholars have long understood that differences of opinion and perspective are healthy and important for groups. Some level of disagreement is necessary for groups to make good decisions and engage in creative and innovative thinking. However, disagreement has the potential to develop into unhealthy conflict, which can lead to dysfunctional group interaction and stymie task accomplishment. Moreover, group conflict can negatively impact group member relationships and can lead groups to form cliques or ostracize particular members (Wittenbaum et al., 2010).

Conflict is also related to group cohesion, which is the extent to which group members feel connected to each other. In group research, cohesion is typically seen as positive. Yet, highly cohesive groups are at risk of developing norms that discourage disagreement. Groups that avoid conflict by suppressing dissent can have disastrous outcomes, as evidenced by case studies of groupthink, such as the Watergate scandal (Janis, 1972). Silencing of dissent can create a false consensus in the group, which not only leads to faulty decision making but also a negative affective climate in the group. Some level of relational closeness and cohesion is important to create a positive group climate. However, groups should also work to develop group norms that engage conflict ethically and appropriately by balancing group cohesion with rigorous analysis of relevant information.

A large body of research has explored how individuals differ in their approaches to conflict. **Conflict management styles** are categorized as competing, collaborating, cooperating, accommodating, and avoiding. Competition emphasizes winning the argument and making sure one's own needs are met. In contrast, people with accommodating or avoiding styles tend to de-emphasize their own needs to preserve the relationship or avoid exacerbating the conflict. The cooperating style prioritizes compromise, where each person in the conflict is willing to give up something to meet some of their needs. Compromise emphasizes fairness, but it presumes that group member's positions can be divided into distributable outcomes. In contrast, a collaborative style attempts to transform conflicts by looking at underlying interests, rather than positions, and focusing on problem solving in ways that integrate both perspectives.

While there are hundreds of studies examining these styles (see Tehrani & Yamini, 2020 for a recent meta-analysis), virtually all conclude that collaborating and cooperating styles are considered most appropriate and effective, while competing and avoiding styles are perceived as inappropriate and least effective, especially in the long term. Nonetheless, each style may be appropriate under specific circumstances, and it is helpful for group members to continuously reflect on the group's circumstances to determine the best approach to conflict.

Group members can learn skills to help them engage in conflict constructively. Individual group members can work on developing their skills such as active listening, paraphrasing other people's perspectives, asking open-ended questions, and explaining their perspective clearly and nonjudgmentally. These skills help group members build shared understanding, which is important for collaborative conflict management. Groups can also work together to manage conflicts by learning to recognize conflict early and developing processes for communicating about and managing conflicts when they arise. For example, groups benefit from creating guidelines or agreements about work processes, even before they begin their projects. Such group contracts typically focus on task-related issues but can also include conflict management processes. Groups can also develop feedback systems so that members receive information about their work on an ongoing basis, which can help prevent issues from growing into larger conflicts.

Another important area of research on how group members express and manage conflict has to do with **conflict framing**. Framing is a process of drawing boundaries around something, and the idea of framing has been used to help understand how people view what is important in a conflict (Black, 2013; Brummans et al., 2008; Putnam, 1990). Traditional work on framing uses the metaphor of a picture frame that is around a piece of art. The frame creates a kind of boundary around the art and helps tell the viewer what to notice, where to look, what matters, and so on. Framing can be understood as an interpretive process because we use frames to make sense of a situation (Goffman, 1974). In a conflict situation, we have a sense for what events led to the conflict, when the conflict started, what the conflict is about, and so on. People who are engaged in a conflict might frame the conflict differently from each other and those differences can have an impact on how the conflict is expressed and experienced in a group.

Framing is inherently communicative. We engage in conflict framing by the way we communicate during a conflict, including our word choice, nonverbal expression, and choice of communication medium. How people characterize a conflict not only demonstrates their perspectives but also has a tangible impact on what happens. For example, a conflict that is framed as an opportunity for creative problem solving will have a far different feel to it and will present a wider range of options for a response than will a conflict that is framed as a personal threat or a conflict that is framed as a struggle over who is right and who is wrong.

Brummans et al. (2008) show that framing is accomplished through several communicative practices. First, people involved in conflict use labels or metaphors for the conflict itself and by indicating why the conflict is happening and what is at stake. For example, a conflict might be described as a "battle," a "personal issue," or a "minor disagreement." It could develop in response to a "crisis" or it may be seen as an "ongoing problem." Second, conflict framing involves the communication that people use to describe themselves, other people in the conflict, and the actions that people have taken. Conflict framing includes language about who is right and who is wrong, what caused the conflict, what actions during the conflict were most important, and why people took those actions.

For instance, someone involved in a conflict might describe themselves as "being reasonable" and the other group member as "too emotional," which supports their frame of the conflict as a "misunderstanding" that can be easily resolved if the other person will stop "overreacting." In contrast, the other party might describe the first group member as "insensitive" or "cruel" and could frame the conflict as a problem of power imbalance that requires structural changes to the group to adequately address the conflict. Group members who are actively involved in leading the group might see infrequently contributing members as "slackers" or social loafers, while those who are contributing less might see the leaders as authoritarians who will not listen or take feedback.

These labels matter as part of the conflict framing process because they indicate a deeper sense of meaningfulness for the people engaged in conflict. Simply changing the wording will not easily resolve conflicts but paying attention to the words people use to describe the conflict can help tap into larger understandings of the situation. Group research on conflict framing shows how conflicts can be addressed through highlighting the frames that are in play and using them to build a new, shared understanding. This reframing can sometimes happen through informal group processes such as asking group members to share their personal stories about the issue at hand (Black, 2013).

For longstanding or intractable conflicts, reframing can happen through formal processes such as negotiation (Putnam, 1990) or **mediation** (Hullman, 2020). Negotiation is a communication process in which people attempt to resolve their conflict by working toward agreement. Negotiation often involves some kind of bargaining, where disputants lay out their grievances and demands, and then work toward a mutually agreeable solution. Group members can approach negotiation distributively, where negotiators attempt to maximize their individual gains, or integratively, where they attempt to integrate the interests of all parties and find solutions that are mutually beneficial (Putnam, 1990; Weingart & Okhelms, 2004). Some formal approaches to negotiation use a moderator to maintain fairness in the process. But group members can engage in negotiation informally within their group, if they do not have access to an outside party to lead the negotiation process.

Conflict mediation is "a communication process in which a neutral third party assists participants" in resolving their conflict (Hullman, 2020, p. 180). Mediators play an important role by structuring the communication process, ensuring fairness, and helping disputants share their perspectives and listen to each other. While most research on negotiation tends to be framed instrumentally, in terms of group members' goals, tactics, and tasks, mediation focuses on conflict framing and relationships.

Mediation involves a neutral party who takes on a particular role to help group members find an agreeable solution to the conflict. Conflict mediators and negotiation moderators are tasked with helping people involved in a conflict find workable solutions that they can all agree to. Yet, mediators also work to highlight the underlying conflict frames and help disputants re-frame the conflict in productive ways. To transform conflict in this way, mediators need to acknowledge and address the emotion involved in conflict (Jameson et al., 2010). Additionally, both negotiation and mediation should take cultural norms into account, especially when conflict occurs within culturally diverse groups.

Conflict and Diversity in Groups

Group scholars have long recognized the value of diversity. Culturally diverse groups can generate more creative ideas, make better decisions, and generally outperform homogenous groups, but to achieve these outcomes groups must communicate in ways that actively include everyone and are mindful of the challenges that can accompany diversity (McLeod et al., 1996; Oetzel, 2002; Zheng & Wei, 2018). Diverse groups can experience conflict in ways that are exacerbated by different cultural expectations, power differences, and differences in communication style (see Chapter 8 for more details). As Moaz and Ellis note, research on conflict resolution has "tended to privilege 'rationality' by foregrounding communication that involves the orderly exchange of ideas and opinion and backgrounding emotions, power asymmetries, and the importance of culture and class" (2006, p. 186). Consequently, traditional conflict management strategies overlook important aspects of diversity and are insufficient for productive conflict engagement in diverse groups.

Intercultural communication and conflict research indicate several important things groups can do to engage diversity appropriately (Broome & Collier, 2012). First, groups should recognize the potential for faultlines, which are "hypothetical dividing lines splitting a group into homogenous subgroups based on the distribution of demographic attributes" (Meyer et al., 2011, p. 257). Groups can mitigate conflict by paying attention to and acknowledging any faultlines that are evident in their group, and reflecting together on why they are occurring in their group. Sometimes groups avoid talking about diversity because they want to develop team cohesion and they seem to think that observing differences between group members will create division. But ignoring faultlines does not make them go away. If conflict develops between cultural subgroups, the conflict is difficult to address until the group can consider how it, perhaps inadvertently, creates or reinforces faultlines.

Second, diverse groups can develop norms that honor diversity and support inclusion. This means that groups should make sure that leaders value diversity (Schölmerich et al., 2016) and understand how to engage people effectively across cultural differences. Group members should develop deeper understandings of how power is related to diversity (Norander & Galanes, 2014), and should embrace, rather than suppress, cultural and social identity differences (Frantell et al., 2019). Diverse groups can manage conflict more successfully if they develop norms that encourage learning from mistakes (Rupert et al., 2019), rather than seeing errors as failures.

Finally, diverse groups are more successful when members develop their intercultural communication skills (Oetzel, 2002; Xu et al., 2019; Zheng & Wei, 2018). In particular, group members should develop their **intercultural conflict competence** (Ting-Toomey, 2009). In general terms, communication competence means communicating in a way that is both effective (i.e., accomplishes goal) and appropriate (i.e., fits the situation and people involved). In an intercultural context, competence also involves adaptability. This means that to communicate across cultural lines, group members need to recognize when to shift the way they are listening and talking to better fit the situation and the context. Intercultural conflict competence involves three components. First, group members should develop *culture-sensitive knowledge*. This means that people should recognize their own cultural expectations and develop knowledge about other cultures. The second component is *mindfulness*, which Ting-Toomey (2009) describes as attending to one's internal communication assumptions, cognitions, and emotions and at the same time, becoming attuned to the other's communication assumptions, cognitions, and emotions. This kind of mindfulness is essential in helping group members develop understanding of themselves and others, which is key to engaging in conflict productively. Finally, group members should develop *constructive conflict communication skills*. This includes skills described earlier, such as active listening, mindful reframing, de-escalation, and collaborative conflict management styles. In intercultural contexts, group members can also develop skills to communicate clearly within and between different sub-groups, such as translation or code-switching, which is the "intentional learning and moving between culturally ingrained systems of behavior" (Ting-Toomey, 2009, p. 103). In sum, diversity is an asset to groups that are enhanced through negotiating conflict in ways that center on mindfulness and cultural competence.

Evidence-Based Recommendations for Practice

As we have argued in this chapter, conflict is a normal part of group life. Although conflict can be uncomfortable, many groups now acknowledge the inevitability of conflict and are working to design group meetings to foster its positive potential. One promising approach is dialogue, which is an evaluated approach to conflict that involves exploratory conversations where facilitators help group members develop mutual understanding. As Black and Wiederhold note, dialogue involves "a structure that encourages people to communicate in ways that are open, respectful, and egalitarian" by promoting "mutual exploration and appreciation of diverse perspectives" (2014, p. 286). Dialogue is "focused on helping groups of people explore ideas deeply and build shared understanding of a common concern… [and helping] transform understandings of a divisive conflict so that groups can work toward collaboration" (2014, p. 287).

Dialogue has been implemented in organizational, educational, and community settings to help groups work through conflicts based on deeply held values (Barge & Andreas, 2013). Dialogue typically involves small groups working closely with facilitators who "provide group guidelines such as 'listen for understanding,' 'respect each other,' or 'everyone should be able to speak,' to help frame the meeting as dialogic" (Black & Wiederhold, 2014, p. 287). Dialogue sessions are carefully designed to prompt group members to think reflectively and listen deeply to one another. Facilitators prepare creative agendas that include open-ended questions that ask group members to reflect on their personal experiences and explore how they developed their understanding of the conflict. Dialogue sessions might involve a combination of reflective writing, talking with partners, going around the circle so each person speaks before engaging in any back-and-forth discussion, or meeting in a variety of smaller subgroups to listen deeply and work through guided questions.

There are a variety of practical approaches to dialogue, and dialogue professionals have recently developed a large community of practice (see National Coalition for Dialogue and Deliberation as an example). Some organizations have adopted dialogue training to help employees manage conflicts (Black, 2005) or address underlying tensions faced by diverse groups. Intergroup dialogue (Frantell et al., 2019) has been used in schools and universities to help diverse groups learn from one another and develop intercultural conflict competence. Similar approaches have been used to mitigate interethnic political conflicts (Moaz & Ellis, 2006) and help build relationships among young people from opposite sides of the conflict. In community settings, nonprofit organizations have developed specific dialogue processes to help groups transform values-based conflicts or address specific local issues and work toward community development and structural change. Community organizations such as school boards and local nonprofit boards frequently face difficult conflicts (Gillispie & Chispeels, 2008; Kerwin et al., 2011; Tracy, 2007) and some engaged group scholars have facilitated dialogues in their local communities to help such groups ethically and effectively address community conflicts (Black, 2020).

These examples point to the importance of intentionally designing group processes that promote dialogic communication. Drawing on Aakhus's (2007) idea of "communication as design," Barge and Andreas (2013) argue that communication scholars can closely study how groups engage in conflict, describe what works and what doesn't, and use those studies to articulate normative ideals of how groups *should* aim to address conflict. The design process is both descriptive and normative and works to create interactional structures that promote new ways of communicating. Designing for dialogue means disrupting the typical conflict interactions, slowing down the conversation, and using dialogic processes to help groups deepen their mutual understanding and transform the conflict frame. The facilitator plays an important role in designing the group process, monitoring how the process is going, and intervening to redirect the group if needed. Unlike mediators who take an active role in finding mutually workable solutions, facilitators help groups to develop their skills so the group members themselves can collaborate on conflict management processes.

Conclusion

This chapter has described how conflict is a natural part of group interaction. Although people often consider conflict to be unpleasant, engaging in conflict can be beneficial for groups. To understand the benefits and challenges of group conflict, it's helpful to identify different kinds of conflict, such as task, relational, and process conflicts. It's also important to remember that people involved in a conflict are likely to frame it differently. This means that people in conflict view the issue, the relationship, themselves, and the other person in particular ways, and those conflict frames can shape how the conflict unfolds in a group. Conflict involves emotion, even if the conflict is ostensibly about a task or process. Conflict also involves power, and this power dynamic can be especially evident in diverse groups.

Often conflict in groups is rooted in group members misunderstanding each other, having different assumptions about group tasks, and failing to communicate with each other about the problem. In most cases, conflict can be addressed by helping group members develop greater communication competence and more complete and nuanced understandings of the conflict. However, sometimes conflict occurs because of some kind of unethical behavior, such as abuse of power, bullying, and/or harassment. These are complicated and very serious problems that can go far beyond the more mundane group conflicts based in misunderstanding. The conflict skills and communication processes we have discussed in this chapter may be helpful in these situations, but ideally such abuse of power should be dealt with as soon as it is detected and will most likely require intervention from an authority figure such as a team leader, manager, HR representative, or teacher.

How conflict is managed often depends on the group members' communication skills, attitudes toward conflict, and the group's norms. Individual group members should develop awareness of their own communication styles and level of comfort with conflict. Group members can also improve their communication skills and develop flexibility in their conflict style. But effective group conflict requires more than members individually developing skills. The group should work together to set shared goals regarding conflict and develop group norms that support constructive conflict engagement. This means the group should set clear expectations for their work, including how group members will hold each other accountable for accomplishing tasks, and how group members should ask for help when they need it.

Groups should also build a supportive group climate of openness and listening, which improves their ability to manage conflict. One way to do this is by developing intercultural communication competence, which helps group members develop awareness of diversity, group member identity, and cultural differences. Group members can minimize misunderstanding and mitigate conflicts by learning about cultural differences and the potential faultlines in their group. Additionally, groups can work together to address conflict productively by developing self-awareness and shifting from competitive to collaborative conflict management approaches.

Sometimes groups need help from an outsider to address the conflict. There are many productive ways to engage conflict, including negotiation, mediation, and dialogue. All of these rely on setting agreements/guidelines about how people involved in the conflict will talk to each other,

Box 10.1   Addressing Identity Faultlines and Conflict in Workshops on Gender in Pakistan

One of the authors of this chapter, Rizvan Saeed, spent several years working with local communities in Pakistan on issues of toxic masculinity and violence against women. These group workshops involved engaging a diverse array of participants including police officers, journalists, members of NGOs, and people who worked in businesses. As organizers, Rizvan and his colleagues made special efforts to include representation from members of marginalized communities. Diversity in these groups also included differences in ethnicities, socio-economic statuses, and political and religious ideologies.

With such diversity in the group, it is perhaps unsurprising that they experienced conflict when discussing gender-based violence. Talk about gender identity highlighted faultlines in the group between participants identifying as men and those identifying as women. These faultlines created rifts in the groups and an "us" versus "them" mentality. Over time, the participants formed cliques based on shared opinions about the acceptability of violence against marginalized groups and its link to toxic masculinity. The views among group members were dramatically different, with some participants even claiming that discrimination or violence against women did not exist. Oppositional viewpoints led to conflict, so facilitators acknowledged participants' feelings through reflective listening and named the conflict happening in the group. Then, they engaged the group in activities designed to help develop empathetic understanding of the different viewpoints around violence against women.

One of the activities involved dividing participants into subgroups based on gender identity. In these subgroups, participants were asked to recall the first time they were made conscious of their gender identity, and to write down their age, who the conversation was with, where they were, and their feelings about the experience. After sharing their stories, participants collated their responses on a large piece of paper, to avoid singling out anyone's response.

Then, the full group came back together and each subgroup shared the summaries they had written. Most of the women shared that they were made aware of their gender and the implications of being a girl around eight or ten years old. Their awareness of femininity coincided with puberty and came along with restrictions on movement and new expectations of how to dress, sit, walk, and present themselves in public. These restrictions made them angry, sad, and confused. In contrast, the men shared that they felt happy, proud, and confident when first becoming aware of their masculinity.

We then asked participants to discuss when and how they started to experience gender segregation. Participants described gender-based separation very early in their lives, including in their families, in games, in school, what clothing was acceptable to wear, and where they were allowed to go as children. During this discussion, we encouraged empathic listening and a group climate of support. This exercise helped participants see issues around violence against women from different perspectives. From this discussion, the *tension between the groups shifted frames, moving from the ways they differed as individuals to an understanding of the social context, which defined their gender identities*. The participants come from different cultural backgrounds, so their level of discomfort with this type of exercise varied. Still, reframing their experiences as socially constructed made gender expectations into something that they all shared. Having this new frame helped reduce the identity-based conflicts and mended some of the faultlines that had developed in the group. Ultimately, the group engaged in a more interactive and constructive discussion.

how they will listen, what kind of outcomes are possible/desirable, and who will decide on the outcome. Creating new communication structures can help group members talk about the conflict in new ways and can help groups transform their understandings of the specific conflict they are facing. These approaches to conflict management can also help groups learn how to approach future conflicts in more productive ways.

Finally, although this chapter has focused predominantly on conflict within groups that meet face to face, it is worth noting that technology has an impact on group conflict. Group research consistently finds that managing conflict in virtual teams is more challenging than in-person settings (Garner, 2022). Frequently cited reasons for this are that technology can take away nonverbal communication, or that people become less concerned with maintaining face for themselves and other group members when shielded behind a computer screen. This consensus about conflict and technology arose from research conducted primarily in an era before video conferencing became part of daily life in many contexts due to the COVID-19 pandemic. Contemporary research (i.e., Karl et al., 2021; Klonek et al., 2022) suggests that using synchronous audio and video technology platforms can lead to successful conflict management, particularly when coupled with intentionally designed communication processes. Technology features shape how people communicate, and group members' response to conflict is impacted by which communication channel people use to express dissent (Garner, 2017). There is a need for future research that considers how conflict is affected by whether the technology used by a group is (a)synchronous, and whether it enables the use of text, audio, and/or video. Further, research should investigate situations where groups employ more than one mode (e.g., group chat and video conferencing) or meet in hybrid in-person/online modes.

Further Readings

Barge, J. K., & Andreas, D. (2013). Communication, conflict, and the design of dialogic conversations. In J. Oetzel & S. Ting-Toomey (Eds.), *The SAGE handbook of conflict management* (2nd ed., pp. 609–634). Sage.

Garner, J. T. (2022). Group conflict. In S. Beck, M. S. Poole, & J. Keyton (Eds.), *The Emerald handbook of group and team communication research* (pp. 245–259). Emerald Publishing.

Nicotera, A. M., & Jameson, J. K. (2021). Conflict in organizations and organizing. In *Oxford research encyclopedia of communication*. Oxford University Press. https://doi.org/10.1093/acrefore/9780190228613.013.1275

Glossary

Conflict framing   An interpretive and communicative process of characterizing what someone believes is important in a conflict. Conflict framing includes how someone sees the cause of the conflict, the people involved, the relationship between the people, and what outcomes are possible. People involved in a conflict can have different frames.

Conflict management styles   Different ways that people address, engage in, and resolve conflict. Styles vary in how much emphasis they place on personal needs versus the needs of the other person involved in the conflict. Example styles are competitive, cooperative, avoidant, accommodating, and collaborative. Individuals tend to have a preferred style but can learn skills to become more flexible and use other styles.

Intercultural conflict competence   The ability to manage conflicts effectively and appropriately in intercultural contexts. Intercultural conflict competence requires that group members develop culture-sensitive knowledge, remain mindful of their own and other group's cultural assumptions about communication, and develop constructive conflict communication skills.

Mediation   An approach to conflict management that involves a neutral third party to assist the participants in resolving their conflict. Mediators use specific communication processes to ensure fairness and help disputants find a mutually agreeable solution to the conflict.

References

Aakhus, M. (2007). Communication as design. *Communication Monographs, 74,* 112–117. https://doi.org/10.1080/03637750701196383

Black, L. W. (2005). Building connection while thinking together: By-products of employee training in dialogue. *Western Journal of Communication, 69,* 273–292. https://doi.org/10.1080/10570310500202421

Black, L. W. (2020). Catalyzing deliberation: How engaged scholarship helped surface community values and transform conflict in local school facilities planning. In P. Kellett, S. Connaughton, & G. Cheney (Eds.), *Transforming conflict and building peace: Community engagement strategies for communication scholarship and practice* (pp. 35–58). Peter Lang Publishers.

Black, L. W. (2013). Framing democracy and conflict through storytelling in deliberative groups. *Journal of Public Deliberation, 9*(1). https://doi.org/10.16997/jdd.153

Black, L. W., & Wiederhold, A. (2014). Discursive strategies of civil disagreement in public dialogue groups. *Journal of Applied Communication Research, 42,* 285–306. https://doi.org/10.1080/00909882.2014.911938

Bodker, A. M., & Jameson, J. K. (2001). Emotion in conflict formation and its transformation: Application to organizational conflict management. *The International Journal of Conflict Management, 12,* 259–275. https://doi.org/10.1108/eb022858

Broome, B. J., & Collier, M. J. (2012). Culture, communication, and peacebuilding: A reflexive, multi-dimensional contextual framework. *Journal of International and Intercultural Communication, 5,* 245–269. http://dx.doi.org/10.1080/17513057.2012.716858

Brummans, B. H. J. M., Putman, L., Gray, B., Hanke, R., Lewicki, R. J., & Wiethoff, C. (2008). Making sense of intractable multiparty conflict: A study of framing in four environmental disputes. *Communication Monographs, 75,* 1–24. https://doi.org/10.1080/03637750801952735

Frantell, K. A., Miles, J. R., & Ruwe, A. M. (2019). Intergroup dialogue: A review of recent empirical research and its implications for research and practice. *Small Group Research, 50,* 654–695. https://doi.org/10.1177/1046496419835923

Garcia-Prieto, P., Bellard, E., & Schneider, S. C. (2003). Experiencing diversity, conflict, and emotions in teams. *Applied Psychology, 52,* 413–440. https://doi.org/10.1111/1464-0597.00142

Garner, J. T. (2017). An examination of organizational dissent events and communication channels: Perspectives of a dissenter, supervisors, and coworkers. *Communication Reports, 30,* 26–38. https://doi.org/10.1080/08934215.2015.1128454

Gillispie, J., & Chispeels, J. H. (2008). Us and them: Conflict, collaboration, and the discursive negotiation of multishareholder roles in school district reform. *Small Group Research, 39,* 397–437. https://doi.org/10.1177/1046496408319877

Goffman, E. (1974). *Frame analysis: An essay on the organization of experience.* Harvard University Press.

Hullman, G. A. (2020). Practicing mediation as an engaged scholar: A personal memoir. In P. M. Kellett, S. L. Connaughton, & G. Cheney (Eds.), *Transforming conflict and building peace: Community engagement strategies for communication scholarship and practice* (pp. 179–192). Peter Lang Publishers.

Jameson, J. K., Bodtker, A. M., & Linker, T. (2010). Facilitating conflict transformation: Mediator strategies for eliciting emotional communication in a workplace conflict. *Negotiation Journal, 26,* 25–48. https://doi.org/10.1111/j.1571-9979.2009.00252.x

Janis, I. L. (1972). *Victims of groupthink: A psychological study of foreign-policy decisions and fiascoes.* Houghton Mifflin.

Jehn, K. A. (1995). A multimethod examination of the benefits and detriments of intragroup conflict. *Administrative Science Quarterly, 40,* 256–282. https://doi.org/10.2307/2393638

Karl, K. A., Peluchette, J. V., & Aghakhani, N. (2021). Virtual work meetings during the COVID-19 pandemic: The good, bad, and ugly. *Small Group Research,* Online First Publication. https://doi.org/10.1177/10464964211015286

Kerwin, S., Doherty, A., & Harman, A. (2011). "It's not conflict, it's differences of opinion": An in-depth examination of conflict in nonprofit boards. *Small Group Research, 42,* 562–594. https://doi.org/10.1177/1046496411398395

Klonek, F. E., Kanse, L., Wee, S., Runneboom, C., & Parker, S. K. (2022). Did the COVID-19 lockdown make us better at working in virtual teams? *Small Group Research, 53,* 185–206. https://doi.org/10.1177/10464964211008991

McLeod, P. L., Lobel, S. A., & Cox, T. H., Jr. (1996). Ethnic diversity and creativity in small groups. *Small Group Research, 27*, 248–264. https://doi.org/10.1177/1046496496272003

Meng, J., Fulk, J., & Yuan, Y. C. (2015). The roles and interplay of intragroup conflict and team emotion management on information seeking behaviors in team contexts. *Communication Research, 42*, 675–700. https://doi.org/10.1177/0093650213476294

Meyer, B., Shemla, M., & Schermuly, C. C. (2011). Social category salience moderates the effect of diversity faultlines on information elaboration. *Small Group Research, 42*, 257–282. https://doi.org/10.1177/1046496411398396

Moaz, I., & Ellis, D. G. (2006). Facilitating groups in severe conflict: The case of transformational dialogue between Israeli-Jews and Palestinians. In L. R. Frey (Ed.), *Facilitating group communication in context: Innovations and applications with natural groups* (pp. 183–203). Hampton Press.

Norander, S., & Galanes, G. (2014). "Bridging the gap": Difference, dialogue, and community organizing. *Journal of Applied Communication Research, 42*, 345–365. http://dx.doi.org/10.1080/00909882.2014.911939

Oetzel, J. G. (2002). The effects of culture and cultural diversity on communication in work groups. In L. R. Frey (Ed.), *New directions in group communication* (pp. 121–137). Sage.

Putnam, L. L. (1990). Reframing integrative and distributive bargaining: A process perspective. In B. H. Sheppard, M. H. Bazerman, & R. J. Lewicki (Eds.), *Research on negotiations in organisations* (Vol. 2). JAl Press.

Putnam, L. L. (2013). Definitions and approaches to conflict and communication. In J. G. Oezel & S. Ting-Toomey (Eds.), *The SAGE handbook of conflict communication* (2nd ed., pp. 1–40). Sage.

Putnam, L. L., & Poole, M. S. (1987). Conflict and negotiation. In F. M. Jablin, L. L. Putnam, K. H. Rogerts, & L. W. Porter (Eds.), *Handbook of organizational communication: An interdisciplinary perspective* (pp. 549–599). Sage.

Rupert, J., Homan, A. C., Jehn, K. A., & Blomme, R. J. (2019). Diversity composition and team learning: The moderating role of error culture. *Group Decision and Negotiation, 28*, 695–722. https://doi.org/10.1007/s10726-019-09626-5

Schölmerich, F., Schermuly, C. C., & Deller, J. (2016). How leaders' diversity beliefs alter the impact of faultlines on team functioning. *Small Group Research, 47*, 177–206. https://doi.org/10.1177/1046496416630960

Tehrani, H. D., & Yamini, S. (2020). Personality traits and conflict resolution styles: A meta-analysis. *Personality and Individual Differences, 157*, 109794. https://doi.org/10.1016/j.paid.2019.109794

Ting-Toomey, S. (2009). Intercultural conflict competence as a facet of intercultural competence development: Multiple conceptual approaches. In D. K. Deardroff (Ed.), *The SAGE handbook of intercultural competence* (pp. 100–119). Sage.

Tracy, K. (2007). The discourse of crisis in public meetings: Case study of a school district's multimillion dollar error. *Journal of Applied Communication Research, 35*, 418–441. https://doi.org/10.1080/00909880701617133

Weingart, L. R., & Okhelms, M. (2004). Communication process in negotiation: Frequencies, sequences, and phases. In M. J. Gelfand & J. M. Brett (Eds.), *The handbook of negotiation and culture* (pp. 143–157). Stanford University Press.

Wittenbaum, G. M., Shulman, H. C., & Braz, M. E. (2010). Social ostracism in task groups: The effects of group composition. *Small Group Research, 41*, 330–353. https://doi.org/10.1177/1046496410363914

Woody Collins, J. (2021). *Affect Theory and racial health inequities: Sparkly feelings making new maps for public health organizing* [Doctoral dissertation, Ohio University].

Xu, N., Chiu, C., & Treadway, D. C. (2019). Tensions between diversity and shared leadership: The role of team political skill. *Small Group Research, 50*, 507–538. https://doi.org/10.1177/1046496419840432

Zheng, W., & Wei, J. (2018). Linking ethnic composition and performance: Information integration between majority and minority members. *Small Group Research, 49*, 357–387. https://doi.org/10.1177/1046496417749727

11 Relational Communication in Groups

Joann Keyton and Stephenson J. Beck

Chapter Objectives

- Distinguish the difference between relational and task messages in group conversations.
- Appreciate the interdependent influence of task and relational dimensions of messages in group conversations.
- Become aware of the variety of relational outcomes associated with group communication.

Relational Communication in Groups

Communication among group members is comprised of verbal and nonverbal messages. Although these messages have a variety of influential dimensions, two primary message orientations are task and relational (Bales, 1950). The focus of this chapter is on **relational messages**, which is based on Keyton's (1999b) definition of relational communication. That is,

> relational communication in groups refers to the verbal and nonverbal messages that create the social fabric of a group by promoting relationships between and among group members. It is the affective or expressive dimension of group communication, as opposed to the instrumental, or task-oriented dimension.
>
> (p. 192)

Teams and groups are often first thought of as *doing something* (e.g., completing a work task, making a decision, playing softball). But group members also rely on their relationships with and among group members to accomplish these tasks (Keyton, 1999b). Relational communication among members creates a group's **communication climate**, cohesion, and identification that are experienced and communicated among group members. While task communication may appear to be most important, relational messages *and* relational outcomes are both central to a group's task interaction and task completion (Paskewitz, 2022).

The verbal and nonverbal messages contributed by members in a group's conversation drive the formation of these relational constructs. However, relational messages among group members are often not as straightforward as **task messages**. Indeed, interpretation of relational messages can be quite complex.

Whereas task messages in group interaction can be straightforward, interpretation of relational messages depends on many additional factors, including who delivers the message, how the message is delivered, the history of the group (including how long the group has been together), and other contextual factors (see Dillard & Solomon, 2000). Additionally, each group member may interpret messages in unique ways, in large part based on (1) the relational history each group member

DOI: 10.4324/9781003227458-13

has with other group members (see Gastil, 2010; Paskewitz, 2022), and (2) individual group members' history with this or other similar groups. These perceptual differences may not appear in a group's earliest interactions, but they will manifest as group members work toward group outcomes.

Studies of group and team development explain why group members' relationships are central to task achievement (see Chapter 6 in this volume). Wheelan et al.'s (1994) review and synthesis of the group development literature found five distinct phases of group interaction: (1) group member formation, (2) dependency of groups members on one another while working on the group tasks, (3) resolution of both relational and task conflict, (4) task interaction, and (5) task completion and relationship resolution. Like other group development models (e.g., Bales, 1950; Tuckman, 1965), these phases can be found in nearly all types of groups. Stages may differ in length, intensity, and focus, yet all groups move through these phases but not necessarily in the same order. More recently, Poole and Dobosh (2010) discovered that group interaction develops simultaneously on three different tracks; these are (1) interpersonal communication, (2) problem solving, and (3) decision making.

For example, many groups develop and organize around task or instrumental goals (e.g., surgery teams, city councils, manufacturing work groups) with relational goals as secondary. However, some types of groups are organized around relational goals (e.g., support groups, friendship groups) with task goals as secondary. Early group research tended to focus on *what the group does*, or its task, rather than *how group member relationships develop and influence* task completion. Indeed, Keyton (1999b) provided a conceptual map of relational communication in groups, which draws attention to the importance of relational communication regardless of the task focus of the group or team. Some messages are task focused; other messages are relationally focused. Relational messages influence variables at both the individual- and group-level (see Figure 11.1).

We tend to consider relational goals as secondary to a group's task goals. However, in practice, relational messages influence both the group task and how group member relationships develop and are sustained.

Researchers have investigated the relational dimension of communication by focusing on different variables and processes. This chapter explores three of these, specifically looking at relational messages, relational groups, and relational outcomes. Additionally, several general methodological approaches used in group and team research are described, with a synthesis on how these approaches represent relational communication in the last section.

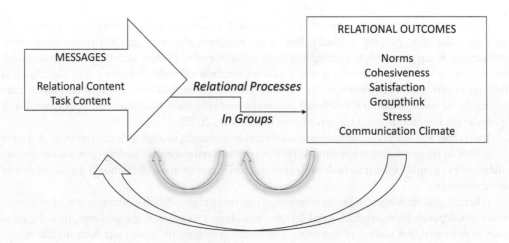

Figure 11.1   Relational Messages, Processes, and Outcomes in Groups (Keyton, 1999b)

Relational Aspects of Messages

The development of all relational dynamics in a group starts with the communication process—that is, group members' messages and interactions. Generally, we tend to evaluate group member interactions as positive or negative. However, it is unlikely that any group member would interact with other group members with only positive messages or only negative messages. More realistically, group members are likely to exchange both types of messages. The ratio of positive and negative relational messages sets a tone for the group's conversation (e.g., mostly friendly, somewhat friendly, neutral, somewhat unfriendly, mostly unfriendly). Of course, group or team members are not only using relational messages, as they are also using task-oriented messages to achieve the group or team's goal. Thus, group members' group interaction is multidimensional.

This is what makes interpretation complex, as group members may use a variety of message dimensions as the basis for determining the meaning and understanding of subsequent interaction. Task messages are often what we consider to be the *work* of a group, and can involve arguments, discussion, clarification, disagreements, and anything else that directly leads to the accomplishment of the group goal. In contrast, the relational dimension is geared toward the social fabric of the group, the underlying relationships, and the requisite relational maintenance essential to group functioning.

In the past, the relational dimension has been considered secondary; however, it is often this aspect of messages and groups that leads to dysfunction. As an example, Keyton (1999a) describes a group member who plays the role of the *primary provoker* as the "group member at the center of the group's negative attention" (p. 494). Unfortunately, other group members can be swept up in the negative tone or comments of one member and actively support—sometimes unknowingly—the provoker's interaction to the extent that other group members become embroiled in negative and dysfunctional behavior as well.

A variety of studies and coding schemes (e.g., Bales, 1950) have relied on the task/relational distinction to investigate group interaction. Many investigations are of necessity isolating one dimension over another. Group interaction is always multidimensional, in that group communication is both task-oriented and relationally-oriented. In others words, labeling a message as primarily task or relational has value, as the surface-level meaning of the message may be quite explicit. But of course, labeling all messages as multidimensional also suggests that all messages have task (i.e., what the message is about) and relational (i.e., how the message is delivered) dimensions, which is also quite true (Keyton, 1999b; Watzlawick et al., 1967).

Just as words can have different meanings, the relational dimension of messages is not static and can refer to many different types of relational influence. For example, there can be direct statements of affinity or support (e.g., "You're are a great teammate!"). There can also be statements that support group identity and comradery (e.g., "I'm glad to be working with this group."). But there is also the relational foundation upon which all interaction is predicated. If you were going to ask for a favor from a group of friends as opposed to your work team, you would certainly prepare your communication differently (for a summary of the different approaches to considering relational messages in groups, see Paskewitz, 2022). And this may very well be a task-oriented message on the surface (e.g., "Would you cover the graveyard shift?"); however, the interpretation of the message may be dependent upon (a) relationships with other members of the group, and/or (b) how the message is perceived as relationally positive or relationally negative. Thus, the relational and task dimensions of messages are interdependent; one cannot fully consider one without the other.

There are a variety of relational message types, or messages that have a predominantly relational and communicative orientation. Early in the study of groups, Bales (1950) distinguished between the task and relational functions of group members' messages in the Interaction Process

Table 11.1 Interaction Process Analysis Functional Codes

Social-emotional area: Position reactions

1   Shows solidarity/seems friendly: Any act that shows positive feelings toward another person
2   Shows tension release/dramatizes: Any act that reduces the anxiety that a person or group may be experiencing
3   Agrees: Any act that shows acceptance of what another person has said

Task area: Attempted answers

4   Gives suggestions: Any act that offers direction/action for how to engage the task
5   Gives opinions: Any act that advances a belief or value that is relevant to the task
6   Gives orientation/information: Any act that reports factual observations or experiences

Task area: Questions

7   Asks for orientation/information: Any act that requests factual observations or experiences
8   Asks for opinions: Any act that requires a belief or value that is relevant to the task
9   Asks for suggestions: Any act that requests direction/action for how to engage the task

Social-emotional area: Negative reactions

10 Disagrees: Any act that shows rejection of what another person has said
11 Shows tension: Any act that indicates that a person is experiencing anxiety
12 Shows antagonism/seems unfriendly: Any act that shows negative feelings toward another person

---

Source: Adapted from Bales (1950).

Analysis (IPA) model. See Table 11.1. The coding scheme developed from the theoretical model allows each message in a group's interaction to be identified as a task function or a relational function. Group interaction messages that serve a task function are: (1) give/ask for suggestions, (2) give/ask for opinions, and (3) give/ask for suggestions. Alternatively, group interaction messages that serve a relational function are those that (1) seem friendly/seem unfriendly, (2) show tension/tension release, and (3) express agreement/disagreement.

Bales IPA coding scheme has been widely used across social science disciplines (see Keyton, 2018), often because it allows researchers to consider how relational messages are used in interaction. In IPA methodology, each members' interactions are coded at the individual level but interpreted at the group level.[1] That is, the meaning of member C's message is dependent on the messages from members A and B that precede member C speaking. In other words, IPA asks us to consider what each message is doing in this group's interaction? What is the goal of this message?

Once a transcript is coded in IPA, it can be compared to other types of group interaction. In Beck's (2008) dissertation, he coded and analyzed three very different types of groups (i.e., a breast cancer support group, a city council, and weekly nonprofit meeting), and found that regardless of type of group, *give orientation/information* messages were most frequent, and *shows antagonism/ seems unfriendly* and *asks for suggestions* were least frequent.

Now, let's look at how relational messages were integrated into the conversations of a weekly breast cancer support group in this same sample. Of the relational messages, positive comments (52.2%) were triple that of negative comments, and "slightly more than half (53.85%) of relational codes were situated between task talk creating segments of task-relational-task talk sequences" (Keyton & Beck, 2009, p. 20). Thus, in this context, relational messages were rarer than task messages, but this does not mean they were less influential. The way they are embedded with task messages suggests that a few relational messages may be quite powerful.

Across many studies using IPA methodology, task communication is more frequent than relational communication in many group types, but that may suggest that frequency is not the same thing as influence. Relational communication is the *glue that holds the group together* as the group works on its task. Without messages that demonstrate agreement, solidarity, friendliness, and without messages to break tension or disagreement or show humor, conversations among group members become terse and tense. Relational communication allows members to be vulnerable and open to information and opinions from others. Most importantly, relational messages allow relationships among group members to emerge and develop. Even human-robot interaction is being evaluated and programmed to mimic group members' relational communication (Laitinen et al., 2021). The IPA coding scheme was used to explore how team members interact with a team-bot. The authors concluded that (a) human-bot communication episodes were shaped by the bot's responses toward more socioemotional and personal functions, and (b) that a team-configured social bot can both display and facilitate relational team communication. Thus, even in human-machine team interaction, relational messages remain important.

Relational communication is also being addressed in online groups (see Chapter 10 in this volume). Early on, Walther and Burgoon (1992) observed that computer-mediated group communication did "develop and evolve in relationally positive directions" (p. 76). More recent research suggests that online environments can be quite dynamic but may require longer time to convey relational cues or appropriately match media to the task (Ledbetter, 2014; Walther, 1996). Pena and Hancock (2006) found that more experienced members of online multiplayer video games used more relational messages in their game playing, suggesting a greater need to account for relationships even while participating in a game based on fighting. Certainly the COVID-19 pandemic resulted in increased use of virtual formats for group interaction, and conveying relational messages through digital formats with their multimodal options (e.g., visual, chat, screen share, options to mute audio or video) can be tricky (Blanchard, 2021).

Relational Groups

Certain groups have overarching relational purposes or goals. In other words, the primary task of the group is creating and maintaining relationships among group members. In this sense, relational groups are like any other group that is trying to accomplish the group's purpose. Since relationships are not something accomplished or complete, relational groups may have goals that cannot be easily measured or assessed. For example, families are certainly a relational group as Barker et al. (2000) pointed out and should be studied as a unit. And there may be goals that a family sets or accomplishes (e.g., saving money for a new car, cleaning the garage). However, social relations among family members, and maintaining those relationships, are often considered the purpose of the family, and these goals may not have an easily identifiable, final outcome. Interestingly, a family's relational goals may be, and often are, assessed throughout the family relationship (e.g., How could our family be more supportive of one another?), but there is often no deadline for such a goal. Thus, maintaining positive relationships among family members is the general task of this group.

Other relational groups do not have an overarching group goal, but instead come together in order to facilitate the accomplishment of individual goals. Social support groups, of which there are more than 500,000 in the United States (Community Tool Box, n.d.), are good examples of such a group. Social support groups "are composed of members who are experiencing a similar disease or condition and desire further help from those who understand their difficulties" (Beck & Keyton, 2014, p. 37). Individuals become a member of these groups to receive information, emotional assistance, or tangible resources (Cutrona, 1996). In fact, one of the benefits of these groups is that not only can members receive support from others in similar situations, but helping others can also be cathartic to the giver. Note that in social support groups, there is not an easily identifiable group goal; rather, group members collectively share the goal of helping each other accomplish their individual goals. Thus, sometimes it takes facilitators with a unique skillset to run these groups (Paskewitz & Beck, 2018). Kang (2017) investigated an online social support group and found that support group members give more support than ask for support, and that support group members are more likely to send positive messages rather than negative ones, which supports earlier findings by Keyton and Beck (2009). Further, Kang found members who included a visual representation of themselves received more positive and supportive messages than members who remained visually anonymous.

The following excerpt comes from data in Keyton and Beck's (2009, p. 2014) breast cancer support group studies and illustrates how relational groups use both task-oriented and relationally-oriented talk in their weekly support group meeting. Teresa has been in the support group the longest, and serves as the unofficial leader of the group. Teresa tends to informally lead the group by encouraging each member to have the opportunity to talk during their weekly one-hour meetings.

Lisa: I'm Lisa. A year ago September 25th, I had a mastectomy, and then August 25th of this year, I had the left mastectomy and I'm just happy to be here with people who've had 11 years. [Lisa is reflecting on the conversation before she spoke in which a member revealed she has survived breast cancer for 11 years.]

Teresa: And your? … everythings done? Your surgeries and your [reconstruction]?

Lisa: Everything's done.

Teresa: How do you feel?

Lisa: I'm beginning to feel well. I'm beginning to have some energy.

Teresa: You're not back to the school …

Lisa: No, I'm not back to school yet. I'm going to try to go back on Monday. Wish me luck.

Prior to this excerpt, other group members were *checking in* with the group. Some provided health updates; other members said hello to the group by describing what happened that week, such as medical appointments and community breast cancer events. The unstated format of this support group is that everyone present is allowed to *check in* before extended and more interactive exchanges among members begin. This type of opening format contributes to the positive relational function of the group. Also notice how Teresa's comments to Lisa express concern and demonstrate solidarity—two common elements of relational communication. See End-of-Week Business Meeting for another example related to task-oriented groups.

Unlike task-oriented groups that are given or choose a task that all members work toward, social groups (i.e., a group of friends) are different. Each group member has personal needs, and a group goal may be difficult to identify and assess. Moreover, membership in the group may be more fluid. Still, group members will have varying types of influences. For example, Goins (2011) examined the rich interaction that occurred in a friendship group of Black women. This study revealed that in their group interaction with friends, multiple topics of conversation were meaningful, including conversations about financial issues, satisfaction with their appearance (style of dress, hair, makeup), and racial language acceptance. Thus, the group discussion was a "safe homeplace of their friendship groups," which helped them "to manage societal tensions … by simultaneously showing their connection to and distance from the dominant discourses of U.S. society" (p. 543). As another example of relational communication in friend groups, Adams (2013) found that members of a role-playing group fulfilled some social needs as their conversations addressed issues of democracy, friendship, extraordinary experiences, and ethics.

End-of-Week Business Meeting

Consider the following excerpt. This end-of-the week business meeting is an opportunity for team members to describe to others what they accomplished and to make others aware of changes in their business.

Jim: Well, let's stop adding people to the list.
Katie: Okay, that's sort of what I was going to recommend.
Jim: Your paperwork is going to need to change.
Don: Let it phase itself out?
Jim: Yeah, so Beth—Beth, you're going to have to get rid of the ACH payment thing.
Katie: And the Web will also need to
Jim: And we take credit cards only, and that's it.
Katie: Right. But, it can be a ...

Do you see the differences in this transcript as compared to the breast cancer support group? In the business meeting, members are giving suggestions, opinions, and information to one another. Only the "okay" and "right" are signaling relational support from one member to others.

Relational Communication in Organizational Task Groups

Relational communication is also found in organizational groups and teams (i.e., task-oriented) which have been the focus of most communication research. Early on, Larson and LaFasto (1989) identified a collaborative climate as a characteristic of high performing work groups. For communication scholars, **relational constructs** such as cohesion, satisfaction, and a positive communication climate illustrate the role of relational communication in task-oriented groups. Susskind and Odom-Reed (2019) reported from their study of 12 project teams that team cohesion developed in the early months and/or the last four months positively influenced team member performance.

Relational Outcomes

While using transcripts of group meetings is often the primary way to examine group interaction, not all research can be conducted by recording, observing, and/or listening to a group's conversation. In such instances, researchers rely on questionnaires to capture group members' perceptions of relational constructs. In these instances, group members are reporting on their overall perception of a relational outcome at the end of a group's meeting or at the conclusion of the group. Thus, the constructs presented in this section refer to attitudes and evaluative perceptions group members have about the totality of the group communication experience. Each group member responds to the same questionnaire and then scores are created for each group member and each group. These constructs include: cohesion, communication climate, satisfaction, trust, and norms.

Cohesion

Cohesion (or cohesiveness) is achieved when the group's conversation encourages group members to remain a member of the group. That is, each group member has a desire to be a group member and be committed to the group's task (Whitton & Fletcher, 2014). Both task cohesion and social cohesion are important. Social cohesion is based on the quality of relationships among group members, whereas task cohesion is based on commitment to the group's task (Hackman, 1992).

For example, sports teams desire a cohesive team environment (Turman, 2003, 2008). Why? When team members are cohesive, they are using communication to create and develop social relationships that can be leveraged to improve the physical tasks required in sport performance. Indeed Cranmer et al. (2020) point out that when coaches encourage student athletes to further develop their physical skills, doing so confirms for them (and others) of their potential and thereby signals their role on and their value to the team. Thus, student athletes become more confident, which leads to a greater rate of winning and a greater sense of cohesion.

Cohesion among group members is developed from the verbal and nonverbal messages team members share in a group; interestingly, the role of language mimicry among group members has also been reported as evidence of cohesion (Gonzales et al., 2010). Knowing how to contribute to cohesion in a group is one goal; knowing how to counteract the negative effects of bullying and whining on cohesiveness is also helpful as Henningsen and Henningsen (2020) found that whining and bullying reduce group cohesiveness.

Satisfaction

Much like cohesion, group member satisfaction develops during a group's interaction events. The decision to spend time with other group or team members is often based on how satisfied one is with the interaction in that group or team. Thus, satisfaction is "a holistic, affective response to the success of behaviors that are selected based on group members' expectations" (Marston & Hecht, 1988, p. 236). However, when Keyton (1991) asked research participants to describe their satisfaction with a group interaction, they clearly distinguished between behaviors that were satisfying (e.g., everyone supports each other) and behaviors that were dissatisfying (e.g., group members have a tendency to talk at the same time). This outcome suggested that satisfaction was not a one-dimensional construct on which a group member would score high (indicating satisfaction) or low (indicating dissatisfaction). Moreover, participants' data revealed greater consistency when evaluating the dissatisfying statements. That is, people *know* more specifically when they are dissatisfied than when they are satisfied in group interaction.

Communication Climate

Addressing a group or team's communication climate is another way to acknowledge how messages from group members to one another create an overall ambience or tone (Gibson & Gibbs, 2006). Groups can develop a defensive or negative climate if group members send messages that express strategic or superiority intent. Likewise, defensive messages are those that explicitly or implicitly control or evaluate other group members. Finally, defensive messages can also be neutral (i.e., a group member refuses to express an opinion) or express certainty (e.g., a group member announces he or she is correct and will not entertain other alternatives).

Alternatively, a group will develop a supportive or positive communication climate if group members send messages that describe rather than evaluate problems. Taking a problem orientation in group discussions is supported by the expression of spontaneity, empathy, equality, and provisionalism (Gibson & Gibbs, 2006). A positive communicate climate exists when culturally diverse team members feel comfortable in speaking up and participating in a group's activities and goals. This type of positive team climate encourages group members to share information that they uniquely hold to become part of the group discussion. Creating a positive communicate climate is especially important when group members are culturally diverse. When culturally diverse individuals are comfortable speaking up and participating in decision making, the group has created an environment that provides a psychologically safe communication climate. When a positive climate is present, diversity among team members leads to greater innovation among group members (Gibson & Gibbs, 2006). While groups will vary in their need for a supportive climate, all groups require some level of supportiveness to maintain interdependence among members to accomplish the group task or activity.

An alternative approach is to adopt Oetzel et al.'s (2012) conceptualization and label of *interaction climate*. Although developed and tested in intercultural group settings, the underlying foundation of interaction climate is both communicatively based and outcome driven. Moreover, interaction climate includes "several communication behaviors that are associated positively with task and relational outcomes: cooperative conflict, respectful communication, consensus decisions making, and participation" (Oetzel et al., 2012, p. 148). This more recent conceptualization is attractive as it captures "the general tone of the group's interaction in terms of cooperation, participation, and respect" (p. 148). Indeed, in a later study conducted on physician teams in a simulated environment, Kirschbaum et al. (2015) examined the interaction of medical teams and found that physicians who increased interdependence and decreased independence were likely to "engage in communication that contributes to positive climate and participatory teamwork" (p. 324).

Group Norms

As group and team members communicate and make progress toward their goals, group norms, or expectations about group members' behavior, develop that are specific to their particular group (Manata, 2019). Groups develop communication norms as they interact. Although some group norms, such as being on time for meetings and participating in discussion, are considered common to all groups, if and how norms are expressed and evaluated by a group tend to be group specific. For example, a work group can be strict about members attending group meetings and arriving on time; a group of friends that meet regularly may be looser with their attendance norm and know that a quick text to a member of the group will excuse their lateness.

One of the more problematic norms in group and team meetings is when two members have a side conversation. These dyadic conversations can have either a positive or negative influence on the group conversation. For example, when group unity is needed to make progress on their goal, "the absence of dyadic communication results in a stronger focus on the group.... However, in problem-solving tasks that benefit from faction-forming, the mere presence of dyadic communication opportunities leads to increased openness to unique information, disagreement, and group performance" (Swaab et al., 2008, p. 384). Thus, the norm of holding dyadic side conversations in group meetings is evaluated based on the group or team's context. For example, holding side conversations in informal meetings may be acceptable, but doing so in more formal meetings may be discouraged (Kauffeld & Lehmann-Willenbrock, 2012).

Evidence-Based Recommendations for Practice

The material in this chapter highlighting the complexity of task and relational messages suggests many implications for group members and facilitators of groups. For example, Paskewitz and Beck (2018) conducted a study exploring how member-leader behaviors helped support and facilitate an online discussion board dedicated to depression. The research found that although leaders used primarily task-oriented messages when interjecting into group discussion, these messages were geared toward helping others attribute meaning and establish a sense of self. In other words, these task-oriented messages were accomplishing multiple objectives, including those with relational goals and outcomes. Instead of focusing on the facilitation of the material on the discussion board, the member-leaders instead focused on encouraging others to consider other people's perspectives. Thus, task messages can have task and relational outcomes, and group members should consider these multiple influences when developing their messages.

Other studies have also looked precisely at how relational messages were used in face-to-face support groups. In the instance of a breast cancer support group, Keyton and Beck (2009) investigated specific relational messages that support group leaders used to facilitate discussion. They found that relational messages were used in conjunction with task messages to accomplish a myriad of facilitation functions, including showing agreement and disagreement and showing solidarity with other group members. Clearly task and relational messages are used interdependently to accomplish a host of task and relational outcomes. Importantly, Keyton and Beck also pointed out that frequency of these message types does not have to be high to be influential. For example, task messages were the dominant message type in these groups, but the uniqueness or more rare nature of relational messages add to their influence. The overall tone of these meetings was supportive, suggesting that relational messages were successful in creating a positive climate. Since they are more rare and potentially more influential, group members may need to be more intentional in remembering to share relational messages. Of course, too many positive relational messages could potentially have a counteracting effect on the climate.

In groups, the sequential flow of group interaction certainly plays an important role in relational influence and outcomes. Group members develop norms about the positive or negative tone of their messages to one another. When an alternating pattern of friendly-then-unfriendly communication persists, "group members were more likely to identify their group as dysfunctional and to identify that dysfunction with one group member" (Keyton, 1999a, p. 513). Thus, **interaction patterns** created by the group and team members are important. Dysfunctional interaction in groups and teams can manifest as negative feelings, reduced trust, and member withdrawal from the group's interaction (Felps et al., 2006). If group norms include dysfunctional relational communication patterns, facilitators may need to intervene and steer the group toward better norms.

Perhaps the overarching finding is that task and relational messages, processes, and outcomes are intrinsically linked. The managing of such interdependent dynamics is essential for groups to function well, and group members are always balancing these dynamics in all types of tasks, whether explicitly relational or not. Given the complexity of navigating this type of interaction, group facilitators may be especially important. In fact, facilitation may be defined in terms of balancing task and relational dynamics of group interaction to accomplish a variety of goals acceptable to all parties. Studies suggest that success in achieving stronger connections among group members lead to more effective and dynamic outcomes (Seddon & Biasutti, 2009). The task and relational framework can be helpful for understanding group successes and failure in accomplishing these outcomes. There are many ways that groups can develop these closer connections. Bormann (1985) portrays storytelling as a primary way for groups to develop this rapport, with such experiences leading to higher cohesion among group members (Zanin et al., 2016). More recently, Paskewitz (2022) highlighted four important stages of relational development of groups that can be examined through group interaction. These are investigating, initiating, integrating, and interconnecting.

Importantly, the way scholars consider relational aspects of relational communication determines their methodological choices. If interested in how group members perceive the group in terms of climate or satisfaction or trust, then closed-ended survey questions and subsequent quantitative analysis are in order. If the consideration of how group members negotiate relational dynamics is of interest, then an analysis of specific messages and message sequences is required.

Communication scholars are especially adept at considering the latter, often through message-based analyses (e.g., content analysis, interaction analysis, conversational analysis). Finally, relational constructs can be measured at the individual and/or aggregated to the group level (Bonito & Keyton, 2019). Some relational constructs such as satisfaction "can be expressed toward the task, individual members in the group, or the group as a whole" (p. 3). Thus, when conceptualizing and operationalizing relational constructs, researchers should be clear in what they are measuring, and if they are interested in measurement at the individual or group level.

We encourage scholars to not neglect message-based analysis, and to limit claims about relational communication when only considering retrospective measurements of relational variables. Combining the two would be a helpful avenue for future research.

Summary

There are relational aspects to all message, whether in the message itself or the foundation upon which it is predicated. Some groups are relational by their very nature, and other times they are task-oriented with an essential relational groundwork upon which communication is predicated. Of course, there are also relational outcomes, which often are how a group's long-term success is determined. The interdependent nature of the task and relational aspect of messages, processes, and outcomes are important to navigate for group success, both for members and leaders. Groups that are successful in navigating these have shown to be more effective and satisfied.

Note

1 The content of the message can be the target of a secondary analysis once a group's conversation is first coded with IPA. For example, these constructs include affinity, cohesion, communication climate, group identity, group member relationships, relationship maintenance, satisfaction, and social support.

Further Readings

Burgoon, J. K., & Hale, J. L. (1984). The fundamental topoi of relational communication. *Communication Monographs, 51*(3), 193–214. https://doi.org/10.1080/03637758409390195
Lehmann-Willenbrock, N., Meyers, R. A., Kauffeld, S., Neininger, A., & Henschel, A. (2011). Verbal interaction sequences and group mood: Exploring the role of team planning communication. *Small Group Research, 42*(6), 639–668. https://doi.org/10.1177/1046496411398397

Glossary

Communication climate   Communication climate is the overall ambience, or mood, of the group. A group's communication climate can be positive or negative and develops from group members' relative balance of positive or negative messages.
Interaction patterns   Interaction patterns are the sequential flow of team members' interaction. Patterns may be positive or negative.
Relational constructs   Relational constructs are group attributes that describe and/or assess the type and direction of relational communication among group members. Positive relational constructs include cohesion, satisfaction, and positive group communication climate. Relational constructs emerge through group members' relational messages.
Relational messages   Relational messages are those that create and maintain relationships among group members. These messages are dependent on several factors, including who delivers the

message, how the message is delivered, and the history of the group. Relational messages are interdependent with task messages.

Task messages   Task messages are verbal and nonverbal communication about the activity or goal of the group. These messages are the work of the group. Task messages are interdependent with relational messages.

References

Adams, A. S. (2013). Needs met through role-playing games: A fantasy theme analysis of Dungeons & Dragons. *Kaleidoscope: A Graduate Journal of Qualitative Communication Research*, *12*, 69–86.

Bales, R. F. (1950). *Interaction process analysis*. Addison-Wesley.

Barker, V. E., Abrams., J. R., Tiyaamornwong, V., Seibold, D. R., Duggan, A., Park, H. S., & Sebastian, M. (2000). New contexts for relational communication in groups. *Small Group Research*, *31*(4), 470–503. https://doi.org/10.1177/104649640003100405

Beck, S. J. (2008). *The communicative creation of meetings: An interaction analysis of meeting thought units and meeting activities in three natural meeting contexts* [Dissertation and theses]. ProQuest (3311376).

Beck, S. J., & Keyton, J. (2014). Facilitating social support: Member-leader communication in a breast cancer support group. *Cancer Nursing*, *37*, E36–43. https://doi.org/10.1097/NCC.0b013e3182813829

Blanchard, A. L. (2021). The effects of COVID-19 on virtual working within online groups. *Group Processes & Intergroup Relations*, *24*(2), 290–296. https://doi.org/10.1177/1368430220983446

Bonito, J. A., & Keyton, J. (2022). A valence-based account of group interaction and decision making. *Communication Monographs*, *89*(2), 260–280. https://doi.org/10.1080/03637751.2021.1998565

Bormann, E. G. (1985). Symbolic convergence theory: A communication formulation. *Journal of Communication*, *35*(4), 128–138. https://doi.org/10.1111/j.1460-2466.1985.tb02977.x

Community tool box. (n.d.). https://ctb.ku.edu/en/table-of-contents/implement/enhancing-support/peer-support-groups/main

Cranmer, G., Ash, E., Fontana, J. L., & Mikkilineni, S. (2020). Communication for the win: Task benefits of coach confirmation in collegiate athletics. *Communication Quarterly*, *68*(5), 539–559. https://doi.org/10.1080/01463373.2020.1850491

Cutrona, C. E. (1996). *Social support in couples*. Sage.

Dillard, J. P., & Solomon, D. H. (2000). Conceptualizing context in message-production research. *Communication Theory*, *10*(2), 167–175. https://doi.org/10.1111/j.1468-2885.2000.tb00186.x

Felps, W., Mitchell, T. R., & Byington, E. (2006). How, when, and why bad apples spoil the barrel: Negative group members and dysfunctional groups. *Research in Organizational Behavior*, *27*, 175–222. https://doi.org/10.1016/S0191-3085(06)27005-9

Gastil, J. (2010). *The group in society*. Sage.

Gibson, C. B., & Gibbs, J. L. (2006). Unpacking the concept of virtuality: The effects of geographic dispersion, electronic dependence, dynamic structure, and national diversity on team innovation. *Administrative Science Quarterly*, *51*(3), 451–495. https://doi.org/10.2189/asqu.51.3.451

Goins, M. (2011). Playing with dialectics: Black female friendship groups as a homeplace. *Communication Studies*, *62*(5), 531–546. https://doi.org/10.1080/10510974.2011.584934

Gonzales, A. L., Hancock, J. T., & Pennebaker, J. W. (2010). Language style matching as a predictor of social dynamics in small groups. *Communication Research*, *37*(1), 3–19. https://doi.org/10.1177/0093650209351468

Hackman, J. R. (1992). *Group influences on individuals in organizations*. Consulting Psychologists Press.

Henningsen, D. D., & Henningsen, M. L. M. (2020). Nuanced aggression in group decision making. *International Journal of Business Communication*, *57*(1), 145–158. https://doi.org/10.1177/2329488417704951

Kang, K. K. (2017). Anonymity and interaction in an online breast cancer social support group. *Communication Studies*, *68*(4), 403–421. https://doi.org/10.1080/10510974.2017.1340902

Kauffeld, S., & Lehmann-Willenbrock, N. (2012). Meetings matter: Effects of team meetings on team and organizational success. *Small Group Research*, *43*(2), 130–158. https://doi.org/10.1177/1046496411429599

Keyton, J. (1991). Evaluating individual group member satisfaction as a situational variable. *Small Group Research*, *22*(2), 200–219. https://doi.org/10.1177/1046496491222004

Keyton, J. (1999a). Analyzing interaction patterns in dysfunctional teams. *Small Group Research*, *30*(4), 491–518. https://doi.org/10.1177/104649649903000405

Keyton, J. (1999b). Relational communication in groups. In L. R. Frey, D. S. Gouran, & M. S. Poole (Eds.), *The handbook of group communication theory & research* (pp. 192–222). Sage.

Keyton, J. (2018). Interaction process analysis (IPA). In E. Brauner, M. Boos, & M. Kolbe (Eds.), *Cambridge Handbook of group interaction analysis* (pp. 441–449). Cambridge University Press.

Keyton, J., & Beck, S. J. (2009). The influential role of relational messages in group interaction. *Group Dynamics: Theory, Research and Practice*, *13*(1), 14–30. https://doi.org/10.1037/a0013495

Kirschbaum, K. A., Rask, J. P., Fortner, S. A., Kulesher, R., Nelson, M. T., Yen, T., & Brennan, M. (2015). Physician communication in the operating room. *Health Communication*, *30*(4), 317–327. https://doi.org/10.1080/10410236.2013.856741

Laitinen, K., Laaksonen, S.-M., & Koivula, M. (2021). Slacking with the bot: Programmable social bot in virtual team interaction. *Journal of Computer-Mediated Communication, Advance Article*. https://doi.org/10.1093/jcmc/zmab012

Larson, C. E., & LaFasto, F. M. (1989). *Teamwork: What must go right/what can go wrong*. Sage.

Ledbetter, A. M. (2014). The past and future of technology in interpersonal communication theory and research. *Communication Studies*, *65*(4), 456–459. https://doi.org/10.1080/10510974.2014.927298

Manata, B. (2019). The structural effects of team density and normative standards on team member performance. *Human Communication Research*, *45*(3), 309–333. https://doi.org/10.1093/hcr/hqz003

Marston, P. J. & Hecht, M. L. (1988). Group satisfaction. In R. S. Cathcart & L. A. Samovar (Eds.), *Small group communication: A reader* (pp. 236–246). Brown.

Oetzel, J., McDermott, V., Torres, A., & Sanchez, C. (2012). The impact of individual differences and group diversity on group interaction climate and satisfaction: A test of the effective intercultural workgroup communication theory. *Journal of International & Intercultural Communication*, *5*(2), 144–167. https://doi.org/10.1080/17513057.2011.640754

Paskewitz, E. A. (2022). Creating and maintain group relationships. In S. J. Beck, J. Keyton, & M. S. Poole's (Eds.), *The Emerald handbook of group and team communication research* (pp. 289–302). Emerald.

Paskewitz, E. A., & Beck, S. J. (2018). Exploring member-leader behaviors and interaction in an online support group. *Small Group Research*, *49*(4), 452–474. https://doi.org/10.1177/1046496418763889

Pena, J., & Hancock, J. T. (2006). An analysis of socioemotional and task communication in online multiplayer video games. *Communication Research*, *33*(1), 92–109. https://doi.org/10.1177/0093650205283103

Poole, M. S., & Dobosh, M. (2010). Group decision-making. In C. Berger, M. Roloff, & D. Roskos-Ewoldsen (Eds.), *Handbook of communication science* (2nd ed., pp. 381–397). Sage.

Seddon, F. A., & Biasutti, M. (2009). Modes of communication between members of a string quartet. *Small Group Research*, *40*(2), 115–137. https://doi.org/10.1177/1046496408329277

Susskind, A. M., & Odom-Reed, P. R. (2019). Team member's centrality, cohesion, conflict, and performance in multi-university geographically distributed project teams. *Communication Research*, *46*(2), 151–178. https://doi.org/10.1177/0093650215626972

Swaab, R. I., Phillips, K. W., Diermeier, D., & Husted Medvec, V. (2008). The pros and cons of dyadic side conversations in small groups: The impact of group norms and task type. *Small Group Research*, *39*(3), 372–390. https://doi.org/10.1177/1046496408317044

Tuckman, B. W. (1965). Developmental sequences in small groups. *Psychological Bulletin*, *63*(6), 384–399. https://doi.org/10.1037/h0022100

Turman, P. D. (2003). Coaches and cohesion: The impact of coaching techniques on team cohesion in the small group sport setting. *Journal of Sport Behavior*, *26*, 86–103.

Turman, P. D. (2008). Coaches' immediacy behaviors as predictors of athletes' perceptions of satisfaction and team cohesion. *Western Journal of Communication*, *72*(2), 162–179. https://doi.org/10.1080/10570310802038424

Walker, R. C., Cardon, P. W., & Aritz, J. (2018). Enhancing global virtual small group communication skills. *Journal of Intercultural Communication Research*, *47*(5), 421–433. https://doi.org/10.1080/17475759.2018.1475292

Walther, J. (1996). Computer-mediated communication: Impersonal, interpersonal and hyperpersonal interaction. *Communication Research*, *23*(1), 3–42. https://doi.org/10.1177/009365096023001001

Walther, J. B., & Burgoon, J. K. (1992). Relational communication in computer-mediated interaction. *Human Communication Research*, *19*(1), 50–88. https://doi.org/10.1111/j.1468-2958.1992.tb00295.x

Watzlawick, P., Beavin, J., & Jackson, D. (1967). *Pragmatics of human communication: A study of interactional patterns, pathologies, and paradoxes*. Norton.

Wheelan, S. A., McKeage, R. L., Verdi, A. F., Abraham, M., Krasick, C., & Johnton, F. (1994). Communication and development patterns in a system of interacting groups. In L. R. Frey (Ed.), *Group communication in context: Studies of natural groups* (pp. 153–180). Erlbaum.

Whitton, S. M., & Fletcher, R. B. (2014). The Group Environment Questionnaire: A multilevel confirmatory factor analysis. *Small Group Research*, *45*(1), 68–88. https://doi.org/10.1177/1046496413511121

Zanin, A. C., Hoelscher, C. S., & Kramer, M. W. (2016). Extending symbolic convergence theory: A shared identity perspective of a team's culture. *Small Group Research*, *47*(4), 438–472. https://doi.org/10.1177/1046496416658554

12 Language and Social Influence

Lyn M. van Swol, Chen-Ting Chang, and Runzhi Mary Lu

Chapter Objectives

- Understand language analysis as a methodological tool to analyze group processes.
- Connect group inputs, processes, and outputs to language use in groups.
- Explore how language in a group can have implications for social influence.

Introduction

Group members communicate and influence each other to reach outcomes that add value to individual members, the group itself, and community in which groups live (McGrath et al., 2000). Communication is essential to the development of group processes and **emergent states**, which are cognitive, affective, and behavioral characteristics that develop from group interaction into a collective level attribute that affect the outputs from group interaction. Integral to communication is language. In other words, the way members communicate and the language they use uncovers much about what is going on in the group. To study groups, understanding how communication unfolds through use of language is important. The study of language in group communication and processes has often been difficult and time-consuming, but technological advancements in the transcription and encoding of group communication have facilitated the study of language in group communication.

Research in the 1950s involved multiple observers taking notes and coding in order to categorize communication in interacting groups (Bales, 1950). Starting in the 1980s with the beginning of less expensive and more portable recording technology, researchers could record group interactions to transcribe and code at a later time, with the option to review the interaction multiple times. Still, the human labor of transcription and accurate coding limited this research. Because of these constraints, research directly examining language patterns in groups was often limited, both in terms of the sophistication of the coding scheme and the amount of group discussions that could be analyzed. Rather, researchers focused on how inputs like the configuration of individual member information and opinions could indirectly affect outputs in the group (e.g., Davis, 1973; Laughlin & Ellis, 1986; Stasser & Titus, 1985). However, a methodological transformation has been underway in the study of group communication with the availability of online group communication, cheap and semi-automated transcription, and the availability of software for coding language in groups. With these new methods, theory is changing to adapt to the influx of data that is now available to researchers. In this chapter, we specifically focus on using language software to analyze group communication. First, we provide an overview of some of the software programs available to researchers. Second, we introduce theory on group processes and emergent states that can help understand the effects of language in groups on social influence and group outputs, such as team

DOI: 10.4324/9781003227458-14

performance and member satisfaction. Last, we specifically review some of the language variables that are especially important for social influence in groups, including pronoun use, language matching and similarity, complexity of language, and emotional language.

Research Methods

Research is driven by the interplay of three forces: theory, available methods, and empirical data (Brinberg & McGrath, 1985). Methods are the "instruments, techniques, and procedures" available to gather and interpret empirical data (McGrath, 1984, p. 28). While methods are often in the background, methods can limit what empirical data is available and what theories one can operationalize into testable hypotheses. McGrath (1984, p. 28) notes "you can't pound a nail if you don't have a hammer." For example, in the 1970s and 1980s, given the methodological limitations of obtaining interacting group empirical data, research on group interaction was limited. Changes in group communication research in the last decade have been driven by methodological advances, which have changed what empirical data is available and what hypotheses can now be tested. In the following, we provide an overview of some methods for analyzing language in group communication.

Methods for Language Analysis in Groups

Researchers can use questionnaire methods with forced-choice or free-response self-report questions to understand factors like emotions in group communication, but questionnaire self-report data has several disadvantages. Participants may be primed by questions, such that the question itself (e.g., Please rate how happy you feel) can elicit the emotion, or participants may be unable to label their emotions in open-ended questions. Computer software can overcome challenges to understanding the emotional valence and sentiment in verbal communication in a reliable fashion. In addition, computer software tools can code for frequency of other types of language, like use of specific pronouns or language complexity. Tools like the **Linguistic Inquiry Word Count (LIWC)** can help researchers analyze semantic features in verbal communication automatically. In the following, we discuss LIWC in more detail as it is the most commonly used program.

LIWC is a software program that analyzes words in a transcript by comparing every word with the software's validated internal dictionaries of up to 74 linguistic categories, ranging from function words like pronouns to content words such as adjectives and verbs (Pennebaker et al., 2015). In addition, LIWC has composite measures that combine several language categories; these include categories that measure amount of clout or authenticity in language. A high score of clout language indicates the speaker is confident, and authenticity signifies the speaker is honest and the discourse is personal (Pennebaker et al., 2015). After running a transcript through LIWC, the output produces a percentage of words in each category. For example, the category "negative emotion" includes words like angry, hurt, and crying, and the category "family" includes words like daughter, aunt, and dad. Thus, if someone says to a person, "My dad was very angry at me because I hurt my cousin Judy. He scolded me and made me cry," This text would score high in the category "negative emotion," "family," as well as "I" pronouns, since the speaker used "my," "I," and "me" several times. The analysis shows that the speaker experienced and conveyed negative emotions and the event involved familial relationships. When analyzing transcripts in LIWC, one can analyze at the group level or create a separate file for each group member. The LIWC user guide is short and easy to understand, and a novice could read through the user guide and be ready to run files through LIWC in a couple hours. In fact, if you want to try LIWC, you can even cut and paste text into their website (https://www.liwc.app/demo) to test it. For example, we cut and pasted this paragraph into LIWC and found that it was high in negative emotional tone. See Box 12.1 for another example comparing two samples of text.

Box 12.1   Language Use under Intimacy and Information Conditions

In the study by van Swol et al. (2022), researchers found that fostering intimacy in groups can increase the group's ability to reach consensus in online discussions on polarized topics like climate change. In the study, before groups discussed a solution for climate change, some groups first engaged in a conversation that fostered intimacy (intimacy condition), whereas other groups only talked about information on climate change (information condition). Following is a transcript excerpt from each condition.

Discussion in Intimacy Condition

Participant A: I personally think that the government should have no intervention in climate change. It should be the individual choice in the matter, you can only force someone or a company to play along until they begin to strike back.
Participant B: That is true, public transportation doesn't reach all areas. We all know people that will drive down the street instead of walking to the corner store.
Participant C: Yeah, I agree.

Discussion in Information Condition

Participant D: Climate change will affect everyone, and will only get worse. This is something that needs to be addressed, but it is not immediate to our survival within the next 5–10 years.
Participant E: I don't think it's too complicated to tackle environmental issues as well as others at the same time.
Participant F: I agree. The article even states that won't affect us for hundreds and even thousands of years from now.

The excerpts have approximately the same word count and, from casual observation, do not seem much different. Yet, text analysis from the LIWC website (https://www.liwc.app/) showed that participants in the intimacy condition used more social and analytic words. There was also more use of clout and authenticity language, and the emotional tone was more positive in the intimacy condition (see Table 12.1).

Table 12.1 Results of LIWC Text Analysis of the Two Transcript Excerpts from van Swol et al. (2022)

LIWC variables	Intimacy condition (69 words)	Information condition (72 words)
I-pronouns (I, me, my)	2.9	2.8
Social words	11.6	4.2
Positive emotions	4.3	2.8
Negative emotions	0.0	1.4
Cognitive processes	18.8	15.3
Analytic	67.8	27.9
Clout	71.9	33.8
authenticity	80.2	58.1
Emotional tone	93.6	51.8

Note: The first four variables reflect percentage of total words within the text. The last four variables have been converted to 100-point scales where 0 = very low along the dimension and 100 = very high. Emotional tone is scored such that higher numbers are more positive and upbeat and lower numbers are more negative.

LIWC provides a simple procedure for linguistic semantic analysis, but it has limitations that can be overcome by using other programs. The Sentiment Analysis and Social Cognition Engine (SEANCE) is an automatic tool that includes indices related to social cognition and social order (Crossley et al., 2017). Social cognition words in SEANCE are related to the psychological processes that enable people to make sense of the behaviors of others and situations in a social group. Social order words indicate status, dominance, and social hierarchy within the group. Researchers interested in understanding the nuances of emotions can benefit from the Geneva Affect Label Coder (GALC), which recognizes 36 affective categories, such as amusement, anxiety, compassion, disappointment, fear, hope, lust, pride, sadness, and shame (for a complete list of categories, see Scherer, 2005).

These software programs are inexpensive or free and generally only require minimal training to use. Paired with the availability of transcripts from online groups and availability of cheap online transcription services for face-to-face groups, analysis of language in groups is within reach of even beginning group scholars. Further, as more and more groupwork is done online with less access to nonverbal cues, language will be even more important than in face-to-face groups as a vehicle through which members can communicate their emotions. Yet, this surfeit of empirical data born of this new methodology poses a new problem: how to interpret the data? Language analysis of group transcripts can produce dozens to hundreds of language variables. Without a priori theory and hypotheses, it can be difficult to interpret this empirical data and easy to fall prey to type one error and seduced by the occasional significant result found within a long list of variables. Thus, methodology and empirical data need theory, which we examine in the next section. In addition, no method in and of itself is complete. Methods allow collection of empirical data but also limit what is collected. In other words, "all methods are flawed, but all are valuable" (McGrath, 1984, p. 31). Thus, collection and analysis of interaction data in groups should not rely solely on automated language analysis but should be triangulated with other methods such as qualitative coding (e.g., Bloomfield et al., 2020) or questionnaire data (e.g., van Swol et al., 2022). Triangulating with multiple methods allows the weakness of one method to be offset by the other. For example, if participants feel it is inappropriate to express their strong emotions in a group discussion, emotions might be measured more accurately privately with a questionnaire than language software, although we acknowledge our earlier point that questionnaire data can be subject to priming or people may have trouble labeling their emotional states for a questionnaire. Further, language software may not pick up on subtle contextual nuances that could be analyzed with a more qualitative method.

Conceptual Framework

A theoretical framework can suggest what language variables can be useful for understanding group communication when designing a study and developing hypotheses before data collection. van Swol et al. (2021, p. 10) state that "language can help us take the temperature of a group" by giving us a window into processes and emergent states like cohesion, focus of attention, emotions, differentiation, cognitive complexity, and conflict. Here we focus on the **input-processes-output model** (Ilgen et al., 2005) that van Swol and Kane (2019) applied to language use in groups (see Figure 12.1). Emergent states are variable and dynamic in that they develop over time as a function of group inputs and processes as group members interact (Marks et al., 2001). We focus on group processes and emergent states with implications for social influence.

van Swol and Kane (2019) used an input-process-output model to explain how group processes and emergent states are reflected in language use in a group. Before a discussion, group members have inputs that they will bring into the group. These inputs include differences in status, opinions, or expertise. During discussion, these inputs could be reflected in the language used. For

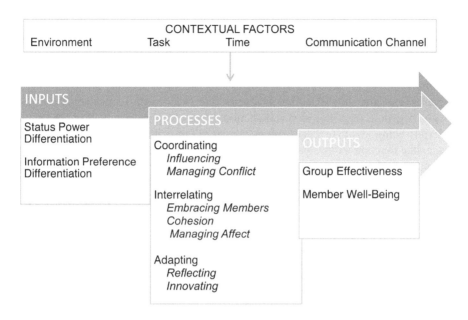

Figure 12.1 The Input-Process-Output Model of Understanding Group Communication. From van Swol and Kane (2019). Copyright of Sage.

example, low status members tend to use more first-person pronouns (Brewer & Gardner, 1996; Jetten et al., 2003; Kacewicz et al., 2014; Rink & Ellemers, 2011) or are more likely to match other's language style (Jones et al., 2014; Muir et al., 2016, 2017). However, during discussion, communication and language can lead to new group processes and emergent states. For example, a group member may become more influential during discussion, and their increasing influence could then be reflected in their use of more clout language which signifies confidence, leadership, and expertise, or lower use of first-person pronouns. Emergent states and group processes can affect the language used by group members, or language used by a group may shape group processes and emergent states. Finally, language can affect group outputs. For example, if group members are more influential when using more complex language or more "we" pronouns, their influence could be reflected in the group decision. Using this conceptual framework, in the next section, we focus on language categories with implications for social influence in groups.

Language in Groups and Social Influence

McGrath (1984, p. xiv of preface) defines groups as "vehicles for delivering social influence." Group members communicate to translate their individual inputs, like member preferences, into group outputs, such as a group decision, and in this process, group members influence each other, reflect on information and opinions presented, engage in conflict, and come together in agreement. During these processes, "language is the bedrock" (Kane & van Swol, 2022, p. 126). In the following, we summarize research on specific language variables and how they relate to social influence.

While language by itself is not interaction, language is a fundamental part of social interaction, and to examine the role of language in social interaction, it is important to focus on language that is specific to the context of the interaction and language that is more non-contextual. Language can be split up into content words which communicate meaning, usually nouns (e.g., daughter, dime), verbs (e.g., run, drink), and adjectives (e.g., expensive, short). Content words are usually specific to the context of the discussion. For example, words related to family would usually be limited to discussions about that context. On the other hand, function words are words that have little lexical meaning and are used across different contexts, with the purpose to create grammatical or structural relationships. Function words include non-contextual words, such as prepositions (e.g., for, before), conjunctions (e.g., because, but), articles (e.g., an, the), personal pronouns (e.g., I, him), auxiliary verbs (e.g., are, should), common adverbs (e.g., very, really), impersonal pronouns (e.g., it, these), and negations (e.g., not, never). Function words comprise over half of the language that we use, despite being less than 1% of our vocabulary (Tausczik & Pennebaker, 2010). Focusing on language, like function words, that is non-contextual allows the researcher to examine concepts beyond the context of the discussion, which can increase generalizability and the ability to examine and compare language use across different topics and contexts.

Pronouns

Use of pronouns indicates where one is directing their attention during an interaction, either toward self or others. Pronouns can point to the cognitive status of the speaker, and reveal the relative ranks among individuals in groups (Brown & Levinson, 1987; Kacewicz et al., 2014). Pronouns can be useful when examining conflict, status, and influence. *We* pronouns can imply a collective focus and signify inclusion in a group (Pennebaker, 2011). There is a positive relationship between group cohesiveness and use of *we* pronouns (Lieberman et al., 2005; Matthews et al., 2015; although see Gonzales et al., 2010). Group members use more *we* pronouns when they have something in common, such as a support group of people with similar medical conditions (Lieberman et al., 2005). Newcomers can find more acceptance in a group discussion when proposing new innovations and ideas when the newcomers use integrating pronouns like *we*, rather than differentiating pronouns, like *I* and *you* (Kane & Rink, 2015; Rink et al., 2013). Group members generally are more attached and committed to groups when there is higher use of *we* pronouns (Lieberman et al., 2005; Matthews et al., 2015), although no claim can be made for a causal relationship. In addition, leaders and higher status members use more *we* pronouns (Cassell et al., 2006), and leaders who use more *we* pronouns are more influential (Steffens & Haslam, 2013), possibly because they tend to focus on the group rather than themselves. This research suggests that use of *we* pronouns has positive implications for influencing others. Indeed, use of *we* pronouns was found to be an indicator for perspective-taking (van Swol et al., 2021). In contrast, a higher level of *I* pronoun use among those in a support group reflects more self-focus and is related to more negative emotions as a result of nonconstructive rumination of one's own problem (Shaw et al., 2008). Likewise, group members that are ostracized use fewer *we* pronouns and more *I* pronouns (Klauke & Kauffeld, 2020).

Collective pronouns, like *they*, can prime group affiliation and perpetuate intergroup biases because they designate an in-group and out-group membership (Perdue et al., 1990). Martin and Hewstone (2001, p. 214) state "A majority should encourage individuals to focus their attention on the relationship between themselves and members of the majority (interpersonal focus), while a minority should lead to greater attention being focused on the content of the minority's message (message focus)." Majorities often have an impact through normative influence, which is influence from social norms and expectations of the majority (Meyers & Brashers, 1999) because of their greater numbers, while minorities have to rely on the quality and consistency of their message. Because majorities have more members, they comprise an in-group and could make members of the numerical minority feel part of the out-group. Because of this, majorities may use pronouns like *they* to highlight the distinction between in-group majority members and out-group minority members to exert this normative influence (van Swol & Carlson, 2017). Other research has also found that use of third-person pronouns can highlight conflicting factions that form within groups, as a faction within a group uses third-person pronouns to refer to the other group members not within that faction (Swaab et al., 2008).

You pronouns, however, signal a focus on oneself in relation to others. Pennebaker (2011, p. 175) argued that *you* pronouns are "the equivalent of pointing your finger" at others; there is more use of you pronouns in high conflict conversations and when people are angry (Pennebaker, 2011). *You* pronouns in a conversation indicate blaming others and differentiation from others, especially when used excessively (Kane & Rink, 2015; Simmons et al., 2008). However, sometimes an increase of *you* pronouns signifies personal connections in the group (Pennebaker & Chung, 2013), especially when use of *I* pronouns decreased, indicating less self-centered thinking and more caring about others (Alpers et al., 2005). Although use of *you* pronouns sometimes suggests there is an increased interest in others, when trying to influence others in a group, use of *you* pronouns may be counter-productive (Kane & Rink, 2015). For example, van Swol et al. (2022) found a relationship between increased feelings of ostracism and more use of *you* pronouns. van Swol et al. (2016) found that members who held their beliefs more rigidly and felt more superior about their opinions used more *you* pronouns in a group discussion, and the more *you* pronouns they used, the less influential they were.

Language Matching

When people desire to build a good relationship with another member in the group or wish to achieve communication effectiveness, they may adjust the way they speak to converge with the speech style of their communication partner (Beebe & Giles, 1984). The magnitude of linguistic accommodation behaviors varies, from subtle adjustment (e.g., changing speech rate, pitch, volume) to more drastic changes such as code-switching, the action of shifting between different languages (Beebe & Giles, 1984). In multilingual groups, group performance is dependent on group members' ability to communicate in a common language (Ahmad & Widén, 2018). Team members in multilingual groups may experience misunderstandings, discord, and conflict due to language diversity, especially when group members lack the linguistic skills to overcome language barriers (Henderson, 2005). Code-switching allows group members to mitigate the negative impact of group diversity and reap the benefits diversity brings (Ahmad & Widén, 2018), although it may cause feelings of exclusion and polarize in-group and out-group identities when used around members with limited language skills (Harzing & Feely, 2008).

Language matching in monolingual groups, on the other hand, is usually less substantial and often involves more subtle accommodation behaviors. By examining use of different types of function words, researchers can identity someone's linguistic style (Gonzales et al., 2010). Comparison between group members can determine whether members are matching each other's linguistic styles. **Linguistic style matching (LSM)** is an equation that can be used with LIWC output to assess language mimicry by measuring the degree to which communicators are producing similar rates of nine different function words (e.g., negations, prepositions, person pronouns, conjunctions) in their dialogue (Gonzales et al., 2010; Müller-Frommeyer & Kauffeld, 2022). It is one measure of language matching or language convergence, although there are other measures (e.g., Huffaker et al., 2011). Communicators regulate social interactions through matching (or mimicry, mirroring) to improve shared understanding (Burgoon et al., 1995; Giles & Coupland, 1991). Matching is a potent mechanism that holds a group together because it can strengthen social bonds, foster group safety, and improve team performance (Kozlowski & Ilgen, 2006; van Baaren et al., 2004). People are more likely to mimic one another and produce similar styles of speech when there is high rapport (Giles & Coupland, 1991). Research has shown that LSM reflects social dynamics in small groups, such that LSM is associated with cohesiveness, as well as task performance in groups (Gonzales et al., 2010). For example, Heuer et al. (2020) studied research teams in multiple disciplines and found that, while higher level of LSM indicated more mutual social support, it was negatively correlated to one's perception of team performance. Given LSM's relationship with rapport and cohesion, it has implications for social influence. For example, people who are more successful in a negotiation task were found to engage in more language matching (Huffaker et al., 2011). Given the well-established finding that we are more influenced by those who are similar to us (Cialdini, 2007), language matching could be a vehicle to establish that similarity and increase influence. Other research has found that group members are more likely to match the language of a group member whose opinion differs from others (Danescu-Niculescu-Mizil et al., 2013; Muir et al., 2016; Yilmaz & Peña, 2015) and that lower status members are more likely to move away from their baseline style of language to match the language of higher status members (Jones et al., 2014; Muir et al., 2016, 2017). In both cases, matching the language of another may be a tactic to make a good impression and gain influence. However, this strategy is more effective when members have lower status and have a collaborative attitude. Group members who think their opinions are more correct than others (van Swol et al., 2016) or are uncooperative (Yilmaz, 2016) are less influential when they match the language of other members. High status group members are also perceived more negatively when they accommodate the language of lower status members, possibly because they are not expected to engage in linguistic convergence (Curhan & Pentland, 2007; Muir et al., 2017).

Language Complexity

Another dimension of language is complexity. Language complexity, as defined by linguistic measures like LIWC's measure of analytical thinking, words per sentence, or use of conjunctions, which can signify stronger, more well thought out arguments and more analytical thinking about an issue. It is related to reported perspective-taking activity in a group conversation (van Swol et al., 2021). When people express ideas with linguistic complexity, they are more influential in the group, possibly because linguistic diversity signifies competence (Huffaker, 2010). As noted, people often focus their attention on a minority member's arguments and reasoning, which is especially important since minority members cannot exert normative influence (Martin & Hewstone, 2001). van Swol and Carlson (2017) found that minority member's influence on the final group decision increased when they used more causation words, which are a linguistic indicator of complex thinking. Sapru and Bourlard (2013) found that members in more important team roles who led the conversation used more causation language. Language complexity is important for social influence, especially when arguments are high quality, but can be counter-productive when arguments are not convincing. For example, when group members who believed their opinions were more correct than others used more complex language to explain their reasoning, their influence decreased, possibly because it became evident that they overestimated their confidence (van Swol et al., 2016). Some research indicates that language complexity may indicate more task-based and less social interactions between group members (Scholand et al., 2009).

Emotional Language

Emotions can be expressed both nonverbally and through language. Words about positive feelings (e.g., like, happy, thank) and valence (e.g., nice, beautiful) indicate positive emotions, whereas words about negative feelings (e.g., worried, mad, anxious) and valence (e.g., bad, nasty) indicate negative emotions (Scherer, 2005; Tausczik & Pennebaker, 2010). In group communication, emotional expressions can indicate members' status and emergent states (van Swol & Kane, 2019). For example, lower status members use more emotional language (Dino et al., 2009), especially expression of positive emotions (Reysen et al., 2010), whereas higher status members tend to show more negative emotion because they are not penalized as much as lower status members for expressing themselves (Paletz & Schunn, 2011). Felt emotions are contagious through the expression of emotional language, and a group member using emotional language, especially negative emotional language and when the member has more status, can influence the emotional language used by other group members and then their felt emotion (Kane & van Swol, 2021).

Negative emotional language in a group can indicate conflict and dissent (Brett et al., 2007; Huffaker et al., 2011), whereas positive emotional and assenting language is associated with more positive interpersonal behavior (Fischer et al., 2007), such as reaching consensus and supporting each other (Huffaker et al., 2011; Sapru & Bourlard, 2013; Yilmaz & Peña, 2015). Groups perform better when there is a positive group climate (Fischer et al., 2007; van Swol et al., 2022; Yoo & Kim, 2014). For example, van Swol et al. (2022) found that, when group members fostered intimate environments by engaging in a conversation about shared identity and values, they were more likely to reach an agreement in subsequent discussions on polarized topics like climate change, and this ability to reach consensus was mediated by their use of positive emotional language.

Evidence-Based Recommendations for Practice

Language use impacts other important dimensions of group interactions such as social influence. To gain influence in a group, members should be mindful of the language they use and pay attention to how language is reflecting and affecting group processes and output. For example, if the group's goal is to coordinate and reach consensus, members should use more positive emotional language and less other-focused pronouns. To gain influence, members can use more *we* pronouns and accommodate the language of other members, especially if they are new to the group. The effectiveness of these tactics depends on the member's status and attitude, however. Group members can make a good impression when they match the language style of other members, if they have lower status, are cooperative, and not assertive. Similarly, when members use language that signals complexity, they are more influential because they appear to be competent, but only when they are not overconfident about their opinions.

When conducting research to examine the influence of language on group processes and emergent states, the input-process-output model (Figure 12.1) established by van Swol and Kane (2019) provides a theoretical framework. Researchers can use software programs like LIWC, SEANCE, and GALC to analyze the language used by each individual and at group level. Researchers can measure or manipulate inputs (e.g., opinions before discussion, initial status, level of intimacy) and also measure processes, emergent states, and outputs to understand their relationship with language use. However, to reach causal conclusions about language, researchers may have to manipulate the language itself, which is difficult without the use of confederates. This has been done in computer-mediated environments. For example, to study emotional contagion, Kane and van Swol (2021) had a participant interact with a chat bot that used either predominantly positive or negative emotional language and then measured how this affected perceived conflict. They found that even when holding opinions and other content the same, more use of negative emotional language increased perception of both task and interpersonal conflicts.

Conclusion

Language can reflect important processes in groups like status, ability to reach consensus, emotional tone, and collective focus. As researchers have more access to transcripts of group discussions, the ability to analyze how language group members use affects social influence within the group can increasingly be studied. When determining what methods could help answer research questions and which variables are relevant, theories can guide researchers to build frameworks and design studies. While existing theories like the input-process-output model can help direct research, developing theory to guide an increasing amount of data driven by new methodological tools will be key.

Further Readings

Pennebaker, J. W. (2011). *The secret life of pronouns: What our words say about us.* Bloomsbury Press.
Pennebaker, J. W., Booth, R. J., Boyd, R. L., & Francis, M. E. (2015). *Linguistic inquiry and word count: LIWC2015.* Pennebaker Conglomerates (www.LIWC.net).
van Swol, L. M., & Kane, A. A. (2019). Language and group processes: An integrative, interdisciplinary review. *Small Group Research, 50*(1), 3–38. https://doi.org/10.1177/1046496418785019

Glossary

LIWC   Linguistic Inquiry Word Count is a software program that analyzes the frequency that words in certain categories, like personal pronouns, appear in text.
Linguistic style matching   Linguistic style matching examines how much people match each other on nine function word categories for a measure of linguistic mimicry.
Input-processes-output model   A model of group interaction that sees group interaction comprising the inputs that group members bring to the discussion, like their opinions or status. Then, processes and emergent states are behaviors and perceptions that emerge, like influence and cohesion, as group members communicate. Finally, from interaction, groups produce outputs, like problem-solving, member well-being, or a consensual decision.
Emergent state   The emergent state is the group atmosphere that emerges during the processes of group interactions, such as cohesion, focus of attention, emotions, differentiation, cognitive complexity, and conflict. Emergent states are variable and dynamic in that they develop over time as a function of group inputs and processes as group members interact.

References

Ahmad, F., & Widén, G. (2018). Knowledge sharing and language diversity in organisations: Influence of code switching and convergence. *European Journal of International Management, 12*(4), 351–373. https://doi.org/10.1504/EJIM.2018.092839
Alpers, G. W., Winzelberg, A. J., Classen, C., Roberts, H., Dev, P., Koopman, C., & Taylor, C. B. (2005). Evaluation of computerized text analysis in an Internet breast cancer support group. *Computers in Human Behavior, 21*, 361–367. http://doi.org/10.1016/j.chb.2004.02.008
Bales, R. F. (1950). Interaction process analysis: A method for the study of small groups. Addison-Wesley Press. https://ia902609.us.archive.org/32/items/interactionproce00bale/interactionproce00bale.pdf
Beebe, L. M., & Giles, H. (1984). Speech-accommodation theories: A discussion in terms of second-language acquisition. *International Journal of the Sociology of Language, 1984*(46), 5–32. https://doi.org/10.1515/ijsl.1984.46.5
Bloomfield, E. F., van Swol, L. M., Chang, C. T., Willes, S., & Ahn, P. H. (2020). The effects of establishing intimacy and consubstantiality on group discussions about climate change solutions. *Science Communication, 42*(3), 369–394. https://doi.org/10.1177/1075547020927017
Brett, J. M., Olekalns, M., Friedman, R., Goates, N., Anderson, C., & Lisco, C. C. (2007). Sticks and stones: Language, face, and online dispute resolution. *Academy of Management Journal, 50*, 85–99. http://doi.org/10.5465/AMJ.2007.24161853
Brewer, M. B., & Gardner, W. (1996). Who is this "we"? Levels of collective identity and self-representations. *Journal of Personality and Social Psychology, 71*, 83–93. http://doi.org/10.1037/0022-3514.71.1.83

Brinberg, D., & McGrath, J. E. (1985). *Validity and the research process.* Sage.

Brown, P., & Levinson, S. (1987). *Politeness: Some universals in language usage.* Cambridge University Press.

Burgoon, J., Stern, L., & Dillman, L. (1995). *Interpersonal adaptation: Dyadic interaction patterns.* Cambridge University Press.

Cassell, J., Huffaker, D., Tversky, D., & Ferriman, K. (2006). The language of online leadership: Gender and youth engagement on the internet. *Developmental Psychology, 42,* 436–449. http://doi.org/10.1037/0012-1649.42.3.436

Cialdini, R. (2007). *The psychology of influence.* Harper Collins.

Crossley, S. A., Kyle, K., & McNamara, D. S. (2017). Sentiment analysis and social cognition engine (SEANCE): An automatic tool for sentiment, social cognition, and social order analysis. *Behavior Research Methods, 49*(3), 803–821. http://doi.org/10.3758/s13428-016-0743-z

Curhan, J. R., & Pentland, A. (2007). Thin slices of negotiation: Predicting outcomes from conversational dynamics within the first 5 minutes. *Journal of Applied Psychology, 92,* 802–811. http://doi.org/10.1037/0021-9010.92.3.802

Danescu-Niculescu-Mizil, C., Sudhof, M., Jurafsky, D., Leskovec, J., & Potts, C. (2013). A computational approach to politeness with application to social factors. *Proceedings of the Annual Meeting of the Association of Computational Linguistics, 51,* 250–259. http://aclweb.org/anthology/P/P13/P13-1025.pdf

Davis, J. H. (1973). Group decision and social interaction: A theory of social decision schemes. *Psychological Review, 80*(2), 97–125. http://doi.org/10.1037/h0033951

Dino, A., Reysen, S., & Branscombe, N. R. (2009). Online interactions between group members who differ in status. *Journal of Language and Social Psychology, 28,* 85–93. http://doi.org/10.1177/0261927X08325916

Fischer, U., McDonnell, L., & Orasanu, J. (2007). Linguistic correlates of team performance: Toward a tool for monitoring team functioning during space missions. *Aviation Space and Environmental Medicine, 78*(Suppl. 1), B86–B95. https://pubmed.ncbi.nlm.nih.gov/17547309/

Giles, H., & Coupland, N. (1991). *Language: Contexts and consequences.* Brooks/Cole.

Gonzales, A. L., Hancock, J. T., & Pennebaker, J. W. (2010). Language style matching as a predictor of social dynamics in small groups. *Communication Research, 37*(1), 3–19. https://doi.org/10.1177/0093650209351468

Harzing, A. W., & Feely, A. J. (2008). The language barrier and its implications for HQ-subsidiary relationships. *Cross Cultural Management: An International Journal, 15*(1), 49–61. https://doi.org/10.1108/13527600810848827

Henderson, J. K. (2005). Language diversity in international management teams. *International Studies of Management & Organization, 35*(1), 66–82. https://doi.org/10.1080/00208825.2005.11043722

Heuer, K., Müller-Frommeyer, L. C., & Kauffeld, S. (2020). Language matters: The double-edged role of linguistic style matching in work groups. *Small Group Research, 51*(2), 208–228. https://doi.org/10.1177/1046496419874498

Huffaker, D. (2010). Dimensions of leadership and social influence in online communities. *Human Communication Research, 36,* 593–617. http://doi.org/10.1111/j.1468-2958.2010.01390.x

Huffaker, D. A., Swaab, R., & Diermeier, D. (2011). The language of coalition formation in online multiparty negotiations. *Journal of Language and Social Psychology, 30*(1), 66–81. https://doi.org/10.1177/0261927X10387102

Ilgen, D. R., Hollenbeck, J. R., Johnson, M., & Jundt, D. (2005). Teams in organizations: From input-process-output models to IMOI models. *Annual Review of Psychology, 56,* 517–543. https://doi.org/10.1146/annurev.psych.56.091103.070250

Jetten, J., Branscombe, N. R., Spears, R., & McKimmie, B. M. (2003). Predicting the paths of peripherals: The interaction of identification and future possibilities. *Personality and Social Psychology Bulletin, 29,* 130–140. http://doi.org/10.1177/0146167202238378

Jones, S., Cotterill, R., Dewdney, N., Muir, K., & Joinson, A. (2014). Finding Zelig in text: A measure for normalising linguistic accommodation. *Proceedings of the International Conference on Computational Linguistics, 25,* 455–465. Retrieved from http://www.aclweb.org/anthology/C14-1044

Kacewicz, E., Pennebaker, J. W., Davis, M., Jeon, M., & Graesser, A. C. (2014). Pronoun use reflects standings in social hierarchies. *Journal of Language and Social Psychology, 33*(2), 125–143. https://doi.org/10.1177/0261927X13502654

Kane, A. A., & Rink, F. (2015). How newcomers influence group utilization of their knowledge: Integrating versus differentiating strategies. *Group Dynamics: Theory, Research, and Practice, 19*(2), 91. https://doi. org/10.1037/gdn0000024

Kane, A., & van Swol, L. M. (2021, July). *Are text-based linguistic emotional displays more contagious from a peer than a manager?* [Conference session: "We Second that Emotion: Collective Affect in Organizations"]. 81st Annual Meeting of the Academy of Management.

Kane, A., & van Swol, L. M. (2022). Language use in groups. In M. Dehghani & R. L. Boyd (Eds.), *The atlas of language analysis in psychology*. Guilford Press.

Klauke, F., & Kauffeld, S. (2020). Does it matter what i say? Using language to examine reactions to ostracism as it occurs. *Frontiers in Psychology, 11*, 1–11. https://doi.org/10.3389/fpsyg.2020.558069

Kozlowski, S. W. J., & Ilgen, D. R. (2006). Enhancing the effectiveness in work groups and teams. *Psychological Science, 7*, 77–124. https://doi.org/10.1111/j.1529-1006.2006.00030.x

Laughlin, P. R., & Ellis, A. L. (1986). Demonstrability and social combination processes on mathematical intellective tasks. *Journal of Experimental Social Psychology, 22*(3), 177–189. https://doi.org/10.1016/0022-1031(86)90022-3

Lieberman, M. A., Wizlenberg, A., Golant, M., & Di Minno, M. (2005). The impact of group composition on internet support groups: Homogeneous versus heterogeneous Parkinson's groups. *Group Dynamics: Theory, Research, and Practice, 9*(4), 239–250. https://doi.org/10.1037/1089-2699.9.4.239

Marks, M. A., Mathieu, J. E., & Zaccaro, S. J. (2001). A temporally based framework and taxonomy of team processes. *The Academy of Management Review, 26*(3), 356–376. https://doi.org/10.2307/259182

Martin, R., & Hewstone, M. (2001). Conformity and independence in groups: Majorities and minorities. In M. A. Hogg & R. S. Tindale (Eds.), *Blackwell handbook of social psychology: Group processes*. Blackwell Publishing.

Matthews, T., Mahmud, J. U., Chen, J., Muller, M., Haber, E., & Badenes, H. (2015). They said what?: Exploring the relationship between language use and member satisfaction in communities. *Proceedings of the 18th ACM Conference on Computer Supported Cooperative Work & Social Computing*, 819–825. https://doi.org/10.1145/2675133.2675150

McGrath, J. E. (1984). *Groups: Interaction and performance*. Prentice-Hall.

McGrath, J. E., Arrow, H., & Berdahl, J. L. (2000). The study of groups: Past, present, and future. *Personality and Social Psychology Review, 4*, 95–105. https://doi.org/10.1207/S15327957PSPR0401_8

Meyers, R. A., & Brashers, D. E. (1999). Influence processes in group interaction. In L. R. Frey, D. S. Gouran, & M. S. Poole (Eds.), *The handbook of group communication theory and research* (pp. 288–312*)*. Sage.

Muir, K., Joinson, A., Cotterill, R., & Dewdney, N. (2016). Characterizing the linguistic chameleon: Personal and social correlates of linguistic style accommodation. *Human Communication Research, 42*, 462–484. http://doi.org/10.1111/hcre.12083

Muir, K., Joinson, A., Cotterill, R., & Dewdney, N. (2017). Linguistic style accommodation shapes impression formation and rapport in computer-mediated communication. *Journal of Language and Social Psychology, 36*, 525–548. http://doi.org/10.1177/0261927X17701327

Müller-Frommeyer, L. C., & Kauffeld, S. (2022). Capturing the temporal dynamics of language style matching in groups and teams. *Small Group Research, 53*(4), 503–531. https://doi.org/10.1177/10464964211073347

Paletz, S. B. F., & Schunn, C. D. (2011). Assessing group-level participation in fluid teams: Testing a new metric. *Behavioral Research Methods, 43*, 533–536. http://doi.org/10.3758/s13428-011-0070-3

Pennebaker, J. W., & Chung, C. K. (2013). Counting little words in big data: The psychology of individuals, communities, culture, and history. In J. P. Forgas, O. Vincze, & J. László (Eds.), *Social cognition and communication* (pp. 25–42). Psychology Press.

Perdue, C. W., Dovidio, J. F., Gurtman, M. B., & Tyler, R. B. (1990). Us and them: Social categorization and the process of intergroup bias. *Journal of Personality and Social Psychology, 59*(3), 475. https://doi.org/10.1037/0022-3514.59.3.475

Reysen, S., Lloyd, J. D., Katzarska-Miller, I., Lemker, B. M., & Foss, R. L. (2010). Intragroup status and social presence in online fan groups. *Computers in Human Behavior, 26*, 1314–1317. http://doi.org/10.1016/j.chb.2010.04.003

Rink, F., & Ellemers, N. (2011). From current state to desired future: How compositional changes affect dissent and innovation in work groups. In J. Jetten & M. J. Hornsey (Eds.). *Rebels in groups: Dissent, deviance, difference and defiance* (pp. 54–72). Blackwell. http://doi.org/10.1002/9781444390841.ch4

Rink, F., Kane, A. A., Ellemers, N., & Van der Vegt, G. S. (2013). Team receptivity to newcomers: Five decades of evidence and future research themes. *Academy of Management Annals*, *7*, 245–291. https://doi.org/10.5465/19416520.2013.766405

Sapru, A., & Bourlard, H. (2013). Investigating the impact of language style and vocal expression on social roles of participants in professional meetings. *Proceedings of the Humaine Association Conference on Affective Computing and Intelligent Interaction*, 324–329. https://doi.org/10.1109/ACII.2013.60

Scherer, K. R. (2005). What are emotions? And how can they be measured. *Social Science Information*, *44*(4), 695–729. https://doi.org/10.1177/0539018405058216

Scholand, A. J., Tausczik, Y. R., & Pennebaker, J. W. (2009). *Quantifiable and objective approach to organizational performance enhancement: Examining social structure and linguistic content during collaborative group work from a network perspective (SAND2009-5975)*. Sandia National Laboratories. Retrieved https://www.researchgate.net/profile/Andrew_Scholand/publication/255206763_Quantifiable_and_objective_approach_to_organizational_performance_enhancement/links/0a85e53ab1d3b737f8000000.pdf

Shaw, B. R., Han, J. Y., Hawkins, R. P., McTavish, F. M., & Gustafson, D. H. (2008). Communicate about self and others within an online support group for women with breast cancer and subsequent outcomes. *Journal of Health Psychology*, *13*, 930–939. https://doi.org/10.1177/1359105308095067

Simmons, R. A., Chambless, D. L., & Gordon, P. C. (2008). How do hostile and emotionally overinvolved relatives view relationships?: What relatives' pronoun use tells us. *Family Process*, *47*(3), 405–419. https://doi.org/10.1111/j.1545-5300.2008.00261.x

Stasser, G., & Titus, W. (1985). Pooling of unshared information in group decision making: Biased information sampling during discussion. *Journal of Personality and Social Psychology*, *48*(6), 1467–1478. https://doi.org/10.1037/0022-3514.48.6.1467

Steffens, N. K., & Haslam, S. A. (2013). Power through "us": Leaders' use of we-referencing language predicts election victory. *PLoS One*, *8*(10), e77952. http://doi.org/10.1371/journal.pone.0077952

Swaab, R. I., Phillips, K. W., Diermeier, D., & Husted Medvec, V. (2008). The pros and cons of dyadic side conversations in small groups: The impact of group norms and task type. *Small Group Research*, *39*(3), 372–390. https://doi.org/10.1177/1046496408317044

Tausczik, Y. R., & Pennebaker, J. W. (2010). The psychological meaning of words: LIWC and computerized text analysis methods. *Journal of Language and Social Psychology*, *29*(1), 24–54. https://doi.org/10.1177/0261927X09351676

van Baaren, R. B., Holland, R. W., Kawakami, K., & Van Knippenberg, A. (2004). Mimicry and prosocial behavior. *Psychological Science*, *15*(1), 71–74. https://doi.org/10.1111/j.0963-7214.2004.01501012.x

van Swol, L. M., Ahn, P. H., Prahl, A., & Gong, Z. (2021). Language use in group discourse and its relationship to group processes. *SAGE Open*, *11(1)*. https://doi.org/10.1177/21582440211001852

van Swol, L. M., Ahn, H., Prahl, A., & Gong, Z. (2022). Language use and feelings of ostracism in an online chat group. *Communication Reports*, *35*(2), 65–77. https://doi.org/10.1080/08934215.2021.2008461

van Swol, L. M., Bloomfield, E. F., Chang, C. T., & Willes, S. (2022). Fostering climate change consensus: The role of intimacy in group discussions. *Public Understanding of Science*, *31*(1), 103–118. https://doi.org/10.1177/09636625211020661

van Swol, L. M., & Carlson, C. L. (2017). Language use and influence among minority, majority, and homogeneous group members. *Communication Research*, *44*, 512–529. https://doi.org/10.1177/0093650215570658

van Swol, L. M., Prahl, A., Kolb, M., Acosta-Lewis, E. E., & Carlson, C. (2016). The language of extremity: The language of extreme members and how the presence of extremity affects group discussion. *Journal of Language and Social Psychology*, *35*, 603–627. https://doi.org/10.1177/0261927X16629788

Yilmaz, G. (2016). What you do and how you speak matter: Behavioral and linguistic determinants of performance in virtual teams. *Journal of Language and Social Psychology*, *35*, 76–97. http://doi.org/10.1177/0261927X15575772

Yilmaz, G., & Peña, J. (2015). How do interpersonal behaviors and social categories affect language use? The case of virtual teams. *Communication Quarterly*, *63*, 427–443. http://doi.org/10.1080/01463373.2015.1058285

Yoo, J., & Kim, J. (2014). Can online discussion participation predict group project performance? Investigating the roles of linguistic features and participation patterns. *International Journal Artificial Intelligence in Education*, *24*, 8–32. http://doi.org/10.1007/s40593-013-0010-8

13 Participation and Information Sharing

Gwen M. Wittenbaum and Joseph A. Bonito

Chapter Objectives

- Recognize a hidden profile task and its importance for understanding information sharing.
- Identify the conditions that enhance the demonstrability of a group task.
- Understand how each task demonstrability condition relates to group member participation and information sharing.
- Apply participation and information sharing concepts to a case study.

Introduction

Most important decisions are entrusted to groups rather than individuals because of the assumption that groups are better problem solvers and decision makers than individuals (Collins & Guetzkow, 1964). Over half of organizations in the United States use teams to perform work or solve problems (Devine et al., 1999). Juries render verdicts in criminal and civil trials and health care teams collaborate on care management for patients. Groups have the potential to generate better solutions and make better decisions than one person working alone, but they sometimes fall short (Pavitt, 2003). The key to what goes wrong in groups often results from who talks and what information they share (e.g., Wittenbaum, Hollingshead, & Botero, 2004). That is, group member participation in discussion and what information they choose to tell other members provide a window into why groups perform well or not. This chapter explores these processes of participation and information sharing in decision-making and problem-solving groups.

We have used the term *information* a bit loosely to describe both data that one might have in his or her possession, and something contributed to discussion. Propp (1999), among others, made the distinction between knowledge and information. The root of *knowledge* is "know" and that for *information* is "inform." Thus, knowledge refers to a cognitive element or structure including where to find information, and information describes a process by which knowledge is transformed to a public- or group-level resource via discussion (Larson & Egan, 2020). This is not a trivial distinction because the problem of information sharing concerns whether and how knowledge is contributed to discussion–knowledge kept "on the sideline" isn't much help to a group, as it doesn't function to inform other members. Consider the case of a private nursing home's admissions board (Sigman, 1984), whose charge was to determine which applicants would be admitted to the facility – there were usually more applicants than beds/space. At least one committee member was charged with knowing bed availability (including how many and when openings were expected), and that knowledge would seem pertinent to mention as information during discussion when the issue of space is relevant. Group members who have the skills to apply their specialized knowledge to specific contexts to solve problems are known as *experts* with *expertise*.

DOI: 10.4324/9781003227458-15

Scholars who study information sharing begin with the assumption that, prior to discussion, knowledge is distributed among group members along multiple dimensions, the first of which is quantity. Members often differ in the amount of task-relevant knowledge each possesses (Letzring et al., 2006). The second dimension is overlap, which refers to the proportion of knowledge some or all members have in common. In some studies or situations, members know or possess all of the same information, as was true in Hirokawa's (1987) study, in which all participants read the same essay describing winter survival tactics before working in groups on the Winter Survival Problem. In other studies, some degree of knowledge is unshared, or uniquely held by a single group member, as was true of the nursing home admissions board mentioned earlier (Sigman, 1984). A meta-analysis by Lu et al. (2012) identified several studies in which approximately 75% of task-relevant data were distributed uniquely among group members. Finally, *information interdependence* describes the degree to which individual or distinct knowledge items might be related to others (Fraidin, 2004). For example, knowing that a candidate football coach has a career winning record is mitigated somewhat if he had losing seasons the past four years – it gives the impression that the candidate's performance is on a downward trajectory. Importantly, interdependent items can overlap completely (everyone knows them) or not at all (only one person knows them) and can be partially distributed such that the item about career record is known by one person but the recent spate of losing seasons known by another.

An Input-Process-Output Model

One way of understanding participation and information sharing in groups is through the lens of an input-process-output (IPO) model (Pavitt, 2014; Wittenbaum, Hollingshead, Paulus, et al., 2004). This model is a common way to characterize group decision making and problem solving in which inputs (e.g., task, member characteristics) influence process (e.g., issues discussed, elimination of alternatives), which in turn leads to or produces some type of output (e.g., group decision, affective orientations toward the group and its members). Regarding information sharing specifically, input consists of, among other things, what information participants have in their possession or have access to, process concerns the extent to which information is contributed to discussion and how groups evaluate it, and the output is the group decision (Propp, 1999). Although not addressed here, it is important to note that the IPO model assumes a linear process in which inputs affect process, which in turn produces outcomes, but it is not uncommon for process to create a feedback loop of sorts on relevant inputs. For example, mentioning a bit of information not known by other members during discussion (e.g., bed availability in a nursing home), among other things, updates what other members know (Larson, 1997) and renders irrelevant some information at that point in the discussion (e.g., no bed availability means it is pointless to discuss which applicants to admit to the nursing home). Bonito (2007) proposed a local management model of information sharing to address the correspondence between relevance as a feature of discussion and information resources distributed among group members.

A useful IPO model for understanding participation and information sharing in groups is the revised model of **task demonstrability** by Bonner et al. (2021) (see Figure 13.1 for a revision of the Nomological Network of Revisited Demonstrability as applied to information sharing). Task demonstrability is the degree to which the group can find the best or correct answer for a given task (also see Chapter 15). We can imagine cases when demonstrability is high, for example, when a jury has sufficient evidence beyond a reasonable doubt to determine the guilt of a defendant; this is known as an *intellective task*. Alternatively, with low demonstrability, the jury may be missing key evidence that makes certain determination of guilt beyond a reasonable doubt not possible or a matter of judgment, which is known as a *judgmental task*. Laughlin (1980) originally proposed

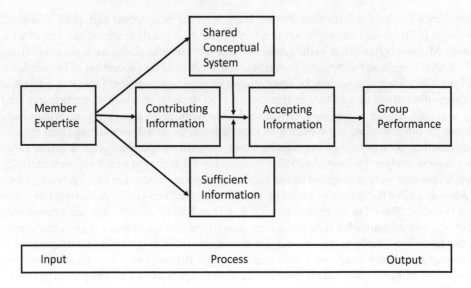

Figure 13.1 Summary of the Task Demonstrability Model of Bonner et al. (2021) as Applied to Information Sharing.

four conditions necessary for a group task to be solvable, and Bonner et al. (2021) applied these four conditions to organizational teams working on complex problems. These four conditions are: (a) a shared conceptual system, (b) sufficient information, (c) contributing truth, and (d) accepting truth. We will relabel the latter two conditions as "contributing information" and "accepting information" to apply to information sharing contexts. We summarize each of the four conditions and the model in the following.

First, the *shared conceptual system* refers to whether the team has a shared consensus on a verbal or mathematical system to solve the problem (see Box 13.1). This can include the symbolic systems and operations related to the task, such as formal logic (e.g., mathematical operations). It is similar to a team having a shared understanding of what the problem is and how to approach it. In organizations, this can be facilitated by training team members across different roles to gain perspective of others' operations and expertise (e.g., Marks et al., 2002). A shared conceptual system is the foundation of demonstrability on which the other components rest, as it defines agreement on what constitutes necessary information for solving a problem. Second, there must be *sufficient information* for a solution within the shared conceptual system. Is the distribution of expertise the right mix, in terms of both knowledge held by members in the group and the knowledge members can access within their networks outside of the team to solve the problem? Third, members who are key experts must have sufficient ability, motivation, and time to demonstrate the *merits of their preferences* to others, also known as *contributing information*. The key here is to create an environment in which team members with the best ideas within the shared system are compelled to speak up, participate, and share their information. Finally, team members have sufficient knowledge within the shared conceptual system to recognize and accept better ideas proposed by other members. That is, members are susceptible to persuasion based on the merit of argument, *affording appropriate weighting* to the best arguments, also known as *accepting information*. When all factors are in place, task demonstrability is "the dynamic that allows groups to detect the signal of truth within the noisy environment of a group interaction, thus improving performance" (Bonner et al., 2021, p. 2). As shown in Figure 13.1, group member expertise is the input contributing to the four task-demonstrability "process" conditions, which leads to the output of group performance. Next, we will illustrate group participation and information sharing processes across the four demonstrability conditions as applied to the hidden profile task.

Hidden Profile

Imagine a puzzle where each group member has different pieces that must be assembled collaboratively to complete the puzzle. One member's puzzle pieces are not sufficient to complete the puzzle. The solution requires each member to bring unique puzzle pieces to the table, integrate them with others' puzzle pieces, and cooperatively discover the solution. This example implies an intellective task that has a single correct solution. The ***hidden profile task*** is similar to the puzzle example. Some information, known as *shared information*, is known by all group members. Additionally, each group member holds different knowledge in the form of pieces of ***unshared information***, each piece known uniquely by a single member. In a hidden profile, the shared information biases group members toward a suboptimal solution, whereas the unshared information points to the best solution. The group can realize the best solution if all members pool their unshared information. Unfortunately, research shows a *discussion bias* whereby group members tend not to pool their unshared information sufficiently and instead tend to discuss more shared than unshared information (for reviews see Larson & Egan, 2020; Stasser & Titus, 2003; Wittenbaum, Hollingshead, & Botero, 2004; Wittenbaum & Stasser, 1996). The consequence for the hidden profile task is that the group often fails to discover the best solution to the problem (for reviews see Lu et al., 2012; Mesmer-Magnus & DeChurch, 2009; Reimer et al., 2010; Sohrab et al., 2015; also see Chapter 15). Note that the best solution in a hidden profile task is not only the one supported by the total pool of information but also the one that groups favor when each member has complete information (e.g., Stasser & Stewart, 1992). The task demonstrability model can provide a framework to understand why the potential intellective properties of the hidden profile task fail to be realized.

Shared Conceptual System

A group task is more solvable if group members have a common understanding about the task, how it is structured, and the method of solving it. In the typical study where groups work on a hidden profile task, members do not know how the task is structured. Information is distributed to members such that each holds both shared and unshared information. Members may receive minimal instructions about this information distribution, for example, that they may know some information that others do not. Sometimes, groups are told that all members have the same total amount of information despite knowing some different information. Based on our experiences running a hidden profile exercise among student groups in the classroom with subsequent debriefing and graphics showing the information distribution among members, it still is difficult for students to understand the task structure and communication strategy for how to solve it. Stasser et al. (1995) revealed more about the task to student participants by informing them of their own area of expertise and that of other members prior to group discussion, which improved information sharing and group decision quality. When members have knowledge about the knowledge of members (i.e., meta-knowledge) and who is expert, they are more likely to discuss unshared information and reach better decisions (Stasser & Abele, 2020). Without a bird's eye view of how the information is distributed in the group, but even with it, members may find it difficult to form a shared understanding of the task and how to solve it. This results in reduced demonstrability and likelihood of discussing unshared information.

Information Sufficiency

In the hidden profile task, the group has sufficient information to determine the optimal solution. However, the group may not be aware of this. As a manipulation of task demonstrability, Stasser and Stewart (1992) told groups solving a hypothetical homicide case that they either did or did not have sufficient information to solve the case and determine which of three suspects was guilty. Groups whose members believed that the group had sufficient information to solve the murder case were more likely to discuss unshared information and correctly solve the case. This finding is consistent with a meta-analysis of many studies showing that higher demonstrability in the hidden profile task fosters information sharing, and lower demonstrability is detrimental to information sharing and group decision quality (Lu et al., 2012). Because this meta-analysis coded each study's task as either high or low in demonstrability, such coding could have included perceptions of the first two conditions of demonstrability (e.g., the Stasser & Stewart, 1992, study was coded as high in demonstrability despite the information sufficiency manipulation therein). So, this meta-analysis suggests that a shared conceptual system, sufficient information, or both combined support information sharing and group decision quality.

The artificial nature of the hidden profile task ensures that the group is composed of members who together possess all information necessary to solve the problem, even though they may not be aware of this fact. We can imagine that natural groups in organizations may not be aware of whether the group has the right mix of people with sufficient expert knowledge and access to additional knowledge from those outside of the group but within their social networks. Thus, natural work groups need to consider how to compose their groups to ensure that the group has access to needed information. If members realize that the group is missing an important area of expertise, they may recruit an additional member who brings that body of knowledge to the group or find the information themselves. The key is that group members need both (a) sufficient information to solve the problem via group member knowledge and social network connections and (b) awareness that the group has sufficient information to perform well. Information sufficiency helps to foster the information sharing process of the final two demonstrability conditions: members contributing information and accepting others' information when shared.

Contributing Information

In the hidden profile task, pooling unshared information is key to solving the task. The unshared information represents the pieces of "truth" that each member knows, which need to be pieced together collaboratively to solve the puzzle. Therefore, members must have sufficient ability, motivation, and time to mention their unshared information during group discussion for the group to perform well. This requires that members participate in the group discussion. However, the central, persistent, and robust finding is that some group members speak more than others during discussion, and in many cases group outcomes reflect the preferences of the most frequent speakers (Bottger, 1984; Sorrentino & Boutillier, 1975). If the main goal of researchers is to improve group decision making, it makes sense to say that unequal participation creates the potential for suboptimal decision making because it is possible that infrequent participators have important things to contribute but, for a variety of reasons, choose not to. Sometimes, infrequent participators don't have much to say (Bonito, 2001). It is likely that in the hidden profile task, all members possess valuable unshared information that is critical for effective group performance. To understand when group members speak up during discussion and mention their unshared information, we must consider two contributing factors: (a) individual differences and (b) communicative context.

Individual Differences

Group members differ from one another in many ways, such as personality, status, knowledge, and roles. These differences predict variation between members in their likelihood of participating in group discussion and mentioning unshared information. One notable personality difference is introversion/extraversion. Introverts get their energy from alone time whereas extraverts feel energized from positive social experiences. Not surprisingly, introverts are less likely to participate in group discussion compared to extraverts (Lambregts, 2020). In a hidden profile task where members hold unshared information, it is important to encourage introverts to speak up because their information may be critical for making a good group decision. Members also differ in status – the regard, rank and prestige each member holds. Wittenbaum (1998, 2000) composed groups of both high-status members (those with prior task experience) and low-status members (those without prior task experience). Results showed that low-status members displayed the discussion bias favoring shared over unshared information during group discussion, whereas high-status members did not. Like introverts, low-status members may participate less in group discussion, which makes creating space for them to speak and share their unshared information critical for successful group performance.

Another important individual difference is that group members differ in how much knowledge they share with the rest of the group. Members who are *cognitively central* have a lot of overlapping knowledge with other group members, whereas members who are *cognitively peripheral* have little knowledge in common with other group members (Kameda et al., 1997). Research by Sargis and Larson (2002) showed that cognitively peripheral members engaged in fewer speaking turns and contributed less information compared to cognitively central members. Members who are on the knowledge outskirts of the group may need encouragement to speak up in the group discussion and share what they know. Finally, group members differ in the roles that they play in the group. Roles identify the types of behaviors group members expect of members who hold particular positions in the group. For example, the group's leader is expected to guide the group toward accomplishing its goals and possibly facilitating the group's discussion. Leaders can play an important role in highlighting the contributions of members and helping the group to consider unshared information. Research using the hidden profile task has shown that leaders repeat unshared information over time, ensuring that the group adequately has considered the unique contributions of its members (Larson et al., 1996, 1998). Ensuring that the group has a leader may help the group to focus on the unshared information when it is critical for effective decision making.

Communicative Context

Aside from member qualities, features of the group's context can influence member communication. This includes the group's climate and norms guiding expected behavior, external constraints such as time pressure, and incentives for cooperating. An important aspect of the group's climate for fostering participation and information is its degree of team psychological safety. *Team psychological safety* is the shared belief among members that it is okay to make mistakes, take risks, and express disagreement (Edmondson, 1999). Edmondson showed that in teams with psychological safety, low-status members were more likely to speak up and voice concerns, even questioning the leader. In doing so, teams were more likely to identify decision errors and potentially correct mistakes. Communicating unshared information can be risky given that, in a hidden profile task, it challenges the prevailing leaning of the group and cannot be validated by other members (Wittenbaum & Park, 2001). Therefore, promoting a team climate of psychological safety may increase participation among low-status members and increase the likelihood that they communicate valuable unshared information.

If the team climate is one of psychological safety, members must also have the time to speak up and share their information. In this regard, time pressure hurts information sharing and longer discussions help. Bowman and Wittenbaum (2012) found that when groups discussed a hidden profile task from memory (rather than having it for reference), high time pressure groups showed a stronger discussion bias favoring shared over unshared information and engaged in shorter discussions. Larson and colleagues have shown that unshared information is more likely to be discussed in groups the longer the discussion lasts (Larson et al., 1994, 1996, 1998). Group discussion focuses more on shared information early on, but members mention unshared information as the discussion progresses. Schulz-Hardt and Mojzisch (2012) concluded that group decisions are higher quality when (a) the discussion tendency to favor shared over unshared information is minimized, and (b) groups engage in longer discussions that bring out more total information (referred to as *discussion intensity*).

Finally, the standard hidden profile task assumes that group members are cooperative communicators, willing to share any information that comes to mind (Wittenbaum, Hollingshead, & Botero, 2004). However, groups in natural settings often have a mixture of both cooperative and competitive goals (Sohrab et al., 2015; Wittenbaum, Hollingshead, & Botero, 2004). The incentive system may reward members who withhold their unshared information from others. For example, members may personally benefit from the group choosing a particular option or solution and therefore choose to conceal information that counters that aim. Some researchers have developed theories of how group members are strategic in selecting what information to share during group discussion (Hollingshead et al., 2007; Toma & Butera, 2015), but research on strategic information sharing is scarce. Given that member goals and incentives influence members' willingness to share what they know, we encourage additional research in this area.

In summary, the hidden profile task is more demonstrable when members contribute their unshared information. In a hidden profile task, contributing information requires that members have sufficient motivation and time to mention their unshared information. Leaders can invite low-status, introverted, and cognitively peripheral members to share their unshared information and create a climate of team psychological safety and cooperative norms to enable such sharing. By repeating unshared information that others mention and taking the time (if possible) for longer discussions that unveil more information, leaders can foster effective group decision making and problem solving in a hidden profile task.

Accepting Information

To correctly solve the hidden profile task, group members must understand the shared conceptual system well enough to accept arguments proposed by other members that are persuasive based on reasoning and logic within the system. This means that when a group member mentions unshared information that is important for solving the task yet contrary to members' preferences, other members must entertain the merits of this new information and accept it for revising their preferences. The key to accepting information is that group members are influenced by the merit of argument (Vinokur & Burnstein, 1978) rather than social pressure or communicator status, which may not be indicative of a communicator's accuracy or competency.

As tasks become more solvable (e.g., because of a shared conceptual system and sufficient information), then a single group member who is willing to contribute critical information and logic for solving the problem tends to influence the group choice. That is, for intellective tasks, groups tend to use a "truth wins" process for combining member preferences into a group choice whereby the single member with the correct solution gets their solution adopted by the group (Laughlin & Ellis, 1986; Zarnoth & Sniezek, 1997; also see Chapter 15). Confident group members are more influential in the group when working on intellective tasks, in part because such members tend to be accurate. "Confidence is correlated with accuracy on intellective tasks, and accuracy, in turn, is directly responsible for the increase in social power" (Zarnoth & Sniezek, 1997, p. 361).

When groups work on a hidden profile task, having just one member of the group favor the correct solution increases the likelihood that the group chooses that solution. Schulz-Hardt et al. (2006) had three-person groups work on a hidden profile task where pooling unshared information was critical for determining the best solution. When all three group members favored the same wrong option before discussion, groups selected the correct option only 7% of the time. However, when the group was composed of two members who preferred a wrong option and a third member who preferred the correct one, groups' solutions were correct 65% of the time. This situation fostered thorough group discussion and sharing of information. Although one group member often has an uphill battle to influence most other members in a group (Wittenbaum, 2013), it is easier for other members to accept this member's unshared information and arguments when the member prefers the correct solution and the task is intellective, such as this hidden profile task.

One of the challenges in the hidden profile task and with group information sharing in general, is a phenomenon known as the *mutual enhancement* effect (Wittenbaum et al., 1999). This occurs when group members evaluate both themselves and other group members more positively (in terms of competence, knowledge, and credibility) when they communicate shared information rather than unshared information. Group members may view unshared information and those who communicate it with suspicion because they cannot validate its accuracy (Wittenbaum & Bowman, 2004). The hidden profile task is one that requires group members to accept the accuracy of those communicating critical unshared information, but the mutual enhancement effect compromises members' ability to see the merits of unshared information when mentioned. Although mutual enhancement could compromise the quality of group decisions in a hidden profile task, it may ease member relations by validating shared knowledge.

Some conditions may enhance group members' willingness to accept as true and retain the unshared information of others. For example, when communicating unshared information, high-status members who felt task competent were more likely to have their unshared information remembered and accepted by lower status members (Wittenbaum, 2000). Likewise, when members' expertise was made explicit to the group, members were more likely to remember others communicated unshared information, suggesting greater acceptance in the validity of this information (Stewart & Stasser, 1995).

Acceptance of communicated critical unshared information may hinge on the intellectual humility of members. Ballantyne (2021) outlined many different definitions of *intellectual humility*. Most of these definitions converge on the notion that intellectual humility involves recognizing that one's beliefs might be wrong and right sizing these beliefs by searching for information to falsify them (Leary, 2018; Schwarz, 2022). Intellectual humility "is a way for us to manage information that's relevant to our pursuit of truth and avoidance of error" (Ballantyne, 2021, p. 5). For groups to solve the hidden profile task, members must show this intellectual humility. At the start of discussion, members may all favor a suboptimal solution supported by shared information. Unshared information, when mentioned, will counter this prevailing preference, and therefore challenge members' beliefs. For members to accept the validity of unshared information, they must realize that their preferences may be wrong and be open to new information that questions their beliefs. Although there is no research relating intellectual humility with acceptance of unshared information's validity during group discussion, we see such an avenue to be fruitful.

In summary, group members are more likely to accept unshared information from others that points toward the truth when (a) the task is demonstrable based on a shared conceptual system with sufficient information to solve it, (b) the contributing member is confident and perceived as credible, and (c) group members are willing to entertain that they might be wrong and are open to logical arguments to determine the veracity of their beliefs.

Recommendations for Practice

Everyone works in groups to make decisions and solve problems. Key to performing well in groups is fostering participation and information sharing from all members. This is especially the case for hidden profile tasks. But any group will not know if the task that they are working on is a hidden profile or not. We recommend assuming that it could be and that participation and information sharing from all members will help the group to perform well regardless.

To make the group task more solvable and promote effective group work, we recommend interventions that address the four conditions of task demonstrability. First, determine each group member's expertise (e.g., via group training, Moreland & Myaskovsky, 2000). This helps members to understand how knowledge is distributed, thus informing a shared conceptual system of how to integrate disparate knowledge to solve a problem. Second, a well-composed group of diverse members will help to ensure that the knowledge available within the group is sufficient for solving the problem. Group members may also brainstorm about sources of technology or people outside of the group which may be helpful for providing sufficient information. For example, human members of online groups sometimes consider a technological agent (e.g., a bot or artificial intelligence) to be a group member who provides unshared information (Yan et al., 2019). Third, ensure that the group has a leader who will encourage quieter members to participate by fostering a culture of psychological safety, cooperation, and patience. Any one member may have critical unshared information that deserves consideration. Fourth, be open minded to members who speak with conviction, logic, and new ideas that challenge the prevailing group norm, as this new information may be key to solving the problem. A socially diverse team (in terms of race or culture) may help members to show open mindedness because they anticipate differences in opinion and more diligent work to achieve consensus (Phillips et al., 2014). Keeping the four task demonstrability conditions in mind – a shared conceptual system, sufficient information, members contributing and accepting information – will provide a roadmap for how to improve information sharing and group performance.

Conclusion

This chapter promotes understanding of participation and information sharing in decision-making groups through the framework of task demonstrability, or how solvable a group task is. Participation and information sharing have the potential to improve group performance as the group task becomes more solvable. To this end, fostering a shared conceptual system for completing the task, ensuring access to sufficient information, encouraging members to contribute important unshared information, and being open to such information, will help groups to make the best decisions. The hidden profile task is one that is potentially solvable under these four conditions of task demonstrability. This chapter provides recommendations for how to improve hidden profile task performance in groups by supporting the facilitating conditions of task demonstrability, of which group member participation and information sharing are critical.

Box 13.1   Moneyball: A Case Study

The concepts in this chapter are nicely illustrated in a scene from the sports film, *Moneyball* (Miller, 2011), which is based on the true story of how the Oakland Athletics baseball team created a winning season in 2002 by recruiting unexpected players. At the time, conventional wisdom in American baseball was to recruit top-paid superstar players to compose a winning team. Billy Beane (played by Brad Pitt), the Athletics' general manager, invited Pete Brand (played by Jonah Hill), a young Yale University economics graduate, to attend the meeting with the scouts to determine which players to recruit to the team. Pete was unknown to the scouts and recommended an unconventional approach to recruiting players based on statistics from in-game activity: Recruit less-expensive players who could get on base and whose collective performance equaled one outstanding player. As Billy led the group discussion during the meeting, one scout asked who Pete was and whether he needed to be there. Billy replied, "Yes, he does" (Miller, 2011, 33:01). With each unexpected player Billy recommended to recruit, the scouts pushed back with arguments for why the suggested players were washed up. Billy instead gave voice to Pete, allowing him to share his novel argument for recruiting players. After the meeting, an angry scout confronted Billy:

> You don't put a team together with a computer, Billy…Baseball isn't just numbers. It's not science. If it was, then anyone could do what we're doing. But they can't because they don't know what we know. They don't have our experience and they don't have our intuition… You've got a kid in there that's got a degree in economics from Yale. You got a scout here with 29 years of baseball experience. You're listening to the wrong one. Now, there are intangibles that only baseball people understand. You're discounting what scouts have done for 150 years, even yourself.
>
> (Miller, 2011, 47:20)

The scouts did not have a shared conceptual system with Billy and Pete for understanding how to recruit baseball players. The scouts questioned Pete's task competence and credibility and even his legitimacy to attend the meeting. Pete's unshared information challenged the prevailing preferences among the scouts and was discounted. Billy gave Pete, a low-status member, the opportunity to speak, but high-status scouts were not open to his critical unshared information and the possibility that they might be wrong. Pete contributed information through data and logical argument, but the scouts did not accept it. If Billy had caved to the scouts' wishes and ignored Pete's unshared information, the Athletics would not have gone on to win the league division that season.

Further Readings

Stasser, G., & Abele, S. (2020). Collective choice, collaboration, and communication. *Annual Review of Psychology*, *71*, 589–612. https://doi.org/10.1146/annurev-psych-010418-103211

Stasser, G., & Titus, W. (2003). Hidden profiles: A brief history. *Psychological Inquiry*, *14*(3), 304–313. https://doi.org/10.1207/S15327965PLI1403&4_21

Glossary

Hidden profile task   Information that is needed to solve the problem is unequally distributed across members.
Task demonstrability   The degree to which a group task is solvable allows the group to find the best or correct answer. It is fostered by four conditions: a shared conceptual system, sufficient information to solve the problem, and members contributing information and accepting it when communicated.
Unshared information   This is information known by a single member in the group about which others will not know unless communicated by the knowledgeable member.

References

Ballantyne, N. (2021). Recent work in intellective humility: A philosopher's perspective. The *Journal of Positive Psychology*, 1–21. https://doi.org/10.1080/17439760.2021.1940252

Bonito, J. A. (2001). An information-processing approach to participation in small groups. *Communication Research*, 28(3), 275–303. https://doi.org/10.1177/009365001028003002

Bonito, J. A. (2007). A local model of information sharing in small groups. *Communication Theory*, 17(3), 252–280. https://doi.org/10.1111/j.1468-2885.2007.00295.x

Bonner, B. L., Shannahan, S., Bain, K., Coll, K., & Meikle, N. L. (2021). The theory and measurement of expertise-based problem solving in organizational teams: Revisiting demonstrability. *Organization Science*. Advance online publication. https://doi.org/10.1287/orsc.2021.1481

Bottger, P. C. (1984). Expertise and air time as bases of actual and perceived influence in problem-solving groups. *Journal of Applied Psychology*, 69(2), 214–221. https://doi.org/10.1037/0021-9010.69.2.214

Bowman, J. M., & Wittenbaum, G. M. (2012). Time pressure affects process and performance in hidden-profile groups. *Small Group Research*, 43, 295–314. https://doi.org/10.1177/1046496412440055

Collins, B. E., & Guetzkow, H. S. (1964). *A social psychology of group processes for decision making*. John Wiley and Sons.

Devine, D. J., Clayton, L. D., Philips, J. L., Dunford, B. B., & Meiner, S. B. (1999). Teams in organizations: Prevalence, characteristics, and effectiveness. *Small Group Research*, 30(6), 678–711. https://doi.org/10.1177/104649649903000602

Edmondson, A. (1999). Psychological safety and learning behavior in work teams. *Administrative Science Quarterly*, 44(2), 350–383. https://doi.org/10.2307/2666999

Fraidin, S. N. (2004). When is one head better than two? Interdependent information in group decision making. *Organizational Behavior and Human Decision Processes*, 93(2), 102–113. https://doi.org/10.1016/j.obhdp.2003.12.003

Hirokawa, R. Y. (1987). Why informed groups make faulty decisions: An investigation of possible interaction-based explanations. *Small Group Behavior*, 18(1), 3–29. https://doi.org/10.1177/104649648701800101

Hollingshead, A. B., Jacobsohn, G. C., & Beck, S. J. (2007). Motives and goals in context: A strategic analysis of information sharing in groups. In K. Fiedler (Ed.), *Frontiers of social psychology: social communication* (pp. 257–280). Psychology Press.

Kameda, T., Ohtsubo, Y., & Takezawa, M. (1997). Centrality in sociocognitive networks and social influence: An illustration in a group decision-making context. *Journal of Personality and Social Psychology*, 73, 296–309. https://doi.org/10.1037/0022-3514.73.2.296

Lambregts, M. G. (2020). *Introverts and extraverts collaborating: The influence on participation, transactivity and group work perceptions during an online discussion*. [Master thesis, University of Twente] https://purl.utwente.nl/essays/85145

Larson, J. R. Jr. (1997). Modeling the entry of shared and unshared information into group discussion: A review and basic language computer program. *Small Group Research*, 28(3), 454–479. https://doi.org/10.1177/1046496497283007

Larson, J. R. Jr., Christensen, C., Abbott, A. S., & Franz, T. M. (1996). Diagnosing groups: Charting the flow of information in medical decision-making teams. *Journal of Personality and Social Psychology, 71(2)*, 315–330. https://doi.org/10.1037/0022-3514.71.2.315.

Larson, J. R. Jr., Christensen, C., Franz, T. M., & Abbott, A. S. (1998). Diagnosing groups: The pooling, management, and impact of shared and unshared case information in team-based mediated decision making. *Journal of Personality and Social Psychology, 75*, 93–108.

Larson, J. R., & Egan, J. R. Jr. (2020). Information sharing within groups in organizations. In L. Argote & J. M. Levine (Eds.), *The Oxford handbook of group and organizational learning* (pp. 127–154). Oxford University Press.

Larson, J. R. Jr., Foster-Fishman, P. G., & Keys, C. B. (1994). Discussion of shared and unshared information in decision-making groups. *Journal of Personality and Social Psychology, 67*(3), 446–461. https://doi.org/10.1037/0022-3514.67.3.446

Laughlin, P. R. (1980). *Social combination processes of cooperative problem-solving groups on verbal intellective tasks.* In M. Fishbein (Ed.), *Progress in social psychology* (pp. 127–155). Erlbaum.

Laughlin, P. R., & Ellis, A. L. (1986). Demonstrability and social combination processes on mathematical intellective tasks. *Journal of Experimental Social Psychology, 22*, 177–189. https://doi.org/10.1016/0022-1031(86)90022-3

Leary, M. R. (2018). *The psychology of intellectual humility.* John Templeton Foundation.

Letzring, T. D., Wells, S. M., & Funder, D. C. (2006). Information quantity and quality affect the realistic accuracy of personality judgment. *Journal of Personality and Social Psychology, 91*(1), 111–123.

Lu, L., Yuan, Y. C., & McLeod, P. L. (2012). Twenty-five years of hidden profiles in group decision making: A meta-analysis. *Personality and Social Psychology Review, 16*(1), 54–75.

Marks, M. A., Sabella, M. J., Burke, C. S., & Zaccaro, S. J. (2002). The impact of cross-training on team effectiveness. *Journal of Applied Psychology, 87(1)*, 3–13. https://doi.org/10.1037/0021-9010.87.1.3

Mesmer-Magnus, J. R., & DeChurch, L. A. (2009). Information sharing and team performance: A meta-analysis. *Journal of Applied Psychology, 94*(2), 535–546. https://doi.org/10.1037/a0013773

Miller, B. (2011). *Moneyball.* Columbia Pictures.

Moreland, R. L., & Myaskovsky, L. (2000). Exploring the performance benefits of group training: Transactive memory or improved communication? *Organizational Behavior and Human Decision Processes, 82*, 117–133. https://doi.org/10.1006/obhd.2000.2891

Pavitt, C. (2003). Colloquy: Do interacting groups perform better than aggregates of individuals? Why we have to be reductionists about group memory. *Human Communication Research, 29*(4), 592–599.

Pavitt, C. (2014). An interactive input–process–output model of social influence in decision-making groups. *Small Group Research, 45*(6), 704–730. https://doi.org/10.1177/1046496414548353

Phillips, K. W., Medin, D., Lee, C. D., Bang, M., Bishop, S., & Lee, D. N. (2014). How diversity works. *Scientific American, 311*(4), 42–47. https://doi.org/10.1038/scientificamerican1014-42

Propp, K. M. (1999). Collective information processing in groups. In L. R. Frey, M. S. Poole, & D. S. Gouran (Eds.), *The handbook of group communication theory and research* (pp. 225–250). Sage.

Reimer, T., Reimer, A., & Czienskowski, U. (2010). Decision-making groups attenuate the discussion bias in favor of shared information: A meta-analysis. *Communication Monographs, 77*, 121–142.

Sargis, E. G., & Larson, J. R. Jr. (2002). Information centrality and member participation during group decision making. *Group Processes and Intergroup Relations, 5(4)*, 333–347. https://doi.org/10.1177/1368430202005004005

Schulz-Hardt, S., Brodbeck, F. C., Mojzisch, A., Kerschreiter, R., & Frey, D. (2006). Group decision making in hidden profile situations: Dissent as a facilitator for decision quality. *Journal of Personality and Social Psychology, 91*, 1080–1093. https://doi.org/10.1037/0022-3514.91.6.1080

Schulz-Hardt, S., & Mojzisch, A. (2012). How to achieve synergy in group decision making: Lessons to be learned from the hidden profile paradigm. *European Review of Social Psychology, 23(1)*, 305–343. https://doi.org/10.1080/10463283.2012.744440

Schwarz, N. (2022). Humility in inquiry. *The Journal of Positive Psychology*, https://doi.org/10.1080/17439760.2022.2155225

Sigman, S. J. (1984). Talk and interaction strategy in a task-oriented group. *Small Group Research, 15*(1), 33–51. https://doi.org/10.1177/104649648401500102

Sohrab, S. G., Waller, M. J., & Kaplan, S. (2015). Exploring the hidden profile paradigm: A literature review and analysis. *Small Group Research, 46(5)*, 489–535. https://doi.org/10.1177/1046496415599068

Sorrentino, R. M., & Boutillier, R. G. (1975). The effect of quantity and quality of verbal interaction on ratings of leadership ability. *Journal of Experimental Social Psychology, 11*(5), 403–411. https://doi.org/10.1016/0022-1031(75)90044-X

Stasser, G., & Abele, S. (2020). Collective choice, collaboration, and communication. *Annual Review of Psychology, 71*, 589–612. https://doi.org/10.1146/annurev-psych-010418-103211

Stasser, G., & Stewart, D. (1992). Discovery of hidden profiles by decision-making groups: Solving a problem versus making a judgment. *Journal of Personality and Social Psychology, 63(3)*, 426–434. https://doi.org/10.1037/0022-3514.63.3.426

Stasser, G., Stewart, D. D., & Wittenbaum, G. M. (1995). Expert roles and information exchange during discussion: The importance of knowing who knows what. *Journal of Experimental Social Psychology, 31*, 244–265. https://doi.org/10.1006/jesp.1995.1012

Stasser, G., & Titus, W. (2003). Hidden profiles: A brief history. *Psychological Inquiry, 14*(3), 304–313. https://doi.org/10.1207/S15327965PLI1403&4_21

Stewart, D., & Stasser, G. (1995). Expert role assignment and information sampling during collective recall and decision making. *Journal of Personality and Social Psychology, 69(4)*, 619–628. https://doi.org/10.1037/0022-3514.69.4.619

Toma, C., & Butera, F. (2015). Cooperation versus competition effects on information sharing and use in group decision-making. *Personality and Social Psychology Compass, 9(9)*, 455–467. https://doi.org/10.1111/spc3.12191

Vinokur, A., & Burnstein, E. (1978). Novel argumentation and attitude change: The case of polarization following group discussion. *European Journal of Social Psychology, 8(3)*, 335–348. https://doi.org/10.1002/ejsp.2420080306

Wittenbaum, G. M. (1998). Information sampling in decision-making groups: The impact of members' task-relevant status. *Small Group Research, 29*, 57–84. https://doi.org/10.1177/1046496498291003

Wittenbaum, G. M. (2000). The bias toward discussing shared information: Why are high status group members immune? *Communication Research, 27*, 379–401. https://doi.org/10.1177/009365000027003005

Wittenbaum, G. M. (2013). The opinion of one can persuade a group: A case of minority influence. In C. Liberman (Ed.), *Casing persuasive communication* (pp. 87–98). Kendall Hunt.

Wittenbaum, G. M., & Bowman, J. M. (2004). A social validation explanation for mutual enhancement. *Journal of Experimental Social Psychology, 40(2)*, 169–184. https://doi.org/10.1016/S0022-1031(03)00091-X

Wittenbaum, G. M., Hollingshead, A. B., & Botero, I. C. (2004). From cooperative to motivated information sharing in groups: Moving beyond the hidden profile paradigm. *Communication Monographs, 71*(3), 286–310. https://doi.org/10.1080/0363452042000299894

Wittenbaum, G. M., Hollingshead, A. B., Paulus, P. B., Hirokawa, R. Y., Ancona, D. G., Peterson, R. S., Jehn, K. A., & Yoon, K. (2004). The functional perspective as a lens for understanding groups. *Small Group Research, 35*, 17–43. https://doi.org/10.1177/1046496403259459

Wittenbaum, G. M., Hubbell, A. P., & Zuckerman, C. (1999). Mutual enhancement: Toward an understanding of the collective preference for shared information. *Journal of Personality and Social Psychology, 77*, 967–978. https://doi.org/10.1037/0022-3514.77.5.967

Wittenbaum, G. M., & Park, E. S. (2001). The collective preference for shared information. *Current Directions in Psychological Science, 10*, 70–73. https://doi.org/10.1111/1467-8721.00118

Wittenbaum, G. M., & Stasser, G. (1996). Management of information in small groups. In J. L. Nye & A. M. Brower (Eds.), *What's social about social cognition? Social cognition research in small groups* (pp. 3–28). Sage.

Yan, B., Kim, Y. J., Hollingshead, A. B., & Brandon, D. P. (2019). Conceptualizing online groups as multidimensional networks. In A. Attrill-Smith, C. Fullwood, M. Keep, & D. J. Kuss (Eds.), *The Oxford handbook of cyberpsychology* (pp. 306–327). Oxford University Press. https://doi.org/10.1093/oxfordhb/9780198812746.013.15

Zarnoth, P., & Sniezek, J. A. (1997). The social influence of confidence in group decision making. *Journal of Experimental Social Psychology, 33*, 345–366. https://doi.org/10.1006/jesp.1997.1326

14 Transactive Memory Systems and Learning

Leila Bighash and Michael Farzinpour

Chapter Objectives

- Define transactive memory systems (TMS) and explain the computer network metaphor used to illustrate TMS.
- Distinguish between and identify elements of the development, processes, and outcomes of TMS, particularly as related to communication.
- Recognize the role of diversity and technology in TMS within each of the stages.

Introduction

Have you ever been a part of a group that worked together seamlessly? Every member knew each other so well that they knew exactly who could best help accomplish specific tasks. No time was wasted on figuring out who could answer questions or carry out tasks, because everyone *just knows* how to reroute problems. All work was completed efficiently, like a well-oiled machine. If you have experienced this (or at least can envision what it would be like), then you already intuitively know something about transactive memory systems (TMS) theory.

TMS theory emerged out of the early theories of *group* mind that were criticized for relying on supernatural rather than scientific explanations since there is no tangible group mind to access (Hollingshead et al., 2011), unlike an individual's memory that exists within an individual's physical brain. Daniel Wegner and colleagues (1985) tried to address this criticism by initially conceptualizing TMSs in terms of dyadic processes, later explicating for groups using the metaphor of a computer network (Wegner, 1995).

The computer network metaphor illustrates how memory can form among a group of people without their minds being physically or telepathically connected, instead using communicative transactions and network connections to access one another's information stores and accomplish tasks (Hollingshead et al., 2011). Each group member can be thought of as a separate computer with its own files in its memory (i.e., the hard drive). All computers are connected through a network, like the internet. This connection allows the computers to communicate to retrieve information from the other computers' memories. To make this retrieval process more efficient, each computer updates a directory of the contents of its memory and keeps a directory of the contents of the other computers' memories, indicating which categories of information are available to allow for easier access.

Similarly, in groups, each member has their own informational expertise in their memory. People in groups are connected through social networks and their communication (i.e., transactions) allows them to make judgments about the expertise of others in a network. Then, through a combination of their own intentional learning and/or group communicative processes, they can

DOI: 10.4324/9781003227458-16

update their mental directories based on their observations and communication. The "location," that is, who stores that knowledge, and "labels," that is, the categories of knowledge, exist within the transactive memory of individuals (Hollingshead et al., 2011), while the transactive memory *system* is the collective group memory facilitated by the collectivity of connections and transactions between all group members (Ren & Argote, 2011). When groups have developed TMSs, this means they have established a system for encoding, processing, storing, and retrieving information, such that there is a division of labor among group members based on their area(s) of expertise (Hollingshead, 1998a; Ren & Argote, 2011). TMSs can reduce the cognitive load of individual members by directing knowledge needs and tasks to others, allowing each person to focus on their own expertise areas (Hollingshead et al., 2011). See Figure 14.1 for a visual representation of this conceptual framework.

In the forthcoming sections, we follow previous scholars' work in reviewing TMS (e.g., Ren & Argote, 2011; Yan et al., 2021) and examine TMS at three different stages: development, processes, and outcomes. When discussing development, we focus on the antecedents that lead to a working TMS. In the processes section, we primarily focus on actions that occur once TMSs have been established. Finally, for outcomes, we discuss the results of TMS for groups. We emphasize that

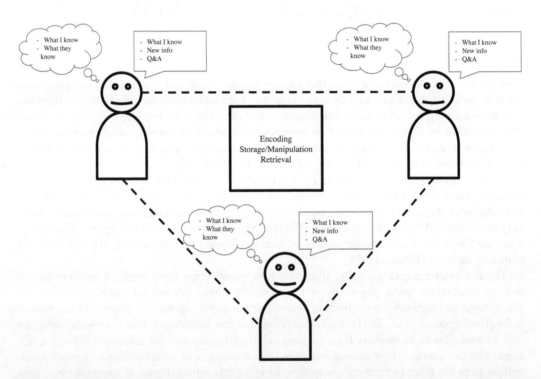

Figure 14.1 A TMS Among Members in a Three-Person Group.

This is a simplified visual representation of a three-person group that developed a TMS. The thought bubbles on the left of each group member represent their internal individual memories and transactive memories, or their directories, which would indicate the location and label of information. The callouts on the right of each group member represent their communication with other group members, including discussing their own expertise and the expertise of others, discussing any new information (and then subsequently allocating that information to new teammates), and asking for/retrieving information. The dotted lines between the group members represent their network connections. All group members are connected to each other in a social network.

some concepts discussed influence the different stages differently. Within each section, we highlight the nature of communication and the role of diversity and technology where applicable. As we review TMS concepts in this chapter, we refer to empirical work that relies on experiments establishing causality, as well as surveys, observational work, and qualitative work (e.g., interviews) examining this theory in the context of real-world groups and teams.

TMS Development

TMSs have been researched thoroughly to determine how they become functional. Group members must learn how to work together. Some of the earliest work in transactive memory studied dyads, particularly romantic couples who develop intuitive, intimate, and cohesive relationships where information storage and expertise allocation are clearly established (Barnier et al., 2018; Wegner et al., 1985). Later, scholars began examining how small groups of three or more have emergent properties, such that "the whole is greater than the sum of its parts." In other words, if each member's independent contributions were added up, this would not be equal to what the group together can accomplish when interacting with one another.

A critical aspect of TMS is that group members eventually "[rely] on other members as their external memory aids" (Peltokorpi & Hood, 2019, p. 645). This reliance on others can be described as "interdependence" (Wegner et al., 1985), where one person's outcomes depend on the outcomes of the rest of the group members (Ren & Argote, 2011). Cognitive interdependence occurs when people depend on others for information and is one of the most important features of a group for a TMS to develop (Brandon & Hollingshead, 2004; Hollingshead, 2001). Hollingshead (2001) experimentally studied how cognitive interdependence and convergent expectations (i.e., sharing the perceptions with group members on the expertise of others) are two necessary elements to developing a TMS among people who had no past interactions with one another. People must start to identify who is associated with specific expertise areas, which is called the location of knowledge (Wegner et al., 1985). How do group members do this? As you may have guessed, communication is key.

Communication is the very action that makes TMS possible: information "transactions" occur when people communicate in some way. Communication allows members to move from simple heuristics about the expertise of others that may be inaccurate, like gender-based stereotypes (Hollingshead & Fraidin, 2003), to more detailed and accurate representations of others' expertise (Hollingshead & Brandon, 2003). For example, an experimental study found that two strangers could quickly begin to develop a TMS by explicitly communicating about who should remember what for a collective recall task (Hollingshead, 1998b). As such, communication about expertise (Lewis et al., 2005) and gaining familiarity with other group members (Lewis, 2004) are key to developing functioning TMSs. Familiarization often relies on time; members need to spend time with one another to gain that familiarity (Lewis, 2004; Olabisi & Lewis, 2018). A study examining virtual teams found that it took several weeks for group members to feel comfortable enough to trust one another and coordinate their specialized information (Kanawattanachai & Yoo, 2007). Training/ practice can also increase familiarity, as explored by Liang et al. (1995) who randomly assigned participants to either individual training or group training to assemble part of a radio in groups of three people of the same sex. Group training strengthened the TMS, which, in turn, improved their performance. Other aspects of communication examined that influence TMS development include quality and frequency (Peltokorpi & Hood, 2019). We recommend Yan and colleagues' (2021) review for a more thorough examination of how communication has been explored in recent TMS research.

Despite these studies demonstrating the importance of communication in TMS development, some have argued that communication is instead a detriment to group functioning. For example,

Pavitt (2003) argued that, based on cumulatively reading previous findings, "communication does not allow us to function optimally in group settings" (p. 598) and instead discourages groups from engaging in behavior like pooling information resources. However, as Hollingshead and Brandon (2003) point out, the literature Pavitt examined involved groups that were strangers rather than longer-term groups that are more likely to form functional TMSs. Others argued that communication internal to the group is not always *necessary* for TMS development because groups can be exogenously told about the expertise of others (e.g., Hollingshead, 1998a; Moreland & Myaskovsky, 2000). Additionally, communication errors may result in less developed and less converged TMSs (Hollingshead et al., 2010), where at least some group members have not agreed on the structure and use of the TMS (Brandon & Hollingshead, 2004). Inconsistent results have been uncovered in several studies related to TMS and communication (Yan et al., 2021, p. 10). Though more work needs untangle the role of communication at the development stage, communication is important at various points in the life of TMSs (Hollingshead & Brandon, 2003). A TMS is "about more than learning, storing, and remembering information; it is also about knowledge transmission and knowledge generation, which involve communication" (Hollingshead et al., 2011, p. 429).

The communication environment – or the context in which group members interact – also influences TMS development. This environment could include (1) whether the group is face-to-face or technologically mediated, (2) whether the group is primarily distributed or collocated, and (3) how many members are in the group, among other environmental characteristics. Some research has found that frequent in-person communication results in a better developed TMSs compared to communication via communication technologies (Hollingshead, 1998d; Lewis, 2004), suggesting that communication technologies did not allow for the full range of important communicative behaviors (e.g., nonverbal). More advanced communication technologies (e.g., video calls and virtual reality) may not follow this trend, which researchers should continue to examine.

Other research has shown that TMSs can form through technologically mediated communication as evidenced by work examining virtual teams (Kanawattanachai & Yoo, 2007; Yoo & Kanawattanachai, 2001). While newly formed virtual teams may need several weeks to develop the trust and recognition of others' expertise, they are still able to form functioning TMSs (Kanawattanachai & Yoo, 2007). Ren and Argote (2011) suggested in their review that perhaps the different study outcomes concerning mediated communication were because of different contexts. Fully distributed teams did well with developing TMSs because there was no other choice but to rely on computer-mediated communication. Likewise, in groups that are required to be technologically mediated, certain information technology tools can be helpful in creating a sense of awareness about distribution of expertise, among other aspects of the group (Choi et al., 2010; Schreiber & Engelmann, 2010; Yuan et al., 2007). For example, having access to digital concept mapping software may enhance the accuracy and agreement of knowledge of others' expertise (Schreiber & Engelmann, 2010). Additionally, specific affordances (i.e., perceived use possibilities) of social media can lead to different outcomes for the sharedness, accuracy, and validation of TMS among remote teams (Yoon & Zhu, 2022). For example, the affordances of visibility and searchability led to more accuracy, while awareness and pervasiveness led to more sharedness. Research on geographically distributed teams has found that TMS can develop but should be aided by setting standards, guidelines, and templates across sites (Oshri et al., 2008), along with managing cross-national differences and building in support (Cordery & Soo, 2008). Group size also plays a role in TMS development. As team size increases size, it becomes less likely that a TMS will develop because members cannot communicate with every other member, reducing both accuracy of expertise recognition and knowledge differentiation (Palazzolo et al., 2006). Smaller groups are expected to be better equipped to handle the necessary communication with all members to develop a TMS. Finally, environmental volatility is positively associated with TMS development because it amplifies a team's information processing demands and the need to coordinate and integrate among group members (Bachrach et al., 2019).

Not only does communicating with other group members help individuals learn the location of "initially distributed expertise" (Lewis, 2004, p. 1521), it also allows members to decide which areas of knowledge to focus on themselves (Hollingshead, 2001). Members can differentiate themselves further by specializing in specific expertise areas (Lewis et al., 2005). Thus, diversity is a key element of TMSs in the development stage. Task incentives can help create a group atmosphere that encourages people to remember their unique knowledge, further emphasizing and leveraging the diversity that exists (Hollingshead, 2001). Surprisingly, however, a meta-analysis found that both demographic (i.e., gender) and informational diversity negatively influenced TMS development, perhaps because gender diversity led to stereotyping or other misperceptions, while informational diversity produced problems with miscommunication, among other issues (Bachrach et al., 2019). Todorova (2021) argues that relationship conflict arises between those with vastly different expertise areas, leading to less developed TMSs.

Group tasks also influence how TMSs develop. Brandon and Hollingshead (2004) argued that members' knowledge of group tasks is as important as knowing the type and location of expertise because group members interpret the structure, nature, and breakdown of a task determining how knowledge gets translated to tasks (pp. 635–636). The task-expertise-person (TEP) unit – or the "triadic unit relating three labeled 'objects'" (Brandon & Hollingshead, 2004, p. 637) – helps understand how people in a group develop their individual mental models and eventually build a shared mental model about the TMS structure, meaning "all group members have similar TEP units and arrange those units in a similar fashion" (p. 638). Individuals develop their perception of TEP units in three cycles: (1) *construction* where initial TEPs are created in individuals' minds, (2) *evaluation* where individuals evaluate the credibility of those initial TEPs, and (3) *utilization* where individuals use the information in TEPs to do something in the group, like ask a question. As group members interact, they discover if their individual mental models of the TEPs and how they are organized overlaps with others, leading to further convergence. To determine how developed the TMS is, scholars suggest examining the accuracy (i.e., expertise perceptions match with actual expertise), sharedness (i.e., mental models are similar to one another), and validation (i.e., how well perceptions match with who is accomplishing what) within the team (Brandon & Hollingshead, 2004).

Tasks also influence TMS development. For example, Baumann and Bonner (2011) found in their experiment that group members altered their information use about expertise depending on task. Others have theoretically explored how different aspects of task types may influence the development of a TMS, including task processes, structural qualities, and relevance (Lewis & Herndon, 2011). Tasks that required groups to produce many alternative ideas benefited from diverse knowledge resources, problem-solving tasks benefited from specialization and reduced cognitive load on any member, and execution tasks were most reliant on all aspects of a well-developed TMS (Lewis & Herndon, 2011, p. 1259). Regardless of the task type, research has found that having conflict revolving around tasks can enhance TMS development because people become aware of others' expertise (Todorova, 2021).

TMS Processes

An "active" TMS can be recognized based on three interrelated "manifestations" (Lewis, 2003, p. 590; Liang et al., 1995): (1) members have specialized expertise and decided on a division of labor, (2) members trust others' expertise areas, (3) and groups can work together to accomplish tasks. Lewis (2003) developed a validated survey measure of TMS including these three factors, calling them specialization, credibility, and coordination, respectively. This indirect measure of TMS is commonly used in the literature, with more than 1300 citations at the time of writing. However, these latent factors are not TMS components themselves (Lewis & Herndon, 2011). When possible, employing direct measures to evaluate actual TMS structure and processes "enable[s] researchers to draw valid conclusions…about the TMSs as a whole" (Lewis & Herndon, 2011, p. 1257).

As groups maintain TMSs, they engage in several processes. **Transactive encoding**, storage/ modification, and retrieval of information occur at the group level, with related subprocesses including **directory updating**, information allocation, and retrieval coordination (Hollingshead et al., 2011).

Transactive encoding occurs when new information enters the group, and group members discuss that information to make decisions about with whom information should be held within the group (Wegner, 1987). For example, Hollingshead (1998a) found that strangers assigned responsibility for different knowledge categories by overtly discussing their expertise and who should be responsible for what. Information allocation, or the actual assignment of information to be stored by specific group member(s), results in continued differentiation and specialization among the people within the group (Hollingshead et al., 2011; Wegner, 1995). When groups have developed TMSs, they are able to engage in encoding and allocation efficiently, as initially shown by studies examining strangers compared to romantic partners (Wegner et al., 1991), and later found in studies of three-person groups trained together (Rulke & Rau, 2000). Individuals were able to focus on their own expertise while knowing either explicitly or implicitly in which areas their partners or group members would specialize. Diversity of storage (i.e., the location of information within individual group members) becomes more prominent and distinct as TMSs engage in internal processes.

Once TMSs are functioning, an important feature of groups is that members have knowledge of who knows what (i.e., the expertise of others) and who knows who (i.e., their network connections). These "metamemories about what others know" (Hollingshead et al., 2011, p. 424) are the directories that individuals develop to facilitate efficient group processes. Directory updating, or determining who is an expert in which areas, must happen consistently so that there is an accurate representation of expertise. Individuals learn and update their own perceptions of the distribution and location of expertise in the group. Communication technologies like information repositories can also help with directory updating and storage, "[diminishing the] need for accurate individual expertise directories" (Yuan et al., 2007, p. 137).

Finally, information retrieval is the communication process that members undertake to access the information encoded and stored in the group-level system. At its simplest, information retrieval occurs when an individual obtains needed information, either by remembering the information themselves or asking another group member (Hollingshead, 1998b). Information retrieval can be influenced by factors, such as whether group members have positive relationships (Neff et al., 2014). In other words, if group members do not like one another, they are less likely to request information from each other. Additionally, a social network study of 12 organizational work teams found group members were more likely to retrieve information from perceived experts because they are most likely to have the information they need (Palazzolo, 2005). Transactive retrieval can also happen through a communicative process where group members discuss a problem and try to **interactively cue** each other to remember the needed information (Hollingshead & Brandon, 2003; Wegner et al., 1985), also called "transactive information search" (Hollingshead, 1998d). For example, an experimental study found intimate couples were better at information retrieval than strangers in many instances, in part because they used nonverbal and paralinguistic communication to succeed (Hollingshead, 1998d, p. 669).

Communication technologies/repositories can act as another source for information, aiding retrieval (Yuan et al., 2007). In fact, some scholars from **sociomateriality** perspectives argue that "non-human actors" should be brought into human systems theories like TMS and that "the association between perceptions of expertise and retrieval should occur not only among people, but also between people and technologies" (Contractor et al., 2011, p. 710). This is especially true with online groups, where members can include "intelligent technologies" (Yan et al., 2019). Organizational intranets can be used as another means of finding, storing, and retrieving knowledge (Hollingshead et al., 2002). To not include these technologies may be disregarding a key component in how groups work together synergistically. Reliance on technology for functioning TMSs may also be a vulnerability. Some groups have become dependent on technologies to accomplish their goals. How would they operate during volatile situations, like power or internet outages? Would TMSs be obsolete without technological tools at their disposal? Extreme weather events or environments with less reliable infrastructure may provide opportunities to test this proposition.

Information retrieval does not happen without first coordination. **Retrieval coordination** involves group members deciding whether any information they have can be used to address a problem, accomplish a task, or answer a question. If they do not have the information within the group, they may decide to obtain that information from outside the group. During retrieval coordination, members figure out "how to organize the search process during retrieval so as to maximize both the speed of the search and its likelihood of finding the needed information" (Wegner, 1995, p. 333). This individual process "happens inside the head of each group member" (p. 335). Coordination at the group level also greatly influences performance. For example, a study on virtual teams found that communication becomes unimportant over time while task-knowledge coordination becomes the most important predictor of team performance, possibly because teams are better able to accomplish goals without needing to overtly communicate about tasks (Kanawattanachai & Yoo, 2007).

The aforementioned interrelated processes are key for TMSs to maintain their functioning. Without engaging in these processes, groups will lose their ability to effectively utilize the varied expertise available to them.

TMS Outcomes

When the TMS processes discussed earlier occur among group members, the TMS can produce many positive outcomes, including improved group coordination and efficiency, optimized decision making, enhanced group performance, greater knowledge diversity and transfer, and increased flexibility, among other outcomes. For example, TMSs may benefit groups by enabling them to better withstand the loss of group members (Siegel Christian et al., 2014), though in general losing group members can lead to the degradation of the TMS and can reduce performance because teams often continue to utilize previous members' TMS structure leading to inefficiencies in TMS processes (Lewis et al., 2007). TMSs can also increase organizations' flexibility and competitive advantage over competitors through the building, reconfiguring, and integrating of knowledge assets (Argote & Ren, 2012).

A TMS may result in increased knowledge transfer, a critical element to achieve goals that require multiple people's expertise. For example, two dimensions of TMS, specialization and credibility, were found to play an integral role in knowledge transfer and better team performance (Wang et al., 2018). Additionally, groups with TMSs can coordinate more effectively than groups without TMSs. For example, research on teams performing in high stress situations (e.g., police tactical teams) has found that a well-functioning TMS can lead to better implicit coordination (i.e., coordination that involves anticipation and flexible adaptation) even during nonroutine tasks because TMS involves implicit division of labor which can allow teammates to quickly rely on the expertise of others (Marques-Quinteiro et al., 2013). Teams that have TMS may also be better able to harness the resources of members that are "boundary spanners," or those who must find and integrate knowledge from outside the team (Olabisi & Lewis, 2018). This is expected to positively influence coordination not just within teams, but also between teams.

TMSs can enable organizations to perform better in terms of creativity, task performance, and affective performance (Bachrach et al., 2019). Creativity uniquely requires divergent thinking to generate idea novelty compared to convergent thinking required to accomplish task-based goals, both of which can be amplified with TMSs (Bachrach et al., 2019). Within the context of social media, for example, groups with TMSs had more team creative efficacy (i.e., shared belief that the team is collectively capable of being creative) leading to more creative outcomes (Ali et al., 2019). While TMS theory often predicts better group performance with a more differentiated structure (little overlap of information between group members) because of the emphasis on harnessing diversity, Gupta and Hollingshead (2010) found that groups with integrated structure (more informational overlap between group members) were better at intellective tasks that involve finding a correct answer because of the potential for more accuracy and efficiency. They found that integrated group members helped each other, corrected errors, and worked together. Similarly, Ali and colleagues (2019) did not find a relation between the specialization dimension and creativity. However, TMSs allow groups to respond to "uncertain and changing conditions" and can reduce task-related errors, though few studies have focused on TMS and innovation (Argote & Guo, 2016).

Evidence-Based Recommendations for Practice

Decision-makers must consider many facets of the environment, situation, and internal group dynamics to help facilitate TMS development, maintenance, and positive outcomes. There are several questions decision-makers should ask:

- What are the tasks?
- What are the group goals?
- What is the makeup of the group?
- What is the environment within which the group is embedded?

Researchers have suggested several implications for team leads, managers, coaches, and other decision-makers based on TMS findings. TMS development and maintenance can be fostered in several ways. Managers can provide incentives, encouraging groups to emphasize each member's specialized expertise (Hollingshead, 2001). For example, in sports when negotiating bonuses for individual players on their contract, terms could include specialized skills incentives (e.g., rebounds or steals) rather than simply winning overall. Additionally, incentives framed as burdens could produce better performance by groups (Bonner et al., 2017). Some may be tempted to maximize, rather than optimize, the division of labor within a team. However, an effort should be made to integrate team members and not *over*emphasize expertise diversity which can lead to lower levels of innovation (Vestal & Mesmer-Magnus, 2020) and reduced performance on intellective tasks (Gupta & Hollingshead, 2010). Interdisciplinary teams need shared experience, or they often fail to reach their full potential (Vestal & Mesmer-Magnus, 2020). Finding the right balance between expertise differentiation and integration is of key importance, and decision-makers should consider both expertise and shared experience. For example, when deciding whether to replace a redundant team member with someone who is more differentiated, ask whether the disruption to familiarity and integration is worth the added unique expertise. When emphasizing differentiation, encourage communicative exchanges to enable members to not only familiarize themselves with each other's expertise but also gain trust (Lewis, 2003; Liang et al., 1995). Groups should cultivate an environment of credibility, where group members trust each other to give them the needed expertise (Lewis, 2003; Liang et al.,

Box 14.1   Transactive Memory Systems in Sports Teams

What do you think of when someone mentions the 1996 Chicago Bulls of the National Basketball Association (NBA)? Those familiar with this team's extraordinary success would likely say, "The talented superstar player Michael Jordan!" However, a TMS scholar might point to the seeming mind-reading that occurred between teammates during their games or the way the team relied on specific people for certain duties (e.g., Scottie Pippen's steals or Dennis Rodman's rebounding). Similarly, Major League Baseball teams strongly focus on individual player statistics to determine who should be on the team or play in a game, but what if TMS scholars are right and players should instead be examined as collectives? For example, the Los Angeles Dodgers did not win a World Series simply because they hired the most talented players; instead, they had to become familiar with one another over several years before becoming champions. How do these teams work *together* to achieve wins with specific *configurations* of players?

Even though people often associate sports team success with talented superstar players, developing a strong TMS could be an even better predictor of success. Sports teams' members are highly interdependent and need each other, after all, to win. Research has shown that past associations and shared information among team members improve knowledge retrieval regarding member expertise. Team members learn who the experts are and who among a team will be best to accomplish specific tasks through communicative processes, such as directory updating, information allocation, and retrieval, which ultimately should enhance team coordination and team success.

A study published in *Nature Human Behaviour* by Mukherjee et al. (2019) examined the aforementioned contention. They analyzed basketball (NBA), football (i.e., soccer; EPL), baseball (MLB), cricket (IPL), and online gaming ("Defense of the Ancients 2") matches in the 2000s and 2010s to determine whether successful prior interactions among teammates impacted the likelihood of winning for teams. While TMS theory was only briefly mentioned in their article, the researchers discussed how successful teamwork is built on relationships that form over time ("social bonding") and can be impacted by the positive or negative interactions that occur.

They argue that team wins experienced together with teammates can be a proxy for accrual of positive information about teammates and information about the opponents (e.g., strengths/weaknesses), which TMS scholars would say are part of the encoding and directory updating processes of TMSs. To determine the strength of the TMS, the researchers first counted the number of times each pair of teammates was part of a shared win. Then, they determined the team's summed past successful interactions based on which teammates were part of each match. They found that average prior shared success (e.g., positive prior interactions) within a team predicted team wins, whereas having highly talented players (operationalized as individual game-relevant statistics) did not necessarily lead to wins. This was true across the different types of sports/games.

The researchers rightly note that they did not consider individual tasks that lead to wins, like drills or interactions during practice. So, while this study helps us understand how prior interactions during competition lead to positive outcomes, there is still work to be done to understand how TMSs may work in sports teams in terms of how team members learn about the expertise of their fellow teammates and utilize that during matches (and perhaps during other interactions that teams may have, like in the locker room and team meetings).

1995). Training among group members can help build TMS leading to greater team performance, especially if they are trained together (Hollingshead, 1998c; Moreland, 1999; Moreland & Myaskovsky, 2000). Additionally, training about *team* skills (not just task-based skills), like role clarification and goal setting, can be a practical way to increase team performance quickly rather than waiting for teams to develop their team skills over time (Prichard & Ashleigh, 2007).

Conclusion

In this chapter, we have introduced readers to TMSs or group-level information-processing systems that divide labor among group members for information storage and task completion. We discussed the metaphor of a computer network used to illustrate the working of a TMS among groups of people (and technologies if we consider them group members). We turned to the development of TMSs and went into detail about several factors that can influence TMS emergence. The processes that group members engage in were then discussed, particularly focusing on the terminology that TMS scholars use to describe the functioning of a TMS. Finally, we considered the various outcomes that TMSs can foster and some practical suggestions for those building and managing groups.

Further Readings

Leo, F. M., González-Ponce, I., García-Calvo, T., & Sánchez-Oliva, D. (2019). The relationship among cohesion, transactive memory systems, and collective efficacy in professional soccer teams: A multilevel structural equation analysis. *Group Dynamics: Theory, Research, and Practice, 23*(1), 44. https://doi.org/ 10.1037/gdn0000097

Todorova, G. (2021). Expertise diversity and transactive memory systems: Insights from a conflict perspective. *Small Group Research, 52*(3), 316–340. https://doi.org/10.1177/1046496420957103

Yan, B., Hollingshead, A. B., Alexander, K. S., Cruz, I., & Shaikh, S. J. (2021). Communication in transactive memory systems: A review and multidimensional network perspective. *Small Group Research, 52*(1), 3–32. https://doi.org/10.1177/1046496420967764

Glossary

Directory updating   Group members learn and update their perceptions of the distribution and location of expertise in the group. This may also involve updating perceptions of who knows who, who has access to what, and how tasks are related to people and expertise.

Interactive cueing   A communicative process by which group members help each other remember the needed information for a group task.

Retrieval coordination   Group members decide whether they have the information necessary, or if they need to find that information from someone else within the group.

Sociomateriality   An approach that entangles the social and material. In the context of Transactive Memory Systems (TMS), technologies are considered part of the group, similar to another group member.

Transactive encoding   When new information enters the group, the group members discuss that information to make decisions about with whom information should be held within the group.

References

Ali, A., Wang, H., & Khan, A. N. (2019). Mechanism to enhance team creative performance through social media: A transactive memory system approach. *Computers in Human Behavior, 91*, 115–126. https://doi.org/10.1016/j.chb.2018.09.033

Argote, L., & Guo, J. M. (2016). Routines and transactive memory systems: Creating, coordinating, retaining, and transferring knowledge in organizations. *Research in Organizational Behavior*, *36*, 65–84. https://doi.org/10.1016/j.riob.2016.10.002

Argote, L., & Ren, Y. (2012). Transactive memory systems: A microfoundation of dynamic capabilities. *Journal of Management Studies*, *49*(8), 1375–1382. https://doi.org/10.1111/j.1467-6486.2012.01077.x

Bachrach, D. G., Lewis, K., Kim, Y., Patel, P. C., Campion, M. C., & Thatcher, S. M. B. (2019). Transactive memory systems in context: A meta-analytic examination of contextual factors in transactive memory systems development and team performance. *Journal of Applied Psychology*, *104*(3), 464–493. https://doi.org/10.1037/apl0000329

Barnier, A. J., Klein, L., & Harris, C. B. (2018). Transactive memory in small, intimate groups: More than the sum of their parts. *Small Group Research*, *49*(1), 62–97. https://doi.org/10.1177/1046496417712439

Baumann, M. R., & Bonner, B. L. (2011). The effects of expected group longevity and expected task difficulty on learning and recall: Implications for the development of transactive memory. *Group Dynamics: Theory, Research, and Practice*, *15*(3), 220–232. https://doi.org/10.1037/a0023615

Bonner, B., Baumann, M. R., & Romney, A. C. (2017). Working outside of your wheelhouse: Effects of incentives and framing on transactive memory systems and performance. *Group Processes & Intergroup Relations*, *20*(6), 894–908. https://doi.org/10.1177/1368430215612223

Brandon, D. P., & Hollingshead, A. B. (2004). Transactive memory systems in organizations: Matching tasks, expertise, and people. *Organization Science*, *15*(6), 633–644. https://doi.org/10.1287/orsc.1040.0069

Choi, S. Y., Lee, H., & Yoo, Y. (2010). The impact of information technology and transactive memory systems on knowledge sharing, application, and team performance: A field study. *MIS Quarterly*, *34*(4), 855–870. https://doi.org/10.2307/25750708

Contractor, N., Monge, P., & Leonardi, P. M. (2011). Network theory | Multidimensional networks and the dynamics of sociomateriality: Bringing technology inside the network. *International Journal of Communication*, *5*, 682–720.

Cordery, J. L., & Soo, C. (2008). Overcoming impediments to virtual team effectiveness. *Human Factors and Ergonomics in Manufacturing & Service Industries*, *18*(5), 487–500. https://doi.org/10.1002/hfm.20119

Gupta, N., & Hollingshead, A. B. (2010). Differentiated versus integrated transactive memory effectiveness: It depends on the task. *Group Dynamics: Theory, Research, and Practice*, *14*(4), 384–398. https://doi.org/10.1037/a0019992

Hollingshead, A. B. (1998a). Communication, learning, and retrieval in transactive memory systems. *Journal of Experimental Social Psychology*, *34*(5), 423–442. https://doi.org/10.1006/jesp.1998.1358

Hollingshead, A. B. (1998b). Distributed knowledge and transactive processes in decision-making groups. In M. A. Neale, E. A. Mannix, & D. H. Gruenfeld (Eds.), *Research on managing groups and teams* (Vol. 1, pp. 105–125). JAI Press.

Hollingshead, A. B. (1998c). Group and individual training: The impact of practice on performance. *Small Group Research*, *29*(2), 254–280. https://doi.org/10.1177/1046496498292006

Hollingshead, A. B. (1998d). Retrieval processes in transactive memory systems. *Journal of Personality and Social Psychology*, *74*(3), 659–671. https://doi.org/10.1037/0022-3514.74.3.659

Hollingshead, A. B. (2001). Cognitive interdependence and convergent expectations in transactive memory. *Journal of Personality and Social Psychology*, *81*(6), 1080–1089. https://doi.org/10.1037/0022-3514.81.6.1080

Hollingshead, A. B., & Brandon, D. P. (2003). Potential benefits of communication in transactive memory systems. *Human Communication Research*, *29*(4), 607–615. https://doi.org/10.1111/j.1468-2958.2003.tb00859.x

Hollingshead, A. B., Brandon, D. P., Yoon, K., & Gupta, N. (2010). Communication and knowledge-sharing errors in groups. In H. E. Canary & R. D. McPhee (Eds.), *Communication and organizational knowledge: Contemporary issues for theory and practice* (1st ed., pp. 133–150). Routledge.

Hollingshead, A. B., & Fraidin, S. N. (2003). Gender stereotypes and assumptions about expertise in transactive memory—ScienceDirect. *Journal of Experimental Social Psychology*, *39*(4), 355–363. https://doi.org/10.1016/S0022-1031(02)00549-8

Hollingshead, A. B., Fulk, J., & Monge, P. (2002). *Fostering intranet knowledge sharing: An integration of transactive memory and public goods approaches*. http://psycnet.apa.org.libproxy1.usc.edu/psycinfo/2002-17012-014

Hollingshead, A. B., Gupta, N., Yoon, K., & Brandon, D. P. (2011). Transactive memory theory and teams: Past, present, and future. In E. Salas, S. M. Fiore, & M. P. Letsky (Eds.), *Theories of team cognition: Cross-disciplinary perspectives* (pp. 421–455). Taylor & Francis Group. http://ebookcentral.proquest.com/lib/uaz/detail.action?docID=957246

Kanawattanachai, P., & Yoo, Y. (2007). The impact of knowledge coordination on virtual team performance over time. *MIS Quarterly, 31*(4), 783–808. https://doi.org/10.2307/25148820

Lewis, K. (2003). Measuring transactive memory systems in the field: Scale development and validation. *Journal of Applied Psychology, 88*(4), 587–604. https://doi.org/10.1037/0021-9010.88.4.587

Lewis, K. (2004). Knowledge and performance in knowledge-worker teams: A longitudinal study of transactive memory systems. *Management Science, 50*(11), 1519–1533. https://doi.org/10.1287/mnsc.1040.0257

Lewis, K., Belliveau, M., Herndon, B., & Keller, J. (2007). Group cognition, membership change, and performance: Investigating the benefits and detriments of collective knowledge. *Organizational Behavior and Human Decision Processes, 103*(2), 159–178. https://doi.org/10.1016/j.obhdp.2007.01.005

Lewis, K., & Herndon, B. (2011). Transactive memory systems: Current issues and future research directions. *Organization Science, 22*(5), 1254–1265. https://doi.org/10.1287/orsc.1110.0647

Lewis, K., Lange, D., & Gillis, L. (2005). Transactive memory systems, learning, and learning transfer. *Organization Science, 16*(6), 581–598. https://doi.org/10.1287/orsc.1050.0143

Liang, D. W., Moreland, R., & Argote, L. (1995). Group versus individual training and group performance: The mediating role of transactive memory. *Personality and Social Psychology Bulletin, 21*(4), 384–393.

Marques-Quinteiro, P., Curral, L., Passos, A. M., & Lewis, K. (2013). And now what do we do? The role of transactive memory systems and task coordination in action teams. *Group Dynamics: Theory, Research, and Practice, 17*(3), 194–206. https://doi.org/10.1037/a0033304

Moreland, R. L. (1999). Transactive memory: Learning who knows what in work groups and organizations. In L. L. Thompson, J. M. Levine, & D. M. Messick (Eds.), *Shared cognition in organizations: The management of knowledge* (pp. 3–31). Lawrence Erlbaum Associates Publishers.

Moreland, R. L., & Myaskovsky, L. (2000). Exploring the performance benefits of group training: Transactive memory or improved communication? *Organizational Behavior and Human Decision Processes, 82*(1), 117–133.

Mukherjee, S., Huang, Y., Neidhardt, J., Uzzi, B., & Contractor, N. (2019). Prior shared success predicts victory in team competitions. *Nature Human Behaviour, 3*(1), 74–81. https://doi.org/10.1038/s41562-018-0460-y

Neff, J. J., Fulk, J., & Yuan, Y. C. (2014). Not in the mood? Affective state and transactive communication. *Journal of Communication, 64*(5), 785–805. https://doi.org/10.1111/jcom.12109

Olabisi, J., & Lewis, K. (2018). Within- and between-team coordination via transactive memory systems and boundary spanning. *Group & Organization Management, 43*(5), 691–717. https://doi.org/10.1177/1059601118793750

Oshri, I., van Fenema, P. C., & Kotlarsky, J. (2008). Knowledge transfer in globally distributed teams: The role of transactive memory. In J. Kotlarsky, I. Oshri, & P. C. van Fenema (Eds.), *Knowledge processes in globally distributed contexts* (pp. 24–52). Palgrave Macmillan. https://doi.org/10.1057/9780230582408_2

Palazzolo, E. T. (2005). Organizing for information retrieval in transactive memory systems. *Communication Research, 32*(6), 726–761. https://doi.org/10.1177/0093650205281056

Palazzolo, E. T., Serb, D. A., She, Y., Su, C., & Contractor, N. S. (2006). Coevolution of communication and knowledge networks in transactive memory systems: Using computational models for theoretical development. *Communication Theory, 16*(2), 223–250. https://doi.org/10.1111/j.1468-2885.2006.00269.x

Pavitt, C. (2003). Colloquy: Do interacting groups perform better than aggregates of individuals? *Human Communication Research, 29*(4), 592–599. https://doi.org/10.1111/j.1468-2958.2003.tb00857.x

Peltokorpi, V., & Hood, A. C. (2019). Communication in theory and research on transactive memory systems: A literature review. *Topics in Cognitive Science, 11*(4), 644–667. https://doi.org/10.1111/tops.12359

Prichard, J. S., & Ashleigh, M. J. (2007). The effects of team-skills training on transactive memory and performance. *Small Group Research, 38*(6), 696–726. https://doi.org/10.1177/1046496407304923

Ren, Y., & Argote, L. (2011). Transactive memory systems 1985–2010: An integrative framework of key dimensions, antecedents, and consequences. *The Academy of Management Annals, 5*(1), 189–229. https://doi.org/10.1080/19416520.2011.590300

Rulke, D. L., & Rau, D. (2000). Investigating the encoding process of transactive memory development in group training. *Group & Organization Management, 25*(4), 373–396. https://doi.org/10.1177/1059601100254004

Schreiber, M., & Engelmann, T. (2010). Knowledge and information awareness for initiating transactive memory system processes of computer-supported collaborating ad hoc groups. *Computers in Human Behavior, 26*(6), 1701–1709. https://doi.org/10.1016/j.chb.2010.06.019

Siegel Christian, J., Pearsall, M. J., Christian, M. S., & Ellis, A. P. J. (2014). Exploring the benefits and boundaries of transactive memory systems in adapting to team member loss. *Group Dynamics: Theory, Research, and Practice, 18*(1), 69–86. https://doi.org/10.1037/a0035161

Vestal, A., & Mesmer-Magnus, J. (2020). Interdisciplinarity and team innovation: The role of team experiential and relational resources. *Small Group Research, 51*(6), 738–775. https://doi.org/10.1177/1046496420928405

Wang, Y., Huang, Q., Davison, R. M., & Yang, F. (2018). Effect of transactive memory systems on team performance mediated by knowledge transfer. *International Journal of Information Management, 41*, 65–79. https://doi.org/10.1016/j.ijinfomgt.2018.04.001

Wegner, D. M. (1987). Transactive memory: A contemporary analysis of the group mind. In *Theories of group behavior* (pp. 185–208). Springer. https://doi.org/10.1007/978-1-4612-4634-3_9

Wegner, D. M. (1995). A computer network model of human transactive memory. *Social Cognition, 13*(3), 319–339. https://doi.org/10.1521/soco.1995.13.3.319

Wegner, D. M., Erber, R., & Raymond, P. (1991). Transactive memory in close relationships. *Journal of Personality and Social Psychology, 61*(6), 923–929. https://doi.org/10.1037/0022-3514.61.6.923

Wegner, D. M., Giuliano, T., & Hertel, P. T. (1985). Cognitive interdependence in close relationships. In W. Ickes (Ed.), *Compatible and incompatible relationships* (pp. 253–276). Springer. https://doi.org/10.1007/978-1-4612-5044-9_12

Yan, B., Kim, Y. J., Hollingshead, A. B., & Brandon, D. P. (2019). Conceptualizing online groups as multidimensional networks. In *The Oxford handbook of cyberpsychology* (pp. 306–327). Oxford University Press. https://doi.org/10.1093/oxfordhb/9780198812746.001.0001

Yoo, Y., & Kanawattanachai, P. (2001). Developments of transactive memory systems and collective mind in virtual teams. *The International Journal of Organizational Analysis, 9*(2), 187–208. https://doi.org/10.1108/eb028933

Yoon, K., & Zhu, Y. (2022). Social media affordances and transactive memory systems in virtual teams. *Management Communication Quarterly, 36*(2), 235–260. https://doi.org/10.1177/08933189211032639

Yuan, Y. C., Fulk, J., & Monge, P. R. (2007). Access to information in connective and communal transactive memory systems. *Communication Research, 34*(2), 131–155. https://doi.org/10.1177/0093650206298067

15 Group Decision Making

Torsten Reimer, Nathanael Johnson,
and Juan Pablo Loaiza-Ramírez

Chapter Objectives

- Understand the role of communication in exchanging and sharing information and constituting common ground.
- Describe combination-based, communication-based, alternative-based, and cue-based decision strategies and the role of communication in implementing these strategies.
- Provide examples for and describe the role of meta-communicative processes for group decision making.

Introduction

Decision making is a common activity that occurs in many groups and is involved in many aspects of daily life. From government committees and courtroom juries to healthcare teams, group decisions impact all aspects of public life (Beck et al., 2022; Frey et al., 1999). Group communication plays a central role in group decision making. In decision-making deliberation, individuals work together to establish goals and to gather, share, and analyze information, in order to form decisions that help attain their goals. Communication and the exchange of relevant information is a key prerequisite of good group decisions. Group miscommunication can have dire consequences as demonstrated by the well-documented cases of the tragedy of the Titanic (see Box 15.1), the Challenger disaster (Gouran et al., 1986), and the preventable death of Jesica Santillan, who received a transplant that did not match her blood type (Diflo, 2006; Russell & Reimer, 2015; also see Chapter 22). In all three cases, groups failed to exchange and attend to information highly relevant for their decisions: The crew of the Titanic ignored multiple warnings of icebergs. The Challenger disaster could have been prevented had the team responsible for the start of the space shuttle listened to concerns related to the low temperatures at the day of the take-off. Jesica Santillan's tragedy could have been prevented had the hospital's team exchanged and paid attention to information about the blood type of the organ donor. At times, particularly when groups face challenging and ill-defined decision tasks that they have not encountered before, it is important that groups develop shared meta-knowledge and engage in meta-communication that involves plans about how important messages can be delivered. Meta-knowledge is a form of meta-cognition that includes group members' knowledge about who knows what in their group that guides many group processes (see Chapters 3 and 14). In addition to conveying relevant information, it is key that group members attend to and weigh critical information appropriately in their deliberation. If done well, group communication not only helps groups make good decisions but can also enhance the commitment with a group's decision (Forsyth, 2018), increase learning (Huber, 2003), strengthen the bonds and relationships among members (Keyton, 1999), and facilitate building trust among members (Driscoll, 1978).

DOI: 10.4324/9781003227458-17

Box 15.1 Titanic, a Group Communication and Decision-Making Tragedy?

Messages have to be attended to, processed, and passed on to the key deciders in a group to be effective. What happened to the "unsinkable" ship on the night of April 15, 1912, has been an inspiration to movies, books, songs, and memorials. The Royal Mail Ship (RMS) Titanic, the famous British steamship and arguably the largest ship at the time, sunk after a collision with an iceberg the night before. Out of the approximately 2,200 people on the ship, more than 1,500 passengers and crew died, making the tragedy the deadliest sinking in maritime history up to that point (Yu, 2012). Several circumstances contributed to this tragedy. The lookouts did not have binoculars at hand (Yu, 2012), not enough lifeboats were at the ship's disposal (Kerby & Baguley, 2022), nearby ships did not pay attention to the Titanic's distress rockets (Zinkova, 2021), and the steel used for its construction could have had better mechanical properties (Leighly et al., 2001). Each of these circumstances involved flawed decision making. Arguably, though, the tragedy of the Titanic was first and foremost a *communication* tragedy that prevented the captain from steering the ship away from the iceberg. The tragedy could have been avoided if the captain and crew had paid close attention to multiple warnings of icebergs that reached the ship throughout the day and made the decision to reduce the ship's speed and change course. The steersman did not turn the boat in the right direction (Boyle, 2012).

On the day of the crash, Titanic's telegram operators received consecutive warnings regarding floating icebergs from other ships. According to Yu (2012), the first warning came at 09:00 a.m. from the Caronia ship. This message reached the Titanic's captain Edward John Smith, who treated iceberg warnings as routine messages, but did not take any action. Later warnings never left the Titanic's telegram room. The final notice was received at 10:30 p.m. from the ship California. This time, the radio operator Jack Phillips, working with Cape Race wireless station for a commercial message, responded angrily, "Shut up!" and dismissed the alert (Danigelis, 2012).

The decisions of the radio operators and the captain to systematically ignore the warnings, either because they were fixing some equipment or transmitting other messages to passengers, caused the Titanic to continue at almost full speed (Yu, 2012). When the lookouts spotted the iceberg ahead, it was too late. The tragedy of the Titanic teaches an important lesson on group communication and decision making that resonates with empirical studies: For critical information (iceberg warnings) to affect a groups' decisions (speed and course of the Titanic), it is not sufficient that a member of the group has access to this information (multiple warnings reached the telegram room), but critical information has to be passed on, attended to, and identified as critical information by the group.

In the remainder, we will introduce a basic taxonomy of group decision tasks and describe task-specific decision strategies that are commonly used by groups. The described tasks have in common that groups have access to a clearly defined choice set that is described by multiple attributes. We also describe approaches to group decision making in situations in which groups face ill-defined decision tasks in that the choice alternatives, the criteria to evaluate decision outcomes, or the members of the group are not clearly identified. Throughout the chapter, we highlight the role of communication in the group-decision process. While a central function of communication is the sharing of task-relevant information and preferences, the chapter also highlights the role of meta-communicative discourses for group decision making.

Classification of Group Decision Tasks

Group decision making refers to the decision processes that are employed and the decisions that are formed by interdependent members of a group who share some common goal. The term *group decision* is typically defined more narrowly and refers to a joint decision that is formed by a group. Examples of group decisions include a jury that either convicts or acquits a defendant, a college search committee that selects a candidate from a pool of applicants for an open position, or a stock club that chooses a stock for their investments. Group decision making also includes the case of the Titanic (see Box 15.1), which can be characterized by a series of decisions of individual crew members that were consequential for their group goals. Typically, research on group decision making has focused on situations in which group members are all motivated to achieve a good group outcome (for an overview of mixed motive groups, in which group members have competing goals, see Davis et al., 1976; also see Wittenbaum et al., 2004). Because group processes and decision outcomes greatly vary depending on the decision task a group faces, we first introduce a basic taxonomy of decision tasks. Subsequently, we discuss common decision strategies that are used by groups for each of the introduced task types. The literature on individual decision making offers two basic distinctions that are also useful to classify group decisions: inferences versus preferences and choices versus judgments (e.g., Hastie & Dawes, 2010). Based on these distinctions, four classes of decision tasks can be defined: inferential choices, inferential judgments, preferential choices, and preferential judgments. Table 15.1 provides examples for each of the four types of tasks (for other classifications of group tasks including group decisions, see Chapter 4; Forsyth, 2018; Hirokawa, 1990).

Table 15.1 Decision-Making Tasks and Common Strategies

	Inference	Preference
Choice		
Tasks	1 Which grade will we receive for our group paper that we just turned in (an A, B, or C)?	1 Which of the discussed topics shall we pick for our class project?
	2 Who scored the most goals in the 2022 Soccer World Cup, Messi, Mbappe, or Giroud?	2 Which marketing medium do we prefer for our new product, social media or cable/television?
	3 Which of the following planets rotates in a clockwise direction, the Earth, Venus, or Mars?	3 Do we want to travel by plane or by car to our next vacation site?
Strategies	*Truth wins*, Take-the-best	*Majority voting*, Unit weight model
Judgment		
Tasks	1 How long will it take us to finish our group project?	1 How long should our project meetings be?
	2 What is the average annual salary of a person with a Ph.D. in the social and behavioral sciences?	2 How much do we like the internet service we are using?
	3 How successful will our company be if we hire this manager?	3 How much money do we want to spend to renovate the entrance to our business?
Strategies	*Best member rule*, QuickEst	*Averaging*, Weighted additive model

Note: The first task of each decision type refers to a typical task in a group working on a project. Unlike judgment tasks, inference tasks have a correct answer. Group processes may depend on whether a group perceives a task solution as being demonstrable or not. The demonstrability of an inference task can be construed as a continuum (see Chapter 4). Combination-based strategies are written in italics.

Inferences Versus Preferences

Inferences are related to tasks for which the correctness of a decision can be determined using some normative criterion (e.g., a mathematical problem or the estimation of the age of a person). Conversely, preferences refer to tasks that lack objective criteria to evaluate the correctness of a decision (e.g., preferences for an ice cream flavor or a movie). In group contexts, inference tasks are often called *intellective tasks*, and preference tasks are called *judgmental tasks* (see Forsyth, 2018). We use the terms *inference* and *preference* in this chapter, as using the same terminology for the same types of tasks for individuals and groups helps one see commonalities between individual and group decision making (see Reimer & Hoffrage, 2012b, for a systematic comparison of decision strategies for individuals and groups). As Stasser and Abele (2020) pointed out, group processes can greatly vary depending on whether group members *believe* a task can be objectively evaluated and the right answer can be demonstrated or not. The *demonstrability* of an inference task, that is a group's capacity to demonstrate which answer is correct, depends on contextual variables (e.g., the amount of available information and perceived time pressure) as well as the ability and motivation of group members (also see Chapters 4).

Choices Versus Judgments

A second basic distinction of decisions refers to choices versus judgments. Choice tasks are when a decider is asked to pick one alternative out of a set of alternatives. Examples for choice tasks include multiple-choice items on a test and a group that is selecting a candidate for an open position. Conversely, judgment tasks require an estimation or evaluation of a decision alternative. Examples include the assessment of attitudes towards an object (e.g., how much does a visitor like a vacation site?), as well as numerical estimations (e.g., a prediction of tomorrow's temperature). Whereas choices always involve several objects among which a decider must choose (e.g., choosing among a set of cameras in a store), judgments involve only one object that is evaluated (e.g., the evaluation of one camera).

The distinction between inferences and preferences and that between choices and judgments can be used to define four different types of tasks: Inferential choices, inferential judgments, preferential choices, and preferential judgments. We invite readers to generate some examples for each task type and consider how a group would go about forming a decision in each case: What procedure could a group use to make a decision in each scenario? Which information would group members exchange during discussion? Would members form individual decisions first? Table 15.1 lists a number of examples for each of the four types of decision tasks. In the following section, we describe decision strategies for each decision type that are often used by groups. The strategies differ in the procedure they use and which information they capitalize on.

Classification of Group Decision-Strategies

Generally speaking, groups can reach a collective decision by adopting or integrating the decisions of individual group members or by discussing and integrating what the group knows about the decision alternatives: *Social-combination rules* base the group's decision on the decisions that are formed by individual group members. Conversely, *social-communication rules* form a group decision based on information about choice alternatives that are exchanged during group discussions. The decision strategies differ in the information that is processed by the group, the order in which information is processed, and their communication demand (for the distinction between social-combination and social-communication rules, see Baron et al., 1992).

While describing the decision strategies, we refer to the following scenario (see Table 15.2): Consider, a committee of five group members (members G, R, O, U, and P) with different

Table 15.2 Distribution of Information Regarding Two Finalists (Mrs. Abby S. and Mrs. Kayla T.) for a Sales Manager Position in Two Committees with Five Members (Group Members G, R, O, U, and P)

Committee Member	Knowledge about Mrs. Abby S.	Knowledge about Mrs. Kayla T.
Committee 1		
Senior sales manager (G),	1 (+), 2 (+), 3 (+),	1 (+), 2 (+),
Human resource manager (R)	7 (–), 8 (–)	7 (–), 8 (–), 9 (–), **10 (–)**
Committee chair (O)	1 (+), 2 (+),	1 (+), 2 (+), 3 (+),
	7 (–), 8 (–), 9 (–)	7 (–), 8 (–)
Lawyer (U),	1 (+), **4 (+), 5 (+), 6 (+)**,	1 (+), 2 (+), 3 (+),
CFO (P)	7 (–), 9 (–)	7 (–), 9 (–), **10 (–), 11 (–), 12 (–)**
Committee 2		
Senior sales manager (G),	1 (+), **4 (+)**,	1 (+), 2 (+), 3 (+),
Human resource manager (R)	7 (–), 8 (–), 9 (–)	7 (–), **10 (–)**
Committee chair (O)	2 (+), **5 (+)**,	1 (+), 2 (+), 3 (+),
	7 (–), 8 (–), 9 (–)	8 (–), **11 (–)**
Lawyer (U),	3 (+), **6 (+)**,	1 (+), 2 (+), 3 (+),
CFO (P)	7 (–), 8 (–), 9 (–)	9 (–), **12 (–)**
Group Knowledge	1 (+), 2 (+), 3 (+), **4 (+), 5 (+), 6 (+)**,	1 (+), 2 (+), 3 (+),
	7 (–), 8 (–), 9 (–)	7 (–), 8 (–), 9 (–), **10 (–), 11 (–), 12 (–)**

Note: Unique attributes are written in bold. Positive attributes: (1) Reliable (+), (2) hard-working (+), (3) business degree (+), **(4) kind (+), (5) tension tamer (+)**, and **(6) knows company well (+)**. Negative attributes: (7) Sometimes sloppy (–), (8) does not always work well under time pressure (–), (9) sometimes late at work (–); **(10) likes to tattle (–), (11) resentful (–)**, and **(12) sometimes moody (–)**.

Overall, Mrs. Abby S. has six positive attributes and three negative attributes, whereas Mrs. Kayla T. has three positive and six negative attributes. *Group Knowledge* displays the information items that are known to the committees as a whole. The Attributes 1, 2, 3, 7, 8, and 9 pertain to both candidates and are common between both candidates, whereas the Attributes 4, 5, 6, and 10, 11, 12 are unique. Unique attributes are written in bold throughout. The information distribution in Committee 2 displays a hidden-profile task, in which the profile of the superior candidate, Mrs. Abby S., is hidden to the individual group members. Members G and R have access to the same information and so have U and P. The numbers of information items that are known to the group and to the individual group members as well as the two candidates' sum scores are constant across the two committees.

organizational roles (e.g., manager, employees, and human resource liaison) that is charged with evaluating internal applications for a new sales manager position in a large company. For the sake of simplicity, let us assume the company has conducted an internal search and has already pre-selected two finalists for their open position, *Mrs. Abby S.* and *Mrs. Kayla T.* Each of the two candidates is described by attributes including specific skills, past experiences, and personality traits based on evaluations from co-workers and supervisors. The columns in Table 15.2 list the attributes for each candidate that are known to the committee, and the first three rows depict the particular set of knowledge that each group member has about the candidates. Often, group members differ in their task-specific knowledge and information about the choice alternatives, for example, due to differences in expertise. To study which information is used and exchanged in the group-decision process, experiments on information sharing in decision-making groups often control for group members' specific knowledge about the choice alternatives by distributing information about the choice alternatives among group members in a systematic way. In the schematic example of Table 15.2, group members G and R have identical information about the candidates as do U and P; however, the samples of information that G/R, O, and U/P have differ from each other.

The last row of Table 15.2 (*Group Knowledge*) describes the information that is known to the group as a whole. Attributes include positive (e.g., reliable or kind) as well as negative (e.g., resentful or moody) characteristics. As is indicated by the cells of Table 15.2, some information items are *shared* by group members—that is, they are known to all group members—whereas other items are only known to individual group members and are, thus, *unshared*. For example, all members of Committee 2 know that Mrs. Abby S. is sometimes late at work (shared information), whereas only the committee chair knows that she is also a tension tamer (unshared information). Typically, groups also have *partially shared information*, that is information that is known to several but not all group members. For example, group members U and P in Committee 1 know that Mrs. S is kind—a piece of information that is unknown to the remaining members G, R, and O. The information distribution in Table 15.2 provides a schematic and simplified situation. Search committees typically have access to many more information items when making hiring decisions, including application and recommendation letters, detailed information about an applicant's work history, and, at times, personality and aptitude tests. However, as in our example, group members typically do not have the same information at their disposal which renders questions about information sharing important. *Information sharing* denotes the information that is shared among group members at the outset as well as the process of sharing information during group deliberation (see Chapter 13).

For demonstration purposes, we describe four different decision tasks that Committee 1 may be charged with and look at each task independently: (1) Choose the candidate that you would hire (preferential choice); (2) judge on a scale from 1 to 5 how much you would welcome each candidate as a member of your project team (preferential judgment); (3) predict which candidate would boost their unit's sales more during their first year if both were hired (inferential choice); (4) estimate on a scale from 1 to 10 how much each candidate is liked by their current co-workers and supervisors (inferential judgment) (see Table 15.1 for additional examples of tasks). The following section illustrates some common strategies that the committee could use to make these decisions.

Social-Combination Rules

Choice Tasks

Social-combination rules integrate individual decisions into one group decision. The most prominent social-combination rule for choice tasks is the *majority rule*. It predicts that the group will choose the option that is favored by a majority of group members (or by most members—the plurality rule). Majority rule is often used as a default strategy when groups have to make a joint decision but cannot reach consensus. It can be applied without knowledge of group members' expertise or accuracy (Hastie & Kameda, 2005).

Majority rule can be used for preferential as well as inferential choice tasks. Members of Committee 1 may form individual preferences by tallying the pros and cons for each candidate. If they all use this individual decision strategy, we would expect that members G, R, U, and P will decide in favor of Mrs. S, whereas the committee chair O will decide in favor of T, for whom O has more positive evidence. During group deliberation, the committee may become aware that there is no consensus in their group as not all group members have the same preference. In this situation, majority rule would predict that the group will recommend hiring Mrs. S. The majority rule typically describes *preferential* choices in groups very well (e.g., see Forsyth, 2018).

With notable exceptions, majority rule also often describes *inferential* choices well (but see Chapter 3 and Ladbury & Hinsz, 2009, for exceptions). For example, if most members of Committee 1 think that Mrs. S has a better prospect to increase sales than Mrs. T, the group may predict that Mrs. S will increase sales more if both candidates are hired. Using the majority rule for inferences can improve group accuracy compared to the accuracy of individual members when group members form their choices independently (e.g., before knowing the opinions of other members and discussing the case) and tend to form correct choices in a task (e.g., group members tend to get a true/false question right in more than 50% of the cases). Under these circumstances, majority rule yields inferences that are typically better than the inferences of an average group member (for a theoretical analysis, see Shapley & Grofman, 1984; for a review of empirical work, see Kerr & Tindale, 2004; Reimer & Katsikopoulos, 2004).

Other combination-based rules are the *leader rule* and the *expert rule*. As the labels suggest, according to the leader rule, the group choice will follow the choice of the (formal or informal) leader of a group, and according to the expert rule, the group's choice will accord with the choice of the member with the highest (actual and/or perceived) expertise. Committee 1, for example, could follow the recommendation of the committee chair (*leader rule*) or the recommendation of the senior sales manager, as this may be the person with the highest level of expertise (*expert rule*). The expert rule requires that group members can judge the expertise of their group members and identify members who have high expertise. The literature provides mixed evidence on how well group members can recognize expertise in their group (Bonner & Baumann, 2012). Participation is related to expertise even though experts do not always speak up more (Bonito, 2007; Larson et al., 1996). At times, group members who have power (Forsyth, 2018), task-specific expertise (Bonner et al., 2022), or personal experience with the task (Oh et al., 2023) are more influential in the group-decision process.

A special form of the expert rule in inference tasks is the so-called *truth-wins rule*. Consider an inference task in which the majority is wrong. Can the minority (and even a single member) sway the majority? Laughlin (2011) and his collaborators have shown that a minority can overcome the majority in such a situation if the expert can *demonstrate* the correctness of the inference. To begin with, it is important that group members perceive the task as an inference task for which a correct answer can potentially be demonstrated within their group setting. Demonstrability involves that the group member favoring the correct answer has the necessary ability, motivation, information, and time to demonstrate the correct solution and that other members have sufficient understanding that they recognize the correct answer (Laughlin & Ellis, 1986; also see Chapter 4). Consider Committee 1 aimed to predict which of the two candidates would boost their unit's sales more during their first year if both were hired (inferential choice). Based on the knowledge of Committee 1 displayed in Table 15.2, it would be unlikely that the chair O could make a strong case in favor of Mrs. T, as the chair does not have any relevant information about the candidates that the other group members do not possess. This could be different, though, if the chair had additional relevant information about Mrs. T and Mrs. S—for example, sales numbers from the past or other relevant information that could be used to support the claim that Mrs. T will boost the unit's sales more than Mrs. S. While the majority rule can be used for inferential as well as preferential choice tasks, the truth-wins rule, by definition, only applies to inferential choice tasks that have a correct answer or solution.

Judgment Tasks

Judgment tasks refer to situations in which a group is asked to come up with one joint evaluation (preferential judgment) or estimation (inferential judgment; see Table 15.1 for examples). Different from tasks that have a set of plausible outcomes, judgments provide a numerical estimation or assessment of only one alternative that is to be judged. Thus, unlike the leader and expert rules, the majority rule cannot be used for judgment tasks (unless several members form identical judgments). As in choice tasks, the group may follow the leader or expert and adopt their judgment as the group judgment. The most prominent combination-based rule for judgments is *averaging* (Mannes et al., 2014). The averaging rule takes the mean score across the individual group members' judgments. Averaging systematically outperforms the average accuracy of group members under the condition that group members' estimations are independent from each other and the errors that members make while providing an estimation are random. This wisdom of crowd effect—higher accuracy of group members' average estimation than the average accuracy of the individual members' estimations—has been observed across a variety of tasks, from guessing the number of jellybeans in a jar to guessing the weight of an ox (see Mannes et al., 2014).

As with choice tasks, experts are at times more influential in judgment tasks also in that groups weigh expert's judgments or estimates more heavily (e.g., the weighted average; see Bonner et al., 2022). For example, to come up with a joint group judgment on how much the group would welcome each of the two candidates as a member of their project team, Committee 1 may average the judgments of the five committee members on the five-point scale (preferential judgment). The committee could also average their individual estimation of how much the candidates are liked by others (inferential judgment). Alternatively and to the extent that the task to infer how much a candidate is liked by others is being perceived as an inference task, the committee may give more weight to the judgment of the senior sales manager (G) or the human resource manager (R) on their team or adopt the judgment of G or R assuming that G and/or R are being perceived as more knowledgeable on providing an estimation of how much each of the candidates is liked by other employees of the company (see Bonner et al., 2022, for the test of social influence models).

Social-Communication Rules

Choice Tasks

Communication-based rules do not integrate preferences or estimations of individual group members but are based on the joint exchange and integration of information on the choice alternatives during group deliberation. Communication-based rules describe group members as integrating their knowledge about the choice alternatives. Two general classes of communication-based strategies for choice tasks are alternative-based and cue-based decision strategies that are often used by individuals who face a multi-attribute decision task (for an overview, see Gigerenzer and Todd, 1999; Hastie & Dawes, 2010; Pachur, 2022). Groups can use these strategies by compiling, sharing, and integrating information that is distributed in their group (Reimer & Hoffrage, 2012b). Even though there is much more empirical evidence for the use of combination-based rules, as only few studies have looked at and considered communication-based rules in the literature, we briefly describe these rules, as they have several interesting characteristics from a prescriptive as well as descriptive perspective. Moreover, as combination- and communication-based strategies suggest identical decisions in many cases (see Reimer & Hoffrage, 2012b), it may well be that groups apply communication-based rules more often than has been acknowledged in the literature.

Alternative-based strategies involve evaluating each option separately and choosing the one that is judged to be the best. This process involves considering the attributes of each alternative one at a time and forming a judgment on each alternative before moving on to the next alternative. The final decision is based on the alternative that receives the highest overall evaluation. Two well-studied alternative-based decision strategies in individuals are the weighted additive model (WADD) and the unit weight linear model (UWM) (see Gigerenzer et al., 1999; Todd et al., 2012).

In a group context, the WADD and UWM require that group members exchange information about the individual choice alternatives (see Reimer & Hoffrage, 2012a). The group has to keep score and jointly decide which alternative has the highest overall score. To apply the strategies and make a joint hiring decision, Committee 1 has to tally the positive and negative characteristics for each of the two finalists. Overall, Mrs. S has a better overall score (four positive – two negative characteristics) than Mrs. T (three positive – five negative characteristics). Thus, if Committee 1 used the UWM strategy, they would choose Mrs. S. In addition to considering the number of positive and negative characteristics, groups may weigh attributes by their importance and put, for example, a stronger weight on the attribute *hard working* than on the attribute *tattles at times* (see Reimer & Hoffrage, 2012b, for details). Note that both alternative-based strategies, WADD and UWM, require that group members compile their knowledge about the candidates by exchanging unshared information that is not known to all group members. Whereas all members know that Mrs. S is reliable (Attribute 1), only U and P know that Mrs. S is kind, a tension tamer, and knows the company well (Attributes 4, 5, and 6). The alternative-based strategies require that U and P share their unique knowledge about the candidates and that the group integrates this information into their evaluation of choice alternatives.

A second class of communication-based strategies for choices consists of cue-based strategies such as the Take-the-best heuristic (TTB). **Cue-based strategies** entail the selection of one attribute at a time and a comparison of alternatives on this attribute (Gigerenzer et al., 1999). The strategies systematically differ in their frugality, that is, the amount of information they consider. As a consequence, they also systematically differ in the amount of information that has to be exchanged during discussion. (Typically, characteristics of choice alternatives such as *reliable* or *kind* in our example, are called *cues* in inference tasks and *attributes* in preference tasks.) TTB involves selecting one attribute at a time and comparing the available alternatives on that attribute. If one choice alternative stands out as the best on the focal attribute, the decision-making process stops and that option is chosen. If the options have identical values on the focal attribute, the next most important attribute is considered. Thus, cue-wise strategies are more frugal than alternative-wise strategies as alternative-wise strategies integrate all available information. Cues are typically processed in order of their predictive validities and attributes are processed in order of their perceived importance. *Cue validity* is defined as the relative frequency with which a cue makes a correct prediction when looking at all possible pairs of objects for which it can be used (Gigerenzer et al., 1999; Reimer & Hoffrage, 2006). Consider that Committee 1 believes that it is most important that a candidate is hard working (Attribute 2). This attribute, though, does not discriminate between the two candidates, as both candidates are characterized as hard workers. If the group chooses as the next most important attribute that a candidate knows the company well (Attribute 6), the group should decide in favor of Mrs. S, as this characteristic only pertains to her. Note that cue-based strategies require that group members exchange and pool information on attributes while comparing alternatives.

Judgment Tasks

The alternative-based choice strategies UWM and WADD discussed earlier require that groups form individual judgments on each candidate. Thus, both strategies can also be used to make *judgments* about an individual choice alternative. This holds for preferences as well as for inferences. When using the strategies to answer the question of how much the committee would welcome a candidate on their project team, an additional step is needed to transform the overall sum score onto the scale that is used to express how much the team welcomes a candidate. There are several ways how that can be done. As a standard method in research, a regression equation is often used for this purpose that yields a criterion value (the to be estimated variable) based on the weights and values of the considered attributes (Gigerenzer et al., 1999). Following this research logic, Gigone and Hastie (1993) conducted a study to determine if the weights that groups assign to cues in an inference task differ from the weights that individual members use and if cues that are shared by members receive more weight. The authors asked their participants to make an inferential judgment about the grades received by each of 32 students in an introductory psychology course. As cues, participants had access to each student's high school GPA, SAT test, self-reported attendance of lectures and recitations, self-rated enjoyment of class, academic anxiety, and workload in other classes. As expected, groups put more weight on shared cues than on unshared cues. There are also estimation heuristics, such as QuickEst, that describe individual estimations and could be used by groups as a communication-based strategy (see Hertwig et al., 1999). The QuickEst heuristic (Hertwig et al., 1999) is based on the insight that many variables are J-shaped (e.g., when rank ordering cities of a country according to their population and displaying the number of inhabitants on the y-axis.) The heuristic is sequentially checking cues (e.g., is a capital [yes/no], has a major university [yes/no]) until a cue with a positive value is found (e.g., if a city is a capital) and by assigning estimates to relevant categories of cues.

An interesting feature of communication-based strategies is that they can facilitate consensus—a decision that all group members agree upon—as group members collaboratively integrate information regarding the choice alternatives. Importantly, groups can discuss if and how attributes should be weighted or rank ordered. The combination- and communication-based decision strategies described earlier differ in the information that is processed by the group, in the order in which information is processed, in their frugality, and in their communication demand, that is, the amount of information that has to be exchanged to form a decision (see Chapter 4). The application of communication-based strategies requires that group members share all pieces of information that are relevant to apply the strategy during discussion. At times, this information may include unshared pieces of information (i.e., information that is only known to some group members at the outset).

As was discussed while applying the various decision strategies to the introduced tasks, one insight of this exercise is that not every strategy can be used for every type of task. Moreover, there are ways to integrate strategies, for example, by judging each alternative separately and choosing the alternative with the highest overall evaluation. Likewise, group members may exchange information and opinions before they decide and vote. Another insight is that strategies will yield the same decisions in many situations—at times, there is overlap in the choices that different strategies suggest (see Pachur, 2022; Reimer & Katsikopoulos, 2004). For example, in situations in which the majority includes the most expert and the leader of the group and favors the correct choice in an inference task, majority rule, the truth-wins principle, the expert rule, and the leader rule all yield the same choice. Likewise, in situations in which group members have a similar background and have access to the same information, individual group members will often favor the same alternatives (also see Pavitt, 2003; Phillips et al., 2014; Propp, 1999). In Committee 1, for example, most of the available information favors Mrs. S, and this is also represented in the partial information of all group members except member O. In a case like this in which one alternative is clearly better and in which group members have a great deal of overlapping information, asking a group to form a joint decision does not provide much room for improvement over the individual group members. This looks very different in the situation of Committee 2 (see Table 15.2).

Synergies in Hidden-Profile Tasks

Unlike the first committee, the information in Committee 2 regarding the two candidates is distributed among group members in a way such that the dominance of Mrs. S is not preserved in the knowledge set of the individual committee members. As indicated by the last row of Table 15.2 (*Group Knowledge*), Mrs. S is better suited for the position than Mrs. T, as Mrs. T does not have *any* positive attributes that do not pertain to Mrs. S also and Mrs. S does not have any negative attributes that do not pertain to Mrs. T. If each group member had access to all available information, we would expect that they preferred Mrs. S. However, unlike in Committee 1, in Committee 2 the information is distributed among group members such that all the information items about positive attributes regarding Mrs. T, as well as the negative items regarding Mrs. S, are *shared* among group members, whereas the positive attributes on Mrs. S and the negative attributes regarding Mrs. T are *unshared* (possessed or known by only one member). As a consequence, in Committee 2, the individual group members are likely to favor Mrs. T based on their individual information. Such a task is called a *hidden-profile task*, as the superior profile of Mrs. S is hidden from each individual group member (see Stasser & Titus, 1985). Most research on the hidden-profile effect suggested that groups are not good at solving this task, as members fail to exchange and consider their unshared information items and focus on group members' preferences without considering a choice alternative that is not favored by any group member (e.g., see Stasser & Abele, 2020). The hidden-profile effect refers to the observation that the mere distribution of information among members can strongly affect the decision that a group forms. Committee 1 and Committee 2 likely form different decisions, even though both committees have access to the same information. It turns out, though, that groups can detect hidden profiles under conditions that encourage the use of communication-based strategies.

Reimer et al. (2010b) reasoned that groups employing a social-combination rule will not be able to connect the dots when facing a hidden profile. While all combination-based strategies discussed earlier (including majority rule) fail to discover hidden profiles, groups applying the cue-based strategy would choose Mrs. S. The authors discovered that one factor arguably facilitated the use of a cue-based strategy and substantially altered the groups' choices in a hidden-profile task-namely, whether group members received their information before the group discussion or at the onset of their group meeting. When groups received their information *before* the group deliberation as in previous research, members entered discussions with strong preferences and most groups used a combination-based rule. As a consequence, groups preferred the inferior alternative (Mrs. T in the example of Committee 2). Conversely, when group members received their information about the candidates *at the beginning* of their group meeting and, thus, group members entered group discussions without choice preferences, they exchanged more of their unshared information and focused more on the information that the group had available. Groups had more time available than they needed to complete the task, ruling out time pressure as a possible explanation of why group members did not form individual preferences. Arguably, distributing information at the beginning of the group meeting facilitated the use of a cue-based strategy. As a consequence, all groups connected the dots and discovered the hidden profile in this condition (Mrs. S in the example of Committee 2). This study provides a documented case in which all groups displayed a strong synergy effect (see Larson, 2010) in that they discovered something new that had not been known to any group member beforehand.

Robust Empirical Findings

Studies that model group decision making in laboratory settings typically use the same or similar designs (see Gigone & Hastie, 1993; Hinsz et al., 1997): Groups are given information about the decision task and are asked to deliberate and make a joint decision. Typically, group members make individual decisions before the group deliberation phase. These individual data are used to formulate predictions about what the decision in the group would look like if they applied a certain strategy. For example, the decision strategies described earlier can be used to make predictions about the decisions of Committees 1 and 2. These predictions can be compared with the actual group decisions to assess how well each strategy describes a group's actual behavior (e.g., see Reimer & Katsikopoulos, 2004; Kaemmer et al., 2014, for examples; also see Hinsz et al., 1997). To see if the group discussion altered members' views, members' individual decisions are typically ascertained a second time after the group deliberation process.

Based on this methodology, research on group decision making has identified several reliable findings: Groups hardly ever select a choice alternative that is not proposed by at least one member. Synergy effects in hidden-profile tasks are an exception to this rule (see Reimer et al., 2010b). Regarding the role of communication during the group-decision process, groups show a tendency to discuss, emphasize, and attend more to information items that are known to group members at the expense of unshared information, and shared information also has more impact than unshared information on members' individual decisions as well as group decisions (e.g., Larson & Egan, 2020; Lu et al., 2012). Stasser and Titus (1987) presented a model that enables the estimation of the anticipated sampling advantage for shared information when group members select information randomly and exhibit no variance in participation rates. This model, known as the *Information Sampling Model*, can be used as a reference point for assessing whether groups accentuate or diminish the discussion bias. Based on an analysis utilizing this model in published studies, Reimer et al. (2010a) found that the sampling advantage of shared information was smaller than what would be expected if information items were sampled at random. Groups exchanged more of their shared than their unshared information. However, the sampling advantage of shared information was attenuated as groups exchanged a smaller portion of their shared information than expected by a random sampling process, which held in particular in hidden-profile tasks, in which unshared information is particularly relevant (see Reimer et al., 2010a for details).

Importantly, when looking at group decision making from the perspective of decision strategies described earlier, it becomes clear that information exchange can be construed as a function of the decision strategies that are employed rather than providing a goal in itself. According to this perspective, the specifics of a decision strategy guide the order and content of group discussions, analogous to the sequence of information processing in individuals (see Riedl et al., 2008). The communication needs for the alternative-based and the cue-based strategies, for example, differ substantially from each other as they capitalize on different pieces of information. From this perspective, it is key that groups exchange and consider information that is critical for the application of the respective decision strategy (e.g., information on discriminating attributes when using the Take-the-best strategy).

Research suggests that group choices in well-defined tasks often follow the majority rule (Forsyth, 2018; also see Ladbury & Hinsz, 2009, and Chapter 3). Even though the majority rule predicts group outcomes well in many situations (particularly in preference tasks), it is not clear how groups manage to implement the majority rule and how often groups follow a communication-based decision strategy when forming majority decisions (see Reimer et al., 2022, for a detailed discussion). More research is needed to test specific process models used by groups, including the described communication-based rules, to form a joint group decision.

When groups deliberate, group members tend to exchange information and argue in favor of their initial preferences (Burnstein & Vinokur, 1977). As a consequence, group discussions often generate considerably more arguments and share more information in favor of the majority position in a group than on dissenting views. Thus, majorities are often larger and majority members are more confident in their preferences after than before group discussions. This informational influence can contribute to group polarization along with normative influence, that is, influence to conform to the group based on our need to belong and to be liked by others.

Group polarization refers to the tendency of groups when forming judgments to form more extreme decisions as a group than their average group members (Lamm & Myers, 1978; Sunstein & Hastie, 2015). Whereas majorities in groups can exert normative as well as informational influence, minorities have to resort to influencing majority members by using good arguments and providing new, unshared pieces of information that demonstrate the correctness of inferences (see Forsyth, 2018).

Meta-Communicative Approaches

From a decision-making perspective, group discussions can affect and alter the decision strategies that are used by groups (e.g., whether an alternative-based or cue-based strategy is used), the attributes that are considered (including the rank order of attributes), and knowledge about attribute values (e.g., to which choice alternatives an attribute pertains) (see Reimer et al., 2012). These influences can occur implicitly (at times even unnoticed), or they can be the outcome of meta-cognitive and meta-communicative discourses. Meta-cognition in groups may be construed as the knowledge group members have about their group and their task, and as the way group members monitor and control their information processing and actions (see Chapter 3), while meta-communication refers to a group's conversations about how to structure their discussions. The implementation of a devil's advocate by a group who is invited to speak up during group deliberation would be an example of meta-cognitive and meta-communicative discourses. Meta-cognition and meta-communication have been shown to play an important role in group functioning, including decision making. For example, research indicates that it is important for effective and efficient group interactions, that group members share mental models (Wittenbaum & Park, 2001), and research on transactive memory systems (Brandon & Hollingshead, 2004; also see Chapter 14) highlights that group communication and performance often hinge on group members' adequate understanding and knowledge of who knows what in a group. Meta-knowledge about how information is distributed has the potential to facilitate information exchange (Stasser & Abele, 2020) and group decision making (Brandon & Hollingshead, 2004) (see Chapter 3 for additional examples).

Meta-cognitive discourses are particularly important in situations in which groups face *ill-defined decision tasks*, including situations in which groups have to develop decision criteria and set their own goals (e.g., see Frey et al., 1999; Gouran, 1999; Poole & Hirokawa, 1996). For example, it may not be clear what the choice set looks like (e.g., a research and development team in a tech company that creates a new product) and groups may have to search for information on attributes (e.g., a medical team that has to perform blood tests to be able to form a diagnosis; see Chapter 22). It might also be that the criteria for a good decision may not be clear at the outset (e.g., it may be important that the implementation of a decision is feasible). Particularly in ill-defined decision environments, it is important for groups to engage in meta-cognitive discussions, including a discussion about which strategy should be employed by the group, how the decision process should be structured, whether additional information should be acquired and searched for, and if additional members should be added to the team. All these are examples of *meta-communication*. Meta-cognitive and meta-communicative discourses entail a discussion about what to discuss and the structure of discussions. Developing procedures can be particularly useful when groups must form several decisions in a sequence, or when members have a history and future together and must face the consequences of their joined decision.

Hirokawa (1990) developed a task-contingency perspective that focuses on the role of discussion in problem solving and decision making. He identified task dimensions that are crucial for effective group discussions and achieving positive outcomes. These dimensions include task complexity, information requirement, and evaluation demand. Simple tasks have clear goals, a shared understanding of necessary steps, minimal steps, and few obstacles, while complex tasks have unclear goals, disagreement on how to proceed, and many obstacles. The information requirement dimension focuses on the amount and distribution of information among group members necessary to solve a problem, and whether the information necessitates significant or minimal processing (also see Sanders & Bonito, 2010). For instance, in jury trials, jurors are typically presented with a vast amount of evidence and testimony, which is available to all members, but may require division of labor for effective processing. Lastly, the evaluation demand dimension refers to the level of effort required by the group to validate their chosen solution. This includes the number of viable solutions, the clarity of decision-making criteria, and the objective verifiability of the chosen solution.

Orlitzky and Hirokawa (2001) conducted a meta-analysis on the relationship between group communication and decision performance and found an association between problem analysis and criteria establishment. In a pioneering study on group dynamics, Gouran (1976) discovered that groups capable of making high-quality decisions engage in effective communication. Effective communication is defined as addressing relevant issues, analyzing information, amplifying diverse contributions, establishing clear goals, evaluating evidence, exhibiting strong leadership, and ensuring equal participation among group members (also see Hirokawa & Laybon, 2022).

Among the many influences on decision making that have been identified (Hirokawa & Johnston, 1989), the *process* that a group follows in arriving at a decision is widely regarded as one of the most important (Hirokawa & Laybon, 2022). In laboratory-based studies, communication is mainly conceptualized as the medium of group interaction (Hirokawa & Laybon, 2022). Additionally, communication can also be viewed as constitutive of group decisions—that is, the means for creating the social reality within which collective decisions are made (Bonito et al., 2014; Poole & Hirokawa, 1996). Gouran and Hirokawa (1996) discovered that group interaction can have a significant impact on the quality of a group's social context and, ultimately, on its decision-making performance. They identified four specific ways in which interaction influences group decision making, where group interactions involve meta-cognitive discourses: (1) shaping the group's understanding of the problem at hand, (2) defining the group's goals and objectives, (3) determining the options available, and (4) evaluating the pros and cons of each option (see also Hirokawa & Salazar, 1999).

Planning group discussions and decision procedures can be helpful: According to Tschan (2002), groups that implement an ideal cycle of action regulation, in which they orient themselves, plan their actions, execute the plan, closely monitor its progress, and evaluate its effectiveness, tend to be more successful. Groups greatly vary in their decision-making sequences. Poole et al. (2022) reviewed a large number of studies on naturally occurring groups and found that only approximately 25% of these groups followed a structured and idealized sequence of decision-making stages.

Evidence-Based Recommendations for Practice

The literature on group communication and decision making offers a variety of evidence-based recommendations for practice. Decision making can be evaluated on various dimensions, including the accuracy and quality of the decision, the fairness and satisfaction with the decision process, and other process variables (e.g., efficiency). Several outcome variables, including members' satisfaction, are enhanced when group members are convinced that the decision process follows rules of procedural justice (see Forsyth, 2018), are invested in the group decision process, actively participate in the group deliberation, and are committed to the group's decision. This is particularly important in situations in which the implementation of a decision is challenging (Vroom, 1976).

If a group faces a new problem or decision task that is not well defined, it is advisable to consider the phases that are suggested by the functional theory of group decision making, including the orientation, discussion, decision, and implementation phases (Gouran & Hirokawa, 1996). It is advisable to reflect on the following questions: Is the decision task a preference or an inference task? Does the group have enough information to form a decision and is the choice set inclusive of all available options? Which decision strategy should the group use? If the group has decided to use a given decision strategy, is the strategy applied correctly (e.g., do group members share relevant information)? In situations in which group members tend to form suboptimal or poor decisions, majority vote should be avoided. In these situations, it is important to provide opportunities for the most knowledgeable members in the group to exert informational influence and demonstrate why certain decisions are better than others or to employ a communication-based strategy. To the extent that a task can be construed as an inference task, the demonstrability of the correct solution should be explored (see Chapter 3). Transparency and explainability increase not only accuracy but also learning, which is particularly useful in situations in which groups form similar decisions in the future (e.g., in a medical context; see Chapter 22).

It is possible to take precautions that reduce the risk and extent of group polarization and groupthink phenomena in groups (Sunstein & Hastie, 2015). One major intervention to reduce group polarization consists in increasing the diversity of a group, as group polarization is most pronounced in highly homogeneous groups, in which group members share similar views (see Phillips et al., 2014). At the same time, increasing diversity in terms of values and general beliefs can also increase unproductive conflicts in groups (see Chapters 8 and 10). As with the selection of decision strategies, a large part of the art of good group decision making consists in making choices that match the requirements of the task and the context. Diversifying a group's expertise and knowledge can help attenuate tendencies of group polarization and groupthink, spur productive conflicts and discussions, and boost the generation of creative and innovative decisions. At the same time, groups in which members greatly vary in their basic values can cause challenges to constructive discussions and joint decision making, prevent groups from achieving consensus, and impair the identification with and implementation of decisions. The key to good decision making is the ability to adapt to contextual constraints, challenges, and characteristics of the information environment. In case groups face ill-defined decision tasks, it is important to engage in meta-cognitive and meta-communicative interactions.

Conclusion

There are various reasons for delegating a decision to a group, such as the prospect for a more informed decision, shared responsibility among the deciders, and the representation and involvement of stakeholders. The group serves a representative role, which is especially crucial when the goal is to promote acceptance, satisfaction, or commitment to a decision, particularly in situations where the group is tasked with making preferential decisions (Stasser & Abele, 2020).

Even though we are far from having a complete picture of how groups form decisions, group decision making is one of the best studied areas in group research. Research on group decision making described impaired decision making (e.g., Sunstein & Hastie, 2015) and also highlighted the quality of group decisions (Forsyth, 2018; Kerr & Tindale, 2004), including scholarship on the bounded rationality of groups (Reimer & Hoffrage, 2012b; Reimer & Katsikopoulos, 2004; Reimer et al., 2020) and scholarship that described situations in which groups are indispensable to make decisions (Hirokawa & Salazar, 1999; Poole & Hirokawa, 1996).

Promising future research directions consist in furthering the identification of decision strategies in group deliberation that can be augmented by new data science tools and new developments in the use of automated text analysis and machine learning (see Chapter 12). These technological advances can help understand contingencies among task characteristics as well as scaling up the coding of group discussions, which has the potential to provide inferences about group deliberation and strategy use. Another promising research area is the study of communication-based decision rules that were discussed in this chapter. The described decision strategies often make identical predictions. Future research might further delineate which strategies groups use in which situations and describe the role of communication and meta-communicative interactions in group decision making. While most research on group decision making focuses on the quality of decisions, it is important to examine a variety of outcome variables including not just accuracy, but also the feasibility of decisions, as well as group members' participation, satisfaction, and commitment. Another promising and important field of study refers to the integration of AIs in group decision making. Researchers have started to analyze and describe the role of AI in group decision making, which invites a variety of conceptual and ethical questions (see Chapter 24). Research on group decision making is very applicable and can—if utilized in the right way—help reduce the risk of decision-making tragedies.

Further Readings

Hirokawa, R. Y., & Laybon, A. (2022). Communication and group decision making processes. In S. Beck, J. Keyton, & S. Poole (Eds.), *The handbook of group and team communication research* (pp. 191–208). Emerald Publishing.

Reimer, T., Barber, H., & Dolick, K. (2020). The bounded rationality of groups and teams. In R. Viale (Ed.), *Routledge handbook on bounded rationality* (pp. 535–547). Routledge.

Glossary

Alternative-based decision strategy   Alternative-based strategies (such as the unit weight linear model or the weighted additive model) process information alternative-wise. They perform a summary evaluation of each alternative by looking at all attributes of each alternative. The strategies choose the alternative that receives the highest overall evaluation.

Cue-based decision strategy   Cue-based strategies (such as Take-the-best) process information cue-wise by comparing choice alternatives on one cue or attribute at a time. Cues (attributes) are processed in the order of their validity (cues) or perceived importance (attributes). Once a processed cue or attribute discriminates among choice alternatives, the alternative with the highest value is chosen.

Group polarization   Group polarization refers to the tendency of homogeneous groups to form more extreme decisions as a group than their average group members.

References

Baron, R. S., Kerr, N. L., & Miller, N. (1992). *Group process, group decision, group action*. Thomson Brooks/ Cole Publishing Co.

Beck, S., Keyton, J., & Poole, S. (Eds.). (2022). *The handbook of group and team communication research*. Emerald Publishing.

Bonito, J. A. (2007). A local model of information sharing in small groups. *Communication Theory, 17*, 252–280.

Bonito, J., Gastil, A., Ervin, J., & Meyers, J. N. (2014). At the convergence of input and process models of group discussion: A comparison of participation rates across time, persons, and groups. *Communication Monographs, 81*(2), 179–207.

Bonner, B. L., & Baumann, M. R. (2012). Leveraging member expertise to improve knowledge transfer and demonstrability in groups. *Journal of Personality and Social Psychology, 102*, 337–350.

Bonner, B. L., Soderberg, A. T., Meikle, N. L., & Overbeck, J. R. (2022). The effects of experience, expertise, reward power, and decision power in groups. *Group Dynamics: Theory, Research, and Practice, 26*, 309–321.

Boyle, A. (2012). *10 causes of the Titanic tragedy*. NBC News. https://www.nbcnews.com/sciencemain/ 10-causes-titanic-tragedy-620220

Brandon, D. P., & Hollingshead, A. B. (2004). Transactive memory systems in organizations: Matching tasks, expertise, and people. *Organization Science, 15*(6), 633–644.

Burnstein, E., & Vinokur, A. (1977). Persuasive arguments and social comparison as determinants of attitude polarization. *Journal of Experimental Social Psychology, 13*(4), 315–332.

Danigelis, A. (2012). *Wireless could have saved lives on Titanic.* NBC News. https://www.nbcnews.com/id/wbna47018360

Davis, J. H., Laughlin, P. R., & Komorita, S. S. (1976). The social psychology of small groups: Cooperative and mixed-motive interaction. *Annual Review of Psychology, 27*, 501–541.

Diflo, T. (2006). The transplant surgeon's perspective on the bungled transplant. In K. Wailoo, J. Livingston, & P. Guarnaccia (Eds.), *A death retold: Jesica Santillan, the bungled transplant, and paradoxes of medical citizenship* (pp. 70–81). University of North Carolina Press.

Driscoll, J. W. (1978). Trust and participation in organizational decision making as predictors of satisfaction. *Academy of Management Journal, 21*, 44–56.

Forsyth, D. R. (2018). *Group dynamics.* Thomson Wadsworth.

Frey, L. R., Gouran, D. S., & Poole, M. S. (Eds.). (1999). *The handbook of group communication theory and research.* Sage.

Gigerenzer, G., & Todd, P. M. (1999). Fast and frugal heuristics: The adaptive toolbox. In G. Gigerenzer, P. M. Todd, & The ABC Research Group (Eds.), *Simple heuristics that make us smart* (pp. 3–34). Oxford University Press.

Gigerenzer, G., Todd, P. M., & The ABC Research Group (1999). *Simple heuristics that make us smart.* Oxford University Press.

Gigone, D., & Hastie, R. (1993). The common knowledge effect: Information sharing and group judgment. *Journal of Personality and Social Psychology, 65*(5), 959–974.

Gouran, D. S. (1976). The Watergate cover-up: Its dynamics and its implications. *Communication Monographs, 43*(3), 176–186.

Gouran, D. S. (1999). Communication in groups: The emergence and evolution of a field of study. In L. R. Frey, D. S. Gouran, & M. S. Poole (Eds.), *The handbook of group communication theory and research* (pp. 3–36). Sage.

Gouran, D. S., & Hirokawa, R. Y. (1996). Functional theory and communication in decision-making and problem-solving groups: An expanded view. In R. Y. Hirokawa & M. S. Poole (Eds.), *Communication and group decision making* (pp. 55–80). Sage.

Gouran, D. S., Hirokawa, R. Y., & Martz, A. E. (1986). A critical analysis of factors related to decisional processes involved in the challenger disaster. *Central States Speech Journal, 37*, 119–135.

Hastie, R., & Dawes, R. M. (2010). *Rational choice in an uncertain world: The psychology of judgment and decision making* (2nd ed.). Sage Publications, Inc.

Hastie, R., & Kameda, T. (2005). The robust beauty of majority rules in group decisions. *Psychological Review, 112*(2), 494–508.

Hertwig, R., Hoffrage, U., & Martignon, L. (1999). Quick estimation: Letting the environment do the work. In G. Gigerenzer, P. M. Todd, & The ABC Research Group (Eds.), *Simple heuristics that make us smart* (pp. 209–234). Oxford University Press.

Hinsz, V. B., Tindale, R. S., & Vollrath, D. A. (1997). The emerging conceptualization of groups as information processors. *Psychological Bulletin, 121*(1), 43–64.

Hirokawa, R. Y. (1990). The role of communication in group decision-making efficacy: A task-contingency perspective. *Small Group Research, 21*(2), 190–204.

Hirokawa, R. Y., & Johnston, D. D. (1989). Toward a general theory of group decision making: Development of an integrated model. *Small Group Behavior, 20*(4), 500–523.

Hirokawa, R. Y., & Laybon, A. (2022). Communication and group decision making processes. In S. Beck, J. Keyton, & S. Poole (Eds.), *The Emerald handbook of group and team communication research* (pp. 191–208). Emerald Publishing.

Hirokawa, R. Y., & Salazar, A. J. (1999). Task-group communication and decision-making performance. In L. R. Frey, D. S. Gouran, & M. S. Poole (Eds.), *The handbook of group communication theory and research* (pp. 167–191). Sage.

Huber, G. L. (2003). Processes of decision-making in small learning groups. *Learning and Instruction, 13*, 255–269.

Kaemmer, J., Gaissmaier, W., Reimer, T., & Schermuly, C. C. (2014). The adaptive use of recognition in group decision making. *Cognitive Science*, *38*(5), 911–942.

Kerby, M., & Baguley, M. (2022). When death gave way to glory: Philip Gibbs, RMS Titanic and the Western front. *International Journal of Maritime History*, *34*(1), 46–62.

Kerr, N. L., & Tindale, R. S. (2004). Group performance and decision making. *Annual Review of Psychology*, *55*, 623–655.

Keyton, J. (1999). Relational communication in groups. In L. R. Frey, D. S. Gouran, & M. S. Poole (Eds.), *The handbook of group communication theory and research* (pp. 192–222). Sage.

Ladbury, J. L., & Hinsz, V. B. (2009). Individual expectations for group decision processes: Evidence for overestimation of majority influence. *Group Dynamics: Theory, Research, and Practice*, *13*(4), 235–254.

Lamm, H., & Myers, D. G. (1978). Group-induced polarization of attitude and behavior. *Advances in Experimental Social Psychology*, *11*, 145–195.

Larson, J. R. (2010). *In search of synergy in small group performance*. Psychology Press.

Larson, J. R., Christensen, C., Abbott, A. S., & Franz, T. M. (1996). Diagnosing groups: Charting the flow of information in medical decision-making teams. *Journal of Personality and Social Psychology*, *71*, 315–330.

Larson, J. R., & Egan, A. C. (2020). Information sharing within groups in organizations: Situational and motivational influences. In L. Argote & J. M. Levine (Eds.), *The Oxford handbook of group and organizational learning* (pp. 127–153). Oxford University Press.

Laughlin, P. R. (2011). *Group problem solving*. Princeton University Press.

Laughlin, P. R., & Ellis, A. L. (1986). Demonstrability and social combination processes on mathematical intellective tasks. *Journal of Experimental Social Psychology*, *22*, 177–189.

Leighly, H. P., Bramfitt, B. L., & Lawrence, S. J. (2001). RMS Titanic: A metallurgical problem. *Practical Failure Analysis*, *1*(2), 10–13.

Lu, L., Yuan, C., & McLeod, P. L. (2012). Twenty-five years of hidden profiles in group decision making: A meta-analysis. *Personality and Social Psychology Review*, *16*(1), 54–75.

Mannes, A. E., Soll, J. B., & Larrick, R. P. (2014). The wisdom of select crowds. *Journal of Personality and Social Psychology*, *107*(2), 276–299.

Oh, J., Reimer, T., & Park, E. (2023). The effects of prior sensory experience on group decision making. *Paper presented at the 73rd annual conference of the International Communication Association*, Toronto, Canada.

Orlitzky, M., & Hirokawa, R. Y. (2001). To err is human, to correct for it divine: A meta-analysis of research testing the functional theory of group decision-making effectiveness. *Small Group Research*, *32*(3), 313–341.

Pachur, T. (2022). Strategy selection in decisions from givens: Deciding at a glance? *Cognitive Psychology*, *136*, 101483.

Pavitt, C. (2003). Colloquy: Do interacting groups perform better than aggregates of individuals? Why we have to be reductionists about group memory. *Human Communication Research*, *29*(4), 592–599.

Phillips, K. W., Medin, D., Lee, C. D., Bang, M., Bishop, S., & Lee, D. N. (2014). How diversity works. *Scientific American*, *311*(4), 42–47.

Poole, M., Dobosh, M., & Keyton, J. (2022). Group communication theory: New theories and perspectives. In S. Beck, J. Keyton, & S. Poole (Eds.), *The Emerald handbook of group and team communication research* (pp. 45–52). Emerald Publishing.

Poole, M. S., & Hirokawa, R. Y. (1996). Introduction: Communication and group decision making. In R. Y. Hirokawa & M. S. Poole (Eds.), *Communication and group decision making* (pp. 3–18). Sage.

Propp, K. M. (1999). Collective information processing in groups. In L. R. Frey, D. S. Gouran, & M. S. Poole (Assoc. Eds.), *The handbook of group communication theory and research* (pp. 225–250). Sage.

Reimer, T., Barber, H., & Dolick, K. (2020). The bounded rationality of groups and teams. In R. Viale (Ed.), *Routledge handbook on bounded rationality* (pp. 535–547). Routledge.

Reimer, T., Dolick, K., Barber, H., & Oh, J. (2022). What methodologies are needed to study group communication? A bounded-rationality perspective. In S. Beck, J. Keyton, & S. Poole (Eds.), *The Emerald handbook of group and team communication research* (pp. 545–558). Emerald Publishing.

Reimer, T., Hertwig, R., & Sipek, S. (2012). Probabilistic persuasion: A Brunswikian theory of argumentation. In R. Hertwig, U. Hoffrage, & The ABC Research Group (Eds.), *Simple heuristics in a social world* (pp. 33–55). Oxford University Press.

Reimer, T., & Hoffrage, U. (2006). The ecological rationality of simple group heuristics: Effects of group member strategies on decision accuracy. *Theory and Decision, 60*(4), 403–438. https://doi.org/10.1007/s11238-005-4750-2

Reimer, T., & Hoffrage, U. (2012a). Simple heuristics and information sharing in groups. In R. Hertwig, U. Hoffrage, & The ABC Research Group (Eds.), *Simple heuristics in a social world* (pp. 266–286). Oxford University Press.

Reimer, T., & Hoffrage, U. (2012b). Ecological rationality for teams and committees: Heuristics in group decision making. In P. M. Todd, G. Gigerenzer, & The ABC Research Group (Eds.), *Ecological rationality: Intelligence in the world* (pp. 335–359). Oxford University Press.

Reimer, T., & Katsikopoulos, K. (2004). The use of recognition in group decision-making. *Cognitive Science, 28*(6), 1009–1029.

Reimer, T., Reimer, A., & Czienskowski, U. (2010a). Decision-making groups attenuate the discussion bias in favor of shared information: A meta-analysis. *Communication Monographs, 77*(1), 121–142.

Reimer, T., Reimer, A., & Hinsz, V. (2010b). Naïve groups can solve the hidden-profile problem. *Human Communication Research, 36*(3), 443–467.

Riedl, R., Brandstaetter, E., & Roithmayr, F. (2008). Identifying decision strategies: A process- and outcome-based classification method. *Behavior Research Methods, 40*, 795–807.

Russell, T., & Reimer, T. (2015). Risk communication in groups. In H. Cho, T. Reimer, & K. A. McComas (Eds.), *The Sage handbook of risk communication* (pp. 272–287). Sage Publications.

Sanders, R. E., & Bonito, J. A. (2010). Speaking for the institution: A fourth production site for group members' influence attempts. *Small Group Research, 41*(4), 427–451.

Shapley, L., & Grofman, B. (1984). Optimizing group judgmental accuracy in the presence of interdependencies. *Public Choice, 43*(3), 329–343.

Stasser, G., & Abele, S. (2020). Collective choice, collaboration, and communication. *Annual Review of Psychology, 71*, 589–612.

Stasser, G., & Titus, W. (1985). Pooling of unshared information in group decision making: Biased information sampling during discussion. *Journal of Personality and Social Psychology, 48*(6), 1467–1478.

Stasser, G., & Titus, W. (1987). Effects of information load and percentage of shared information on the dissemination of unshared information during group discussion. *Journal of Personality and Social Psychology, 53*, 81–93.

Sunstein, C. R., & Hastie, R. (2015). *Wiser: Getting beyond groupthink to make groups smarter*. Harvard Business Review Press.

Todd, P. M., Gigerenzer, G., & The ABC Research Group (Eds.). (2012). *Ecological rationality: Intelligence in the world*. Oxford University Press.

Tschan, F. (2002). Ideal cycles of communication (or cognitions) in triads, dyads, and individuals. *Small Group Research, 33*(6), 615–643.

Vroom, V. H. (1976). Can leaders learn to lead? *Organizational Dynamics, 4*(3), 17–28.

Wittenbaum, G. M., Hollingshead, A. B., & Botero, I. C. (2004). From cooperative to motivated information sharing in groups: Moving beyond the hidden profile paradigm. *Communication Monographs, 71*(3), 286–310.

Wittenbaum, G., & Park, E. (2001). The collective preference for shared information. *Psychological Science, 10*(2), 70–73.

Yu, F. L. T. (2012). The sinking of the unsinkable Titanic: Mental inertia and coordination failures. *Human Systems Management, 31*(3–4), 177–186.

Zinkova, M. (2021). The Titanic's 'low-lying', silent distress rockets explained. *International Journal of Maritime History, 33*(4), 761–772.

16 Creativity and Innovation in Groups

Roni Reiter-Palmon and Payge Japp

Chapter Objectives

- Define and understand creativity and innovation in general and in teams.
- Understand cognitive processes that influence creativity and innovation.
- Understand how communication influences creativity and innovation processes in teams.

Introduction

There has been an increase in research and popular press books and articles on **creativity** and **innovation** in organizations over the last couple of decades. Rapid changes in the marketplace, technological advancements, globalization, and the COVID-19 pandemic have all underscored the need of organizations to develop creative solutions and products (Reiter-Palmon et al., 2021). A recent report by IBM and MIT (Fleming et al., 2019) analyzed jobs and tasks from 2010 to 2017, and found that tasks that could be conducted by machines, including AI and machine learning, were disappearing at a higher rate from job descriptions. For example, Fleming et al. (2017) suggested that tasks such as scheduling and credential validation, that can be conducted by machines, are not showing up as frequently. On the other hand, tasks that required intellectual skill, knowledge, and creativity showed an increase in demand, such as the tasks required for those in the design industry. In addition, the World Economic Forum (2020) notes that skills necessary for workers in 2025 include critical thinking, problem-solving, creativity, and innovation among the top five skills. These two reports together indicate that creativity is critical for employees and organizations.

The use of teams in the workplace to address complex problems has increased, and with it, the interest in team creativity. A number of research streams have emerged to understand how teams capitalize on individual creativity and develop creative products or ideas. Specifically, work regarding team creativity has focused on team cognition, or how team members think and develop shared cognition that leads to creative solutions (Harvey, 2014). A second stream focuses on the social processes that emerge in teams during team interactions and how those facilitate or inhibit team creativity (Reiter-Palmon et al., 2011). This dual focus has resulted in fragmented independent streams of research. However, it is important to note that creativity and innovation in teams cannot occur without communication. Team members must communicate with each other regarding their cognitions, such as how they frame the problem, discuss solutions, or share needed knowledge.

In this chapter, we will start by defining creativity and innovation. We will follow with a discussion of cognitive processes associated with team creativity and those associated with team innovation. We will further discuss how communication influences these cognitive processes with specific attention to **information sharing**. Finally, the chapter includes practical recommendations to improve creativity and innovation in teams.

DOI: 10.4324/9781003227458-18

Creativity and Innovation

Within this context of organizations, creativity has been defined as a "novel product, idea, or problem solution that is of value to the individual and/or the larger social group" (Hennessey & Amabile, 2010, p. 572). This definition suggests that for an idea or solution to be creative, two conditions must be met. First, the idea needs to be novel – that is unique or original. This aspect of creativity is the one that most people attend to. However, a second condition must be met – the idea needs to have value, must be useful, solve the problem at hand, or be effective. The dual criteria of novelty and usefulness thus define creative ideas or solutions. The distinction between creativity and innovation focuses on the processes associated with each. Creativity is viewed as the generation of ideas and solutions, whereas innovation is defined as the implementation of these ideas and solutions in the organization (West, 2002). In an organizational setting, generating ideas is only the beginning. Implementing those ideas is critical for organizational success (West, 2002).

It is also important to disentangle the relationship between creative problem-solving (creativity), general problem-solving, and critical thinking. The distinction between creativity and general forms of problem-solving and critical thinking is based on the desired outcome. When the focus is on creativity, the desired outcome is that of a creative idea or solution, then the dual aspects of novelty and usefulness are required. In contrast, when focusing on general problem-solving or critical thinking, the focus is only on usefulness. Further, creative ideas tend to be generated to ill-defined problems (Schraw et al., 1995). Ill-defined problems are problems that are ambiguous, tend to have multiple and potentially conflicting goals, and multiple possible solutions. Additionally, these problems often do not have correct or incorrect answers, rather, they have solutions that solve the problem better compared to others. Ill-defined problems because they are ambiguous and have multiple possible solutions, allow for creativity. Many problems facing organizations are ill-defined. An example of such a problem is when a business needs to manage the shortage of workers. The problem may have different and multiple causes such as low pay relative to other jobs, difficult job, skill and educational requirements place by the organization, to name a few. Organizations may respond in different ways as well (as we have seen) from boosting pay, improving work conditions, reducing educational requirements, and adding automation. Typically, these problems do not have a specific structure or known solution, which will allow (but does not require) creativity. Well-defined problems, by contrast, are characterized by a known and correct answer. For example, geometry puzzles are often considered well-defined, such that they often have a clearly specified goal and instructions clearly state out the necessary information. In addition, well-defined problems allow for only pre-specified way to solve them. As such, well-defined problems require problem-solving and critical thinking only, whereas creativity can only occur when the problem is ill-defined. Between these two extremes, problems can have a specified general goal, that is still somewhat ambiguous (write a poem), specific ways of solving however, new ways may be found, and so on.

Models of team cognition for creativity and innovation suggest that teams may follow similar processes to those of individuals (Mumford et al., 1991; Reiter-Palmon et al., 2008). Specifically, early processes include **problem identification and construction** and idea generation. The later processes are viewed as innovation processes and include idea evaluation and the selection of the idea to implement (see Figure 16.1). These models of creative problem-solving can also be used to understand general problem-solving and critical thinking. It has been suggested that the cognitive processes associated with creativity are the same as those associated with general problem-solving, with the difference being one of increased emphasis on certain processes for creative problem-solving, and a focus on the outcome of creative ideas or solutions (Reiter-Palmon & Illies, 2004).

Figure 16.1 Overview of Creative Problem-Solving Process.

The double-sided arrows denote that the creative processes can co-occur. These processes may cycle back to one another, alternation between problem construction, idea generation, idea evaluation, and idea selection.

Creativity in Teams: Early Cognitive Processes

Problem Identification and Construction

Problem identification and construction is viewed as the first step in creative problem-solving (Reiter-Palmon et al., 2008). Problem identification and construction is defined as the process of identifying that a problem exists and identifying the goals and parameters of the problem-solving effort (Reiter-Palmon & Robinson, 2009), and has emerged as an important factor for creative problem-solving (Abdulla et al., 2020). Getzels (1982) provided an example of problem construction. An automobile traveling on a deserted road and blows a tire. The passengers find that there is no jack, and define their dilemma by posing the following problem: "Where can we get a jack?". Effective communication regarding problem construction can be done simply by summarizing the said problem and by restating what is known about the problem in different ways. Another way to construct the problem is also suggested "how can we lift the car so we can change the tire." Importantly, once the problem is constructed by the team, it would lead to different solutions. One reason problem identification and construction may be particularly important is because problems that face organizations as well as teams that require creativity are complex and ill-defined. The ambiguity and complexity resulting from ill-defined problems increase the likelihood of communication errors, misunderstandings, lack of coordination, and conflict (Okhuysen & Bechky, 2009). These breakdowns and difficulties in communications can lead to errors and time delays, and reduce creativity. Important ways in which communication influences problem construction in teams are discussed as follows.

Research on problem identification and construction in teams has focused on the extent to which team members share a similar understanding of the problem and construct it in the same way. Obtaining shared mental models has shown to be important in team problem identification and construction, because it allows for team members to coordinate attention, understand the common goals, and communicate and collaborate effectively (Jonker et al., 2010). Cronin and Weingart (2007) coined the term rGap to denote differences in how individual team members understand the problem and structure it. In interdisciplinary teams in particular, rGaps can be larger. Interdisciplinary teams include diverse team members that represent different departments in the organization and different educational backgrounds. Interestingly, large rGaps have been found to both facilitate creativity (Weingart et al., 2008) and to hinder creativity (Weingart et al., 2005). Whether large rGaps lead to creative ideas is dependent on effective communication. When teams discuss the differences in understanding the problem early and integrate the different conceptualizations of the problem into a coherent whole, creative ideas follow. For example, consider the aforementioned automobile problem. Effective communication may occur when the passengers state the problem of lacking a jack to fix the tire, acknowledge other existing problems (e.g., nowhere nearby to obtain a jack), and collectively map out a plan towards an attainable solution. However, team communication failures result in lower creativity. Communication failures can occur when teams fail to discuss their different conceptualizations, when teams communicate later in the process, or when teams fail to integrate the different constructions.

Surprisingly, individuals are not aware of their own problem constructions and it tends to occur in an automatic fashion (Mumford et al., 1994). In teams, individual team members are not typically aware that others view the problem differently (Leonardi, 2011). It has been suggested that one reason for conflict during creative problem-solving efforts in teams is that different team members view the problem differently, but are not aware of that (Reiter-Palmon et al., 2011). However, effective communication between team members early in the problem-solving effort can mitigate the conflict (Toader et al., 2019). For example, to identify differences in problem representation, team members can engage in summarization of the problem, break the problem down into smaller pieces, and are open to different ways in which other team members think about the problem. Additionally, when team members are instructed to discuss the different conceptualizations prior to developing creative ideas and integrate different conceptualizations, and have leaders that facilitate such effective discussions and communication, creativity of the solutions increases. Further, these teams also report less conflict and more satisfaction with the process and outcome (Reiter-Palmon & Murugavel, 2018).

Taken together, these studies indicate that communication and sharing of information, regardless of the mechanism by which it occurs (instructions, leadership, and naturally occurring), are important mechanisms by which teams reach a shared understanding of the nature of the problem and can resolve discrepancies in problem identification and construction. This is especially important for diverse teams which are more likely to have different understandings of the problem. Diverse teams that bring different perspectives and come from different backgrounds are often more creative, because their ability to integrate different points of view is enhanced (Hundschell et al., 2020). However, discussion about these different problem constructions is not sufficient. Teams must find a way to combine and integrate these divergent problem representations and not just compromise or conform for the sake of expediency. Research on how team members gain these integrative perspectives, beyond just discussing the different perspective, is lacking.

Idea Generation and Brainstorming

One cognitive process that has been investigated extensively at the team level is that of idea generation or brainstorming. In fact, idea generation has become equated with creativity and innovation, even though the idea generation process is only one of multiple processes that are required for creativity (Reiter-Palmon & Paulus, 2020). Work on brainstorming has started with Osborn (1953), who not only coined the term but also suggested four specific rules for effective brainstorming. First, ideas should not be evaluated or criticized during the brainstorming session. The purpose of this rule was to focus on generation with the notion that debate and refinement will occur later. Second, quantity of ideas is important, as quantity will lead to quality. Third, all ideas should be suggested, even if they are outrageous. The goal here was to avoid self-censure and be able to use ideas that are not workable as stepping stones for other ideas. Fourth, participants in the brainstorming session should build upon ideas that have already been suggested, creating synergy.

Nemeth et al. (2004) evaluated Osborn's rules and found that teams that engaged in debate generated more ideas compared to those working under the traditional rules. They suggested that the instructions to debate may be liberating and allow participants to offer more ideas as a result. Supporting the notion that debate may be beneficial for brainstorming and creativity, research suggests that some level of task conflict, or conflict that involves disagreement about the problems, solutions, or decisions regarding working tasks, facilitates creativity (Petrou et al., 2019). It has been found that a moderate level of task conflict is most beneficial, whereas when task conflict is too low or too high, creativity is reduced. These studies suggest that the no debate rule may not be beneficial for creativity; however, teams should be careful about the degree of conflict or

---

Box 16.1   Creativity in Design Teams

In 2011, Leonardi studied teams in an automobile manufacturer, Autoworks, located in the United States (US). Leonardi focused on creative-problem-solving process and communication within teams. The study included two different specialties: designers and engineers. Designers are responsible for creating the parts with a computer-aided drafting software (CAD) and assigning it vehicle coordinates that indicate where that part belongs. The engineers are then responsible for assembling the CAD parts, as well as for testing the performance of the vehicle on various parameters (e.g., crashworthiness, noise, and heat transfer). See Leonardi (2011) for more information.

In this study, the author focused on a technology that was developed to aid engineers testing crashworthiness. Leonardi (2011) defines crashworthiness as "the vehicles ability to absorb energy through structural deformation" (p. 350). In other words, in order for a car to be legally sellable in the US, there are various crashworthiness standards that must be met. With attempt to reduce time and standardize the process, a computer simulation technology, CrashLab, was used to make predictions about how a vehicle structure would respond to a crash event.

Leonardi interviewed those who were involved in the CrashLab development, to understand the process of how CrashLab was developed. A total of 58 interviews, with 36 informants, from six different departments, about the development of CrashLab. Employees were asked about their role in the development processes, as well as more specific questions about the development and the changes that occurred in the organization over time. Additionally, archival data, such as reports, e-mails, and previous presentations were used to further analyze the development of CrashLab. By analyzing the interview information, as well as the archival data, Leonardi (2011) was able to construct a narrative of how the events unfolded from the perspective of each department.

Once Leonardi (2011) had determined the development process for each department, the creative problem-solving process in the teams was examined using coding of the interview and archival data. For four different departments, it was found that each team shared a common goal at the lower level, but each team developed a distinct understanding of what the problem was and what strategies should be used to solve the problem. For example, teams identified four different problems being, (1) accuracy, (2) speed, (3) capacity, and (4) credibility. While all teams shared the goal of moving the simulation analysis into a central role of the vehicle development process, each team believed a different problem needed to be solved in order to achieve the overarching goal.

The study made clear that teams from different departments disagreed about the features that the technological artifact should have, and the author notes that the teams were often blind to the reasons why others disagreed with them. These findings highlight the importance of communication in creative problem-solving in teams. As team members failed to acknowledge that other team members may view the problem differently, it is possible that effective communication at the beginning of this process could have been resolved. In other words, this study demonstrates how effective discussion and communication during early stages of the creative problem-solving process can lead to teams to more effective performance.

---

debate, as too much can hurt creative performance. A debate about how to accomplish a task, what are the important outcomes, and which solution is best, can be beneficial for creativity, as it allows team members to critically think about the solution and develop better solutions. However, it is important that this debate or task conflict does not become too extensive or personal, where team members insult each other for example.

The rule of increasing quantity of ideas has been responsible for the focus of creativity research on idea quantity over other metrics such as idea originality and usefulness (Reiter-Palmon et al., 2019). Research suggests that it is important to provide more specific quantity goals to ensure an increase in the number of ideas generated (Litchfield, 2009), that is a specific number of ideas. Previous research has suggested that goal-setting initiative will increase the probability of more creative ideas being generated (Paulus et al., 2011). Similarly, setting a specific goal for originality or novelty results in improved novelty of the ideas generated (Litchfield et al., 2011). Paulus et al. (2011) found support for Osborn's notion that quantity will increase the creativity of the ideas generated; however, other work has suggested that a focus on quantity may not be an effective approach. First, research has not supported the notion that more ideas would lead to more creative or higher quality ideas (Mouchiroud & Lubart, 2001). Further, there is some evidence that more ideas can lead to confusion and result in selection of less creative or less optimal ideas (Mumford et al., 2001).

The last two rules, of suggesting outrageous or unusual ideas and building upon the ideas suggested, have to do with capitalizing on group synergy stemming from exposure to the ideas of others. While research in this area is limited, studies have found that exposure to the ideas of others can result in stimulation and more effective idea generation and brainstorming (Korde & Paulus, 2017; Nijstad et al., 2002). Other work has focused on idea elaboration in teams, which is similar to what Osborn describes as building on ideas. When team members build on and elaborate on already suggested ideas, the creativity of the ideas or solutions generated increases (Mumford et al., 2001). For example, asking another team member to expand on a suggested solution, or by suggesting additional details to an existing solution, may promote idea elaboration and increase creativity.

Additional support for the role of synergy in effective idea generation and brainstorming comes from research focusing on team diversity. Team diversity has long been suggested as important for creativity and innovation because it would lead synergy across different domains and expertise (Reiter-Palmon et al., 2011). An assumption regarding team diversity and creativity is that diverse knowledge and experiences of the team members would lead to the generation of different ideas, and through synergy, more creative ideas (McLeod et al., 1996).

Research indicates that team diversity in knowledge or expertise among team members (functional diversity) does have positive effects on innovation, but demographic diversity does not have as clear an effect (Bell et al., 2011; Hulsheger et al., 2009). One issue is whether demographic diversity is related to the task at hand. In fact, when demographic diversity is related to differences in knowledge or experience relevant to the task, positive effects of diversity can be observed, especially when groups have a positive attitude towards diversity (Nakui et al., 2011; Paulus & van der Zee, 2015).

A review of the early research focusing on idea generation and brainstorming in teams suggests that nominal groups (when information from individuals working alone is combined) tend to outperform teams when the criterion is the number of ideas generated (Mullen et al., 1991). This surprising finding dubbed process loss, led to research focusing on the factors that affect process loss and ways to overcome them (Diehl & Stroebe, 1987). Process loss can be inherent in the process of communication between team members. When working face-to-face, team members cannot all speak at the same time. As a result, process loss may occur as team members wait to take turns. This wait can result in less time to present ideas, as well as in idea loss. One of the most common approaches to dealing with such process loss is the use of technology to facilitate idea generation, known as electronic brainstorming (EBS, Dennis & Williams, 2003; Gallupe et al., 1992). EBS is beneficial as it allows team members to simultaneously introduce ideas without having to wait. EBS has been found to be effective for tasks requiring divergent thought (Kerr & Murthy, 2004) and for larger teams (DeRose et al., 2007).

Creativity in Teams: Late Stage Processes

The late stage processes of creativity are viewed as innovation. These processes of idea evaluation and idea selection are important when multiple ideas have been generated. Mumford et al. (2002) proposed that idea evaluation and selection include three major activities: (1) forecasting possible outcomes of selecting and implementing an idea; (2) judging how well the characteristics of an idea fit with specific standards and criteria; and (3) choosing, revising, or rejecting the idea as a solution. The first two aspects focus on idea evaluation, whereas the last focuses on idea choice or idea selection. The generation of creative ideas alone does not necessarily ensure that individuals or teams will effectively evaluate, select, and implement a creative solution (Cropley, 2006; Rietzschel et al., 2006).

Idea Evaluation

During the idea evaluation process, individuals and teams focus on determining the possible outcomes of ideas or solutions proposed, and whether these outcomes will address the specific problem identified (Mumford et al., 2002). Idea evaluation can occur when teams identify the pros and cons of possible ideas and the likelihood that it will solve the problem at hand. Take the aforementioned automobile problem. If one passenger has generated the idea of walking to a local store to call a tow truck, the passengers will evaluate this idea by assessing the outcomes of this idea. For example, the passengers may suggest that this idea will not actually solve the problem, seeing as they would no longer have a ride. Research on idea evaluation is limited and results are mixed (Mumford et al., 2001; Rietzschel et al., 2006). As the Osborn rules calls for a distinct differentiation between idea generation and idea evaluation, it has been of interest whether this differentiation is indeed useful.

Harvey and Kou (2013) explored various modes of brainstorming and idea evaluation over several meetings and interactions among four teams developing innovative health information technology policy. Harvey and Kou identified two different approaches to how teams cycled between idea generation and idea evaluation. Some teams focused on generation first, generated multiple ideas, and then evaluated all of the ideas they generated to determine feasibility and whether the ideas solved the problem. Other teams evaluated each idea as it was generated, and if the idea was viewed favorably, team members then proceeded to elaborate and develop the idea. Generation-centered teams generated more ideas than the evaluation-centered teams; however, evaluation-centered teams often agreed upon and accepted more idea recommendations in the evaluation process than did generation-centered groups. Harvey and Kou suggested that engagement in evaluation processes supports the development of a shared framework for the problem at hand and directs collective attention to ideas to guide feedback and decisions of how well ideas address the problem.

Similar results were found in an experimental study by McIntosh et al. (2021). In this study, individuals were asked to develop ideas and a plan for a new restaurant. One manipulation in the study focused on the timing of evaluation. Participants were either asked to evaluate and forecast potential outcomes as they were generating the ideas (idea generation followed immediately by evaluation) or they first generated all the ideas, and then were asked to evaluate the ideas they generated. Participants were also asked to either focus on positive outcomes, negative outcomes, or both positive and negative outcomes during the evaluation process. When participants were asked to evaluate immediately after they generated the idea, they were more effective in their idea evaluations, replicating the findings by Harvey and Kou. In addition, participants produced better evaluations when they were asked to focus on both positive and negative outcomes. That is, focusing on both the pros and cons of each idea resulted in evaluations that were more complete.

The effectiveness of the idea evaluation process is a critical determinant of a person's ability to choose the best or most creative idea. Individuals are able to accurately evaluate ideas for originality and/or quality, with creative individuals being more likely to recognize creative ideas (Basadur et al., 2000). Further, it has been suggested that creative individuals are more likely to recognize and accurately evaluate creative ideas (Berg, 2016). In addition, teams can be more accurate in their evaluations when they are given guidance or training in how to evaluate ideas (Reiter-Palmon et al., 2018). For example, when teams receive examples, practice, and detailed rubrics for evaluation training, this increases their evaluation accuracy (Reiter-Palmon, 2018). While idea evaluation can be exemplified by expressing like or dislike in ideas, teams move to selection when they begin rejecting ideas. Some research has debated the sequence of these processes, with some research suggesting that these processes flow sequentially (Basadur, 1994), and others suggesting that these processes may co-occur. For example, Mumford et al. (1991) has suggested that processes may cycle back to one another, alternating between idea generation, idea evaluation, and selection. However, the majority of the research on these later stage process focused on idea selection. Additional research is needed to determine when teams move from idea evaluation to idea selection and the specific content of discussions during idea evaluation.

Idea Selection

The general finding of idea selection, both at the individual and team level, is that people typically do not choose the most creative ideas (Reiter-Palmon, 2018; Zhu et al., 2020). Multiple reasons have been identified as to why this phenomenon may occur. First, individuals and teams may be reluctant to choose creative ideas as these ideas tend to be viewed as too risky (Blair et al., 2007). Creative ideas, in general, are viewed as risky as the solutions have not been tried. Therefore, there is a greater likelihood of failure. Johnson and D'Lauro (2018) found that when teams were instructed to select their best ideas, they typically focused on the feasibility of the idea and were less likely to select original ideas.

Second, it has been suggested that social cues may be critical in selecting ideas. When those selecting ideas have access to information about how others view these ideas, that information plays an important role in idea selection. Mueller et al. (2018) studied idea selection where participants were told to choose an idea for winning a creative idea competition. Participants were told either that their opinion will be taken into consideration when the decision about ideas is made or that they are among a set of judges in choosing the winning idea. Participants were also provided information about whether others judged the ideas favorably or not. Those who were told that their decisions carried more weight, that they were part of the judging team, turned to information about the evaluations of others, and as a result choose less original ideas.

Third, it has been suggested that inaccurate evaluation may be responsible for choosing less creative ideas. Accuracy of idea evaluation is typically identified as ideas that are evaluated as creative (or not) when experts identify them as such. Kennel and Reiter-Palmon (2012) evaluated both idea evaluation and idea selection, and determined that more accurate idea evaluation led to better idea selection. Teams that more accurately evaluated the quality of the solutions chose ideas of higher quality to solve the problem, while teams who more accurately evaluated the originality of the solutions chose ideas of higher creativity (i.e., originality and quality) to solve the problem. In terms of idea selection though, only 55% of the teams selected ideas that were either creative or high quality (but not creative). That is, 45% of the teams selected sub-optimal ideas for implementations.

What is less clear is how team communication patterns influence idea evaluation or idea selection. While communication among team members is necessary to share thoughts about which ideas would be best and why, research has not sought to identify whether specific communication patterns or types are especially effective or ineffective during these processes.

Information Sharing

The discussion of the main creative problem-solving processes in teams highlights the importance of communication. One important role of the communication processes within teams and with others is sharing information that would aid in the creative problem-solving process. Whether the information provides a shared understanding of the problem (problem construction), sharing of ideas (idea generation), or discussing pros and cons of different ideas to determine which idea to select for implementation, team communication focuses on information sharing. It is important to note that information sharing is relevant to all the processes of creative problem-solving that have been discussed.

Information sharing or knowledge sharing has been positively related to team creativity and innovation (Damanpour, 1991; Howell & Shea, 2006). Information sharing can take place both with members outside the group (external knowledge sharing) and within the group (internal knowledge sharing). External knowledge sharing focuses on the role of team members in obtaining knowledge that is not available to the team internally. Internal knowledge sharing focuses on sharing of knowledge within the team, such that team members inform each other. While external knowledge sharing is important, the focus of this chapter is on internal team communication.

Meta-analyses by Damanpour (1991) and Hulsheger et al. (2009) found that internal communication was positively related to creativity and innovation. In these meta-analyses, all forms of internal communication within a team were combined. De Dreu and West (2001) suggested that when diverse groups share information, they have a higher opportunity to integrate their possibly conflicting viewpoints and to generate more creative ideas. Drach-Zahavy and Somech (2001) and Moser et al. (2019) found that sharing information measured as a general tendency to communicate and share information within a team was positively related to team innovation. Chen and Agrawal (2017), evaluating student teams, found that information sharing, especially early in the creative problem-solving process, was especially important for developing effective communication, overcoming communication barriers, and resulting in more creative solutions.

Research focusing on the conditions under which team members will be more likely to share information indicates that information that is available to all team members prior to team discussion is more likely to be discussed, while information that is not available to all or most team members is less likely to be discussed (Mesmer-Magnus & DeChurch, 2009). In order to increase the likelihood of this information to be shared, team members or the leader can ask fellow team members about their thoughts regarding the information and can share the information presented to them. Furthermore, a study on the effect of functional diversity on team performance in business unit management teams (Bunderson & Sutcliffe, 2002) found that having a degree of overlap in experiences and functions between team members facilitated information-sharing and team performance. They argued that the overlap in information provides a common ground that facilitates information sharing by allowing for easier communication.

Teams that are specifically asked to discuss information prior to reaching a decision are more likely to discuss previously unshared information (Stewart & Stasser, 1995). In addition, social processes that promote open discussion and cooperation allow team members to overcome the tendency to share only information that is already known to all team members (Mesmer-Magnus & DeChurch, 2009). Psychological safety and trust are important social processes that facilitate open and honest discussion (Reiter-Palmon & Millier, in press). Finally, group members who were designated as experts tended to discuss more information, including previously unshared information, especially when the group was aware of their expert status (Franz & Larson, 2002; Stasser & Stewart, 1992). It has been suggested that experts may feel more confident in speaking up in the group setting, and when group members know that someone is an expert they are more likely to seek their input. In interdisciplinary teams, all members have their own area of expertise and therefore are more likely to communicate unshared information.

However, it must be noted that the nature of the communication, whether collaborative or contentious, is critical (Lovelace et al., 2001). This study suggests that collaborative communication – that is, communication that is positive and intended to find mutually beneficial solutions – was related to higher creativity and innovation. On the other hand, contentious communication – that is communication that is less positive and focuses on win-lose situations – was related to lower creativity and innovation. Further, the effect of contentious communication was found to be particularly detrimental when frequency of information exchange is high. It is important to note that contentious communication focusing on win-lose is not the same as debate or task conflict discussed before. Debate can include constructive criticism and an open discussion about ideas without a framework of win-lose, but rather a win-win approach.

Evidence-Based Recommendations for Practice

This chapter provides an overview of the role communication plays in the effective facilitation of team creative problem-solving. As such a number of practical recommendations can be derived from the research described. First and foremost, developing effective communication within the team is critical. Team members must feel comfortable discussing their own points of view, even when they are in conflict with the rest of the team. This notion of being able to speak up, address concerns, and openly and honestly discuss issues within the team has been called psychological safety and has been found to be critical for creativity and innovation (Edmondson, 1999). Furthermore, this concept of psychological safety is critical for many reasons. Because creativity requires novel, divergent, and non-normative thoughts, it is essential that team members feel comfortable and safe sharing these thoughts. Without psychological safety in teams, team members may be as though they may be viewed as deviant or foolish for verbalizing these original ideas. That said, psychological safety can help to mitigate and concerns of those who are willing to openly express creative ideas.

More specifically, effective communication within each creative process will look somewhat differently. The problem construction and identification process tends to be automatic, and as such, individuals will immediately move to developing solutions, without much thought about how the problem is framed (Reiter-Palmon et al., 2011). Therefore, an important recommendation is to actively engage in this process by explicitly discussing how different team members understand the problem and the important goals and constraints. Any disagreement at this problem construction stage must be resolved through integration of the different points of view. Specifically, if a team is able to find a way to reframe and construct the problem in a way that takes into account multiple perspectives, this will lead to improved creativity.

At the idea generation stage, it is important to engage in healthy debate, building up on ideas generated by other team members, and attending to the diversity of the various points of view. From a practical perspective, it is important to have a diverse team, which includes members who will have different perspective about the problem and how to solve it, and bring in unique knowledge and expertise. However, as noted regarding problem construction, it is important to integrate the different perspectives, as opposed to ignoring them. In addition, it is important to encourage an open discussion regarding the merits of ideas, and ensuring that all team members can voice their opinion. One way this can be achieved is by ensuring that all team members have a chance to voice their opinion, and even calling upon those who have not provided their point of view. Finally, for idea evaluation and idea selection, it is important to discuss how and in what way ideas should be evaluated. Discussion of the criteria by which ideas should be judged and developing a shared understanding of those criteria is critical for effective evaluation and therefore ideas selection. Specifically, if creativity and innovation are desired, this should be made explicit.

Conclusion

In this chapter, we have provided a review of the role that communication plays in team creativity and innovation. We have examined a number of core cognitive process that facilitates creativity and innovation: problem construction and identification, idea generation, and idea evaluation and selection. Effective engagement in these core processes is critical for team success for creativity and innovation, and communication plays an important role in this process. Team members must engage in positive and effective communication strategies, sharing knowledge and information, and integrating the different points of view expressed for creativity and innovation to emerge.

Further Readings

Edmondson, A. (1999). Psychological safety and learning behavior in work teams. *Administrative Science Quarterly*, *44*, 350–383.

Reiter-Palmon, R., & Robinson, E. J. (2009). Problem identification and construction: What do we know, what is the future? *Psychology of Aesthetics, Creativity, and the Arts*, *3*, 43–47.

Petrou, P., Bakker, A. B., & Bezemer, K. (2019). Creativity under task conflict: The role of proactively increasing job resources. *Journal of Occupational and Organizational Psychology*, *92*, 305–329.

Glossary

Creativity   The development of a product, idea, or problem solution that is both novel (original) and useful (effective).

Information sharing   A team activity where team members share knowledge and expertise within the team and with others within the organization.

Innovation   The implementation of creative ideas and solutions in the organization.

Problem identification and construction   The process of identifying that a problem exists and identifying the goals and parameters of the problem-solving effort.

References

Abdulla, A. M., Paek, S. H., Cramond, B., & Runco, M. A. (2020). Problem finding and creativity: A meta-analytic review. *Psychology of Aesthetics, Creativity, and the Arts*, *14*(1), 3–14. http://dx.doi.org/10.1037/aca0000194

Basadur, M. (1994). Managing the creative process in organizations. In M. A. Runco (Ed.), *Problem finding, problem solving, and creativity* (pp. 237–268). Ablex.

Basadur, M., Runco, M. A., & Vega, L. A. (2000). Understanding how creative thinking skills, attitudes, and behaviors work together: A causal process model. *Journal of Creative Behavior*, *34*, 77–100.

Bell, S. T., Villado, A. J., Lukasik, M. A., Belau, L., & Briggs, A. L. (2011). Getting specific about demographic diversity variable and team performance relationships: A meta-analysis. *Journal of Management*, *37*(3), 709–743. https://doi.org/10.1177/0149206310365001

Berg, J. M. (2016). Balancing on the creative highwire: Forecasting the success of novel ideas in organizations. *Administrative Science Quarterly*, *61*(3), 433–468. https://doi.org/10.1177/0001839216642211

Blair, C. S., & Mumford, M. D. (2007). Errors in idea evaluation: Preference for the unoriginal? The Journal of Creative Behavior, 41(3), 197–222. https://doi.org/10.1002/j.2162-6057.2007.tb01288.x

Bunderson, J. S., & Sutcliffe, K. M. (2002). Comparing alternative conceptualizations of functional diversity in management teams: Process and performance effects. *Academy of Management Journal*, *45*, 875–893.

Chen, M., & Agrawal, S. (2017). Do communication barriers in student teams impede creative behaviors in the long run? A time-lagged perspective. *Thinking Skills and Creativity*, *26*, 154–167. https://doi.org/10.1016/j.tsc.2017.10.008

Cronin, M. A., & Weingart, L. R. (2007). Representational gaps, information processing, and conflict in functionally diverse teams. *Academy of Management, 32*(3), 761–773. https://doi.org/10.5465/amr.2007.25275511

Cropley, A. (2006). In praise of convergent thinking. *Creativity Research Journal, 18*(3), 391–404. https://doi.org/10.1207/s15326934crj1803_13

Damanpour, F. (1991). Organizational innovation: A meta-analysis of effects of determinants and moderators. *Academy of Management, 34*(3), 555–590.

De Dreu, C. K. W., & West, M. A. (2001). Minority dissent and team innovation: The importance of participation in decision making. *Journal of Applied Psychology, 86*(6). https://doi.org/10.1037//0021-9010.86.6.1191

Dennis, A. R., & Williams, M. L. (2003). Electronic brainstorming: Theory, research, and future directions. In P. B. Paulus & B. Nijstad (Eds.), *Group creativity: Innovation through collaboration* (pp. 160–178). Oxford University Press.

DeRose, D. M., Smith, C. L., & Hantula, D. A. (2007). The medium matters: Mining the long-promised merit of group interaction in creative idea generation tasks in a meta-analysis of the electronic group brainstorming literature. *Computers in Human Behavior, 23*, 1549–1581. https://doi.org/10.1016/j.chb.2005.07.003

Diehl, M., & Stroebe, W. (1987). Productivity loss in brainstorming groups: Toward the solution of a riddle. *Journal of Personality and Social Psychology, 53*, 497–509.

Drach-Zahavy, A., & Somech, A. (2001). Understanding team innovation: The role of team processes and structures. *Group Dynamics: Theory, Research, and Practice, 5*(2), 111–123. https://doi.org/10.1037//1089-2699.5.2.111

Fleming, M., Clarke, W., Das, S., Phongthiengtham, P., & Reddy, P. (2019). The future of work: How new technologies are transforming tasks. *MIT-IB Watson AI Lab.*

Franz, T. M., & Larson, J. R., Jr. (2002). The impact of experts on information sharing during group discussion. *Small Group Research, 33*(4), 383–411.

Gallupe, R. B., Dennis, A. R., Cooper, W. H., Valacich, J. S., Bastianutti, L. M., & Nunamaker, J. F. (1992). Electronic brainstorming and group size. *Academy Management Journal, 35*(2), 350–369.

Getzels, J. W. (1982). The problem of the problem. In *New directions for methodology of social and behavioral science: Question framing and response consistency* (Vol. 11, pp. 37–49).

Harvey, S. (2014). Creative synthesis: Exploring the process of extraordinary group creativity. *Academy of Management, 39*(3), 324–343.

Harvey, S., & Kou, C. Y. (2013). Collective engagement in creative tasks: The role of evaluation in the creative process in groups. *Administrative Science Quarterly, 58*, 346–386. https://doi.org/10.1177/0001839213498591

Hennessey, B. A., & Amabile, T. M. (2010). Creativity. *Annual Review of Psychology, 61*, 569–598. https://doi.org/10.1146/annurev.psych.093008.100416

Howell, J. M., & Shea, C. M. (2006). Effects of champion behavior, team potency, and external communication activities on predicting team performance. *Group and Organization Management, 31*, 180–211.

Hulsheger, U. R., Anderson, N., & Salgado, J. F. (2009). Team-level predictors of innovation at work: A comprehensive meta-analysis spanning three decades of research. *Journal of Applied Psychology, 94*(5), 1128–1145. https://doi.org/10.1037/a0015978

Hundschell, A., Razinskas, S., Backmann, J., & Hoegl, M. (2020). The effects of diversity on creativity: A literature review and synthesis. *Applied Psychology*, 1–37. https://doi.org/10.1111/apps.12365

Johnson, B. R., & D'Lauro, C. J. (2018). After brainstorming, groups select an early generated idea as their best idea. *Small Group Research, 49*(2), 177–294. https://doi.org/10.1177/1046496417720285

Jonker, C. M., Van Riemsdijk, M. B., & Vermeulen, B. (2010, August). Shared mental models: A conceptual analysis. In International *workshop on coordination, organizations, institutions, and norms in agent systems* (pp. 132–151). Springer Berlin Heidelberg.

Kennel, V., & Reiter-Palmon, R. (2012, August). *Teams and creativity: Accuracy in idea evaluation and selection.* In Paper presented at the 120th American Psychological Association Conference in Orlando, FL.

Kerr, D. S., & Murthy, U. S. (2004). Divergent and convergent idea generation in teams: A comparison of computer-mediated and face-to-face communication. *Group Decision and Negotiation, 13*, 381–399.

Korde, R., & Paulus, P. B. (2017). Alternating individual and group idea generation: Finding the elusive synergy. *Journal of Experimental Social Psychology, 70*, 177–190. https://doi.org/10.1016/j.jesp.2016.11.002

Leonardi, P. M. (2011). Innovation blindness: Culture, frames, and cross-boundary problem construction in the development of new technology concepts. *Organization Science*, *22*(2), 347–369. https://doi.org/10.1287/orsc.1100.0529

Litchfield, R. C. (2009). Brainstorming rules as assigned goals: Does brainstorming really improve idea quantity? *Motivation and Emotion*, *33*, 25–31.

Litchfield, R. C., Fan, J., & Brown, V. C. (2011). Directing idea generation using brainstorming with specific novelty goals. *Motivation and Emotion*, *35*, 135–143. https://doi.org/10.1007/s11031-011-9203-3

Lovelace, K., Shapiro, D. L., & Weingart, L. R. (2001). Maximizing cross-functional new product teams' innovativeness and constraint adherence: A conflict communications perspective. *Academy of Management*, *44*(4), 779–793.

McIntosh, T., Mulhearn, T. J., & Mumford, M. D. (2021). Taking the good with the bad: The impact of forecasting timing and valence on idea evaluation and creativity. *Psychology of Aesthetics, Creativity, and the Arts*, *15*(1), 111.

McLeod, P. L., Lobel, S. A., & Cox, T. H. (1996). Ethnic diversity and creativity in small groups. *Small Group Research*, *27*(2), 248–264.

Mesmer-Magnus, J. R., & DeChurch, L. A. (2009). Information sharing and team performance: A meta-analysis. *Journal of Applied Psychology*, *93*(2), 535–546. https://doi.org/10.1037/a0013773

Moser, K. S., Dawson, J. F., & West, M. A. (2019). Antecedents of team innovation in health care teams. *Creativity and Innovation Management*, *28*(1), 72–81.

Mouchiroud, C., & Lubart, T. (2001). Children's original thinking: An empirical examination of alternative measures derived from divergent thinking tasks. *The Journal of Genetic Psychology*, *162*(4), 382–401. https://doi.org/10.1080/00221320109597491

Mueller, J., Melwani, S., Loewenstein, J., & Deal, J. J. (2018). Reframing the decision-makers' dilemma: Towards a social context model of creative idea recognition. *Academy of Management Journal*, *61*, 94–110.

Mullen, B., Johnson, C., & Salas, E. (1991). Productivity loss in brainstorming groups: A meta-analytic integration. *Basic and Applied Psychology*, *12*, 3–24.

Mumford, M. D., Feldman, J. M., Hein, M. B., & Nagao, D. J. (2001). Tradeoffs between ideas and structure: Individuals versus group performance in creative problem solving. *Journal of Creative Behavior*, *35*(1), 1–23.

Mumford, M. D., Mobley, M. I., Reiter-Palmon, R., Uhlman, C. E., & Doares, L. M. (1991). Process analytic models of creative capacities. *Creativity Research Journal*, *4*(2), 91–122. https://doi.org/10.1080/10400419109534380

Mumford, M. D., Reiter-Palmon, R., & Redmond, M. R. (1994). Problem construction and cognition: Applying problem representations in ill-defined domains. In M. Runco (Ed.), *Problem finding, problem solving, and creativity* (pp. 3–39). Ablex.

Mumford, M. D., Scott, G. M., Gaddis, B., & Strange, J. M. (2002). Leading creative people: Orchestrating expertise and relationships. *The Leadership Quarterly*, *13*(6), 705–750. https://doi.org/10.1016/s1048-9843(02)00158-3

Nakui, T., Paulus, P. B., & van der Zee, K. I. (2011). The role of attitudes in reactions toward diversity in workgroups. *Journal of Applied Social Psychology*, *41*(10), 2327–2351. https://doi.org/10.1111/j.1559-1816.2011.00818.x

Nemeth, C. L., Personnaz, B., Personnaz, M., & Goncalo, J. A. (2004). The liberating role of conflict in group creativity: A study in two countries. *European Journal of Social Psychology*, *34*, 365–374. https://doi.org/10.1002/ejsp.210

Nijstad, B. A., Stroebe, W., & Lodewijkx, H. F. M. (2002). Cognitive stimulation and interference in groups: Exposure effects in an idea generation task. *Journal of Experimental Social Psychology*, *38*, 535–544. http://dx.doi.org/10.1016/S0022-1031(02)00500-0

Okhuysen, G. A., & Bechky, B. A. (2009). Coordination in organizations: An integrative perspective. *Academy of Management Annals*, *3*(1), 462–502. https://doi.org/10.5465/19416520903047533

Osborn, A. F. (1953). *Applied imagination*. Creative Education Foundation.

Paulus, P. B., Kohn, N. W., & Arditti, L. E. (2011). Effects of quantity and quality instructions on brainstorming. *Journal of Creative Behavior*, *45*(1), 38–46. https://doi.org/10.1002/j.2162-6057.2011.tb01083.x

Paulus, P. B., & van der Zee, K. (2015). Creative processes in culturally diverse teams. In S. Otten, K. van der Zee, & M. B. Brewer (Eds.), *Current issues in work and organizational psychology. Towards inclusive organizations: Determinants of successful diversity management at work* (pp. 108–131). Psychology Press.

Reiter-Palmon, R. (2018). Creative cognition at the individual and team level: What happens before and after idea generation. In R. Sternberg & J. Kaufman (Eds.), *The nature of human creativity* (pp. 184–208). Cambridge Press. https://doi.org/10.1017/9781108185936.015

Reiter-Palmon, R., Forthmann, B., & Barbot, B. (2019). Scoring divergent thinking tests: A review and systematic framework. *Psychology of Aesthetics, Creativity, and the Arts, 13*(2), 144–152. https://doi.org/10.1037/aca0000227

Reiter-Palmon, R., Herman, A. E., & Yammarino, F. (2008). Creativity and cognitive processes. A multi-level linkage between individual and team cognition. In M. D. Mumford, S. T. Hunter, & K. E. Bedell-Avers (Eds.), *Multi-level issues in creativity and innovation* (Vol. 7, pp. 203–267). JAI Press.

Reiter-Palmon, R., & Illies, J. J. (2004). Leadership and creativity: Understanding leadership from a creative problem-solving perspective. *The Leadership Quarterly, 15*(1), 55–77. https://doi.org/10.1016/j.leaqua.2003.12.005

Reiter-Palmon, R., & Millier, M. (in press). Psychological safety and creativity: The glue that binds a creative team. In Z. Ivcevic, J. D. Hoffmann, & J. C. Kaufman (Eds.), *Cambridge handbook of creativity and emotion*. Cambridge University Press.

Reiter-Palmon, R., & Murugavel, V. (2018). The effect of problem construction on team process and creativity. *Frontiers Psychology: Performance Science, 9,* https://doi.org/10.3389/fpsyg.2018.02098

Reiter-Palmon, R., & Paulus, P. (2020). Cognitive and social processes in team creativity. In M. D. Mumford (Ed.), *Creativity and innovation in organizations* (pp. 161–190). Taylor and Francis.

Reiter-Palmon, R., Royston, R., & Mitchell, K. (2021). Improving creativity in organizational settings. In *Creativity: An introduction* (pp. 242–271). https://doi.org/10.1017/9781108776721.014

Reiter-Palmon, R., Wigert, B., & de Vreede, T. (2011). Team creativity and innovation: The effect of team composition, social processes, and cognition. *Handbook of organizational creativity, 295–326.* Academic Press.

Rietzschel, E. F., Nijstad, B. A., & Stroebe, W. (2006). Productivity is not enough: A comparison of interactive and nominal brainstorming groups on idea generation and selection. *Journal of Experimental Social Psychology, 42,* 244–251.

Schraw, G., Dunkle, M. E., & Bendixen, L. D. (1995). Cognitive processes in well-defined and ill-defined problem solving. *Applied Cognitive Psychology, 9*(6), 523–538. https://doi.org/10.1002/acp.2350090605

Stasser, G., & Stewart, D. (1992). Discovery of hidden profiles by decision-making groups: Solving a problem versus making a judgment. *Journal of Personality and Social Psychology, 63*(3), 426–434.

Stewart, D. D., & Stasser, G. (1995). Expert role assignment and information sampling during collective recall and decision making. *Journal of Personality and Social Psychology, 69*(4), 619–628. https://doi.org/10.1037/0022-3514.69.4.619

Toader, A. F., Cantor, U., & Kessler, T. (2019). The effect of team mental models divergence on creative performance during situational changes. *Creativity Research Journal, 31*(1), 40–51. https://doi.org/10.1080/10400419.2019.1577206

Weingart, L. R., Cronin, M. A., Houser, C. J. S., Cagan, J., & Vogel, C. M. (2005). Functional diversity and conflict in cross-functional product development teams: Considering representation gap and task characteristics. *Research in Management, 4,* 89–110.

Weingart, L. R., Todorova, G., & Cronin, M. A. (2008). *Representation gaps, team integration, and team creativity: The mediating roles of conflict and coordination.* In Paper presented at the conference of the Academy of Management, Anaheim, CA.

West, M. A. (2002). Sparkling fountains or stagnant ponds: An integrative model of creativity and innovation implementation in work groups. *Applied Psychology: An International Review, 51,* 355–387.

World Economic Forum (2020, October). *These are the top 10 job skills of tomorrow and how long it takes to learn them.* https://www.weforum.org/agenda/2020/10/top-10-work-skills-of-tomorrow-how-long-it-takes-to-learn-them/

Zhu, Y., Ritter, S. M., & Dijksterhuis, A. P. (2020). Creativity: Intrapersonal and interpersonal selection of creative ideas. *The Journal of Creative Behavior, 54*(3), 626–635. https://doi.org/10.1002/jocb.397

17 Social Networks and Groups

Seungyoon Lee and Bailey C. Benedict

Chapter Objectives

- Explain how the structure of communication within and across groups can be examined through social network perspectives.
- Describe key assumptions and terminologies of social network analysis (SNA) approaches.
- Explain main features and functions of within- and across-group networks through highlighting relevant theoretical lenses, methodological approaches, and toopics of research in organizational and group communication.
- Discuss evidence-based recommendations, based on social network approaches, for nurturing positive environments in and across groups of various forms.

Introduction

Human nature drives people together to form groups and live interdependently with each other (Frey, 1996; Lewin, 1951). Groups are built when individuals share and co-create their "life-space" with others by interacting with them (Lewin, 1951). In addition, groups themselves are surrounded by other groups and the external environment. Theories and methods about social networks have emerged as useful frameworks for understanding relationships and interactions within and across groups. Social networks are defined as a set of entities such as people, groups, companies, and neighborhoods tied by one or more types of relations such as communicating, forming alliances, and competing (Wasserman & Faust, 1994). Social network analysis (SNA) focuses on understanding the features, determinants, and implications of the structural patterns of these relations.

This chapter introduces fundamental concepts of social networks with examples relevant to group and team settings. Major topics introduced include communication patterns, information and knowledge sharing, transactive memory system, leadership, multi-team systems (MTSs), and conflict and negative ties. This chapter offers an overview of the theoretical and methodological perspectives for examining group networks. Network studies on contemporary issues in group communication (e.g., technology, virtual teams, and diversity) are also discussed, together with ideas about how we can harness the potential of various relationships that bring people and groups together.

Key Properties of Social Network Analysis

The social world is comprised of relations between entities, such as people, groups, and organizations. A group of people (e.g., players on an intramural sports team) can form relations, as can a group of groups (e.g., teams in an intramural sports league). Social network theories and methods offer many opportunities for making sense of group communication in the social world.

DOI: 10.4324/9781003227458-19

The entities in a social network are called *nodes*, also known as actors, points, players, or vertices. When a social network is visualized, nodes are represented by symbols, such as triangles for coaches and squares for players or simply dots for all the entities. In the field of SNA relevant to group communication, nodes can represent individual people as well as groups of people or organizations.

To determine what nodes should be included in a social network, a network boundary must be established. There are many approaches to defining a network boundary, such as position-based, relation-based, and event-based approaches (Laumann et al., 1983). The position-based approach includes actors in the network who hold particular positions or attributes (e.g., all the employees in the design group of a company).The relation-based approach focuses on actors with relationships of a particular type, beginning with a small set of actors whose contact chains are traced to include others connected to them. For example, a business could create a network of all the employees who worked together to develop a specific marketing plan, which may grow in size as the project develops. The event-based approach includes actors who participated in a particular event or activity (e.g., all the employees who attended a product launch).

The relations between entities (i.e., nodes) in a social network are called *edges*, also called ties, links, arcs, or lines. When a social network is visualized, edges are represented using lines and arrows. An edge can be directed (i.e., pointing in a direction) or undirected (i.e., sender and receiver are not distinguished from each other). There are four types of relationships between entities: similarities, social relations, interactions, and flows (Borgatti et al., 2009). Similarities exist when the entities have a shared location, membership, or attribute, like being the same age or participating in the same club. Social relations are based on the roles people occupy, like coworker, friend, and enemy, and their perceptions of others. Examples of social relations include relationships like kinship (i.e., between family members) and friendship, as well as liking, disliking, or knowing someone. While usually undirected, relations based on roles can still be directed, such as the role relation between the employees and their manager. Interactions are based on behaviors, such as when two people brainstorm with each other (i.e., undirected) or are dating (i.e., undirected) or when a crush is unreciprocated (i.e., directed). Flows are marked by the exchange or transfer of a belief, such as agreement with a piece of fake news, or resource, such as social support or money. Flows typically have a direction (e.g., when a student receives financial assistance from their parent), which in some cases can be reciprocated (e.g., when roommates provide each other emotional support).

Four defining properties characterize the field of SNA (Freeman, 2011). First, SNA focuses on the relationships among social actors as opposed to the attributes or behaviors of the actors themselves. Since relationships between entities in the network are not independent of each other, considering the network as a whole when trying to understand a single relationship is important. For example, an adversarial relationship between two members of Greek life could be due to a simple difference in opinion or the result of complex dynamics within their organization. In addition, when people have similar attitudes or behaviors, these attributes could be due to their relationships or position within the network, such as when we copy our friends' mannerisms or take on a politician's beliefs after following them on social media. Second, the field employs collecting and analyzing data which record relations among entities. Third, SNA frequently utilizes visualizations which display the structural patterns of relationships. Last, the field increasingly dedicates efforts for developing mathematical, statistical, and computational models to analyze network structures.

Conceptual Foundations of Social Network Analysis

In this section, the fundamental concepts and measures used in SNA are explained. Measurements allow for the assessment of the entities, the relationships, and the overall structure and composition of the network. Table 17.1 summarizes key measures relevant to group communication at the node-, dyad-, subgroup-, and network-level (see Box 17.1 for an example).

Table 17.1 Summary of Network Measures at Multiple Levels

	Measure	Definition and Implications	Key References
Node level	Degree centrality	Considers a given node's number of direct connections. Nodes high in degree centrality have many immediate exchanges of information.	Borgatti (2005)
	Closeness centrality	Considers the average shortest path from a given node to all other nodes in the network. Nodes high in closeness centrality can reach all the other nodes in the network in a small number of steps and, therefore, can be efficient in accessing or sharing information.	Wasserman & Faust (1994)
	Betweenness centrality	Considers the extent to which a given node is positioned between other nodes on their shortest paths, or geodesics. Nodes high in betweenness centrality can serve as a bridge to transport information or control the interactions between other nodes.	Freeman (1977) and Wasserman & Faust (1994)
	Eigenvector centrality	Considers the centralities of a given node's neighbors. Nodes high in eigenvector centrality are more influential than nodes which have a large number of connections to less central nodes.	Bonacich (2007)
Dyad level	Direction and reciprocity	Shows whether a tie between node i and node j can be distinguished by its origin and destination. A tie can be undirected (i.e., absence of distinction between origin and destination), directed and one-way (i.e., a tie points in only one direction), or directed and two-way (i.e., a directed tie is reciprocated in the opposite direction).	Gouldner (1960)
	Weight or Strength	A weighted tie considers the strength of ties. Strength is measured by indicators such as frequency, duration, and reciprocity. In contrast, a binary tie only considers the existence or absence of ties.	Granovetter (1973) and Wasserman & Faust (1994)
	Sign	Whether a tie is positively valenced (e.g., like, collaborate, friendship) or negatively valenced (e.g., dislike, conflict, avoidance).	Labianca (2014)
	Multiplexity	Considers the extent to which multiple relationship types overlap between node i and node j.	Lazega & Pattison (1999)
Subgroup and overall network level	Triads	A group of three nodes among which ties might be present or absent. Representative types include transitive triads (when there is a tie from i to j, and also from j to k, then there is a tie from i to k) and cyclical triads (when there is a tie from i to j, and also from j to k, then there is a tie from k to i).	Wasserman & Faust (1994)
	Clique	A cohesive subgroup of nodes that are all directly connected to all others in the group. Members in a clique have constraints in accessing nonredundant information if they do not have ties to nodes outside of the clique.	Hanneman & Riddle (2005)
	Community structure	Structures of densely connected subsets of nodes. Represents social groupings, impacting the flow of information within and across those boundaries.	Girvan & Newman (2002)
	Diameter	Measures the distance between the two nodes furthest apart in the network. Represents the maximum distance a piece of information needs to travel in a network.	Yamaguchi (1994)

(Continued)

Table 17.1 (Continued)

Measure	Definition and Implications	Key References
Mean geodesic distance	Measures the average number of shortest steps between pairs of nodes. Reflects the overall connectivity of a network and impacts the extent to which information can be shared among nodes in few steps.	Hanneman & Riddle (2005)
Density	Measures the proportion of total possible ties that are actually present.	Hanneman & Riddle (2005)
Centralization	Measures the extent to which the distribution of ties is unequal across nodes (e.g., how heterogeneous node centralities are)	Wasserman & Faust (1994)

Box 17.1   Group and Network Dynamics Surrounding the Impressionist Movement

In the second half of the 19th century in France, a new school of painting emerged from the periphery of the fine arts field. They faced opposition from the dominant actors including the Salon, a competitive exhibition held by the Royal Academy of Painting and Sculpture. To appeal their controversial innovation to the audience, about 30 artists formed a group called the "Société Anonyme Coopérative." In 1874, they organized the first exhibition of their 165 artworks in Paris. This group of artists was diverse in their backgrounds and painting styles. Yet, the group strengthened solidarity to achieve the collective goal of advocating for and selling their artwork. Conceptualized as a loosely coordinated coalition, this emergent network of artists is characterized by various relational ties both within and across groups, as Delacour and Leca (2017) and Farrell (2003) detail in their analysis.

Multiplex ties existed between many individuals. Some members, including Monet, Renoir, Sisley, and Bazille, studied with the same teacher in the early 1860s. This group of artists was inspired by the revolutionary style expressed in Manet's "The Luncheon on the Grass." Many artists also worked together under open sky and gathered at Café Guerbois and other cafes and bars of Paris to discuss their work and find inspiration. Some had close friendship ties, visiting and spending time at each other's places. There were people who played brokerage roles. For instance, Caillebotte invited Pissarro to dinner so that he could meet other artists such as Degas and Manet. Cézanne was a classmate of novelist Émile Zola and introduced him to painters including Pissarro and Manet. Zola became close friends with many painters and joined their conversations at cafes and held gatherings at his home. He both presented the Impressionists in his writing and was influenced by their work (Hemmings, 1958). Two female painters, Morisot and Cassatt, exhibited highly esteemed work but were relatively distant from the dense social circle of artists who met regularly at cafes (Meyers, 2005; Moran, 2021).

Outside of the group, there were supporters of the movement, including a network of groups consisting of dealers, museums, commercial galleries, and critics (Wijnberg & Gemser, 2000). The dealers organized exhibitions in commercial galleries, promoted the work of Impressionists, and provided money advances. Paul Durand-Ruel was the main art dealer, who bought large amounts of Impressionists' works and later became a bridge (i.e., high in betweenness centrality) for attracting other collectors

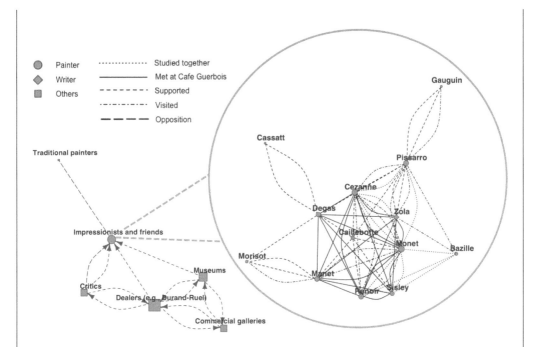

Figure 17.1 Illustration of Networks Among Painters and Other Groups During the Early Stage of the Impressionist Movement.

and organizing an international network of galleries and exhibitions. Increasingly, Impressionist's exhibitions became an important source of income for museums. Critics promoted the innovative art style so that artists and dealers could be seen as valuable. At the same time, critics themselves gained legitimacy by proving their capacity to recognize the newest styles and artists. Some supporters utilized their social position, as in the case of a well-connected celebrity patron, Mrs. Charpentier, whose role was critical in supporting Renoir's exhibit of his work at the Salon.

Artwork is often seen as a product of individual artists but the ebbs and flows of early Impressionism illustrate complex group and network dynamics. Figure 17.1 portrays some of the key relationships, both positive and negative, between painters and surrounding individuals at the early stage of the Impressionist movement. Over time, relationships were formed and severed, and groups were assembled, disassembled, and reassembled. These formal and informal social interactions involving many people and groups explain the rise of a modern art movement.

Node-Level Measures

Node-level measures provide information about the individual entities in a network. First, the attributes of nodes can be used to describe the composition of the network. For example, attributes of the members of a work group often include demographic information (e.g., gender, age, or years of service) but can also include more specific characteristics, such as attitude toward a new initiative.

Second, **centrality** is a node-level measure, related to being in a powerful or influential position in a network. Power or influence can be derived from several different structural features.

Envisioning a stereotypical social network of the friendship ties among high school students in their senior year can help illustrate the differences between four measures of centrality.

- *Degree centrality* measures the number of direct connections to other nodes. These connections can function as a conduit of interactions such as sharing information, as well as providing and seeking support. In the example, the node with the highest degree centrality (i.e., the person with the most friendship ties) may be the most popular student in the class, possibly the class president or the person who is nice to everyone. Depending on context, degree centrality can be relevant to other traits or behaviors of the node such as one's level of expertise.
- *Closeness centrality* is also based on the number of connections. But in contrast to degree centrality, closeness also considers indirect connections such as being two or more steps away from another node. If a node can reach all other nodes in the network in a small number of steps, it is high in closeness centrality. Members who are high in closeness centrality can quickly communicate their messages to the entire network. They may be the "floaters," also called the "drifters" or the "clique jumpers," who can connect with various other students in relatively few steps. For example, a new student who moved schools in their senior year would probably want to find someone with high closeness centrality to tell them about all the different social groups among the seniors.
- *Betweenness centrality* measures how much a node is "in-between" other nodes. A group member high in betweenness centrality is the only person, or one of the few people, who ties disconnected network members together, which allows them to control the flow of information. For example, the hockey team and the football team might have a rivalry because they compete for time in the weightlifting room, so the student who plays both hockey and football and is friends with all their teammates would have high betweenness centrality and might help negotiate the weightlifting schedule.
- *Eigenvector centrality* considers the extent to which a node is tied to other central nodes in the network. Group members might not have extensive ties but are in advantageous positions if they have a few ties to prominent members. In the stereotypical high school, the yearbook editor who is friends with all the team captains and club presidents would have high eigenvector centrality, because they are connected to other students who occupy important positions.

Figure 17.2 illustrates an example of a network of 14 nodes, wherein the size of node represents each of the four centrality measures. In this network, Node 4 is the highest in degree centrality, but Node 8 is the highest in closeness centrality because it has quicker access to the relatively isolated cluster composed of Nodes 10, 11, 12, and 14.

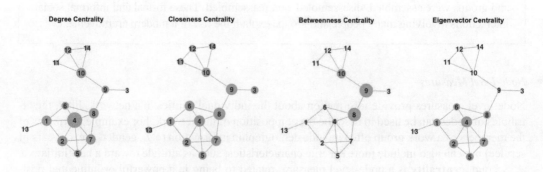

Figure 17.2 Illustration of Four Types of Centrality Measures (Lee et al., 2019).

Dyad-Level Measures

Dyad-level measures help us understand the relationship (e.g., edge) between two entities in the network. Edges can be explained by their direction. Directed ties have a specified direction indicated using a one-headed arrow, while undirected ties are typically represented with a line without arrow (e.g., two corporate groups in an alliance). A directed tie can be one-way (e.g., group member A seeks advice from B, but B does not seek advice from A) or two-way (i.e., mutual) when reciprocity occurs (e.g., two interest groups endorse each other's campaign). However, two-way ties are different from undirected ties in the sense that there is a notion of sender and receiver, even though one node can play both roles.

Edges can also be characterized by their strength. Approaches to measuring tie strength span a wide spectrum, including frequency, amount of interaction, duration, emotional intensity, reciprocity, and the relationship type (e.g., Granovetter, 1973). In addition, edges can be categorized based on their valence: positive, neutral, or negative. Positive ties have associated forces which bind people together and negative ties have dissociative forces which make people avoid each other (Labianca, 2014). Structural equivalence is another measure which can be measured at the dyadic level, referring to the extent to which two nodes occupy similar structural positions in the network. Returning to the stereotypical high school example, two students from different friend groups who each have one best friend and one "frenemy" (i.e., friend-enemy or fake friend) in their friend group can be considered to be similar in their structural position.

When more than one type of edge connects nodes in a network, multiplexity arises. For example, two members in a work group might be colleagues and friends at the same time. People might form these overlapping relations because each type of tie offers different resources such as technical advice and emotional support, respectively. The co-presence of these two types of ties between two people could be an indication of their close relationship. However, some people might attempt to avoid creating multiplex ties to minimize their dependence on a particular person. It is well known that the Medici dynasty during the Italian Renaissance intentionally discouraged families marrying other families with whom they did business so that the obligations from two spheres can be kept independent from each other (Padgett & Ansell, 1993).

Subgroup- and Network-Level Measures

A triad refers to a group of three nodes. Triads can be arranged in many ways, which have implications for the triad's functioning (Faust, 2010). For example, if a student must serve as a bridge between two otherwise unconnected students in a group project, a communication delay can be expected. Triads can be transitive, in which one person becomes friends with their friend's friend. When these ties are formed across multiple triads, a larger friend group will be built. A cyclical triad resembles a chain, in which values flow in one direction. If student *i* interviews student *j*, student *j* interviews student *k*, and student *k* interviews student *i* as part of a class project to improve interviewing skills, there is cyclicality in the triad.

Stereotypical high schools often contain identifiable "cliques." A clique is colloquially understood to be a small group of students who are not really friends with anybody other than the members of their clique. Cliques are often thought of as exclusionary and hard to infiltrate. However, the term "clique" is neutral in SNA. A clique is a group of nodes in which every node is directly connected to each other. The concept can be used in a relaxed manner (e.g., *n*-clique if all members are connected to each other in *n* or fewer steps). In addition to triads and cliques, various conceptualizations exist to describe the community structure of a network.

Network-level measures give insight into the overall network. Several measures at the network level are derived from the concept of a path, which is a linked sets of edges connecting one node to another. Geodesic distance refers to the shortest path or shortest linked set of edges between two nodes. Diameter refers to the distance across the network, or the longest of the geodesic distances (i.e., shortest paths). In other words, diameter measures the number of edges between the two nodes in the network that are furthest apart from each other. For example, if we assume that a rumor can start from any given student in a group, diameter shows how many steps it takes for a rumor to be exchanged between two students who are the most distant from each other in the communication network.

Centralization has been popularly examined in the study of networks in groups as a predictor of group task performance. Centralization is different from centrality. Centralization measures the extent to which a network, as a whole, is organized around one or few central nodes.

Theoretical Approaches for Studying Social Networks in and Across Groups

Many theories can be used to explain social networks in and across groups. For example, people's basic human needs, such as the need for love and belonging, described in Maslow's (1970) Hierarchy of Needs can explain *why* people *form* social networks. *Why* people *use* their social networks can be explained with numerous theories, including uncertainty reduction (Berger & Calabrese, 1975) and uncertainty management (Brashers, 2001) theories, the theory of planned behavior (Ajzen, 1991), and the communication theory of resilience (Buzzanell, 2019). *How* relationships with members of a social network *change* over time can be explained through social penetration theory (Altman & Taylor, 1973), Tuckman's (1965) stages of group development, and evolutionary theories (Monge et al., 2011). There are three broader theoretical frameworks that commonly guide the study of group communication using network perspectives.

Systems theory, as discussed in Chapter 7, approaches groups as systems, or as assemblages of parts or components (Poole, 2014). The nodes and edges of a network can be understood as the components of system. Systems theory acknowledges the processual nature of interaction, whereby resources move into and throughout the network using an input, process, and output pattern. Exchange, as an important concept of systems theory, recognizes that the network is embedded within an environment that influences its existence and functioning. Furthermore, feedback relations among the nodes underscore the interdependence of the system's components.

Networks of a system are also an important facet of structuration theory (Giddens, 1976). Structuration theory describes how social systems are produced and reproduced through interaction, wherein "structuration" is the process of creating structures (McPhee et al., 2014). Structures consist of the rules (i.e., principles or routines guiding an activity) and resources (i.e., material and nonmaterial things that facilitate activity) that people depend on for their activities (Giddens, 1984). For example, Whitbred et al. (2011) found that internal structures were more influential than external structural rules in the emergence of communication networks. In other words, how organizational networks form is dictated more by factors internal to the network than factors external to the network.

Using a multi-theoretical multi-level (MTML) approach is particularly useful when the network is complex. The MTML framework helps analyze relationships between entities using multiple theoretical viewpoints and at multiple levels, with attention given to inferential, rather than only descriptive, analyses (Monge & Contractor, 2003). The MTML approach considers both the attributes of nodes and multiple types of relations among nodes to model how networks are formed, maintained, and dissolved over time. For example, the emergence of adversarial ties among athletes in a team could be explained by their personality and pressure to win, as well as various relations (e.g., trust, social support, rivalry) among them and with others, such as coaches or players of other teams.

History and Major Themes of Research on Social Networks in and Across Groups

Studies of group structure have been an essential research area since the inception of SNA. One of the earliest studies of group networks was pioneered by Chevaleva-Janovskaja (1927), in which preschool teachers observed the interaction of 276 preschool children in 888 spontaneous groups. She found age and sex homogeneity in the groups, and boys were more likely to interact in groups than girls were (Freeman, 1996). A highly productive era of group networks research dates to the 1940s and 1950s, when Kurt Lewin formed the Research Center for Group Dynamics at Massachusetts Institute of Technology (Freeman, 2004). Alex Bavelas, a graduate student of Lewin, created a new research center: the Group Networks Laboratory. Research at the lab examined how group communication structure impacted group performance through a series of experiments. A formal model of centrality measures was also developed in the lab (Freeman, 2004). Katz et al. (2004) explain that research on networks in groups was relatively slow in the 1970s and 1980s, until there was a resurgence in the 1990s and 2000s. Studies expanded beyond the laboratory settings and utilized field data collection from work groups and organizations. The substantive research questions also expanded in several ways: moving the focus beyond identifying optimal structure for group functioning to examining factors which influence the emergence of networks; considering not just people but also tasks and organizational tools as nodes; and examining the influences of groups' external ties on performance (Katz et al., 2004). Social network research offers useful applications to a wide range of group processes.

Communication Patterns

Studying communication patterns in groups has been a key research topic since Bavelas' experiments. An example includes Cummings and Cross (2003), who examined informal communication network structure within work groups. Hierarchy (i.e., a tree-like structure that is ordered and asymmetrical), core-periphery (i.e., a network with a dense core and sparsely connected periphery), and structural holes of leaders (i.e., a leader who bridges otherwise unconnected nodes) were negatively related to group performance. These effects existed after controlling for the overall frequency of group communication and leader communication, showing the value of considering the network properties of groups. In the context of product development projects, Sosa et al. (2015) examined the structure of triads consisting of two interdependent design teams and a common third party. They found that the direction of communication flow within the triad, measured based on which team(s) received technical information from which team(s), impacts the likelihood of communication and coordination between teams.

Information and Knowledge Sharing

Studies have increasingly suggested conceptualizing **multidimensional networks** in which the sources of information and knowledge include nonhuman sources such as digital knowledge repositories (Contractor et al., 2011). Group members' tendency to seek information from human and nonhuman sources is shaped by network factors, such as interpersonal relationships, awareness of colleagues' expertise, and ease of access (Su & Contractor, 2011). A relevant stream of research is on transactive memory systems, which examines how perceptions of group members' expertise influence information allocation and retrieval (e.g., Hollingshead, 1998). Network analysis methodologies can help unpack the complexities of transactive memory system by conceptualizing information seeking as a relation between a seeker and a source. In a study of work teams, Su (2021) showed that various surrounding relationships such as communication, trust, and perceived competition were associated with the likelihood of some members withholding knowledge from others.

Leadership

Network studies emphasize leadership as flexible and emergent, not prescribed as part of a fixed organizational hierarchy. There could be multiple leaders, and leaders may be constructed based on group members' perceptions. For example, Emery's (2012) study examined whom group members perceived to be the task leaders and relationship leaders. By differentiating between dimensions of emotional abilities, the study found that being able to perceive and manage emotions predicts a person's emergence as a relationship leader, while being capable of using and understanding emotions facilitates becoming a task leader. Lungeanu et al. (2022) examined the extent to which leadership is enacted by multiple team members and whether the leaders rely on one another. The study suggested that various types of connected or fragmented leadership structures have differential impact on the development of team mental models (Mohammed et al., 2010) regarding how task elements are related with each other. In particular, shared leadership styles in which all team members collectively enact leadership had the strongest impact on members developing a common understanding about their task and work environments.

Group leaders typically play central roles in their group's networks. Team performance in advice-giving networks is influenced by the formal leader's centrality positively in larger teams and negatively in smaller teams, and the relationship between team performance and leader centrality is moderated by member collaboration in smaller teams (Yuan & Van Knippenberg, 2022). A possible explanation for the relationship between leader centrality and team performance is leader charisma, which has been found to influence team performance (Balkundi et al., 2011). In advice-giving networks, leaders who are viewed as charismatic by subordinates are likely to occupy a central position, and leaders who occupy central positions are viewed as charismatic (Balkundi et al., 2011). However, having centrality in advice-giving networks on its own may not be enough. Having a leader with multiplex centrality (i.e., centrality in the advice and friendship networks) predicted more team performance change over time than a leader with simplex centrality (i.e., centrality in either the advice or friendship networks; Clarke et al., 2022). Further, for informal leadership, higher network centrality influences greater leadership emergence for men more so than for women (Neubert & Taggar, 2004). Therefore, demographic characteristics and diversity are important considerations, too.

Multi-Team Systems

The concept of MTSs emphasizes that teams are embedded in a complex and interdependent system of teams and external organizations (Contractor, 2013). These teams interact with each other to achieve collective goals. The study of MTS performance highlights the role of both within- and cross-team ties. Oh et al. (2004) found that an ideal network structure for enhanced team outcomes involves high density in within-team networks and the presence of bridging connections which span intergroup boundaries. Sosa et al. (2015) studied an MTS in which 60 teams that design engine components are nested within subsystems of teams, which work together on an aircraft engine development. The findings show that the location of the common third party in the triadic communication structure influences communication between two teams. For instance, when the common third party was positioned in the middle in a transitive triad, the likelihood of the two interdependent teams exchanging knowledge with each other increased.

Conflict and Negative Ties

While SNA has more often examined ties with positive connotations (e.g., collaboration, sharing information, and support), negative ties are not rare in groups. Labianca (2014) offers a thorough review of research on negative ties in organizations and provides a broad definition of negative ties as "relatively enduring relationships inducing negative affect (feelings), judgments about others, and/or behavioral intentions directed toward others" (p. 242). Negative thoughts and feelings toward others (e.g., hatred, disliking, annoyance, and distrust) and negative communication behaviors (e.g., hate speech, gossip, disapproval, and avoidance) can be understood as negative ties. Membership in opposing groups (such as conflicting gangs), negative social relations (such as attacker and victim), and denial of resource exchange (such as evictions) are other examples of negative ties. Understanding the many potential negative ties is crucial for addressing consequences such as poor well-being of group members, low organizational identification, turnover, and reduced performance. In children's peer groups, detecting negative ties may help support potential victims of bullying.

The study of negative ties in group settings has a long history, including the widely known ethnographic study by Sampson (1969) on relationships among monks preparing to enter a New England monastery. The study identified clusters of novices based on four types of negative ties: disesteem, disliking, negative influence, and blame. The social interactions and leadership structure within clusters helped explain the conflicts and crises in the monastery, including some monks leaving or being expelled (Reitz, 1988).

Recent theorizing about negative ties is applicable to group contexts. One surrounds the evolution of negative ties. Labianca (2014) suggests that reciprocity is less likely to exist for negative ties than positive ties because negative ties deviate from organizational norms. In addition, studies suggest a more nuanced approach to theorizing the consequences of negative ties. For example, the impact of negative ties on outcomes might be larger than the impact of positive ties (Labianca & Brass, 2006). Negative ties, such as conflict relations, might in fact provide positive benefits to the neighboring contacts who are not directly involved, due to the support they offer to those in need and the ability to derive value from being in that position of power (Marineau et al., 2016).

The topics introduced so far are frequently studied in traditional work or organizational settings. Yet, many of these topics can apply to a plethora of non-work contexts, including children's peer groups, online communities, health-related support groups, ethnic groups in multicultural societies, and civic groups such as neighborhood associations and mutual aid groups. Relatedly, groups that are emergent and lack pre-defined boundaries are becoming prevalent in modern societies. The power of emergent groups is illustrated in cases such as online activist groups, Twitter users who collectively mobilize "hashtagged" social movements, and a group of loosely tied Reddit users and amateur traders who drove the GameStop rally against the Wall Street in 2021. There is much to be known about the structure and dynamics of coordination networks that empower these fluid groups.

Research Methods for Studying Networks in and Across Groups

Researchers use various methods to collect social network data in and across groups. Name generator techniques, where individuals are asked about the people in their social network, are commonly paired with survey data collection. Interviews, focus groups, and experiments are other methods of generating social network data. Archival datasets and datasets collected using qualitative methods are also utilized. For example, network data can be extracted from texts, such as local newspapers, as was done by Comfort and Haase (2006) to illustrate the network of organizations responding to Hurricane Katrina. Trace data can also be captured from online group interactions such as through recording the messages sent among team members (Pilny et al., 2016).

Various qualitative and quantitative methods exist for analyzing social networks, with mixed methods approaches growing in popularity (Rice et al., 2014). Descriptive statistics are often used to characterize the attributes of the nodes, edges, and overall networks. Visual network analysis provides one descriptive option (Decuypere, 2020), where the researcher uses their trained eye to derive insights about the network. Inferential statistics can be used to make formal predictions about outcome variables based on the characteristics of the nodes, edges, and overall network. These methods can stand alone or work in conjunction with other methodological approaches.

Methodologies and tools for SNA are quickly evolving. New developments cater to the more diverse and complex ways in which networks are conceptualized. Many of these methods are highly applicable for studying networks in group contexts. Exponential random graph models (ERGMs) are used to test whether networks have unique structural signatures (Robins et al., 2007). For example, ERGM can show whether the formation of collaboration ties in a work group is more likely to be driven by geographical proximity or similarity of previous work experiences. Relational event models (REMs) have been used for studying sequence of interactions in groups (Pilny et al., 2016). An example is shown in Pilny et al. (2020) for analyzing episodic communication networks in teams. With increasing attention to negative ties or disruptive ties, new approaches have been developed to measure network structural features such as centrality and cliques for negative tie networks as well as networks which have a mixture of both positive and negative ties (e.g., Everett & Borgatti, 2014).

Evidence-Based Recommendations for Practice

Considering the social networks in and across groups recognizes the interconnectedness of the social world and the value in the relationships that bring people together. Valente (2012) presents a series of network intervention strategies for facilitating change in various social contexts, which can be consulted by those interested in taking network-informed approaches to managing groups. Capturing the complexity of real-world groups using network perspectives can help generate practical implications for better group functioning. For instance, multidimensional networks in groups consider multiple types of nodes and ties. Nodes can include both human and nonhuman entities. Nodes can be tied together for a variety of reasons in many positive and negative ways simultaneously, which is especially relevant to two important issues facing contemporary groups: technology and diversity.

Technology

Technology is a core element of group processes, especially with the growing prevalence of virtual and remote work arrangements. The different media used by members are especially important to the study of group communication. Haythornthwaite's (2005) media multiplexity theory argues that people in stronger relationships use more channels of communication to sustain the relationship. An example of group communication research using media multiplexity theory and network perspectives found that, in a network of 137 third-year high school students, strong ties (i.e., close friends) used many media to communicate with each other, while weak ties preferred communicating face-to-face or via social media (Van Cleemput, 2010). A recent study examined how online recommender systems that suggest potential new collaborators through algorithms impact team assembly mechanisms (Twyman et al., 2022). The study found that team members' choice of sending invitation messages to potential teammates was influenced by recommendations generated from the technological platform only when they did not have prior collaboration with the person.

In addition, with the increasing prominence of online social networks in people's lives, understanding the types of structures that motivate members to join online groups and facilitate the group's growth has important implications (Backstrom et al., 2006). For example, by examining the network structure of online groups, group organizers and moderators can find insights for developing group identity (Benedict, 2022) and encouraging the growth and maintenance of groups. Urbanoski et al. (2017) examined communication patterns among members through posts in an online support group for problematic drinking. Like other studies on online support groups, the authors found an asymmetry in members' participation level. There were a small number of highly active members and a majority of members whose participation was low. The highly active members connected with peripheral members and played an important role in sustaining the community. In the context of a large multiplayer online video game, a network of players and roles filled by the players were analyzed based on three positive ties (e.g., trade) and three negative ties (e.g., armed aggression; Szell et al., 2010). These relations can both facilitate and constrain the functioning of the network and impact group outcomes.

Diversity

Diversity can be considered both outside of groups and within groups. Diversity present in groups impacts members' interactions, and diverse network ties outside of the group facilitate accessing new information sources and innovation potentials (Reagans et al., 2004). The presence of sociodemographic diversity in groups has typically been tested from the theoretical perspective of homophily, which suggests that people with similarities are more likely to form ties with each other.

Two contrasting explanations exist for the origins of homophily (Kossinets & Watts, 2009): people voluntarily choose others who are similar to them (i.e., choice homophily) or people may be limited in the choice of potential contacts, often due to demographic distribution (i.e., induced homophily). For example, residential segregation of ethnic groups in urban cities could be observed through both perspectives. Homophily, in this case, is likely a function of a recursive process stemming from both systemic and institutional mechanisms of segregation as well as individuals' preference to interact with those of the same ethnicity. Such selection processes and strengthened ingroup–outgroup boundaries bring similar individuals closer, possibly through triadic closure, which subsequently impacts the choice of others who are connected to these individuals (Kossinets & Watts, 2009).

Demographic diversity, or the lack of homophily, is widely studied in groups. A meta-analysis of research on organizational demography and diversity from the 1950s to the 1990s revealed two important findings (Williams & O'Reilly, 1998). First, the composition of groups (e.g., based on characteristics such as age, gender, and race and ethnicity) has important implications for group processes and group performance. Second, increased diversity at the group level "typically has negative effects on the ability of the group to meet its members' needs and to function effectively over time" (p. 116).

A paradox exists for groups with diversity. Groups with demographic diversity are assumed to benefit from varying perspectives and unique approaches to problems; however, research reveals demographic diversity can yield social divisions and worse performance for groups (Mannix & Neale, 2005). These pessimistic views of demographic diversity often are informed by theories such as the similarity-attraction phenomenon and self-categorization and social identity paradigms, which posit that individuals magnetize toward similar others and have more cohesion among homophilic groups (Mannix & Neale, 2005). Network perspectives offer insights to limitations of demographically diverse groups: increasing demographic diversity results in a tradeoff of increased external range (with more diverse connections outside the group) but reduced internal density (with fewer connections within the group; Reagans et al., 2004).

In a recent study, Cross et al. (2021) reveal findings on how new hires of different gender, race, and ethnicity were integrated into workplace networks differently. Black women and Latino men were less likely to create early network ties within their functional groups and also had fewer ties across functions and geographies. Black men and Asian women tended to develop more cohesive internal ties with members of their ingroup. The study also showed that the patterns of network structure employees created were correlated with retention and promotion. One prominent finding was that creating early ties and having less insular networks (i.e., having more cross-cutting ties to other functional groups or geographic locations) were predictors of staying longer in the organization and being promoted quickly. Therefore, examining connectivity patterns of diverse subpopulations within groups is meaningful for understanding the positive influence of demographic diversity in groups and assessing and progressing in diversity, equity, and inclusion efforts. Additional findings on group diversity are discussed in Chapter 8.

Conclusion

With human nature driving people together to form groups, considering the interactions among group members and their situatedness in the larger environments can enhance group communication. Network theories, methods, and analysis present opportunities for people interested in group communication to recognize the many potentials of the complex webs of relationships present in our everyday interaction in and across groups.

Further Readings

Hanneman, R. A., & Riddle, M. (2005). *Introduction to social network methods*. University of California, Riverside. http://faculty.ucr.edu/~hanneman/nettext/
Katz, N., Lazer, D., Arrow, H., & Contractor, N. (2004). Network theory and small groups. *Small Group Research, 35*, 307–332. https://doi.org/10.1177/1046496404264941

Glossary

Centrality   A measure of power or influence in a network.
Edges   Relations which connect entities in a network.
Multidimensional networks   Networks with multiple types of nodes and edges.
Nodes   Entities in a network (e.g., people, computers).
Subgroup   A subset of network nodes (e.g., people) which are relatively well connected.

References

Ajzen, I. (1991). The theory of planned behavior. *Organizational Behavior and Human Decision Processes, 50*(2), 179–211. https://doi.org/10.1016/0749-5978(91)90020-T
Altman, I., & Taylor, D. (1973). *Social penetration: The development of interpersonal relationships*. Holt.
Backstrom, L., Huttenlocher, D., Kleinberg, J., & Lan, X. (2006, August). Group formation in large social networks: Membership, growth, and evolution. In *Proceedings of the 12th ACM SIGKDD international conference on knowledge discovery and data mining* (pp. 44–54). https://doi.org/10.1145/1150402.1150412
Balkundi, P., Kilduff, M., & Harrison, D. A. (2011). Centrality and charisma: Comparing how leader networks and attributions affect team performance. *Journal of Applied Psychology, 96*(6), 1209. https://doi.org/10.1037/a0024890
Benedict, B. C. (2022). Entanglements of identity and resilience in the Camp Fire's network of disaster-specific Facebook groups. *Media and Communication, 10*(2), 5–17. https://doi.org/10.17645/mac.v10i2.5038
Berger, C. R., & Calabrese, R. J. (1975). Some explorations in initial interaction and beyond: Toward a developmental theory of interpersonal communication. *Human Communication Research, 1*(2), 99–112. https://doi.org/10.1111/j.1468-2958.1975.tb00258.x

Bonacich, P. (2007). Some unique properties of eigenvector centrality. *Social Networks*, *29*(4), 555–564. https://doi.org/10.1016/j.socnet.2007.04.002

Borgatti, S. P. (2005). Centrality and network flow. *Social Networks*, *27*(1), 55–71. https://doi.org/10.1016/j.socnet.2004.11.008

Borgatti, S. P., Mehra, A., Brass, D., & Labianca, G. (2009). Network analysis in the social sciences. *Science*, *323*, 892–895.

Brashers, D. E. (2001). Communication and uncertainty management. *Journal of Communication*, *51*, 477–497. https://doi.org/10.1111/j.1460-2466.2001.tb02892.x

Buzzanell, P. M. (2019). Communication Theory of Resilience in everyday talk, interactions, and network structures. In S. Wilson & S. Smith (Eds.), *Reflections on interpersonal communication research* (pp. 65–88). Cognella.

Chevaleva-Janovskaja, E. (1927). Groupements spontanés d'enfants à l'age préscolaire. *Archives de Psychologie*, *20*, 219–223.

Clarke, R., Richter, A. W., & Kilduff, M. (2022). One tie to capture advice and friendship: Leader multiplex centrality effects on team performance change. *Journal of Applied Psychology*, *107*(6), 968–986. https://doi.org/10.1037/apl0000979

Comfort, L. K., & Haase, T. W. (2006). Communication, coherence, and collective action: The impact of Hurricane Katrina on communications infrastructure. *Public Works Management & Policy*, *10*(4), 328–343. https://doi.org/10.1177/1087724X06289052

Contractor, N. (2013). Some assembly required: Leveraging Web science to understand and enable team assembly. *Philosophical Transactions of the Royal Society A: Mathematical, Physical and Engineering Sciences*, *371*(1987), 20120385. https://doi.org/10.1098/rsta.2012.0385

Contractor, N., Monge, P. R., & Leonardi, P. (2011). Multidimensional networks and the dynamics of sociomateriality: Bringing technology inside the network. *International Journal of Communication*, *5*, 682–720.

Cross, R., Oakes, K., & Cross, C. (2021). Cultivating an inclusive culture through personal networks. *MIT Sloan Management Review*, *62*(4), 33–37.

Cummings, J. N., & Cross, R. (2003). Structural properties of work groups and their consequences for performance. *Social Networks*, *25*(3), 197–210. https://doi.org/10.1016/S0378-8733(02)00049-7

Decuypere, M. (2020). Visual network analysis: A qualitative method for researching sociomaterial practice. *Qualitative Research*, *20*(1), 73–90. https://doi.org/10.1177/1468794118816613

Delacour, H., & Leca, B. (2017). The paradox of controversial innovation: Insights from the rise of impressionism. *Organization Studies*, *38*(5), 597–618. https://doi.org/10.1177/0170840616663237

Emery, C. (2012). Uncovering the role of emotional abilities in leadership emergence: A longitudinal analysis of leadership networks. *Social Networks*, *34*(4), 429–437. https://doi.org/10.1016/j.socnet.2012.02.001

Everett, M. G., & Borgatti, S. P. (2014). Networks containing negative ties. *Social Networks*, *38*, 111–120. https://doi.org/10.1016/j.socnet.2014.03.005

Farrell, M. P. (2003). *Collaborative circles: Friendship dynamics and creative work*. University of Chicago Press.

Faust, K. (2010). A puzzle concerning triads in social networks: Graph constraints and the triad census. *Social Networks*, *32*(3), 221–233. https://doi.org/10.1016/j.socnet.2010.03.004

Freeman, L. C. (2004). *The development of social network analysis: A study in the sociology of science*. Empirical Press.

Freeman, L. C. (2011). The development of social network analysis–with an emphasis on recent events. *The Sage Handbook of Social Network Analysis*, *21*(3), 26–39. https://doi.org/10.4135/9781446294413.n3

Freeman, L. C. (1977). A set of measures of centrality based on betweenness. *Sociometry*, 35–41. https://doi.org/10.2307/3033543

Freeman, L. C. (1996). Some antecedents of social network analysis. *Connections*, *19*(1), 39–42.

Frey, L. R. (1996). Remembering and "re-membering": A history of theory and research on communication and group decision making. In R. Y. Hirokawa & M. S. Poole (Eds.), *Communication and group decision making* (2nd ed., pp. 19–54). Sage.

Giddens, A. (1976). *New rules of sociological method: A positive critique of interpretative sociologies*. Basic Books.

Giddens, A. (1984). *The constitution of society: Outline of the theory of structuration*. University of California Press.

Girvan, M., & Newman, M. E. (2002). Community structure in social and biological networks. *Proceedings of the National Academy of Sciences, 99*(12), 7821–7826. https://doi.org/10.1073/pnas.122653799

Gouldner, A. W. (1960). The norm of reciprocity: A preliminary statement. *American Sociological Review, 25*(2), 161–178. https://doi.org/10.2307/2092623

Granovetter, M. (1973). The strength of weak ties. *American Journal of Sociology, 78*, 136–1380.

Haythornthwaite, C. (2005). Social networks and Internet connectivity effects. *Information, Community & Society, 8*(2), 125–147. https://doi.org/10.1080/13691180500146185

Hemmings, F. W. J. (1958). Zola, Manet, and the Impressionists (1875-80). *PMLA, 73*(4-Part1), 407–417. https://doi.org/10.2307/460259

Hollingshead, A. B. (1998). Communication, learning, and retrieval in transactive memory systems. *Journal of Experimental Social Psychology, 34*(5), 423–442. https://doi.org/10.1006/jesp.1998.1358

Kossinets, G., & Watts, D. J. (2009). Origins of homophily in an evolving social network. *American Journal of Sociology, 115*(2), 405–450. https://doi.org/10.1086/599247

Labianca, G. J. (2014). Negative ties in organizational networks. In *Contemporary perspectives on organizational social networks, research in the sociology of organizations* (Vol. 40, pp. 239–259). Emerald Group Publishing Limited.

Labianca, G., & Brass, D. J. (2006). Exploring the social ledger: Negative relationships and negative asymmetry in social networks in organizations. *Academy of Management Review, 31*, 596–614. https://doi.org/10.5465/amr.2006.21318920

Laumann, E. O., Marsden, P. V., & Prensky, D. (1983). The boundary specification problem in network analysis. In R. S. Burt & M. J. Minor (Eds.), *Applied network analysis: A methodological introduction* (pp. 18–34). Sage.

Lazega, E., & Pattison, P. E. (1999). Multiplexity, generalized exchange and cooperation in organizations: A case study. *Social Networks, 21*(1), 67–90. https://doi.org/10.1016/S0378-8733(99)00002-7

Lee, S., Wittrock, Z., & Benedict, B. (2019). Who Dunnit: The party mystery game for analyzing network structure and information flow. *Connections, 39*(1), 1–18. DOI:10.21307/connections-2019-005.

Lewin, K. (1951). *Field theory in social science*. Harper.

Lungeanu, A., DeChurch, L. A., & Contractor, N. S. (2022). Leading teams over time through space: Computational experiments on leadership network archetypes. *The Leadership Quarterly*, 101595. https://doi.org/10.1016/j.leaqua.2021.101595

Mannix, E., & Neale, M. A. (2005). What differences make a difference? The promise and reality of diverse teams in organizations. *Psychological Science in the Public Interest, 6*(2), 31–55.

Marineau, J. E., Labianca, G. J., & Kane, G. C. (2016). Direct and indirect negative ties and individual performance. *Social Networks, 44*, 238–252. https://doi.org/10.1016/j.socnet.2015.09.003

Maslow, A. H. (1970). *Motivation and personality*. Harper & Row.

McPhee, R. D., Poole, M. S., & Iverson, J. (2014). Structuration theory. *The SAGE handbook of organizational communication: Advances in theory, research, and methods* (3rd ed., pp. 1–15). Sage Publications. https://us.sagepub.com/en-us/nam/the-sage-handbook-of-organizational-communication/book235059#contents

Meyers, J. (2005). *Impressionist quartet: The intimate genius of Manet and Morisot, Degas and Cassatt*. Houghton Mifflin Harcourt.

Mohammed, S., Ferzandi, L., & Hamilton, K. (2010). Metaphor no more: A 15-year review of the team mental model construct. *Journal of Management, 36*(4), 876–910.

Monge, P. R., & Contractor, N. S. (2003). *Theories of communication networks*. Oxford University Press.

Monge, P., Lee, S., Fulk, J., Frank, L., Margolin, D., Schultz, C., Shen, C., & Weber, M. (2011). Evolutionary and ecological models. In V. D. Miller, M. S. Poole, D. R. Seibold, & Associates, Advancing research in organizational communication through quantitative methodology. *Management Communication Quarterly, 25*(1), 4–58. https://doi.org/10.1177/0893318910390193

Moran, C. (2021). Minor intimacies and the art of Berthe Morisot: Impressionism, female friendship and spectatorship. *Dix-Neuf, 25*(2), 137–157.

Neubert, M. J., & Taggar, S. (2004). Pathways to informal leadership: The moderating role of gender on the relationship of individual differences and team member network centrality to informal leadership emergence. *The Leadership Quarterly*, *15*(2), 175–194. https://doi.org/10.1016/j.leaqua.2004.02.006

Oh, H., Chung, M. H., & Labianca, G. (2004). Group social capital and group effectiveness: The role of informal socializing ties. *Academy of Management Journal*, *47*(6), 860–875. https://doi.org/10.2307/20159627

Padgett, J. F., & Ansell, C. K. (1993). Robust action and the rise of the Medici, 1400-1434. *American Journal of Sociology*, *98*(6), 1259–1319. https://doi.org/10.1086/230190

Pilny, A., Dobosh, M., Yahja, A., Poole, M. S., Campbell, A., Ruge-Jones, L., & Proulx, J. (2020). Team coordination in uncertain environments: The role of processual communication networks. *Human Communication Research*, *46*(4), 385–411. https://doi.org/10.1093/hcr/hqz020

Pilny, A., Schecter, A., Poole, M. S., & Contractor, N. (2016). An illustration of the relational event model to analyze group interaction processes. *Group Dynamics: Theory, Research, and Practice*, *20*(3), 181.

Poole, M. S. (2014). Systems theory. In L. L. Putnam & D. K. Mumby (Eds.), *The SAGE handbook of organizational communication* (pp. 49–74). Sage.

Reagans, R., Zuckerman, E., & McEvily, B. (2004). How to make the team: Social networks vs. demography as criteria for designing effective teams. *Administrative Science Quarterly*, *49*(1), 101–133. https://doi.org/10.2307/4131457

Reitz, K. P. (1988). Social groups in a monastery. *Social Networks*, *10*(4), 343–357.

Rice, E., Holloway, I. W., Barman-Adhikari, A., Fuentes, D., Brown, C. H., & Palinkas, L. A. (2014). A mixed methods approach to network data collection. *Field Methods*, *26*(3), 252–268. https://doi.org/10.1177/1525822X13518168

Robins, G., Pattison, P., Kalish, Y., & Lusher, D. (2007). An introduction to exponential random graph (*p**) models for social networks. *Social Networks*, *29*(2), 173–191. https://doi.org/10.1016/j.socnet.2006.08.002

Sampson, F. (1969). *A Novitiate in a period of change: An experimental and case study of social relationships* [Doctoral dissertation]. Cornell University.

Sosa, M. E., Gargiulo, M., & Rowles, C. (2015). Can informal communication networks disrupt coordination in new product development projects? *Organization Science*, *26*(4), 1059–1078. https://doi.org/10.1287/orsc.2015.0974

Su, C. (2021). To share or hide? A social network approach to understanding knowledge sharing and hiding in organizational work teams. *Management Communication Quarterly*, *35*(2), 281–314. https://doi.org/10.1177/0893318920985178

Su, C., & Contractor, N. (2011). A multidimensional network approach to studying team members' information seeking from human and digital knowledge sources in consulting firms. *Journal of the American Society for Information Science and Technology*, *62*(7), 1257–1275. https://doi.org/10.1002/asi.21526

Szell, M., Lambiotte, R., & Thurner, S. (2010). Multirelational organization of large-scale social networks in an online world. *Proceedings of the National Academy of Sciences*, *107*(31), 13636–13641. https://doi.org/10.1073/pnas.1004008107

Tuckman, B. W. (1965). Developmental sequence in small groups. *Psychological Bulletin*, *63*(6), 384. https://doi.org/10.1037/h0022100

Twyman, M., Newman, D. A., DeChurch, L., & Contractor, N. (2022). Teammate invitation networks: The roles of recommender systems and prior collaboration in team assembly. *Social Networks*, *68*, 84–96. https://doi.org/10.1016/j.socnet.2021.04.008

Urbanoski, K., Van Mierlo, T., & Cunningham, J. (2017). Investigating patterns of participation in an online support group for problem drinking: A social network analysis. *International Journal of Behavioral Medicine*, *24*(5), 703–712. https://doi.org/10.1007/s12529-016-9591-6

Valente, T. W. (2012). Network interventions. *Science*, *337*(6090), 49–53. https://doi.org/10.1126/science.1217330

Van Cleemput, K. (2010). "I'll see you on IM, text, or call you": A social network approach of adolescents' use of communication media. *Bulletin of Science, Technology & Society*, *30*(2), 75–85. https://doi.org/10.1177/0270467610363143

Wasserman, S., & Faust, K. (1994). *Social network analysis: Methods and applications*. Cambridge University Press.

Whitbred, R., Fonti, F., Steglich, C., & Contractor, N. (2011). From microactions to macrostructure and back: A structurational approach to the evolution of organizational networks. *Human Communication Research*, *37*(3), 404–433. https://doi.org/10.1111/j.1468-2958.2011.01404.x

Wijnberg, N. M., & Gemser, G. (2000). Adding value to innovation: Impressionism and the transformation of the selection system in visual arts. *Organization Science*, *11*(3), 323–329. https://doi.org/10.1287/orsc.11.3.323.12499

Williams, K. Y., & O'Reilly, C. A. III (1998). Demography and diversity in organizations: A review of 40 years of research. *Research in Organizational Behavior*, *20*, 77–140.

Yamaguchi, K. (1994). The flow of information through social networks: Diagonal-free measures of inefficiency and the structural determinants of inefficiency. *Social Networks*, *16*(1), 57–86. https://doi.org/10.1016/0378-8733(94)90011-6

Yuan, Y., & Van Knippenberg, D. (2022). Leader network centrality and team performance: Team size as moderator and collaboration as mediator. *Journal of Business and Psychology*, 1–14. https://doi.org/10.1007/s10869-021-09745-4

Part III

Contexts of Group Communication

18 Groups in Organizations

Johny T. Garner

Chapter Objectives

- Understand the ways in which group members negotiate identity in an organizational context.
- Understand the complexities of organizational and group leadership in workgroups.
- Understand the importance of maintaining a moderate amount of task conflict while minimizing or eliminating relationship conflict.

Introduction

Groups exist in a variety of contexts, from families to schools to therapy to politics. Particularly noteworthy, groups and teams are ubiquitous in contemporary organizations as globalization, pressure to democratize, and diversifying organizational forms have increased the ways in which organizations rely on teams (Seibold et al., 2014). As organizations grapple with more information, they often turn to workgroups to process that information (Seibold et al., 2009). Groups are often responsible for planning organizational strategies, solving problems, quality control, developing products and services, customer service, and myriad other tasks. Increasingly, employees may be compensated for team performance as much as for organizational outcomes (Conroy & Gupta, 2016). For the purposes of this chapter, a *workgroup* is a small, interdependent subset of organizational members centered on one or more organizational goals. Workgroups could include project teams, self-managing teams, departmental groups, and a variety of other types of collaborations. These groups could be permanent, long-standing such as a board of directors or short-term teams associated with specific goals like developing a new product or service. Seibold et al. (2014) described work teams as embedded in organizations, highlighting the ways in which organizational structures shape workgroups and simultaneously drawing attention to the ways in which workgroup members' communication constitutes organizations. While it is natural to see the group as a subset of the organization and thus influenced by organizational norms, groups are often how employees and others engage with the organization. This reciprocal influence model emphasizes communication as workgroup communication can create and give meaning to the structures, identities, and experiences that group members associate with the organization. Scholars have long understood that communication creates and sustains organizations, and some have argued that group meetings are the mechanism through which communication constitutes organizations (Tracy & Dimock, 2004). Organizational work often occurs in the context of group meetings (Beck & Keyton, 2009).

Organizations bring people together in groups because they assume that people with different skills and expertise working together will produce better outcomes that individuals working independently. A project team comprised of someone with production experience, someone with marketing experience, and someone with sales experience may be ideally equipped to launch a new

DOI: 10.4324/9781003227458-21

product line because the diverse expertise enables the group to better anticipate problems and solve any obstacles they encounter. Of course, those varied backgrounds can also create conflict because each member may see the task from a different point of view with different values and mental models. For example, a group member with a sales background might have a different perspective in a product development team than someone with a production background, who might also differ from someone with a finance background. Functional diversity refers to differences in group members' backgrounds and roles. Johnson et al. (2018) found that functional diversity affected team performance, but that the effect depended upon how the team managed interpersonal conflict. Johnson et al. studied health care groups comprised of multiple specialties. When the team had effective interpersonal conflict management processes in place, functional diversity was associated with improved performance as measured by supervisors' ratings. This means that group processes are integral to organizations effectively using teams to improve organizational outcomes, and that conflict management norms are vitally important in organizational groups.

This chapter covers the points at which group processes and organizational structures seem most likely to intersect, where the group being embedded in an organization is most likely to affect either the group or the organization. The first section examines issues of identity both in terms of a group's identity relative to the organization as well as how members navigate group and organizational identifications. The next section considers **group leadership** as organizational status issues play out in group members' roles and relationships with each other. Following that, the chapter considers conflict and uses one specific type of conflict, dissent, to explore junctures between organizational and group conflict. Finally, the chapter covers issues of group diversity and virtual teams before closing with the practical applications of this research for groups in organizational contexts.

Group and Organizational Identity

Identity is an important issue in any context. Identity can refer to either a core attribute of an entity or how that entity relates to the environment around it (see Cheney et al., 2014). In the first sense, identity is something an organization, a group, or an individual has, something that seems enduring as the organization, group, or individual interacts with others. On the other hand, many communication scholars see identity as a process, where an organization, group, or individual is becoming something. For example, Scott et al. (1998) used structuration theory to explore how individuals might use their identity (e.g., I am the kind of person who is a team player) to construct identification (e.g., I want to be part of this group). That identification then recreates the individual's identity. In that example, the individual might sacrifice autonomy for the group because that is what team players do, reinforcing their identity of team player. From a communication, identity is less something that a person has and more something that they do through communication.

Relatedly, identity is contextual. One might have one identity at work and another identity at home. Some mistakenly think of identity as "real" or "fake" as in circumstances where someone is their fake self at work and their real self at home. Tracy and Trethewey (2005) challenged this dichotomy and conceptualized identity as crystalized, where individuals have multiple identity facets (e.g., work, family, hobbies). Scott et al. (1998) used structuration theory to understand these facets of identity as regionalized, a term which recognizes how multiple identities might be relevant in different ways in different contexts. For example, members of a community choir could describe their identities in terms of the choir itself as well as music broadly or family activities (Meisenbach & Kramer, 2014).

The ongoing and contextual aspects of identity are important in thinking about the identity of workgroup members individually, the identity of the workgroup collectively, and the ways in which group members perceive connections between the group's identity and the organization's identity.

Workgroup members must see themselves as a group, perhaps adopting a team name or using pronouns like "we;" others in the organization should also recognize that these members are working together (Seibold et al., 2014). Those perceptions provide a language from which the group's identity emerges. The organization may also promote the group's identity, encouraging members to be "team players." At the same time, the group's boundaries must be permeable because the group is embedded in and thus interdependent with the organization. The group may depend on the organization more broadly for information or other resources. Others within the organization may be responsible for executing the group's plan or provide the funds that the group uses to accomplish its work. Group members may hold membership in other groups, further complexifying group boundaries. Thus, one task confronting group members is sifting through these memberships as they think through their identity at the individual, workgroup, and organizational levels.

A significant factor in each of those identities is the boundary of the group. Group boundaries are constituted through communication as members negotiate how to engage with members and nonmembers. Part of identifying as part of a group is deciding how to communicate about and toward nonmembers. Somech and Khalaili (2014) examined the ways in which a workgroup defined its own boundaries as well as how it then engaged with other organizational groups. They termed these two activities as boundary-tightening (e.g., explicitly communicating about who is in and who is not in the group) and boundary-loosening (e.g., communication that coordinates with other workgroups). They found that the degree to which the team perceived its goals aligned with organizational goals and the diversity of organizational roles on the team positively predicted boundary-loosening activities and that organizational role diversity negatively predicted boundary-tightening activities. When group members perceived their team's goals aligned with the organization's goals, they likely saw others in the organization as part of that alignment. Likewise, organizational role diversity may also help the group think beyond its borders. Importantly, both boundary tightening and loosening led to increased innovation. The researchers concluded that examining both internal and external relationships were important for innovation in organizational groups. Importantly, team leaders may also liaise between the group and others in the organization.

Interestingly, because groups are embedded in organization, the connection between **group identity** and organizational identity may not be straightforward. An employee may identify as a member of their organization and as a member of a particular workgroup within that organization. However, those identifications may not always be salient at all times. In other words, the employee may feel more strongly about one of those identities versus the other. Silva and Sias (2010) found that group identity was more salient than organizational identity and that group membership became a substitute for organizational membership. That is to say that individuals saw their group membership as foreground and organizational experiences apart from their group as background. For example, a workgroup could develop such type bonds that members identify with their group but not with the larger organization in which the group is embedded. Group members may perceive that their group "gets it" and is essentially to the organization, picking up the slack left when others in the organization "can't keep up." Lammers et al. (2013) found that group identification reduced certain aspects of burnout while organizational identification had no effect on burnout. They went on to suggest that employees felt they could be themselves more authentically in their workgroup than in other organizational contexts and that group members distanced themselves from organizational experiences apart from their group.

Especially if an employee's daily interactions are mostly with workgroup members, it can be easy for those relationships to matter more to that employee than others in the organization. Of course, the danger is that the employee or the group as a whole begins to see themselves as independent of rather than interdependent with the organization. Essentially, the group may forget its embeddedness, that it depends on the organization as much as the organization depends on the group. This can lead to insular silos and negatively affects the organizations. For example, if a sales team sees itself as superior to the rest of the organization, it might act in detrimental ways because it underappreciates communication from others in the organization. Thus, although it is natural and desirable for group members to form strong bonds with each other, it is also important for the group to maintain its sense of connection to the organization.

Group Leadership in Organizational Contexts

Another interesting question when thinking about groups or teams in organizational contexts is the question of leadership. Because most organizations are hierarchical, organizational groups may include members with equal positions, but that is not always the case. One member may have considerably more or less organizational status than another member either because of hierarchical position or informal influence. A group could include some number of coworkers and their supervisor. Another group could include a mix of employees across hierarchical levels within the organization. One member might be an organizational leader but not a group leader, a group leader but not an organizational leader, or an organizational leader who also leads a workgroup. This interplay between organizational and group leadership means that leaders and members must manage both organizational and group status, and researchers must also unpack the intersection of these influences.

Employees easily perceive status differences when supervisors are present for workgroup meetings, either as regular attendees or as special visitors (Shumski Thomas et al., 2018). Employees withhold their feelings and opinions when supervisors are present, leading meetings to be less effective than meetings without supervisors. Particularly in organizations that emphasize hierarchical position and power differences between supervisors and subordinates, group members may simply comply with supervisors' directives rather than actively and independently participating in group decisions (Chernikova et al., 2017), which can defeat the reason to have a group. One way to counter this tendency is for group leaders, particularly those with higher organizational positions or influence than other team members, to withhold opinions to encourage others to share ideas. Group leaders might also intentionally solicit feedback from members who could be hesitant to voice their ideas.

Sometimes, the nature of a group's work may be entirely orthogonal to traditional organizational hierarchy. Jahn and Black (2017) examined wildland firefighting teams. High reliability organizing necessary for firefighting teams is predicated on flatter organizational structures where hierarchical positions and power differences are minimized because such structures enable organizations to more quickly adapt to unpredictable circumstances. However, those teams may exist in traditional, vertical hierarchies that value hierarchy and associate status with hierarchical position. Jahn and Black found that supervisors who sought feedback from subordinates and who communicated big picture concerns improved team communication because subordinates were more likely to share critical information with the team. Put another way, organizational groups that include members across various hierarchical levels may benefit when supervisors deemphasize their position using behaviors such as feedback solicitation and information sharing because other team members may feel less inhibited in sharing information.

At other times organizational groups may even exist outside a traditional hierarchy. Organizations have historically been hierarchical where subordinates report to a supervisor. By contrast, some organizations organize employees into teams where members are accountable only to the team rather than a supervisor; authority is invested in the group rather than a supervisor. These self-managing teams plan and execute their work, making decisions, solving problems, and even evaluating members' performance (Lawler, 1986). Because group members have diverse experiences and expertise and because members are involved in both strategic planning and executing organizational production or services, self-managing teams may often improve organizational effectiveness (Cooney, 2004; Wall et al., 1986). At the same time, such autonomy can come at a price. Research on a phenomenon known as concertive control demonstrates that self-managing teams can be more oppressive than traditional hierarchical supervision (Barker, 1993; Barker et al., 1993). Concertive control argues that these teams may develop formal rules and procedures that reflect managerial interests. In such cases, group members perceive a false sense of autonomy because they participated in developing the rules and procedures.

Group Conflict in Organizations

Conflict is unavoidable in groups. In fact, some conflict is desirable and should be welcomed (Janis, 1982). Instead of eliminating conflict, researchers often focus on whether conflict helps or hinders the group's progress toward accomplishing its goal. One prototypical stream of research from this perspective is that of task conflict versus relationship conflict. Jehn (1995) distinguished between **task conflict**, which included disagreements related to the group's goal ("That solution is too costly"), and relationship conflict, which included interpersonal disagreements ("Your ideas are always terrible"). Jehn found that a moderate amount of task conflict could lead to better decision making in groups, but any relationship conflict was likely to interfere with group productivity. Groups need some task conflict to avoid groupthink and make optimal decisions, but too much task conflict can create relationship conflict as members mistake task-related disagreements as personal affronts (Guenter et al., 2016). When task conflict is moderate, strong team identification can prevent task conflict from generating relationship conflict (Schaeffner et al., 2015).

Closely related to task conflict is dissent. Dissent has been examined in organizations and in groups, but these literatures rarely inform each other. Organizational dissent focuses on one or more subordinates expressing disagreement with policies or practices (Garner, 2013; Kassing, 2011). The central aspect of organizational dissent is an employee questioning a particular policy, suggesting an alternative to the way their organization functions, or by disagreeing with particular instructions given by management. For example, an employee might want the ability to work from home and challenge a policy requiring all employees to be physically present in an office. Group dissent is generally defined as a member or small group of members challenging the opinions or assertions of the majority (e.g., De Dreu & West, 2001; Garner & Iba, 2017; Schulz-Hardt et al., 2006). For example, a group might develop a solution to a problem, but a group member questions whether the solution is cost-effective.

Interesting and important connections between these ideas emerge when an organizational context is overlaid on a group context. If the majority of a workgroup favors an organizational policy, a dissenting group member would be expressing both organizational and group dissent. A group member disagreeing with the group majority about something other than an organizational policy or practice would be group dissent but not organizational dissent. A group member dissenting about an organizational policy or practice when the group majority does not have a position on that policy or practice would be organizational dissent but not group dissent. Garner (2022) also highlighted how a group majority can disagree with an organizational policy, making the workgroup an organizational dissenter. While underexplored in academic research, connections between organizational and group dissent are important for at least two reasons. First, they illustrate how groups in organizations complicate discrete definitions of organizational and group dissent. Second, dissent is vitally important for organizations and for groups. Dissent can lead to greater problem solving and creativity (De Dreu & West, 2001; Mitchell et al., 2009), increased productivity (Detert et al., 2013; Ng & Feldman, 2012), increased job satisfaction (Lutgen-Sandvik et al., 2011), and decreased turnover (Spencer, 1986).

Box 18.1   Firefighters and Organizational Communication

Jahn and Black (2017) offered an interesting case study of groups in organizational contexts that illustrates many of the principles in this chapter. Jahn and Black surveyed 574 wildland fire fighters. These fire fighters worked in groups across three federal agencies to deploy and extinguish fires in areas that are difficult to access. This type of work fits into what scholars call high reliability organizations (HRO), where failure is more costly than traditional organizations. HRO theory offers several guiding principles for these organizations to limit catastrophic incidents including a preoccupation with the possibility of failure, information sharing across the organization, resiliency, and deference to expertise (Weick & Sutcliffe, 2015). Jahn and Black used these principles to demonstrate how communication processes in firefighting groups leads to successful organizational outcomes.

Government agencies generally, and fire departments more specifically, are often highly structured and hierarchical. Chain of command is an important value in these organizations. However, as previously mentioned, HROs expect members to defer to expertise to optimize decision making and reduce the likelihood of errors. That deference means that decisions may need to be made outside the formal hierarchy, creating a tension between norms that privilege a rigid organizational structure and norms that privilege seeking expertise outside that structure. As part of that tension, Jahn and Black (2017) noted that wildland firefighting supervisors needed to solicit input from group members and encourage dissenting viewpoints. Organizational leadership overlapped with the formal leadership of the group, but the nature of HRO work meant that supervisors had to be open to a group member with a lower organizational position taking on group leadership responsibilities.

Given the hours of strenuous work, it is hardly surprising that members of wildland firefighting teams developed strong bonds. They had to learn to trust each other in challenging and dangerous circumstances. At the same time, these teams were highly interdependent on others in the organization for information, coordination, and assistance in fighting fires. Team leaders needed to serve as liaisons to people outside the group in order to facilitate cross-level communication.

Finally, wildland firefighting groups had to encourage task conflict to ensure optimal performance and reduce the likelihood of errors in decision making while also minimizing or eliminating relationship conflict. As previously mentioned, supervisors needed to encourage group members to express opposing points of view, particularly when those members had necessary expertise, which entailed task conflict. By contrast, Jahn and Black (2017) explained that effective HRO communication requires "trust, respect, honesty, and attention to each other" (p. 364). These characteristics are the opposite of relationship conflict. To be effective when failure would be catastrophic, these groups must maintain appropriate task conflict while eliminating relationship conflict.

Diverse Groups in Organizations

Importantly, a person rarely chooses their coworkers, which means that employees often work in groups with members they did not choose. Among other things, this can lead to greater diversity in workgroups than in other types of groups or teams. Indeed, for the organization to harness the power of varied expertise and skill, the group needs to be comprised of diverse members. Group members with varied backgrounds and experiences are more likely to bring unique knowledge and expertise to the group, enabling the group to more effectively solve problems.

On the other hand, diversity in organizational groups can also lead to tensions. Hentschel et al. (2013) found that, when group members perceive that their group is diverse in terms of age, gender, nationality, or other aspects, they may be less identified with the group and experience more relationship conflict. In such cases, social group identifications override workgroup identifications. One key for successfully managing diversity is to emphasize the value of diversity itself. Group members may resent people who are different. That might be particularly true if group members perceive diversity being forced upon them (e.g., new members being added as part of organizational diversification efforts). On the other hand, other groups may see the addition of diverse members as an opportunity to widen a pool of expertise and experiences. Hentschel et al. argued that group members' beliefs about the value of diversity and the overall affective tone of the group moderated the negative relationships among diversity and identification and conflict. Organizational groups that believe diverse membership adds value to the team and that approach team dynamics with positive attitudes were less likely to experience decreases in identification and increases in conflict due to perceptions of diversity. That could be because groups that resent diversification efforts or members from different groups may not communicate in ways that allow those members to contribute ideas and information. In that case, the diversity does not benefit the group's decision making. It is only when a group can leverage information disparities across subgroups that diversity can positively affect team performance (Zheng & Wei, 2018).

Virtual Teams in Organizations

Certainly the Covid-19 pandemic has accelerated many organizations' use of virtual teams even though the idea is hardly a recent one. Teams have been able to "meet" via telephone conference calls for decades when one or more group member was not physically present. Following increasing costs and security concerns after the 9/11 attacks in the United States, more and more organizations shifted to virtual meetings rather than asking employees to travel to meet with other team members. During the quarantine lockdowns due to Covid-19, such virtual meetings became the norm. Even in organizational groups that meet face-to-face, virtual connections through email afford group members the opportunity to better share information, co-construct meaning, and resolve conflict (Erhardt et al., 2016). Erhardt et al. (2016) found that email provided group members with the opportunity to better process information as they had time to reflect on what questions needed to be asked, how questions should be answered, what resources were needed to solve problems, and how misunderstandings might be corrected. Organizations have increasingly used intranets to allow employees the opportunity to share ideas and build relationships, and group members' support through these intranets contributes to a greater sense of community (Uysal, 2016).

More narrowly though, the term virtual group usually refers to a group that rarely or never meets face-to-face. Purvanova and Kenda (2018) argued that a variety of paradoxes confront virtual groups. For example, although technology provides rich data to group members, that technology can also overwhelm members with data. Geographic dispersion can isolate members but can also afford them increased flexibility. Purvanova and Kenda argued that leadership in virtual groups was fundamentally about managing paradoxes. Such leadership can be challenging for group leaders who previously relied on watching members to measure performance, and those leaders may need to shift to performance measures based on outcomes rather than observable processes. Relationships among workgroup members may also take longer to develop. Without a face-to-face component, it can be challenging to build rapport with group members, but familiarity with group members remains vitally important as a foundation for processing information (Maynard et al., 2019). In face-to-face groups, members build that familiarity through small talk outside of group meetings and informal greetings in passing. Without those opportunities, virtual groups must find other ways to establish rapport. Groups might use chat functions alongside video meeting tools or develop other informal communication media. Ultimately, some virtual groups may never develop the familiarity that can come through face-to-face interactions.

Evidence-Based Recommendations for Practice

I have mentioned some recommendations throughout the chapter, but I want to highlight two that are particularly important for groups in contemporary organizations. First, identification with one's group is highly advantageous as it may lead to better group relationships and greater commitment to the group and the organization. Using language and stories that are unique to the group as well as first-person plural pronouns can strengthen group identification. At the same time, group identification can lead to silos, where group members feel isolated from others in the organization and lose sight of their interdependence with the rest of the organization. To guard against such isolationism, group members should remind each other of how the group connects with the rest of the organization. Group members who are members of other groups might describe the work of those outside the group. Boundary spanners can emphasize coordination with others, describing how the group's work depends on and facilitates the work of other units within the organization. It is important that group members maintain a sense of the organization even if their main connection to the organization is the group.

A second practical application of this research is the need for moderate amounts of task conflict. Some groups try to avoid conflict, thinking that the absence of conflict is an indicator of group cohesion. However, research indicates that a moderate level of task conflict is critical for organizational groups to make optimal decisions. That means that organizational and group leaders should create a group climate where members feel free to challenge the status quo and voice dissenting opinions. Certainly that entails not sanctioning those who disagree, but groups also might consider ways to foster task conflict such as appointing someone to raise objections to group ideas. At the same time, it is important for the group to recognize the difference between task and relationship conflict. When conflicts become personal, they tend to lead toward decreased group satisfaction and performance, rather than improving group performance. Groups might proactively stop relationship conflict, recognizing personal disputes, and calling on parties to reconcile.

Conclusion

Groups are one of the fundamental features of contemporary organizations, and that seems unlikely to change. It is, therefore, important to understand the ways in which group processes shape and are shaped by the organizational environment. Processes of identification, leadership, and conflict are particularly noteworthy as moments where group and organizational influences intersect. The diversity of the group is also important in organizational contexts. Finally, the increase in virtual teams calls attention to the need for understanding how organizational groups accomplish their tasks in the absence of face-to-face interactions.

Further Readings

Garner, J. T., & Ragland, J. P. (2019). Tabling, discussing, and giving in: Dissent in workgroups. *Group Dynamics: Theory, Research, and Practice, 23*, 57–74. https://doi.org/10.1037/gdn0000098

Koeslag-Kreunen, M., van den Bossche, P., Hoven, M., van der Klink, M. R., & Gijselaers, W. (2018). When leadership powers team learning: A meta-analysis. *Small Group Research, 49*(4), 475–513. https://doi.org/10.1177/1046496418764824

Magpili, N. C., & Pazos, P. (2018). Self-managing team performance: A systematic review of multilevel input factors. *Small Group Research, 49*(1), 3–33. https://doi.org/10.1177/1046496417710500

Glossary

Group identity   Group identity includes how members identify themselves with a group as well as how the group as a whole identifies itself to nonmembers. These identities are created as group members communicate with each other and with nonmembers.

Group leadership   The group leader is a person who has formal or informal authority over the group. This could be someone formally designated to be in charge, or it could be someone who assumes leadership responsibilities for the group. Sometimes, but not always, group leadership overlaps with organizational leadership such that the group leader has a higher position on the organization's hierarchy than other members.

Task conflict   Task conflict is related to the group accomplishing its goal. This is opposed to relationship conflict, which includes interpersonal disagreements. Research suggests that while both types of conflict may be uncomfortable, moderate amounts of task conflict can improve decision making.

Workgroup   A workgroup is a small subset of organizational members focused on one or more organizational goals. The workgroup is interdependent with other parts of the organization.

References

Barker, J. R. (1993). Tightening the iron cage: Concertive control in self-managing teams. *Administrative Science Quarterly*, *38*, 408–437. https://doi.org/10.2307/2393374

Barker, J. R., Melville, C. W., & Packanowsky, M. E. (1993). Self-directed teams at Xel: Changes in communication practices during a program of cultural transformation. *Journal of Applied Communication*, *21*, 297–312. https://doi.org/10.1080/00909889309365375

Beck, S. J., & Keyton, J. (2009). Perceiving strategic meeting interaction. *Small Group Research*, *40*(2), 223–246. https://doi.org/10.1177/1046496408330084

Cheney, G., Christensen, L. T., & Dailey, S. L. (2014). Communicating identity and identification in and around organizations. In L. L. Putnam & D. K. Mumby (Eds.), *The SAGE handbook of organizational communication: Advances in theory, research, and methods* (3rd ed., pp. 695–716). Sage.

Chernikova, M., Lo Destro, C., Pierro, A., Higgins, E. T., & Kruglanski, A. W. (2017). A multilevel analysis of person–group regulatory-mode complementarity: The moderating role of group–task interdependence. *Group Dynamics: Theory, Research, and Practice*, *21*(2), 108–120. https://doi-org.ezproxy.tcu.edu/10.1037/gdn0000067

Conroy, S. A., & Gupta, N. (2016). Team pay-for-performance: The devil is in the details. *Group & Organization Management*, *41*(1), 32–65. https://doi.org/10.1177/1059601115607746

Cooney, R. (2004). Empowered self-management and the design of work teams. *Personnel Review*, *33*, 677–692. https://doi.org/10.1108/00483480410561556

De Dreu, C. K. W., & West, M. A. (2001). Minority dissent and team innovation: The importance of participation in decision making. *Journal of Applied Psychology*, *86*, 1191–1201.

Detert, J. R., Burris, E. R., Harrison, D. A., & Martin, S. R. (2013). Voice flows to and around leaders: Understanding when units are helped or hurt by employee voice. *Administrative Science Quarterly*, *58*(4), 624–668. https://doi.org/10.1177/0001839213510151

Erhardt, N., Gibbs, J., Martin-Rios, C., & Sherblom, J. (2016). Exploring affordances of email for team learning over time. *Small Group Research*, *47*(3), 243–278. https://doi.org/10.1177/1046496416635823

Garner, J. T. (2013). Dissenters, managers, and coworkers: The process of co-constructing organizational dissent and dissent effectiveness. *Management Communication Quarterly*, *27*, 373–395. https://doi.org/10.1177/0893318913488946

Garner, J. T. (2022). Exploring collective and multi-audience dissent in organizational meetings. *Management Communication Quarterly*, *36*, 736–760. https://doi.org/10.1177/08933189221088297

Garner, J. T., & Iba, D. L. (2017). Why are you saying that? Increases in gaze duration as responses to group member dissent. *Communication Studies*, *68*, 353–367. https://doi.org/10.1080/10510974.2017.1334147

Garner, J. T., & Poole, M. S. (2013). Perspectives on workgroup conflict and communication. In J. G. Oetzel, & S. Ting-Toomey (Eds.), *The Sage handbook of conflict communication: Integrating theory, research, and practice* (2nd ed., pp. 321–347). Sage.

Guenter, H., Emmerik, H., Schreurs, B., Kuypers, T., Iterson, A., & Notelaers, G. (2016). When task conflict becomes personal. *Small Group Research*, *47*(5), 569. https://doi.org/10.1177/1046496416667816

Hentschel, T., Shemla, M., Wegge, J., & Kearney, E. (2013). Perceived diversity and team functioning: The role of diversity beliefs and affect. *Small Group Research*, *44*(1), 33–61. https://doi.org/10.1177/1046496412470725

Jahn, J. L. S., & Black, A. E. (2017). A model of communicative and hierarchical foundations of high reliability organizing in wildland firefighting teams. *Management Communication Quarterly*, *31*(3), 356–379. https://doi.org/10.1177/0893318917691358

Janis, I. L. (1982). *Groupthink* (2nd ed.). Houghton Mifflin.

Jehn, K. A. (1995). A multimethod examination of the benefits and detriments of intragroup conflict. *Administrative Science Quarterly*, *40*, 256–282.

Johnson, A., Nguyen, H., Groth, M., & White, L. (2018). Reaping the rewards of functional diversity in healthcare teams: Why team processes improve performance. *Group & Organization Management*, *43*(3), 440–474. https://doi.org/10.1177/1059601118769192

Kassing, J. W. (2011). *Dissent in organizations*. Polity.

Lammers, J. C., Atouba, Y. L., & Carlson, E. J. (2013). Which identities matter? A mixed-method study of group, organizational, and professional identities and their relationship to burnout. *Management Communication Quarterly*, *27*(4), 503–536. https://doi.org/10.1177/0893318913498824

Lawler, E. E. (1986). *High-involvement management: Participative strategies for improving organizational performance*. Jossey-Bass.

Lutgen-Sandvik, P., Riforgiate, S., & Fletcher, C. (2011). Work as a source of positive emotional experiences and the discourses informing positive assessment. *Western Journal of Communication*, *75*, 2–27. https://doi.org/10.1080/10570314.2010.536963

Maynard, M. T., Mathieu, J. E., Gilson, L. L., Sanchez, D., & Dean, M. D. (2019). Do i really know you and does it matter? Unpacking the relationship between familiarity and information elaboration in global virtual teams. *Group & Organization Management*, *44*(1), 3–37. https://doi.org/10.1177/1059601118785842

Meisenbach, R. J., & Kramer, M. W. (2014). Exploring nested identities: Voluntary membership, social category identity, and identification in a community Choir. *Management Communication Quarterly*, *28*, 187–213. https://doi.org/10.1177/0893318914524059

Mitchell, R., Nicholas, S., & Boyle, B. (2009). The role of openness to cognitive diversity and group processes in knowledge creation. *Small Group Research*, *40*, 535–554. https://doi.org/10.1177/1046496409338302

Ng, T. H., & Feldman, D. C. (2012). Employee voice behavior: A meta-analytic test of the conservation of resources framework. *Journal of Organizational Behavior*, *33*(3), 216–234. https://doi.org/10.1002/job.754

Purvanova, R., & Kenda, R. (2018). Paradoxical virtual leadership: Reconsidering virtuality through a paradox lens. *Group & Organization Management*, *43*(5), 752–786. https://doi.org/10.1177/1059601118794102

Schaeffner, M., Huettermann, H., Gebert, D., Boerner, S., Kearney, E., & Song, L. J. (2015). Swim or sink together: The potential of collective team identification and team member alignment for separating task and relationship conflicts. *Group & Organization Management*, *40*(4), 467–499. https://doi.org/10.1177/1059601114561059

Schulz-Hardt, S., Brodbeck, F. C., Mojzisch, A., Kerschreiter, R., & Frey, D. (2006). Group decision making in hidden profile situations: Dissent as a facilitator for decision quality. *Journal of Personality and Social Psychology*, *91*, 1080–1093.

Scott, C. R., Corman, S. R., & Cheney, G. (1998). Development of a structurational model of identification in the organization. *Communication Theory*, *8*, 298–336. https://doi.org/10.1111/j.1468-2885.1998.tb00223.x

Seibold, D. R., Hollingshead, A. B., & Yoon, K. (2014). Embedded teams and embedding organizations. In L. L. Putnam & D. K. Mumby (Eds.) *The SAGE handbook of organizational communication: Advances in theory, research, and methods* (3rd ed., pp. 327–349). Sage.

Seibold, D. R., Kang, P., Gailliard, B. M., & Jahn, J. (2009). Communication that damages teamwork: The dark side of teams. In P. Lutgen-Sandvik & B. Davenport Sypher (Eds.), *Destructive organizational communication: Processes, consequences, and constructive ways of organizing* (pp. 267–289). Routledge/ Taylor & Francis.

Shumski Thomas, J., Olien, J. L., Allen, J. A., Rogelberg, S. G., & Kello, J. E. (2018). Faking it for the higher-ups: Status and surface acting in workplace meetings. *Group & Organization Management, 43*(1), 72–100. https://doi.org/10.1177/1059601116687703

Silva, D., & Sias, P. M. (2010). Connection, restructuring, and buffering: How groups link individuals and organizations. *Journal of Applied Communication Research, 38*, 145–166. https://doi.org/10.1080/00909881003639510

Somech, A., & Khalaili, A. (2014). Team boundary activity: Its mediating role in the relationship between structural conditions and team innovation. *Group & Organization Management, 39*(3), 274–299. https://doi.org/10.1177/1059601114525437

Spencer, D. G. (1986). Employee voice and employee retention. *Academy of Management Journal, 29*, 488–502. https://doi.org/10.2307/256220

Tracy, K., & Dimock, A. (2004). Meetings: Discursive sites for building and fragmenting community. In P. J. Kalbfleisch (Ed.), *Communication yearbook* (vol. 28, pp. 127–165). Lawrence Erlbaum.

Tracy, S. J., & Trethewey, A. (2005). Fracturing the real-self↔fake-self dichotomy: Moving toward "crystallized" organizational discourses and identities. *Communication Theory, 15*, 168–195.

Uysal, N. (2016). Social collaboration in intranets: The impact of social exchange and group norms on internal communication. *International Journal of Business Communication, 53*(2), 181–199. https://doi.org/10.1177/2329488415627270

Wall, T. D., Kemp, N. J., Jackson, P. R., & Clegg, C. W. (1986). Outcomes of autonomous workgroups: A long-term field experiment. *Academy of Management Journal, 29*, 280–304. https://doi.org/10.2307/256189

Weick, K. E., & Sutcliffe, K. M. (2015). *Managing the unexpected: Sustained performance in a complex world* (3rd ed.). John Wiley.

Zheng, W., & Wei, J. (2018). Linking ethnic composition and performance: Information integration between majority and minority members. *Small Group Research, 49*(3), 357–387. https://doi.org/10.1177/1046496417749727

19 Function of Groups Within Society

Justin Reedy and Elizabeth H. Hurst

Chapter Objectives

- Understand how various types of groups form and function in a democratic society.
- Provide examples of groups shaping our society.
- Grasp on the role that dialogue and deliberation plays in the functioning of groups, and how group dialogue shapes our larger social system.

Introduction

Since early hunter-gatherer days, humans have come together as a means for survival. The formation of groups is, in and of itself, a function of society. Consider your own life. How many groups do you belong to? Your family unit is a group, you may belong to clubs and organizations at school, or you may participate at a place of worship. You may also be a member of a political group. Or march with a group formed to make political change, such as the Black Lives Matter movement. All of these groups, both the smaller personal groups, like the family unit, and the larger social groups, like a political party, shape both our personal lives and society at large. *Society,* as defined by Aberle and colleagues in the 1950s, is "a group of human beings sharing a self-sufficient system of action which is capable of existing longer than the life-span of an individual, the group being recruited at least in part by the sexual reproduction of its members" (Aberle et al., 1950, p. 101). Within societies, we follow a system of rules in the form of laws and cultural norms, and these rules and norms are passed down from generation to generation. Members of society are either born into that society or immigrate into the society. From a systems perspective, the individuals within the society, along with the groups, and organizations within the society, shape society itself.

In a democratic society, groups are especially important. Though we can think of society as a large group of people, there are numerous small groups, organizations, and other collective social entities of all sizes contained therein, often nested within each other. Those social groupings are often key to democratic participation, which is often based in social interaction in some way. For example, an individual may be part of a family group that discusses political issues, as well as having a group of friends who are politically active and are all members of an organization trying to get young college students registered to vote.

Democratic systems may look slightly different across the globe; however, they all rely on civic engagement. In many democracies, one way in which individuals can practice civic engagement is through voting for leaders, who are in turn expected to govern on behalf of the people (Schumpeter, 1942). Voting is the most direct form of civic engagement and is a key civic action for the running of a democracy. As Gastil (2008) puts it, "a political system cannot begin to call itself democratic unless its citizens, one and all, have the right to vote" (p. 3). Because citizens have the power to make change in a democratic society, the coming together of groups becomes catalysts for that

DOI: 10.4324/9781003227458-22

change. Groups may form to address social problems or to raise awareness regarding social problems. Groups also enable discussion and deliberation on both micro and macro levels. The forming of in-person groups in town halls and protests or the forming of large social groups online shapes **dialogue** and **deliberation** in the larger public sphere. In a democratic system, groups are often key to political action and stability, but can also become the basis for social change.

In this chapter, we discuss ways in which groups constitute and shape our democratic society. First, we discuss the formation of **social movements**. Here, we explain how and why social movements form. Next, we discuss how and why groups in society maintain a shared sense of identity. We then go on to discuss the importance of group identity for smaller localized groups, as well as large social movements. Following the section on maintaining a shared identity, we describe where groups form; in particular, we discuss groups that exist on local, regional, national, and global scales. We also discuss the use of technology as a space for group functions, groups meeting in-person, and non-formal groups that meet in "third spaces" outside of the home and workspaces. Finally, we describe ways in which groups enable collective dialogue and deliberation, as well as how that dialogue and deliberation shapes the larger society. At the end of the chapter, we overview deliberative democratic practices that may improve group functioning. By reading this chapter, students will have a firmer understanding of the important role groups play in a democratic society, and the role of dialogue and deliberation within those groups.

Formation of Social Movements

Social movements are organized groups of people (or social collectives, hence "social" movements) who purposefully come together to work toward a common political or societal goal. When small groups or organizations working on political or social change form on a mass scale, creating a social movement, they have the potential to change the very fabric of history. Consider the changes that happened after the Civil Rights Movement. The movement ultimately led to the Civil Rights Act of 1964, which ended segregation in public spaces and banned employment discrimination. Real, tangible societal changes were made through the mass collection of individuals gathering in different places across the country, at various events, for a common cause. The goals for social movements may differ: some may wish to create societal change or form in resistance to societal change, while others may form in response to an injustice, providing a voice for those who are disenfranchised or building awareness of some societal problem. They may be working to create change for themselves and people like them, as with the many Black members of the Civil Rights Movement, or they may be working to help others, such as the mixed-race groups of Freedom Riders who rode buses in the segregated South to challenge racial segregation laws and practices. Alternatively, they may be organizing to change some potential problem in society, such as anti-war movements or movements to address environmental problems. Movements can also be reactionary responses to social change, such as protests against minority groups that have been granted new freedoms. Weber et al. (2018) explain that social movements "reflect dissatisfaction with sociopolitical environments and are a platform for communicating dissent" (p. 2290). Through collective action, large numbers of people can come together to voice dissent and work to make change (Weber et al., 2018). These processes can have one or more of many potential aims in their collective actions: building solidarity within an oppressed group, expressing resistance to injustice, challenging existing rules and social norms, raising awareness of a problem among specific groups or the public at large, and building support for policy changes, to name a few.

Sometimes preexisting groups shift their focus in response to various actions taken by governments or organizations that have had negative consequences on members of the society. For example, environmental groups and organizations have long existed as part of a broader environmental movement seeking protection of the environment. Larger environmental organizations or environmental justice efforts often focus on more localized cases with the goal of encouraging public participation for environmental decision making (Endres, 2012). Following the British Petroleum's (BP) 2010 Deepwater Horizon oil spill in the Gulf of Mexico, environmental groups like Greenpeace and the Sierra Club joined in forming the Hands Across the Sand Campaign to protect coastlines from fossil fuel pollution. The group continues to fight against pollution from drilling, with its mission statement being to:

> Bring together individuals and organizations to promote a clean energy future across the world and end our dependence on dirty fuels. Gather thousands of Americans and global citizens at beaches and cities to draw metaphorical and actual lines in the sand; human lines in the sand against fossil fuels that threaten our future. Move local, state, national and world leaders to adopt policies encouraging the growth of clean and renewable energy. An opportunity of national and global importance. Now is the time for citizens across the globe to join hands and steer our energy policy away from our dependence on fossil fuels and towards clean energy and renewables.
>
> (Hands Across the Sand, 2021, Mission Statement)

In this case, following the BP Deep Horizon oil spill, larger environmental movements shifted their focus to a localized case. Through this shift, a whole new group was formed. Following the attempted clean-up and ramifications of the spill in 2010, the new group continued its work, with the ultimate goal of encouraging clean and renewable energy sources around the world.

While some social groups are offshoots of other larger groups within a social movement, others form from the ground up. A movement around a crisis dubbed Missing and Murdered Indigenous Women (MMIW), now MMIWG (to include both women *and* girls) formed in response to generations of Indigenous women and girls being the victims of violent crimes, going missing, and murdered, with little or uneven response from authorities. Rather than being a response to a single event, like the BP oil spill example, MMIWG formed in response to a long history of transgressions against a group. The group formed in 2015 in Canada as a **grassroots movement**, or a movement started from the ground up by a dedicated core group of activists, but has since gained traction across the United States (Native Hope, 2022). Today, the group works to inform the public and elected officials on injustices to native women, and fight for new legislation to protect Indigenous women and girls in North America.

Social movements often form in response to some action. They may be formed in response to legislative action (or lack of action), to social injustices, or in response to harm done by a big corporation. They seek to raise awareness or social and legislative consciousness on an issue, to promote social change, and to promote changes in legislation. According to deprivation theory, some groups are formed when societal members feel that they are not receiving equal resources as compared to other group members, that is to say, that a segment of society feels it is being deprived of a resource that others in the society have, or that they themselves feel they deserve or expect to have. Contrary to deprivation theory, resource mobilization theory posits that when group members feel political or societal dissatisfaction, they come together to mobilize various resources to resolve the issue (Kerbo, 1982). In comparing the two theories, Kerbo (1982) explains:

> In place of the deprivation assumption, the resource mobilization perspective focuses attention on the ability of social movement promoters to gain and manipulate resources of power, to organize, to recruit members from exiting voluntary association networks, and to provide individual incentives or coercion in motivating participation in social movement activities.
>
> (p. 646)

Resources may be "feet on the ground" to raise consciousness around an issue, raise money for advertising or to hire lobbyists, or gain media coverage as intermediate goals to an end. Ultimately, the end goal of a social movement is to create social or political change (Coglianese, 2001).

Box 19.1 Historical Snapshot: *The Suffragettes*

Recall, one way in which social movements may create change is through legislative action. Social movements may work toward changing laws to be more socially just. This is exactly what the women's suffrage movement managed to do.

Suffragettes were members of 20th-century activist movements which marched under the banner "Votes for Women," fighting for women to have the right to vote in public elections. Part of the suffrage movement formed in response to the "Cult of True Womanhood." This worldview was related to a woman's subservience and obedience to her husband and place in the household, with the women's four primary virtues to be: "piety, purity, submissiveness, and domesticity" (Welter, 1966, p. 152). As such, this pervasive belief that women should be second to men meant that women did not have the right to be civically engaged.

In response to the beliefs surrounding "True Womanhood," Elizabeth Cady Stanton and Lucretia Mott organized with friends at a summer tea party in 1848, where the group began planning a meeting for women's rights (National Park Services, 2019). After placing an ad in the newspaper, the Seneca Falls convention was organized. Here the Declaration of Sentiments was outlined. Within its opening sentences, this document begins:

> We hold these truths to be self-evident; that all men *and women* are created equal; that they are endowed by their Creator with certain inalienable rights; that among these are life, liberty, and the pursuit of happiness; that to secure these rights governments are instituted, deriving their just powers from the consent of the governed. Whenever any form of Government becomes destructive of these ends, it is the right of those who suffer from it to refuse allegiance to it, and to insist upon the institution of a new government, laying its foundation on such principles, and organizing its powers in such form as to them shall seem most likely to effect their safety and happiness.
>
> (Declaration of Sentiments, 1848)

While some states allowed women to vote following the 15th Amendment, which was ratified in 1870 granted African American men to vote,* it would not be until August of 1920 when women were granted voting rights with the ratification of the 19th Amendment. The Voting Rights Act of 1965 would not be passed for another 45 years, which provided Black women with the right to vote.

What started as a small-group meeting, a tea party among friends, grew into a national movement, eventually becoming the National American Woman Suffrage Association and later the National Woman's Party. The small group that turned into a social movement changed the very fabric of American democracy, allowing women the right to vote.

It should be noted, Jim Crow era laws and norms overturned much of this work, and the vision for a multi-racial democracy was not yet accomplished.

Maintaining a Shared Identity

Larger social movements and more localized community movements alike must share common goals and have shared sense of unity to survive. Even at the small-group level, a shared sense of identity or group belonging is necessary for the group to function. Likewise, collective or group identities have been examined by social scientists as being key elements of social movements, because a collective identity can act as a catalyst for resource mobilization and acts as the glue holding social movements together (Polletta & Jasper, 2001). Collective identities are the feelings of "we-ness" within a social group. It is the perception of sharing a label. No longer does the individual view themselves as working independently, but rather, within the group they view themselves as members of something larger. Collective identities are passed down and expressed through cultural means, such as the sharing of beliefs and values, enacting various rituals, and sharing social norms (Polletta & Jasper, 2001).

Collective identity and social identity are very similar, and both may shape how social groups work; however, they are not synonymous. Like collective identity, social identity causes the individual to stop thinking in terms of "me" and move to thinking in terms of "we." The social category becomes part of the self-concept (Hogg et al., 1995). Tajfel and Turner's (1979) social identity theory describes how individuals define themselves in social terms, often based on larger-scale societal divisions like race, ethnicity, class, and geography. Individual members also gain self-esteem and a sense of worth – at both the individual and group level – by identifying strongly with a group. This higher sense of self and group increases our commitment to the group and motivates us to work harder for the group. One key process that can occur due to social identity is that of in-grouping and out-grouping. Unlike collective identity, where members can be a part of the group without comparing themselves to others, social identity theory describes how groups use relevant out-groups to define themselves. Put differently, groups can be defined not just by who they "are," but by who they "are not" (Brewer, 2001). Take the People for Bernie Sanders movement, a grassroots movement made up from veteran organizers of the Occupy Wall Street movement that supported Bernie Sanders as a presidential candidate (Kasperkevic, 2015). In a statement, the group said: "Our goal is to establish a government that carries out the will of the people, rather than one that serves to increase the profits of the wealthiest 1% at the expense of the rest of us" (Kasperkevie, 2015, para. 16). Like the Occupy Wall Street Movement that came before it, the 1% becomes an identifiable out-group, an "other," which helps to foment social unrest and motivate the group. The group is driven by *not* being the 1%, by having another group to point to as an enemy, in addition to being defined by being part of the "other 99%" of society that is not in that wealthiest 1%.

Shared identity can in some cases be important for group success, especially for larger groups that constitute social movements; it may be less pivotal for smaller groups like community action committees or ad hoc movements trying to accomplish more modest goals. In order to maintain membership in a large ongoing movement, groups must work to maintain a sense of "we-ness," which at the small-group level would translate to entitativity or a shared sense of the group as a collective entity. Though the sense of togetherness is important for group membership, in-grouping and out-grouping can provide members with a feeling of purpose, creating the perception of need for collective action. Finally, sharing a common goal, along with shared values, help unify groups, bonding them together (Polletta & Jasper, 2001).

Where Do Groups Form?

In the previous sections, we have discussed how and why larger social movements form, along with the importance of maintaining a shared group identity. Here, we will discuss how various types of social groups form in various locations, from the small and localized groups to the larger national and global social movements. Furthermore, we will discuss the nature of groups forming and moving between online or virtual spaces to in-person settings. Finally, we will discuss how third spaces create an additional place where dialogue happens in the public sphere.

People form groups to make change at various levels within society. At the *local level*, you may see groups form to distribute flyers and pamphlets, groups of people meet in town-hall meetings to discuss local issues, and small-group meeting in coffee shops or at the local gas station to talk about political issues. If you take time to look around your own community, you may find a variety of groups forming to create political or social change. *Regional level* groups might only act within a state or region. The TogetherOK group, for example, is a grassroots coalition of Oklahoma citizens who work for the best educational, family, and economic outcomes for their local communities through political advocacy and education. At the *national level*, people from across the country take part. Often times, sister chapters exist in major cities across the country. Consider the Occupy Wall Street Movement, which began in Zuccotti Park in New York City. The more localized Occupy Wall Street Movement started at the local level, and though it was influenced by people who were not "locals" per se, it started as a smaller movement, with very structured deliberative communication practices, such as open discussion of group decisions among all meeting attendees (sometimes hundreds of people), volunteer moderators running discussions, and a requirement of near consensus for decisions to be made (Min, 2015). The movement was started by a Canadian magazine, *Adbusters,* as a call for protest against social and economic inequality. Word of the movement spread through the public sphere giving rise to the larger Occupy movement. The Occupy movement became a national movement, giving rise to the "We are the 99%" slogan is used in various locales. A movement that began in New York saw sister movements and protests launch in cities such as Washington, D.C., Houston, Austin, Tampa, and San Francisco. Finally, groups can grow to a *global level*. These groups seek change across international borders. Groups like Greenpeace and PETA have formed large nongovernmental organizations that seek change on a global scale. Groups may begin as more localized, but grow to become a larger movement, as seen in the Occupy Movement example. As the group boundaries grow, from local to regional, or from national to global, so does the complexity of communication and organizational structure (see Figure 19.1).

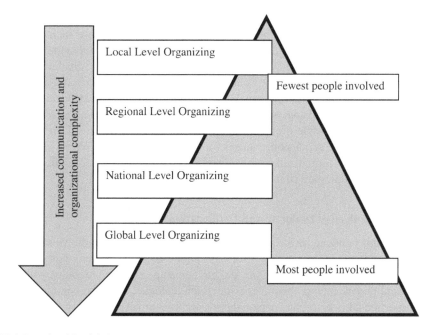

Figure 19.1 Levels of Social Groups.

Regardless of the level, or how big the group is, groups need to have a place to share ideas, form bonds, and make plans. In today's digital society, technology plays a major role in *where* groups are meeting. In her book, *Twitter and Tear Gas: The Power and Fragility of Networked Protest*, Zeynep Tufekci (2017) examines the role of the internet in organizing massive protests and maintaining social movements. Tufekci (2017) describes the role of virtual space in finding like-minded people, planning events, organizing materials and costs, protecting others, and raising consciousness. She explains that the internet played a major role in many modern-day movements, such as the Mexican Zapatista uprising, the Occupy Movement, and the Arab Spring.

Technology allows for both online and offline meeting. Organizers can use social media, such as Twitter or Facebook, to send members to different locations. Tufekci uses the Tea Party movement in the United States as an example. On April 15, 2009, social media was used to organize in-person protests across the country. Social media is also important in the formation of new movements, as, it provides a space to find like-minded people. During the Arab Spring, members from across the Middle East and North Africa were able to draw strength from one another before the protests broke out in late 2010 and 2011. While their political regimes were discouraging environments for political activists, they were able to form groups online, and find friendly allies (Tufekci, 2017). Digital technology is an important tool for groups as they gather members, organize movements, and disseminate messages to a broader audience.

Digital technology allows for the organization of private meetings as well. While some groups may form with the clear goal of creating broad social change, other groups may form to provide a space for like-minded individuals to discuss current events. A study conducted by Emily Van Duyn (2018) titled, "Hidden Democracy: Political Dissent in Rural America," examined a group of rural women who met in secret to talk about politics because they feared the ramifications of "coming out" as liberal in rural conservative hometowns. While digital technology helped members to find meeting places, members met in-person, finding comradery in like-minded others. Rather than practicing political expression in public forums, the women decided to find private spaces to express their political beliefs with others. Essentially a secret political group was formed which met in places like corn fields, where political dissent could take place.

Groups do not have to be large in order to shape the greater public sphere. Recall, voting is a fundamental tenet of democratic systems (Gastil, 2008). Political decisions, such as voting, made on the individual level are influenced through social interactions, people *doing* the work of politics together through political discourse (Van Duyn, 2018). The formation of smaller non-formalized groups, with the purpose of political talk, is an important element of democratic political systems. Political talk does not always occur in formalized groups. Political talk may occur in third spaces. First spaces (home) and second spaces (work) are often spaces for casual political talk, but so too are third spaces, such as lifestyle groups or sporting groups. Groups formed for reasons outside of political or social change can become spaces for political organizing (Wright et al., 2016). The formation of groups, from formalized national level social groups to non-formalized small groups taking place in third spaces, play an important role in shaping our society.

Groups Enabling Collective Dialogue and Deliberation

In addition to groups being an important site for organizing social and political movements, they are also vital for helping citizens gather to discuss public issues. Citizens might gather in-group settings to engage in dialogue on some issue that has come up in their community, with the hope of building a shared understanding about this issue. Such dialogue, in which commonalities are explored, introspection takes place, and personal positionalities are explored may also provide spaces for peacebuilding (Ron et al., 2020), and provide voices or affirmation of special ownership and belonging to marginalized groups (Marceau & Martin, 2020). Note that such dialogue may be formal or informal. Groups of citizens may form to engage in more casual conversations about political issues, a situation that sadly has become more fraught as the United States has become more politically polarized in recent years (Johnson et al., 2019). Citizens might also get involved in formal processes of group deliberation focused on solving a public problem or making a recommendation on a policy question.

These formal and informal types of group conversations serve several important purposes. They may aid in decision-making processes through increasing understanding, helping people to engage in perspective taking and increase empathy for others, building consensus, solving problems, and encouraging collective action around an issue. Group conversations in the form of dialogue or deliberation can help people learn more about a topic by hearing from experts and fellow citizens who may have more knowledge in some areas than they do. For example, learning was an important outcome when an American Indian (AI) health system brought together a group of tribal citizens to discuss the future of biomedical research and treatment with the advent of genomic medicine (Reedy et al., 2020). Though this was a new area for the tribe's health system, the group deliberations on these topics helped give leaders insight into community members' thoughts and concerns about this growing field, and helped citizens learn more about a deeply technical and scientific issue that will become more common in the future. This project was part of a larger research consortium supported by a National Institutes of Health grant that centers on AI and Alaska Native (AN) perspectives, which have been marginalized from much of the practice of biomedical research. In this deliberative forum and two others, believed to be the first such forums on genomics held entirely in Indigenous communities, the Western democratic model of deliberative discussion (described in more detail below) was adapted to fit the context of AI/AN social and cultural norms of conversation, such as offering greater deference to tribal Elders in discussion rather than having strictly egalitarian relations between discussants. The process of developing, conducting, and evaluating these deliberative community forums is described in more detail by Blacksher et al. (2021).

Group discussions might also help people engage in perspective taking, which is when members try to take on the perspective of another member of the group with whom they might disagree. Groups might also help people build a better understanding of other members' views and values, as people share what they think about a public issue and why. Both perspective taking and trying to understand others' views, for example, are key exercises in some group discussions organized by Braver Angels, a non-profit in the United States that is trying to help bridge the widening gap between Democrats and Republicans through thoughtful conversation (Baron et al., 2021).

Group discussions of public issues might also help people persuade others or make up their own mind on an issue, which are important for ensuring that a democratic society moves forward with some policy choices. Such outcomes of persuasion and choice-making are often seen when groups are discussing an issue that is ripe for a decision, like when friends gather ahead of an upcoming election to hear how others plan to vote (Reedy et al., 2016) or when a community needs to decide on a direction for their future (Fung, 2015).

Public groups can also help a community find an outcome or output around which it can build consensus through thoughtful and collaborative discussion. This process of consensus building can give credibility and legitimacy to the output chosen by the community members. For example, community deliberative forums called Consensus Conferences bring together citizens with experts and policy makers to analyze some public issue – often related to some new technology, like the use of biotech in food production – and identify key concerns and core values shared by the public (Einsiedel & Eastlick, 2000). Similar structures can be used to create reports of the forum participants' shared concerns and findings of fact on public issues, as is the case with deliberative forums on genetic sample repositories in Canada (O'Doherty & Burgess, 2009).

Groups of citizens can also be oriented toward problem solving and encouraging collective action, both of which can be particularly challenging for some kinds of public issues like environmental problems, highly technical and risk-related topics, and especially thorny problems. For instance, a community forum on environmental issues related to a changing climate in the coastal region of South Carolina focused the participants on developing potential solutions to climate-related problems in their region, rather than on conflicts over the politics of climate change (Reedy & Anderson, 2019). This community forum utilized deliberative small-group discussions with moderators, and participants listened to experts in the field before discussion. This design aided in the overall success of the forum. Moderators, for example, helped keep conversations from becoming polarized, overly politicized, or one-sided, and helped ensure that all participants could contribute. Discussion goals were provided to keep the group on track. A qualitative analysis of this deliberative forum revealed that through this deliberative forum, rather than feeling politically divided on the issue, participants moved toward a sense of togetherness or "we-ness" related to the risks of climate change and potential solutions (Hurst et al., 2022). The use of deliberative models in public forums, as seen in this example, offers solutions for navigating group community discussions and solving problems related to polarizing topics.

Evaluating and Improving Group Political Discussions

As group political conversations, especially formal discussions aimed at building understanding or solving public problems, have been studied by social scientists more in recent years, one key question has been how such groups work well together – or don't, in some circumstances. Some researchers have turned to political and democratic theories for guidance. But others have looked to theories of group discussion and dynamics, such as the Functional Groups Perspective (Gastil, 2010; Gouran & Hirokawa, 1996). This theoretical perspective laid out five key functions of communication that help a group work well together and reach a good decision or outcome. First, group discussion can build a solid information base about the problem they are facing, so they can best understand their situation; that is, they can assess what they know about the problem and the type of solution they want to arrive at. This first function involves understanding what the desired outcome is. Second, their conversation could try to determine the key values at stake in this context; doing so helps the group to better determine what a "good" outcome looks like for the people involved. Third, the group discussion could identify a broad range of solutions to ensure the group is really considering all of its options and not settling too quickly on a choice that is not optimal. Some choices may be *acceptable,* but not the *best* solution. By identifying a range of solutions, members can determine what option best fits their needs. Fourth, they should also weigh the pros and cons and tradeoffs between solutions to evaluate their options with respect to the information and values they have discussed. Last, they should use some fair procedures to make the best decision possible. Through procedures, such as deliberative democracy, egalitarian decision-making processes can occur through respectful and informed discussion where all group members have a voice and a variety of perspectives are considered, which generally leads to decisions more in line with what the group values (Burkhalter et al., 2002).

Deliberative democracy scholar John Gastil used this perspective as a starting point for his foundational framework for analyzing group political deliberation (2008), applying these five concepts to the context of political conversation and other political processes. Citizens deliberating on a community problem should try to enact these five functions through their deliberative process, Gastil argued. For example, after gathering relevant information about the problem and determining the key values at stake in this area, they should spend part of their discussion brainstorming possible solutions to that problem and earnestly consider those solutions. And it is not enough for a group to settle on a solution that they prefer – they should ensure they are evaluating those possible solutions with respect to key political information and to the political values of the community members. This might involve each member sharing their thoughts and opinions, seeking outside speakers or *experts* on a topic to come talk with the group, or reading and sharing sources online which show multiple perspectives. Unlike work organizations where a manager or owner might make a final choice, such groups should make decisions in a democratic way, Gastil says, through voting or some other process of opinion expression. All of these elements make up what Gastil refers to as the Analytic Process of group political deliberation, which focuses on policy problems and the effectiveness and legitimacy of their solutions.

But there is much more to group interaction than simply the effectiveness of a group's discussions and the solutions it develops. There is also the quality of the communication that occurs in that group and the social relations between its members. This also holds true for political discussion groups, which led Gastil to creating a typology of several communicative functions that he calls the Social Process of group deliberation. Political groups should not just have an environment in which people are free to speak up, he argues, but rather should ensure equitable speaking opportunities for everyone. People should take turns when speaking and perhaps consider other actions, like relying on a facilitator, or asking some members to yield their time to others who have not yet had a chance to speak. The group should ensure mutual comprehension in the discussion, speaking in plain language and without technical jargon, and allowing for clarification when some members are confused or have misunderstood a point. Group members should consider other ideas and experiences, by listening well and earnestly to their fellow members and truly considering what they have to say about an issue even if – and especially when – they disagree at the outset. Last, group members should respect other participants in the discussion, starting from an assumption of good intentions and acknowledging useful contributions – again, even and especially when those participants may be ideological opponents. This last function can seem especially challenging during an era of extreme political polarization, but strong communicative processes – such as an assertive moderator, norms of mutual respect and thoughtful conversation, turn taking practices, and the like – can help ensure that participants act with good intentions and that deliberations are productive despite strong ideological differences (Gastil & Knobloch, 2020).

Evidence-Based Recommendations for Practice

Frameworks like Gastil's, which enumerate the analytic and social processes that can occur within vibrant group political conversations, can be useful for multiple applications. As seen in some recent studies of governance processes and collaborative decision-making efforts, such frameworks can help scholars and practitioners evaluate a public engagement process and determine how well it did in reaching some of the ideals of "good" democracy. For instance, when the state of Oregon decided to run a pilot test of a process called the Citizens' Initiative Review (CIR) to let groups of citizens advise their fellow voters on upcoming ballot measures, they relied on a team led by Gastil to help evaluate the pilot test and determine whether it was a good process that was worth continuing (Gastil & Knobloch, 2020). The evaluative framework used on the first CIR processes in 2010 built on Gastil's original framework, giving an A to F letter grade (i.e., collecting the ratings of how frequently each major segment of the process accomplished these functions, as applicable) to each of the two forums on the several criteria above, as well as two additional criteria geared to the specific mission of the CIR (Knobloch et al., 2013). As Gastil and Knobloch wrote about in their 2020 book "Hope for Democracy," this evaluation was instrumental in helping the CIR become an official political institution in Oregon for several election cycles, serving as a source of unbiased, citizen-developed guidance on what can sometimes be very confusing policy questions faced by voters in the state.

In addition to being useful in evaluating group political discussions from the ideals of deliberative democracy, normative frameworks like Gastil's and others (i.e., theoretical frameworks that put forward an ideal for which to strive) can be useful for trying to build new discussion groups or improve existing discussion. For instance, when a group is first forming and wants to try to enact democratic ideals in a practical way, these kinds of frameworks can help guide organizers as they design the discussion and decision-making practices that will be used as the group develops (Gastil, 1993; Reedy et al., 2020). Alternatively, organizations and institutions looking to improve existing discussion procedures can try to incorporate elements from these frameworks to bolster the deliberative quality of their processes, though such reforms are not always easy (Stromer-Galley et al., 2012). For example, groups may look for ways to be more inclusive in who is involved in decision-making processes and seek out formats where voting on decisions is encouraged. Groups may also assign a member to act as a moderator, to keep topics on track and to ensure that everyone, or at least all perspectives, get to share. It is important to note that frameworks like Gastil's can be useful for a broad range of contexts beyond politics, such as classrooms, workplaces, and voluntary and social organizations – nearly any setting in which groups of people are engaging in discussion and collective decision making.

For people and groups engaging in social and political organizing, many years of scholarship and practical work in these areas offers some tips for success. The reality of modern organizing via the internet and social media offers a lot of promise, but Tufekci (2017) and others argue that online platforms are not the only necessary element to success in organizing. Rather, such online settings give people and groups affordances, or possibilities of actions that can be taken using the tools of the online world, like communicating quickly with a spread-out group of people or broadcasting a protest action to the rest of the world. Using those tools creatively and to their full potential is also important. Unimaginative and non-interactive forms of media use seem to be less effective in engaging people than efforts to utilize the interactivity of online spaces (Wells, 2015). In addition, successful movements often require more than just online engagement: they often require in-person activities like meetings, marches, and sit-ins to help effect change more broadly. In-person performative actions, such as ritualized performance of meetings and sit-ins, binds group members together, creating a sense of belongingness (Power, 2009). Regardless of what groups individuals form a sense of belonging to, the *feeling* of belonging promotes both psychological and physical well-being (Hagerty et al., 1996). In addition, such in-person activities are often higher in public profile and more confrontational to the existing political order than entirely online activities like hashtag activism, in which people post messages of support for a movement but may not take any in-person action (Tufekci, 2017). Finally, social and political groups seem to be on the rise again in recent years after long declines during the 20th century (Putnam, 2001). Students interested in trying to bring about positive social change may not realize there are groups in their area working on a wide range of issues; seeking out such causes can give people a great opportunity to get involved on an issue that matters to them.

Conclusion

In this chapter, we provided a review of some of the ways that small groups can be a vital location for social and political organizing and for collective discussion and decision making. The sections on organizing provided insight into key theories of social and political movements, such as the deprivation and resource motivation theories, the social identity perspective, and online organizing. The sections on collective discussion and decision making helped define and explain the concept of deliberation in a democratic society, and laid out the ways that groups of people may self-organize or be brought together through a formal public process to deliberate on some topic and reach a decision. Last, we provided several evidence-based recommendations for practical attempts to get involved in social and political movements and make them more successful, as well as ways to apply the ideals of democracy to evaluating deliberative processes and to improving existing organizations and practices. Students reading this chapter should have a better understanding of these different contexts in which groups can help shape society, both politically and socially, and be able to provide some examples of these kinds of groups. Students should also have a sense of how group dialogue and deliberation can help influence society through informal talk and formal processes of discussion and decision making.

Additional Resources From the National Park Services

https://www.nps.gov/articles/declaration-of-sentiments.htm#_ftn1
https://www.nps.gov/wori/learn/historyculture/declaration-of-sentiments.htm
https://www.nps.gov/articles/000/did-women-earn-the-right-to-vote-on-august-18-1920.htm

Further Readings

Gastil, J., & Knobloch, K. R. (2020). *Hope for democracy: How citizens can bring reason back into politics.* Oxford University Press.
Polletta, F., & Jasper, J. M. (2001). Collective identity and social movements. *Annual Review of Sociology,* 27, 283–305. https://doi.org/10.1146/annurev.soc.27.1.283
Tufekci, Z. (2017). *Twitter and tear gas: The power and fragility of networked protest.* Yale University Press.

Glossary

Deliberation   Deliberation is a group-level process that allows us to examine issues, topics, and problems; think about options and trade-offs; and make collective decisions. The end goal of deliberation is to solve a problem (or problems) or make decisions. Through thoughtful and careful group discussion, deliberative processes allow for multiple perspectives in the decision-making process.

Dialogue   Dialogue is a discussion process that allows people to share their perspectives and experiences with each other often times regarding difficult topics. Rather than having the end goal of making a decision or solving a problem, as is the case with deliberation, dialogue carries the goals of exploring commonalities, re-examining personal positions, and discovering new ways of thinking. Dialogue can occur at the interpersonal, small group, organizational, or larger mass level.

Grassroots movement   A movement started from the ground up by a dedicated core group of activists.

Social movements   Social movements are organized groups of people who purposefully come together to work toward a common goal through collective action. The goal of a social movement is to make change, either political or social change, or to empower disempowered or oppressed populations.

Society   A group of people, recruited at least in part by the sexual reproduction of its members, sharing a self-sufficient system of action that is capable of existing longer than the life-span of an individual.

References

Aberle, D. F., Cohen, A. K., Davis, A. K., Levy, M. J. Jr., & Sutton, F. X. (1950). The functional prerequisites of a society. *Ethics, 60,* 100–111.

Baron, H., Blair, R., Choi, D. D., Gamboa, L., Gottlieb, J., Robinson, A. L., Rosenzweig, S., Turnbull, M., & West, E. A. (2021). *Can Americans depolarize? Assessing the effects of reciprocal group reflection on partisan polarization.* OSF Preprints. https://doi.org/10.31219/osf.io/3x7z8

Blacksher, E., Hiratsuka, V. Y., Blanchard, J. W., Lund, J. R., Reedy, J., Beans, J. A., Saunkeah, B., Peercy, M., Byars, C., Yracheta, J., Tsosie, K. S., O'Leary, M., Ducheneaux, G., & Spicer, P. G. (2021). Deliberations with American Indian and Alaska native people about the ethics of genomics: An adapted model of deliberation used with three tribal communities in the United States. *AJOB Empirical Bioethics*, 1–15. https://doi.org/10.1080/23294515.2021.1925775

Brewer, M. B. (2001). Ingroup identification and intergroup conflict: When does ingroup love become outgroup hate. In R. D. Ashmore, L. Jussim, & D. Wilder (Eds.), *Social identity, intergroup conflict, and conflict reduction* (pp. 17–41). Oxford University Press.

Burkhalter, S., Gastil, J., & Kelshaw, T. (2002). A conceptual definition and theoretical model of public deliberation in small face-to-face groups. *Communication Theory*, *12*, 398–422. https://doi.org/10.1111/j.1468-2885.2002.tb00276.x

Coglianese, C. (2001). Social movements, law, and society: The institutionalization of the environmental movement. *University of Pennsylvania Law Review*, *150*(1), 85–118. https://doi.org/10.2307/3312913

Declaration of Sentiments. (1848, July 19). The First Women's Rights Convention. Seneca Falls, NY. "Declaration of Sentiments." National Park Services. Retrieved August 1, 2023, from https://www.nps.gov/wori/learn/historyculture/declaration-of-sentiments.htm

Einsiedel, E. F., & Eastlick, D. L. (2000). Consensus conferences as deliberative democracy: A communications perspective. *Science Communication*, *21*(4), 323–343. https://doi.org/10.1177/1075547000021004001

Endres, D. (2012). Sacred land or national sacrifice zone: The role of values in the Yucca Mountain participation process. *Environmental Communication*, *6*(3), 328–345. https://doi.org/10.1080/17524032.2012.688060

Fung, A. (2015). Putting the public back into governance: The challenges of citizen participation and its future. *Public Administration Review*, *75*(4), 513–522. https://doi.org/10.1111/puar.12361

Gastil, J. (1993). *Democracy in small groups: Participation, decision making and communication.* New Society Publishers.

Gastil, J. (2008). *Political communication and deliberation.* Sage Publications.

Gastil, J. (2010). *The group in society.* Sage.

Gouran, D. S., & Hirokawa, R. Y. (1996). Functional theory and communication in decision-making and problem-solving groups: An expanded view. In *Communication and group decision making* (2nd ed., pp. 55–80). Sage Publications. https://doi.org/10.4135/9781452243764.n3

Hagerty, B., Williams, R., Coyne, J., & Early, M. (1996). Sense of belonging and indicators of social and psychological functioning. *Archives of Psychiatric Nursing*, *10*(4), 235–244. https://doi.org/10.1016/S0883-9417(96)80029-X

Hands Across the Sand. (2021). Mission Statement. https://handsacrossthesand.org/

Hogg, M. A., Terry, J., & White, K. M. (1995). A tale of two theories: A critical comparison of identity theory with social identity theory. *Social Psychology Quarterly*, *58*(4), 255–269. https://doi.org/10.2307/2787127

Hurst, E. H., Trujillo-Falcón, J. E., Reedy, J., & Anderson, C. (2022). Citizen deliberation at South Carolina's 'Our Coastal Future Forum': Talking through risk related to climate change. *Journal of Risk Research*, *25*(6), 764–777. https://doi.org/10.1080/13669877.2021.2020882

Johnson, A. J., Bostwick, E. N., & Cionea, I. A. (2019). Talking Turkey: Effects of family discussions about the 2016 election over the thanksgiving holiday. *Journal of Family Communication*, *19*(1), 63–76. https://doi.org/10.1080/15267431.2018.1543688

Kasperkevic, J. (September 16, 2015). Occupy Wall Street: Four years later. *The Guardian.* https://www.theguardian.com/world/ng-interactive/2015/sep/16/occupy-wall-street-four-years-later-timeline

Kerbo, H. R. (1982). Movements of "crisis" and movements of "affluence": A critique of deprivation and resource mobilization theories. *Journal of Conflict Resolution*, *26*(4), 645–663. https://doi.org/10.1177/0022002782026004004

Knobloch, K. R., Gastil, J., Reedy, J., & Cramer Walsh, K. (2013). Did they deliberate? Applying an evaluative model of democratic deliberation to the Oregon Citizens' initiative review. *Journal of Applied Communication Research*, *41*, 105–125. https://doi.org/10.1080/00909882.2012.760746

Marceau, S. G., & Martin, P. M. (2020). 'Dialogue divides if it is not fair': Québec First Nations' youth call for responsive spaces of citizenship. *Social and Cultural Geography*, *21*(6), 767–787. https://doi.org/10.1080/14649365.2018.1514648

Min, S. (2015). Occupy Wall Street and deliberative decision making: Translating theory to practice. *Communication, Culture, and Critique*, *8*(1), 73–89. https://doi.org/10.1111/cccr.12074

National Park Services. (2019). Women's Rights National Historical Park – New York. https://www.nps.gov/wori/index.htm

Native Hope. (2022). Missing and murdered indigenous women (MMIW). https://www.nativehope.org/missing-and-murdered-indigenous-women-mmiw

O'Doherty, K. C., & Burgess, M. M. (2009). Engaging the public on Biobanks: Outcomes of the BC Biobank deliberation. *Public Health Genomics*, *12*(4), 203–215. https://doi.org/10.1159/000167801

Polletta, F., & Jasper, J. M. (2001). Collective identity and social movements. *Annual Review of Sociology*, 27, 283–305. https://doi.org/10.1146/annurev.soc.27.1.283

Power, J. (2009). Rites of belonging: Grief, memorial and social action. *Health Sociology Review*, *18*(3), 260–272. https://doi.org/10.5172/hesr.2009.18.3.260

Putnam, R. (2001). *Bowling alone: The collapse and revival of American community*. Simon and Schuster.

Reedy, J., & Anderson, C. (2019). Group communication and security—small groups for good or ill: Developing a group communication approach to security. In B. C. Taylor & H. Bean (Eds.), *The handbook of communication and security*. Routledge.

Reedy, J., Blanchard, J. W., Lund, J., Spicer, P. G., Byars, C., Peercy, M., Saunkeah, B., & Blacksher, E. (2020). Deliberations about genomic research and biobanks with citizens of the Chickasaw nation. *Frontiers in Genetics*, *11*. https://doi.org/10.3389/fgene.2020.00466

Reedy, J., Gastil, J., & Moy, P. (2016). From the secret ballot to the public vote: Examining voters' experience of political discussion in vote-by-mail elections. *Political Communication*, *33*(1), 39–58. https://doi.org/10.1080/10584609.2014.969462

Ron, Y., Suleiman, C., & Maoz, I. (2020). Women for peace: Promoting dialogue and peace through Facebook? *Social Media + Society*, *6*(4), 1–11. https://doi.org/10.1177/2056305120984461

Schumpeter, P. (1942). *Capitalism, socialism, and democracy*. Harper & Brothers.

Stromer-Galley, J., Webb, N., & Muhlberger, P. (2012). Deliberative e-rulemaking project: Challenges to enacting real world deliberation. *Journal of Information Technology & Politics*, *9*(1), 82–96. https://doi.org/10.1080/19331681.2012.635971

Tajfel, H., & Turner, J. C. (1979). An integrative theory of intergroup conflict. In W. G. Austin & S. Worshel (Eds.), *Social psychology of intergroup relations* (pp. 33–47). Brooks, Cole.

Tufekci, Z. (2017). *Twitter and tear gas: The power and fragility of networked protest*. Yale University Press.

Van Duyn, E. (2018). Hidden democracy: Political dissent in rural America. *Journal of Communication*, *68*(5), 965–987. https://doi.org/10.1093/joc/jqy042

Weber, K., Dejmanee, T., & Rhode, F. (2018). The 2017 Women's March on Washington: An analysis of protest-sign messages. *International Journal of Communication* (Online), 2289–2313. https://ijoc.org/index.php/ijoc/article/view/8043

Wells, C. (2015). *The civic organization and the digital citizen: Communicating engagement in a networked age*. Oxford University Press.

Welter, B. (1966). The cult of true womanhood: 1820-1860. *American Quarterly*, *18*(2), 151–174. https://doi.org/10.2307/2711179

Wright, S., Graham, T., & Jackson, D. (2016). Third space, social media, and everyday political talk. In A. Bruns, G. Enli, E. Skogerbø, A. Olof Larsson, & C. Christensen (Eds.), The Routledge companion to social media and politics (1st ed., pp. 74–88). Routledge. https://doi.org/10.4324/9781315716299-6

20   Online Communities and Big Data

Jeremy Foote and Sohyeon Hwang

Chapter Objectives

- Understand the key features of online communities.
- Understand how group processes are influenced by the features of online communities.
- Understand how digital trace data can be used (and misused) in studying online communities.

Introduction

In January of 2021, a number of members of the Reddit community "r/wallstreetbets" argued that stock in the retail video game store GameStop was underpriced. Perhaps more importantly, they pointed out that wealthy hedge funds had "shorted" the stock. When shorting a stock, a hedge fund borrows shares of the stock from a broker and sells them immediately, hoping to buy the stock later at a lower price so they can return the shares to the broker and pocket the difference. Members of r/wallstreetbets argued that if the community banded together to buy GameStop shares then they could drive the stock price up. This would force the hedge funds into a "short squeeze" where they would have to buy the stock back at the new higher price, driving the price up even further. Thus, community members could both make money *and* stick it to the wealthy hedge funds.

Amazingly, their plan mostly worked. As r/wallstreetbets members bought GameStop stock the price rose sharply and when deadlines for the hedge funds to return the borrowed stock grew closer, r/wallstreetbets members convinced each other to avoid selling the stock (and cashing in on their gains). In the end, a number of hedge funds lost a lot of money and a number of r/wallstreetbets members made a lot of money (Phillips et al., 2021) – although like many bubbles, the price eventually fell and other community members lost money. The chaos created by the community's actions led to emergency stock freezes, Congressional hearings, and class-action lawsuits.

So how did a group of strangers, communicating through a simple web forum, manage to coordinate and motivate their members to the point that they were willing to take huge financial risks? The case of r/wallstreetbets is in many ways an anomaly, but it serves as a clear example of the impact and potential of online communities. Countless other online communities serve as important gathering places for people to socialize, seek and share information, and collaborate on shared projects. Millions of people spend millions of hours writing code, editing articles, and engaging in public conversations. In this chapter, we talk about what online communities are, some key features that influence how they operate as groups, and how the data from online platforms is enabling exciting new group-based research.

DOI: 10.4324/9781003227458-23

What Are Online Communities?

We define online communities as virtual spaces where people freely and voluntarily convene around a shared interest. A virtual "space" is a communal online interface that allows interaction between group members, such as forums, wikis, or GitHub projects. In online communities, the shared space is often (but not always) public and all group members experience it in basically the same way. Communities vary in their particular social structure and size, as well as in what interface they use to communicate.

Contemporary online communities take many different forms, which is part of what makes them so interesting. In addition to Reddit and other online forums, question and answer sites like Yahoo! Answers or StackOverflow, teams of online gamers, online learning platforms like Scratch, or even the comment sections of news articles, gaming streams, or blogs could all be considered online communities. Despite this diversity, not all online interactions happen in online communities. For example, two other prominent types of online interactions include: virtual teams, which are distributed work teams who coordinate and communicate using online tools, but are obligated to do so as part of their employment; and social media (like Instagram, Snapchat, or TikTok), where individuals experience a personalized "stream" of content.

Attributes of Online Communities

One way of thinking about how groups work is the Input-Process-Output model (Ilgen et al., 2005). According to this model, groups have a set of inputs, including their skills, attributes, resources, and raw materials. Through communication and other group processes, they transform these inputs into outputs. We use this model as a way of organizing some of the key features of online communities. In *inputs*, we discuss why and how people participate in online communities; in *processes*, we discuss the social and technical processes underpinning interactions and why those matter; and in *outputs*, we discuss the typical outcomes and consequences of online communities.

Input

The primary inputs of a group are its members' time, skills, knowledge, and contributions, such as posts, comments, or messages. Online communities differ wildly from many other types of groups when it comes to how difficult it is to participate, how visible membership is to others, who is allowed to participate, and what motivations group members have.

Degrees of Engagement

Often, joining an online community is as easy as clicking a button. The low barriers to entry and exit in online communities necessitate a broad definition of participation and membership. In face-to-face groups, for example, it is very clear who is present and participating in a group. In online communities, on the other hand, membership can be basically invisible. Indeed, often the vast majority of participants of online communities are **lurkers** who consume content without posting in the community (Nonnecke & Preece, 2000). Even among those who do contribute content, there are stark differences in degrees of engagement. While most participants contribute very little, a few participants may spend hours each day contributing content to a community. This pattern of participation inequality is surprisingly consistent across online communities (see Figure 20.1). It is tempting to see lurkers and low-effort contributors as free-riders who benefit from the efforts of others (c.f., Olson, 1965). In many contexts, those free-riding on group efforts may be subject to

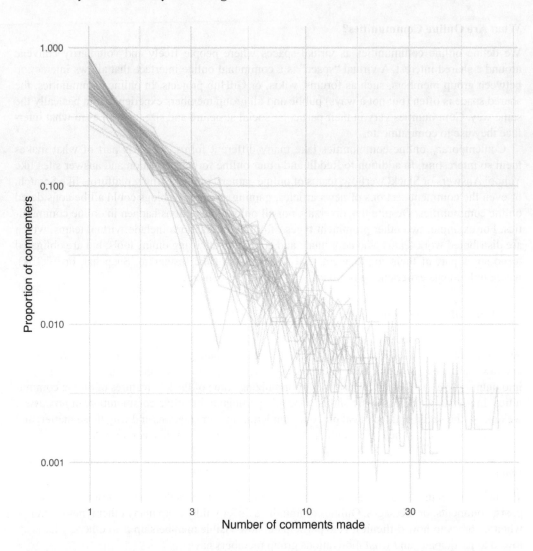

Figure 20.1 Number of Comments in Subreddits (From Foote, 2022).

This figure from Foote (2022) shows the number of comments per person for 100 randomly selected subreddits active in January 2017, with the most prolific 5% of users removed. The *x*-axis shows the number of comments, and the *y*-axis is the proportion of commenters making that number of comments. In every single case, the vast majority of contributors make only a few contributions. Both axes are logged, so the distribution is even more unequal than it looks.

social or formal sanctions, but the relative invisibility of lurkers and the low barriers to exit make some types of sanctions both more difficult and less effective in online communities (Gibbs et al., 2021). On the other hand, lurkers may be seen as the "audience" for the content produced and a larger audience can encourage greater participation by active participants (Zhang & Zhu, 2011).

Low costs of joining and leaving – combined with the fact that communities often exist on platforms – enable people to participate in *multiple* communities much more easily than is possible in face-to-face groups. This mode of engagement is also substantively different from participation in virtual teams, where team membership is typically more restricted and less flexible. One implication of this is that just as it is difficult to draw a clear line around who is a member of an on-line community it is also difficult to draw clear lines between different communities – the bounda-ries between them can be indistinct as conversations and members move between communities.

Anonymity and Pseudonymity

The virtual nature of online spaces makes it possible for participants to be **pseudonymous** (or even entirely anonymous) in ways that are usually impossible in other kinds of groups. While we might think that this would simply make relationships more difficult and norms more difficult to enforce, the influence of anonymity is complicated. In some cases, anonymity does have a disinhibition effect, leading to anti-social behavior (Suler, 2004). However, anonymity can also help people to control what aspects of their identity they reveal, and to whom, allowing them to participate in groups that they don't yet want to attach to their offline identities (e.g., LGBTQ+ groups providing support for people who haven't yet come out) (Ammari et al., 2019). We discuss additional impacts of anonymity on group processes in the *process* section below.

Motivations for Participation

One argument behind why online communities succeed is that they are able to harness the contribu-tions of people who contribute for very different reasons (Benkler, 2002). *Uses and gratifications theory* proposes that people intentionally seek out multiple types of media in order to satisfy dif-ferent needs (Ruggiero, 2000). Researchers have found that participants seek out different online communities to fit their diverse needs (TeBlunthuis et al., 2022). Broadly speaking, researchers have identified many different motivations for participating in online communities, including connect-ing with others, information-seeking and -sharing, entertainment, and feeling a sense of belonging (Lampe et al., 2010; Ren et al., 2012). It's important to note one motivation that is missing – while most production-oriented offline groups (like work teams) use financial compensation as a primary motivation, even in online communities focused on production financial compensation is rare.

Process

Most groups are trying to do something. This might be as simple as entertaining other group mem-bers, or as complicated as building software or designing rockets. In order to meet those goals, groups need to coordinate who does what, make group decisions, socialize newcomers, etc. In offline groups, much of this work happens through synchronous meetings and interactions. In online communities, processes are often remote and asynchronous, mediated by user interfaces, algorithms, and platforms, and participated in by a rotating host of volunteers.

Communication Tools

Much of the communication in an online community happens directly, through posts, comments, and talk pages. Treem and Leonardi (2013) argue that online communication tools have four attrib-utes that have the potential to dramatically influence how groups organize: visibility, persistence, editability, and association. Visibility refers to the fact that conversations and actions are often accessible and searchable by others, providing new ways to share knowledge about who knows what, also called "transactive memory" (Wegner, 1987). Persistence refers to the way that commu-nications can remain available long after they were created, making them valuable shared public repositories that can be retrieved and built upon over time. Editability refers to both the ability of group members to think carefully and edit messages before making them visible as well as the ability in most group software to edit communications after posting. This can help group members to control how they present themselves and how they are perceived by others. Finally, association refers to the visibility of connections between different group members or between group members and content. Treem and Leonardi (2013) argue that among other influences, association can make social relationships more likely and increase social capital.

Shared, persistent content provides another unique communicative opportunity for online communities called **stigmergic communication**. Stigmergy is the idea that communication can happen through an artifact itself (Heylighen, 2016). This is most obvious for open source software or wiki communities, where the community has a clear shared artifact they are working on together. For example, a wiki community member might make a link to a non-existing page to signal that someone should create it. Stigmergy-like interactions occur even in conversation-based communities, where interactions are often mediated by algorithms. For example, many conversation-based communities like Reddit rely on non-linguistic communication in the form of reactions and likes, upvotes/downvotes, or sharing in order to determine what content to prioritize or to hide. At times the primary interaction of online communities may in fact not be interpersonal communication but instead interaction with the shared digital artifact.

Structure and Hierarchy

In firms and other kinds of offline groups, one role of hierarchy is to coordinate actions and to make sure the organization is moving in the same direction (Coase, 1937). Even very large production-based online communities like Wikipedia almost completely lack a formal structure for assigning work: members work on what they want, when they want. Researchers have found that contributors often self-select into various "roles," performing actions like copy-editing, cleaning up after vandals, or welcoming newcomers (Welser et al., 2011). Although there are failures (Champion & Hill, 2021), this process works surprisingly well. One explanation is that the vast scale and low barriers to entry allow those with expertise to identify where improvements are needed and to make them (Benkler, 2002).

An important exception to the formal structurelessness of online communities is the role of moderators. One result of low barriers to entry and anonymity is that many online communities deal with many newcomers and bad-faith actors, and some community members act as moderators, who use powerful technical tools like bans and deletion of content. Often, moderator decisions are without recourse or appeal, and online communities can act as fiefdoms (Schneider, 2022). Even when moderators are chosen via more democratic means, those with the time and interest hold outsized power as measured by contributing to policy or having their contributions valued (Matei & Britt, 2017).

Of course, groups also undergo other emergent processes to shape norms and make decisions. Gibbs et al. (2021) argue that many online communities are able to exert "concertive control" on their members. The original theory of concertive control explained how in some conditions members of a work group will surveil each other, sanctioning norm violators and reinforcing rule-followers without management intervention (Barker, 1993). Gibbs et al. (2021) argue that the persistent visibility of interactions as well as technical tools like voting provide ways for online communities to develop and enforce norms even without strong interpersonal relationships or top-down moderation.

Algorithms and Bots

The communication and behavior of online community members is deeply influenced by the technical aspects of the platforms on which they reside. In particular, the algorithms driving and prioritizing certain posts and content over others can alter the context in which group communication happens and how it is perceived. For example, many communities include a voting system which automatically hides comments which have been downvoted by others or which come from untrusted users (Lampe & Resnick, 2004). It is easy to see how systems like this shape which voices have influence.

Another distinct dynamic in online communities is the role of automated agents (i.e., bots). While there are some malignant bots, bots also act as beneficial, semi-visible group members, helping to moderate content, welcome newcomers, and enforce group norms (Seering et al., 2018). For example, a number of bots on Wikipedia identify and block vandals, fix typos, and alert contributors to possible problems (Geiger & Halfaker, 2013). By both contributing and shaping content in online communities, bots substantially change how communication flows within and across members of groups.

Scale

The software and self-organizing processes of online communities allow them to exist across very different scales. While most communities are very small (Hwang & Foote, 2021), the same "space" can grow to accommodate hundreds of thousands of members (or more). How easily a group can scale depends on its goals and the software it uses. Voting-based conversation communities like Reddit may just need to add more moderators to handle a greater number of vandals while an open-source software project may need to add additional processes to manage contributions and ensure quality.

Output

Online communities frequently have outputs that are distinct from those of other types of groups. The tools of text-based, asynchronous communication which are the backbone of most online groups mean that many community outputs are also text-based, collaborative information goods, like wikis, open source software, or curated conversations. However, online communities also have relational and emotional outputs and produce impacts beyond their virtual spaces.

Information Goods

For some communities, the production of a shared artifact – a **public information good** (Fulk et al., 1996) – is the explicit goal. Fan communities on sites like Fandom, for example, collate information about the media content (e.g., television series or comics) they are fans of, recording detailed backstories and histories of characters as well as creating pages on other world-building aspects of the media such as fictional locations and creatures (Mittell, 2009). Other online communities facilitate the production of open source software, such as those on GitHub (Dabbish et al., 2012), or serve as important spaces for learning, such as those on StackOverflow or Reddit centered around specific skills like programming and design (Cheng et al., 2022).

Just like many face-to-face groups, some types of online communities do not produce clearly identifiable shared artifacts. However, online communities almost always produce a digital record of their interactions. In other words, by storing informational exchanges, online communities inadvertently produce a persistent, searchable public informational archive that may benefit later viewers, in addition to any coordinated efforts that come out of the community.

Attachment and Identity

Distinct from the information or entertainment that online community artifacts and conversations provide, they can also produce social outputs just like many other kinds of groups, including support, camaraderie, and friendship (Ren et al., 2012). Because online community members are often strangers to one another and, in many cases, pseudoanonymous to each other, early news articles and books about online communities expressed shock and surprise that people could actually form meaningful relationships and a shared identity simply through text (Rheingold, 1993; Seabrook, 1998).

However, although dyadic friendships appear to be rare even in small online communities (Hwang & Foote, 2021), people can still form a strong sense of group identity, trust each other, and find both informational and emotional support from groups of online strangers (Ren et al., 2012). As we hinted at earlier, there are aspects of online communities that may actually make forming a group identity easier. One is that groups are often focused on very specific and niche topics, which can appeal to individuals who already have a deep interest in the topic and are looking to find like-minded others. Other groups are explicitly centered on identity, such as the AAPI communities examined by Dosono and Semaan (2019). Second, the social identity model of deindividuation effects (SIDE) model suggests that pseudonymity and text-based communication can actually help people to focus less on the individual members of a group and to form a deeper relationship with the group as a whole (Reicher et al., 1995). Another possible explanation for the cohesion in many online communities is that the barriers to leaving are so low – those who disagree with a group decision or norm may just leave rather than creating schisms in the group (Hirschman, 1970).

Offline Outcomes

Online communities can influence people's beliefs and behaviors beyond interactions in the online space, including members' opinions on social issues as well as their willingness to participate in offline activism (Greijdanus et al., 2020). For example, Salehi et al. (2015) describe how Dynamo, a community platform designed to support Amazon Mechanical Turk workers, enabled community members to form publics around issues and mobilize collective campaigns to make their needs visible and to improve working conditions.

Unfortunately, online communities can also influence their members in destructive ways. Hannah (2021) argues that the QAnon conspiracy theory – which has led to multiple violent crimes – was enabled thanks in part to the way that anonymous online communities can provide legitimacy to conspiratorial thinking. More broadly, Massanari (2017) describes how the design, algorithms, and politics of a community platform can enable "toxic technocultures" that foster harassment campaigns including hate speech, doxxing, and threats of harm. On the other hand, platforms can take actions that lead to less toxic and destructive content as described in Box 20.1.

Implications for Group Communication

In summary, online communities are typically composed of an ever-changing group of pseudonymous strangers with little formal hierarchy or direction, embedded in a complex ecosystem of related communities. Researchers have devoted significant attention to some aspects of how online community features influence group processes and group communication. For example, researchers have shown the importance of technological affordances in shaping how people in online groups communicate with one another (Kraut et al., 2012). At the same time, many aspects of group communication research have not been addressed explicitly and new theories and researches are needed, especially around online community platforms as interdependent, self-organizing, multi-group systems. As we argue in the next section, the large-scale data from online communities is ideal for addressing this and other group communication topics.

Box 20.1 The Effect of Community Bans

While we have focused this chapter on the positive aspects of online communities, many individuals and entire communities engage in racism, political extremism, misogyny, or bigotry. One common approach platforms take to dealing with problematic communities is a ban, when the community space is removed from the platform.

Does this work, or do members of a banned community simply move to different communities and behave in the same way? In 2015, Reddit changed their platform policies and unexpectedly banned a large number of their most troublesome subreddits. Chandrasekharan et al. (2017) looked at what happened, finding that the ban was effective: users who had been active in toxic communities and stayed on Reddit reduced their use of toxic language dramatically, and there was not a significant uptick in toxic language in the other communities that they joined.

This is great news for platforms, but we might ask the same question at the platform level: if a community is banned, do its users simply migrate to a new platform? Ribeiro et al. (2021) studied two cases where users from banned communities created their own new standalone sites. They found that these new communities were much less popular, with fewer users, posts, and new recruits. However, in one of the two cases studied users on the new platform showed increased linguistic markers of toxicity and radicalization.

There are a few lessons that we might take from this research, some of which echo arguments from this chapter. One lesson is the power of sociotechnical tools: banning turned out to be a simple but effective tool. Another lesson is the importance of group norms to shape behavior; users who behaved badly in a toxic community changed their behavior when participating in spaces with more prosocial norms.

Finally, there seems to be a lesson about the importance of platforms of related communities. If we imagine online communities like digital "clubs" with meet in digital "rooms," a ban is like kicking a club out of its meeting place. Even though finding a new digital place to meet seems relatively cost-free, when a community is banned, the "club" typically disbands and only a fraction of its users find a way to coalesce in a new space.

Data From Online Communities

In addition to being novel empirical settings for studying groups, online communities are also exciting to researchers due to the type and scale of the data they produce. Simply as part of their operation, online platforms like Wikipedia, Reddit, and Github store billions of time-stamped actions and interactions. As discussed earlier, these actions can be made visible and can contribute to the informational public goods produced by a community. They can also be used to study social science questions: As actions like joining a new community or sending a message to another user are naturally archived, they become **digital trace data** that can be both qualitatively and quantitatively analyzed to study social behaviors in these spaces.

What is so special about online data? Among other attributes, online data is often large-scale, longitudinal, and granular. Large-scale can be massive. For example, publicly available Reddit comment data includes *billions* of comments in *millions* of communities. This is especially exciting for group researchers, because it is possible to use this data to study many groups at once, to study groups that might otherwise be too small to meaningfully identify and sample from (Welles,

2014), and to study relationships between groups (Hill & Shaw, 2017). Online community data is also longitudinal, meaning that it's tracked over time. For most platforms, data gathering is "always on" – actions are tracked constantly over extended periods. Finally, online data is often very granular, with full-text data that can be tied to individual users, letting researchers study within-group and within-individual processes.

Of course, there are also some characteristics of online community data which are problematic either for researchers or for community members. In the following section, we discuss some of the ethical considerations, and later on we discuss some of the technical challenges.

Ethical Questions in Researching Online Communities

Although large-scale online community data presents exciting opportunities for social science research, it also poses ethical questions around privacy and consent.

While the fine-grained nature of some digital trace data is a boon for researchers, it raises privacy concerns at both the community level and the individual level. Technically, the content of many online communities is public, and it could be argued that research using this data is similar to researchers observing people in a public park. However, norms around how to do research using this data (and whether researchers even *should* use this data) are evolving (Fiesler & Proferes, 2018; Hallinan et al., 2020).

One example of these debates focuses on a method of data collection called web scraping. Through web scraping, a researcher uses a custom code script to access and collect anything that they could access through a browser, including private forums or personal information from friends. The scale and reach of this automated process makes it much harder to argue that it is analogous to observing a public space. These concerns become amplified when researchers are studying vulnerable or marginalized communities where unwanted attention can put members at risk. On the other hand, web scraping can also be a powerful tool to audit how online community platforms' algorithms and design choices affect their users. Through web scraping, researchers can study aspects of corporate platforms that corporations would rather keep hidden (Bandy, 2021).

When it comes to consent, online data gathering is equally fraught. Technically, when people create accounts on platforms, they consent to having their content made public. However, online communities are not spaces intended for research: many community members participate in communities with no idea that their clicks, likes, and comments might be used as data. Some community members may feel that their activity being used as data affects the integrity of their communal space, especially if the topic being discussed is sensitive; others may feel like the community is being exploited for research purposes, especially when the research involves experiments that manipulate user experiences. An infamous case is the 2014 study on emotional contagion on Facebook, where researchers manipulated which posts appeared in users' newsfeeds to see whether users would post more positively or negatively after being exposed to more or less positive content (Kramer et al., 2014). In addition to the ethical implications of attempting to manipulate peoples' emotions, the experiment caused an uproar because the users were not aware that they had been experimented on until the study was published.

In short, research using online community data has enormous promise, but also new challenges and opportunities for harm that do not always have clear-cut answers on how to proceed. This chapter covers just the tip of the iceberg as an introduction to studying online communities, but it is imperative that any researcher of online communities carefully considers what the relationship of their research is with the communities being studied. Researchers should seek to increase the benefits of research to communities – for example, by conducting participatory research *alongside* community members, in order to explicitly help communities meet their goals (Matias, 2019). They should also seek to reduce the potential for harms by obfuscating details of participants and their communities (even for public accounts and public data), reporting data in aggregate, and working with community members and other researchers to think through the implications of proposed research (Vitak et al., 2016). When done well, online community research can yield findings that are ultimately helpful for society and for online communities.

Online Community Research

In this section, we give examples of how large-scale data can be used to research online communities. Much of the research on online communities does not require large-scale data; methods like surveys, participant observation, experiments, interviews, and ethnography have generated much of our understanding of how and why online communities work. However, because large-scale online datasets are opening up new avenues of inquiry, we focus on a few exciting approaches and opportunities enabled by them.

Observational Studies

The first approach is observational studies. This typically involves gathering digital trace data about individuals or groups, creating measures from that data that correspond to theoretical constructs, and then using statistical analyses to test hypotheses about the relationship between those constructs. Researchers can focus on individuals, groups, or ecosystems of groups. Work at the individual level looks at how members interact with and are influenced by a group that they belong to. For example, Danescu-Niculescu-Mizil et al. (2013) use natural language-processing (NLP) tools to look at the longitudinal dynamics of beer-rating online communities. They show that the community's linguistic norms changed over time, and that newer members of a community were more willing to adapt to linguistic shifts (e.g., using "aroma" instead of "smell"), while older members left when the norms changed too much.

At the group level, researchers have looked at things like how the structure of the communication networks in a group predict the group's longevity or productivity (Foote et al., 2023). Comparing across groups can be powerful. For example, TeBlunthuis et al. (2018) look at how hundreds of popular wikis changed in size over time; they find a general pattern where wikis would grow for a few years followed by a gradual decline in activity. Researchers have also begun examining "ecosystems" of communities. Given how easy it is for people to move between communities or participate in multiple communities, it can be illuminating to study the relationships that communities have with each other. For example, researchers showed that the amount of overlap that a community has with other communities – either in membership or topic – has an inverse-U ($\frown$) relationship with the community's activity level and survival (Zhu et al., 2014).

Natural Experiments

One special case of observational research is natural experiments. In a natural experiment, researchers look for times when external, unexpected "shocks" impact a system. Then, due to the "always on" nature of online data, researchers go back in time to look at the influence of the shock. For example Zhang and Zhu (2011) identified a time when the Chinese government blocked Wikipedia for nearly a year without warning, dramatically reducing the size of the Chinese Wikipedia community. According to some theories, as group size grows so does the temptation to free ride, so we would expect people to increase their contributions when the community shrank (Olson, 1965). On the other hand, perhaps people contribute partially because it feels good to help others (the "warm glow theory"), and so a larger group of readers and co-contributors would encourage one to contribute more (Andreoni, 1990). Zhang and Zhu (2011) found that individuals who were active before the block (but not blocked themselves) actually contributed less during the block, providing evidence for the "warm glow theory" that people are motivated in part by the knowledge that they are helping others.

Experiments

Online data can also be leveraged for participants doing "real" experiments. For example, Matias (2019) worked with moderators of the very popular "r/science" subreddit to show a "stickied" comment containing the community rules at the top of a random selection of posts. Newcomers who participated on those posts that had a comment were both more likely to participate and were more likely to communicate according to group norms. This kind of approach enables researchers to create large-scale experiments at a much lower cost than lab-based experiments. In the case of the Reddit experiment, Matias (2019) studied nearly 63,000 newcomer participants. Always-on data also means that the behavior of those in experiments can be tracked both before and after the experiment, allowing for longitudinal and long-term analyses.

Computational Text Analysis

Online data often includes the text of thousands or millions of interactions. Qualitative methods like content analysis or ethnography are designed to make meaning out of texts, but when dealing with the equivalent of hundreds of thousands of pages of text, these methods are impossible. Instead, researchers often use NLP tools which use computation to summarize text in some way. LIWC is a popular utility that defines a list of terms that correspond to psychological constructs and counts how often they occur in a text or set of texts (Tausczik & Pennebaker, 2010). For example, Hamilton et al. (2017) showed that Reddit users who used more personal pronouns and affect words were less likely to quit a community. More advanced NLP approaches include topic modeling, which seeks to recover different "topics" that are used in large sets of texts, based on how often words co-occur within texts (Blei, 2012). Some recent research seeks to build best-of-both-worlds processes that combine automated steps done by a computer and interpretive steps done by humans. Nelson (2020) suggests "Computational Grounded Theory," an approach which uses topic modeling or other NLP steps to identify patterns in the data and to identify texts which are representative of those patterns. The next step involves a "computationally-guided deep reading," intended to contextualize, question, and interpret the key texts identified in the first step. These two inductive steps help to build theories which can then be tested using other computational methods (like LIWC). Ideally, this approach builds on the strengths of both humans and computers and allows for a rich understanding of even very large datasets.

Evidence-Based Recommendations for Researchers

Each of the research approaches that we have outlined opens up exciting new opportunities for studying group communication phenomena by taking advantage of the scale and granularity of online community data. There are, of course some drawbacks to working with online data. In addition to some of the ethical and conceptual difficulties discussed above, working with this type of data also requires computational and statistical training.

For some datasets, even obtaining and storing the data requires significant computational expertise. In order to gather a sufficient longitudinal dataset, researchers must consistently and securely collect, clean, and store data in a reliable manner. In some cases, platforms make large datasets available for download, but often researchers must write and maintain code that runs for an extended period of time on a server. Researchers benefit from developing well-documented data collection pipelines. Doing so can also strengthen the robustness and validity of one's work and analyses because it can enable replication as well as visibility into the strengths and limitations of the data collection process.

More broadly, there are a number of challenges when working with large-scale online data, including ensuring a match between data measures and theoretical constructs, successfully applying approaches like large-scale natural experiments or NLP, and accounting for changes to online platforms (Salganik, 2017); each of these can require fairly advanced computational skills. For example, one common challenge is detecting bots in digital trace data. If a researcher wants to know about human behaviors, it's important to distinguish which posts and comments are by humans and which are by bots. While some bots are obviously labeled or detectable because of behavioral patterns (posting too fast, always writing the same message, etc.), some are not. Failing to sufficiently account for non-human contributions can paint a misleading picture of how people interact online. Because of the scale of the data, filtering out bots can require researchers to take approaches like building or applying classification algorithms to predict if a user in their data is a bot.

Fortunately, many of the skills needed can be learned in a few semesters through publicly available learning resources or through tailored courses. Alternatively, this area of work offers an exciting opportunity for researchers to build interdisciplinary collaborations with computer scientists.

Conclusion

Online communities have emerged as an important new way of organizing groups. From business to politics to culture, online communities are increasingly influencing how people perceive and act in the world: they produce powerful and popular software, gather and produce knowledge, and organize and persuade. Because groups are digital – with interactions that are timestamped and stored – they can be studied with more depth than we can study groups in other contexts. Online communities offer an incredible chance to understand how communication technologies are transforming group communication in evolving empirical settings as well as to revisit fundamental questions about how individuals in groups can effectively interact, organize, and communicate with one another. Only through understanding the dynamics of online communities better will we be able to shape the role that they play in society.

Further Readings

Bruckman, A. S. (2022). *Should you believe Wikipedia?: Online communities and the construction of knowledge*. Cambridge University Press.

Kraut, R. E., Resnick, P., & Kiesler, S. (2012). *Building successful online communities: Evidence-based social design*. MIT Press.

Salganik, M. J. (2017). *Bit by bit: Social research in the digital age*. Princeton University Press.

Glossary

Digital trace data   As people participate in online communities, data and metadata about what they are doing is stored. This data is often visible to other users and/or made available to researchers.

Lurkers   People who consume the content on a community but don't actively participate. For most online communities, lurkers represent the vast majority of community members.

Pseudonymous   Many online communities allow for pseudonyms – persistent identifiers like usernames which are not tied to a users real identity.

Public information good   A shared information repository. Many online communities produce explicit information goods, like wikis or software. Stored conversations can also serve as public information goods.

Stigmergic communication   Communication that happens through modifying the environment rather than through typical communication channels.

References

Ammari, T., Schoenebeck, S., & Romero, D. (2019). Self-declared throwaway accounts on Reddit: How platform affordances and shared norms enable parenting disclosure and support. *Proceedings of the ACM on Human- Computer Interaction, 3*(135), 1–30. https://doi.org/10.1145/3359237

Andreoni, J. (1990). Impure altruism and donations to public goods: A theory of warm-glow giving. *The Economic Journal, 100*(401), 464–477.

Bandy, J. (2021). Problematic machine behavior: A systematic literature review of algorithm audits. *Proceedings of the ACM on Human-Computer Interaction, 5*(74), 1–34. https://doi.org/10.1145/3449148

Barker, J. R. (1993). Tightening the iron cage: Concertive control in self-managing teams. *Administrative Science Quarterly, 38*(3), 408–437. https://doi.org/10.2307/2393374

Benkler, Y. (2002). Coase's penguin, or, Linux and the nature of the firm. *Yale Law Journal, 112*(3), 369–446. https://doi.org/10.2307/1562247

Blei, D. M. (2012). Probabilistic topic models. *Communications of the ACM, 55*(4), 77–84. https://doi.org/10.1145/2133806.2133826

Bruckman, A. S. (2022). *Should you believe Wikipedia?: Online communities and the construction of knowledge*. Cambridge University Press.

Champion, K., & Hill, B. M. (2021). Underproduction: An approach for measuring risk in open source software. *2021 IEEE international conference on software analysis, evolution and reengineering (SANER)*, 388–399. https://doi.org/10.1109/SANER50967.2021.00043

Chandrasekharan, E., Pavalanathan, U., Srinivasan, A., Glynn, A., Eisenstein, J., & Gilbert, E. (2017). You can't stay here: The efficacy of Reddit's 2015 ban examined through hate speech. *Proceedings of the ACM on Human-Computer Interaction, 1*(31), 1–22. https://doi.org/10.1145/3134666

Cheng, R., Dasgupta, S., & Hill, B. M. (2022). How interest-driven content creation shapes opportunities for informal learning in scratch: A case study on novices' use of data structures. *Proceedings of the 2022 CHI conference on human factors in computing systems*, 1–16. https://doi.org/10.1145/3491102.3502124

Coase, R. H. (1937). The nature of the firm. *Economica, 4*(16), 386–405. https://doi.org/10.1111/j.1468-0335.1937.tb00002.x

Dabbish, L., Stuart, C., Tsay, J., & Herbsleb, J. (2012). Social coding in GitHub: Transparency and collaboration in an open software repository. *Proceedings of the ACM 2012 conference on computer supported cooperative work - CSCW'12*, 1277. https://doi.org/10.1145/2145204.

Danescu-Niculescu-Mizil, C., West, R., Jurafsky, D., Leskovec, J., & Potts, C. (2013). No country for old members: User lifecycle and linguistic change in online communities. *Proceedings of the 22nd international conference on world wide web – WWW'13*, 307–318. https://doi.org/10.1145/2488388.2488416

Dosono, B., & Semaan, B. (2019). Moderation practices as emotional labor in sustaining online communities: The case of AAPI identity work on Reddit. *Proceedings of the 2019 CHI conference on human factors in computing systems*, 1–13. https://doi.org/10.1145/3290605.3300372

Fiesler, C., & Proferes, N. (2018). "Participant" perceptions of Twitter re-search ethics. *Social Media + Society, 4*(1), 2056305118763366. https://doi.org/10.1177/2056305118763366

Foote, J. (2022). A systems approach to studying online communities. *Media and Communication, 10*(2), 29–40. https://doi.org/10.17645/mac.v10i2.5042

Foote, J., Shaw, A., & Hill, B. M. (2023). Communication networks do not predict success in attempts at peer production. *Journal of Computer-Mediated Communication*. https://doi.org/10.1093/jcmc/zmad002

Fulk, J., Flanagin, A. J., Kalman, M. E., Monge, P. R., & Ryan, T. (1996). Connective and communal public goods in interactive communication systems. *Communication Theory, 6*(1), 60–87. https://doi.org/10.1111/j.1468-2885.1996.tb00120.x

Geiger, R. S., & Halfaker, A. (2013). When the levee breaks: Without bots, what happens to Wikipedia's quality control processes? *Proceedings of the 9th international symposium on open collaboration (Open-Sym'13)*, 6, 1–6. https://doi.org/10.1145/2491055.2491061

Gibbs, J. L., Rice, R. E., & Kirkwood, G. L. (2021). Digital discipline: Theorizing concertive control in online communities. *Communication Theory*. https://doi.org/10.1093/ct/qtab017

Greijdanus, H., de Matos Fernandes, C. A., Turner-Zwinkels, F., Honari, A., Roos, C. A., Rosenbusch, H., & Postmes, T. (2020). The psychology of online activism and social movements: Relations between online and offline collective action. *Current Opinion in Psychology*, *35*, 49–54. https://doi.org/10.1016/j.copsyc.2020.03.003

Hallinan, B., Brubaker, J. R., & Fiesler, C. (2020). Unexpected expectations: Public reaction to the Facebook emotional contagion study. *New Media & Society*, *22*(6), 1076–1094. https://doi.org/10.1177/1461444819876944

Hamilton, W. L., Zhang, J., Danescu-Niculescu-Mizil, C., Jurafsky, D., & Leskovec, J. (2017). Loyalty in online communities. *arXiv:1703.03386 [cs]*.

Hannah, M. (2021). QAnon and the information dark age. *First Monday*. https://doi.org/10.5210/fm.v26i2.10868

Heylighen, F. (2016). Stigmergy as a universal coordination mechanism I: Definition and components. *Cognitive Systems Research*, *38*, 4–13. https://doi.org/10.1016/j.cogsys.2015.12.002

Hill, B. M., & Shaw, A. D. (2017) Studying populations of online communities. In B. Foucault Welles & S. GonzálezBailón (Eds.), *The Handbook of Networked Communication*. New York: Oxford University Press.

Hirschman, A. O. (1970). *Exit, voice, and loyalty: Responses to decline in firms, organizations, and States*. Harvard University Press.

Hwang, S., & Foote, J. (2021). Why do people participate in small online communities? *Proceedings of the ACM on Human-Computer Interaction*, *5*(CSCW2), 1–25. https://doi.org/10.1145/3479606

Ilgen, D. R., Hollenbeck, J. R., Johnson, M., & Jundt, D. (2005). Teams in organizations: From input-process-output models to IMOI models. *Annual Review of Psychology*, *56*(1), 517–543. https://doi.org/10.1146/annurev.psych.56.091103.070250

Kramer, A. D. I., Guillory, J. E., & Hancock, J. T. (2014). Experimental evidence of massive-scale emotional contagion through social networks. *Proceedings of the National Academy of Sciences*, *111*(24), 8788–8790. https://doi.org/10.1073/pnas.1320040111

Kraut, R. E., Resnick, P., & Kiesler, S. (2012). *Building successful online com-munities: Evidence-based social design*. MIT Press.

Lampe, C., & Resnick, P. (2004). Slash(dot) and burn: Distributed moderation in a large online conversation space. *Proceedings of the SIGCHI conference on human factors in computing systems* (pp. 543–550). https://doi.org/10.1145/985692.985761

Lampe, C., Wash, R., Velasquez, A., & Ozkaya, E. (2010). Motivations to par-ticipate in online communities. *Proceedings of the 28th international conference on human factors in computing systems* (pp. 1927–1936). https://doi.org/10.1145/1753326.1753616

Massanari, A. (2017). #Gamergate and The Fappening: How Reddit's algorithm, governance, and culture support toxic technocultures. *New Media & Society*, *19*(3), 329–346. https://doi.org/10.1177/1461444815608807

Matei, S. A., & Britt, B. C. (2017). *Structural differentiation in social media: Adhocracy, entropy, and the "1% effect"*. Springer.

Matias, J. N. (2019). Preventing harassment and increasing group participation through social norms in 2,190 online science discussions. *Proceedings of the National Academy of Sciences*, *116*(20), 9785–9789. https://doi.org/10.1073/pnas.1813486116

Mittell, J. (2009). Sites of participation: Wiki fandom and the case of Lostpedia. *Transformative Works and Cultures*, *3*. https://doi.org/10.3983/twc.2009.0118

Nelson, L. K. (2020). Computational grounded theory: A methodological framework. *Sociological Methods & Research*, *49*(1), 3–42. https://doi.org/10.1177/0049124117729703

Nonnecke, B., & Preece, J. (2000). Lurker demographics: Counting the silent. *Proceedings of the SIGCHI conference on human factors in computing systems* (pp. 73–80). https://doi.org/10.1145/332040.332409

Olson, M. (1965). *The logic of collective action: Public goods and the theory of groups*. Harvard University Press.

Phillips, M., Lorenz, T., Bernard, T. S., & Friedman, G. (February 7, 2021). The Hopes That Rose and Fell With GameStop. *The New York Times*.

Reicher, S. D., Spears, R., & Postmes, T. (1995). A social identity model of deindividuation phenomena. *European Review of Social Psychology*, *6*(1), 161–198. https://doi.org/10.1080/14792779443000049

Ren, Y., Harper, F., Drenner, S., Terveen, L., Kiesler, S., Riedl, J., & Kraut, R. (2012). Building member attachment in online communities: Applying theories of group identity and interpersonal bonds. *Management Information Systems Quarterly*, *36*(3), 841–864.

Rheingold, H. (1993). *The virtual community: Homesteading on the electronic frontier*. Addison Wesley Publishing Company.

Ribeiro, M. H., Jhaver, S., Zannettou, S., Blackburn, J., Stringhini, G., De Cristofaro, E., & West, R. (2021). Do platform migrations compromise content moderation? Evidence from r/The_Donald and r/Incels. *Proceedings of the ACM on Human-Computer Interaction*, *5*(316), 1–24. https://doi.org/10.1145/3476057

Ruggiero, T. E. (2000). Uses and gratifications theory in the 21st century. *Mass Communication and Society*, *3*(1), 3–37. https://doi.org/10.1207/S15327825MCS0301_02

Salehi, N., Irani, L. C., Bernstein, M. S., Alkhatib, A., Ogbe, E., Milland, K., & Clickhappier. (2015). We are dynamo: Overcoming stalling and friction in collective action for crowd workers. *Proceedings of the 33rd annual ACM conference on human factors in computing systems*, 1621–1630. https://doi.org/10.1145/2702123.2702508

Salganik, M. J. (2017). *Bit by bit: Social research in the digital age*. Princeton University Press.

Schneider, N. (2022). Admins, mods, and benevolent dictators for life: The implicit feudalism of online communities. *New Media & Society*, *24*(9), 1965–1985. https://doi.org/10.1177/1461444820986553

Seabrook, J. (1998). *Deeper*. Simon and Schuster.

Seering, J., Flores, J. P., Savage, S., & Hammer, J. (2018). The social roles of bots: Evaluating impact of bots on discussions in online communities. *Proceedings of the ACM on Human-Computer Interaction*, *2*(CSCW), 1–29. https://doi.org/10.1145/3274426

Suler, J. (2004). The online disinhibition effect. *CyberPsychology & Behavior*, *7*(3), 321–326. https://doi.org/10.1089/1094931041291295

Tausczik, Y. R., & Pennebaker, J. W. (2010). The psychological meaning of words: LIWC and computerized text analysis methods. *Journal of Language and Social Psychology*, *29*(1), 24–54. https://doi.org/10.1177/0261927X09351676

TeBlunthuis, N., Kiene, C., Brown, I., Levi, L., McGinnis, N., & Hill, B. M. (2022). No community can do everything: Why people participate in similar online communities. *Proceedings of the ACM on Human-Computer Interaction: Computer Supported Cooperative Work*, *6*, 1–25. https://doi.org/10.1145/3512908

TeBlunthuis, N., Shaw, A., & Hill, B. M. (2018). Revisiting "The rise and decline" in a population of peer production projects. *Proceedings of the 2018 CHI conference on human factors in computing systems*, 355, 1–7. https://doi.org/10.1145/3173574.3173929

Treem, J. W., & Leonardi, P. M. (2013). Social media use in organizations: Exploring the affordances of visibility, editability, persistence, and association. *Annals of the International Communication Association*, *36*(1), 143–189. https://doi.org/10.1080/23808985.2013.11679130

Vitak, J., Shilton, K., & Ashktorab, Z. (2016). Beyond the Belmont principles: ethical challenges, practices, and beliefs in the online data research community. *Proceedings of the 19th ACM conference on computer-supported cooperative work & social computing*, 941–953. https://doi.org/10.1145/2818048.2820078

Wegner, D. M. (1987). Transactive memory: A contemporary analysis of the group mind. In B. Mullen & G. R. Goethals (Eds.), *Theories of group behavior* (pp. 185–208). Springer. https://doi.org/10.1007/978-1-4612-4634-3

Welles, B. F. (2014). On minorities and outliers: The case for making Big Data small. *Big Data & Society*, *1*(1), 2053951714540613. https://doi.org/10.1177/2053951714540613

Welser, H. T., Cosley, D., Kossinets, G., Lin, A., Dokshin, F., Gay, G., & Smith, M. (2011). Finding social roles in Wikipedia. *Proceedings of the 2011 iConference*, 122–129. https://doi.org/10.1145/1940761.1940778

Zhang, X. M., & Zhu, F. (2011). Group size and incentives to contribute: A natural experiment at Chinese Wikipedia. *American Economic Review*, *101*(4), 1601–1615. https://doi.org/10.1257/aer.101.4.1601

Zhu, H., Chen, J., Matthews, T., Pal, A., Badenes, H., & Kraut, R. E. (2014). Selecting an effective niche: An ecological view of the success of online communities. *Proceedings of the SIGCHI conference on human factors in computing systems*, 301–310. https://doi.org/10.1145/2556288

21 Groups in Health Contexts

Online Health Communities

Stephen A. Rains

Chapter Objectives

- Recognize the social implications of experiencing a chronic or serious health condition.
- Identify forms of distress relevant to online health community participation.
- Understand the technological affordances salient in online health communities.
- Consider digital coping activities in online health communities.

Introduction

Although groups play an important role in many aspects of life, they can be especially critical in health contexts. Experiencing a chronic or serious health condition can create a myriad of personal, social, professional, and financial challenges. Gaining access to other people who have had similar experiences can be a vital coping resource. By virtue of facing related challenges and having similar needs, peers are uniquely situated to offer information and comfort. In the past few decades, people experiencing illness have begun coming together online in communities dedicated to specific health conditions.

Online health communities are a space where groups of people concerned about the same health condition interact to give and receive aid. Although they regularly appear on stand-alone websites dedicated to one or more health conditions, online health communities also form on social media platforms like social networks sites (e.g., Facebook) and microblogs (e.g., Twitter). These communities are marked by several characteristics. Participation is typically open and open-ended, meaning that anyone with an interest in the topic may join and the group persists as long as members actively contribute. Online health communities are unbounded in size and may range from a few people to thousands of members. There is typically no appointed leader, although some communities have moderators who ensure that conversations remain on topic and follow established standards. The activity level of individual members varies. Core members participate regularly, and peripheral members may visit only a few times or even a single time. Lurkers, involving people who read content posted to the community but do not actively contribute, also may be common. Conversations are structured in discussion threads consisting of an original post made by one community member followed by a series of responses to the initiating post. Messages contributed to the community can be seen and may be responded to by any other member. Communities tend to develop their own unique norms for behavior.

Although the preceding characteristics are common to all types of communities appearing online, health communities are distinct in that they are illness focused. They are typically populated by people who have experienced or are experiencing a health condition along with their loved ones. Much of the discussion activity in these community centers around seeking and providing

DOI: 10.4324/9781003227458-24

aid in the form of social support. A meta-analysis summarizing more than 40 studies examining the message shared in online health communities showed that emotional and informational support were the most common (Rains et al., 2015). Whereas emotional support involves efforts to provide comfort for emotional distress, informational support involves advice, feedback, and situation appraisals (Cutrona & Suhr, 1992). Health communities are a place where people cope with their illness experiences collectively.

This chapter examines the implications of online health communities for groups of people experiencing illness. The goals are to help readers gain insights about why people join these communities, how they are used as a coping resource, and the role played by technology. The chapter proceeds with a brief review of background information about illness and groups. The digital coping model (Rains, 2018) will then be described and serve as a theoretical framework to organize our exploration of online health communities. Common forms of distress experienced by people who decide to join online heath communities, unique technological affordances of online communities, and digital coping activities are next discussed. The chapter concludes with some recommendations for practice.

Illness and Community

For people who have generally been healthy most of their lives, it can sometimes be difficult to fully understand the experiences of people facing a chronic or serious physical or mental health condition. The notion of illness goes beyond the functioning of specific organs like the heart or systems such as the cardiovascular system and encapsulates the beliefs and experiences that mark one's state of being related to a health condition (Kleinman, 1988). Illness can bring a great deal of uncertainty about medical issues related to symptoms and treatment. It can make it difficult or impossible to participate in activities such as work or hobbies that are central to our identity. Serious illness can disrupt personal relationships, requiring family members to become caregivers, and isolate people from their social networks. Ultimately, serious illness can untether people from their preexisting lives. Bury (1982) describes this phenomenon as a state of biographical disruption in which the narrative people had been constructing and telling about themselves is interrupted. People are forced to reorganize how they think about themselves. They must modify their story of who they are and what they might become to account for illness.

Given the substantial challenges posed by illness, it is not surprising that people turn to peers facing similar circumstances for assistance. Support groups dedicated to a variety of health conditions have been studied for more than half a century (e.g., Riessman, 1965). Perhaps the most well-known group, Alcoholics Anonymous, began during 1934 as a way for people experiencing problems with alcohol to be helped by and help peers dealing with the same challenges (Tiebout, 1944). For people facing a health condition, connecting with others experiencing similar circumstances can be a valuable resource. Despite their best intentions, family and friends may not fully understand the depth and breadth of difficulties posed by chronic illness (Wright & Miller, 2010). Beyond the intricacies of symptoms, diagnoses, medications, and all of the technical components involved in treatment, living with illness can be a profoundly unsettling experience. Being able to share insights and experiences with others in similar circumstances can be helpful.

Although many groups continuing meeting face-to-face even today, the dramatic growth in home Internet access during the late 1990s created significant opportunities for the formation of online communities. Rather than being limited to meeting with others who live or work in the same geographic area, the Internet made it possible for people to connect with people from around the world who were experiencing or had experienced the same condition. Notable public interest in online health communities is documented in one of the first surveys of Internet use in the United

States conducted during 2000 (Rainie & Fox, 2000). Among people who sought health information online, 9% reported participating in an online support community. Although most online health communities continue to operate on websites containing discussion forums, the diffusion of social media during the past decade has resulted in communities emerging on networks of blogs, social networks sites, and related platforms. All of these online health groups or communities – defined as collections of people held together by a common focus on one or more health conditions and who interact using one or more communication technologies – offer important opportunities for digital coping.

Digital Coping and Online Health Communities

The digital coping model (Rains, 2018), which is illustrated in Figure 21.1, was developed to help explain the implications of communication technologies for people experiencing illness. It builds on prior models of stress and coping (Lazarus, 1966, 2012) by considering the role of communication technologies ranging from email to contemporary forms of social media. **Digital coping** is defined as the use of communication technologies in responding to the challenges posed by illness. Communication technologies include virtually any means of communicating beyond face-to-face interaction, ranging from letters and landline telephones to email and instant messaging along with contemporary forms of social media. This project focuses on online health communities. The starting point for the digital coping model is the notion that people facing chronic illness experience different classes of distress like emotional upset, inadequate information, deficits in companionship, and other issues. These forms of distress serve as primary appraisals involving assessments of the personal relevance of an event. In the digital coping model, they reflect recurring threats that tend to appear along with chronic or serious illness.

The different forms of distress in the digital coping model give rise to secondary appraisal involving communication technologies (Rains, 2018). Following prior work in the domain of stress and coping (Lazarus, 1966, 2012), secondary appraisals involve a person's ability to respond to a threat. In the case of the digital coping model, the affordances of communication technologies are considered as a means of evaluating response options. An **affordance** involves the way a technology is perceived and used by people (Gibson, 1977; Markus & Silver, 2008). It includes the potential for action people perceive a technology to facilitate. As a secondary appraisal, communication technology affordances represent ways that technology may be used to respond to different forms of illness-related distress. The ability to conceal one's physical appearance from others in online

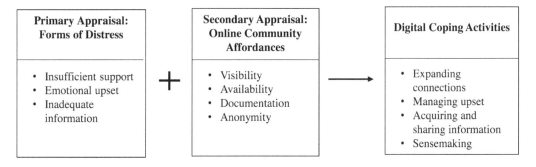

Figure 21.1 The Digital Coping Model Applied to Online Health Communities. (Adapted from Rains (2018). The original figure appeared in Rains, Stephen A., *Coping with Illness Digitally*, ©2018 Massachusetts Institute of Technology, published by the MIT Press.)

communities, for example, may foster the affordance of anonymity. This affordance can allow online community members to feel more comfortable sharing information that is personal or embarrassing and acquiring aid from others.

The final element of the digital coping model concerns digital coping activities (Rains, 2018). As in prior theorizing (Lazarus, 1966, 2012), the nature of a stressor (i.e., primary appraisal) and communication technology affordances (i.e., secondary appraisal) shape efforts at coping or responding to illness. Common coping activities in the digital coping model include acquiring and sharing information, sensemaking, reinforcing social connections, and other possibilities. These activities are shaped by the nature of the distress and communication technology affordances. People undertake these coping activities in an effort to remedy their distress. Several examples of the connection between affordances and coping activities are provided in applying the model to online health communities.

The digital coping model offers a framework to better understand how and why people use online health communities. It suggests that there are common forms of distress, technological affordances, and coping activities that are particularly relevant to online health communities. In an effort to systematically evaluate online health communities, I dedicate the remaining sections of this chapter to each of these three dimensions from the digital coping model.

Forms of Distress Relevant to Online Health Community Participants

The first major element of the digital coping model involves common forms of distress experienced by people facing illness (Rains, 2018). Three forms of distress are particularly relevant to people who participate in online health communities: insufficient support, emotional upset, and inadequate information. All three forms of distress present unique challenges stemming from serious or chronic illness.

Social support generally involves the connection between social relationships and wellbeing. A wealth of research shows that people tend to fair better when they have meaningful social relationships. Indeed, a review examining almost 150 studies focused on mortality rates found that people with stronger social relationships had a greater likelihood of survival (Holt-Lunstad et al., 2010). A lack of support is a prevalent form of distress among people experiencing illness. It is marked by the absence of support providers or the presence support providers who possess inadequate motivation or ability to effectively offer aid.

Illness can be isolating by making people feel disconnected or set apart from others. People coping with obesity, for example, reported feeling as if they were dismissed by society (Dickins et al., 2016). Illness can also physically separate people from their existing support networks. Symptoms or treatments may make people unable to get together with friends and family or participate in activities like work that previously provided regular social interaction. People experiencing early onset Alzheimer's disease may be forced to retire early from work or required to discontinue driving and feel physically isolated from others (Rodriquez, 2013).

Even when others are available, they may be ill equipped to be an effective support resource. The most well-intention friends and family members may not fully appreciate what it means to experience illness. That was the case for members of an online fertility community who indicated that their loved ones were unable to completely understand their condition and the anxiety they felt (Malik & Coulson, 2008). This lack of understanding may lead friends and family to be unable or unwilling to provide helpful information, comfort, or other types of support. Wright and Miller (2010) explain that some people even develop and enduring preference for support from weak ties – people who are not interpersonally close like friends and family but from whom resources can be drawn. This preference develops due to the potential for role conflict in which a spouse may become a care provider, because people feel more comfortable sharing with peers who may be more understanding, and because peers are more likely to provide novel information that is helpful in responding to illness.

A second form of distress experienced by people who participate in online health communities involves emotional upset. Negative emotions like fear, anger, sadness, and several more general aversive states like frustration and discontent are common among people facing illness. Negative emotions can stem stressors ranging from day-to-day challenge in completing routine tasks and the toll taken by changing symptoms to concerns with mortality and the disruption caused by illness to long-term plans. Women in an online breast cancer community discussed feelings of exhaustion, loneliness, and fear (Høybye et al., 2005). Resentment (Mirivel & Thombre, 2010) and anger (Bar-Lev, 2008) were common in communities dedicated to HIV/AIDS and burn survivors.

A third and final source of distress relevant to online support communities involves inadequate information. Serious illness can create tremendous uncertainty (Brashers et al., 2000). One major source of uncertainty involves technical or medical aspects of illness related to its etiology, symptoms, long-term prognosis, and other factors. In studies of people experiencing breast cancer or prostate cancer (Kirschning & von Kardorff, 2008) and multiple sclerosis (Colombo et al., 2014), information about diagnoses, causes, treatments, and disease trajectory were important. Uncertainty about these topics left people worried about negative outcomes and undermined their sense of agency to shape the trajectory of their health condition. People may also experience uncertainty about what illness means for their lives. People may have questions, for example, how illness may affect their fertility or if they will be able to hold a full-time job in the future. People diagnosed with multiple sclerosis, for example, faced information deficits about how to deal with aspects of everyday life like managing fatigue, how to give an injection without producing bruising that would be noticeable to others, and bladder disturbances (Colombo et al., 2014).

Technological Affordances of Online Health Communities

The second major element of the digital coping model involves communication technology affordances (Rains, 2018). Affordances are distinct from the features of a technology and capture the opportunities for actions perceived by users (Gibson, 1977; Markus & Silver, 2008). Email, for example, is a text-based technology in which all messages appear and persist written form. This feature – being text-based and composed of written language – may be leveraged by users in a documentation affordance. Rather than calling, patients may prefer to email their doctor so that they may have a written record of their interaction that could be referred to in the future. In other words, patients may see the written form of email as an opportunity to document and maintain records of their interactions with their doctor. In the case of online health communities, affordances refer to the opportunities for action made possible by unique features of online communities. Four affordances are particularly relevant in this context (Rains, 2018): visibility, availability, documentation, and anonymity.

The visibility affordance involves the potential to observe the behavior of others and have one's behavior observed. Online communities make it possible to witness other people in similar circumstances respond to a health condition. It is possible to read about challenges and concerns faced by others due to a health condition and, in many cases, see how that person responded and the outcomes of their response. In this way, the visibility of online health communities can make them a valuable resource for learning about how others cope. That was the case for members of online health communities dedicated to infertility (Malik & Coulson, 2008) and breast cancer (Montali et al., 2021). Observing others was a valuable learning experience that led some people to feel more informed and empowered to manage their health condition. The visibility affordance also makes it possible for people to have their behavior observed. This can be critical in help seeking. By virtue of posting in a public space on the community, people can have their problems seen by others who may be able to provide aid. Rather than suffering in silence, visibility offers the potential for an individual's voice to be heard by others in similar circumstances and potentially acquire assistance.

A second affordance relevant to online health communities involves availability. Availability concerns the potential to gain access to resources like information and people when they are most needed. Online health communities are typically asynchronous, which means that there is a lag between when messages are sent and receive. Unlike a telephone conversation where an utterance by one person is followed by the immediate response of the other person, some period of time elapses between when people post a message to an online community and when others respond. This affordance is valuable because it allows people to participate at their own convenience. It makes it possible for people from all over the globe to share insights and feedback. Indeed, the potential to share their concerns at any time of day or night was noted as an important advantage of online communities in several studies (Coulson, 2015; Malik & Coulson, 2008). This is especially important for people who experience mobility impairments, have a rare condition, or live in rural areas where face-to-face groups dedicated to their health condition may not exist. Among people experiencing physical disabilities, the potential to acquire social support online was a valuable coping resource (Braithwaite et al., 1999).

Documentation is a third affordance that is particularly relevant to online health communities. As previously discussed, documentation concerns the potential to create a written record of interactions. Because online health communities are text-based, records are often automatically created for all interactions that occur in the community. All of the questions asked, experiences shared, challenges faced and overcome, and so forth are documented in a relatively permanent digital record. This documentation affordance can result in a rich archive containing the collective intelligence accrued by the community. It can provide a wealth of information for users, making it possible to evaluate a wide range of possible issues and potentially multiple accounts of those issues. In one study of people who searched online after an appointment with a health care provider, more than 80% of participants reporting reading posts in an online community made by people who had similar concerns (Bell et al., 2011).

A fourth affordances of online communities involves anonymity or the potential to conceal one's identity. By virtue of allowing users to create screen names that are not linked to their legal identity and not requiring portraits of users, online communities offer a potentially high degree of anonymity (Kang, 2017). It is possible for users to participate in the community without others learning their legal identity. Anonymity is an important affordance because of the stigma associated with many health conditions. Stigma involves a discrediting attribute that may lead to social rejection. Any type of health condition has the potential to be a source of stigma because it can be perceived by others to indicate non-normal functioning (Scambler, 2009). By virtue of allowing people to withhold their identity, anonymity may make people feel more comfortable participating in online health communities. In a survey of online health community members, anonymity was particularly important to people who perceived greater levels of stigma associated with their health condition (Tanis, 2008). Because comments cannot be traced back to their legal identity, people may feel less inhibited by stigma and less worried about social rejection – and ultimately more likely to share their feelings and concerns.

Digital Coping Activities in Online Health Communities

The final element of the digital coping model (Rains, 2018) involves specific coping activities. The forms of distress and affordances give rise to digital coping activities in online communities.

Box 21.1 Anorexia Support Groups

Although online health communities can facilitate several types of digital coping that are likely to foster positive outcomes, it is possible for deleterious effects to occur. Haas and colleagues (2011) examined pro-anorexia online communities dedicated to promoting unhealthy eating behavior and developed a grounded model of what they refer to as online negative enabling support groups. They identified four themes about these communities that promote anti-health attitudes and behavior related to anorexia. Notably, three of the themes they identified stemmed directly from community participation. One involved the co-construction of a personal identity as an "ana" in which community norms encouraged documenting eating and exercise behavior consistent with anorexia. Users communicated a shared commitment to anorexia as a part of their identity. A second theme involved group encouragement. This included posting messages articulating commitment to the group and particular (unhealthy) eating behaviors. It also involved encouraging others who pursued community ideals and attacking outsiders who were seen as a threat to the "ana" ideal. A third theme the researchers identified involved information sharing. The online community served as a resource for how to engage in unhealthy eating and how to deal with outsiders in social situations. The community functioned as a repository of instructions for how to perform and sustain behavior consistent with anorexia. Despite the potential benefits of online health communities, Hass and colleagues' research offers a powerful reminder that the same mechanisms of community that bring about health benefits can also be used to undermine health or foster unhealthy behavior.

Four activities particularly relevant in this context involve expanding social connections, managing upset, sensemaking, and acquiring and sharing information. Each of these four activities will be considered in the following paragraphs with a focus on the role of communities.

Online health communities can be a valuable resource for expanding social connections. Because they can bring together people from all over the globe who are interested in the same health condition, online communities offer the potential for people to connect with similar others. The shared experiences of online community members involving symptoms, prognoses, difficulties with health care providers and institutions, occupational and familial concerns as well as several other nuances of serious illness are particularly important to help address feelings of isolation. By virtue of facing similar difficulties, online community members can truly empathize with what others are going through. Participants in an online community dedicated to arthritis, for example, indicated feeling that members of their community were uniquely prepared to understand what they were experiencing (Hadert & Rodham, 2008). This may be particularly valuable for people who believe that their family and friends are unable or unwilling to serve as a support resource.

Perhaps more important, online communities offer a sense of membership in a broader movement – people feel part of something larger than themselves. This sense of membership can produce feelings of inclusion and trust in the community as well as reduce concerns with evaluation. Especially in cases of health conditions that may be stigmatized, feeling solidarity with others can be critical. People participating in a community addressing self-harm, for example, reported being heartened by learning that they are not alone in their experiences but part of a broader group (Haberstroh & Moyer, 2012). The knowledge that other people in the world face the same challenges can be comforting.

A second digital coping activity relevant to online health communities is managing upset. On-line communities can be used to cope with negative emotions. Sharing one's feelings can allow people work through those feelings among an empathetic audience. This may take the form of articulating one's negative experiences as a means of venting and/or in order to receive feedback from community members. In one study examining a breast cancer online community over time, the researchers found that participants reported increased posttraumatic growth involving a new understanding of their experiences (Lieberman & Goldstein, 2006). Participating in the community helped people to grow from the challenges caused by breast cancer. Additionally, witnessing others work through their distress can be valuable. Other community members can serve as a model from which people can draw conclusions about responses to distress that are more and less helpful.

Although online health communities can be a valuable resource for managing upset, they also have some limitations that should be noted. One involves the negative implications of exposure to others' distress. In studies of online communities, at least some people reported that learning about the problems experienced by other community members was anxiety provoking (Hadert & Rodham, 2008; Holbrey & Colson, 2013). Reading about the difficulties faced by others can be dis-tressing. Another negative consequence involves social comparison in which people use others as a reference point to evaluate their own experiences or behavior. Hearing about the successes experi-enced by others may make people who are doing poorly have greater negative feelings about their circumstances. A final potential limitation of online communities for managing distress involves the potential of people to become hyper-focused on their health condition. The time spent learning about others' experiences with the condition can lead to rumination and exacerbate distress.

Acquiring and sharing information is a third digital coping activity relevant to online communi-ties. The common experiences with a health condition that mark membership in online communities can make them a potentially valuable information resource. Indeed, online health communities can be a particularly helpful repository of experiential information involving how others cope with a health condition. For example, one study showed that young women diagnosed with breast cancer were especially interested in acquiring information relevant to their role as mothers of young chil-dren and professionals aiming to maintain a career (Balka et al., 2010). This type of information goes beyond the technical aspects of a health condition that might be addressed in a doctor's office and concerns navigating life-with-illness. By virtue of providing access to others who may have had similar experiences, online communities can be a unique information resource for addressing such issues. The lived experiences of community members can provide a valuable guide or refer-ence point for others responding to similar health challenges.

Online communities can also be beneficial as a means for people facing illness to be help pro-viders. Online health communities are a space where one's own experiences can provide valuable information to others. People coping with cancer in one study indicated disclosing their experi-ences online in the hope that it might benefit others facing similar challenges (Chiu & Hsieh, 2013). Sharing information can help people feel connected to other members and may lead them to see value in the challenges they have faced. The difficulties they experienced can serve to improve the lives of others.

Despite the potential benefits of acquiring and sharing information in online health communi-ties, this form of coping may have some unexpected and deleterious outcomes that deserve note. One involves the potential for information overload. People may become overwhelmed by the sheer volume of information available about their health condition. The second is the potential for exposure to upsetting information. Researchers have shown that, although information seek-ing can make people feel a greater sense of efficacy to manage their own condition or reassurance about their circumstances, it can also lead to anxiety and confusion (Laurent et al., 2012; Medlock et al., 2013). Potential exposure to misinformation is another possibility. However, researchers evaluating the quality of medical information appearing in online health communities have found that false or misleading information tends to be relatively rare and is often corrected by community members (Cole et al., 2016; Esquivel et al., 2006).

A final digital coping activity relevant to online heath communities is sensemaking. Illness can be a source of intense and enduring distress that may create a need to give voice to one's feelings. Traumatic events like serious illness can challenge one's foundational beliefs about the world and encourage efforts to restore order. Expressing negative thoughts and feelings in an online support community offers the opportunity to make sense of those experiences. Reflection was an important motivation for sharing in a study of people experiencing chronic pain (Ressler et al., 2012). At a very basic level, the act of putting experiences into words can create structure. It allows people to order their past actions, thoughts, and feelings into a coherent narrative that explains their lives with illness. It also offers a means for people to revise the narrative of their lives that was disrupted by illness. People can incorporate illness as a chapter – or perhaps an entire volume – in the broader story of their lives. The social nature of online community participation plays a critical role in these sensemaking efforts. Other community members have the potential to provide knowing feedback based on their shared difficulties with a health condition.

Evidence-Based Recommendations for Practice

The digital coping model offers a nuanced approach to better understand online health communities. The preceding review examined forms of distress, affordances, and digital coping behaviors especially relevant to online health communities and their members. These factors have several implications for practice. For people participating in these communities and the people operating them, the digital coping model suggests the importance of considering the degree to which the affordances that mark these online communities are being leveraged effectively. Users and moderators alike, for example, might ask to what degree the community is perceived by users to be anonymous and what implications that has for their comfort in talking about health experiences. Following the documentation affordance, the potential for the community to be indexed and searched could similarly influence the degree to which users are able to acquire helpful information. It might be further possible to identify affordances unique to a community and explore how they contribute to coping behavior.

More broadly, the digital coping model underscores the importance of community and groups in coping with illness. A theme throughout this chapter involves the ways in which people experiencing similar health circumstances come together as a novel support resource. In addition to learning that one is not alone, communities provide a sense of connection as well as information to help better understand and navigate chronic or serious illness. Online communities serve as a space for people to collectively cope with their illness experiences. Finally, it is important to keep in mind that these communities are social constructions that are the product of the communication behavior that occurs within them. Online health communities are a perpetually evolving space where people come together and make sense of what it means to experience illness.

Conclusion

The goal of this chapter has been to evaluate the implications of online health communities for people experiencing illness. To this end, we first considered what it means to experience serious or chronic illness. We next examined three forms of distress, four communication technology affordances, and four types of digital coping behavior relevant to people participating in online health communities. This review collectively provided insights about why and how online health communities are used by people experiencing illness. It is my hope that readers are able to systematically evaluate the promise as well as pitfalls of online health communities as a coping resource.

Further Readings

Rains, S. A. (2018). *Coping with illness digitally*. MIT Press.

Wright, K. (2016). Communication with online social support groups for individuals facing health concerns: A review of theory and research on supportive interactions and their implications online for health outcomes. *Review of Communication Research*, *4*, 65–87. https://rcommunicationr.org/index.php/rcr/article/view/19

Yeshua-Katz, D., & Hård af Segerstad, Y. (2020). Catch 22: The paradox of social media affordances and stigmatized online support groups. *Social Media + Society*, *6*(4), 1–12. https://doi.org/10.1177/2056305120984476

Glossary

Affordance   An affordance involves the way a technology is perceived and used by people. It involves the potential for action users perceive in a technology.

Digital coping   Digital coping involves the use of communication technologies in responding to the challenges posed by illness.

Online health community   A loosely structured collection of people who share a common interest in one or more health conditions and interact using communication technologies.

References

Balka, E., Krueger, G., Holmes, B. J., & Stephen, J. E. (2010). Situating internet use: Information-seeking among young women with breast cancer. *Journal of Computer-Mediated Communication*, *15*(3), 389–411. https://doi.org/10.1111/j.1083-6101.2010.01506.x

Bar-Lev, S. (2008). "We are here to give you emotional support": Performing emotions in an online HIV/AIDS support group. *Qualitative Health Research*, *18*(4), 509–521. https://doi.org/10.1177/1049732307311680

Bell, R. A., Hu, X., Orrange, S. E., & Kravitz, R. L. (2011). Lingering questions and doubts: Online information-seeking of support forum members following their medical visits. *Patient Education and Counseling*, *85*(3), 525–528. https://doi.org/10.1016/j.pec.2011.01.015

Braithwaite, D. O., Waldron, V. R., & Finn, J. (1999). Communication of social support in computer-mediated groups for people with disabilities. *Health Communication*, *11*(2), 123–151. https://doi.org/10.1207/s15327027hc1102_2

Brashers, D. E., Neidig, J. L., Haas, S. M., Dobbs, L. K., Cardillo, L. W., & Russell, J. A. (2000). Communication in the management of uncertainty: The case of persons living with HIV or AIDS. *Communications Monographs*, *67*(1), 63–84. https://doi.org/10.1080/03637750009376495

Bury, M. (1982). Chronic illness as biographical disruption. *Sociology of Health & Illness*, *4*(2), 167–182. https://doi.org/10.1111/1467-9566.ep11339939

Chiu, Y. C., & Hsieh, Y. L. (2013). Communication online with fellow cancer patients: Writing to be remembered, gain strength, and find survivors. *Journal of Health Psychology*, *18*(12), 1572–1581. https://doi.org/10.1177/1359105312465915

Cole, J., Watkins, C., & Kleine, D. (2016). Health advice from Internet discussion forums: How bad is dangerous? *Journal of Medical Internet Research*, *18*(1), e4–e4. https://doi.org/10.2196/jmir.5051

Colombo, C., Mosconi, P., Confalonieri, P., Baroni, I., Traversa, S., Hill, S. J., Synnot, A. J., Oprandi, N., & Filippini, G. (2014). Web search behavior and information needs of people with multiple sclerosis: Focus group study and analysis of online postings. *Interactive Journal of Medical Research*, *3*(3), e3034. https://doi.org/10.2196/ijmr.3034

Coulson, N. (2015). Patterns of engagement with inflammatory bowel disease online support groups. *Gastroenterology Nursing*, *38*(5), 348–353. https://doi.org/10.1097/SGA.0000000000000131

Cutrona, C. E., & Suhr, J. A. (1992). Controllability of stressful events and satisfaction with spouse support behaviors. *Communication Research*, *19*(2), 154–174. https://doi.org/10.1177/009365092019002002

Dickins, M., Browning, C., Feldman, S., & Thomas, S. (2016). Social inclusion and the fatosphere: The role of an online weblogging community in fostering social inclusion. *Sociology of Health & Illness*. https://doi.org/10.1111/1467-9566.12397

Esquivel, A., Meric-Bernstam, F., & Bernstam, E. V. (2006). Accuracy and self correction of information received from an internet breast cancer list: Content analysis. *BMJ*, *332*(7547), 939–942. https://doi.org/10.1136/bmj.38753.524201.7C

Gibson, J. J. (1977). A theory of affordances. In R. Shaw & R. Bransford (Eds.), *Perceiving, acting, and knowing: Toward an ecological psychology* (pp. 67–82). Lawrence Erlbaum Associates.

Haas, S. M., Irr, M. E., Jennings, N. A., & Wagner, L. M. (2011). Communicating thin: A grounded model of online negative enabling support groups in the pro-anorexia movement. *New Media & Society*, *13*(1), 40–57. https://doi.org/10.1177/1461444810363910

Haberstroh, S., & Moyer, M. (2012). Exploring an online self-injury support group: Perspectives from group members. *The Journal for Specialists in Group Work*, *37*, 113–132. https://doi.org/10.1080/01933922.2011.646088

Hadert, A., & Rodham, K. (2008). The invisible reality of arthritis: A qualitative analysis of an online message board. *Musculoskeletal Care*, *6*(3), 181–196. https://doi.org/10.1002/msc.131

Holbrey, S., & Colson, N. S. (2013). A qualitative investigation of the impact of peer to peer online support for women living with polycystic ovary syndrome. *BMC Women's Health*, 13. https://doi.org/10.1186/1472-6874-13-51

Holt-Lunstad, J., Smith, T. B., & Layton, J. B. (2010). Social relationships and mortality risk: A meta-analytic review. *PLOS Medicine*, *7*(7), e1000316–e1000316. https://doi.org/10.1371/journal.pmed.1000316

Høybye, M. T., Johansen, C., & Tjørnhøj-Thomsen, T. (2005). Online interaction. Effects of storytelling in an Internet breast cancer support group. *Psycho-Oncology*, *14*(3), 211–220. https://doi.org/10.1002/pon.837

Kang, K. K. (2017). Anonymity and interaction in an online breast cancer social support group. *Communication Studies*, *68*(4), 403–421. https://doi.org/10.1080/10510974.2017.1340902

Kirschning, S., & von Kardorff, E. (2008). The use of the Internet by women with breast cancer and men with prostate cancer-results of online research. *Journal of Public Health*, *16*(2), 133–143. https://doi.org/10.1007/s10389-007-0134-0

Kleinman, A. (1988). *The illness narratives: Suffering, healing, and the human condition*. Basic Books.

Laurent, M. R., Cremers, S., Verhoef, G., & Dierickx, D. (2012). Internet use for health information among haematology outpatients: A cross-sectional survey. *Informatics for Health & Social Care*, *37*(2), 62–73. https://doi.org/10.3109/17538157.2011.606481

Lazarus, R. S. (1966). *Psychological stress and the coping process*. McGraw-Hill.

Lazarus, R. S. (2012). Evolution of a model of stress, coping, and discrete emotions. In V. H. Rice (Ed.), *Handbook of stress, coping, and health* (pp. 199–225). Sage.

Lieberman, M. A., & Goldstein, B. A. (2006). Not all negative emotions are equal: The role of emotional expression in online support groups for women with breast cancer. *Psycho-Oncology*, *15*, 160–168. https://doi.org/10.1002/pon.932

Malik, S. H., & Coulson, N. S. (2008). Computer-mediated infertility support groups: An exploratory study of online experiences. *Patient Education and Counseling*, *73*, 105–113. https://doi.org/10.1016/j.pec.2008.05.024

Markus, M. L., & Silver, M. S. (2008). A foundation for the study of IT effects: A new look at DeSanctis and Poole's concepts of structural features and spirit. *Journal of the Association for Information Systems*, *9*(10/11), 609–632.

Medlock, S., Eslami, S., Askari, M., Sent, D., de Rooij, S. E., & Abu-Hanna, A. (2013). The consequences of seniors seeking health information using the internet and other sources. *Studies in Health Technology and Informatics*, *192*, 457–460. https://doi.org/10.3233/978-1-61499-289-9-457

Mirivel, J. C., & Thombre, A. (2010). Surviving online: An analysis of how burn survivors recover from life crises. *Southern Communication Journal*, *75*(3), 232–254. https://doi.org/10.1080/10417940903377151

Montali, L., Zulato, E., Frigerio, A., Frangi, E., & Camussi, E. (2021). Mirroring, monitoring, modelling, belonging, and distancing: Psychosocial processes in an online support group of breast cancer patients. *Journal of Community Psychology* [Advance online publication]. https://doi.org/10.1002/jcop.22696

Rainie, L., & Fox, S. (2000). *The online health care revolution*. Pew Internet and American Life Project. https://www.pewresearch.org/internet/2000/11/26/the-online-health-care-revolution/

Rains, S. A. (2018). *Coping with illness digitally*. MIT Press.

Rains, S. A., Peterson, E., & Wright, K. B. (2015). Communicating social support in computer-mediated contexts: A meta-analytic review of content analyses examining support messages shared online among individuals coping with illness. *Communication Monographs*, *82*(4), 403–430. https://doi.org/10.1080/03637751.2015.1019530

Ressler, P. K., Bradshaw, Y. S., Gualtieri, L., & Chui, K. K. H. (2012). Communicating the experience of chronic pain and illness through blogging. *Journal of Medical Internet Research*, *14*(5), e143–e143. https://doi.org/10.2196/jmir.2002

Riessman, F. (1965). The "helper" therapy principle. *Social Work*, *10*(2), 27–32. https://doi.org/10.1093/sw/10.2.27

Rodriquez, J. (2013). Narrating dementia: Self and community in an online forum. *Qualitative Health Research*, *23*(9), 1215–1227. https://doi.org/10.1177/1049732313501725

Scambler, G. (2009). Health-related stigma. *Sociology of Health & Illness*, *31*, 441–455. https://doi.org/10.1111/j.1467-9566.2009.01161.x

Tanis, M. (2008). Health-related online forums: What's the big attraction? *Journal of Health Communication*, *13*, 698–714. https://doi.org/10.1080/10810730802415316

Tiebout, H. M. (1944). Therapeutic mechanisms of alcoholics anonymous. *American Journal of Psychiatry*, *100*(4), 468–473. https://doi.org/10.1176/ajp.100.4.468

Wright, K. B., & Miller, C. H. (2010). A measure of weak tie/strong tie support network preference. *Communication Monographs*, *77*(4), 502–520. https://doi.org/10.1080/03637751.2010.502538

22 Groups in Medicine

Franziska Tschan, Sandra Keller, Stephan U. Marsch, Guido Beldi, and Norbert K. Semmer

Chapter Objectives

- Familiarize the reader with concepts related to teamwork discussed in research on teams in medicine.
- Compare three typical teams in medicine – ward teams, ad-hoc emergency teams, and surgical teams – with regard to temporal stability, skill and authority differentiation, task requirements, and the resulting challenges for collaboration and communication.

Introduction

This chapter begins with a brief history of **medical team** research and introduces common concepts in this field. We then discuss three prototypical healthcare teams using Hollenbeck et al.'s (2012) dimensions, which include authority and skill differentiation, as well as temporal stability, to which we add task (coordination) requirements. Finally, we offer recommendations.

History of Medical Team Research and Concepts

Research on healthcare teams is relatively recent (Schaefer & Helmreich, 1994), reflecting the growing emphasis on working in teams in healthcare. The number of publications and topics studied are rapidly growing (Dinh et al., 2019; Mayo et al., 2021). Contributions come from different disciplines, including social and organizational psychology (Kolbe et al., 2014), human factors (Salas et al., 2007), communication (Eisenberg et al., 2005; Woo et al., 2020), medicine (Hunziker et al., 2011), and nursing (Gillespie et al., 2012). Most research is published in medical journals (Dinh et al., 2019).

Historically, team research in medicine originated from patient safety concerns, driven by the realization that many medical errors and mishaps are rooted in communication and collaboration issues (Leape, 1994). Cooperation between aviation/military and medical scholars found similarities between aviation and medical teams (Flin & Maran, 2004); this influenced theories and concepts used. The analysis of the death of an airline pilot and safety specialist's wife during a standard anesthesia induction, which showed that teamwork and communication failures were a main reason for the tragic outcome (Bromiley & Mitchell, 2009), contributed to the popularity of the topic within medicine, but also in the general public.

Conceptual papers, meta-analyses, and reviews on medical teams use either the input-process-output framework (McGrath, 1984) as organizing principle (Dinh et al., 2019; Fernandez et al., 2008; Rosen et al., 2018; Schmutz et al., 2019), or Marks et al.'s (2001) taxonomy of team processes (Dinh et al., 2021). Many papers also enumerate specific aspects to consider, with considerable variety in number and scope (Fernandez et al., 2008; King et al., 2008; Salas et al., 2008). This is not surprising,

DOI: 10.4324/9781003227458-25

given that teamwork in medicine is as complex as teamwork in other domains, and the applicability of general concepts to all types of teams in a uniform way is limited (McGrath et al., 2000).

The following concepts are particularly salient and frequently discussed in medical team research:

- *Non-technical skills* (NTS; soft skills), initially developed for airline pilots, are defined as "cognitive, social and personal resource skills that complement technical skills and contribute to safe and efficient task performance" (Flin et al., 2008, p. 1). Three NTS refer to communication, teamwork, and leadership. NTS are general ("generic") skills, but the critical set varies for different professional roles. For example, within **surgical teams**; surgeons require more leadership NTS (Yule & Paterson-Brown, 2012) compared to anesthetists (Fletcher et al., 2004), or scrub nurses (Mitchell et al., 2012), reflecting the different tasks and roles within the team.
- *(Team) Situation awareness (SA)* refers to the perception of ongoing developments, "knowing what is going on around you" (Flin et al., 2008. p. 17), which helps to anticipate and facilitate coordination. It was first described on the individual level (Flin et al., 2008) and later applied to teams (Wellens, 1993). Team SA overlaps with the concept of shared mental models, transactive memory systems, and other concepts of shared cognition (Mohammed et al., 2017), but emphasizes knowledge and understanding of the *ongoing* process. These concepts characterize teams as information processing systems with communication representing information processing on the team level (Cranach et al., 1986; Hinsz et al., 1997).
- *Closed-loop communication* (CLC) is a communication sequence that assures information is accurately understood (Salas et al., 2008). A message sent (call out) is followed by feedback and acknowledgment (readback) and then followed by a verification of the message by the sender (hearback). This is important in high-risk organizations where small misunderstandings (e.g., confounding left and right) can have severe consequences (e.g., wrong limb amputation).
- *Step-back communication, briefings*: Stepping back from taskwork and reflecting upon one's actions or specifically devoting time to exchanging information improves team performance (Allen et al., 2018; West, 1996). For teams focused on task execution, planned step-backs may be particularly helpful (Fernandez et al., 2008; Schmutz & Eppich, 2017). Examples are patient rounds, team checklists, briefings, and debriefings (Kündig et al., 2020). Step-backs during task execution can help to deal with difficult situations (Rall et al., 2008) or prepare for critical phases (Roberts et al., 2014; Tschan et al., 2022).
- *Psychological safety; speaking up*: Behaviors revealing own vulnerabilities (e.g., asking for help, admitting errors), or challenging others' behavior (i.e., speaking up) carry interpersonal risks, because interaction partners may react negatively. "The shared belief that the team is safe for [such] interpersonal risk taking" (Edmondson, 1999, p. 345) is called *psychological safety*. It is particularly important in teams with strict hierarchies where lower status members may feel hesitant to speak up. It is associated with trust, cohesion, good interpersonal relations, and teamwork quality, and contributes to patient safety (Okuyama et al., 2014).

Three Different Team Types in Medicine and Their Specific Challenges

As an organizing structure, we use Hollenbeck et al.'s (2012) framework to classify teams based on skill and authority differentiation, and temporal stability. *Skill differentiation* refers to "the degree to which members have specialized knowledge or functional capacities" (Hollenbeck et al., 2012, p. 84) within the team. Low skill differentiation allows for easy member exchange because all have similar skills; high differentiation indicates specialized roles that are not interchangeable. *Authority differentiation* is "the degree to which decision-making responsibility is vested in individual members, subgroups of the team or the collective as a whole" (Hollenbeck et al., 2012, p. 84), and describes the team's power and leadership structure. *Temporal stability* pertains to past and future cooperation within a team. Additionally, we consider *task and coordination requirements* as a fourth aspect because tasks differ in behavioral as well as in cooperation requirements that influence optimal communication and coordination within a group (Kerr, 2017; McGrath, 1984; Tschan & von Cranach, 1996).

We discuss three prototypical hospital teams. First, as shown in Table 22.1, **Ward teams** provide 24/7 patient care, team members rotating in shifts. Second, upon an alarm signaling an emergency,

Table 22.1 Temporal Stability, Task Requirements, Skill and Authority Differentiation and Resulting Challenges for Medical Ward Teams, Ad-Hoc Emergency Teams, and Surgical Teams

Team	Temporal Stability	Task Requirements	Skill Differentiation/ Authority Differentiation	Challenges
Ward teams	Moderate temporal stability – temporal frame is the work shift. Stable standing team (high familiarity), but team composition changes each shift.	Provide diagnosis and care for inpatients. Ensure continuation of work across shifts 24/7	Multidisciplinary; nurses and physicians have different skills, socialization, professional culture, status, goals, and responsibilities.	• Multidisciplinary collaboration in a hierarchical environment with status differences • Ensure information transmission across shifts to optimize continuation of care • Ensure integrative decision-making and shared representations
Ad-hoc action teams (cardiopulmonary resuscitation)	High temporal instability – temporal frame is the emergency; teams form ad-hoc around an emergency. Team members may join sequentially. Often low familiarity.	Deal with an acute emergency under high time pressure. Rapid decision-making necessary. Very tight collaboration requirements. Co-presence of team members.	Mono- or multidisciplinary. Team members receive standardized training. Leadership may have to be established ad hoc.	• Establish a functioning team rapidly, integrate sequentially arriving team members • Ensure that the team follows treatment guidelines • Establish leadership and specific roles • Optimize communication and coordination, minimize interruptions
Surgical teams	Temporal instability – temporal frame is an operation. Familiarity often rather low.	Perform a safe operation. Be ready for rapid adaptations. Very tight (manual) collaboration requirements. Co-presence of team members	Multidisciplinary, different skills and responsibilities of different professions. Hierarchical, with core role of surgeon who is performing central task and is team leader	• Ensure optimal coordination in multidisciplinary, often low familiarity team • Minimize communication issues and ensure shared and continued situational awareness • Deal with the double role of the surgeon performing the core manual task and leading the team • Minimize disruptive communication and ensure psychological safety

anyone who happens to be around may respond, forming an **ad-hoc or flash emergency team**, whose members may not know each other. Finally, *surgical teams* are multidisciplinary and assembled for each operation from a pool of personnel (Stucky & De Jong, 2021).

Hospital Ward Teams

Hospital ward teams are responsible 24/7 for inpatients. Tasks are diverse and include diagnostics, treatment, and care. Task cooperation requirements range from independent individual tasks (e.g., administering medication), sequential tasks by different team members (e.g., preparing a patient for a procedure, transporting the patient) to tight temporal-spatial collaboration (e.g., assisting with a change of dressing).

Ward teams have high skill differentiation and are multidisciplinary, with physicians and nurses as the main professions. Their general goals align, and their work is interdependent, but the professions undergo different training and socialization and have different professional cultures and role expectations. Physicians focus on disease and medical treatment while nurses also address patients' needs (care) more generally (Zwarenstein & Reeves, 2002).

Ward teams have high authority differentiation. Although nurses and physicians are organized separately regarding administration and the chain of command, physicians have a higher status (Noyes, 2021). Hierarchies, status differences, diverging role expectations, and intergroup issues are typical and can contribute to friction. Both report higher trust within their own profession (McComb et al., 2017), but nurses perceive more collaboration problems with physicians than vice-versa (House & Havens, 2017). A classic paper by Stein (1967) described how nurses use indirect communication strategies for recommendations to physicians; 25 years later, Stein and colleagues (1990) noted changes in the nurse-physician relationship toward more equality. Despite somewhat flatter hierarchies, nurses still tend to avoid open disagreement with physicians (Noyes, 2021).

Good multidisciplinary collaboration in ward teams improves patient outcomes (Ma et al., 2018) and staff satisfaction (Korner et al., 2015). Recommendations for improving collaboration range from seemingly simple behaviors like signaling respect by mutual greeting, listening, and introduction of new team members to both teams, (McComb et al., 2017), to more complex endeavors, such as structural changes (Glouberman & Mintzberg, 2001) and interdisciplinary team training (Parker et al., 2019).

Ensure Information Transmission Across Shifts

Ward teams are temporally unstable and change twice or three times a day, making continuity of care and information transmission to the next shift important. Handovers are time slots devoted to the transmission of information across teams. Accurate handovers require that the providing team has information and accurately transmits what is important for the receiving team. Receivers have to understand and store the information and link it to future actions. This is a demanding requirement: errors and information loss are frequent during handovers (Webster et al., 2022). Common failures are related to medication, documentation, or inaccurate accounts of interventions (Bogenstatter et al., 2009). Hindrances to accurate handovers can be external (e.g., interruptions and noise), but also arise from insufficient preparation and lack of structure of the handover process. To optimize handovers, structured procedures, such as I-PASS (illness severity – patient summary – action list – situation awareness and contingency planning – synthesis by the receiver) have been developed. Its introduction increased the quality of information transmission (Robertson et al., 2014) and reduced errors, without prolonging handover time (Starmer et al., 2014).

Healthcare has a culture of documenting patient and treatment-related information. The introduction of electronic health records has reduced medication errors and increased guideline adherence (Campanella et al., 2016). However, it also increases administrative load (Holzer et al., 2019; Salminen-Karlsson & Golay, 2022). Physicians and nurses spend about 30% of their time with patient contact but 40% with documentation (Momenipur & Pennathur, 2019). While helpful in principle, electronic health records often have problems in design and usability and may not be adequately adapted to the team member's needs (Salminen-Karlsson & Golay, 2022).

Ensure Integrative Decision-Making and Shared Representations Within the Team

Ward rounds (a team visiting patients regularly) have a long tradition in medicine, offering communication opportunities that serve to collect, update, and transmit information and discuss treatment plans. Interdisciplinary rounds that include both nurses and physicians have a particularly positive influence on team collaboration and quality of care, as patient complications often decrease after introducing interdisciplinary rounds (Arora et al., 2014). Interdisciplinary rounds allow the integration of physician and nursing perspectives (Heip et al., 2022), though differences between professional groups sometimes persist after the introduction (Have & Nap, 2014). Furthermore, establishing interdisciplinary rounds is challenging because of the different working schedules of nurses and physicians, which make it hard to find a suitable time to meet (Heip et al., 2022).

Ad-Hoc Emergency Teams

A patient emergency requires immediate action. Typically, the first person realizing an emergency sounds an alarm, and everyone close rushes to help, creating a short-lived ad-hoc or flash team. We will discuss resuscitation teams (responding to a cardiac arrest) as examples of ad-hoc teams.

Establish a Functioning Team

Forming around an ongoing emergency, ad-hoc emergency teams are temporally unstable in that team composition may be different each time. Members may or may not be of the same profession, may lack previous collaboration experience, and may not know each other's expertise (Hunt et al., 2008; McLeod et al., 2019). As new members often join sequentially, integrating them without interrupting the ongoing treatment can be challenging (Marsch et al., 2004)

Ensure Enacting Treatment Guidelines

For resuscitation teams, evidence-based treatment guidelines specify the steps of the cardiopulmonary resuscitation (CPR) task, which include chest compressions combined with ventilations, defibrillation, and medication (Panchal et al., 2020). CPR has tight coordination requirements; actions have to be coordinated in close physical and temporal proximity on a second-to-second basis to avoid interruptions. Time-pressure is high, as every minute of treatment delays after a cardiac arrest reduces survival chances – for example, patients are 39% likely to survive to be discharged if defibrillated within two minutes as compared to 22% if defibrillation was delayed (Chan et al., 2008).

CPR guidelines are standardized task requirements, and healthcare providers receive regular training. Standardization is an established means of team coordination (Glouberman & Mintzberg, 2001; Okhuysen & Bechky, 2009), creating a shared mental model, which allows for coordinated action even among team members without prior collaboration experiences (Wittenbaum et al., 2002). However, guidelines refer to prototypical situations and teams need to adapt to the specific context to ensure optimal performance (McLeod et al., 2019). Thus, many resuscitation teams take longer than prescribed to initiate critical treatments (Hunt et al., 2008), and treatment delays were the most frequent errors (Ornato et al., 2012). CPR team performance often remains suboptimal, indicating the importance, and the difficulties, of adaptational coordination.

Establish Leadership

Tight coordination requirements under time pressure require rapid and clear decision-making and role and task assignments, and new members need to be informed and integrated. In these situations, a leader can prioritize tasks, assign roles, ensure adherence to the guidelines, balance workload, and encourage team members to speak up (Fernandez et al., 2008; Roberts et al., 2014). However, in ad-hoc teams, it may not immediately be apparent who is the leader, which means authority differentiation may not be established. Lack of leadership is one of the main deficits during resuscitations. Nurses and junior physicians often feel insufficiently prepared to lead, and leaders often fail to assign roles or tasks to team members, resulting in up to a third of team members (many of who are junior) not knowing how they should act (Robinson et al., 2016).

Resuscitations led by trained leaders showed increased guideline adherence and more timely initiation of tasks (Cooper & Wakelam, 1999; Fernandez et al., 2008). A relationship between more leadership and resuscitation performance has also been found in other studies (Hunziker et al., 2010). Specific recommendations on how to communicate as leader include to be direct, give short and clear orders, and address team members by their name (Roberts et al., 2014).

Because ad-hoc teams often do not have a preassigned leader, leadership may be established by explicitly (self-) identifying a team member as leader early in the situation. Unfortunately, this occurs too infrequently and remains a problem even after training (Roberts et al., 2014). Sometimes, leadership is assumed by the first responder (often a nurse) and handed over to a higher-status person arriving later (Tschan et al., 2006). Sometimes, team members assume leadership when it is lacking, as when nurses help physicians with little leadership experience (Janssens et al., 2018).

An interesting issue is whether shared leadership is beneficial in resuscitation teams (Bedwell et al., 2012) – several team members can concurrently lead. Leadership utterances (e.g., directives) can improve coordination independently from who emits them. In general, shared leadership has performance-improving potential (D'Innocenzo et al., 2016) although evidence in medicine is scarce and inconclusive (Janssens et al., 2018). The potential of shared leadership depends on the degree to which it utilizes specific skills or expertise, relieves the leader from overload, or compensates for leader weaknesses. However, the coordination costs of shared leadership may outweigh potential advantages.

Optimize Coordinative Behaviors and Avoid Interruptions

Coordinative behaviors suggested for CPR teams range from general categories (communication, coordination) to more specific behaviors such as listening, information sharing, monitoring, mutual support, and speaking up, to very specific behaviors such as CLC and talking to the room (Roberts et al., 2014). However, communication errors, defined as "communication problems that cause a delay in treatment or affect decision making" (Hunt et al., 2008, p. e38) were observed in 100% of resuscitation teams; good communication was related to resuscitation quality and patient survival (Cant et al., 2016).

CLC is particularly useful in emergencies, which often involve chaotic and noisy situations with several strands of actions going on simultaneously. CLC helps avoid misunderstandings (Salas et al., 2008) and is related to fewer errors and faster completing of requests (El-Shafy et al., 2018). However, despite specific training, it seems difficult to implement and is rarely observed (Hughes et al., 2014). Although we are not aware of any pertinent studies, we surmise that CLC may be experienced as unnatural and awkward, as it contradicts Grice's (Grice, 1975) maxim of quantity, which states to not repeat information that may be known, although such repetitions may have important benefits in emergencies.

CPR guidelines request to *avoid even short interruptions in patient care* (Panchal et al., 2020). Nevertheless, significant interruptions happen in 70% of resuscitations (McInnes et al., 2012). Detailed process analyses showed that treatment interruptions were often caused by all team members engaging in secondary activities (e.g., resolving technical problems), thereby neglecting the primary task (Tschan et al., 2011). This can be interpreted as loss in situational awareness, which often happens in stressful situations, and may explain why team leaders often are not aware of treatment interruptions and thus do not correct them (McInnes et al., 2012).

Surgical Teams

With regard to task requirements and temporal stability, surgical teams are in-between ward and ad-hoc teams. Like ad-hoc teams, surgical teams are assembled around a specific, time-limited task and disband afterward, but they typically are members of a larger team. Surgical procedures have predefined steps known to all team members, and operating requires close temporal-spatial coordination. Like ward teams, they are high in authority and skill differentiation, requiring multidisciplinary coordination.

Most surgical procedures follow predefined steps; thus, team members can prepare before they collaborate, which helps to establish a shared mental model. However, intraoperative modifications of strategies are common, and in case of a non-routine event (e.g., bleeding), rapid adaptation is key. Task complexity can be even higher for emergencies, and cooperation requirements are especially challenging for special techniques, such as robotic surgery (Catchpole et al., 2019).

Operations require particularly close spatial-temporal coordination. The surgeon performs the operation, assisted by colleagues and residents as well as a scrub technician. Within this team, coordination requires close synchronization of movements, as surgeons assist each other in cutting, suturing and other sensorimotor tasks, and scrub technicians hand and take back instruments. Movement synchronization is a matter of fractions of seconds; it works best if team members can anticipate each other's proximal movements (Korkiakangas et al., 2014). Scrub technicians familiar with the procedure and with the surgeon can "think ahead of the surgeon" (Mitchell et al., 2012), and often hand the instrument even before the surgeon explicitly requires it. Such tacit or implicit coordination implies that people anticipate the needs of others; they can reduce communication to short utterances (e.g., "now") or to nonverbal communication (e.g., nodding) (Wittenbaum et al., 2002).

Ensuring Optimal Coordination in Multidisciplinary, Low Familiarity Teams

In surgical teams, *skill differentiation is high, with clear roles and competencies.* Surgeons perform the operation, the scrub technician is responsible for instruments, and anesthesia providers keep the patient in stable condition. Circulators act as the link between the surgical team and the "non-sterile world" by providing material, sending out samples, communicating with externals, and performing administrative tasks.

The tight collaboration requirements, the common goals, and the strong interdependence suggest that surgical teams correspond to the prototypical definition of teams (McGrath, 1984). However, there is often no consensus about one important aspect of being a team, namely the feeling of being a group ("entitativity," Blanchard et al., 2018). Whereas most scrub technicians generally perceive the people present during an operation as one team, surgeons and anesthetists perceive multiple specialized sub-teams cooperating (Undre et al., 2006). Although this reflects the task distribution during the operation, it may also be enforced by stereotypes related to the different professions.

For organizational reasons, the operating team is often composed around the main surgeon for from a pool of scrub technicians, circulators, and anesthetists, implying low team familiarity. This influences team process and team performance because familiar team members have better knowledge of each other's expertise ("transactive memory system"), share information more easily, and thus develop better shared mental models and team situation awareness (Bedwell et al., 2012). Higher familiarity in surgical teams was indeed related to fewer miscommunications, better teamwork quality, shorter turnover times, and shorter duration of operations (Stucky & De Jong, 2021; Xiao et al., 2015). Familiarity decreased the risk of team members suffering needle injuries, indicating that even sensory-motor coordination profits from familiarity (Myers et al., 2016). Patient outcomes related to familiarity include fewer complications, shorter hospital stays, and fewer readmissions (Kurmann et al., 2014; Xiao et al., 2015). Newer research shows that familiarity may not be necessary for the whole team, but seems most important with regard to specific pairings, with horizontal familiarity between peers (i.e., main and second surgeon) being especially important (ElBardissi et al., 2013; Kurmann et al., 2014) as compared to vertical familiarity (i.e., surgeon and circulators) (Avgerinos et al., 2020).

Cooperation and Communication During Operations

Of all medical fields, adverse events are most frequent for surgery, with human factors as main contributor (Zegers et al., 2011). About half of the adverse events are regarded as preventable (Schwendimann et al., 2018). During operations, communication issues are particularly frequent (Hu et al., 2012; Wiegmann et al., 2007). About a third of communication episodes during operations failed (e.g., poor timing, missing or inaccurate information), and more than a third of failures resulted in negative effects for the procedure, the team, or the patient (Lingard, 2004). Although teams dealt with most minor issues without persisting negative effects, communication failures were still the strongest predictor of more severe surgical errors (Wiegmann et al., 2007).

Besides the obvious link between communication failures and subsequent problems, more general aspects of communication and collaboration are important. Across different types of teams and tasks, a meta-analysis found that more (notably task-related) communication was related to higher performance (Marlow et al., 2018). This also applies to surgery, as more information sharing and more task-related communication during operations was related to lower patient mortality and complications (Mazzocco et al., 2009; Tschan et al., 2015).

A majority of communication during operations involved surgeons (Sevdalis et al., 2012); they adapt their communication to the specific collaboration involved, such as more requests (e.g., for instruments) vis-à-vis scrub technicians, and more statements vis-à-vis fellow surgeons. Most communication between scrubs and circulators involved requests (Santos et al., 2012). This corresponds to the specific collaborative tasks of the respective dyads, but also indicates that communication during operations is largely dyadic (Parush et al., 2011), which is consistent with the finding that dyadic exchanges characterize many groups (Parker, 1988). Indeed, during operations, little communication is directed to the whole team (Santos et al., 2012), implying that not all communication contributes to building shared mental models or SA of the whole team. Although one may overhear communication addressed to others, the commonly high levels of noise in the operating room impair communication and concentration (Keller et al., 2016), and parallel tasks of anesthetists and circulators may make it difficult to follow others' conversations.

Thus, *step-back communication*, which provides updates during the operation itself, may foster SA. Well-known step-back communications are surgical safety checklists as advocated by the World Health Organization (WHO) (Haynes et al., 2009) and adopted by most hospitals. Checklists should be completed before anesthesia induction, before skin incision, and before the patient leaves the operating room. The checklists contain items designed to avoid the so-called never-events, such as operating at the wrong site or missing allergies. Correct use of the WHO checklist is related to lower patient complications, reduced communication problems, and better teamwork (Haugen et al., 2019). However, to maintain SA throughout the operation, continuous updates are useful. An intervention study introduced the "StOP?"protocol that requires the surgeon to provide structured step-back communication episodes. The surgeon informs about the current **S**tatus, next **O**bjectives, and potential **P**roblems and (**?**) encourages team members to contribute (Tschan et al., 2022). These regular updates ensure SA and encourage speaking up. Using the StOP? protocol is associated with lower patient complications and lower mortality (Tschan et al., 2022).

Dealing With the Core Role of the Surgeon

Surgical teams are high in authority differentiation, with the surgeon as leader. As surgeons execute the main task and are central for collaboration, including leadership (Pasarakonda et al., 2020), they have "strategic core roles," which are defined as being central with regard to the tasks as well as to the workflow (Humphrey et al., 2009). However, operating itself is a manual task that requires the surgeon to pay close attention to the operative field; this captures concentration (Gallagher et al., 2015) and can limit the attention the surgeon can allocate to team processes. During operations, surgeons engage mostly in functional leadership (Zaccaro et al., 2002), managing aspects critical to the immediate task. Most leadership behavior was addressed to the collaboration partners at the operating table, and even more so during critical events and complex phases (Parker et al., 2014). While this may be functional for the immediate operative task, it can generate a leadership vacuum for less proximal team members such as circulators who are not directly at the operating table.

Supporting team members is part of the leadership role and an NTS for surgeons. It includes establishing rapport within the team, providing constructive criticism, recognition, and respectful communication (Yule & Paterson-Brown, 2012). During operations led by surgeons with a more transformational (inspiring and motivating as opposed to rewarding and punishing) leadership style, team members shared more information and showed more voice behaviors (Hu et al., 2016), supporting the notion that inclusive leadership influences psychological safety (Nembhard & Edmondson, 2006).

Minimizing Disruptive Communication

Tensions and rudeness during operations, most often expressed by surgeons (Keller et al., 2019), are a pervasive issue (Keller et al., 2020); studies reported several tensions per operation (Keller et al., 2019). Explanations for tensions during operations often refer to egotistic behavior, personality, and gender (Jones et al., 2018), based on the stereotype depicting surgeons as male and authoritarian solo players. However, triggers of tensions are often situational, such as coordination problems, threats to patient safety, or poor performance of team members. Tense communication episodes were predominantly a reaction to coordination problems rather than to disagreements and interpersonal dislike (Keller et al., 2019). It is thus important to include coordination problems as triggers of tensions and not fall prey to the fundamental attribution error by regarding disruptive behavior mainly as a personality issue.

Tense communication in the OR can negatively affect team processes and performance. Tense communication need not be clearly rude; displaying impatience was enough to lower technical performance of anesthesia providers (Katz et al., 2019). Moreover, speaking up after a mistake made by a senior surgeon was lower if residents were discouraged to ask questions (Barzallo Salazar et al., 2014).

Being exposed to disruptive behavior consumes attentional resources. Notably, an offense experienced likely focuses attention on concerns about defending one's integrity (Semmer et al., 2019). This may limit individual performance and interfere with emerging states in teams, such as building a transactive memory system (Riskin et al., 2020).

Recommendations for Practice

Medical teams have to overcome specific challenges due to their temporal instability, high authority differentiation, different levels of skill differentiation, and task coordination requirements. In an environment where lives are at stake, small errors can have important consequences, and there is often high time pressure. There are several recommendations. First, healthcare should work toward

---

Box 22.1   Health Team Emergency Situation

At the handover (transferring the responsibility for a patient to a new caretaker), intensive care nurse Hannah is informed that her 62-year-old male patient just underwent a cardiac procedure. While she introduces herself to the patient, the patient monitor displays short episodes of ventricular tachycardia (VT; abnormally rapid heartbeat). Hannah immediately asks two colleagues for help. She only has to say "VT," and Carlo and Lee immediately understand that this is a potential emergency. Although they are all nurses, Hannah takes the lead and asks Carlo to call a physician and Lee to prepare the defibrillator (a device allowing to synchronize VT to normal heartbeat). Shortly thereafter, the patient becomes unresponsive, the monitor shows continuous VT, a life-threatening situation. As Hannah announces, "We need to resuscitate!," the team coordinates without words. Carlo, on the phone, updates the physician, rushes back to the patient and starts cardiac massage as Hannah ventilates and asks Lee to defibrillate. As VT persists after defibrillation, the team changes back to cardiac massage and ventilation. Junior physician Dan arrives, asking "What have you done so far?," and Hannah reports. As physician, Dan is now in charge, takes the lead and tells the team to continue ventilation and cardiac massage and to prepare for further defibrillations. But now the monitor displays a changed heartrate. Dan loudly gives directions to each member of the team: "Asystole, we cannot defibrillate. Lee, prepare 1 mg of epinephrine. Hannah, call the senior. Carlo, continue cardiac massage!" and Dan then steps to the head of the patient to ventilate. Lee administers the medication and says, "1 mg of epinephrine administered." Dan acknowledges, closing this communication loop. While the team continues resuscitation, Dan asks Hannah for background information about the patient when Dawna, senior physician, arrives. Dan informs her about the patient, and they discuss potential causes and treatment. Lee sees that the monitor shows VT again and suggest defibrillating. As none of the physicians reacts, Hannah states loudly, "Defibrillation is suggested," which triggers Dan to order defibrillation. Dawna nods. After defibrillation, normal heartbeat returns and the patient wakes up. The team breaks into a relieved laughter as the instructor announces, "The simulation exercise is over, please come to the debriefing room" (Tschan et al., 2006).

structural and organizational support to establish conditions for good teamwork, for example, real teams, role clarity, temporal stability, psychological safety, and training (Hackman, 2002). Second, the importance of task-related communication and information exchange implies that (structured) communication is an important task on its own right that needs to be considered. Pre-set timeslots for deliberate information exchanges such as handovers, rounds, step-back communication during procedures, briefings, and debriefings should be provided for teams. Treatment guidelines seldom include communication and coordination requirements, these should be added.

The Pivotal Importance of Task and Role Requirements

We added task (coordination) requirements as a fourth category to Hollenbeck et al.'s (2012) taxonomy, acknowledging the crucial role of task-related communication and behaviors in group performance (Kerr, 2017). Many team concepts such as shared mental models or SA refer to tasks, and even tensions often result from task coordination problems. Also, leading implies making sure that necessary tasks actually get done (McGrath, 1962).

Obviously, interpersonal aspects are extremely important, as teams work best in a culture of respect (Leape et al., 2012). However, the association of socio-emotional aspects with tasks often is overlooked. Roles and tasks are part of many people's identity, and "illegitimate tasks" (e.g., "non-nursing activities") may be perceived as offending (Semmer et al., 2019). Therefore, teamwork analysis must consider task requirements.

Training and Interventions

Team training and interventions can improve medical team's teamwork, despite implementation challenges (King et al., 2008). Team training positively impacts learning, transfer, and patient outcomes, and there is evidence for the learning-transfer-results chain (Hughes et al., 2016). Interventions promoting reflection and information sharing such as standardized handoffs and briefings (Allen et al., 2018), step-back communication (Roberts et al., 2014; Tschan et al., 2022), and targeted short instructions guiding attention to specific collaborative behavior (Hochstrasser et al., 2022; Hunziker et al., 2010) showed positive results on medical team processes and outcomes.

Further Readings

Bromiley, M., & Mitchell, L. (2009). Would you speak up if the consultant got it wrong? And would you listen if someone said you'd got it wrong. *Journal of Perioperative Practice*, *19*(10), 326–329. https://doi.org/10.1177/175045890901901004

Gregory, M. E., Hughes, A. M., Benishek, L. E., Sonesh, S. C., Lazzara, E. H., Woodard, L. D., & Salas, E. (2019). Toward the development of the perfect medical team. *Journal of Patient Safety.* https://doi.org/10.1097/pts.0000000000000598

Rosen, M. A., DiazGranados, D., Dietz, A. S., Benishek, L. E., Thompson, D., Pronovost, P. J., & Weaver, S. J. (2018). Teamwork in healthcare: Key discoveries enabling safer, high-quality care. *American Psychologist*, *73*(4), 433–450. https://doi.org/10.1037/amp0000298

Glossary

Ad-hoc emergency teams (also called action teams)   They are temporary groups of experts, often from different disciplines. Formed to rapidly respond to specific emergency situations, such as a cardiac arrest.

Medical teams   They are composed of healthcare professionals with different roles and specialties who collaborate to provide healthcare to patients.

Surgical teams   They are groups of healthcare professionals typically composed of a surgeon, anesthesia provider, a scrub technician, a circulator, and other specialists, depending on the procedure. They collaborate to perform a surgical procedure.

Ward teams   They provide and coordinate patient care 24/7 for patients admitted to a hospital ward. These interprofessional teams are composed of nurses, physicians, and other specialized professionals.

References

Allen, J. A., Reiter-Palmon, R., Crowe, J., & Scott, C. (2018). Debriefs: Teams learning from doing in context. *American Psychologist, 73*(4), 504–516. https://doi.org/10.1037/amp0000246

Arora, N., Patel, K., Engell, C. A., & LaRosa, J. A. (2014). The effect of interdisciplinary team rounds on urinary catheter and central venous catheter days and rates of infection. *American Journal of Medical Quality, 29*(4), 329–334. https://doi.org/10.1177/1062860613500519

Avgerinos, E., Fragkos, I., & Huang, Y. (2020). Team familiarity in cardiac surgery operations: The effects of hierarchy and failure on team productivity. *Human Relations, 73*(9), 1278–1307. https://doi.org/10.1177/0018726719857122

Barzallo Salazar, M. J., Minkoff, H., Bayya, J., Gillett, B., Onoriode, H., Weedon, J., Altshuler, L., & Fisher, N. (2014). Influence of surgeon behavior on trainee willingness to speak up: A randomized controlled trial. *Journal of the American College of Surgeons, 219*(5), 1001–1007. https://doi.org/10.1016/j.jamcollsurg.2014.07.933

Bedwell, W. L., Ramsay, P. S., & Salas, E. (2012). Helping fluid teams work: A research agenda for effective team adaptation in healthcare. *Translational Behavioral Medicine, 2*(4), 504–509. https://doi.org/10.1007/s13142-012-0177-9

Blanchard, A. L., Caudill, L. E., & Walker, L. S. (2018). Developing an entitativity measure and distinguishing it from antecedents and outcomes within online and face-to-face groups. *Group Processes & Intergroup Relations, 23*(1), 91–108. https://doi.org/10.1177/1368430217743577

Bogenstatter, Y., Tschan, F., Semmer, N. K., Spychiger, M., Breuer, M., & Marsch, S. (2009). How accurate is information transmitted to medical professionals joining a medical emergency? A simulator study. *Human Factors, 51*(2), 115–125. https://doi.org/10.1177/0018720809336734

Bromiley, M., & Mitchell, L. (2009). Would you speak up if the consultant got it wrong? And would you listen if someone said you'd got it wrong. *Journal of Perioperative Practice, 19*(10), 326–329. https://doi.org/10.1177/175045890901901004

Campanella, P., Lovato, E., Marone, C., Fallacara, L., Mancuso, A., Ricciardi, W., & Specchia, M. L. (2016). The impact of electronic health records on healthcare quality: A systematic review and meta-analysis. *European Journal of Public Health, 26*(1), 60–64. https://doi.org/10.1093/eurpub/ckv122

Cant, R. P., Porter, J. E., Cooper, S. J., Roberts, K., Wilson, I., & Gartside, C. (2016). Improving the nontechnical skills of hospital medical emergency teams: The team emergency assessment measure (team). *Emergency Medicine Australasia, 28*(6), 641–646. https://doi.org/10.1111/1742-6723.12643

Catchpole, K., Bisantz, A., Hallbeck, M. S., Weigl, M., Randell, R., Kossack, M., & Anger, J. T. (2019). Human factors in robotic assisted surgery: Lessons from studies 'in the Wild'. *Applied Ergonomics, 78*, 270–276. https://doi.org/10.1016/j.apergo.2018.02.011

Chan, P. S., Krumholz, H. M., Nichol, G., & Nallamothu, B. K. (2008). Delayed time to defibrillation after in-hospital cardiac arrest. *New England Journal of Medicine, 358*(1), 9–17.

Cooper, S., & Wakelam, A. (1999). Leadership of resuscitation teams: 'Lighthouse Leadership'. *Resuscitation, 42*(1), 27–45. https://doi.org/10.1016/s0300-9572(99)00080-5

Cranach, M., Ochsenbein, G., & Valach, L. (1986). The group as a self-active system: Outline of a theory of group action. *European Journal of Social Psychology, 16*(3), 193–229.

D'Innocenzo, L., Mathieu, J. E., & Kukenberger, M. R. (2016). A meta-analysis of different forms of shared Leadership–Team performance relations. *Journal of Management, 42*(7), 1964–1991. https://doi.org/10.1177/0149206314525205

Dinh, J. V., Schweissing, E. J., Venkatesh, A., Traylor, A. M., Kilcullen, M. P., Perez, J. A., & Salas, E. (2021). The study of teamwork processes within the dynamic domains of healthcare: A systematic and taxonomic review. *Frontiers in Communication*, 6. https://doi.org/10.3389/fcomm.2021.617928

Dinh, J. V., Traylor, A. M., Kilcullen, M. P., Perez, J. A., Schweissing, E. J., Venkatesh, A., & Salas, E. (2019). Cross-disciplinary care: A systematic review on teamwork processes in health care. *Small Group Research*, *51*(1), 125–166. https://doi.org/10.1177/1046496419872002

Edmondson, A. (1999). Psychological safety and learning behavior in work teams. *Administrative Science Quarterly*, *44*(2), 350–383. https://doi.org/10.2307/2666999

Eisenberg, E. M., Murphy, A. G., Sutcliffe, K., Wears, R., Schenkel, S., Perry, S., & Vanderhoef, M. (2005). Communication in emergency medicine: Implications for patient safety. *Communication Monographs*, *72*(4), 390–413. https://doi.org/10.1080/03637750500322602

ElBardissi, A. W., Duclos, A., Rawn, J. D., Orgill, D. P., & Carty, M. J. (2013). Cumulative team experience matters more than individual surgeon experience in cardiac surgery. *The Journal of Thoracic and Cardiovascular Surgery*, *145*(2), 328–333. http://dx.doi.org/10.1016/j.jtcvs.2012.09.022

El-Shafy, I. A., Delgado, J., Akerman, M., Bullaro, F., Christopherson, N. A. M., & Prince, J. M. (2018). Closed-loop communication improves task completion in pediatric trauma resuscitation. *Journal of Surgical Education*, *75*(1), 58–64. https://doi.org/10.1016/j.jsurg.2017.06.025

Fernandez, R., Kozlowski, S. W., Shapiro, M. J., & Salas, E. (2008). Toward a definition of teamwork in emergency medicine. *Academic Emergency Medicine*, *15*(11), 1104–1112. https://doi.org/10.1111/j.1553-2712.2008.00250.x

Fletcher, G., Flin, R., McGeorge, P., Glavin, R., Maran, N., & Patey, R. (2004). Rating non-technical skills: Developing a behavioural marker system for use in anaesthesia. *Cognition, Technology & Work*, *6*(3), 165–171. https://doi.org/10.1007/s10111-004-0158-y

Flin, R., & Maran, N. (2004). Identifying and training non-technical skills for teams in acute medicine. *Quality & Safety in Health Care*, *13*(Suppl 1), i80–84. https://doi.org/10.1136/qhc.13.suppl_1.i80

Flin, R., O'Connor, P., & Crichton, M. (2008). *Safety at the sharp end. A guide to non-technical skills*. CRC Press; Taylor & Francis Group.

Gallagher, A. G., Satava, R. M., & O'Sullivan, G. C. (2015). Attentional capacity: An essential aspect of surgeon performance. *Annals of Surgery*, *261*(3), e60–61. https://doi.org/10.1097/SLA.0b013e318296c473

Gillespie, B. M., Chaboyer, W., & Fairweather, N. (2012). Interruptions and miscommunications in surgery: An observational study. *AORN Journal*, *95*(5), 576–590. https://doi.org/10.1016/j.aorn.2012.02.012

Glouberman, S., & Mintzberg, H. (2001). Managing the care of health and the cure of disease—Part II: Integration. *Health Care Management Review*, *26*(1), 70–84. http://www.jstor.org/stable/44951311

Gregory, M. E., Hughes, A. M., Benishek, L. E., Sonesh, S. C., Lazzara, E. H., Woodard, L. D., & Salas, E. (2019). Toward the development of the perfect medical team. *Journal of Patient Safety*. https://doi.org/10.1097/pts.0000000000000598

Grice, H. P. (1975). Logic and conversation. In P. Cole & J. Morgan (Eds.), *Syntax and semantics (vol. 9)* (pp. 22–40). Academic Press.

Hackman, J. R. (2002). *Leading teams: Setting the stage for great performances*. Harvard Business School Press.

Haugen, A. S., Sevdalis, N., & Softeland, E. (2019). Impact of the world health organization surgical safety checklist on patient safety. *Anesthesiology*, *131*(2), 420–425. https://doi.org/10.1097/ALN.0000000000002674

Have, E. C., & Nap, R. E. (2014). Mutual agreement between providers in intensive care medicine on patient care after interdisciplinary rounds. *Journal of Intensive Care Medicine*, *29*(5), 292–297. https://doi.org/10.1177/0885066613486596

Haynes, A. B., Weiser, T. G., Berry, W. R., Lipsitz, S. R., Breizat, A. H., Dellinger, E. P., Herbosa, T., Joseph, S., Kibatala, P. L., Lapitan, M. C., Merry, A. F., Moorthy, K., Reznick, R. K., Taylor, B., & Gawande, A. A. (2009). A surgical safety checklist to reduce morbidity and mortality in a global population. *The New England Journal of Medicine*, *360*(5), 491–499. https://doi.org/10.1056/NEJMsa0810119

Heip, T., Van Hecke, A., Malfait, S., Van Biesen, W., & Eeckloo, K. (2022). The effectiveness of interdisciplinary bedsiderounds on patient centeredness, quality of care and team collaboration: A systematic review. *Journal of Patient Safety*, *18*(1), e40–e44. https://doi.org/10.1097/PTS.0000000000000695

Hinsz, V. B., Tindale, R. S., & Vollrath, D. A. (1997). The emerging conceptualization of groups as information processors. *Psychological Bulletin, 121*(1), 43–64. https://doi.org/10.1037/0033-2909.121.1.43

Hochstrasser, S. R., Amacher, S. A., Tschan, F., Semmer, N. K., Becker, C., Metzger, K., Hunziker, S., & Marsch, S. (2022). Gender-focused training improves leadership of female medical students: A randomised trial. *Medical Education, 56*(3), 321–330. https://doi.org/10.1111/medu.14658

Hollenbeck, J. R., Beersma, B., & Schouten, M. E. (2012). Beyond team types and taxonomies: A dimensional scaling conceptualization for team description. *Academy of Management Review, 37*(1), 82–106. https://doi.org/10.5465/amr.2010.0181

Holzer, E., Tschan, F., Kottwitz, M. U., Beldi, G., Businger, A. P., & Semmer, N. K. (2019). The workday of hospital surgeons: What they do, what makes them satisfied, and the role of core tasks and administrative tasks: A diary study. *BMC Surgery, 19*(1), 112. https://doi.org/10.1186/s12893-019-0570-0

House, S., & Havens, D. (2017). Nurses' and physicians' perceptions of nurse-physician collaboration: A systematic review. *Journal of Nursing Administration, 47*(3), 165–171. https://doi.org/10.1097/NNA.0000000000000460

Hu, Y.-Y., Arriaga, A. F., Peyre, S. E., Corso, K. A., Roth, E. M., & Greenberg, C. C. (2012). Deconstructing intraoperative communication failures. *Journal of Surgical Research, 177*(1), 37–42. http://www.sciencedirect.com/science/article/pii/S0022480412003915

Hughes, K. M., Benenson, R. S., Krichten, A. E., Clancy, K. D., Ryan, J. P., & Hammond, C. (2014). A crew resource management program tailored to trauma resuscitation improves team behavior and communication. *Journal of American College of Surgeons, 219*(3), 545–551. https://doi.org/10.1016/j.jamcollsurg.2014.03.049

Hughes, A. M., Gregory, M. E., Joseph, D. L., Sonesh, S. C., Marlow, S. L., Lacerenza, C. N., Benishek, L. E., King, H. B., & Salas, E. (2016). Saving lives: A meta-analysis of team training in healthcare. *Journal of Applied Psychology, 101*(9), 1266–1304. https://doi.org/10.1037/apl0000120

Humphrey, S. E., Morgeson, F. P., & Mannor, M. J. (2009). Developing A theory of the strategic core of teams: A role composition model of team performance. *Journal of Applied Psychology, 94*(1), 48–61. https://doi.org/10.1037/a0012997

Hunt, E. A., Walker, A. R., Shaffner, D. H., Miller, M. R., & Pronovost, P. J. (2008). Simulation of in-hospital pediatric medical emergencies and cardiopulmonary arrests: Highlighting the importance of the first 5 minutes. *Pediatrics, 121*(1), E34–E43. https://doi.org/10.1542/peds.2007-0029

Hunziker, S., Buhlmann, C., Tschan, F., Balestra, G., Legeret, C., Schumacher, C., Semmer, N. K., Hunziker, P., & Marsch, S. (2010). Brief leadership instructions improve cardiopulmonary resuscitation in a high-fidelity simulation: A randomized controlled trial. *Critical Care Medicine, 38*(4), 1086–1091. https://doi.org/10.1097/CCM.0b013e3181cf7383

Hunziker, S., Johansson, A. C., Tschan, F., Semmer, N. K., Rock, L., Howell, M. D., & Marsch, S. (2011). Teamwork and leadership in cardiopulmonary resuscitation. *Journal of the American College of Cardiology, 57*(24), 2381–2388. https://doi.org/10.1016/j.jacc.2011.03.017

Hu, Y. Y., Parker, S. H., Lipsitz, S. R., Arriaga, A. F., Peyre, S. E., Corso, K. A., Roth, E. M., Yule, S. J., & Greenberg, C. C. (2016). Surgeons' leadership styles and team behavior in the operating room. *Journal of the American College of Surgeons, 222*(1), 41–51. https://doi.org/10.1016/j.jamcollsurg.2015.09.013

Janssens, S., Simon, R., Beckman, M., & Marschall, S. (2018). Shared leadership in healthcare action teams: A systematic review. *Journal of Patient Safety.* https://doi.org/htpps://doi.org/10.1097/PTS.0000000000000503

Jones, L. K., Jennings, B. M., Higgins, M. K., & de Waal, F. B. M. (2018). Ethological observations of social behavior in the operating room. *Proceedings of the National Academy of Sciences of the United States of America, 115*(29), 7575–7580. https://doi.org/10.1073/pnas.1716883115

Katz, D., Blasius, K., Isaak, R., Lipps, J., Kushelev, M., Goldberg, A., Fastman, J., Marsh, B., & DeMaria, S. (2019). Exposure to incivility hinders clinical performance in a simulated operative crisis. *BMJ Quality and Safety, 28*(9), 750–757. https://doi.org/10.1136/bmjqs-2019-009598

Keller, S., Tschan, F., Beldi, G., Kurmann, A., Candinas, D., & Semmer, N. K. (2016). Noise peaks influence communication in the operating room. An observational study. *Ergonomics, 59*(12), 1541–1552. https://doi.org/10.1080/00140139.2016.1159736

Keller, S., Tschan, F., Semmer, N. K., Timm-Holzer, E., Zimmermann, J., Candinas, D., Demartines, N., Hubner, M., & Beldi, G. (2019). "Disruptive behavior" in the operating room: A prospective observational study of triggers and effects of tense communication episodes in surgical teams. *PLoS One*, *14*(12), e0226437. https://doi.org/10.1371/journal.pone.0226437

Keller, S., Yule, S., Zagarese, V., & Henrickson Parker, S. (2020). Predictors and triggers of incivility within healthcare teams: A systematic review of the literature. *BMJ Open*, *10*(6), e035471. https://doi.org/10.1136/bmjopen-2019-035471

Kerr, N. L. (2017). The most neglected moderator in group research. *Group Processes & Intergroup Relations*, *20*(5), 681–692. https://doi.org/10.1177/1368430217712050

King, H. B., Battles, J., Baker, D. P., Alonso, A., Salas, E., Webster, J., Toomey, L., & Salisbury, M. (2008). TeamSTEPPS: Team strategies and tools to enhance performance and patient safety. In K. Henriksen, J. B. Battles, & M. A. Keyes (Eds.), *Advances in patient safety: New directions and alternative approaches (Vol. 3 Performance and tools)*. Agency for Healthcare Research and Quality.

Kolbe, M., Grote, G., Waller, M. J., Wacker, J., Grande, B., Burtscher, M. J., & Spahn, D. R. (2014). Monitoring and talking to the room: Autochthonous coordination patterns in team interaction and performance. *Journal of Applied Psychology*, *99*(6), 1254–1267. https://doi.org/10.1037/a0037877

Korkiakangas, T., Weldon, S.-M., Bezemer, J., & Kneebone, R. (2014). Nurse-surgeon object transfer: Video analysis of communication and situation awareness in the operating theatre. *International Journal of Nursing Studies*, *51*(9), 1195–1206. https://doi.org/10.1016/j.ijnurstu.2014.01.007

Korner, M., Wirtz, M. A., Bengel, J., & Goritz, A. S. (2015). Relationship of organizational culture, teamwork and job satisfaction in interprofessional teams. *BMC Health Services Research*, *15*, 243. https://doi.org/10.1186/s12913-015-0888-y

Kündig, P., Tschan, F., Semmer, N. K., Morgenthaler, C., Zimmermann, J., Holzer, E., Huber, S. A., Hunziker, S., & Marsch, S. (2020). More than experience: A post-task reflection intervention among team members enhances performance in student teams confronted with A simulated resuscitation task—A prospective randomised trial. *BMJ Simulation and Technology Enhanced Learning*, *6*(2), 81–86. https://doi.org/10.1136/bmjstel-2018-000395

Kurmann, A., Keller, S., Tschan-Semmer, F., Seelandt, J., Semmer, N. K., Candinas, D., & Beldi, G. (2014). Impact of team familiarity in the operating room on surgical complications. *World Journal of Surgery*, *38*(12), 3047–3052. https://doi.org/10.1007/s00268-014-2680-2

Leape, L. L. (1994). Error in medicine. *Journal of the American Medical Association*, *272*(23), 1851–1857. https://doi.org/10.1001/jama.272.23.1851

Leape, L. L., Shore, M. F., Dienstag, J. L., Mayer, R. J., Edgman-Levitan, S., Meyer, G. S., & Healy, G. B. (2012). Perspective: A culture of respect, part 1: The nature and causes of disrespectful behavior by physicians. *Academic Medicine*, *87*(7), 845–852. https://doi.org/10.1097/ACM.0b013e318258338d

Lingard, L. (2004). Communication failures in the operating room: An observational classification of recurrent types and effects. *Quality and Safety in Health Care*, *13*(5), 330–334. https://doi.org/10.1136/qshc.2003.008425

Ma, C., Park, S. H., & Shang, J. (2018). Inter- and intra-disciplinary collaboration and patient safety outcomes in U.S. Acute care Hospital units: A cross-sectional study. *International Journal of Nursing Studies*, *85*, 1–6. https://doi.org/10.1016/j.ijnurstu.2018.05.001

Marks, M. A., Mathieu, J. E., & Zaccaro, S. J. (2001). A temporally based framework and taxonomy of team processes. *Academy of Management Review*, *26*(3), 356–376. https://doi.org/10.5465/amr.2001.4845785

Marlow, S. L., Lacerenza, C. N., Paoletti, J., Burke, C. S., & Salas, E. (2018). Does team communication represent a one-size-fits-all approach?: A meta-analysis of team communication and performance. *Organizational Behavior and Human Decision Processes*, *144*, 145–170. https://doi.org/10.1016/j.obhdp.2017.08.001

Marsch, S. C., Muller, C., Marquardt, K., Conrad, G., Tschan, F., & Hunziker, P. R. (2004). Human factors affect the quality of cardiopulmonary resuscitation in simulated cardiac arrests. *Resuscitation*, *60*(1), 51–56. https://doi.org/10.1016/j.resuscitation.2003.08.004

Mayo, A. T., Myers, C. G., & Sutcliffe, K. M. (2021). Organizational science and health care. *Academy of Management Annals*, *15*(2), 537–576. https://doi.org/10.5465/annals.2019.0115

Mazzocco, K., Petitti, D. B., Fong, K. T., Bonacum, D., Brookey, J., Graham, S., Lasky, R. E., Sexton, J. B., & Thomas, E. J. (2009). Surgical team behaviors and patient outcomes. *American Journal of Surgery*, *197*(5), 678–685. https://doi.org/10.1016/j.amjsurg.2008.03.002

McComb, S. A., Lemaster, M., Henneman, E. A., & Hinchey, K. R. (2017). An evaluation of shared mental models and mutual trust on general medical units: Implications for collaboration, teamwork, and patient safety. *Journal of Patient Safety*, *13*(7), 237–242. https://doi.org/10.1097/PTS.0000000000000151

McGrath, J. E. (1962). *Leadership behavior: Some requirements for leadership training*. U.S. Civil Service Commission.

McGrath, J. E. (1984). *Groups: Interaction and performance* (Vol. 14). Prentice-Hall.

McGrath, J. E., Arrow, H., & Berdahl, J. L. (2000). The study of groups: Past, present, and future. *Personality and Social Psychology Review*, *4*(1), 95–105. http://psr.sagepub.com/content/4/1/95

McInnes, A. D., Sutton, R. M., Nishisaki, A., Niles, D., Leffelman, J., Boyle, L., Maltese, M. R., Berg, R. A., & Nadkarni, V. M. (2012). Ability of code leaders to recall CPR quality errors during the resuscitation of older children and adolescents. *Resuscitation*, *83*(12), 1462–1466. https://doi.org/10.1016/j.resuscitation.2012.05.010

McLeod, P. L., Cunningham, Q. W., DiazGranados, D., Dodoiu, G., Kaplan, S., Keyton, J., Larson, N., LeNoble, C., Marsch, S. U., O'Neill, T. A., Parker, S. H., Semmer, N. K., Shuffler, M., Su, L., Tschan, F., Waller, M., & Wang, Y. (2019). Hacking teamwork in health care: Addressing adverse effects of ad hoc team composition in critical care medicine. *Health Care Management Review*. https://doi.org/10.1097/HMR.0000000000000265

Mitchell, L., Flin, R., Yule, S., Mitchell, J., Coutts, K., & Youngson, G. (2012). Evaluation of the scrub Practitioners' list of intraoperative non-technical skills system. *International Journal of Nursing Studies*, *49*(2), 201–211. https://doi.org/10.1016/j.ijnurstu.2011.08.012

Mohammed, S., Hamilton, K., Sánchez-Manzanares, M., & Rico, R. (2017). Team mental models and situation awareness. In E. Salas, R. Rico, & J. Passmore (Eds.), *The Wiley-Blackwell handbook of the psychology of team working and collaborative processes* (pp. 369–392). Wiley & Sons.

Momenipur, A., & Pennathur, P. R. (2019). Balancing documentation and direct patient care activities: A study of a mature electronic health record system. *International Journal of Industrial Ergonomics*, *72*, 338–346. https://doi.org/10.1016/j.ergon.2019.06.012

Myers, D. J., Lipscomb, H. J., Epling, C., Hunt, D., Richardson, W., Smith-Lovin, L., & Dement, J. M. (2016). Surgical team stability and risk of Sharps-related blood and body fluid exposures during surgical procedures. *Infection Control and Hospital Epidemiology*, *37*(5), 512–518. https://doi.org/10.1017/ice.2016.12

Nembhard, I. M., & Edmondson, A. C. (2006). Making it safe: The effects of leader inclusiveness and professional status on psychological safety and improvement efforts in health care teams. *Journal of Organizational Behavior*, *27*(7), 941–966. https://doi.org/10.1002/job.413

Noyes, A. L. (2021). Navigating the hierarchy: Communicating power relationships in collaborative health care groups. *Management Communication Quarterly*, *36*(1), 62–91. https://doi.org/10.1177/08933189211025737

Okhuysen, G. A., & Bechky, B. A. (2009). Coordination in organizations: An integrative perspective. *Academy of Management Annals*, *3*, 463–502. https://doi.org/10.1080/19416520903047533

Okuyama, A., Wagner, C., & Bijnen, B. (2014). Speaking up for patient safety by hospital-based health care professionals: A literature review. *BMC Health Services Research*, *14*(1), 61. https://doi.org/10.1186/1472-6963-14-61

Ornato, J. P., Peberdy, M. A., Reid, R. D., Feeser, V. R., Dhindsa, H. S., & Investigators, N. (2012). Impact of resuscitation system errors on survival from in-hospital cardiac arrest. *Resuscitation*, *83*(1), 63–69. https://doi.org/10.1016/j.resuscitation.2011.09.009

Panchal, A. R., Bartos, J. A., Cabanas, J. G., Donnino, M. W., Drennan, I. R., Hirsch, K. G., Kudenchuk, P. J., Kurz, M. C., Lavonas, E. J., Morley, P. T., O'Neil, B. J., Peberdy, M. A., Rittenberger, J. C., Rodriguez, A. J., Sawyer, K. N., Berg, K. M., Adult, B., & Advanced Life Support, W. (2020). Part 3: Adult basic and advanced life support: 2020 American Heart Association Guidelines for Cardiopulmonary Resuscitation and Emergency Cardiovascular Care. *Circulation*, *142*(16_suppl_2), S366–S468. https://doi.org/10.1161/CIR.0000000000000916

Parker, A. L., Forsythe, L. L., & Kohlmorgen, I. K. (2019). TeamSTEPPS((r)): An evidence-based approach to reduce clinical errors threatening safety in outpatient settings: An integrative review. *Journal of Healthcare Risk Management, 38*(4), 19–31. https://doi.org/10.1002/jhrm.21352

Parker, K. C. (1988). Speaking turns in small group interaction: A context-sensitive event sequence model. *Journal of Personality and Social Psychology, 54*(6), 965.

Parker, S. H., Flin, R., McKinley, A., & Yule, S. (2014). Factors influencing surgeons' intraoperative leadership: Video analysis of unanticipated events in the operating room [Research support, non-U.S. Gov't]. *World Journal of Surgery, 38*(1), 4–10. https://doi.org/10.1007/s00268-013-2241-0

Parush, A., Kramer, C., Foster-Hunt, T., Momtahan, K., Hunter, A., & Sohmer, B. (2011). Communication and team situation awareness in the OR: Implications for augmentative information display. *Journal of Biomedical Informatics, 44*(3), 477–485. https://doi.org/10.1016/j.jbi.2010.04.002

Pasarakonda, S., Grote, G., Schmutz, J. B., Bogdanovic, J., Guggenheim, M., & Manser, T. (2020). A strategic core role perspective on team coordination: Benefits of centralized leadership for managing task complexity in the operating room. *Human Factors,* 18720820906041. https://doi.org/10.1177/0018720820906041

Rall, M., Glavin, R., & Flin, R. (2008). The '10-seconds-for-10-minutes principle'-why things go wrong and stopping them getting worse. *Bulletin of the Royal College of Anaesthetists, 51,* 2614–2616. https://doi.org/10.1007/978-3-642-29436-5_13

Riskin, A., Bamberger, P., Erez, A. and Zeiger, A. (2020), "Discrete Incivility Events and Team Performance: A Cognitive Perspective on a Pervasive Human Resource (HR) Issue", Buckley, M.R., Wheeler, A.R., Baur, J.E. and Halbesleben, J.R.B. (Ed.) *Research in Personnel and Human Resources Management* (Research in Personnel and Human Resources Management, Vol. 38), Emerald Publishing Limited, Bingley, pp. 223–258. https://doi.org/10.1108/S0742-730120200000038008

Roberts, N. K., Williams, R. G., Schwind, C. J., Sutyak, J. A., McDowell, C., Griffen, D., Wall, J., Sanfey, H., Chestnut, A., Meier, A. H., Wohltmann, C., Clark, T. R., & Wetter, N. (2014). The impact of brief team communication, leadership and team behavior training on ad hoc team performance in trauma care settings. *American Journal of Surgery, 207*(2), 170–178. https://doi.org/10.1016/j.amjsurg.2013.06.016

Robertson, E. R., Morgan, L., Bird, S., Catchpole, K., & McCulloch, P. (2014). Interventions employed to improve intrahospital handover: A systematic review. *BMJ Quality & Safety.* https://doi.org/10.1136/bmjqs-2013-002309

Robinson, P. S., Shall, E., & Rakhit, R. (2016). Cardiac arrest leadership: In need of resuscitation? *Postgraduate Medical Journal, 92*(1094), 715–720. https://doi.org/10.1136/postgradmedj-2015-133738

Rosen, M. A., DiazGranados, D., Dietz, A. S., Benishek, L. E., Thompson, D., Pronovost, P. J., & Weaver, S. J. (2018). Teamwork in healthcare: Key discoveries enabling safer, high-quality care. *American Psychologist, 73*(4), 433–450. https://doi.org/10.1037/amp0000298

Salas, E., Rosen, M., & King, H. (2007). Managing teams managing crises: Principles of teamwork to improve patient safety in the emergency room and beyond. *Theoretical Issues in Ergonomics Science, 8*(5), 381–394. https://doi.org/10.1080/14639220701317764

Salas, E., Wilson, K. A., Murphy, C. E., King, H., & Salisbury, M. (2008). Communicating, coordinating, and cooperating when lives depend on it: Tips for teamwork. *The Joint Commission Journal on Quality and Patient Safety, 34*(6), 333–341. https://doi.org/10.1016/s1553-7250(08)34042-2

Salminen-Karlsson, M., & Golay, D. (2022). Information systems in nurses' work: Technical rationality versus an ethic of care. *New Technology, Work and Employment.* https://doi.org/10.1111/ntwe.12231

Santos, R., Bakero, L., Franco, P., Alves, C., Fragata, I., & Fragata, J. (2012). Characterization of non-technical skills in paediatric cardiac surgery: Communication patterns. *European Journal of Cardio-Thoracic Surgery, 41*(5), 1005–1012. https://doi.org/10.1093/ejcts/ezs068

Schaefer, H.-G., & Helmreich, R. L. (1994). Team performance in the operating room. In M. S. Bogner (Ed.), *Human error in medicine* (pp. 225–253). Lawrence Erlbaum and Associates.

Schmutz, J. B., & Eppich, W. J. (2017). Promoting learning and patient care through shared reflection: A conceptual framework for team reflexivity in health care. *Academic Medicine, 92*(11), 1555–1563. https://doi.org/10.1097/ACM.0000000000001688

Schmutz, J. B., Meier, L. L., & Manser, T. (2019). How effective is teamwork really? The relationship between teamwork and performance in healthcare teams: A systematic review and meta-analysis. *BMJ Open, 9*(9), e028280. https://doi.org/10.1136/bmjopen-2018-028280

Schwendimann, R., Blatter, C., Dhaini, S., Simon, M., & Ausserhofer, D. (2018). The occurrence, types, consequences and preventability of in-hospital adverse events - a scoping review. *BMC Health Services Research*, *18*(1), 521. https://doi.org/10.1186/s12913-018-3335-z

Semmer, N. K., Tschan, F., Jacobshagen, N., Beehr, T. A., Elfering, A., Kälin, W., & Meier, L. L. (2019). Stress as offense to self: A promising approach comes of age. *Occupational Health Science*, *3*(3), 205–238. https://doi.org/10.1007/s41542-019-00041-5

Sevdalis, N., Wong, H. W. L., Arora, S., Nagpal, K., Healey, A., Hanna, G. B., & Vincent, C. A. (2012). Quantitative analysis of intraoperative communication in open and laparoscopic surgery. *Surgical Endoscopy*, 1–8. https://doi.org/10.1007/s00464-012-2287-3

Starmer, A. J., Spector, N. D., Srivastava, R., West, D. C., Rosenbluth, G., Allen, A. D., Noble, E. L., Tse, L. L., Dalal, A. K., Keohane, C. A., Lipsitz, S. R., Rothschild, J., Wien, M., Yoon, M. F., Zigmont, C. S., Wilson, K. R., O'Toole, K. M., Solan, J. K., Aylor, L. G., & Group, I. P. S. (2014). Changes in medical errors after implementation of a handoff program. *The New England Journal of Medicine*, *371*(19), 1803–1812. https://doi.org/10.1056/NEJMsa1405556

Stein, L. I. (1967). The doctor-nurse game. *Archives of General Psychiatry*, *16*(6), 699–703. https://doi.org/10.1001/archpsyc.1967.01730240055009

Stein, L. I., Watts, D. T., & Howell, T. (1990). The doctor–nurse game revisited. *The New England Journal of Medicine, 322*(8), 546–549. https://doi.org/ 10.1056/NEJM199002223220810

Stucky, C. H., & De Jong, M. J. (2021). Surgical team familiarity: An integrative review. *AORN Journal*, *113*(1), 64–75. https://doi.org/10.1002/aorn.13281

Tschan, F., Keller, S., Semmer, N. K., Timm-Holzer, E., Zimmermann, J., Huber, S. A., Wrann, S., Hubner, M., Banz, V., Prevost, G. A., Marschall, J., Candinas, D., Demartines, N., Weber, M., & Beldi, G. (2022). Effects of structured intraoperative briefings on patient outcomes: Multicentre before-and-after study. *British Journal of Surgery*, *109*(1), 136–144. https://doi.org/10.1093/bjs/znab384

Tschan, F., Seelandt, J. C., Keller, S., Semmer, N. K., Kurmann, A., Candinas, D., & Beldi, G. (2015). Impact of case-relevant and case-irrelevant communication within the surgical team on surgical-site infection. *British Journal of Surgery*, *102*(13), 1718–1725. https://doi.org/10.1002/bjs.9927

Tschan, F., Semmer, N. K., Gautschi, D., Hunziker, P., Spychiger, M., & Marsch, S. U. (2006). Leading to recovery: Group performance and coordinative activities in medical emergency driven groups. *Human Performance*, *19*(3), 277–304. https://doi.org/10.1207/s15327043hup1903_5

Tschan, F., Vetterli, M., Semmer, N. K., Hunziker, S., & Marsch, S. C. (2011). Activities during interruptions in cardiopulmonary resuscitation: A simulator study. *Resuscitation*, *82*(11), 1419–1423. https://doi.org/ 10.1016/j.resuscitation.2011.06.023

Tschan, F., & von Cranach, M. (1996). Group task structure, processes and outcome. In M. West (Ed.), *Handbook of work group psychology* (pp. 95–121). Wiley.

Undre, S., Sevdalis, N., Healey, A. N., Darzi, S., & Vincent, C. A. (2006). Teamwork in the operating theatre: Cohesion or confusion? *Journal of Evaluation in Clinical Practice*, *12*(2), 182–189. https://doi.org/10.1111/j.1365-2753.2006.00614.x

Webster, K. L. W., Keebler, J. R., Lazzara, E. H., Chaparro, A., Greilich, P., & Fagerlund, A. (2022). Handoffs and teamwork: A framework for care transition communication. *The Joint Commission Journal on Quality and Patient Safety*. https://doi.org/10.1016/j.jcjq.2022.04.001

Wellens, A. R. (1993). Group situation awareness and distributed decision making: From military to civilian applications. In N. J. Castellan (Ed.), *Individual and group decision making: Current issues* (pp. 267–291). Lawrence Erlbaum Associates.

West, M. (1996). Reflexivity and work group effectiveness: A conceptual integration. In M. West (Ed.), *Handbook of work group psychology* (pp. 555–579). John Wiley & Sons, Ltd.

Wiegmann, D. A., ElBardissi, A. W., Dearani, J. A., Daly, R. C., & Sundt, T. M. 3rd (2007). Disruptions in surgical flow And their relationship to surgical errors: An exploratory investigation [Research support, N.I.H., Extramural]. *Surgery*, *142*(5), 658–665. http://www.sciencedirect.com/science/article/pii/S0039606007005168

Wittenbaum, G. M., Vaughan, S. I., & Strasser, G. (2002). Coordination in task-performing groups. In R. S. Tindale, L. Heath, I. Edwards, E. I. Posavac, F. B. Bryant, Y. Suarez-Balcazar, E. Henderson-King, & I. Myers (Eds.), *Theory and research on small groups* (Vol. 4, pp. 177–204). Springer.

Woo, D., Miller, L. E., & Lamsen, L. N. (2020). Swift role negotiations: Communicative strategies for enabling rapid role shifts in cross-functional teaming. *Communication Monographs*, *88*(4), 440–462. https://doi.org/10.1080/03637751.2020.1862888

Xiao, Y., Jones, A., Zhang, B. B., Bennett, M., Mears, S. C., Mabrey, J. D., & Kennerly, D. (2015). Team consistency and occurrences of prolonged operative time, prolonged hospital stay, and hospital readmission: A retrospective analysis. *World Journal of Surgery*, *39*(4), 890–896. https://doi.org/10.1007/s00268-014-2866-7

Yule, S., & Paterson-Brown, S. (2012). Surgeons' non-technical skills [review]. *Surgical Clinics of North America*, *92*(1), 37–50. https://doi.org/10.1016/j.suc.2011.11.004

Zaccaro, S. J., Rittman, A. L., & Marks, M. A. (2002). Team leadership. *The Leadership Quarterly*, *12*(4), 451–483. https://doi.org/10.1016/S1048-9843(01)00093-5

Zegers, M., de Bruijne, M. C., de Keizer, B., Merten, H., Groenewegen, P. P., van der Wal, G., & Wagner, C. (2011). The incidence, root-causes, and outcomes of adverse events in surgical units: Implication for potential prevention strategies. *Patient Safety in Surgery*, *5*, 13. https://doi.org/10.1186/1754-9493-5-13

Zwarenstein, M., & Reeves, S. (2002). Working together but apart: Barriers and routes to Nurse–Physician collaboration. *The Joint Commission Journal on Quality Improvement*, *28*(5), 242–247. https://doi.org/10.1016/s1070-3241(02)28024-4

23 Communication in Sports Teams

Jonas Akpetou and Philip Furley

Chapter Objectives

- The present chapter both applies mainstream theorizing in the field of communication to the sports domain and uses the sports domain to provide novel insights into the science of communication.
- Review and integrate a highly diverse body of literature from the domain of sports within a communication perspective.
- Derive evidence-based recommendations on verbal and nonverbal communication when working in the context of sports.

Introduction

Communication is a central aspect of human nature shaping social life as we know it. Generally speaking, it can be viewed as the process of conveying and receiving information linking different parts of the living world (Littlejohn et al., 2011) and thereby enabling us to interact with other individuals. This process can occur explicitly with the intent to affect others' cognitions and behavior or implicitly as an unconscious display of social information (Littlejohn et al., 2011). Furthermore, information can be transmitted in different forms (e.g., verbally or nonverbally). Either way, the relevance of communication extends to all contexts in which some form of social interaction occurs.

An area characterized by the constant need for communication is the domain of team sports. Sport teams act in the pursuit of a common goal and team members are placed in highly complex and dynamic environments in which they have to interact with regard to the team's objectives and the opponent team's actions (Reimer et al., 2006). Thus, team sports hold numerous demands for efficient coordination, instruction, feedback, and the regulation of the social climate within the group (Ishak, 2017). Those demands can be met through direct communication and effective speech aiming at exchanging intentions and plans accordingly. Besides the open verbal and nonverbal exchange between teammates or rivals, many sports have elaborated symbolic communications (e.g., signs in beach volleyball, or baseball indicating the next play) that are intended to maintain the privacy of the content (e.g., game plans, strategies).

As team athletes are interdependent and have to coordinate their actions in the best possible way, the ongoing simultaneous exchange of information between multiple team members (i.e., group communication) is crucial (Eccles & Tran, 2012). Moreover, regular interpersonal communication, for example, between the coach and specific players, constitutes another important part of the interaction within a team. In addition, the interpersonal communication with reporters and fans, making players and coaches available for interviews, is also promoted.

DOI: 10.4324/9781003227458-26

Research points out that effective team performance in dynamic settings is facilitated when members can develop adequate expectations regarding their team mates' roles, actions, and decisions (Blickensderfer et al., 2000). This enhances adaptation to changing demands in the environment. To consolidate the mutual understanding of each athletes' roles in the team extensive communication is necessary.

However, when overt communication between members is impeded, for example, due to time pressure, or the necessity to hide intentions from the opposing team, teammates can't engage in explicit strategic planning but need to draw back on pre-existing knowledge, like, shared mental models. These are knowledge structures that support individuals in understanding how a system operates and what is expected in this context (Hinsz, 1995). Such models become crucial to successful team functioning because they support prediction of team members' actions and needs, allowing them to adjust their behaviors accordingly (Cannon-Bowers & Salas, 1998).

Coaches and athletes depend on good communication skills to successfully share knowledge, to convey technical and tactical ideas, to provide social and mental support (Cherubini, 2019; Ishak, 2017), and to coordinate and adjust their efforts efficiently to ultimately increase the likelihood of winning. As communication in social interaction serves the exchange of thoughts, ideas and feelings with others in a way they will understand (McKenna, 1998) good and efficient communication also implies the reduced likelihood of misunderstandings and miscommunication.

The fact that winning teams tend to communicate considerably more during competition and display more homogenous communication styles (i.e., being more in sync regarding the type of communication patterns that are used; Lausic et al., 2009) reflects the significance of team communication and shared knowledge structures in competitive sports.

According to Ishak (2017), the constant exchange between team members is a critical component in team performance with good communication being a crucial component for team success. Moreover, team sports offer a setting to improve communication efficacy.

Hence, in the present chapter we apply well-established communication theories like the four-sides-model of communication (Schulz von Thun, 1981) or the five **axioms** of communication (Watzlawick et al., 1967) to the sports domain as these are well suited to give guidance to coaches and players in fostering communication skills. By synthesizing a diverse body of literature, we aim at promoting an understanding of group communication in sports teams while also addressing interpersonal aspects of communication in this context. Finally, we derive applicable recommendations for coaches and athletes.

Theoretical Framework for Fostering Communication in Sports

Human communication has evolved to be highly sophisticated, which makes it unique and very useful for regulating interpersonal relations and organizing life in social groups. However, its complexity and multi-layered nature renders communication susceptible for errors and misunderstandings. Every message that is sent encompasses a multitude of informational content which can be interpreted in various ways. Difficulties may, for instance, arise through inadequate coding of messages by the sender or erroneous decoding by the recipient (Schulz von Thun, 1981). Inept wording or unclear formulation (i.e., coding) of a given information by the coach may for instance lead to misinterpretation (i.e., decoding) by the athlete. Such tendencies can be rooted in the composition of different personalities within a team and the relational dynamics among the communicators, who may differ in the way they express and interpret information (e.g., due to socio cultural differences, or language barriers; Sullivan & Callow, 2005). Thus, successful team communication depends on sharing a common code (i.e., a system of rules to exchange information) which is readily understood by everybody who is involved (Athanasios, 2005). In this vein, the

German psychologist and communication expert Friedemann Schulz von Thun (1981) proposed a model illustrating some of the versatility and challenges of human communication. Although, this early model of communication is somewhat dated and similar approaches to viewing communication have been criticized in the past for not fully capturing the complexity of the communication process (e.g., Levinson et al., 2006), it still has utility in fostering an understanding of some of the challenges of human communication. Hence, it has been argued to be a useful framework in applied sport psychology in giving heuristic guidance to coaches and players (Lau, 2020, 2023). In addition, the framework seems to be a promising starting point for structuring and initiating empirical research on interpersonal communication in sport.

The Four-Sides-Model of Communication

The four-sides-model of communication (Schulz von Thun, 1981) facilitates the analysis of social interaction and the identification of potential sources of misunderstandings. Thereby, it helps to understand communication processes and resulting interpersonal dynamics between two or more people clarifying communicational patterns and potentially preventing miscommunication. As the model comprises both verbal as well as nonverbal aspects of communication (Schulz von Thun, 2013) it is considered well suited to account for a great variety of communication behavior in the context of sports.

According to Schulz von Thun (2013), transmission of a message consists of two parts. First, information is transmitted verbally or nonverbally by the sender. It is then up to the recipient to decode and interpret the given information. Each message has four different layers that influence how the information is received: (1) The factual layer represents the raw content of a message and comprises the literal informational data of a statement; (2) The layer of self-disclosure reveals information about the sender. It contains conscious or unconscious accounts of the communicators' motives, emotions, or values; (3) The appeal-layer indicates a demand revealing what the sender of a message wants from the recipient. It can encompass desires, advice, or instructions; (4) The relationship-layer points to the nature (e.g., amicable, or collegiate) and quality (e.g., harmonious, or disharmonious) of the relationship between the sender and the recipient.

Every layer for itself can provide the recipient with a different mode of interpretation for a message. The final reception may depend on situational as well as relational factors and is highly context specific (Schulz von Thun, 2013). Thus, it is the recipient who attributes meaning to the information he or she obtains. The more room for interpretation is left by the sender, the higher is the chance for misinterpretations or misunderstandings (Schulz von Thun, 2013).

The following anecdotal scenario exemplifies the application of the model to the context of sports. During the soccer world cup in 2014 the German national coach Jogi Löw brought 22-year-old Mario Götze into the game in the 88th minute saying: "Show the world that you are better than Lionel Messi. Show that you can decide a match." The factual content of the message was: "Show everybody how good of a soccer player you are and help us win the final." Thereby, Löw revealed the motive: "I want you to play to the best of your abilities." resulting in the demand on the appeal level: "Score the decisive goal." On the relationship level Mario Götze may have heard: "I trust you and your quality as a player and I know that you can make the difference." The communication of trust may have boosted Götze's confidence, contributing to his motivation and subsequent in-game performance. However, depending on the relationship, the para- and nonverbal cues and the situational context of the interaction between coach and player, Götze could also have interpreted Löw's words differently. For instance: "Now is your last chance to prove your worth as a national player. You owe it to our fans. So, show us already that you can be useful for a change." Instead of fostering positive feelings, such an interpretation could have had a more negative impact. Thus, both interpretations of the same message may result in completely different consequences potentially influencing the player's performance, the dynamic in the team and finally the game outcome. Acknowledging that the German victory was not solely due to Jogi Löw's choice of words his message was apparently nevertheless rather well received as Mario Götze made history when he scored the winning goal in the 113th minute granting the German national team its fourth world championship title.

This example illustrates that all sides of a message are subject to personal interpretation and its conception can therefore vary according to each individual. Thus, misunderstandings can easily occur throughout the communication process. Therefore, basic knowledge about the different facets of messages and the relation between the communicators can help analyzing communication patterns within a team. If miscommunication or conflicts arise frequently, taking a closer look at when it occurs and how certain messages are transmitted may reduce occurrence of misunderstandings and improve verbal and nonverbal exchange as well as interpersonal relations (Lau, 2020, 2023). Both are deemed beneficial for collective behavior (Ishak, 2017). While **verbal communication** primarily transports the content of a message (Argyle, 2005), nonverbal behavior (NVB) helps framing verbal communication and clarifying the intention behind what has been said to a certain extent (Schulz von Thun, 2013). It provides the recipient with important cues about the sender's attitudes and emotions. These cues are often elusive and therefore too intricate to be expressed verbally (DePaulo, 1992). Thereby **nonverbal communication** facilitates the interpretation of content, and helps determining the meaning of the verbal aspect of a message (Schulz von Thun, 2013). A friendly facial expression would for instance frame the content of a verbal message differently than a sad or angry face and therefore lead to a diverging interpretation.

Recent theorizing in sport psychology (Lau, 2020, 2023) has combined the four-sides-model of communication (Schulz von Thun, 1981) with the seminal work of Austrian-American psychologist Paul Watzlawick and colleagues who proposed five principles (pragmatic axioms) of interpersonal communication that have a high face validity for understanding communication in sports, as is outlined in the next section.

Five Axioms of Communication

As NVB is an integral part of human interaction importantly affecting interpretation of verbal messages (Argyle, 2005), psychologist and communication theorist Paul Watzlawick and colleagues (1967) have developed five **axioms** explicitly encompassing the nonverbal aspect of communication. Their work serves as an important basis in communication science helping to analyze and understand human interaction.

Axiom 1: One Cannot Not Communicate

According to Watzlawick et al. (1967), communication arises from every perceivable behavior and can happen both consciously and unconsciously. Thus, group communication starts as soon as two or more people perceive each other. Even the absence of an action is interpreted in some form by the observer and therefore conveys social information contributing to the communication process. Team members should therefore be aware that communication is a pervasive process which is not tied to active forms of interaction.

Axiom 2: Every Communication Act Has a Content and a Relationship Aspect

Similar to Schulz von Thun (1981), Watzlawick claims that what is being said is always interpreted according to the relationship of the communicators.

If a coach criticizes an athlete, it depends on the nature of their relation how the criticism is received by the athlete. If the relationship is good the athlete is more likely to accept and to interpret it as a well-intended, possibly beneficial advice. If the relationship is difficult the same criticism may be conceived less favorably increasing the chance of rejection and conflict.

Axiom 3: Communication Is Punctuated

Every communicative act can be regarded as a stimulus as well as a response or reinforcement. Punctuation of communicative sequences is subjective and may differ for each interaction partner. Thus, the perception of the beginning and development of an interaction may vary for each individual potentially resulting in a different interpretation of the same situation.

If a player is not included in the starting formation (stimulus) for a match this may lead to frustration and lack of motivation in training (response). In a conversation to resolve the situation the coach may state that the player's lack of motivation in training (stimulus) is the reason for the non-consideration (response). The individual punctuation of the same situation makes it hard to retrace cause and consequence of the interaction and may lead to opposite perspectives potentially initiating a spiraling conflict. It is important to note that communication transcends the moment (i.e., it doesn't only comprise a given conversation, but may start earlier, e.g., with a certain behavior). This event may be perceived as the start of the communication for one but not necessarily for the other interaction partner. The bigger the group the more perspectives are to be considered which increases the complexity of the communication. Given these differences, it seems beneficial to try to pinpoint one initial point of origin for a communicative situation.

Axiom 4: Communication Involves Digital and Analogous Modalities

Communication encompasses several modalities. According to Watzlawick et al. (1967) the digital modality refers to what we actually say. It mainly relates to verbal forms of interaction (e.g., spoken or written word) which follow a clear syntax. The analog modality refers to how we say something. It comprises paraverbal (e.g., speed, pitch, and tone of voice) and nonverbal (e.g., facial expressions, gestures, posture) properties providing information about inner states (e.g., attitudes and emotions).

Precise unambiguous communication relies on the congruence of both, verbal and nonverbal modalities (Argyle, 2005). If the verbal and nonverbal information sent by the communicator are incongruent, chances of misinterpretation and misunderstandings increase (Argyle, 2005). For instance, a coach verbally expressing his or her dissatisfaction with the team after a loss would be taken less seriously when displaying a happy facial expression. In cases of conflicting verbal and nonverbal information observers tend to rely more on the perceivable NVB (Burgoon et al., 2011).

Athletes and coaches should therefore be aware that both, the verbal and the nonverbal channel, importantly contribute to team communication with verbal communication transporting the factual aspect of a message and nonverbal cues providing meaning by clarifying attitudes, emotions, and intentions.

Axiom 5: Communication Can Be Symmetrical or Complementary

The characteristic of human interaction depends on whether the relationship between the communicators is based on equality or disparity. In a symmetrical relation, both interaction partners are of comparable status. Communication is generally symmetrical if interaction partners are of equal social status or share a similar level of expertise in a specific area of interest. In a complementary constellation social status or knowledge is unequally distributed among the individuals. Differences in status often lead to one interaction partner subordinating to another. However, differences in expertise can also be used to complement one another. A head coach may for instance base decisions on years of experience in a specific field but still profit from fresh ideas provided by the young assistant coach who lacks experience but tends to think more out of the box. Both modes of communication importantly influence the dynamic of an interaction.

All five axioms are considered general communication principles that relate to verbal and nonverbal modes of communication. Both, verbal and nonverbal communication in sport teams will subsequently be focused on in more detail. Therefore, we will review several different lines of investigation within sport psychological research that are related to the outlined, broad theoretical framework on communication.

Verbal and Nonverbal Communication in Sports Teams

The goal of the next section is to integrate a highly diverse body of literature within a communication perspective and, where possible, derive some evidence-based recommendations when working in the context of sports. To this end we have divided the literature review into research on verbal and nonverbal communication in sports.

Verbal Communication

This section is intended to highlight some widely studied topics within sports (e.g., goal-setting, motivation, social support, decision making, or team cohesions) from a communication perspective. In this endeavor, we adopted the term **message-based constructs** from Ishak (2017) to describe the factual layer of the four-sides-model.

Message-Based Constructs of Sports Team Communication

Many of the efforts to manage teams and increase performance are delivered through verbal messages. The following passages intend to highlight how the factual content of some verbal messages have the potential to impact sports team behavior and performance for the better or the worse.

Goal-Setting

An important antecedent of effective team performance are communicatively constructed goals. It is well-established that successful teams need a shared goal to effectively work together (e.g., Katzenbach & Smith, 1993; Kingston & Wilson, 2009; Williams, 2013). An important distinction within the literature on goal-setting in sports has been established between outcome goals, performance, and process goals, but also between training and competition goals, and individual and team goals (Burton & Weiss, 2008; Hall & Kerr, 2001). Hence, an evidence-informed guideline would be to set and communicate a variety of different types of goals across different time scales (e.g., Williams, 2013 for more detail). However, as studies on goal-setting interventions in sports have provided ambiguous results (Williams, 2013 for a review) and have been shown to be highly context-dependent, we refrain from giving recipe-like information on how to communicate about goals in sport teams (Ishak, 2017). Nevertheless, there seems to be a pattern in the literature on goal-setting that points to the importance of acknowledging relationship factors when setting team goals and it seems not advisable of simply having people in leading/high-status positions on a team to dictate goals to the entire teams (e.g., Williams, 2013). Thus, in team communication it seems important to consider relationship and status of the communicators to ensure most efficient transmission of certain types of messages. A principle also indicated in Watzlawick's second and fifth axiom of communication.

Motivation and Motivational Climate

There are several lines of research within the sports literature that indicate how verbal messages can affect motivation of team members and the motivational climate of the whole team. In this respect, a seminal finding in sport psychology has been that task mastery, that is process goals, as opposed to outcome goals can lead to higher satisfaction and intrinsic motivation (Duda & Balaguer, 2007). Hence, sports teams seem well advised in communicating process goals and personal mastery (e.g., improving skills) instead of solely focusing on outcomes like winning championships.

A dominant theory within the sports motivation literature is self-determination theory (Deci & Ryan, 2011; Hagger & Chatzisarantis, 2007). This theory also has some important value concerning communication in sports teams. In a nutshell, the theory assumes that the fulfillment of three basic psychological needs (autonomy, competence, and social relatedness) leads to higher levels of intrinsic motivation with numerous positive outcomes in various sports contexts. Therefore, verbal messages that give athletes and teams the feeling of being competent, autonomous individuals and/or teams will likely be beneficial to individuals and sport teams. On the other hand, highly controlling verbal behavior by coaches is likely to undermine feelings of autonomy within teams and therefore will presumably negatively impact on athlete's motivation (Bartholomew et al., 2009; Occhino et al., 2014). In this respect, Mageau and Vallerand (2003) summarize "hands-on" strategies of how coaches' verbal behavior can increase a sports teams (intrinsic) motivation: (1) giving athletes the opportunity to choose within boundaries; (2) giving a rationale for tasks; (3) acknowledging feelings, valuing perspectives and input; (4) giving opportunities for athletes to take initiative; (5) avoid controlling comments and behaviors; and (6) reducing perception of ego-involvement. Although, these heuristic guidelines might help coaches to keep motivation high in their athletes, it is important to acknowledge that not all athletes will respond equally to verbal feedback as there may be important individual differences in how athletes want to be addressed (e.g., Horn et al., 2011). Referring back to the second axiom of communication (Watzlawick et al., 1967) and Schulz von Thun's model of communication, the influence of the relationship between the communicators needs to be considered when assessing the effect of a certain type of verbal behavior (Schulz von Thun, 2013).

Research on a coach's communication style distinguishes between a mastery-oriented climate or a performance-oriented climate (Horn et al., 2012). A mastery-oriented climate is characterized by defining success by skill-development, by valuing all players on a team, by emphasizing cooperative learning, and viewing mistakes as opportunities for learning. On the other hand, a performance-oriented or ego-involving climate emphasizes competition between team members, sanctioning of mistakes, and values higher-skilled players more than less-skilled players. Several studies (e.g., Barić & Bucik, 2009; Duda & Balaguer, 2007) have provided converging evidence for a variety of more positive outcomes (e.g., higher satisfaction, less drop-out) for a mastery-oriented climate as opposed to a performance-oriented climate.

Social Support

Starting about 20 years ago, there has been a shift regarding coaching behavior in sports that has been summarized as the *"Positive Coaching Movement"* (Denison & Avner, 2011; Thompson,

---

Box 23.1   The Most Memorable Messages Athletes Got From Their Coaches

A study by Cranmer et al. (2017) identified that certain types of verbal messages from a coach were particularly influential and memorable to high school athletes. In this study, messages were collected from 102 former high school athletes via open-ended questionnaires and coded for further analyses. Results indicated that three categories of messages were particularly enduring and influential in supporting athletes. The first category of messages were informational support messages telling them how to play, how to be successful, and how to relate to other team members. The second category were esteem support messages focusing on abilities, encouraging intangibles, and reinforce relationships within the team. The third category were emotional support messages that benefitted the athlete's wellbeing, offered praise, helped them improve performance, and cope with poor performance and failure. The study concludes that coaches' verbal support can take many forms, including praise, advice, instruction, and demonstrations of concern. The three identified classifications of support messages offer a promising starting point for coaches to improve their coaching effectiveness and give support to their athletes.

2003; see Box 23.1). This movement is characterized by a deemphasis of "winning at all costs" to positive development in both sports and other areas of life. In this regard the verbal behavior and communication of coaches during practice and during games has been shown to have a substantial impact on the development of athletes, particularly at younger ages (Thompson, 2003).

Although there has been a shift toward more positive communication in sports, many coaches frequently use negative messaging. One study (Walters et al., 2012) across numerous youth sports found that 35.4% of coaches' comments could be classified as positive (e.g., praise, encouragement) and 21.6% were negative, included scolding, contradicting, ridicule, and correcting without supporting. Although, this type of negative messaging might sometimes succeed to motivate athletes, research (Walters et al., 2012) has shown that negative outcomes (e.g., loss of motivation, frustration, dropping out) are correlated with this type of negative messaging. It seems plausible that such verbal behaviors may provoke a shift in social interaction from more symmetrical to more complementary forms of communication (see Axiom 5; Watzlawick et al., 1967) potentially increasing the perceived status-related social distance between coaches and athletes within a team.

Communication of Roles

A role can be described as a set of behaviors expected from a person who occupies a particular position. Research has shown that a clear communication of roles is an important component of success in sports teams (Eys et al., 2014). Various communication events occur in the process of determining and fulfilling roles. For example, the coach must determine which athlete should fill which role (e.g., field position, leader) and then communicate certain expectation toward the role. Then all players have to accept the allocated roles or negotiate the expectations (Eys et al., 2005). Studies indicate that teams with higher role clarity perform better than teams with lower role clarity (e.g., Bray et al., 2002). In addition, it was shown that teams with higher role ambiguity showed lower levels of cohesion. Hence, roles within a team should be clearly assigned and communicated between coaches and players. The communication model by Schulz von Thun and the five axioms of communication can serve as an orientation pointing out what to consider in order to communicate roles as unambiguously as possible.

All of the message-based constructs presented in this section constitute explicit forms of communication. They generally require attention of teams and team leaders, and are delivered through spoken messages and interaction (Ishak, 2017). In the following section, the focus will be placed on more implicit forms of communication which do not rely on verbal interaction but are also integral for team functioning.

Nonverbal Communication

The importance of NVB in social interaction has been acknowledged for a long time. In fact, the nonverbal share in human communication surpasses the verbal part by far as humans constantly send out nonverbal signals conveying information about inner states (e.g., attitudes, emotions, and intentions; Knapp et al., 2013). Research suggests 65%–95% of face-to-face communication to amount to NVB (Matsumoto et al., 2013). Thus, interpretation of verbal information substantially depends on ongoing processing of nonverbal cues transmitting attitudes, emotions, and intentions (see Axiom 4; Watzlawick et al., 1967) complementing and supporting interpretation of the spoken word (Argyle, 2005).

Nonverbal communication encompasses any form of signaling detached from semantics that can be perceived via sensory pathways. It includes auditory cues referred to as paralanguage (e.g., pitch, tone, speed, and rhythm of voice) and visual cues (e.g., facial expressions, gaze, gestures, and posture) also described as body language (Argyle, 2005). Furthermore, NVB comprises spatial behavior (e.g., interpersonal distance), physical features, and olfactory and haptic signals which can all be categorized as body language in a broader sense (Hess, 2016).

DePaulo (1992) emphasizes NVB to be of notable importance for interpersonal communication for various reasons: (1) In line with Watzlawick's first axiom of communication, people always convey some kind of nonverbal information. Thus, nonverbal cues are pervasive in any form of social interaction. (2) Since certain impressions are elusive and hard to express in words, they can only be conveyed nonverbally. (3) As nonverbal responses are often spontaneous and immediate, they transmit the impression of sincerity. Hence, NVB is perceived to provide rather genuine information about a respective person. (4) Nonverbal expressions are closely linked to internal states and are more accessible to the observer than to the actor. Thus, nonverbal displays can inadvertently expose emotional experience and foster specific impressions.

Even though nonverbals mostly underly some form of regulation, the attempted control is not always conscious and may therefore also unintentionally convey information to others (DePaulo, 1992). An athlete may for instance experience feelings of nervousness or anxiety immediately before a competition. This can manifest in the expression of nonverbal signals like rushing and pacing, or fidgeting gestures with hands or feet. All these behaviors may occur automatically without the athlete noticing. Such cues can readily be perceived by teammates or opponents, and may in turn affect their cognitions and subsequent actions. However, as such behaviors are semi-conscious, athletes can become aware of them and learn to control their nonverbal expressions and suppress unwanted leakage of emotional cues.

Furthermore, NVB communicates status-related social information like dominance and submissiveness which serves clarification of social hierarchies (Martens et al., 2012). A coach could, for example, add authority to a speech by adopting correspondent severe facial expressions and upright resolute posture.

In competitive sports nonverbal communication is of particular importance, as the means of verbal communication are often limited (e.g., due to the size of the court or the amount of noise in a stadium; Moesch et al., 2014). Furthermore, time constraints and other stressors cause players to increasingly rely on nonverbal rather than verbal communication (Eccles & Tran, 2012). Gaze behavior, facial expressions, posture, gestures, spatial behavior, touch, paralanguage, and silence are mentioned to be commonly occurring for the purpose of communication and coordination among athletes and coaches (Renz & Greg, 2000). For instance, athletes use bodily signals to indicate in-game decisions and spontaneous mutual adjustments while coaches make gestures at the sidelines to communicate tactical instructions. A specific benefit of nonverbal communication in sports is that it allows for communicating play calls and tactical adjustments secretly in plain sight. Athletes frequently use predetermined gestures transmitting information to teammates (e.g., signs in baseball, play calls in basketball) while preventing opponents from grasping what is about to happen (Ishak, 2017).

Moreover, performance-related NVB informs on athletes' and coaches' emotional states. On the one hand, successful sports performance is usually followed by celebratory gestures which are often spontaneous outbursts of joy and triumph but at the same time signal strength and dominance to the observer. On the other hand, failure frequently entails shameful bodily expressions conveying impressions of weakness and submission (Tracy & Matsumoto, 2008).

Status-Related Nonverbal Displays

In sports, status-related NVBs frequently occur among athletes and coaches. This includes, for instance, the occupation of more space by adopting an erect posture with a wider stance and expanded chest – a behavior seen countless times during Christiano Ronaldo's infamous freekick preparations. Triumphant gestures like extending the arms from the body or over the shoulders make individuals appear taller signaling confidence and superiority (Matsumoto & Hwang, 2012). Further, showing a clenched fist conveys feelings of anger or pride both of which are dominant signals found to influence the attribution of power (Tracy & Robins, 2007a). All of those NVBs evoke impressions of dominance and strength. In contrast, minimizing occupied space by adopting a more narrow stance and a slouched posture with hanging shoulders and the limbs close to the body conveys more submissive impressions.

Such nonverbals constitute a significant factor in team communication as they have been repeatedly shown to affect cognitive patterns related to sports performance (e.g., Furley & Schweizer, 2014; Furley et al., 2017). For instance, the observation of athletes' dominant nonverbal displays evokes increased confidence and expectations of success among teammates and decreased confidence and success expectancies among opponents (Furley & Schweizer, 2014). This correlation may be explained by the implicit association between dominant body language and positive attributes such as control, expertise, and power (Tracy & Robins, 2007a, 2007b). The observation of dominant body language thereby transmits the impression of an athlete being capable and in control of the situation (Furley et al., 2012) which can push teammates and support individual and team performance (Furley & Schweizer, 2020). In contrast, observation of submissive body language (e.g., slouched posture; head and gaze pointing down; limbs touching the torso; minimizing the occupied space by collapsing the body inwards, shoulders hanging to the front) implicitly linked to low social status, entails converse effects resulting in performance advantages for the opponent (Furley & Dicks, 2012). An observational study conducted by Moll et al. (2010) found dominant post-performance gestures in soccer to be associated with a deterioration of opponents' subsequent performance. More specifically, players performed significantly worse in penalty shootouts after opponents celebrated a goal by extending both arms from the body. Moreover, players extending both arms from the body while clenching both fists were significantly more likely to be in the team that ultimately won the shootout (Moll et al., 2010).

Results suggest that status-related NVB may indeed be an important factor in team communication influencing both teammates and opponents. Athletes and coaches seem well advised to openly display dominant nonverbal signals to (1) evoke positive cognitions in team mates potentially enhancing momentum for team performance and (2) intimidate and discourage opponents decreasing their confidence in successful performance.

Tactile Communication

Another means of nonverbal communication frequently occurring in team sports is physical touch. Recent scientific advances in the domain suggest tactile communication among athletes to potentially affect team performance (e.g., Kraus et al., 2010; Moesch et al., 2013, 2014, 2018). Systematic observation in elite handball showed increased occurrence of physical touch (e.g., low five, high five, high ten, touch shoulders) during post-shot celebrations among teammates when playing well to be related to positive subsequent team performance. In contrast, showing little touch in phases when teams played well-entailed negative subsequent team performance. These findings suggest nonverbal post-shot celebrations in the form of touch after successful periods to be a good strategy for fostering psychological momentum and maintaining good team performance. However, when playing poorly high degrees of tactile team communication was related to negative subsequent team performance whereas low degrees of touch entailed more positive performance. Thus, it is suggested that timing and situational context plays an important role in the impact physical touch has within team communication.

On a more general note, studies report an increase in touching behavior during play-off games and among athletes within winning teams (Moesch et al., 2013, 2014). In a similar vein, in National Basketball Association, increased physical touch among teammates (e.g., fist bumps, high fives, chest bumps, leaping shoulder bumps, chest punches, head slaps, head grabs, low fives, high tens, full hugs, half hugs, and team huddles) in early season was found to predict greater individual and team performance later in the season (Kraus et al., 2010). More specifically, in their observational study, Kraus et al. (2010) found that the touch observed during one game early on in the season predicted enhanced team cooperation, individual, and team performance over the course of the entire season regardless of player status, preseason expectations, and early season performance.

All four studies (i.e., Kraus et al., 2010; Moesch et al., 2013, 2014, 2018) indicate tactile communication to be related to group functioning during competition. It is important to mention that these studies assessed specific patterns of physical touch in specific competitive groups (i.e., basketball and handball teams) and were conducted within a western cultural environment (i.e., Sweden and United States). Furthermore, touching behavior was only investigated within same gender teams. Cultural and gender-related differences (e.g., due to religious beliefs, or mixed gender teams) may play an important role in how touch is perceived and to what extent tactile NVB is accepted. For instance, behavioral rules concerning physical touch may differ between people of the same gender as opposed to individuals of opposite sex. Thereby, occurrence, quality, and effect of tactile NVB may be subject to change depending on the context in which it is implemented.

However, athletes and coaches should note that touch is generally a prosocial behavior highly important for bonding (Kraus et al., 2010). It communicates emotions like gratitude and sympathy and may – when applied adequately – function as positive reinforcement fostering intimacy, and encouraging compliance which is essential to cooperation within groups (Kraus et al., 2010; Moesch et al., 2014). Touch can further promote trust which is a central component of long-term cooperative bonds (Williams & Bargh, 2008). In conclusion, implementing tactile communication (e.g., hugs, high fives, fist bumps, and team huddles) in sports practice seems beneficial as it may strengthen team structure enhancing intra-team cooperation and team functioning (Kraus et al., 2010; Moesch et al., 2018).

Advantages of NVB in Sports

As team sports are characterized by high complexity, time pressure, as well as various simultaneous challenges the necessity to interact quickly and efficiently becomes evident. The swiftness of nonverbal communication, for example, an encouraging touch or gesture, is therefore of great value for team communication. Considerable benefits of NVB also lie in its capacity to transport meanings and emotions that verbal communication cannot (Burgoon et al., 2016). As certain impressions, like the reassuring feeling of a teammate's confident demeanor, are elusive, they are more difficult to verbalize than to express nonverbally (DePaulo, 1992). At the same time, nonverbal information transmitting inner states is perceived as more genuine and reliable than verbal information (Burgoon et al., 2016) which makes NVB particularly valuable for conveying impressions to observers (Argyle, 2005). Finally, an extensive body of NVB is universally comprehensible and can therefore transcend potential barriers of verbal communication (Burgoon et al., 2016) which is a great asset considering the multicultural character of modern sports.

Challenges of NVB in Sports

Despite its various benefits in team communication NVB can also be a source of misunderstandings (Burgoon et al., 2016). Especially when team members do not share the same conception about the interpretation or transmission of specific nonverbal messages (Aly, 2014). Formation of intent to produce a specific NVB is subject to cultural and situational norms (DePaulo, 1992). The overt expression of certain nonverbal displays may be encouraged in some cultures, but not in others. Moreover, there are situational factors dictating which NVBs are appropriate (DePaulo, 1992). Individuals' knowledge about such display rules determines which NVBs are taken into consideration (Furley & Schweizer, 2020). Moreover, translation of self-presentational intentions into nonverbal expressions can be inhibited by several factors. The ability to control NVBs that deviate from habitual displays may for instance be impeded by lack of expressiveness or confidence (Furley & Schweizer, 2020). An anxious or shy athlete wanting to convey signals of dominance might fail to transmit the wanted impression to his or her teammates when acting hesitantly or sending conflicting bodily signals. Therefore, clarification and synchronization of nonverbal means of communication within a team are important. This includes individual knowledge about situationally and culturally appropriate display rules as well as team members' ability to deliberately produce the desired expressions (DePaulo, 1992). However, nonverbally evoking a desired impression at will is taxing. Constraints are imposed by motivational factors, fatigue, and depletion (Matsumoto et al., 2013). Thus, under highly emotional or stressful circumstances – which frequently occur in the context of professional sports – certain expressions may be too difficult to produce or suppress at will (Furley & Schweizer, 2020) leading to failure in transmitting intended impressions or unintentionally leaking emotional cues potentially undermining self-presentational efforts (DePaulo, 1992).

Evidence-Based Recommendations for Practice

As evident from other social domains, good communication is a matter of practice. Also in team sports, the explicit focus on group and interpersonal communication skills can improve player communication competencies (Sullivan, 1993). There is an extensive body of literature claiming that good communication provides sport teams with valuable resources. This includes task-oriented resources (e.g., the exchange of tips and instructions on how to play; Widmeyer & Williams, 1991), as well as motivation prior to, during, and appraisal after competition (Hanin, 1992). Furthermore, it comprehends social resources, like, dealing with emotional messages of affection or anger (Diberardinis et al., 1983) and the acceptance of individual members

(Sullivan, 1993). Concerning the exchange of social support within teams there is a differentiation between tangible (e.g., personal assistance), emotional (e.g., listening support), and informational (e.g., task appreciation support) resources (Rosenfeld & Richman, 1997). These variables have been empirically linked to team cohesion (Widmeyer & Williams, 1991), as well as team (Hanin, 1992) and player performance (Diberardinis et al., 1983). Cherubini (2019) emphasizes that athletes benefit from harmonious and positive communication styles transmitting information with respect, empathy, honesty, and brevity. It can facilitate positive affect, self-determination, on-task behavior, and self-regulation which fosters athletes' potential to thrive both in and outside of the sporting context (Cherubini, 2019).

Also, nonverbal communication can be practiced to be more precise and efficient (Hackfort & Schlattmann, 2002). For athletes, video-based behavioral training to develop appropriate self-presentation has been suggested in the past (Hackfort & Schlattmann, 2002). The plethora of visual data available specifically in professional sports offers extensive possibilities to base NVB training on. Moreover, given that body language extends to every area of social interaction, training awareness, interpretation, and nonverbal expression is possible in specific sporting encounters as well as in general social interaction. However, repeated and deliberate practice is necessary to consolidate acquired abilities (Furley & Schweizer, 2020).

Conclusion

Considering the abundance of variables and relations within a sports team, it is not possible to fully control all aspects of social interaction while performing. However, good communication is an important pillar providing structure and supporting athlete satisfaction (Ishak, 2017). The verbal share in team communication comprehends essential processes like goal-setting, motivation, social support, sharing of knowledge, decision making, and clarification of roles (Ishak, 2017). The nonverbal portion supports these processes to a great extent (Burgoon et al., 2016) and constitutes a major factor in the communication of signals related to emotions and social status also affecting impression formation (Furley & Schweizer, 2020). Hence, fostering the synergy of well-functioning verbal and nonverbal modes of interaction in sport teams is likely to be a good way to advance team coordination, overall performance (Eccles & Tran, 2012) and enhance the sporting experience (Cherubini, 2019).

Further Readings

Eccles, D. W., & Tran, K. B. (2012). Getting them on the same page: Strategies for enhancing coordination and communication in sports teams. *Journal of Sport Psychology in Action*, *3*(1), 30–40.
Ishak, A. W. (2017). Communication in sports teams: A review. *Communication Research Trends*, *36*(4), 4–38.
Jowette, S. E., & Lavallee, D. E. (2007). *Social psychology in sport*. Human Kinetics.

Glossary

Axiom   A statement accepted as an established principle or self-evident truth which is used as the basis for further reasoning or inference.
Message-based constructs   Explicit forms of team interaction that are based on the verbal exchange of information, feedback, and/or knowledge.
Nonverbal communication   The transfer of information by means of body language (e.g., facial expressions, gaze, gestures, and posture) and/or paralanguage (e.g., pitch, tone, speed, and rhythm of voice).
Verbal communication   The conveyance of a message by means of spoken or written words.

References

Aly, E. R. (2014). Communication management among athlete and coaches. *European Scientific Journal, 3*, 1–3.

Argyle, M. (2005). *Körpersprache und Kommunikation* (9th ed.). Junfermann.

Athanasios, L. (2005). Communication problems in professional sports: The case of Greece. *Corporate Communications: An International Journal, 10(3)*, 252–256. https://doi.org/10.1108/13563280510614500

Barić, R., & Bucik, V. (2009). Motivational differences in athletes trained by coaches of different motivational and leadership profiles. *Kineziologija, 41*(2), 181–194.

Bartholomew, K. J., Ntoumanis, N., & Thogersen-Ntoumani, C. (2009). A review of controlling motivational strategies from a self-determination theory perspective: Implications for sports coaches. *International Review of Sport and Exercise Psychology, 2*, 215–233. https://doi.org/10.1080/17509840903235330

Blickensderfer, E. L., Cannon-Bowers, J. A., & Salas, E. (2000). *The relationship between shared knowledge and team performance: A field study*. Paper presented at the Annual Meeting of the American Psychological Society. Miami, FL, June 8–11, 2000.

Bray, S. R., Brawley, L. R., & Carron, A. V. (2002). Role ambiguity, role efficacy, and role performance: Multidimensional and mediational relationships within interdependent sport teams. *Group Dynamics: Theory, Research, and Practice, 6*(3), 229–242. https://doi.org/10.1037/1089-2699.6.3.229

Burgoon, J. K., Guerrero, L. K., & Floyd, K. (2016). *Nonverbal communication*. Routledge.

Burgoon, J. K., Guerrero, L. K., & Manusov, V. (2011). Nonverbal signals. In M. L. Knapp & J. A. Daley (Eds.), *The SAGE handbook of interpersonal communication* (4th ed., pp. 239–280). Sage.

Burton, D., & Weiss, C. (2008). The fundamental goal concept: The path to process and performance success. In T. S. Horn (Ed.), *Advances in sport psychology* (3rd ed., pp. 339–375). Human Kinetics.

Cannon-Bowers, J. A., & Salas, E. (1998). Individual and team decision making under stress: Theoretical underpinnings. In J. A. Cannon-Bowers & E. Salas (Eds.), *Making decisions under stress: Implications for individual and team training* (pp. 17–38). American Psychological Association.

Cherubini, J. (2019). Strategies and communication skills in sports coaching. In M. H. Anshel, T. A. Petrie, & J. A. Steinfeldt (Eds.), *APA handbook of sport and exercise psychology, Vol. 1. Sport psychology* (pp. 451–467). American Psychological Association. https://doi.org/10.1037/0000123-023

Cranmer, G. A., Anzur, C. K., & Sollitto, M. (2017). Memorable messages of social support that former high school athletes received from their head coaches. *Communication & Sport, 5*(5), 604–621. https://doi.org/10.1177/2167479516641934

Deci, E. L., & Ryan, R. M. (2011). Self-determination theory. *Handbook of Theories of Social Psychology, 1*, 416–433.

Denison, J., & Avner, Z. (2011). Positive coaching: Ethical practices for athlete development. *Quest, 63*(2), 209–227. https://doi.org/10.1080/00336297.2011.10483677

DePaulo, B. M. (1992). Nonverbal behavior and self-presentation. *Psychological Bulletin, 111*(2), 203.

Diberardinis, J., Barwind, J., Flaningam, R. R., & Jenkins, V. (1983). Enhanced interpersonal relation as predictor of athletic performance. *International Journal of Sport Psychology, 14*, 243–251.

Duda, J. L., & Balaguer, I. (2007). Coach-created motivational climate. In S. Jowette & D. Lavallee (Eds.), *Social psychology in sport* (pp. 117–130). Human Kinetics.

Eccles, D. W., & Tran, K. B. (2012). Getting them on the same page: Strategies for enhancing coordination and communication in sports teams. *Journal of Sport Psychology in Action, 3*(1), 30–40.

Eys, M. A., Carron, A. V., Beauchamp, M. R., & Brays, S. R. (2005). Athletes' perceptions of the sources of role ambiguity. *Small Group Research, 36*(4), 383–403. https://doi.org/10.1177/1046496404268533

Eys, M. A., Schinke, R. J., Surya, M., & Benson, A. J. (2014). Role perceptions in sport groups. In M. R. Beauchamp & M. A. Eys (Eds.), *Group dynamics in exercise and sport psychology* (pp. 131–146). Routledge.

Furley, P., & Dicks, M. (2012). Hold your head high. The influence of emotional versus neutral nonverbal expressions of dominance and submissiveness in baseball. *International Journal of Sport Psychology, 43*(4), 294.

Furley, P., Dicks, M., & Memmert, D. (2012). Nonverbal behavior in soccer: The influence of dominant and submissive body language on the impression formation and expectancy of success of soccer players. *Journal of Sport and Exercise Psychology, 34*(1), 61–82.

Furley, P., Schnuerch, R., & Gibbons, H. (2017). The winner takes it all: Event-related brain potentials reveal enhanced motivated attention toward athletes' nonverbal signals of leading. *Social Neuroscience.* 12, 448–457. https://doi.org/10.1080/17470919.2016.1182586

Furley, P., & Schweizer, G. (2014). "I'm pretty sure that we will win!": The influence of score-related nonverbal behavioral changes on the confidence in winning a basketball game. *Journal of Sport and Exercise Psychology, 36*(3), 315–319.

Furley, P., & Schweizer, G. (2020). Body language in sport. *Handbook of Sport Psychology*, 1201–1219. https://doi.org/10.1002/9781119568124.ch59

Hackfort, D., & Schlattmann, A. (2002). Self-presentation training for top athletes. *International Journal of Sport Psychology, 33*(1), 61–71.

Hagger, M. S., & Chatzisarantis, N. L. D. (Eds.) (2007). *Intrinsic motivation and self-determination in exercise and sport*. Human Kinetics.

Hall, H. K., & Kerr, A. W. (2001). Goal setting in sport and physical activity: Tracing empirical developments and establishing conceptual direction. In G. C. Roberts (Ed.), *Motivation in sport and exercise* (pp. 183–234). Human Kinetics.

Hanin, Y. (1992). Social psychology and sport: Communication processes in top performance teams. *Sport Science Review, 1*, 13–28.

Hess, U. (2016). Nonverbal communication. In H. S. Friedman (Ed.), *Encyclopedia of mental health* (2nd ed., Vol. 3, pp. 208–218). Academic Press.

Hinsz, V. B. (1995). Mental models of groups as social systems: Considerations of specification and assessment. *Small Group Research, 26*, 200–233.

Horn, T. S., Bloom, P., Berglund, K. M., & Packard, S. (2011). Relationship between collegiate athletes' psychological characteristics and their preferences for different types of coaching behavior. *The Sport Psychologist, 25*(2), 190–211. https://doi.org/10.1123/tsp.25.2.190

Horn, T. S., Byrd, M., Martin, E., & Young, C. (2012). Perceived motivational climate and team cohesion in adolescent athletes. *Sport Science Review, 21*(3–4), 25–48.

Ishak, A. W. (2017). Communication in sports teams: A review. *Communication Research Trends, 36*(4), 4–38.

Katzenbach, J. R., & Smith, D. K. (1993). *The wisdom of teams: Creating the high-performance organization*. Harvard Business School Press.

Kingston, K. M., & Wilson, K. M. (2009). The application of goal setting in sport. In S. D. Mellalieu & S. Hanton (Eds.), *Advances in applied sport psychology: A review* (pp. 75–123). Routledge.

Knapp, M. L., Hall, J. A., & Horgan, T. G. (2013). *Nonverbal communication in human interaction* (8th ed.). Cengage Learning.

Kraus, M. W., Huang, C., & Keltner, D. (2010). Tactile communication, cooperation, and performance: An ethological study of the NBA. *Emotion, 10*(5), 745–749. https://doi.org/10.1037/a0019382

Lau, A. (2020). Interaktion und kommunikation im sport. In J. Schüler, M. Wegner, & H. Plessner (Eds.), *Sportpsychologie* (pp. 427–442). Springer.

Lau, A. (2023). Interaction and communication in sport. In J. Schüler, M. Wegner, H. Plessner, & R. Eklund (Eds.), *Sport and exercise psychology*. Springer.

Lausic, D., Tennebaum, G., Eccles, D., Jeong, A., & Johnson, T. (2009). Intrateam communication and performance in doubles tennis. *Research Quarterly for Exercise and Sport, 80*(2), 281–290.

Levinson, S. (2006). Cognition at the heart of human interaction. *Discourse Studies, 8*(1), 85–93.

Littlejohn, S. W., Foss, K. A., & Oetzel, J. G. (2011). *Theories of human communication*. Waveland Press, pp. 30, 32.

Mageau, G. A., & Vallerand, R. J. (2003). The coach-athlete relationship: A motivational model. *Journal of Sports Science, 21*(11), 883–904.

Martens, J. P., Tracy, J. L., & Shariff, A. F. (2012). Status signals: Adaptive benefits of displaying and observing the nonverbal expressions of pride and shame. *Cognition & Emotion, 26*(3), 390–406.

Matsumoto, D., Frank, M. G., & Hwang, H. S. (2013). Reading people: Introduction to the world of nonverbal behaviour. In D. Matsumoto, M. Frank, & H.S. Hwang (Eds.), *Nonverbal communication: Science and applications* (pp. 3–14). Sage.

Matsumoto, D., & Hwang, H. S. (2012). Evidence for a nonverbal expression of triumph. *Evolution and Human Behavior*, *33*(5), 520–529.

McKenna, C. (1998). *Powerful communication skills*. Career Press.

Moesch, K., Kenttä, G., Bäckström, M., & Mattsson, C. M. (2014). Exploring nonverbal behaviors in elite handball: How and when do players celebrate? *Journal of Applied Sport Psychology*, *27*(1), 94–109. https://doi.org/10.1080/10413200.2014.953231

Moesch, K., Kenttä, G., Bäckström, M., & Mattsson, C. M. (2018). Nonverbal post-shot celebrations and their relationship with performance in elite handball, *International Journal of Sport and Exercise Psychology*, *16*(3), 235–249. https://doi.org/10.1080/1612197X.2016.1216148

Moesch, K., Kenttä, G., & Mattsson, M. C. (2013). *How much means touch? An investigation of touching behaviors among female elite handball players* (pp. 81–81) Abstract from World Congress of Sport Psychology.

Moll, T., Jordet, G., & Pepping, G. J. (2010). Emotional contagion in soccer penalty shootouts: Celebration of individual success is associated with ultimate team success. *Journal of Sports Sciences*, *28*(9), 983–992. https://doi.org/10.1080/02640414.2010.484068

Occhino, J. L., Mallett, C. J., Rynne, S. B., & Carlisle, K. N. (2014). Autonomy-supportive pedagogical approach to sports coaching: Research, challenges, and opportunities. *International Journal of Sports Science & Coaching*, *9*(2), 401–415. https://doi.org/10.1260/1747-9541.9.2.401

Reimer, T., Park, E. S., & Hinsz, V. B. (2006). Shared and coordinated cognition in competitive and dynamic task environments: An information-processing perspective for team sports. *International Journal of Sport and Exercise Psychology*, *4*(4), 376–400.

Renz, M. A., & Greg, J. B. (2000). *Effective small group communication in theory and practice*. Allyn & Bacon.

Rosenfeld, L. B., & Richman, J. M. (1997). Developing effective social support: Team building and the social support process. *Journal of Applied Sport Psychology*, *9*(1), 133–153.

Schulz von Thun, F. (1981). *Miteinander reden, bd.1.[Talking to each other]*. Rowohlt Verlag GmbH.

Schulz von Thun, F. (2013). *Miteinander reden 1: Störungen und Klärungen: Allgemeine Psychologie der Kommunikation* (Vol. 1). Rowohlt Verlag GmbH.

Sullivan, P. A. (1993). Communication skills training for interactive sports. *The Sport Psychologist*, *7*(1), 79–91. https://doi.org/10.1123/tsp.7.1.79

Sullivan, P. J., & Callow, N. (2005). A cross-cultural examination of the factor structure of the scale for effective communication in team sports. *Group Dynamics: Theory, Research, and Practice*, *9*(2), 87.

Thompson, J. (2003). *The double-goal coach: Positive coaching tools for honoring the game and developing winners in sports and life*. Harper Collins.

Tracy, J. L., & Matsumoto, D. (2008). The spontaneous expression of pride and shame: Evidence for biologically innate nonverbal displays. *Proceedings of the National Academy of Sciences*, *105*(33), 11655–11660.

Tracy, J. L., & Robins, R. W. (2007a). Emerging insights into the nature and function of pride. *Current Directions in Psychological Science*, *16*(3), 147–150.

Tracy, J. L., & Robins, R. W. (2007b). The nature of pride. In J. L. Tracy, R. W. Robins, & J. P. Tangney (Eds.), *The self-conscious emotions: Theory and research* (pp. 263–282). The Guilford Press.

Walters, S. R., Schluter, P. J., Oldham, A. R. H., Thomson, R. W., & Payne, D. (2012). The sideline behavior of coaches at children's team sports games. *Psychology of Sport and Exercise*, *13*(2), 208–215. https://doi.org/10.1016/j.psychsport.2011.11.008

Watzlawick, P., Beavin, J. H., & Jackson, D. D. (1967). *Pragmatics of human communication: A study of interactional patterns, pathologies, and paradoxes*. WW Norton & Company.

Widmeyer, W. N., & Williams, J. (1991). Predicting cohesion in a coacting sport. *Small Group Research*, *22*, 548–570.

Williams, K. J. (2013). Goal setting in sports. In E. A. Locke & G. P. Latham (Eds.), *New developments in goal setting and task performance* (pp. 375–396). Routledge.

Williams, L. E., & Bargh, J. A. (2008). Experiencing physical warmth promotes interpersonal warmth. *Science*, *322*, 606–607.

24 Communication in Human-AI Teaming

Wen Duan, Nathan McNeese, and Rui Zhang

Chapter Objectives

- Gain insights into where the state-of-the-science stands with regard to communication in human-AI teaming.
- Learn about the communication behaviors afforded by the current state-of-the-art AI technology and studied in HAT research.
- Learn about how the communication behaviors commonly studied in HAT research impact team processes and outcomes.

Introduction

As artificial intelligence (AI) and machine learning (ML) mature, AI agents are gradually integrated into teams to assist or collaborate with humans in joint task completion, resulting in a concept called **human-AI teaming (HAT)** (McNeese et al., 2018). In HATs, AI agents are not to replace humans, nor are they "tools" for human "operators" to use, rather, they are to complement humans' skill set and achieve synergy through effective cooperation and coordination with humans as "teammates" (Phillips et al., 2011). In manufacturing, healthcare, delivery business and so forth, AI has been implemented to assist human workers to achieve high levels of precision, accuracy, and efficiency. With AI's powerful computational capacity to rapidly and accurately process and analyze data, and humans' adaptivity and flexibility in dynamic and complex task environments, it is expected that humans and AI agents will each provide their unique skills and strengths to achieve unprecedented team outcomes by combining the best of both worlds (Larson & DeChurch, 2020).

It is primarily through communication that team members coordinate and collaborate over shared tasks and develop a sense of team (Salas et al., 2005). However, despite rapid advancements in natural language processing and generation (NLP and NLG), many of the task-oriented AI agents in HAT research have yet to be able to communicate as naturally as humans (Ashktorab et al., 2021). Therefore, research that investigates the role of communication in human-AI teamwork is, first of all, scarce. Much of it remains at the conceptual level, proposing models and methods for assessing communication in HATs by drawing on human communication theories (e.g., Baker et al., 2021). Human communication theories and models may not be readily applicable to human-AI communication (Guzman & Lewis, 2020), nor should they be held as the gold standard against which human-AI communication is judged (Spence, 2019). The current state-of-the-art AI has yet to possess the communication capabilities (both verbal and nonverbal) commensurate to that of humans (at least in HATs), making it difficult to match even basic communication concepts (e.g., field of experience, common ground). Additionally, theories of communication have always conceptualized humans as communicators and technologies (including AI) as the means or

DOI: 10.4324/9781003227458-27

mediators (Guzman, 2018). While they may work well when technology is theorized as a tool to support teamwork (Wallace et al., 2017), so far they do not extend to autonomous agents that can take the role of a communicator and a constituent team member (Phillips et al., 2011).

Empirical research investigating the role of communication in HATs offers a starting point to inductively generate theories unique to HATs. Empirical studies take place in domains where the AI is most needed, and most importantly, needed in *teams*. They characterize what the AI should

---

Box 24.1 Humans' Expectations of the Communication Capabilities of an AI Teammate

Communication is a core element of teamwork, as the interdependent nature of many team tasks requires team members to coordinate and collaborate through communication. As an emerging teaming ecology, the communication capabilities of HATs are not yet mature, and the design of these capabilities requires an understanding of the needs of humans who actually engage in collaborations with AI on a team. In an exploratory study that sought to understand humans' expectations of the communication capabilities of an AI as their teammate, Zhang et al. (2021) conducted interviews with participants who had been on a HAT in primarily game settings.

The study identified several communication strategies and affordances desired by different individuals. Almost all wanted the AI to be able to understand natural human language and communicate verbally. Among these, some would like to use one-way communication to voice command an AI teammate. For instance, one participant noted,

> One way to improve human-AI communication will be making them to understand normal human language, like I get somebody to say like "go", "fall back", or something like that. In Counter-Strike, they should be able to understand how to stick with me or something like that. If I say "follow me", the AI would just follow me.
>
> (P2, male, 22)

For these people, the AI is only expected to act on the voice command, and doesn't need to speak back. Others desired two-way communication with the AI teammate, as this will allow humans to know that their order is acknowledged and acted upon by the AI without needing to check for themselves.

Another desired communication feature of an AI teammate is visual communication, especially in game settings where players' virtual locations are vital to their coordination. For instance, the ping system, a nonverbal communicative alert offered by League of Legends, transfers information by allowing players to mark a location or object on a shared visual environment in-game. Some believed that setting visual markers for an AI teammate on a map would be more effective and efficient than voice commands. As the following quote suggests,

> So it would be cool if they could react to humans. For example, you can say "go here, ping and this", so they can kind of follow your orders, or say, "is there an enemy over here", so they can look in, like set in that direction. I think that would be so sort of helpful. I think ping would be more practical compared to voice communication. I don't know if voice communication would be necessarily better.
>
> (P7, male, 23)

be capable of and look like, on what kind of tasks it is expected to complement or collaborate with humans, what kind of teams it is expected to be implemented into to achieve what goals. These characteristics exhibited in HAT research shape, and to an extent constrain the communication between human and AI teammates. In order to understand where the current state-of-the-science stands, it is therefore imperative to provide a review of the communication behaviors in HAT research, and how they impact certain team processes and outcomes.

This chapter seeks to do this and starts by providing a definition of HAT which delineates the scope of this informal review (see the second section). The third section reviews and categorizes the communication behaviors frequently studied in HAT research, followed by the fourth section that discusses how communication impacts team processes and outcomes.

Definition and Scope of HATs

HAT can be short for Human-Autonomy Teaming, Human-AI Teaming, Human-Agent Teaming. These terms are interchangeably used in HAT research to denote the same teaming ecology where *at least one human and at least one autonomous agent work interdependently to achieve a common goal, and "each human and autonomous agent is recognized as a unique team member occupying a distinct role on the team"* (McNeese et al., 2018; O'Neill et al., 2020, p. 8).

This definition raises the question of when an AI agent may be viewed as a tool as opposed to a legitimate teammate (Phillips et al., 2011). Two overarching criteria exist for an AI agent to be viewed as a teammate: a degree of *interdependence* with other team members regarding their activities and outcomes (Nass et al., 1996), and a degree of autonomy manifested through a level of independence of human control or intervention (O'Neill et al., 2020). It should be noted that much research that used the term "human-AI teams" is not technically HAT research according to these criteria, as the AI in such research either does not exhibit the level of autonomy that requires little or no human operation (Parasuraman et al., 2000), or does not work interdependently with its human team members to achieve a shared goal (e.g., Bansal et al., 2021). This chapter also intentionally excludes human-robot teaming research involving a physically embodied robot, but notes that a review of robots in groups and teams can be found in Sebo and colleagues (2020).

We begin by reviewing and categorizing the communication behaviors commonly studied and identified in HAT research.

Communication Behaviors in HATs

In this section, we introduce two main communication behaviors that are of particular interest to HAT research and have gathered a body of literature to synthesize: anticipatory information pushing (AIP), and **AI transparency** and **explainable AI (XAI)**; as well as other types of communication behaviors such as verbal anthropomorphism. We describe what these behaviors are, how they were developed as concepts and examined in HAT research.

Anticipatory Information Pushing

AIP refers to the preemptive behavior of a teammate who anticipates another teammate's information needs and provides the necessary information before they request it (Baker et al., 2021). AIP is highly specific to the task scenario taking place in the CERTT (Cognitive Engineering Research on Team Tasks Unmanned Aerial System Synthetic Task Environment) simulation environment that hosted a majority of HAT research (e.g., Gorman et al., 2019; Grimm et al., 2018). In the simulation, three interdependent teammates need to coordinate and collaborate effectively and efficiently to take good photos for critical waypoints, with each teammate designated a different task role: Air Vehicle Operator (AVO or pilot) who controls the UAV in regard to heading, altitude, and airspeed; Data Exploitation, Mission Planning, and Communications (DEMPC or navigator) who provides a dynamic flight plan, speed and altitude restrictions; and Payload Operator (PLO or photographer) who monitors sensor equipment, negotiates with the AVO, and takes photographs of target waypoints. Communication content, style, and directionality in this simulation environment are highly templated and rigid, dictated by the role, and the task for each role. For instance, the navigator sends information about the target to the pilot, the pilot then communicates with the photographer about the target's altitude and airspeed restrictions with the goal of adjusting camera settings, and finally the photographer provides feedback on whether an acceptable photo was acquired (McNeese et al., 2018). Despite the rigidity in content and style, to our knowledge, this environment affords the closest to natural human language interactive communication among HAT research.

In this task environment, three types of communication occur: "Information" (I), the navigator provides information about the upcoming target waypoint information to the pilot; "Negotiation" (N), the photographer and the pilot negotiate the appropriate altitude and airspeed for the target's required camera settings; and "Feedback" (F), the photographer provides feedback about the status of the target photo (Demir et al., 2015). Each team member will need to communicate in a timely and effective manner to ensure team performance (i.e., taking as many good photos as possible).

This concept was developed through a sequence of studies attempting to categorize the communication behaviors taking place in the CERTT task. Demir and colleagues (2016) first developed a typology of communication behaviors involving: general status update, repeated requests, inquiry about status of others, planning ahead, suggestions, negative communication, positive communication, and unclear communications. In a later study, Demir and colleagues (2017) further grouped the verbal behaviors into pushing (general status update, suggestions, planning ahead) and pulling (repeated requests, inquiry about status of others) of information. They subsequently (Demir et al., 2019) examined the relationship between pushing and pulling of information and team task performance and effectiveness, under various complex circumstances (e.g., types of failures). Their insights informed the development of a series of training techniques that encourages human participants to push critical information, calibrate their expectations of the AI agent and their communication with it (Johnson et al., 2020, 2021).

Most of the studies conducted in the CERTT environment use **Wizard of Oz** technique (Riek, 2012). This technique makes human participants believe they are interacting with an autonomous computer system (real AI) but in fact the system is operated by a research confederate. Those that used a real AI agent (e.g., Demir et al., 2018; McNeese et al., 2018) found that the volume of communication in HAT was only half that in all-human teams, and that the AI agent did not engage in information pushing as much as humans did, suggesting a weakness in the AI (at least that applied in HAT research by the current state-of-the-technology) to anticipate the information needs of its teammates.

Transparency and Explainability

While HAT research studying the two-way interactive communication between humans and their AI teammates is scarce, the study of how AI communicates its intent and reasoning process behind its decision, prediction, and recommendation to humans has received extensive attention in the past decade. This results in an exponentially growing body of research on AI transparency and XAI (e.g., Liao et al., 2020).

XAI emerged as a means to make AI systems more understandable to humans (Gunning et al., 2019) and reduce the mystery of the "black box" to keep humans in the loop (Adadi & Berrada, 2018), making it extremely important for HATs in which effective and successful collaboration and coordination between human and AI teammates premises on understanding one another's intention, action and reasoning.

This emerging field involves several concepts sometimes interchangeably used and preferred by different scientific communities, such as interpretability, explainability, understandability and transparency (Adadi & Berrada, 2018). In an effort to distinguish these concepts, Verhagen and colleagues (2021, 2022) treated them as different communication styles, referring to *transparency* as the disclosure of information for users to analyze and exploit, and to *explainability* as the clarification of the disclosed information by providing reasoning and causality. Specifically, they operationalized transparent communication as the AI teammate disclosing its world knowledge, actions, decisions, and suggestions. For explainable communication, in addition to the disclosed information, it clarified it by providing explanations for the intended actions, decisions, and suggestions. Both communication styles were better than no communication in improving the human's understanding, but no significant difference was found between explainable and transparent communication.

Providing uncertainty information is a common method of increasing AI transparency (Selkowitz et al., 2015). Kox and colleagues (2022) investigated the AI teammate's *uncertainty communication* and apology in a collaborative house search task in which the AI warned its human teammate about potential dangers ahead. Uncertainty communication was manipulated as the presence or absence of the percentage of certainty in the AI's danger or clearance detection. Providing uncertainty information was found to mitigate trust loss when the AI failed to warn participants of a danger. In other words, when participants were informed about the imperfect reliability of the AI beforehand, their trust was less affected by the AI's subsequent error.

Overall, there have been mixed findings and trade-offs concerning the transparency of an AI teammate. While high levels of transparency are related to better understanding of the AI teammate (Harbers et al., 2011), better performance (e.g., Mercado et al., 2016) and higher trust (Boyce et al., 2015); higher transparency may nevertheless increase workload (Wright et al., 2016), as it requires certain cognitive efforts to process the information and reasoning provided by transparency. Additionally, higher transparency may induce complacency in human teammates who may become less vigilant in questioning the AI teammate's work (Sadler et al., 2016). This often happens in cognitively demanding multitasking environments, where the human teammate may attend to one task while entrusting the less than perfectly reliable AI to carry out another, believing that it knows what it's doing since it provides high transparency.

Other Communication Behaviors

Aside from AIP, transparency and XAI that have gathered a body of knowledge to synthesize, other types of communication behaviors in most HAT research remain scattered. Additionally, while a striking majority investigated the AI's communication behavior toward their human teammates, very few studied the human's communication behavior toward the AI teammate. One attempt is Cohen and colleagues (2021) who investigated the human's "verbal anthropomorphism" toward their AI teammate. They were able to match patterns of verbal anthropomorphism onto self-reports of perceived anthropomorphism, over a course of collaboration and coordination involving failures. This suggests a novel way of measuring perceived anthropomorphism through analyzing team communication behaviors in real-time. According to the authors, gendered pronouns, language that attributed human-like states to the AI (e.g., What do you feel?), and politeness markers such as "Please," "Sorry" were indicators of verbal anthropomorphism; whereas objectifying communication such as referring to the agent by "it" or as an "agent" indicated the opposite of anthropomorphizing. They found that declines in verbal anthropomorphism, trust in the AI and team performance in the face of AI failure coincided, suggesting that verbal anthropomorphism may be an indicator of the human's evolving perceptions of the AI's competency. In other words, the gradual awareness of the AI's inability to overcome failures may have made humans perceive the AI teammate as less human-like. This adds to a muddy realm of findings regarding the relationship between perceived human-likeness of the AI and its competence and trustworthiness. While some suggest a positive correlation (e.g., Jensen et al., 2020), others (e.g., Salem et al., 2013) suggest AI that makes errors may appear more human and "alive." The next section dives deeper into the effects of different communication behaviors on several team processes and outcomes.

How Communication Impacts Team Processes and Outcomes in HATs

In this section, we discuss three variables that are most frequently studied in HAT research: performance, situation awareness, and trust. We first describe how these variables were measured and then detail how communication attributes such as quantity, modality, and behavior were found to affect each of the team processes or outcomes. By doing so, we identify both trends and inconsistencies in the findings, which opens up opportunities for future research.

Performance

Team and individual performance is the most dominant dependent variable studied by HAT research. Measures of performance vary widely and heavily depend on the task on which human and AI teammates collaborate. Most studies used objective measures embedded in the simulation, such as identifying and handling threats, taking good photos of targets, destroying enemy units, time to task completion, often automatically calculated into a score by the system (e.g., Bogg et al., 2021; Demir et al., 2016). Some used subjective perceptions of team and individual performance (e.g., Liang et al., 2019). Overall, HAT research (e.g., Demir et al., 2016) suggests that the volume of communication can greatly impact team performance in HATs. By using the Wizard of Oz technique, human and AI team members were allowed to communicate freely in natural language. This significantly increased the quantity of communication among them, which in turn resulted in enhanced team performance (McNeese et al., 2018, 2021). However, communication quantity is not always an indicator of better team performance. In fact, higher communication frequency could indicate confusion, misunderstandings, and inefficiency (Macmillan et al., 2002), and a greater number of messages shared among HAT was found in other studies that used similar task environment (Cooke et al., 2016) to be associated with lower performance. Given the mixed findings regarding communication quantity, a look at different types of communication behaviors can provide a nuanced understanding of how communication impacts team performance.

Using the typology of information pushing and pulling (see the definitions in the subsection *Anticipatory Information Pushing*), it was found that information pushing from the AI teammate was a predictor of positive team performance for HATs (Demir et al., 2016) but the relationship between information pulling and team performance was not observed (Demir et al., 2017). Demir and colleagues (2019) did a preliminary study exploring how communication training (i.e., encouraging information pushing and pulling) can help HATs overcome various failures, which concluded that constructive and timely communication is essential in joint coordination to be aware of failures and come up with solutions. Johnson and colleagues (2020) further developed coordination training in which participants were "coached to push critical information in order to improve team coordination," and calibration training that calibrated participants' expectation of the agent to encourage them to be persistent in communicating with it. Teams that received coordination training pushed information more frequently compared to teams that received calibration training, and were more likely to overcome failures attributed to the AI teammate's cognitive capacities, resulting in better team performance. Additionally, coordination training was also found to improve task efficiency (Johnson et al., 2020). The authors coined the term and the measure of "team communication anticipation ratio," which "was calculated by dividing the number of information pushes by the number of pulls." Greater anticipation ratio indicates more effective information sharing (MacMillan et al., 2004). They found that the change in the communication behavior of a single team member (the AI teammate played by a confederate) resulted in significant improvement in anticipation ratios and processing efficiency of the team as a whole, suggesting that the behaviors of an AI teammate can have a widespread impact on the behaviors of its teammates, which in turn impact emergent team-level processes and performance beyond the dyadic interaction level (Johnson et al., 2021).

Situation Awareness

Situation awareness is often measured through two means: an indirect approach using completion of additional tasks as behavioral indicators, or direct assessment using Situation Awareness Global Assessment Technique (SAGAT; Endsley, 1988) tailored to the specific task environment. Situation awareness is closely related to an AI teammate's transparency, as the latter is designed to support the human's situation awareness by communicating the agent's status, intent, and understanding of the current environment, the reasoning behind an action or recommendation, and outcome predictions (Chen et al., 2018). It is thus expected that higher transparency will lead to better situation awareness. Indeed, Verhagen and colleagues (2022) showed how both transparent and explainable communication styles resulted in significantly better situation awareness compared to not communicating what the AI teammate was doing and why. Communication involving information pushing (rather than pulling) behaviors was also found to be associated with better team situation awareness (Demir et al., 2016), though causality was not established. It was unclear whether it was the better situation awareness that made team members more effectively anticipate one another's information needs to push the right information in a timely manner, or the other way around. Wright and colleagues (2022) showed that human participants' situation awareness did not differ significantly for when the AI teammate responded to or did not respond to their interpretation of events in a cordon-and-search task, partly because the feedback was simply agreement or disagreement with no additional information. Bogg and colleagues (2021) found that voice communication did not outperform text communication or even no communication in improving participants' situation awareness even though performance was improved.

Trust

Trust is most often measured using subjective scales, but the measurements used in HAT research range widely from organizational trust (Mayer & Davis, 1995), to trust scale for XAI (Hoffman et al., 2018), trust in robots (Charalambous et al., 2016), trust in automated systems, automation and machines (e.g., Jian et al., 2000; Körber, 2018; Lyons et al., 2016). Some also used behavioral indicators such as acceptance of AI's decision or a combination of many measures. Inconsistency in trust measures might obstruct the synthesis of findings. In fact, Wohleber and colleagues (2017) used two subjective trust measures that yielded different results. Specifically, the human-human trust measure (Mayer & Davis, 1995) revealed no significant effect of AI transparency. There was only a trend toward a slightly greater trust when the AI teammate highlighted a parameter of the human's chosen plan that was not satisfied (critical communication framing) than when it highlighted a parameter that was optimal (complimentary communication framing). This is reasonable as the human-human trust measure emphasizes the interpersonal aspects of trust that are more sensitive to the manipulation of communication framing than to the task-oriented manipulation of AI transparency that primarily provides various levels of reasoning information. On the other hand, the human-automation trust measure (Jian et al., 2000) used in the same study deals with humans' trust in automation and machines. It thus yielded a significant main effect of transparency, with higher transparency associated with greater trust, and no significant effect concerning communication framing. This example underscores a challenge for future HAT research to develop appropriate measures of humans' trust in their communicative AI teammate that embodies both the interpersonal and technological qualities.

Measuring trust using trust scale for XAI (Hoffman et al., 2018), Verhagen and colleagues (2022) showed that the presence of the AI teammate's communication, rather than being silent, resulted in significantly higher human trust in it. But no significant difference was found for the effect of transparent or explainable or adaptive communication on trust.

Kox and colleagues (2022) studied the effect of uncertainty communication and apology and compared the trust of two populations (civilian and military) in the AI teammate. They demonstrated that the AI teammate's uncertainty communication lessened the decline in civilians' trust in the AI teammate following its mistake, suggesting that advice accompanied by an uncertainty measure can alleviate the severity of trust depletion compared to that without a notion of uncertainty. This finding echoes some previous work (e.g., Kraus et al., 2020) that suggested when humans were reminded of the imperfection of the autonomous system by providing transparency prior to the interaction, their trust was less affected by the errors made by the system. Additionally, the civilian participants regained their trust in the AI teammate after the trust violation, both when it offered an apology and when it did not, with trust levels increased considerably more for the former compared to the latter. However, these effects were not observed for military participants, to whom, a minor mistake could mean life-or-death. Further, an apology can affect trust negatively, partly because it explicitly focuses the attention on error (Fahim et al., 2021), to which military people appeared to be more sensitive, being immersed in a house search mission (Kox et al., 2022). Moreover, apologies may not often be acceptable or at least not a common practice in the military context, which defines the organizational norms including that of communication. For an AI to be accepted as a teammate, and to be part of an organization, it requires that it adheres to the norms that govern that group's behavior. Their findings therefore highlight the need to design the AI's communication behaviors and styles that should be compatible with the culture, norms, and expectations of the organization or team in which the agent will be implemented (Matthews et al., 2021).

Johnson and colleagues (2021) found that humans' trust in their AI teammate did not improve after receiving coordination training, even though the training did encourage AIP and increased task efficiency. It appeared that focusing on effective information sharing alone was not enough to overcome failures, which required the team to be adaptable and flexible in communication: improvise, step outside of the routine communication process, request necessary information from a teammate who does not routinely provide it, or route information through a different teammate. None of these adaptive measures of communication were captured by emphasizing AIP.

Evidence-Based Recommendations for Practice

AI teammates in HATs need to be equipped with NLP and NLG capabilities closely coupled with its task completion capabilities to effectively collaborate with human team members. In most HAT research, the AI is programmed to perform a specific task, the completion of which is by no means affected by its communication (or lack thereof) with humans. In other words, the AI's task completion does not take input from its communication with humans, which is not realistic of team collaboration. This lack of incorporation of communication into task completion may render the findings on the effects of communication unreliable.

More HAT research on the role of communication is needed outside of the military domain. As it currently stands, HAT research predominantly uses military tasks to examine teaming processes and outcomes. While this reflects where HATs are most needed, given the value of AI in performing highly risky and dangerous tasks, HATs are and will be present in various other domains (e.g., healthcare, emergency crisis management) that merit investigations. The communication content, styles, modalities, and directionalities, as well as how they impact team coordination and outcomes in these domains will certainly vary. HAT research on communication also needs to step outside of simulation laboratories. To gain a nuanced understanding of the contextual needs of stakeholders in future HATs, researchers should consider various other methodologies including in-depth interviews, field research, participatory design, etc.

Conclusion

HAT is an emerging yet rapidly growing type of teamwork that has the potential to benefit all people working various professions in various sectors and realms around the world. However, this review of the empirical research on HAT revealed that the AI implemented into teams where it was programmed to perform a specific task was far from communicative. It has yet to be able to engage in bidirectional naturalistic communication with human team members and incorporate the communication into task completion. This highlights the need for future HAT research to closely couple the AI's task completion capability with communication capability by enabling it to not only understand but also act on natural language. Further, HAT research was predominantly conducted in the military domain, using experimental methods in simulation environments, with teams performing execution tasks. These characteristics have restricted the communication behaviors in HATs to a narrow range. Future work should exploit a wide array of methods appropriate for understanding humans' needs from their AI teammate with regard to communication in team collaboration. Zhang and colleagues (2021) work represents a good example, but other methods such as participatory design, field research in workplaces where workers are already collaborating with AI on a daily basis may be beneficial.

Further Readings

Hauptman, A. I., Duan, W., & McNeese, N. J. (2022). *The components of trust for collaborating with AI colleagues* [Conference session]. Companion Publication of the 2022 Conference on Computer Supported Cooperative Work and Social Computing (pp. 72–75). https://doi.org/10.1145/3500868.3559450
Schelble, B. G., Flathmann, C., McNeese, N. J., Freeman, G., & Mallick, R. (2022). Let's think together! Assessing shared mental models, performance, and trust in human-agent teams. *Proceedings of the ACM on Human-Computer Interaction*, 6(GROUP), 1–29. https://doi.org/10.1145/3492832
Zhang, R., Duan, W., Flathmann, C., McNeese, N. J., Freeman, G., & Williams, A. (2023). Investigating AI teammate communication strategies and their impact in human-AI teams for effective teamwork. *Proceedings of the ACM on Human-Computer Interaction*, 7, CSCW2, Article 281 (October 2023), 31. https://doi.org/10.1145/3610072
Zhang, R., McNeese, N. J., Freeman, G., & Musick, G. (2021). "An ideal human": Expectations of AI teammates in human-AI teaming. *Proceedings of the ACM on Human-Computer Interaction*, 4(CSCW3), 1–25. https://doi.org/10.1145/3432945

Glossary

AI transparency   The quality of an interface pertaining to its abilities to afford a human's comprehension about an AI agent's intent, performance, future plans, and reasoning process.
Explainable AI (XAI)   Explainable artificial intelligence is one that produces details or reasons to make its functioning, decisions, and predictions clear or easy to understand.

Human-AI teaming (HAT)   A teaming ecology where at least one human and at least one AI agent work interdependently to achieve a common goal, and each human and AI agent is recognized as a unique team member occupying a distinct role on the team.

Wizard of Oz   In the field of human–computer interaction, the Wizard of Oz method is used in experiments in which participants interact with a computer system that participants believe to be autonomous, but is actually operated or partially operated by an unseen research confederate.

References

Adadi, A., & Berrada, M. (2018). Peeking inside the black-box: A survey on explainable artificial intelligence (XAI). *IEEE Access*, 6, 52138–52160. https://doi.org/10.1109/ACCESS.2018.2870052

Ashktorab, Z., Dugan, C., Johnson, J., Pan, Q., Zhang, W., Kumaravel, S., & Campbell, M. (2021). Effects of communication directionality and AI agent differences in human-AI interaction. *Proceedings of the 2021 CHI conference on human factors in computing systems*, 1–15. https://doi.org/10.1145/3411764.3445256

Baker, A. L., Fitzhugh, S. M., Huang, L., Forster, D. E., Scharine, A., Neubauer, C., Lematta, G., Bhatti, S., Johnson, C. J., Krausman, A., Holder, E., Schaefer, K. E., & Cooke, N. J. (2021). Approaches for assessing communication in human-autonomy teams. *Human-Intelligent Systems Integration*, 3(2), 99–128. https://doi.org/10.1007/s42454-021-00026-2

Bansal, G., Wu, T., Zhou, J., Fok, R., Nushi, B., Kamar, E., Ribeiro, M. T., & Weld, D. (2021, May). Does the whole exceed its parts? The effect of AI explanations on complementary team performance. In *Proceedings of the 2021 CHI conference on human factors in computing systems* (pp. 1–16). Association for Computing Machinery.

Bogg, A., Birrell, S., Bromfield, M. A., & Parkes, A. M. (2021). Can we talk? How a talking agent can improve human autonomy team performance. *Theoretical Issues in Ergonomics Science*, 22(4), 488–509. https://doi.org/10.1080/1463922X.2020.1827080

Boyce, M. W., Chen, J. Y., Selkowitz, A. R., & Lakhmani, S. G. (2015). Effects of agent transparency on operator trust. In *Proceedings of the tenth annual ACM/IEEE international conference on human-robot interaction extended abstracts* (pp. 179–180). Association for Computing Machinery.

Charalambous, G., Fletcher, S., & Webb, P. (2016). The development of a scale to evaluate trust in industrial human-robot collaboration. *International Journal of Social Robotics*, 8(2), 193–209.

Chen, J. Y. C., Lakhmani, S. G., Stowers, K., Selkowitz, A. R., Wright, J. L., & Barnes, M. (2018). Situation awareness-based agent transparency and human-autonomy teaming effectiveness. *Theoretical Issues in Ergonomics Science*, 19(3), 259–282. https://doi.org/10.1080/1463922X.2017.1315750

Cohen, M. C., Demir, M., Chiou, E. K., & Cooke, N. J. (2021). The dynamics of trust and verbal anthropomorphism in human-autonomy teaming. *2021 IEEE 2nd international conference on human-machine systems (ICHMS)*, 1–6. https://doi.org/10.1109/ICHMS53169.2021.9582655

Cooke, N. J., Demir, M., & McNeese, N. (2016). *Synthetic teammates as team players: Coordination of human and synthetic teammates*. Cognitive Engineering Research Institute Mesa United States.

Demir, M., McNeese, N. J., & Cooke, N. J. (2016). Team communication behaviors of the human-automation teaming. *2016 IEEE international multi-disciplinary conference on cognitive methods in situation awareness and decision support (CogSIMA)*, 28–34. https://doi.org/10.1109/COGSIMA.2016.7497782

Demir, M., McNeese, N. J., & Cooke, N. J. (2017). Team situation awareness within the context of human-autonomy teaming. *Cognitive Systems Research*, 46, 3–12. https://doi.org/10.1016/j.cogsys.2016.11.003

Demir, M., McNeese, N. J., & Cooke, N. J. (2018). The impact of perceived autonomous agents on dynamic team behaviors. *IEEE transactions on emerging topics in computational intelligence*, 2(4), 258–267. https://doi.org/10.1109/TETCI.2018.2829985

Demir, M., McNeese, N. J., & Cooke, N. J. (2019). The evolution of human-autonomy teams in remotely piloted aircraft systems operations. *Frontiers in Communication*, 4, 50. https://doi.org/10.3389/fcomm.2019.00050

Demir, M., McNeese, N. J., Cooke, N. J., Ball, J. T., Myers, C., & Frieman, M. (2015). Synthetic teammate communication and coordination with humans. *Proceedings of the Human Factors and Ergonomics Society Annual Meeting*, 59(1), 951–955. https://doi.org/10.1177/1541931215591275

Endsley, M. R. (1988). Situation awareness global assessment technique (SAGAT). *Proceedings of the IEEE 1988 National Aerospace and Electronics Conference*, *3*, 789–795. https://doi.org/10.1109/NAECON.1988.195097

Fahim, M. A. A., Khan, M. M. H., Jensen, T., Albayram, Y., & Coman, E. (2021). Do integral emotions affect trust? The mediating effect of emotions on trust in the context of human-agent interaction. *Designing Interactive Systems Conference 2021*, 1492–1503. https://doi.org/10.1145/3461778.3461997

Gorman, J. C., Demir, M., Cooke, N. J., & Grimm, D. A. (2019). Evaluating sociotechnical dynamics in a simulated remotely-piloted aircraft system: A layered dynamics approach. *Ergonomics*, *62*(5), 629–643. https://doi.org/10.1080/00140139.2018.1557750

Grimm, D., Demir, M., Gorman, J. C., & Cooke, N. J. (2018). The complex dynamics of team situation awareness in human-autonomy teaming. *2018 IEEE conference on cognitive and computational aspects of situation management (CogSIMA)*, 103–109. https://doi.org/10.1109/COGSIMA.2018.8423990

Gunning, D., Stefik, M., Choi, J., Miller, T., Stumpf, S., & Yang, G. Z. (2019). XAI—Explainable artificial intelligence. *Science Robotics*, *4*(37), eaay7120.

Guzman, A. L. (2018). What is human-machine communication, anyway. In *Human-machine communication: Rethinking communication, technology, and ourselves* (pp. 1–28). Peter Lang. https://lccn.loc.gov/2017053385

Guzman, A. L., & Lewis, S. C. (2020). Artificial intelligence and communication: A human–machine communication research agenda. *New Media & Society*, *22*(1), 70–86. https://doi.org/10.1177/1461444819858691

Harbers, M., Bradshaw, J. M., Johnson, M., Feltovich, P., van den Bosch, K., & Meyer, J. J. (2011). Explanation and coordination in human-agent teams: A study in the BW4T testbed. In *2011 IEEE/WIC/ACM international conferences on web intelligence and intelligent agent technology, 3*, 17–20. IEEE.

Hoffman, R. R., Mueller, S. T., Klein, G., & Litman, J. (2018). Metrics for explainable AI: Challenges and prospects. *arXiv preprint arXiv:1812.04608*. https://doi.org/10.48550/arXiv.1812.04608

Jensen, T., Khan, M. M. H., & Albayram, Y. (2020, July). The role of behavioral anthropomorphism in human-automation trust calibration. In *International conference on human-computer interaction* (pp. 33–53). Springer.

Jian, J. Y., Bisantz, A. M., & Drury, C. G. (2000). Foundations for an empirically determined scale of trust in automated systems. *International Journal of Cognitive Ergonomics*, *4*(1), 53–71.

Johnson, C. J., Demir, M., McNeese, N. J., Gorman, J. C., Wolff, A. T., & Cooke, N. J. (2021). The impact of training on human–autonomy team communications and trust calibration. *Human Factors*, *0*(0). https://doi.org/10.1177/00187208211047323

Johnson, C. J., Demir, M., Zabala, G. M., He, H., Grimm, D. A., Radigan, C., Wolff, A. T., Cooke, N. J., McNeese, N. J., & Gorman, J. C. (2020). Training and verbal communications in human-autonomy teaming under degraded conditions. *2020 IEEE conference on cognitive and computational aspects of situation management (CogSIMA)* (pp. 53–58). https://doi.org/10.1109/CogSIMA49017.2020.9216061

Körber, M. (2018). Theoretical considerations and development of a questionnaire to measure trust in automation. In *Congress of the international ergonomics association* (pp. 13–30). Springer.

Kox, E. S., Siegling, L. B., & Kerstholt, J. H. (2022). Trust development in military and civilian human–agent teams: The effect of social-cognitive recovery strategies. *International Journal of Social Robotics*, *14*(5), 1323–1338. https://doi.org/10.1007/s12369-022-00871-4

Kraus, J., Scholz, D., Stiegemeier, D., & Baumann, M. (2020). The more you know: Trust dynamics and calibration in highly automated driving and the effects of take-overs, system malfunction, and system transparency. *Human Factors*, *62*(5), 718–736.

Larson, L., & DeChurch, L. A. (2020). Leading teams in the digital age: Four perspectives on technology and what they mean for leading teams. *The Leadership Quarterly*, *31*(1), 101377.

Liang, C., Proft, J., Andersen, E., & Knepper, R. A. (2019). Implicit communication of actionable information in human-AI teams. In *Proceedings of the 2019 CHI conference on human factors in computing systems*, 1–13. https://doi.org/10.1145/3290605.3300325

Liao, Q. V., Gruen, D., & Miller, S. (2020). Questioning the AI: Informing design practices for explainable AI user experiences. In *Proceedings of the 2020 CHI conference on human factors in computing systems* (pp. 1–15). https://doi.org/10.1145/3313831.3376590

Lyons, J. B., Koltai, K. S., Ho, N. T., Johnson, W. B., Smith, D. E., & Shively, R. J. (2016). Engineering trust in complex automated systems. *Ergonomics in Design*, *24*(1), 13–17.

Macmillan, J., Entin, E. E., & Serfaty, D. (2002). A framework for understanding the relationship between team structure and the communication necessary for effective team cognition. In *Team cognition: Process and performance at the inter- and intra-individual level* (pp. 112–139). American Psychological Association. https://doi.org/10.1177/154193120204600338

MacMillan, J., Entin, E. E., & Serfaty, D. (2004). Communication overhead: The hidden cost of team cognition. In E. Salas & S. M. Fiore (Eds.), *Team cognition: Understanding the factors that drive process and performance* (pp. 61–82). American Psychological Association.

Matthews, G., Hancock, P. A., Lin, J., Panganiban, A. R., Reinerman-Jones, L. E., Szalma, J. L., & Wohleber, R. W. (2021). Evolution and revolution: Personality research for the coming world of robots, artificial intelligence, and autonomous systems. *Personality and Individual Differences*, *169*, 109969.

Mayer, R. C., & Davis, J. H. (1995). An integrative model of organizational trust. *The Academy of Management Review*, *20*(3), 709–734.

McNeese, N. J., Demir, M., Chiou, E. K., & Cooke, N. J. (2021). Trust and team performance in human–autonomy teaming. *International Journal of Electronic Commerce*, *25*(1), 51–72. https://doi.org/10.1080/10864415.2021.1846854

McNeese, N. J., Demir, M., Cooke, N. J., & Myers, C. (2018). teaming with a synthetic teammate: Insights into human-autonomy teaming. *Human Factors: The Journal of the Human Factors and Ergonomics Society*, *60*(2), 262–273. https://doi.org/10.1177/0018720817743223

Mercado, J. E., Rupp, M. A., Chen, J. Y., Barnes, M. J., Barber, D., & Procci, K. (2016). Intelligent agent transparency in human–agent teaming for multi-UxV management. *Human Factors*, *58*(3), 401–415.

Nass, C., Fogg, B. J., & Moon, Y. (1996). Can computers be teammates? *International Journal of Human-Computer Studies*, *45*(6), 669–678. https://doi.org/10.1006/ijhc.1996.0073

O'Neill, T., McNeese, N., Barron, A., & Schelble, B. (2020). Human–autonomy teaming: A review and analysis of the empirical literature. *Human Factors: The Journal of the Human Factors and Ergonomics Society*, 1–35. https://doi.org/10.1177/0018720820960865

Parasuraman, R., Sheridan, T. B., & Wickens, C. D. (2000). A model for types and levels of human interaction with automation. *IEEE Transactions on Systems, Man, and Cybernetics-Part A: Systems and Humans*, *30*(3), 286–297.

Phillips, E., Ososky, S., Grove, J., & Jentsch, F. (2011). From tools to teammates: Toward the development of appropriate mental models for intelligent robots. *Proceedings of the Human Factors and Ergonomics Society Annual Meeting*, *55*(1), 1491–1495.

Riek, L. D. (2012). Wizard of Oz studies in HRI: A systematic review and new reporting guidelines. *Journal of Human-Robot Interaction*. 1, 119–136. https://doi.org/10.5898/JHRI.1.1.Riek

Sadler, G., Battiste, H., Ho, N., Hoffmann, L., Johnson, W., Shively, R., Lyons, J., & Smith, D. (2016). Effects of transparency on pilot trust and agreement in the autonomous constrained flight planner. In *2016 IEEE/AIAA 35th digital avionics systems conference (DASC)* (pp. 1–9). IEEE.

Salas, E., Sims, D. E., & Burke, C. S. (2005). Is there a "Big Five" in teamwork? *Small Group Research*, *36*(5), 555–599. https://doi.org/10.1177/1046496405277134

Salem, M., Eyssel, F., Rohlfing, K., Kopp, S., & Joublin, F. (2013). To err is human (-like): Effects of robot gesture on perceived anthropomorphism and likability. *International Journal of Social Robotics*, *5*(3), 313–323.

Sebo, S., Stoll, B., Scassellati, B., & Jung, M. F. (2020). Robots in groups and teams: A literature review. *Proceedings of the ACM on Human-Computer Interaction*, *4*(CSCW2), 1–36. https://doi.org/10.1145/3415247

Selkowitz, A., Lakhmani, S., Chen, J. Y., & Boyce, M. (2015). The effects of agent transparency on human interaction with an autonomous robotic agent. *Proceedings of the Human Factors and Ergonomics Society Annual Meeting*, *59*(1), 806–810. https://doi.org/10.1177/1541931215591246

Spence, P. R. (2019). Searching for questions, original thoughts, or advancing theory: Human-machine communication. *Computers in Human Behavior*, *90*, 285–287.

Verhagen, R. S., Neerincx, M. A., & Tielman, M. L. (2021). A two-dimensional explanation framework to classify AI as incomprehensible, interpretable, or understandable. In *International workshop on explainable, transparent autonomous agents and multi-agent systems*. (pp. 119–138). Springer.

Verhagen, R. S., Neerincx, M. A., & Tielman, M. L. (2022). The influence of interdependence and a transparent or explainable communication style on human-robot teamwork. *Frontiers in Robotics and AI, 9*, 993997. https://doi.org/10.3389/frobt.2022.993997

Wallace, J. R., Oji, S., & Anslow, C. (2017). Technologies, methods, and values: Changes in empirical research at CSCW 1990-2015. *Proceedings of the ACM on Human-Computer Interaction, 1*(CSCW), 1–18.

Wohleber, R. W., Stowers, K., Chen, J. Y. C., & Barnes, M. (2017). Effects of agent transparency and communication framing on human-agent teaming. *2017 IEEE international conference on systems, man, and cybernetics (SMC)*, 3427–3432. https://doi.org/10.1109/SMC.2017.8123160

Wright, J. L., Chen, J. Y. C., Barnes, M. J., & Hancock, P. A. (2016). Agent reasoning transparency's effect on operator workload. *Proceedings of the Human Factors and Ergonomics Society Annual Meeting, 60*(1), 249–253. https://doi.org/10.1177/1541931213601057

Wright, J. L., Lakhmani, S. G., & Chen, J. Y. C. (2022). Bidirectional communications in human-agent teaming: The effects of communication style and feedback. *International Journal of Human–Computer Interaction*, 1–14. https://doi.org/10.1080/10447318.2022.2068744

Zhang, R., McNeese, N. J., Freeman, G., & Musick, G. (2021). "An ideal human": Expectations of AI teammates in human-AI teaming. *Proceedings of the ACM on Human-Computer Interaction, 4*(CSCW3), 1–25. https://doi.org/10.1145/3432945

Glossary

Adaptive structuration (Chapter 5)   A theory that focuses on how organizations and groups utilize technology, focusing on the structures of the technology and the way users appropriate those structures.

Ad-hoc emergency teams (Chapter 22)   (also called action teams) They are temporary groups of experts, often from different disciplines. Formed to rapidly respond to specific emergency situations, such as a cardiac arrest.

Affordance (Chapter 21)   An affordance involves the way a technology is perceived and used by people. It involves the potential for action users perceive in a technology.

AI transparency (Chapter 24)   The quality of an interface pertaining to its abilities to afford a human's comprehension about an AI agent's intent, performance, future plans, and reasoning process.

Alternative-based decision strategy (Chapter 15)   Alternative-based strategies (such as the unit weight linear model or the weighted additive model) process information alternative-wise. They perform a summary evaluation of each alternative by looking at all attributes of each alternative. The strategies choose the alternative that receives the highest overall evaluation.

Axiom (Chapter 23)   A statement accepted as an established principle or self-evident truth which is used as the basis for further reasoning or inference.

Centrality (Chapter 17)   A measure of power or influence in a network.

Collaborative climate (Chapter 6)   Climate where group members share positive feelings, perceptions, and relationships that make them want to work together to achieve a common goal or objective.

Communication climate (Chapter 11)   Communication climate is the overall ambience, or mood, of the group. A group's communication climate can be positive or negative and develops from group members' relative balance of positive or negative messages.

Conflict framing (Chapter 10)   An interpretive and communicative process of characterizing what someone believes is important in a conflict. Conflict framing includes how someone sees the cause of the conflict, the people involved, the relationship between the people, and what outcomes are possible. People involved in a conflict can have different frames.

Conflict management styles (Chapter 10)   Different ways that people address, engage in, and resolve conflict. Styles vary in how much emphasis they place on personal needs versus the needs of the other person involved in the conflict. Example styles are competitive, cooperative, avoidant, accommodating, and collaborative. Individuals tend to have a preferred style but can learn skills to become more flexible and use other styles.

Conventional thinking (Chapter 7)   The idea that social phenomenon like groups can be best understood by looking at and optimizing their individual parts (e.g., group member attributes, technologies).

Creativity (Chapter 16)   The development of a product, idea, or problem solution that is both novel (original) and useful (effective).

Cue-based decision strategy (Chapter 15)   Cue-based strategies (such as Take-the-Best) process information cue-wise by comparing choice alternatives on one cue or attribute at a time. Cues (attributes) are processed in the order of their validity (cues) or perceived importance (attributes). Once a processed cue or attribute discriminates among choice alternatives, the alternative with the highest value is chosen.

Cybernetics (Chapter 7)   An interdisciplinary field of study that explores the communication and control mechanisms in systems. Some core concepts include feedback (i.e., information about a system's behavior), communication (i.e., exchange of information between components of a system), and control (e.g., adjustments to behavior based on feedback). Cybernetics provides a framework for understanding how systems work, how they can be designed and controlled, and how they interact with their environment.

Deliberation (Chapter 19)   Deliberation is a group-level process that allows us to examine issues, topics, and problems; think about options and trade-offs; and make collective decisions. The end goal of deliberation is to solve a problem (or problems) or make decisions. Through thoughtful and careful group discussion, deliberative processes allow for multiple perspectives in the decision-making process.

Dialogue (Chapter 19)   Dialogue is a discussion process that allows people to share their perspectives and experiences with each other often times regarding difficult topics. Rather than having the end goal of making a decision or solving a problem, as is the case with deliberation, dialogue carries the goals of exploring commonalities, re-examining personal positions, and discovering new ways of thinking. Dialogue can occur at the interpersonal, small group, organizational, or larger mass level.

Digital coping (Chapter 21)   Digital coping involves the use of communication technologies in responding to the challenges posed by illness.

Digital trace data (Chapter 20)   As people participate in online communities, data and metadata about what they are doing is stored. This data is often visible to other users and/or made available to researchers.

Directory updating (Chapter 14)   Group members learn and update their perceptions of the distribution and location of expertise in the group. This may also involve updating perceptions of who knows who, who has access to what, and how tasks are related to people and expertise.

Discursive leadership (Chapter 9)   A perspective that sees communication as the starting point for creating leadership and organizational life.

Diversity (Chapter 8)   Diversity is heterogeneity among members of a group with respect to some attribute. It is a multidimensional concept that can imply variety, separation, and disparity. Some diversity dimensions are surface-level and visible, while others are deep-level and less visible.

Double-edged sword metaphor (Chapter 8)   This metaphor is frequently used in diversity research to capture the simultaneous existence of opportunities and challenges of diversity.

Edges (Chapter 17)   Relations which connect entities in a network.

Emergent leadership (Chapter 9)   A group's temporary perception that a certain individual appears to be a leader, despite a lack of formal authority.

Emergent state (Chapter 12)   The emergent state is the group atmosphere that emerges during the processes of group interactions, such as cohesion, focus of attention, emotions, differentiation, cognitive complexity, and conflict. Emergent states are variable and dynamic in that they develop over time as a function of group inputs and processes as group members interact.

Entitativity (Chapter 2)   The perception of being a single, unified entity rather than a set of independent and unrelated pieces.

Experiment (Chapter 4)   A specific type of study that in base form compares control and treatment groups. Participants are randomly assigned to either the treatment or control. The researcher manipulates the independent variable, which changes the conditions under which participants experience the study.

Explainable AI (XAI) (Chapter 24)   Explainable artificial intelligence is one that produces details or reasons to make its functioning, decisions, and predictions clear or easy to understand.

Fieldwork (Chapter 4)   Research that takes place away from the laboratory. In most cases, the purpose is to observe groups as they go about their normal activities on any given day.

Generalizability (Chapter 4)   Is the extent to which study results obtained from a sample can be used to describe characteristics of a population.

Goal clarity (Chapter 6)   Clear understanding of the performance objective the group wants to achieve, phrased in a concrete way such that it is possible to tell whether or not that performance objective has been met.

Grassroots movement (Chapter 19)   A movement started from the ground up by a dedicated core group of activists.

Group identity (Chapter 18)   Group identity includes how members identify themselves with a group as well as how the group as a whole identifies itself to nonmembers. These identities are created as group members communicate with each other and with nonmembers.

Group leadership (Chapter 18)   The group leader is a person who has formal or informal authority over the group. This could be someone formally designated to be in charge, or it could be someone who assumes leadership responsibilities for the group. Sometimes, but not always, group leadership overlaps with organizational leadership such that the group leader has a higher position on the organization's hierarchy than other members.

Group polarization (Chapter 15)   Group polarization refers to the tendency of homogeneous groups to form more extreme decisions as a group than their average group members.

Group support systems (Chapter 5)   Networked computer information systems that facilitate group work through structured communication (e.g., information exchange, planning, problem solving, decision making, and conflict resolution).

Hidden profile task (Chapter 13)   Information that is needed to solve the problem is unequally distributed across members.

Holism (Chapter 7)   Because groups as systems consist of complex and interdependent webs of relationships, they cannot be reduced to the sum of its parts (i.e., reductionism). Holism is based on the idea that such complex interactions in groups will create a higher-level entity that needs to be understood by analyzing such interactions rather than individual components of the groups.

Homophily (Chapter 2)   The tendency to seek out or associate and bond with similar others.

Human-AI teaming (HAT) (Chapter 24)   A teaming ecology where at least one human and at least one AI agent work interdependently to achieve a common goal, and each human and AI agent is recognized as a unique team member occupying a distinct role on the team.

Inclusive leadership (Chapter 9)   Words, deeds, and communication from leaders that invite and appreciate others' contributions.

Information and communication technologies (Chapter 5)   A broad term referring to the devices, media, applications, hardware, and software that allow users to distribute, receive, process, store, retrieve, and utilize digital information.

Information elaboration (Chapter 8)   Information elaboration refers to systematic exchange, discussion, and examination of the content of communication. Group task performance is thought to benefit from diversity through the elaboration of knowledge contributed by members.

Information sharing (Chapter 16)   A team activity where team members share knowledge and expertise within the team and with others within the organization.

Innovation (Chapter 16)   The implementation of creative ideas and solutions in the organization.

Interdependency (Chapter 7) The mutual reliance and influence that exists between two or more individuals, groups, or systems. In interdependent relationships, the actions and decisions of one group member have an impact on the outcomes of the other group member involved.

Input-processes-output model (Chapter 12)   A model of group interaction that sees group interaction comprising the inputs that group members bring to the discussion, like their opinions or status. Then, processes and emergent states are behaviors and perceptions that emerge, like influence and cohesion, as group members communicate. Finally, from interaction, groups produce outputs, like problem-solving, member well-being, or a consensual decision.

Interaction patterns (Chapter 11)   Interaction patterns are the sequential flow of team members' interaction. Patterns may be positive or negative.

Interactive cueing (Chapter 14)   A communicative process by which group members help each other remember the needed information for a group task.

Intercultural conflict competence (Chapter 10)   The ability to manage conflicts effectively and appropriately in intercultural contexts. Intercultural conflict competence requires that group members develop culture-sensitive knowledge, remain mindful of their own and other group's cultural assumptions about communication, and develop constructive conflict communication skills.

Interdependence (Chapter 2)   A state of mutual dependence or reliance; the ways in which individuals influence each other through their interactions.

Linguistic Inquiry Word Count (LIWC) (Chapter 12)   Linguistic Inquiry Word Count is a software program that analyzes the frequency that words in certain categories, like personal pronouns, appear in text.

Linguistic style matching (Chapter 12)   Linguistic style matching examines how much people match each other on nine function word categories for a measure of linguistic mimicry.

Lurkers (Chapter 20)   People who consume the content on a community but don't actively participate. For most online communities, lurkers represent the vast majority of community members.

Media richness (Chapter 5)   A theory that focuses on how communication media have varying levels of richness for carrying messages, and that certain technologies have set characteristics that do not change which must be considered.

Mediation (Chapter 10)   An approach to conflict management that involves a neutral third party to assist the participants in resolving their conflict. Mediators use specific communication processes to ensure fairness and help disputants find a mutually agreeable solution to the conflict.

Medical teams (Chapter 22)   They are composed of healthcare professionals with different roles and specialties who collaborate to provide healthcare to patients.

Message-based constructs (Chapter 23)   Explicit forms of team interaction that are based on the verbal exchange of information, feedback, and/or knowledge.

Metacognition (Chapter 3)   Metacognition in groups refers to knowledge group members have about themselves and other group members, about their group, their task, and their group interactions, and the way group members monitor and control their information processing and actions.

Monitoring and controlling (Chapter 3)   Metacognitive processes that are important for the application of group communication theories. Monitoring refers to the assessment of group processes and controlling refers to regulating and changing processes and group interactions and behavior.

Multicommunication (Chapter 5)   A behavior occurring when individuals simultaneously engage in two or more conversations that require speaking turns.

Multidimensional networks (Chapter 17)   Networks with multiple types of nodes and edges.

Nodes (Chapter 17)   Entities in a network (e.g., people, computers).

Nonverbal communication (Chapter 23)   The transfer of information by means of body language (e.g., facial expressions, gaze, gestures, and posture) and/or paralanguage (e.g., pitch, tone, speed, and rhythm of voice).

Norms (Chapter 6)   Rules or standards of behavior that are shared by members of the group.

Online health community (Chapter 21)   A loosely structured collection of people who share a common interest in one or more health conditions and interact using communication technologies.

Positive and negative feedback (Chapter 7)   Positive feedback is deviation amplifying in that such communication leads to further behavior reinforcement (e.g., past success of groups creates future success). Negative feedback is deviation reducing feedback in that such communication leads to a change in behavior (e.g., an information sharing intervention leads to group success).

Problem identification and construction (Chapter 16)   The process of identifying that a problem exists and identifying the goals and parameters of the problem-solving effort.

Process (Chapter 6)   How group members go about doing their work and completing their task.

Pseudonymous (Chapter 20)   Many online communities allow for pseudonyms – persistent identifiers like usernames which are not tied to a user's real identity.

Public information good (Chapter 20)   A shared information repository. Many online communities produce explicit information goods, like wikis or software. Stored conversations can also serve as public information goods.

Relational constructs (Chapter 11)   Relational constructs are group attributes that describe and/or assess the type and direction of relational communication among group members. Positive relational constructs include cohesion, satisfaction, and positive group communication climate. Relational constructs emerge through group members' relational messages; but the construct is attributed to the group.

Relational messages (Chapter 11)   Relational messages are those that create and maintain relationships among group members. These messages are dependent on several factors, including who delivers the message, how the message is delivered, and the history of the group. Relational messages are interdependent with task messages.

Retrieval coordination (Chapter 14)   Group members decide whether they have the information necessary, or if they need to find that information from someone else within the group.

Role coordination (Chapter 9)   It occurs when group members' different roles, subcultures, and expertise work together to facilitate organizational performance.

Roles (Chapter 6)   Specific behaviors expected of group members who occupy specific positions in the group.

Social categorization (Chapter 8)   People's tendency to place themselves and others into different social groups based on socially meaningful categories such as demographics, professional or personal interests, political, religious, or professional affiliations, among others. Social categorization processes can lead to intergroup bias, which can disrupt knowledge sharing processes and task performance.

Social movements (Chapter 19)   Social movements are organized groups of people who purposefully come together to work toward a common goal through collective action. The goal of a social movement is to make change, either political or social change, or to empower disempowered or oppressed populations.

Sociality (Chapter 2)   The urge or tendency to aggregate, associate in groups, and develop social connections.

Society (Chapter 19)   A group of people, recruited at least in part by the sexual reproduction of its members, sharing a self-sufficient system of action that is capable of existing longer than the life-span of an individual.

Sociomateriality (Chapter 14)   An approach that entangles the social and material. In the context of Transactive Memory Systems (TMS), technologies are considered part of the group, similar to another group member.

Stigmergic communication (Chapter 20)   Communication that happens through modifying the environment rather than through typical communication channels.

Structure (Chapter 6)   It refers to the norms and roles of the group.

Subgroup (Chapter 17)   A subset of network nodes (e.g., people) which are relatively well connected.

Surgical teams (Chapter 22)   They are groups of healthcare professionals typically composed of a surgeon, anesthesia provider, a scrub technician, a circulator, and other specialists, depending on the procedure. They collaborate to perform a surgical procedure.

Survey research (Chapter 4)   A study technique that captures self-reports from participants using a set of questions that measure a construct (e.g., satisfaction), experiences (e.g., time spent working in small groups), or demographic information.

Systems thinking (Chapter 7)   The idea that social phenomenon-like groups can be best understood by looking at and optimizing their complex interactions (e.g., relationships between group members, interactions with other groups).

Task conflict (Chapter 18)   Task conflict is related to the group accomplishing its goal. This is opposed to relationship conflict, which includes interpersonal disagreements. Research suggests that while both types of conflict may be uncomfortable, moderate amounts of task conflict can improve decision making.

Task demonstrability (Chapter 13)   The degree to which a group task is solvable allows the group to find the best or correct answer. It is fostered by four conditions: a shared conceptual system, sufficient information to solve the problem, and members contributing information and accepting it when communicated.

Task messages (Chapter 11)   Task messages are straightforward verbal and nonverbal communication about the activity or goal of the group. These messages are the work of the group. Task messages are interdependent with relational messages.

The META mnemonic (Chapter 3)   META stands for *M*onitor, *E*xplain, *T*est, and *A*ssess. The application of group communication theories requires group members to go through a continuous process to *monitor* the specific situation and group behaviors, *explain* this situation in terms of a group theory, *test* out an intervention informed by the theory, and *assess* the impact it has on group functioning.

Transactive encoding (Chapter 14)   When new information enters the group, the group members discuss that information to make decisions about with whom information should be held within the group.

Transformational leadership (Chapter 9)   It refers to a leader's ability to motivate group members to do something they never thought they could do.

Unshared information (Chapter 13)   This is information known by a single member in the group about which others will not know unless communicated by the knowledgeable member.

Verbal communication (Chapter 23)   The conveyance of a message by means of spoken or written words.

Ward teams (Chapter 22)   They provide and coordinate patient care 24/7 for patients admitted to a hospital ward. These interprofessional teams are composed of nurses, physicians, and other specialized professionals.

Wizard of Oz (Chapter 24)   In the field of human–computer interaction, the Wizard of Oz method is used in experiments in which participants interact with a computer system that participants believe to be autonomous, but is actually operated or partially operated by an unseen research confederate.

Workgroup (Chapter 18)   A workgroup is a small subset of organizational members focused on one or more organizational goals. The workgroup is interdependent with other parts of the organization.

Index

Note: *Italicized*, **bold** and ***bold italics*** refer to figures, tables and boxes, respectively. Page numbers followed by "n" refer to notes.